ADULT INCAPACITY

AUSTRALIA
LBC Information Services—Sydney

CANADA and USA
Carswell—Toronto

NEW ZEALAND
Brooker's—Auckland

SINGAPORE and MALAYSIA
Sweet & Maxwell Asia
Singapore and Kuala Lumpur

ADULT INCAPACITY

Adrian D. Ward, MBE, LL.B.
Solicitor, Turnbull & Ward, Barrhead

W. GREEN/Sweet & Maxwell Ltd
EDINBURGH
2003

Published in 2003 by W. Green & Son Ltd
21 Alva Street
Edinburgh EH2 4PS

Reprinted 2005

Typeset by J.P.Price, Chilcompton, Somerset
Printed and bound in Great Britain by
Athenaeum Press Ltd, Gateshead, Tyne & Wear

No natural forests were destroyed to make this product;
only farmed timber was used and replanted

A CIP catalogue record for this book is available from the
British Library

ISBN 0 414 01472 3

© W. Green & Son Ltd 2003

All rights reserved. UK statutory material in this publication is
acknowledged as Crown copyright.

No part of this publication may be reproduced or transmitted in any form or by any means, or stored in any retrieval system of any nature without prior written permission, except for permitted fair dealing under the Copyright, Designs and Patents Act 1988, or in accordance with the terms of a licence issued by the Copyright Licensing Agency in respect of photocopying and/or reprographic reproduction. Application for permission for other use of copyright material including permission to reproduce extracts in other published works shall be made to the publishers. Full acknowledgment of author, publisher and source must be given.

PREFACE

Adult incapacity can raise issues in almost every area of law, and sooner or later for most families. Practising lawyers are increasingly recognising the importance of the subject. Providers of post-qualifying education, and some authors, have responded. However, this wide subject still receives inadequate attention in legal education and literature. This book aims to help reduce that deficit in one specific, but important, area. It addresses situations where adults have impairment of capacity to act, to make decisions or to safeguard their interests in relation to their own personal welfare, or in relation to their assets and financial affairs. It addresses three simple questions. What may people do to provide for any future such impairments of their own capacity? What may be done to deal with such matters where an adult has lost relevant capacity, and has not made anticipatory provision? What may someone making provision for others do to address existing incapacity, or possible future incapacity, of a beneficiary? I categorise the answers to these three questions as, respectively, anticipatory measures, responsive measures and third party measures.

The Adults with Incapacity (Scotland) Act 2000 provides a modern and integrated, but not comprehensive, code of provision in relation to the first two categories, those of anticipatory and responsive measures. It is necessary to consider measures within the Act's provisions and also measures, including third party measures, outwith the Act. Any membrane around the Act's own provisions is permeable in both directions. Measures outwith the Act are influenced by it, and must be taken into account when proceeding under the Act. Likewise, while the Act represents by far the most significant line ever drawn across the many centuries of development of this area of law, and while it puts an end to seriously outmoded measures and procedures and ways of applying them, nevertheless the best lessons from the past, if drawn upon carefully, can be carried across that line to assist us now and in the future.

Such a significant line nevertheless marks a suitable point at which to review and state the law. On and from July 1, 2002 all of the Act's provisions, except for Part 4 and a few minor other exceptions, were fully in force. I endeavour to state the law at October 1, 2002. I have taken account of some features of draft Codes and Regulations for Part 4 issued for consultation on September 6, 2002, and of the Mental Health (Scotland) Bill introduced in the Scottish Parliament on September 16, 2002. I have also had regard to various statements of intent by the Scottish Executive in the context of that Bill.

Discrimination against those of our fellow-citizens whose capacity is or becomes impaired has been commonplace. That discrimination has often extended to arbitrary deprivation of basic human rights and denial of basic justice. Such discrimination is abhorrent to the core values which unite lawyers everywhere, and our society is now committed to breaking it down. Particularly when one places in that setting the three questions posed above, then answering is not as simple as asking them. We are challenged how best to answer them, in each individual case, so as to minimise discrimination, respect human rights, and deliver justice. In the exploration of the answers to those questions I have been hugely helped over many years by far more people than can be thanked individually. I thank in particular those who have given me so much help, encouragement and vital back-up support in writing this book. I thank also those whose specific assistance is acknowledged where appropriate in the text; though the responsibility for what I have written remains solely mine.

The law cannot by itself ensure that we achieve in each individual case the aims of non-discrimination, respect and justice outlined above. Good law provides a helpful framework. It is to the lasting credit of the Scottish Parliament that, in its historic first major piece of legislation, it has given us such a framework. The challenge for all who employ that framework is to do so intelligently and conscientiously, open-mindedly and to the best of their ability. If this book motivates and assists them to meet that challenge, it will have achieved its purpose. Perhaps I may also have conveyed something not only of the human importance of the subject, but of its fascination; of the remarkable privilege of involvement in its unprecedented development at home and abroad over the last quarter of a century, and above all of how fortunate we now are to be able at last to deliver better outcomes for the most vulnerable and deserving members of our society. They—as people, not problems—are central to the subject and to this book.

As one busy practising solicitor, I have written principally for other such practitioners, but also—I hope—with sufficient explanation of the main legal concepts for much of this text to be reasonably accessible to interested lay-people, and to members of all the many other professions which engage with matters of adult incapacity.

Adrian D. Ward
Turnbull & Ward
54 Main Street
Barrhead
Glasgow G78 1RB

CONTENTS

	Page
Preface	v
Table of Cases	xix
Table of Statutes	xxv
Table of Statutory Instruments	xxxvii
Abbreviations and Definitions	xli

Chapter 1

DISABILITIES, CAPACITY AND ASSESSMENT

	Para.
Introduction	1–1
Intellectual impairments and disabilities	1–5
Communication difficulties	1–14
Effects on legal capacity	1–15
Minimising impairment of legal capacity	1–16
Distortions	1–19
Legal significance	1–20
Facility and circumvention; undue influence	1–21
Validity	1–22
Supervening incapacity	1–23
Modified liability, special benefits and special protections	1–24
Anticipatory measures	1–25
Responsive measures	1–26
Third party measures	1–27
Tests of capacity	1–28
Assessment of capacity	1–32
Facility and circumvention; undue influence	1–36
Facility and circumvention	1–37
Undue influence	1–38
Personal welfare matters	1–40
Disability discrimination	1–41
Disabled person	1–42
Provision of goods, facilities and services	1–43
Reasonable adjustments	1–45
Other provisions	1–46
European Convention on Human Rights	1–47

Chapter 2

PROFESSIONAL AND PRACTICAL ISSUES

Introduction	2–1
Identification of potential incapacity	2–3
Non-discrimination and communication	2–6

Principles	2–9
Responsive measure inappropriate	2–10
Who is my client?	2–11
Adult is client	2–12
Adult is not client	2–14
Hybrid situations	2–15
Hard cases	2–17
Anticipatory measures–taking instructions	2–19
Gifts	2–20

CHAPTER 3

THE INCAPACITY ACT–INTRODUCTION AND BACKGROUND

"Old law" and "new law"	3–1
History	3–3
Overview	3–7
Layout	3–10
Regulations	3–12
Codes of Practice	3–14
Commencement	3–19
Jurisdiction, applicable law and private international law	3–20
Jurisdiction	3–21
Applicable law	3–22
Recognition and enforcement	3–26
Criminal offence	3–27
Matters excluded from the Act	3–28
Legal Aid	3–30
Reform of mental health law	3–31
England	3–32

CHAPTER 4

THE INCAPACITY ACT–GENERAL PRINCIPLES AND DEFINITION OF INCAPACITY

Introduction	4–1
Application of general principles	4–2
Intervention	4–3
Consequences of non-compliance	4–4
The first principle (section 1(2))	4–6
"The person responsible for authorising or effecting the intervention"	4–7
"Benefit	4–8
"Such benefit cannot reasonably be achieved without the intervention"	4–9
Wider application	4–10
The second principle (section 1(3))	4–12
Choice of procedure	4–13

Choice of powers	4–14
Exercise of powers	4–15
The third principle (section 1(4)(a))	4–16
The fourth principle (section 1(4)(b)–(d))	4–20
The fifth principle (section 1(5))	4–22
Definition of incapacity (section 1(6))	4–23
First gateway: "mental disorder"	4–24
Second gateway: physical inability to communicate	4–25
The criteria for incapacity	4–27
Appeals	4–29
Good practice–the six levels	4–30
Duty of care and fiduciary duty	4–31
Duty of care	4–35
Fiduciary duty	4–36
The Codes–conflict of interest	4–37
The Codes–confidentiality	4–38

Chapter 5

KEY ROLES AND FUNCTIONS UNDER THE ACT

Introduction	5–1
The sheriff	
General	5–2
Jurisdiction	5–4
Procedure	5–5
General discretionary and ancillary powers	5–6
Safeguarders	5–7
General principles	5–8
Intimation to the adult	5–9
Expenses	5–10
Appeals	5–13
Giving directions	5–14
Orders regarding functions of nearest relative	5–16
Appeal against decisions as to incapacity	5–18
Appeal against decisions as to medical treatment	5–19
Miscellaneous applications, remits and appeals	5–20
Comment	5–21
Court of Session	5–22
Public Guardian	5–23
Mental Welfare Commission	5–28
Changes in Mental Health (Scotland) Bill	5–32
Local authorities	5–33
Other roles and responsibilities	
Chief social work officers	5–35
Medical practitioners (including approved psychiatrists)	5–36
Mental health officers	5–37
Nearest relative	5–38
Primary carer	5–40
Powers applicable to non-Act measures	5–41

Chapter 6

POWERS OF ATTORNEY

Introduction	6–1
Contract or grant?	6–6
The contract interpretation	6–7
The grant model	6–8
Creation and Registration	6–9
Creation	6–11
Certifiers and certificates	6–12
Registration with Public Guardian	6–16
Certificate of registration and copies of power	6–17
Registration in Books of Council and Session	6–18
Grantor	6–19
Attorneys	6–20
Powers	
Powers which cannot be conferred	6–23
Powers which require to be express	6–25
"Statutory powers?"	6–27
Good practice, the Style	6–28
Gifts and tax planning	6–31
Good practice–extraneous matters	6–32
Attorneys' actings and duties	6–33
Solicitor attorneys	6–36
Remuneration and indemnification	6–37
Powers of the sheriff and others	
The sheriff	6–38
Other authorities	6–41
Inter-relationship with other techniques	6–42
Termination	6–43
Effect of termination–third parties	6–46
Attorneys as agents	6–47
Income tax	6–48
English and foreign powers	6–49
English powers	6–50
All non-Scottish powers	6–51
Applicable law	6–53
Transitional provisions	6–54

Chapter 7

OTHER ANTICIPATORY TECHNIQUES

Joint accounts	7–1
Trusts for administration	7–3
Gifts	7–4
Advance directives	7–5
BMA policy	7–6
Taking instructions	7–7
Styles	7–8

Linking to power of attorney	7–9
Use of interdict	7–10
Mental health legislation	7–11
Guardianship and intervention orders	7–12
Statement of wishes and feelings	7–13

CHAPTER 8

AUTHORITY TO INTROMIT AND TRANSFER

Introduction	8–1
Terminology	8–2
Limitations	8–3
Applications–authority to intromit	8–4
Part A	8–5
Countersignature–Part B	8–6
Medical Certificate	8–8
Procedure	8–9
Certificate of authority	8–10
Purposes	8–11
Withdrawer's actings and duties	8–12
Supervision	8–14
Duration and termination	8–15
Transfer of funds	8–17
Related provisions	
Joint Accounts	8–18
Managers of establishments	8–19

CHAPTER 9

MANAGEMENT OF RESIDENTS' FINANCES

Introduction	9–1
Terminology	9–2
Managers	9–3
Limited registration	9–4
Opting out	9–5
Procedure	9–6
Medical examination and certificate	9–8
Management	
Scope	9–9
Duties and functions of managers	9–10
Withdrawal of funds	9–12
Registered establishments–regulation under ROCSA	9–13
Supervision	
Supervisory bodies	9–14
Changes in capacity or residence	
Review of certificate	9–19
Resident regains relevant capacity	9–20
Resident leaves, capacity not regained	9–21
Transitional provisions–MHSA management	9–22

CHAPTER 10

INTERVENTION ORDERS AND GUARDIANSHIP–GENERAL

INTRODUCTION	10–1
THE SUPERSEDED TECHNIQUES–RELEVANT PRINCIPLES AND PRECEDENTS	
Statutory (MHSA) guardians	10–2
Curators bonis	10–5
Historical development	10–7
The "preservation" issue	10–8
The curatory regime	10–10
Tutors-at-law	10–11
Tutors-dative	10–13
Historical development	10–14
Comparative influences	10–17
Revival	10–18
Appointees	10–19
Welfare powers	10–21
Management powers	10–25
CRITERIA, SCOPE AND COMMON PROVISIONS	10–26
Criteria	10–27
Interpretation	10–28
Scope	
Orders	10–29
Combinations	10–30
Limitations	10–31
Summary	10–32
Uses and effect of intervention orders	10–33
Guardianship: uses and powers	10–37
Distinction between welfare and management powers	10–41
Legal representative	10–42
Pursuit and defence of proceedings	10–43
Adult abroad	10–45
Procedure	10–46
Applicants, notice and nominees	10–47
Reports	10–48
Other orders and measures	10–51
Caution	10–52
Registration with the Public Guardian	10–54
Heritable property and accommodation	
Registration of orders relating to heritable properly	10–55
Amendment of registration (guardianship only)	10–57
Protection of third parties	10–58
Accommodation	10–59
Duties, liabilities, supervision	10–60
Records	10–61
Liability	10–62
The sheriff	10–63
The Public Guardian	10–64
Mental Welfare Commission	10–65
Local authority	10–66
Protection of third parties	10–68

Inter-relationship with other techniques 10–70
Termination of authority (including death of adult) 10–71
INTERVENTION ORDERS–FURTHER PROVISIONS
Interim orders 10–72
Variation and recall 10–73
Outlays 10–74
Change of address 10–75
Appointee as "guardian"? 10–76
Intervention orders under criminal procedure 10–77

CHAPTER 11

GUARDIANSHIP–FURTHER PROVISIONS

INTRODUCTION 11–1
GUARDIANS
Individual as guardian 11–2
Chief officer as guardian 11–3
    Responsible officer 11–4
    Change of local authority area 11–5
Joint and concurrent guardians 11–6
Concurrent guardians 11–7
Joint guardians 11–8
    Who may be appointed joint guardians 11–9
    Actings, consultation, disagreement, third parties 11–10
    Additional guardian 11–11
    Removal and resignation of joint guardian 11–13
Substitute guardian 11–14
    Caution 11–15
    Triggering the substitution 11–16
Replacement guardian 11–17
Transitional guardians 11–18
Interim guardian 11–19
DURATION AND RENEWAL
Duration of appointment 11–22
Renewal 11–24
FUNCTIONS, ACTINGS AND DUTIES 11–25
Delegation 11–26
Change of address 11–27
Effect of appointment; transactions of guardian and adult ... 11–28
    Matters outwith scope of the order 11–29
    Management within the scope of the order 11–30
    Personal welfare matters within the scope of the order 11–31
    Matters within scope of power to authorise 11–32
Reimbursement and remuneration of guardian
    Individual as guardian 11–33
    Chief officer as guardian 11–34
    Fixing amount, and payment 11–35
    Forfeiture of remuneration 11–36
Non-compliance with decisions of welfare guardian 11–37
    Procedure under section 70 11–38

MANAGEMENT BY FINANCIAL GUARDIANS
Introduction 11–39
Public Guardian 11–41
Inventory 11–42
   Public Guardian's discretion 11–43
Management plan 11–44
   Restrictions prior to approval of plan 11–45
   Review and variation 11–46
   Directions from sheriff 11–47
   General principles 11–48
Financial guardian's powers etc
   General 11–49
   Money 11–50
   Investment 11–51
   Carrying on of business 11–52
   Purchase or disposal of accommodation 11–53
Gifts 11–55
   Procedure 11–56
   The sheriff 11–59
Powers and duties under other statutes etc 11–60
Accounting and auditing 11–61
   Auditing 11–63
   Approval of accounts 11–64
   Deficiencies 11–65
Discharge 11–66
   The sheriff 11–67
ALTERATIONS AND TERMINATION 11–68
The sheriff 11–69
   Replacement 11–70
   Removal 11–71
   Recall 11–72
   Variation 11–73
   Registration and intimation 11–74
   Remits and appeals 11–75
The Public Guardian, Mental Welfare Commission and local
   authority 11–76
   Procedure 11–77
   The sheriff 11–78
   Notification and intimation 11–79
Resignation 11–80
GUARDIANSHIP UNDER CRIMINAL PROCEDURE (SCOTLAND) ACT 1995
Circumstances in which order competent 11–84
Criteria and procedure 11–86
   Medical Reports 11–87
The order 11–88
Comment 11–89
FOREIGN GUARDIANS
Directions 11–90
Other provisions 11–91
TRANSITIONAL PROVISIONS
Continuation of appointments 11–92
Proceedings relating to previous appointments 11–93
Application of the Act 11–94

Guardians with management powers 11–95
Public Guardian's Guidance Notes 11–96
Former MHSA guardians 11–97
Duration 11–98
Replacement, additional and substitute guardians 11–101
Curators bonis to persons under 16 11–102
Comment 11–103
CHECKLIST 11–104

CHAPTER 12

OTHER RESPONSIVE MEASURES

INTRODUCTION 12–1
Good practice 12–3
MANAGEMENT
Social security benefits
General 12–4
Regulation 33 12–5
Regulation 34 12–8
Regulation 34A 12–9
Regulation 35 (and Schedule 9) 12–10
Vaccine damage payments 12–11
The deed of trust 12–12
Damages payments in the sheriff court 12–13
Damages payments: any competent court 12–15
Criminal injuries compensation 12–16
Miscellaneous statutory methods 12–17
Negotiorum gestio 12–18
Informal voluntary arrangements 12–21
Joint accounts 12–23
Bare trusts 12–24
Judicial factors 12–25
Curators ad litem 12–26
Parens patriae jurisdiction 12–27
PERSONAL WELFARE
Introduction 12–28
MHSA provisions 12–29
Criminal Procedure (Scotland) Act 1995 12–32
Removal under the National Assistance Act 1948 12–33
Parens patriae jurisdiction 12–34
Curators ad litem 12–35

CHAPTER 13

TRUSTS AND OTHER THIRD PARTY MEASURES

Introduction 13–1
Formal private trusts–general description 13–2
Delivery 13–10

Legal rights 13–11
　Calculation 13–12
　The beneficiary with impaired capacity 13–13
Prohibition of accumulations 13–17
Taxation–general 13–19
Income Tax
　Liferent trust (interest in possession) 13–20
　Discretionary trust (non-interest in possession) 13–22
Capital Gains Tax 13–23
Inheritance Tax 13–26
Means-testing 13–31
Other third party measures
　Nominations 13–36
　Gifts and bequests 13–37
　Provisions for management of particular assets 13–38
　Informal voluntary arrangements and bare trusts 13–39

CHAPTER 14

HEALTH-CARE DECISIONS AND MEDICAL RESEARCH

HEALTH-CARE DECISIONS
Introduction 14–1
　Terminology 14–2
Patient's decision 14–3
　Difficulty and debate 14–11
Appointee decisions 14–13
　Source of authority 14–15
　Error in code of practice 14–16
　Sections 16(6) and 64(2) limitations 14–17
　Inter-relationship with other categories 14–21
　General application of the Incapacity Act 14–24
Parens patriae 14–25
Necessity 14–30
　Application of the Incapacity Act 14–34
Part X authority 14–38
Intervention order 14–40
Section 47(2) authority 14–41
　General application of Incapacity Act 14–42
　Procedure and duration 14–43
　Scope of authority 14–44
　Exclusions 14–45
Section 48(3) authority 14–48
　Treatments requiring application to the Court of Session .. 14–49
　Treatment requiring a certificate from an appointed practitioner 14–51
　Emergencies 14–53
Section 50(5) authority 14–54
Judicial determination 14–58
　Persons having an interest 14–59
　Section 50(3) 14–60
　Section 50(6) 14–61

Section 52	14–62
AUTHORITY FOR RESEARCH	14–63
What is research?	14–70
What is wrongful?	14–71

CHAPTER 15

CONSTRUCTING DECISIONS

Constructing Decisions	15–1

APPENDICES

Appendix 1: Adults with Incapacity (Scotland) Act 2000	A1–01
Appendix 2: Statutory Instruments	
Adults with Incapacity (Public Guardian's Fees) (Scotland) Regulations 2001 (SSI 2001/75).	A2–01
Adults with Incapacity (Certificates from Medical Practitioners) (Accounts and Funds) (Scotland) Regulations 2001 (SSI 2001/76).	A2–02
Adults with Incapacity (Supervision of Welfare Attorneys by Local Authorities) (Scotland) Regulations 2001 (SSI 2001/77).	A2–03
Adults with Incapacity (Countersignatories of Applications for Authority to Intromit) (Scotland) Regulations 2001 (SSI 2001/78).	A2–04
Adults with Incapacity (Evidence in Relation to Dispensing with Intimation or Notification) (Scotland) Regulations 2001 (SSI 2001/79).	A2–05
Adults with Incapacity (Certificates in Relation to Powers of Attorney) (Scotland) Regulations 2001 (SSI 2001/80).	A2–06
Adults with Incapacity (Scotland) Act 2000 (Commencement No.1) Order 2001 (SSI 2001/81 (C.2)).	A2–07
Civil Legal Aid (Scotland) Amendment Regulations 2001 (SSI 2001/82).	A2–08
Act of Sederunt (Summary Applications, Statutory Applications and Appeals etc. Rules) Amendment (Adults with Incapacity) 2001 (SSI 2001/142).	A2–09
Adults with Incapacity (Supervision of Welfare Guardians etc by Local Authorities) (Scotland) Regulations 2002 (SSI 2002/95).	A2–10
Adults with Incapacity (Reports in Relation to Guardianship and Intervention Orders) (Scotland) Regulations 2002 (SSI 2002/96).	A2–11
Adults with Incapacity (Recall of Guardians' Powers) (Scotland) Regulations 2002 (SSI 2002/97).	A2–12
Adults with Incapacity (Non-compliance with Decisions of Welfare Guardians) (Scotland) Regulations 2002 (SSI 2002/98).	A2–13

Adults with Incapacity (Scotland) Act 2000 (Commencement
  No.2) Order 2002 (SSI 2002/189 (C.14)).. . . . . A2–14
Adults with Incapacity (Ethics Committee) (Scotland) Regu-
  lations 2002 (SSI 2002/190). A2–15
Adults with Incapacity (Medical Treatment Certificates)
  (Scotland) Regulations 2002 (SSI 2002/208). A2–16
Adults with Incapacity (Specified Medical Treatments)
  (Scotland) Regulations 2002 (SSI 2002/275). A2–17
Appendix 3: Criminal Procedure (Scotland) Act 1995, ss.57,
  58, 58A, 60B and 61 . . . . A3–01
Appendix 4: Part 5 Code of Practice (extract) A4–01
Appendix 5: Style of Power of Attorney A5–01
Appendix 6: Styles: Intervention Order and Guardianship
  Style A: Application for Intervention Order. A6–01
  Style B: Application to replace Guardian. A6–02
  Style C: Application for Guardianship Order. A6–03

Page

Index 553

TABLE OF CASES

AB v CB, 1937 S.C. 408 .... 1–1, 10–43
Aberdeen Railway v Blaikie Bros (1854) 1 Macq. 461 4–36
Ainslie v Arbuthnot and Co., February 7, 1743, 1 Cr. and St. App. 340 6–26
Airedale NHS Trust v Bland [1993] A.C. 789; [1993] 2 W.L.R. 316; [1993] 1 All
  E.R. 821; [1993] 1 F.L.R. 1026; [1993] 14 Med. L.R. 39, HL 7–5, 14–32
Aitken v Hunter (1871) 9 M. 756 4–36
Alexander, unreported, (1992) 10–19
Allan's Trs v Inland Revenue Commissioners. *See* Allan's Trs v Lord Advocate
Allan's Trs v Lord Advocate; sub nom. Allan's Trs v Inland Revenue Commis-
  sioners, 1971 S.C. 45; 1971 S.C. (H.L.) 45; 1971 S.L.T. 62, HL 13–10
Anderson v Croall and Sons Ltd (1903) 6 F. 153; 11 S.L.T. 453 6–40
Anderson's Trs v Skinner, 1871 S.L.R. 325, 1 Div 10–43

B, Re. *See* B (A Minor) (Wardship: Sterilisation), Re
B v Forsey; sub nom. B v F, 1988 S.C. (H.L.) 28; 1988 S.L.T. 572 9–5
B (A Minor) (Wardship: Sterilisation), Re; B, Re [1988] A.C. 199; [1987] 2 W.L.R.
  1213; [1987] 2 All E.R. 206, HL 10–24, 14–25, 14–32, 14–50
B, Miss [2002] 2 All E.R. 449; *The Times*, March 23, 2002 ..... 14–4, 14–7, 14–8, 14–12
B, Petrs, unreported, (2000) 10–19
B's Curator Bonis, Noter, 1996 S.L.T. (Sh. Ct) 27; 1995 S.C.L.R. 671, Sh. Pr 4–8,
                                                                    6–31, 10–7
Bannatine's Trs v Cunningham (1872) 10 M. 319 12–19
Beaney (Deceased), Re; sub nom. Beaney v Beaney [1978] 1 W.L.R. 770; [1978] 2
  All E.R. 595, Ch D 1–28
Beattie v Lord Ebury (1874–75) L.R. 7 HL 102, HL; (1871–72) L. R. 7 Ch. App.
  777, CA in Chancery 6–47
Bennett v Bennett [1969] 1 W.L.R. 430; [1969] 1 All E.R. 539 1–28
Birkin v Wing (1890) 63 L.T. 80 1–32
Black v Cullen (1853) 15 D. 646 6–43
Boyle v Boyle's Executor, 1999 S.C. 479; 1999 G.W.D. 12–584, OH .. 1–28, 1–36, 1–38
Bremner v Bremner (Fraud), 1939 S.L.T. 448, OH 1–36, 1–37
Brenan v Campbell's Trs (1898) 25 R. 423 6–43
Bridges v Willison's Trs (1831) 10 S. 43 6–26
Britton v Britton's Curator Bonis, 1992 S.C.L.R. 947 .... 10–11, 10–48
Brogan v Rennie, 1991 G.W.D. 31–1885 .... 1–32, 1–38
Brogan, Petr, 1986 S.L.T. 420, OH 10–10, 11–4, 11–6
Bryce v Grahame (1828) 6 S. 425; (1828) 3 W and S 323 .... 10–11, 14–26, 14–59
Buchanan, unreported, (1989) 10–18, 10–19
Buchanan v Eaton, 1911 S.C. (HL) 40 4–35
Burns' Curator Bonis v Burns' Trs, 1961 S.L.T. 166, OH 13–14

C (Adult: Refusal of Medical Treatment), Re [1994] 1 W.L.R. 290; [1994] 1 All E.R.
  819, Fam. Div. 7–5, 14–11
CMS Dolphin Ltd v Simonet [2002] B.C.C. 600; [2001] 2 B.C.L.C. 704, Ch D 4–36
Calder v Calder, 1942 S.N. 40 1–28
Cameron v Greater Glasgow Health Board, 1993 G.W.D. 6–433, OH 14–6
Cameron's Trs v Cameron, 1907 S.C. 407 13–10
Campbell v Anderson (1829) 3 W and S 384 6–46
Campbell v Cochrane, 1928 J.C. 25 10–49
Carmichael v Carmichael's Executrix, 1920 S.C. (HL) 195 13–10
Carver v Duncan (Inspector of Taxes); Bosanquet v Allen [1985] A.C. 1082;
  [1985] 2 W.L.R. 1010; 59 T.C. 125, HL 13–22
Chapman, Petrs (Judicial factor: Tutor dative), 1993 S.L.T. 955; 1993 S.C.L.R. 236,
  OH 10–13, 10–25
Chatterton v Gerson [1981] Q.B. 432; [1980] 3 W.L.R. 1003, QBD 14–5
Christie's Curator (1869) 7 M. 1130 10–5
Clark Taylor and Co. Ltd v Quality Site Development (Edinburgh) Ltd, 1981
  S.C. 111; 1981 S.L.T. 308, 1 Div 13–10
Clark's Trs v Inland Revenue Commissioners; sub nom. Clark's Trs v Lord
  Advocate, 1972 S.C. 177; 1972 S.L.T. 190, 2 Div 13–10

Clunie v Stirling (1854) 17 D. 15 1–37
Collins (Deceased), Re [1990] Fam. 56; [1990] 2 W.L.R. 161; [1990] 2 All E.R. 47,
    Fam Div 13–14
Cooper and Son's Judicial Factor, 1931 S.L.T. 26, OH 10–9
Copland v Brogan, 1916 S.C. 277, 1916 1 S.L.T. 13 .... 6–33, 6–40
Cosgrove v Lothian Health Board, 1990 G.W.D. 15–839, OH 14–6
Crabbe v Whyte (1891) 18 R. 1065 4–35
Craig v Glasgow Victoria and Leverndale Hospitals Board of Management,
    unreported, March 23, 1976 14–6

D, Petr, unreported, (1991) 10–24, 10–48
D's Curator Bonis, Noter, 1998 S.L.T. 2; 1997 G.W.D. 13–538, OH ... 4–8, 6–31, 10–7,
    15–27
Dale v Inland Revenue Commissioners [1954] A.C. 11; [1953] 3 W.L.R. 448 4–32
Danish Dairy Co. Ltd v Gillespie, 1922 S.C. 656; 1922 S.L.T. 487, 1 Div 6–26
Dempster v Potts (1836) 14 S. 521 6–26
Dick v Douglas, 1924 S.C. 287; 1924 S.L.T. 578, 1 Div 10–5, 10–15, 10–16, 11–6
Drummond's Trs v Peel's Trs; sub nom. Drummond v Peel's Trs, 1929 S.C. 484;
    1929 S.L.T. 450, 2 Div 12–26
Dunbar v Wilson and Dunlop's Trs (1887) 15 R. 210 12–08
Dunn v Chambers (1897) 2 R. 247 4–36
Durham v Durham; Hunter v Edney (otherwise Hunter); Cannon v Smalley
    (otherwise Cannon) (1885) L.R. 10 P.D. 80, PDAD 1–28

E, Re; sub nom. E v E [1966] 1 W.L.R. 709; [1966] 2 All E.R. 44 13–14
E, Mrs v Eve (1986) 2 S.C.R. 388 14–25
Eadie v MacBean's Curator Bonis (1885) 12 R. 660 1–23
Elias v Black (1856) 18 D. 1225 4–36
Emslie, unreported, (1191) 10–18

F, Re. See F v West Berkshire H.A.
F, Re. See K (Enduring Powers of Attorney), Re
F v West Berkshire H.A.; sub nom. F (Mental Patient: Sterilisation), Re; F, Re
    [1990] 2 A.C. 1; [1989] 2 W.L.R. 1025; [1989] 2 All E.R. 545, HL ... 10–24, 14–32,
    14–33, 14–50
F (Mental Patient: Sterilisation), Re. See F v West Berkshire H.A.
Farrar v Farrars Ltd (1888) 40 Ch. D 395 4–36
Fernie v Robertson (1871) 9 M. 437 12–08
Ferraby v Hobson (1847) 2 Phillips 255 4–36
Finlay v Finlay, 1962 S.L.T. (Sh. Ct) 43; (1962) 78 Sh. Ct. Rep. 62, Sh. Ct
    (Glasgow) 12–26
Forbes v Forbes' Trs (No.1); sub nom. Forbes v Knox, 1957 S.C. 325; 1957 S.L.T.
    102, OH 1–36, 1–38, 1–39
Forbes v Knox. See Forbes v Forbes' Trs (No.1)
Frankland v Inland Revenue Commissioners [1997] S.T.C. 1450; [1997] B.T.C.
    8045; CA; affirming [1996] S.T.C. 735, Ch D 13–24
Fraser v Irvine's Exr, 1924 S.L.T. 114 1–36
Fraser v Paterson. See Fraser v Paterson (No.1)
Fraser v Paterson (No.1); sub nom. Fraser v Paterson, 1987 S.C. 193; 1987 S.L.T.
    562 .... 1–34, 1–35, 4–26, 6–43, 10–6
Freen v Beveridge (1832) 10 S. 727 6–24

G, Petr, unreported, (1992) 10–19, 10–24, 10–48
Gall v Bird (1855) 17 D. 1027 1–36
Gibson v Gibson, 1970 S.L.T. (Notes) 60, OH 10–43
Gibson's Exr v Anderson, 1925 S.C. 774 .... 1–35, 1–37
Gillow v Lord Aberdare (1892) 9 T.L.R. 12, CA 6–43
Gilpin v Martin (1869) 7 M. 807 13–10
Goodall v Bilsland, 1909 S.C. 1152 6–25
Goodwin, Re; Goodwin v Goodwin [1969] 1 Ch. 283; [1968] 3 W.L.R. 558; [1968]
    3 All E.R. 12, Ch D 13–14
Goorkani v Tayside Health Board, 1991 S.L.T. 94, OH 14–6
Gordon's Curator Bonis (1902) 4 F. 577 10–9
Graham v Mauchen's Exrx, 1995 G.W.D. 15–874 1–28

Table of Cases

Graham's Trs v Gillies, 1956 S.C. 437 13–10
Graham (1881) 8 R. 996 10–15
Gray v Binny (1879) 7 R. 332, 1 Div 1–38

Halliburton v Maxwell (1791) M. 16379 10–11
Hall's Trs v McArthur, 1918 S.C. 646 4–36
Hamilton v Wright (1842) 9 Cl. and F. 111; (1842) 1 Bell's App. Cas. 574 4–36
Harrington v Gill (1983) 4 F.L.R. 265, CA 13–14
Hollinworth v Dunbar, January 21, 1813, FC 6–26
Honeyman's Executors v Sharp, 1978 S.C. 223 1–38
Hunter v Bradford Property Trust Ltd, 1970 S.L.T. 173, HL; affirming 1977 S.L.T. (Notes) 33, OH 6–14
Hunter v Hanley; Galloway (or Hunter) v Hanley, 1955 S.C. 200; 1955 S.L.T. 213, 1 Div 14–71

I and I, Petrs, unreported, (1992) 10–19
Inland Revenue v Wilson, 1927 S.C. 733 13–10

Jarvie's Trs v Jarvie's Trs (1887) 14 R. 411 13–10

K, Re; F, Re [1988] 1 All E.R. 358 6–19
K v Department de L'action Sociale et de la Santé A (702) 1992-ASAN 7–11
K (Enduring Powers of Attorney), Re; F, Re [1988] Ch. 310; [1988] 2 W.L.R. 781; [1988] 1 All E.R. 358, Ch D 2–10
Kennedy v Kennedy (1884) 12 R. 275 4–35
Kerr's Trs v Inland Revenue Commissioners, 1974 S.C. 115; 1974 S.L.T. 193, 2 Div 13–10
Knox v Mackinnon (1888) L.R. 13 App. Cas. 753; (1888) 15 R. (HL) 83, HL 4–35
Kolbin and Sons v Kinnear and Co. Ltd (The Altai); Kolbin and Sons v United Shipping Co. Ltd (The Eduard Woermann); sub nom. Kolbin and Sons v Kinnear and Co.; Kolbin and Sons v Kinnear and Co. (S.S Altai) (1931) 40 Ll. L. Rep. 241; 1931 S.L.T. 464, HL 12–19
Kolbin and Sons v United Shipping Co. Ltd. *See* Kolbin and Sons v Kinnear and Co. Ltd (The Altai)

L v L's Curator ad Litem: sub nom. Lawrence, Petr, 1997 S.L.T. 167; (1996) 32 B.M.L.R. 87, OH 10–19, 14–50
LG Chemnitz (11. ZK, Beschluss v. 9.5.2000–11 T 1270/00) 5–15
LG Köln, Beschluss v. 27.4.1992–IT 117/92 5–15
Laing v Taylor, 1978 S.L.T. (Sh. Ct) 59, Sh Pr 1–13
Laird v Laird (1855) 17 D. 984 4–36
Latta, Noter, 1977 S.L.T. 127, OH 10–43
Law Hospital NHS Trust v Lord Advocate, 1996 S.C. 301; 1996 S.L.T. 848; 1996 S.C.L.R. 491, IH 3–29, 5–22, 10–13, 12–34, 14–4, 14–25, 14–26, 14–27, 14–28
Law Hospital NHS Trust v Lord Advocate (No.2), 1996 S.L.T. 869; [1996] 2 F.L.R. 407; 1996 S.C.L.R. 566, OH 14–28
Leishman, unreported, December 17, 1980 6–24
Leslie's Judicial Factor, 1925 S.C. 464 12–25
Life Association of Scotland v Douglas (1886) 13 R. 910 6–43
Lindsay v Watson (1843) 5 D.1194 .... 1–1, 14–5
Linton v Inland Revenue Commissioners, 1928 S.C. 209; 1928 S.L.T. 154, 1 Div 13–10
Liston v Cowan (1865) 3 M. 1041 1–37
Livingston v Johnston (1830) 8 S. 594 6–26

MB (Caesarean Section), Re; sub nom. L (Patient: Non-Consensual Treatment), Re; L (An Adult: Non-Consensual Treatment), Re; MB (Medical Treatment), Re [1997] 2 F.L.R. 426; [1997] 2 F.C.R. 541; [1997] 8 Med. L.R. 217, CA 14–7, 14–8
McDougal v McDougal's Trs. *See* MacDougal v MacDougal's Trs
MacDougal v MacDougal's Trs; sub nom. McDougal v McDougal's Trs, 1931 S.C. 102; 1931 S.L.T. 45, 2 Div 1–31, 1–37
McFarlane v Donaldson (1835) 13 S. 725 .... 10–10, 11–4, 11–6
McGaughey v Livingstone, 1992 S.L.T. 386; 1991 S.C.L.R. 412, OH 10–43

Macgregor v Balfour (1899) 2 F. (Ct. of Sess.) 345; (1899) 7 S.L.T. 273, 1 Div 6–26
Mackay v Campbell 1967 S.C. (H.L.) 53; 1967 S.L.T. 337, HL 1–37
McKenzie v Campbell (1894) 21 R. 904 6–43
McNeil, Rowan and Co. v Dawling (1696) Mor. 10085 6–26
Mags of Aberdeen v University of Aberdeen (1877) 4 R. (HL) 48 4–36
Maule v Graham, 1757 Mor. 329 12–18
Millar, unreported, (1992) 10–19
Millborrow, Applicant (for appointment of guardian to D), unreported, 2000 ... 5–2, 15–19
Millward v Shenton; sub nom. Millward v Shenton and British Empire Cancer Campaign for Research [1972] 1 W.L.R. 711; [1972] 2 All E.R. 1025, CA ... 13–14
Mitchell, 1939 S.L.T. 91 13–14
Moffat v Secretary of State for Social Services, 1992 S.L.T. 393, 1 Div 10–44
Moir, unreported, (2000) 10–20, 10–24
Moodie v Dempster, 1931 S.C. 553; 1931 S.L.T. 324, 1 Div 10–43, 12–26
Moore, Ex p. (1881) 51 L.J. Ch. 72 4–36
Morris (No.2), unreported, (1991) 10–18, 10–19, 10–20
Morris (No.3), unreported, (2002) 10–18
Morris, Petr, unreported, 1986 .... 10–13, 10–18, 10–19, 10–21
Morrison v Maclean's Trs (1862) 24 D. 625 1–37
Morrisons Associated Companies Ltd v James Rome and Sons Ltd, 1964 S.C. 160; 1964 S.L.T. 249, 1 Div 14–71
Moyes v Lothian Health Board, 1990 S.L.T. 444, OH 14–5, 14–6
Munro v Strain (1874) 1 R. 1039 1–37
Murphy v Brentwood D.C. [1990] 3 W.L.R. 414 6–33

Neilson (1865) 3 M. 559 10–9
North of Scotland Banking Company v Behn, Moller and Co. (1881) 8 R. 423 .. 6–46

OLG Bayern (High Court of Bavaria) (3. ZS, Beschluss v. 27.6.1991–BReg. 3 Z 52/91) 5–15
OLG Schleswig (2. ZS Beschluss v. 2.5.1996–2 W 106/95) 5–15
Orbiston v Hamilton (1736) Mor. 4063 .... 6–26, 6–37

Park v Mood, 1919 S.L.T. 170 6–25
Park v Park, 1914 S.L.T. 88 1–28
Parnie v MacLean, unreported 1–37
Pollock v Burns (1875) 2 R. 497 1–13
Pollock v Paterson, December 10, 1811, F.C. 6–3, 6–46
Practice Note No. 11, 1994 10–13
Pretty. See R. (on the application of Pretty) v DPP

Queen, unreported, (1992) 10–25

R. v Responsible Medical Officer Broadmoor Hospital Ex p. Wilkinson. See R. (on the application of Wilkinson) v Broadmoor Hospital
R. (on the application of Pretty) v DPP [2001] UKHL 61; [2002] 1 A.C. 800; [2001] 3 W.L.R. 1598; [2002] 1 All E.R. 1, HL 14–12
R. (on the application of Wilkinson) v Broadmoor Hospital; sub nom. R. (on the application of Wilkinson) v Broadmoor Special Hospital Authority; R. (on the application of Wilkinson) v Responsible Medical Officer Broadmoor Hospital; R. v Responsible Medical Officer Broadmoor Hospital Ex p. Wilkinson [2001] EWCA Civ 1545; [2002] 1 W.L.R. 419, CA 14–38
Regal (Hastings) Ltd v Gulliver [1967] 2 A.C. 134 (Note); [1942] 1 All E.R. 378, HL 4–36
Reid v Reid (1839) 1 D. 400, 1 Div 10–43
Reid v Reid Bros (1887) 14 R. 789 6–40
Rennie v Steven, 1991 G.W.D. 26–1559 1–32
Richmond v Richmond (1914) 111 L.T. 273 1–32
Robertson v Fife Council [2002] UKHL 35; 2002 S.L.T. 951; HL reversing 2001 S.L.T. 708; 1 Div; affirming 2000 S.L.T. 1226, OH 13–34
Robertson v Robertson, 2001 S.L.T. 797 12–25
Russell v Cleland, 1885 S.L.R. 211, 2 Div 6–40

S v S. See S (An Infant) v S
S (Adult: Refusal of Treatment), Re [1993] Fam. 123; [1992] 3 W.L.R. 806; [1992] 4 All E.R. 671, Fam Div 14–7

S (An Infant) v S; W v W; W v Official Solicitor (acting as Guardian Ad Litem for
 a Male Infant Named PHW); sub nom. S v McC (formerly S); S v S [1972]
 A.C. 24; [1970] 3 W.L.R. 366; [1970] 3 All E.R. 107, HL 14–1
S, Petrs, unreported, (2000) 10–19, 10–22, 15–12, 15–13
Sabatini, Re (1969) 114 S.J. 35 .... 1–1, 1–28
St George's Healthcare NHS Trust v S; R. v Collins Ex p. S (No.1) [1998] 3
 W.L.R. 936; [1998] 3 All E.R. 673, CA 14–5, 14–7
Sidaway v Board of Governors of the Bethlem Royal Hospital [1985] A.C. 871;
 [1985] 2 W.L.R. 480, HL 14–3, 14–5, 14–6
Simpson v Simpson (1891) 18 R. 1207 10–11
Sinclair, Moorhead and Co. v Wallace and Co. (1880) 7 R. 874; 1880 S.L.R. 604, 2
 Div 6–26
Skinner's Curator Bonis, Petr; sub nom. Hodge, Petr (1903) 5 F. (Ct. of Sess.) 914;
 (1903) 11 S.L.T.196, 1 Div 13–14
Smith v Bank of Scotland; Mumford v Bank of Scotland, 1997 S.C. (H.L.) 111;
 1997 S.L.T. 1061, HL 1–37, 1–38
Smith v Harding (1877) 5 R. 147 6–37
Smith's Reps v Earl of Winton, 1714 Mor. 9275 12–19
Spring v Martin's Trs, 1910 S.C. 1087 1–36
Stewart v Johnston (1857) 19 D. 1071 6–26
Stiven v Watson (1874) 1 R. 412 .... 6–33, 6–40

T (Adult: Refusal of Treatment), Re; sub nom. T (Consent to Medical Treatment)
 (Adult Patient), Re [1993] Fam. 95; [1992] 3 W.L.R. 782; [1992] 4 All E.R. 649,
 CA 7–5
Taylor v Provan (1864) 2 M. 1226 1–13
Taylor v Tweedie (1865) 3 M. 928 1–37
Templeton v Burgh of Ayr, 1912 1 S.L.T. 421 4–36
Thomas v Walker's Trs (1829) 7 S. 828 .... 6–25, 6–26
Thomson v Devon (1899) 15 Sh. Ct Rep. 209 14–3
Thomson v Fullarton (1842) 5 D. 379 6–26
Tibbert v McColl, 1994 S.L.T. 1227; 1994 S.C.L.R. 285, 2 Div 4–35
Tyler v Logan (1904) 7 F. 123; 12 S.L.T. 466 6–40

Usher's Curator, Petr, unreported, 1989 .... 10–5, 10–19

V, unreported, (1995) 10–19, 10–23
V and V, Petrs, unreported, (1997) 10–19

W, Re. See W (Enduring Power of Attorney), Re
W v L [1974] Q.B. 711; [1973] 3 W.L.R. 859, CA 4–24
W v Official Solicitor [1972] A.C. 24 14–1
W (Enduring Power of Attorney), Re; sub nom. W, Re [2001] Ch. 609; [2001] 2
 W.L.R. 957; [2001] 4 All E.R. 88, CA 1–3, 1–15
W, Petr, unreported, (1997 and 1998) 10–25
Walker v Somerville (1837) 16 S. 217 6–43
Waterman's Will Trusts, Re; sub nom. Lloyds Bank Ltd v Sutton [1952] 2 All E.R.
 1054; [1952] 2 T.L.R. 877 4–35
Watkins, Re; sub nom. Hayward v Chatterton; Watkins, Hayward v Chatterton
 [1949] 1 All E.R. 695; 65 T.L.R. 410, Ch D 13–14
Watkins, Hayward v Chatterton. See Watkins, Re
Weir v Grace (1899) 2 F. (HL) 30 1–38
Wharrie's Judicial Factor, 1916, 1 S.L.T. 345 10–9
Wheelans v Wheelans (Fraud and misrepresentation: Facility and circumven-
 tion), 1986 S.L.T. 164, OH 1–37
Wink v Mortimor (1849) 11 D. 995 .... 2–12, 6–3
Wright v Morgan [1926] A.C. 788, PC (NZ) 4–32, 4–36

X, Petr, Y, Petrs, unreported, (2001) 10–19, 15–19, 15–27

York Buildings Co. v Mackenzie (1795) 3 Pat. 378, HL 4–36
Yule v South Lanarkshire Council (No.1), 1998 S.L.T. 490; (1997–98) 1 C.C.L.
 Rep. 571, OH 13–33

TABLE OF STATUTES

1585	Curators Act (c.18).... 3–11, 10–11, 10–14		1959	Mental Health Act (7 and 8 Eliz. 2 c.72)............ 14–32
1849	Judicial Factors Act (12 and 13 Vict. c.51)..... 10–7, 11–103		1960	Mental Health (Scotland) Act (8 and 9 Eliz. c.61).. 10–4, 10–16
1856	Court of Exchequer (Scotland) Act (19 and 20 Vict. c.56)—			s.2..................... 5–28
				s.29(4)........... 10–2, 10–16
	s.1..................... 10–13		1961	Trusts (Scotland) Act (c.57)—
	s.3..................... 10–13			s.5..................... 13–17
1857	Court of Session (Scotland) Act (20 and 21 Vict. c.57)................. 10–13			Trustee Investments Act (9 and 10 Eliz.2 c.62)...... 10–10
			1963	Offices, Shops and Railway Premises Act (c.41)..... 10–42
	Lunacy (Scotland) Act (20 and 21 Vict. c.71)........ 10–2		1964	Succession (Scotland) Act (c.41)................. 13–11
1862	Lunacy (Scotland) Act (25 and 26 Vict. c.54)....... 10–2		1965	Industrial and Provident Societies Act (c.12)—
1864	Improvement of Land Act (27 and 28 Vict. c.114)... 3–19			s.26................... 12–17
1868	Court of Session Act (31 and 32 Vict. c.100).......... 10–11		1966	Law Reform (Miscellaneous Provisions) (Scotland) Act (c.19)—
	s.101................... 10–11			s.6.................... 13–17
1880	Judicial Factors (Scotland) Act (43 and 44 Vict. c.4) 5–22, 10–7		1967	Police (Scotland) Act (c.77).. 11–37
				Abortion Act (c.87).... 14–4, 14–52
			1968	Social Work (Scotland) Act (c.49)............. 3–19, 9–23
1890	Partnership Act (53 and 54 Vict. c.39)—			s.3................. 5–35, 11–3
	s.32..................... 1–23			s.51B................... 5–35
	s.35(a).................. 1–23			s.87.................... 13–32
1892	Sheriff Courts (Scotland) Extracts Act (55 and 56 Vict. c.17)—			s.94(1)................. 11–37
			1970	Taxes Management Act (c.9)—
	s.9..................... 11–65			s.13(1)................. 6–48
1894	Heritable Securities (Scotland) Act (57 and 58 Vict. c.44).......... 10–42			s.19.................... 6–48
				s.41(6)................. 7–3
				s.42(6).......... 11–60, 13–21
1907	Sheriff Courts (Scotland) Act (7 Edw.7 c.51)......... 12–13			ss.71–73................ 13–20
				s.72.... 6–48, 7–3, 11–60, 13–21
1913	Mental Deficiency and Lunacy (Scotland) Act (3 and 4 Geo.5 c.38)..... 10–2			s.76(2)................. 6–48
				s.78.................... 6–48
				s.83.................... 6–48
	s.11(2)................. 10–2			s.98.................... 6–48
1921	Trusts (Scotland) Act (11 and 12 Geo.5 c.58)......... 11–26			s.118(1)................ 6–48
				Conveyancing and Feudal Reform (Scotland) Act (c.35)—
	s.23..................... 1–23			
1944	Disabled Persons (Employment) Act (7 and 8 Geo. 6 c.10)—			s.9(3)................. 6–50
			1971	Powers of Attorney Act (c.27)—
	s.6..................... 1–42			s.3..................... 6–17
1948	National Assistance Act (11 and 12 Geo.6 c.29)—			s.4..................... 6–50
			1975	Inheritance (Provision for Family and Dependants) Act (c.63)........ 13–14
	s.22................... 13–32			
	s.26................... 13–32		1976	Damages (Scotland) Act (c.13)—
	s.47.......... 3–9, 12–28, 12–33			
1951	National Assistance (Amendment) Act (14 and 15 Geo.6 c.57)..... 12–28, 12–33			Sch.1.................. 14–27
				Divorce (Scotland) Act (c.39)—
				s.11.................... 10–43

1977	Marriage (Scotland) Act (c.15)—		1984	Mental Health (Scotland) Act—cont.	
	s.13(1)(b)	6–24		s.26	12–30
	s.19(2)(b)	6–24		s.26A	12–30
1978	National Health Service (Scotland) Act (c.29)	9–2, 9–3		s.27	12–30
				s.29(4)	5–12
	s.102	9–2		s.30	12–30
	s.108(1)	9–2		ss.35A–35K	12–30
1979	Land Registration (Scotland) Act (c.33)—			s.36(b)	10–4
				ss.36–52	3–31, 10–1, 11–92
	s.19	10–56		s.37(2)(a)	11–4
	Vaccine Damage Payments Act (c.17)	12–11		(3)	10–4
				s.39	11–87
1980	Education (Scotland) Act (c.44)—			s.41(2)	10–3, 11–92
				ss.53–57	5–38
	s.62(2)(c)	3–31		s.55(3)	3–19
	s.135	8–6		s.92(1)	10–47
	Solicitors (Scotland) Act (c.46)—			s.94	3–19, 3–31, 9–1, 9–22, 14–11
	s.65(1)	6–12, 8–6		(1)	9–22, 9–23
1981	Education (Scotland) Act (c.58)	3–2		(2)	9–9, 9–22
				(3)	9–22
	Matrimonial Homes (Family Protection) (Scotland) Act (c.59)	6–32		(3A)	9–22, 9–24
				s.95	3–19
1983	Mental Health Act (c.20)	13–24		s.96(1)	7–11, 14–39
	Pt VII	3–32		s.97	7–11, 14–37, 14–39
	s.8(1)	10–18		(2)	14–5
	s.96	3–32, 10–34		s.98	7–11, 14–37, 14–39
	s.97	3–32		(3)	14–5
	s.142	12–17		s.102	14–37, 14–39
	Mental Health (Scotland) (Amendment) Act (c.39)	10–3		s.103	7–11, 14–39
				s.105	3–27
1984	Inheritance Tax Act (c.51)—			s.106	1–24
	s.3A	13–27		s.107	1–24
	s.49(1)	13–28		s.117(1)	12–31
	s.51(1)	13–28		(2)	12–31
	s.52(1)	13–28		s.118	12–31
	ss.58–69	13–30		s.125	8–6
	ss.80–85	13–30		(1)	5–37, 9–2
	s.89	13–29	1985	Enduring Powers of Attorney Act (c.29)	6–50
	Mental Health (Scotland) Act (c.36)	2–4, 3–9, 3–10, 3–11, 3–30, 3–31, 4–24, 5–2, 5–16, 5–28, 5–37, 7–11, 10–1, 10–4, 10–31, 11–18, 11–37, 11–92, 11–97, 11–100, 12–28, 12–29, 12–30, 12–31, 14–5, 14–25, 14–38, 14–39		s.1(1)(b)	6–50
				(2)	6–50
				s.3(2)	6–50
				(5)	6–50
				s.5	6–50
			1987	Crime and Punishment Act (c.48)—	
				s.10	11–87
	Pt X	10–31, 14–1, 14–3, 14–8, 14–11, 14–18, 14–21, 14–38, 14–45, 14–48, 14–51	1988	Income and Corporation Taxes Act (c.1)—	
				s.59	13–20
	s.1	12–29		s.868	13–22
	(2)	1–9, 4–24		Court of Session Act (c.36)	10–11
	ss.2–6	5–28		Finance Act (c.39)—	
	s.3(2)	5–30		s.24(4)	13–22
	s.9	5–37		s.55(3)	13–22
	(1)	5–37	1990	Law Reform (Miscellaneous Provisions) (Scotland) Act (c.40)—	
	s.12(2)	9–2			
	ss.17–23	12–30			
	s.20	11–87		s.23	8–6
	(1)(b)	5–36, 10–48, 14–2		s.71	2–19, 6–3, 7–3
	s.21(3B)	12–30		Sch.8, para.29(15)	8–6
	s.24	12–30		Sch.9	8–6
	s.25(1)	12–30			
	s.25(2)	12–30			

1991	Mental Health (Detention) (Scotland) Act (c.47)—	1995	Disability Discrimination Act—*cont.*

1991 Mental Health (Detention) (Scotland) Act (c.47)—
    s.1. 12–30
    s.2. 12–30
  Age of Legal Capacity (Scotland) Act (c.50)...... 1–2, 10–11, 10–42, 13–7
    s.1. .... 6–19, 6–22
      (1)(b). 1–2
    s.2. 6–19
    Sch.2. 10–11
1992 Social Security Contributions and Benefits Act (c.4).... 9–9, 9–10
  Social Security Administration Act (c.5)—
    s.15A. 12–9
  Taxation of Chargeable Gains Act (c.12)—
    s.3. .... 13–23, 13–24
    s.4. 13–23
    s.5. 13–23
    s.74. 13–23
    ss.77–79. .... s.260 13–23
    s.689B. 13–22
    Sch.1, para.1. 13–24
      para.2. 13–23
1994 Local Government etc. (Scotland) Act (c.39)—
    s.2. .... 5–33, 8–6, 11–3
    s.45. 5–35
1995 Requirement of Writing (Scotland) Act (c.7)—
    s.8. 6–15
      (1). 6–15
  Environment Act (c.25)—
    Sch.22, para.232(1). 8–6
  Mental Health (Patients in the Community) Act (c.52)—
    s.4. 12–30
  Children (Scotland) Act (c.36). 10–42
    s.11(2)(b). 11–103
    s.13. 12–13
  Disability Discrimination Act (c.50).. 1–24, 1–41, 1–42, 1–43, 1–45, 1–46, 2–6, 9–5
    Pt II. 1–46
    Pt IV. 1–43, 1–46
    Pt V. 1–43, 1–46
    s.1. 1–42
    s.2. 1–42
    s.19. 1–43
      (1). 1–43
      (2)(a). 1–43
        (b). 1–43
      (5). 1–43
    s.20. .... 1–43, 1–44
      (1). 1–43
      (2). 1–43
      (3). 1–44
      (4). 1–44
        (b). 1–44

1995 Disability Discrimination Act—*cont.*
    s.21. .... 1–43, 1–45
      (1). 1–45
      (4). 1–45
      (6). 1–45
      (7). 1–45
      (10). 1–45
    ss.22–28. 1–46
    Sch.1. 1–42
      para.1(1). 1–42
      para.2. 1–42
      para.2(2). 1–42
      para.4(1)(f). 1–42
      para.4(1)(h). 1–42
      para.4(1)(h). 1–42
      para.6. 1–42
      para.8. 1–42
    Sch.2. 1–42
  Criminal Procedure (Scotland) Act (c.46)..... 1–24, 3–9, 3–10, 5–36, 5–37, 10–36, 10–78, 11–2, 11–84, 12–28, 12–32
    Pt VI. 12–32
    s.52. 12–32
    s.53. 12–32
    s.54. 12–32
    s.55. .... 11–84, 12–32
    s.56. .... 11–84, 12–32
    s.57. 11–85
      (1)(a). 11–84, 12–32
        (b). 11–84, 12–32
      (2). 12–32
        (c)... 10–77, 11–84, 11–89
      (4). 11–85
      (6). 11–85
    s.58. .... 11–84, 11–85, 12–32
      (1). 10–77, 11–85
      (1A).... 10–77, 11–85, 11–87
        (a). 11–86, 11–87
        (b). 10–77, 11–86
      (2). 11–84, 12–32
      (3). 11–84, 12–32
      (6)(a). 11–86
        (b). 11–86
        (c). 11–86
        (d). 11–86
      (7). 11–88, 11–89
      (10). 11–84, 12–32
      (11). 11–85
    s.58A. 11–85
      (1). 11–85
        (b). 10–77
      (2). 11–88
        (a). 11–88
        (b). 11–84
        (c). 11–84
        (d). 11–88
      (3). 11–88
      (4). 11–88
      (5). 11–88
      (6). 11–92
    s.59. 12–32
    s.59A. 12–32
    s.60A. 10–77

1995	Criminal Procedure (Scotland) Act—cont.		1998	Human Rights Act (c.42)..... 1–47
	s.60B............ 10–77, 11–86			Sch.1.................. 1–47
	s.61....... 11–85, 11–86, 11–87			Art.5.................... 1–48
	(1).................. 11–87			Art.6..... 1–47, 4–9, 4–12, 5–12,
	(2)................... 11–87			5–21, 9–1, 9–7, 10–37, 10–43
	(3)................. 11–87			Art.8.............. 1–48, 5–23
	(4)................. 11–87			First Protocol, Art.1....... 1–48
	(c)............... 11–87			Scotland Act (c.46)—
	(5)................. 11–87			s.57(2)................ 1–47
	(6)................. 11–87			s.100................. 1–47
	Sch.4, para.1(1).......... 12–32		1999	Disability Rights Commission Act (c.17).......... 1–41
	Criminal Injuries Compensation Act (c.53)........ 12–16			s.2.................... 1–41
1997	Town and Country Planning (Scotland) Act (c.8)—			Mental Health (Amendment) (Scotland) Act (c.32)................... 9–1
	s.75..................... 10–56		2000	Representation of the People Act (c.2)—
1997	Crime and Punishment (Scotland) Act (c.48)—			s.12..................... 6–24
	s.22.................. 10–77			Sch.4.................. 6–24
				Financial Services and Markets Act (c.8).......... 11–51
			2001	Special Educational Needs and Disability Act (c.10).. 1–43

TABLE OF ACTS OF THE SCOTTISH PARLIAMENT

1999	Mental Health (Public Safety and Appeals) (Scotland) Act (asp 1)—		2000	Adults with Incapacity Act (Scotland) Act—cont.
	s.3(1)(a)....... 1–9, 4–24, 12–29			(d).......... 4–20, 11–104
2000	Adults with Incapacity Act (Scotland) Act (asp 4)... 1–14,			(5)... 3–10, 4–22, 9–17, 10–28, 10–39, 11–32
	1–28, 1–35, 1–36, 2–9, 2–17,			(6)..... 1–2, 1–29, 1–30, 3–10,
	2–19, 3–1—3–32, 4–1—4–38			4–23, 4–25, 5–30, 9–6, 10–28,
	Pt 1... 3–10, 10–1, 10–77, 11–85,			10–49, 11–16, 11–104, 11–104,
	14–1			12–16, 14–1, 14–2, 14–41
	s.1... 2–9, 3–8, 3–10, 4–13, 4–18,			(a)–(e).... 4–27, 4–28, 4–30
	4–33, 4–37, 5–9, 5–16, 6–30, 7–2,			(b)................ 15–18
	9–11, 9–12, 10–6, 10–12, 11–37,			(e)................. 6–44
	11–89, 11–103, 14–36, 14–45,			(7).............. 6–1, 11–91
	14–51, 14–57, 15–19, **A1–01**			(b)................. 6–51
	s.1(1)......... 4–2, 4–3, 14–36			(c)................. 6–51
	ss.1(1)–(4)..... 5–8, 5–23, 10–27, 11–38			s.2..................... **A1–02**
	ss.1(1)–(5)......... 6–56, 14–42			(2)................. 5–5, 5–12
	s.1(2) 1–16, 2–5, 3–8, 3–10, 4–6,			(3)................... 5–13
	4–9, 4–10, 4–11, 4–13, 9–10,			s.3.... 5–12, 5–14, 10–48, 10–72,
	9–20, 10–28, 10–52, 11–33,			11–10, 11–21, 11–104, 14–59,
	11–104, 14–16			**A1–03**
	ss.1(2)–(4)...... 8–12, 8–17, 9–6,			(1)..... 4–37, 5–6, 5–8, 10–55,
	9–17, 10–49			11–15, 11–38, 11–88
	s.1(3)...... 1–16, 2–5, 3–8, 3–10,			(2)...... 10–50, 11–38, 11–88
	4–11, 4–12, 4–13, 4–18, 8–1,			(a)......... 5–6, 5–8, 10–66
	9–20, 10–28, 10–32, 11–221,			(b)............ 5–6, 10–48
	11–104			(c)................. 5–6
	(4)..... 3–10, 4–8, 4–16, 10–6,			(d)..... 5–6, 10–29, 10–34,
	10–48			10–48, 10–72, 11–19, 11–21,
	(a) 2–17, 4–16, 4–25, 4–38,			11–104
	5–8, 7–12, 7–13, 11–104			(3)..... 2–3, 4–20, 4–37, 5–14,
	(b)..... 4–20, 5–39, 5–40,			5–23, 5–34, 5–35, 5–36, 5–37,
	11–104			6–21, 6–38, 6–39, 6–41, 6–44,
	(c)............... 11–104			6–52, 6–53, 6–56, 7–2, 8–14,
	(i).... 4–20, 6–51, 11–91			8–17, 9–8, 9–18, 10–35, 10–48,
	(ii)... 4–21, 11–7, 11–104			10–63, 10–66, 10–67, 10–70,
				11–10, 11–15, 11–63, 11–90,
				14–24, 14–42, 14–49, 14–58,
				14–62

Table of Statutes

2000 Adults with Incapacity Act (Scotland) Act—*cont.*
    (b)........... 6–52, 11–90
    (4)..... 3–30, 5–7, 5–8, 10–43,
        11–38
    (5)..... 3–30, 5–7, 5–8, 11–38,
        12–26
    (6).................... 5–6
s.4.. 5–5, 5–16, 5–17, 5–22, 5–38,
        14–10, **A1–04**
    (1)................... 5–17
      (a)................ 5–16
      (b)................ 5–16
      (c)................ 5–16
    (3)................... 5–17
    (4)................... 5–17
s.5..... 3–30, 5–7, 5–22, 14–59,
        A1–05
    (1)................... 10–43
s.6......... 5–23, 11–96, **A1–06**
    (1).. 5–23, 10–10, 11–96, 14–8
      (e)................ 4–37
    (2).......... 10–10, 10–64
      (a)................ 5–23
      (b)................ 5–23
        (i).......... 5–23, 6–16
        (ii).......... 5–23, 6–16
        (iii)..... 5–23, 8–9, 8–13
        (iv) 5–23, 10–54, 10–56,
          10–57, 11–1
        (v).. 5–23, 10–54, 10–56,
          10–75
      (c).. 5–24, 6–41, 6–51, 7–2,
        8–14, 10–64, 11–91
        (i)................ 6–55
      (d) 5–24, 5–41, 6–41, 6–56,
    7–2, 7–3, 8–14, 9–18, 10–64,
        11–104
      (e) 5–24, 6–33, 6–56, 8–12,
        10–60, 11–53
      (f).. 5–23, 5–24, 5–30, 5–34,
        5–41
    (3)................... 6–51
      (a)................ 11–91
s.7.................... **A1–07**
    (1)................... 3–12
      (a)............ 3–12, 5–26
      (b)....... 3–12, 5–26, 6–16
      (c) 3–12, 5–26, 6–16, 11–77
    (2)........ 3–12, 5–26, 8–4
    (3)................... 5–26
s.8.... 5–10, 5–11, 11–96, **A1–08**
    (1)................... 5–10
    (2)................... 5–10
s.9............... 6–56, **A1–09**
    (1)........ 5–29, 6–41, 10–67
      (a)...... 5–29, 5–32, 10–65
      (b) 5–30, 5–32, 5–41, 10–65
      (c).. 5–24, 5–30, 5–34, 5–41
      (d)...... 5–30, 6–41, 6–51,
        10–65, 11–91
      (e) 5–30, 5–32, 5–41, 6–41,
        10–65, 14–42
      (f).. 5–30, 5–32, 5–41, 6–41,
        7–2, 8–14, 9–18

2000 Adults with Incapacity Act (Scotland) Act—*cont.*
      (g) 4–37, 5–31, 6–33, 10–60
    (2).............. 5–31, 5–34
    (3).............. 5–30, 6–51
      (a)................ 11–91
s.10......... 5–33, 6–56, **A1–10**
    (1)(a).... 5–34, 10–66, 10–67
      (b)..... 5–24, 5–30, 5–33,
        5–34, 5–41
      (c)..... 5–34, 6–41, 6–51,
        10–67, 11–91
      (d)..... 5–33, 5–34, 5–41,
        6–41, 10–67, 11–3, 14–42
      (e)..... 4–37, 5–31, 6–33,
        10–60
    (2).............. 5–33, 11–3
    (3)................. 10–67
      (a).......... 5–34, 10–66
      (b)................ 6–38
        (i)........ 5–34, 10–66
        (ii)............. 5–34
    (4)............. 5–34, 6–51
      (a)................ 11–91
s.11 5–5, 5–22, 6–45, 9–7, 10–54,
    11–4, 11–5, 11–12, 11–14,
    11–16, 11–27, 11–53, 11–57,
    11–66, 11–74, 11–77, 11–79,
        11–83, **A1–11**
    (1)... 5–9, 5–25, 6–45, 11–38,
        11–104
    (2).... 5–9, 5–25, 6–34, 6–38,
    6–45, 8–5, 8–9, 11–77, 11–81
s.12........ 8–14, 14–42, **A1–12**
    (1)... 5–24, 5–30, 5–34, 5–41,
        6–41, 10–63
    (2)... 5–24, 5–30, 5–34, 5–41
s.13... 3–14, 6–33, 10–60, **A1–13**
    (1).................... 3–15
    (3)............. 7–2, 11–1
s.14 2–3, 4–29, 5–18, 5–19, 5–36,
    9–8, 14–24, 14–42, 14–58,
        14–62, **A1–14**
Pt 2 2.19, 3–10, 5–23, 6–2, 6–19,
    6–38, 6–58, 14–1, 14–13,
        14–20, 14–59
s.15.... 6–6, 6–7, 6–8, 6–9, 6–43,
        A1–15
    (1)......... 4–28, 6–9, 6–19
    (2)..................... 6–9
    (3)... 6–11, 6–15, 6–18, 6–47
      (a)............ 6–11, 6–18
      (b)............ 6–11, 6–15
      (c) 1–39, 6–11, 6–12, 6–15
        (i)............. 6–12
        (ii)............ 6–13
        (iii)........... 6–14
    (4)................... 6–12
s.16... 6–6, 6–7, 6–8, 6–10, 6–43,
        A1–16
    (1)................... 6–19
s.16(1)–(4)................ 6–55
s.16(3)... 6–11, 6–15, 6–18, 6–47,
        14–16
      (a)........... 6–11, 6–18

2000 Adults with Incapacity Act (Scotland) Act—*cont.*
    (b)........... 6–11, 6–15
    (c)...... 1–39, 1–40, 6–11, 6–12, 6–15
        (i).............. 6–12
        (ii)............. 6–13
        (iii)............ 6–14
  s.16(4)................... 6–12
    (5).................. 6–56
      (a)................ 6–20
      (b)..... 6–10, 6–23, 6–51, 14–9, 14–16
        (i).............. 4–28
        (ii)............. 6–30
    (6)....... 6–51, 6–56, 14–13, 14–15, 14–16, 14–17, 14–17, 14–20, 14–45, 14–53
      (a).......... 6–23, 14–21
      (b).... 4–19, 6–23, 14–19, 14–20
    (7)... 6–19, 6–22, 6–43, 6–55
    (8).................. 6–1
      (a)................ 6–51
      (b)................ 6–51
  s.17......... 6–33, 6–56, **A1–17**
  s.18.... 6–3, 6–6, 6–7, 6–8, 6–10, 6–43, 6–53, 6–54, 6–57, **A1–18**
  s.19...... 6–8, 6–10, 6–18, 6–55, **A1–19**
    (2)(c)...... 5–31, 5–32, 6–17
    (3)......... 6–9, 6–16, 6–18
    (4)............. 6–8, 6–17
    (5)(a)................ 6–17
      (b)................ 6–17
    (6)............. 5–20, 6–16
  s.20..... 6–38, 6–39, 6–41, 6–45, 6–51, 6–53, 6–56, **A1–20**
    (1).................. 2–3
    (2).................. 6–39
      (a)–(d)............. 5–20
      (b)................ 6–33
      (c)................ 5–34
      (d)................ 6–33
      (e) 5–20, 6–38, 6–39, 6–44
        (i)........ 6–43, 10–70
        (ii)............. 6–43
    (3)(a).......... 6–55, 6–56
    (5).............. 6–1, 6–51
  s.21.... 6–33, 6–55, 6–56, **A1–21**
    (6)(g)................ 8–2
  s.22........ 6–55, 10–71, **A1–22**
    (1)................. 6–34
      (d)................ 6–34
    (2).................. 6–45
  s.23.. 6–20, 6–45, 6–55, 7–1, 7–2, **A1–23**
    (1)....... 5–34, 6–45, 11–77
      (c)............. 5–40
    (2).................. 6–45
    (3).................. 6–45
    (4).................. 6–45
      (b)............ 6–7, 6–8
  s.24.............. 6–46, **A1–24**
    (1)... 6–30, 6–43, 6–46, 6–56

2000 Adults with Incapacity Act (Scotland) Act—*cont.*
    (2)... 6–41, 6–43, 6–46, 6–51, 6–56, 10–51, 10–70, 11–104
    (3)................. 6–51
    (4)................. 6–46
  Pt 3..... 3–10, 3–31, 5–23, 5–24, 5–36, 6–2, 6–42, 6–51, 7–2, 8–1, 8–3, 8–12, 8–14, 8–16, 9–12
  s.25.................. **A1–25**
    (1)..... 1–36, 4–28, 7–1, 8–2, 8–3, 9–12
    (2).................. 8–2
  s.26.................. **A1–26**
    (1)(a)................ 8–5
      (b)................ 8–5
      (c)................ 8–6
      (iii)(C)............ 10–49
      (d).......... 5–39, 5–40
      (e)................ 8–5
      (f)................ 8–8
      (g)................ 8–5
    (2).................. 8–4
    (3)......... 5–39, 5–40, 8–9
    (4).................. 8–9
      (a)............... 8–16
    (5)............ 8–10, 8–15
    (6)................ 8–10
    (7)................. 8–9
    (8)............ 5–20, 8–9
    (9)............ 5–20, 8–9
    (10)................. 8–2
  s.27.................. **A1–27**
  s.28............ 8–11, **A1–28**
    (1)................. 8–11
      (d)............... 8–11
    (2)............. 4–8, 8–11
    (4)........... 8–10, 8–11
  s.29.................. **A1–29**
    (1)................ 8–10
    (2)................ 8–16
    (3)......... 8–5, 8–9, 8–10
    (4)............ 5–20, 8–9
  s.30.................. **A1–30**
    (2)................ 8–14
    (3)................ 8–14
    (4)................ 8–14
  s.31.................. **A1–31**
    (1)................ 8–15
    (2)............. 8–5, 8–15
    (3)................ 8–16
    (4)................ 8–16
    (5)................ 8–16
    (6)....... 5–20, 8–15, 8.16
    (7)........ 8–3, 8–16, 10–70
    (8)................ 8–16
  s.32.. 6–2, 7–1, 8–3, 8–18, 12–23, **A1–32**
  s.33.................. **A1–33**
    (1)................. 8–2
    (2)................. 8–2
    (3)................ 5–20
  s.34...... 6–42, 7–2, 8–3, 10–70, **A1–34**
    (1)................. 6–51
    (2)(b).............. 6–51

| 2000 | Adults with Incapacity Act (Scotland) Act—*cont.* | 2000 | Adults with Incapacity Act (Scotland) Act—*cont.* |

2000 Adults with Incapacity Act (Scotland) Act—*cont.*
 Pt 4 ss.35–46. . 3–10, 3–11, 3–15,
  3–19, 4–7, 4–13, 5–24, 5–33,
  5–39, 6–2, 6–42, 6–51, 9–1, 9–2,
  9–3, 9–4, 9–5, 9–7, 9–9, 9–10,
  9–11, 9–12, 9–13, 9–15, 9–18,
  9–21, 9–22, 9–23, 9–24, 10–34,
  14–59
 s.35. . . . . 8–17, 9–3, 9–23, **A1–35**
  (1)(a). 9–2
   (b). 9–2
   (c). 9–2
   (d). 9–2
   (e). 9–2
  (2). 5–5, 9–2, 9–14
  (3). 9–2
  (4). 9–2
  (5). 9–2, 9–3
  (6). 9–2
 s.36. . . . . 9–23, **A1–36**
 s.37. . . . . 9–19, 9–23, **A1–37**
  (1). 9–8, 9–9
  (2). 1–36, 4–7, 4–28, 9–1,
   9–6, 9–7, 9–8, 9–12
  (3). 5–9, 5–39, 9–7
  (4). 5–9, 9–8
  (5). 9–8
  (6). 9–8
  (7)(a) 2–3, 9–10, 9–19, 14–59
   (b). 9–8
  (8). 5–9, 6–45, 9–7, 9–8,
   11–77
  (9). 9–7
 s.38. . . . . 9–23, **A1–38**
 s.39. . 9–6, 9–9, 9–10, 9–19, 9–20,
  9–20, **A1–39**
  (1). 9–9
  (2). 9–10
  (3). 9–9, 9–23
  (4). 9–9
  (5). 9–10
 s.40. . . . . **A1–40**
  (1). 9–2, 9–23
  (2). 5–24, 9–14
  (3). 5–24, 9–14
  (4). 9–2, 9–14
 s.41. . . . . 9–10, 9–14, **A1–41**
  (f). 5–39
 s.42. . . . . 8–19, 9–12, **A1–42**
  (1). 8–19, 9–12
  (2). 8–19, 9–12
  (3). 8–19, 9–12
  (4). 9–12
  (5). 9–12
 s.43. . . . . 9–20, **A1–43**
  (2). 9–20
  (3). 9–21
  (4). 9–21
 s.44. . . . . 9–20, **A1–44**
  (1). 9–20, 9–21
  (2). 9–20, 9–21
  (3). 9–20, 9–21
  (4). 9–21
   (a). 9–20

2000 Adults with Incapacity Act (Scotland) Act—*cont.*
  (b). 5–33
 s.45. . . . . 9–15, **A1–45**
  (1). 9–14
  (3). 9–3, 9–14
  (4). 9–15
  (5). 9–15
  (6). 5–20, 9–15
 s.46. . . . 6–42, 9–9, 10–70, **A1–46**
  (1). 6–51
  (2)(b). 6–51
 Pt 5. . 3–10, 3–15, 4–3, 4–7, 4–14,
  5–14, 5–19, 5–22, 5–36, 6–2,
  10–35, 10–77, 11–85, 11–91,
  14–1, 14–2, 14–13, 14–16, 14–20,
  14–22, 14–24, 14–30, 14–44,
  14–58, 14–59, 14–62
 s.47. . . . . . 6–42, 7–7, 7–9, 14–41,
  14–42, **A1–47**
  (1). 5–19, 14–9, 14–16,
   14–20, 14–43, 14–44
   (a). 4–28
  (2). . . . 4–19, 7–9, 14–1, 14–3,
   14–8, 14–9, 14–15, 14–18, 14–19,
   14–20, 14–23, 14–33, 14–34,
   14–35, 14–41, 14–42, 14–43,
   14–44, 14–45, 14–46, 14–47,
   14–48, 14–51, 14–56, 14–60
  (3). 14–23
  (4). 14–1, 14–44
  (5). 14–43
  (6). 14–43
  (7). 14–45
   (a). 4–19, 14–51
  (8). 14–45
  (9). 14–23, 14–30, 14–35,
   14–45
  (10). 7–10, 14–23, 14–35,
   14–47
 s.48. . . 5–22, 6–23, 14–35, 14–45,
  A1–48
  (1). 6–23, 10–31, 14–17,
   14–18, 14–21, 14–45
  (2). 3–12, 6–23, 10–31,
   10–33, 14–1, 14–17, 14–19,
   14–20, 14–33, 14–45, 14–48,
   14–53
  (3). 14–1, 14–19, 14–23,
   14–33, 14–45, 14–48, 14–51
 s.49 10–70, 14–13, 14–46, **A1–49**
  (2). 14–23, 14–30, 14–35
  (3). 7–10, 14–23, 14–35,
   14–47
 s.50 2–3, 5–19, 5–22, 5–29, 5–31,
  6–51, 6–52, 7–9, 10–13, 11–91,
  14–13, 14–26, 14–46, 14–55,
  14–59, 14–62, **A1–50**
  (1). 7–9, 14–46
  (2). . 6–42, 7–9, 10–70, 14–16,
   14–46, 14–56
  (3). 14–1, 14–35, 14–60,
   14–62
  (4). 14–2, 14–56
  (5). 14–1, 14–8, 14–21,
   14–23, 14–54, 14–57

2000	Adults with Incapacity Act (Scotland) Act—cont.		2000	Adults with Incapacity Act (Scotland) Act—cont.
	(6)......	14–0, 14–35, 14–59, 14–61		s.55............. 10–75, **A1–55**
	(7)..........	14–30, 14–35		s.56............. 10–55, **A1–56**
	(8)......	7–10, 14–35, 14–47, 14–57		(1)................. 10–55
	(9)......	5–31, 14–2, 14–57		(2)................. 10–55
				(3)................. 10–55
	(a)...............	11–91		(4)................. 10–55
	(10)....	14–13, 14–46, 14–54, 14–60		(b)............... 10–56
				(5)................. 10–55
	(b).........	6–51, 14–13		(6)................. 10–55
	s.51..	5–39, 11–91, 14–63, 14–70, 14–71, **A1–51**		(7)................. 10–55
				s.57....... 11–22, 11–73, **A1–57**
	(1).............	4–28, 14–71		(1)....... 2–3, 10–10, 10–47
	(a)...............	14–63		(2)... 2–12, 5–24, 5–33, 5–41, 10–47, 11–3
	(b)...............	14–63		
	(2)(a).............	14–63		(3)..... 10–48, 11–21, 11–24, 11–86, 11–104, 14–16
	(b)...............	14–63		
	(f)...	14–69, 14–71, 14–72		(a)... 4–26, 10–48, 10–50, 11–104
	(3)..................	14–63		
	(a)...............	14–64		(b).... 4–26, 5–35, 10–50, 11–104
	(b)...............	4–19		
	(f).................	5–39		(c)................. 10–49
	(4).......	4–8, 14–63, 14–64		(4)...... 5–35, 10–47, 10–49, 11–104
	(5)................	14–66		
	(6)................	14–66		(5).... 10–20, 10–29, 11–19, 11–20, 11–104
	(7)................	14–66		
	(8)................	14–69		(6).... 11–19, 11–22, 11–23, 11–104
	(a)...............	11–91		
	s.52	2–3, 5–13, 5–19, 5–22, 14–1, 14–24, 14–26, 14–42, 14–58, 14–59, 14–62, **A1–52**		s.58... 4–13, 11–8, 11–19, 11–24, **A1–58**
				(1)....... 4–13, 10–1, 10–27
	Pt 6......	3–10, 3–11, 3–31, 5–3, 5–14, 5–17, 5–23, 5–30, 5–36, 6–2, 6–58, 8–3, 8–16, 9–9, 10–1, 10–18, 10–77, 11–39, 11–60, 11–85, 11–92, 11–95, 11–102, 14–1, 14–13, 14–20, 14–59		(a) 1–36, 1–40, 4–13, 4–28
				(b)..... 8–2, 10–37, 14–42
				(c)................. 10–28
				(d)................ 11–21
				(2)..... 10–30, 10–51, 11–104
				(3) 5–2, 10–30, 10–46, 11–21
	s.53.............	10–77, **A1–53**		(4)..... 10–18, 10–28, 11–22, 11–88, 11–104
	(1)...	2–3, 4–28, 10–1, 10–27, 10–47, 10–77, 14–9		
				(5)....... 10–20, 11–6, 11–7
	(2)............	10–30, 10–51		(6).... 10–10, 10–52, 11–104
	(3)...	2–12, 5–24, 5–33, 5–41, 10–47		(7)....... 10–54, 11–4, 11–5, 11–24, 11–88
	(4)......	5–35, 10–46, 10–47, 10–48		(b)................. 10–54
				(c)................. 10–54
	(5)....	10–29, 10–32, 10–70, 14–15		(d)................ 10–54
				s.59... 5–11, 10–10, 10–36, 11–8, 11–9, 11–14, 11–20, 11–104, **A1–59**
	(a)..	10–32, 10–33, 10–35, 10–49, 10–65, 10–66, 14–9, 14–21, 14–40		
				(1)............. 11–2, 11–34
	(b)..	10–10, 10–32, 10–36, 11–3, 14–9, 14–40		(a).... 10–47, 11–2, 11–11
				(b).......... 11–2, 11–3
	(6)...........	10–58, 10–59		(2)....... 5–11, 11–3, 11–34
	(7)...........	10–10, 10–52		(3)....... 10–49, 11–2, 11–3
	(8)......	5–34, 10–66, 10–73		(3)–(5).. 11–11, 11–17, 11–70
	(9)................	10–33		(4)....... 10–49, 11–2, 11–3
	(10)..............	10–54		(a)................ 10–12
	(11)...............	10–68		(a)–(f).............. 11–2
	(12)...............	10–74		(b)................. 11–3
	(13)...............	10–58		(c)................. 11–3
	(14)....	10–31, 10–45, 10–62, 14–15, 14–21		(d)................ 11–3
				(5)............. 4–33, 11–2
	s.54.............	10–61, **A1–54**		s.60...... 11–24, 11–98, 11–100, **A1–60**

2000 Adults with Incapacity Act
(Scotland) Act—*cont.*
    (1)..... 10–20, 11–23, 11–24,
                                      11–98
    (2)..... 10–47, 11–23, 11–24
    (3).......... 10–48, 11–24
    (4)................. 11–24
        (b)........ 10–18, 11–22
    (5)................. 11–24
  s.61....... 10–55, 10–57, **A1–61**
    (1)................. 10–55
        (a)............... 14–15
    (2)................. 10–55
    (3)................. 10–55
    (4)(b).............. 10–56
    (4)................. 10–55
    (5)................. 10–55
    (6)................. 10–55
    (7)................. 10–55
  s.62.... 10–10, 11–6, 11–8, 11–9,
                              A1–62
    (1)...... 10–20, 11–6, 11–8
        (a).................. 11–8
        (b)... 11–8, 11–11, 11–12,
                              11–101
  s.62(2)........... 10–20, 11–9
        (b)............... 10–31
    (3).......... 11–8, 11–20
    (4)................. 11–11
    (5)................. 11–12
    (6)................. 11–10
    (7)........... 11–7, 11–10
    (8)........... 5–14, 11–10
    (9)................. 11–10
  s.63.. 10–10, 10–20, 11–6, 11–14,
        11–16, 11–101, **A1–63**
    (1).......... 11–14, 11–16
    (2)................. 11–14
    (3)................. 11–14
    (4)................. 11–14
    (5)................. 11–15
    (6)................. 11–14
    (7)................. 11–14
        (a)............... 11–15
    (8).......... 10–71, 11–16
    (9)(b).............. 11–15
    (10)................ 11–16
  s.64............. 11–4, **A1–64**
    (1).. 5–2, 10–1, 10–29, 10–38,
                     10–70, 14–15
        (a)............... 10–32
        (b)........ 10–32, 14–15
        (c)............... 10–32
        (d)............... 10–32
        (e)... 4–22, 10–28, 10–32,
          10–39, 11–32, 11–96, 11–104
    (2)..... 10–31, 10–33, 14–15,
         14–17, 14–19, 14–20,
         14–21, 14–45, 14–53
        (a).... 4–19, 10–31, 14–21
        (b).. 10–13, 10–31, 10–33,
                            14–20
    (3)...... 2–15, 10–42, 10–70
    (4)........... 10–75, 11–27
    (5)........... 11–49, 11–95

2000 Adults with Incapacity Act
(Scotland) Act—*cont.*
    (6)................. 11–26
    (7)...... 5–20, 10–64, 10–67,
                          11–41, 11–95
    (8)................. 11–19
    (9).... 5–9, 6–45, 11–4, 11–5
    (10)... 5–9, 6–45, 11–4, 11–5,
                             11–77
    (11).... 10–31, 10–40, 11–88
    (12)................ 11–39
  s.65............. 10–61, **A1–65**
  s.66... 4–8, 11–56, 11–57, 11–95,
                             A1–66
    (1)................. 11–55
    (7)................. 5–20
    (8)................. 5–20
  s.67..................... **A1–67**
    (1)....... 4–22, 9–11, 10–28,
         10–39, 11–29, 11–30, 11–31,
                   11–32, 14–9
    (2)........... 11–30, 11–95
    (3)..... 10–45, 11–28, 11–91
    (4) 4–5, 10–62, 11–28, 11–91
    (5)......... 10–39, 11–32
    (6).......... 10–68, 11–28
    (7)..... 10–45, 10–62, 11–28,
                             11–91
  s.68... 5–10, 11–7, 11–33, **A1–68**
    (1)............ 11–33, 1–34
    (2).......... 11–34, 11–97
        (a)............... 11–33
    (3).. 5–10, 5–11, 11–3, 11–34,
                             11–97
        (b)............... 11–34
    (4).......... 11–33, 11–34
    (5)................. 11–33
    (6)................. 11–35
    (7)................. 11–35
    (8).......... 5–20, 11–35
  s.69... 2–3, 10–60, 11–36, **A1–69**
  s.70 11–31, 11–37, 11–38, 11–91,
                             A1–70
    (1)(a).............. 11–37
        (b)............... 11–37
    (2)................. 11–37
    (3)................. 11–38
    (4)................. 11–38
    (6)................. 11–91
  s.71 10–57, 11–16, 11–17, 11–69,
        11–82, 11–91, **A1–71**
    (1)...... 2–3, 11–16, 11–69
        (a)... 11–2, 11–70, 11–80,
                          11–101
        (b)............... 11–71
          (i)............. 11–13
          (ii)............ 11–16
        (c)... 11–72, 11–80, 11–82
          (ii)............. 4–13
    (2)............ 11–70, 11–72
    (3)................. 11–74
        (a)............... 10–57
    (4).......... 10–30, 11–72
    (5)................. 11–91
  s.72 10–10, 11–66, 11–95, **A1–72**
  s.72(1)–(5).............. 11–66

2000 Adults with Incapacity Act
(Scotland) Act—cont.
(2). 5–39, 5–40
(5). 5–20, 11–67
(6). 5–20, 11–67
s.73. . 6–45, 10–57, 10–67, 11–77,
A1–73
(1). 2–3, 11–76
(a). 10–67
(2). 11–79
(a). 10–57
(3). 11–76
(a). 10–67
(b). 10–67
(4). 11–79
(5). 5–39, 5–40, 11–77
(7). 11–77
(8). 5–20, 11–78
(9). 5–20, 11–78
(10). 11–77
s.74 10–55, 10–57, 11–15, 11–69,
A1–74
(1). 2–3, 11–69, 11–73
(2). 11–15, 11–73
(3). 11–73
(4). 11–22, 11–73
(5)(a). 10–57, 11–74
s.75. . 6–45, 10–57, 11–16, 11–80,
A1–75
(1). 11–13, 11–16
(2). 11–16
(a)(i). 11–13
(ii). 11–16
(3). 6–45
(a). 10–57
(b). 11–81
(4). 6–45, 11–83
(5). 11–70, 11–82
s.76. . . . . 5–25, 6–45, 11–4, 11–5,
11–27, **A1–76**
(4). 5–9, 11–5
s.77. . . . . 11–91, **A1–77**
(1). 10–71
(2). 10–71
(3). 10–69
(4). 10–58
(5). 11–91
s.78 10–57, 11–74, 11–79, 11–81,
A1–78
s.79. . . . . 10–58, **A1–79**
Pt 7. . . . 3.10, 10–1, 10–77, 11–85
s.80. . 10–1, 10–14, 11–60, 11–92,
11–102, 12–25, 14–25, **A1–80**
s.81. . . . . 3–19, 6–33, 6–56, 8–12,
9–11, 10–60, 11–36, 11–65,
11–95, **A1–81**
s.82 3–10, 3–19, 4–5, 4–13, 4–33,
4–34, 4–36, 4–37, 6–33, 6–33,
6–56, 8–12, 9–11, 10–60, 11–36,
11–65, 11–91, 11–95, **A1–82**
(2)(a). 11–91
(b). 6–51
(c). 6–51
s.83. . . . . 3–27, 6–33, 6–35, 6–52,
6–56, 10–60, 14–42, **A1–83**
s.84. . 10–77, 11–1, 11–85, **A1–84**

2000 Adults with Incapacity Act
(Scotland) Act—cont.
s.85. . . . . 3–20, **A1–85**
s.86. . . . . **A1–86**
(1). 3–12
(2). 3–13
s.87. . . . . 9–2, **A1–87**
(1). 1–6, 1–9, 3–12, 3–31,
4–24, 5–4, 5–33, 5–39,
11–3, 11–27, 14–59
(2). 5–38
(3). 5–38
(4). 6–43
s.88. . . . . 6–36, **A1–88**
(1). 6–58, 11–102
s.89. . . . . **A1–89**
Sch.1. . . . . . . 3–11, 5–5, 9–2, 9–3,
A1–90
para.1. 3–19
para.1(d). 9–3
para.2. . . . . 3–19, 11–47
Sch.2. . . . 3–11, 3–12, 5–20, 5–23,
10–1, 11–39, 11–95, **A1–91**
para.1(1). 11–104
para.1(1)–(3). 1–44
para.1(4). . . 11–20, 11–45,
11–104
para.1(5). 11–45
para.1(6)–(9). 11–46
para.3. 10–10
para.3(1)–(3). 11–42
para.3(2). 3–12
para.3(4). 11–43
para.4. . . . . . 10–10, 11–50
para.5. 10–10
para.5(1)–(4). 11–51
para.5(6). 11–52
para.6. . . . . . 10–59, 11–53
para.6(1)(b). 11–54
para.6(1)–(6). 11–53
para.6(7). 11–54
para.6(8). 11–53
para.6(9). 11–54
para.6(2). 5–39, 5–40
para.7. 11–61
para.7(5). 3–12
para.7(6). 3–12
para.8. 11–61
para.8(1)–(5). 11–64
para.8(6). . . 10–60, 11–36,
11–65
para.8(7). . . 10–60, 11–36,
11–65
para.10. 3–19
para.11. 3–19
Sch.3. . . . 3–11, 3–20, 3–25, 3–26,
6–53, 10–1, **A1–92**
para.1. 3–21
para.1(1). 5–4
para.1(1)(c). 11–21
paras 1(2)–(4). 3–19
para.2. . . . . . . 5–4, 11–104
para.2(1)(c). 11–21
para.2(2). 3–19, 5–4
para.3. . . . . . . 3–25, 11–21
para.3(1). 3–22

2000	Adults with Incapacity Act (Scotland) Act—*cont.*		2000	Adults with Incapacity Act (Scotland) Act—*cont.*	
	para.3(2)	3–22		Sch.6	3–11, 3–19, 10–1, 10–11, 10–47, 11–87, 11–92, 11–103, **A1–96**
	para.3(3)	3–24, 5–5			
	para.3(4)	3–22		Standards in Scotland's Schools etc. (Scotland) Act (asp 6)	1–43
	para.3(5)	3–22			
	para.4	3–25			
	paras 4(1)–(5)	3–24	2001	Regulation of Care (Scotland) Act (asp 8)	3–6, 3–11, 3–19, 9–1, 9–2, 9–13, 9–17, 11–84
	paras 4(6)–(8)	3–23			
	para.5	3–25			
	para.6	3–25		s.2	9–3
	para.6(4)	11–100		(1)	9–3
	para.7(2)(b)	3–19		(3)	9–2
	para.7(2)(e)	3–19		(5)	9–2, 9–3
	paras 7–10	3–26		s.6	9–16
	para.11	3–19		s.7	9–3
	para.12	3–19		(1)	9–2
	Sch.4	3–11, 5–20, 6–58, 10–1, 11–102, **A1–93**		(2)	9–4
				ss.7(3)–(5)	9–4
	para.1	11–92, 14–13		s.8	9–2, 9–4
	para.1(2)	11–102		(1)	9–4
	para.2	11–92		(2)	9–4
	para.3	11–93		(3)	9–4
	para.4	6–3, 6–8, 6–54, 6–57, 14–13		(4)	9–2
				s.9	9–4, 9–16
	para.4(1)	6–55		s.10	9–16
	para.4(2)	6–57		s.11	9–16
	para.4(3)	6–55, 6–57, 6–58		s.12	9–16
				s.13	9–16
	para.4(4)–(7)	6–55, 6–58		ss.14–17	9–16
	para.4(5)	6–58		s.18	5–20, 9–16
	para.4(6)	6–58		s.19	8–16
	para.4(7)	6–58		s.20	9–16
	para.5	3–19		s.24	9–4
	para.5(1)	9–23		s.25(6)	6–27, 10–42
	para.5(2)	9–23		(7)	6–27, 10–42
	para.5(3)	9–23		ss.25–27	9–16
	para.5(4)	9–23		s.28	9–4, 9–16
	para.6	11–94, 11–101, 11–102		s.29	9–13
				(2)	9–17
	para.6(1)	11–101, 11–102		(h)	9–13
	para.6(2)	11–95		(3)	9–17
	para.6(3)	10–18, 11–98, 11–99		(4)	9–16, 9–17
				(6)	9–16
	para.6(6)	11–95		(7)(a)–(f)	9–13
	para.6(7)	5–20, 11–95		(j)	9–3
	para.6(8)	11–94		(10)	9–13
	para.7	11–94		(11)	9–13
	para.7(a)	6–58		s.32	9–16
	para.7(b)	8–16		s.33	9–3
	para.7(c)	8–3		s.59	9–17
	para.7(d)	3–19, 9–9		(1)	9–17
	Sch.5	3–11, 10–42, **A1–94**		s.77(1)	9–2
	para.4	3–19		(2)	9–2
	para.7	10–42		Sch.3, para.23(5)	10–77
	para.9	10–42		para.23(7)	10–77, 11–1
	para.10	9–23		Sch.4	9–23
	para.11	9–23	2002	Community Care and Health (Scotland) Act (asp 5)	13–32
	para.17(22)	3–19			
	para.17(23)	3–19			
	para.26	11–1			
	para.26(3)	10–77			
	para.26(4)	11–87			

TABLE OF STATUTORY INSTRUMENTS

1730 Act of Sederunt Concerning Factors (February 13, 1730).................. 10–7
1972 Premium Savings Bonds Regulations (SI 1972/65)—
    reg.4(3)................. 6–27
    reg.10(2)............... 12–17
    National Savings Bank Regulations (SI 1972/764)—
    reg.7(4)................ 12–17
1983 Act of Sederunt (Ordinary Cause Rules, Sheriff Court) (SI 1983/747)—
    r.36.14..... 12–13, 12–14, 12–15
    rr.36.14-36.17........... 12–13
    r.36.15................. 12–14
    r.36.16................. 12–14
    r.36.17(2)......... 12–13, 12–15
    r.36.17(3)............... 12–15
    Chap.14........... 5–5, 11–24
1987 Income Support (General) Regulations (SI 1987/1967)....... 13–32, 13–35
    reg.38.................. 13–35
    reg.40.................. 13–34
    reg.46.................. 13–34
    reg.51.................. 13–33
    Sch.9, para.15........... 13–35
    Sch.9, para.15(4)......... 13–35
    Sch.9, para.36........... 13–35
    reg.51(2)(a).............. 13–34
    Social Security (Claims and Payments) Regulations (SI 1987/1968)............ 12–4
    reg.33.............. 12–5, 12–7
    reg.34................... 12–8
    reg.4A................... 12–9
    reg.35................... 12–10
    Sch.10................... 12–10
1990 Income Tax (Building Societies) (Dividends and Interest) Regulations (SI 1990/2231)... 12–17
    Income Tax (Deposit-Takers) (Interest Payments) Regulations (SI 1990/2232)............. 12–17
1991 Savings Certificates Regulations (SI 1991/1031)—
    reg.9(4)................ 12–17
    Act of Sederunt (Rules of the Court of Session Amendment No.8) (Discharge of Judicial Factors) (SI 1991/1915)..... 10–10
1992 Act of Sederunt (Judicial Factors Rules) (SI 1992/272).............. 10–10
1992 Income Tax (Building Societies) (Dividends and Interest) (Amendment) Regulations (SI 1992/2915)............. 12–17
    National Assistance (Assessment of Resources) Regulations (SI 1992/2997)............. 13–32
    reg.25................... 13–33
    Sch.3, para.10........... 13–35
    Sch.3, para.29........... 13–35
    Sch.3, para.31........... 13–35
    Income Tax (Deposit-Takers) (Interest Payments) (Amendment) Regulations (SI 1992/3234)... 12–17
1993 Act of Sederunt (Interest in Sheriff Court Decrees and Extracts) (SI 1993/769).............. 11–65
    Act of Sederunt (Sheriff Court Ordinary Cause Rules) (SI 1993/1956).... 12–13
1994 Act of Sederunt (Rules of the Court of Session) (SI 1994/1443)—
    r.14.2(i)......... 10–13, 14–27
    r.14.7(3)................ 10–13
1996 Qualification of Chief Social Work Officers (Scotland) Regulations (SI 1996/515)............ 5–35
    Disability Discrimination (Meaning of Disability) Regulations (SI 1996/1455)............... 1–42
    Act of Sederunt (RCSA No.3) (Miscellaneous) (SI 1996/1756).......... 14–27
    Act of Sederunt (Family Proceedings in the Sheriff Court) (SI 1996/2167)... 12–13
    Civil Legal Aid (Scotland) Regulations (SI 1996/2444)—
    reg.14A................. 3–30
    reg.14A(1)............... 3–30
    reg.14A(2)............... 3–30
    regs.14A(2)(a)-(g)......... 3–30
    reg.14A(2)(b)............. 3–30
    regs.14A(2)(h)-(k)......... 3–30
    regs.14A(2)(l)-(n)......... 3–30
1997 Civil Legal Aid (Scotland) Amendment Regulations (SI 1997/727)..... 3–30
1998 Civil Legal Aid (Scotland) Amendment Regulations (SI 1998/725)..... 3–30

1998	Individual Savings Account Regulations (SI 1998/1870)—	
	reg.13.	11–60
1999	Act of Sederunt (Summary Applications, Statutory Applications and Appeals etc. Rules) (SI 1999/929). .	10–46, 11–1, A2–09
	Chap.3, Pt XVI.	5–5
	r.3.16.1.	6–1
	r.3.16.2.	5–5
	r.3.16.3.	5–5
	r.3.16.4(1).	5–5
	r.3.16.4(1)(ea).	5–5
	r.3.16.4(1)(eb).	5–5
	r.3.16.4(1)(a).	5–5
	r.3.16.4(2).	5–5
	r.3.16.4(3).	5–5
	r.3.16.4(4).	5–5
	r.3.16.4(5).	5–5
	r.3.16.4(6).	10–48
	r.3.16.5(1).	5–9
	r.3.16.5(2).	5–9
	r.3.16.5(3).	5–9
	r.3.16.6.	5–5
	r.3.16.6(2).	5–5
	r.3.16.8(1).	5–5, 11–24
	r.3.16.8(1A).	5–5, 11–24
	r.3.16.8(2).	5–5
	r.3.16.8(3).	5–5
	r.3.16.8(4).	10–48
	r.3.16.9.	5–5
	r.3.16.10.	10–53
	r.3.16.11.	11–19
	r.3.16.13.	11–38
	Sch.4, para.4.	6–1
1999	Scotland Act 1998 (Consequential Modifications) (No.1) Order (SI 1999/1042).	3–30
2001	Individual Savings Account (Amendment) Regulations (SI 2001/908)—	
	reg.7(b).	11–60

TABLE OF SCOTTISH STATUTORY INSTRUMENTS

2000	European Communities (Lawyer's Practice) (Scotland) Regulations (SSI 2000/121)—	
	reg.2.	8–6
	Civil Legal Aid (Scotland) Amendment Regulations (SSI 2000/182).	3–30
2001	Adults with Incapacity (Public Guardian's Fees) (Scotland) Regulations (SSI 2001/75)	3–12, 5–23, 5–26, 8–1, 8–4, **A2–01**
	Adults with Incapacity (Certificates from Medical Practitioners) (Accounts and Funds) (Scotland) Regulations (SSI 2001/76).	8–1, 8–8, **A2–02**
	Adults with Incapacity (Supervision of Welfare Attorneys by Local Authorities) (Scotland) Regulations (SSI 2001/77).	5–34, 6–38, **A2–03**
	Adults with Incapacity (Countersignatories of Applications for Authority to Intromit) Regulations (SSI 2001/78).	8–1, 8–6, **A2–04**
	Adults with Incapacity Evidence in Relation to Dispensing with Intimation or Notification) (Scotland) Regulations (SSI 2001/79).	5–25, **A2–05**
	reg.2(3).	4–26
2001	Adults with Incapacity (Certificates in Relation to Powers of Attorney) (Scotland) Regulations (SSI 2001/80).	**A2–06**
	reg.2.	6–11
	reg.3.	6–11
	reg.4.	6–12
	Sch.1.	6–11
	Sch.2.	6–11
	Adults with Incapacity (Scotland) Act 2000 (Commencement No.1) Order (SSI 2001/81).	3–19, 6–13, 10–1, 11–60, **A2–07**
	Civil Legal Aid (Scotland) Amendment Regulations (SSI 2001/82).	3–30, **A2–08**
	Act of Sederunt (Summary Applications, Statutory Applications and Appeals etc. Rules) Amendment (Adults with Incapacity) (SSI 2001/142).	10–46, 11–1, **A2–09**
	para.3(2).	5–5
2002	Civil Legal Aid (Scotland) Amendment Regulations (SSI 2002/88).	3–30
	Adults with Incapacity (Supervision of Welfare Guardians etc. by Local Authorities) (Scotland) Regulations (SSI 2002/95).	5–34, 10–1, 10–66, 10–67, **A1–10**
	reg.2.	10–66
	reg.2(5).	10–66

2002 Adults with Incapacity (Reports in Relation to Guardianship and Intervention Orders) (Scotland) Regulations (SSI 2002/96). 10–1, 10–48, **A2–11**
    Sch.2. 10–49
    Sch.3. 10–49
    Sch.4. 10–49
    Sch.5. 10–49
    Sch.6. 10–49
    Sch.7. 10–49
    Sch.8. 10–49
    Sch.9. 10–49
    Sch.10. 10–49
Adults with Incapacity (Recall of Welfare Guardian's Powers) (Scotland) Regulations (SSI 2002/97). 10–1, 11–77, **A2–12**
Adults with Incapacity (Non-compliance with Decisions of Welfare Guardians) (Scotland) Regulations (SSI 2002/98). . . 10–1, 11–38, **A2–13**
    reg.2. 11–38
    reg.3. 11–38
    Sch.. 11–38
Adults with Incapacity (Public Guardian's Fees) (Scotland) Amendment Regulations (SSI 2002/131). 3–12, 5–23, 5–26
Act of Sederunt (Summary Applications, Statutory Applications and Appeals etc. Rules) Amendment (No.3) (Adults with Incapacity) (SSI 2002/146). . . . 3–19, 10–46, 11–1
Adults with Incapacity (Scotland) Act 2000 (Commencement No.1) (Amendment) Order (SSI 2002/172). 3–19
Adults with Incapacity (Scotland) Act 2000 (Commencement No.2) Order (SSI 2002/189). . . . 3–19, **A2–14**

2002 Adults with Incapacity (Ethics Committee) (Scotland) Regulations (SI 2002/190). . . . 14–66, **A2–15**
    reg.6. 14–66
Adults with Incapacity (Medical Treatment Certificates) (Scotland) Regulations (SSI 2002/208). . 3–12, 14–43, **A2–16**
Civil Legal Aid (Scotland) Amendment (No.2) Regulations (SSI 2002/254). . . . 3–30
Adults with Incapacity (Specified Medical Treatments) (Scotland) Regulations (SSI 2002/275) (Specified Treatment Regulations) (SSI 2002/275) 1–2, 3–12, 5–22, 6–23, 10–1, 10–13, 10–31, 14–1, 14–2, 14–19, 14–20, 14–33, 14–34, 14–35, 14–45, 14–48, 14–58, 14–59, 14–65, **A2–17**
    reg.2(1). 14–20
    reg.2(2). 14–20, 14–45
    reg.2(3). 14–48
    reg.3. 14–49
    reg.3(1)(b). 14–49
    reg.3(2). 14–49
    reg.4. . . . . 14–2, 14–51
    reg.4(2). 14–2
    reg.5. . . . . . . 12–23, 14–30, 14–35, 14–53
    reg.5(1). 14–35
    reg.5(2). 14–53
    reg.5(3). 7–10, 14–35, 14–47, 14–53
    reg.6. . . . . 14–2, 14–51
    reg.6(1). 14–49
    reg.7. . . . . 14–49, 14–51
    Sch.1. . . . . . 14–20, 14–35, 14–48
    Sch.1, Pt 1. . 4–19, 14–33, 14–49, 14–50, 14–52, 14–59
    Sch.1, Pt 2. . 14–50, 14–51, 14–52
    Sch.2. . . . . 14–19, 14–51
Adults with Incapacity (Specified Medical Treatments) (Scotland) Amendment Regulations (SSI 2002/302). . . . 3–12, 5–22, 10–1, 14–2, 14–48, 14–50, **A2–17**
    reg.3. 4–19

TABLE OF RULES

2001 Solicitors (Scotland) Accounts, Accountants Certificate, Professional Practice and Guarantee Fund Rules

r.8. 6–36
r.23. . . . . **6–36**
r.23(1). 6–36
r.23(2). 6–36
r.23(3). 6–36

ABBREVIATIONS AND DEFINITIONS

Statutes

the Act, Incapacity Act:	Adults with Incapacity (Scotland) Act 2000 (asp 4)
the 1968 Act:	(in Chapter 5) Social Work (Scotland) Act 1968 (c.49)
the 1978 Act:	(in Chapter 9) National Health Service (Scotland) Act 1978
the 1995 Act:	(in Chapters 10, 11 and 12) Criminal Procedure (Scotland) Act 1995 (c.46)
DDA:	Disability Discrimination Act 1995
MHSA:	Mental Health (Scotland) Act: where the context so indicates, either mental health legislation generally or the Mental Health (Scotland) Act 1984 (c.36), which if necessary is referred to more specifically as "MHSA 1984". "New MHSA" refers to the forthcoming legislation expected to follow upon the Mental Health (Scotland) Bill introduced in the Scottish Parliament on September 16, 2002
ROCSA:	Registration of Care (Scotland) Act 2001 (asp 8)

Regulations and Rules

The cumbersome titles of Regulations under the Act are, where appropriate, abbreviated in the text by omitting the Act's title, or the elements thereof. Some have been further abbreviated as follows:

the Reports Regulations:	The Adults with Incapacity (Reports in Relation to Guardianship and Intervention Orders) (Scotland) Regulations 2002 (SSI 2002/96)
the Specified Treatments Regulations:	The Adults with Incapacity (Specified Medical Treatments) (Scotland) Regulations 2002 (SSI 2002/275) as amended by the Adults with Incapacity (Specified Medical Treatments) (Scotland) Amendment Regulations 2002 (SSI 2002/302)
OCR:	Ordinary Cause Rules as contained in first Schedule to Sheriff Courts (Scotland) Act 1907 (7 Edw. 7 c.51) as substituted for causes commenced from January 1, 1994 by SI 1993/1956 as amended, regarding rules referred to, by SI 1996/2167
Rules:	The rules in the Act of Sederunt (Summary Applications, Statutory Applications and Appeals etc Rules) 1999 as amended by SSI 2001/142 and SSI 2002/146, see para.5–5 (except where in context "Rule" clearly applies to other rules, e.g. in para.6–36 and references to OCR (*q.v.*))

Codes of Practice

Local Authority Code: Code of Practice for Local Authorities Exercising Functions under the Act (effective from April 2, 2001, SE/2001/88, March 2001)

Part 2 Code: Code of Practice for Continuing and Welfare Attorneys (effective from April 2, 2001, SE/2001/90, March 2001)

Part 3 Code: Code of Practice for Persons Authorised under Part 3 to Access Funds of an Adult (effective from April 2, 2001, SE/2001/89, March 2001)

Part 5 Code: Code of Practice for Persons Authorised to Carry Out Medical Treatment or Research under Part 5 of the Act (effective from July 1, 2002, due for revision July 1, 2003, SE/2002/73, April 2002)

Part 6 Code: Code of Practice for Persons Authorised under Intervention Orders and Guardians (effective from April 1, 2002, SE/2002/65, March 2002)

Medical Practitioners

approved psychiatrist: a medical practitioner "approved . . . by a health board as having special experience in the diagnosis or treatment of mental disorder" (Mental Health (Scotland) Act 1984, s.20(1)(b))

doctor: any medical practitioner

See also the various definitions in para.14–2.

Other

adult: a person over 16 whose capacity is, or may be, or may at some time become, at least in some respects and in some degree impaired

affairs or welfare: property, financial affairs or personal welfare

the Alliance: the Alliance for the Promotion of the Incapable Adults Bill (later the Adults with Incapacity Bill)

appointees: attorneys, persons authorised under intervention orders, guardians, withdrawers, managers of authorised establishments, or such of them as may be referred to in the provision or context in question

combined powers: welfare powers (*q.v.*) and management powers (*q.v.*) in combination

CPA: continuing power of attorney

the Department: (in paras 12–4 to 12–10) the Department of Work and Pensions, formerly the Department of Social Security

DWP:	Department of Work and Pensions
ECHR:	European Convention on Human Rights, as set out in Schedule 1 to the Human Rights Act 1988 (c.42)
EPA:	enduring power of attorney (England only)
financial guardians, financial guardianship:	guardians and guardianship with powers in relation to property and financial affairs only
limited powers:	powers limited to particular matters, or to particular aspects of an adult's property, financial affairs or personal welfare
management:	acting, transacting and deciding in relation to property and financial affairs
management powers:	powers to act, transact and make decisions in management (*q.v.*) matters
personal decision-making:	acting and making decisions in matters of personal welfare, including the range of matters described in para.3–7
plenary powers:	welfare powers (*q.v.*) to act in all matters of personal decision-making (*q.v.*) and/or management powers (*q.v.*) to act in all management matters (*q.v.*)
relevant authority:	(in paras 11–76 to 11–78) the Public Guardian, Mental Welfare Commission or local authority, as the case may be
relevant matters:	(in Chapter 10) an adult's property, financial affairs or personal welfare
SCRC:	Scottish Commission for the Regulation of Care
SLC Discussion Paper:	Scottish Law Commission Discussion Paper No.94 *Mentally Disabled Adults: Legal Arrangements for Managing their Welfare and Finances,* September 1991
SLC draft Bill:	draft Incapable Adults (Scotland) Bill on pp.168 *et seq.* of the SLC Report (*q.v.*)
SLC Report:	Scottish Law Commission *Report on Incapable Adults* (Report No.151) published September 1995
SP OR:	Scottish Parliament Official Report
welfare guardians, welfare guardianship:	guardians and guardianship with powers in relation to personal welfare only
welfare powers:	powers to act and make decisions in matters of personal welfare, including the range of matters described in para.3–7
WPA:	welfare power of attorney

Note 1: Further definitions are given where appropriate in the text. See in particular paragraphs 3–1, 8–2, 9–2, 10–26, 10–46, 11–1, 13–4, 13–8 and 14–2.

Note 2: Cases (including overseas cases), statutes and statutory instruments are referred to by their various customary methods of citation.

CHAPTER 1

DISABILITIES, CAPACITY AND ASSESSMENT

"I think it hurts inside you, not to be independent"
(See Chapter 10, para.10–12, n.59)

Introduction

Adults are presumed to have legal capacity.[1] That presumption may be rebutted, because various disabilities and conditions may cause impairment of capacity. Legal incapacities imposed as a consequence of a special status, such as the status of prisoners or of bankrupts, are outside the scope of this book. **1–1**

Children's capacity and incapacities, or potential ranges of capacity, are defined by reference to age. The most significant statute in that regard is the Age of Legal Capacity (Scotland) Act 1991, and the most significant age is 16. A person who has attained that age has legal capacity "to enter into any transaction".[2] For the purposes of adult incapacity law, an "adult" is accordingly a person who has attained the age of 16 years. That is the definition adopted for the purposes of this book, and in the Adults with Incapacity (Scotland) Act 2000.[3] It is the age at which the régime of that Act commences.[4] **1–2**

Child law and adult incapacity law have traditionally shared concepts and terminology, but the analogies should be approached with caution, and are often false. In relation to children, the presumption of full capacity is set aside automatically by reference to age, but in relation to adults the presumption is not set aside in any equivalent way by reference to any medical diagnosis or psychological measurement.[5] Issues of capacity are specific to a particular adult, in particular **1–3**

---

[1] Bell, *Principles*, s.2103; Dickson, *Evidence*, para.114(1); McBryde, *The Law of Contract in Scotland* (2nd ed.) para.3–41; *Lindsay v Watson* (1843) 5 D. 1194; *AB v CB*, 1937 S.C. 408 per L.J.-C. Aitchison at 418; *Sabatini, Re* (1969) 114 S.J. 35.
[2] Age of Legal Capacity (Scotland) Act 1991, s.1(1)(b).
[3] s.1(6).
[4] But other ages may have relevance to the Act's régime. For example, a nearest relative other than a spouse must be aged at least 18, see para.5–38 *infra*; on provisions concerning 16 and 17-year olds in the Specified Treatments Regulations, see paras 14–49 and 14–51 *infra*. On an apparent gap in the Ordinary Cause Rules see para.12–13 *infra*. See para.13–17 *infra* for a provision under which minority ends at age 21.
[5] In *In re W (Enduring power of attorney)* [2001] 4 All E.R. 88; [2001] 2 W.L.R. 957, the Court of Appeal in England held that even where there was evidence that the grantor did not understand the nature and effect of an enduring power of attorney, the onus of proof remained upon those challenging its validity, and did not—as had been argued—transfer to an attorney who maintained that it was valid. Upon this *ratio*, evidence of illness or disability, however severe, would not of itself remove the presumptions of capacity and validity so as to reverse the onus of proof. That, it is suggested, would also be the proper approach in Scotland.

circumstances, for a particular purpose, and at a particular time. The concepts of the International Classification of Impairments, Disabilities and Handicaps[6] are as applicable to the legal environment as they are to physical and social surroundings. The Classification helpfully separates the concepts of:

impairment: any loss or abnormality of psychological, physiological or anatomical structure or function;

disability: any restriction or lack of ability to perform an activity;

handicap: a disadvantage that limits or prevents the fulfilment of a role that is normal for the individual.

The consequence of disease, injury or disorder may be an impairment, which produces a disability, and which in turn may result in a handicap. In physical terms, someone with arthritis has the *impairment* of limited range of joint movement, leading to *disabilities* in walking and climbing stairs, and in turn to the *handicap* of reduced ability to remain mobile in the environment. The handicap will be greater living alone on an upper floor of a tenement than if the same person lives in a bungalow with a car available and an able-bodied and supportive spouse who cares for the person, looks after the house and drives the car. The disadvantages and handicaps which a person suffers as a result of disability are thus a product of the interaction between disability and—in the widest sense—environment. This enabled Professor Stephen Hawking, disabled by motor-neurone disease, to write that with a supportive family and a cerebral career in theoretical physics "my disability has not been a serious handicap".[7]

1-4   Substituting *legal incapacity* for *handicap*, the same concepts and sequence apply in the legal environment. A disease, injury or disorder may cause an impairment, resulting in an intellectual disability which may (in particular circumstances, at a particular time and for a particular legal purpose) deprive the adult of legal capacity. Alternatively, an impairment may block communication to the extent that legal capacity is likewise affected.

Intellectual impairments and disabilities

1-5   Intellectual impairments have a range of different causes and are infinitely variable in the nature and degree of resulting disabilities, which in individual cases may or may not cause some degree of legal incapacity. The following brief descriptions of causes of intellectual impairments set a context for this legal text, and are not intended to be comprehensive or scientific.

1-6   *Learning disabilities*[8] are lifelong. They are characterised by (a) intellectual functioning which is significantly below average and (b) marked impairment in ability to adapt to the cultural demands of

---

[6] World Health Organisation, *The International Classification of Impairments, Disabilities and Handicaps—a manual relating to the consequences of disease*, Geneva 1980.

[7] Acknowledgements: *A Brief History of Time*. This quotation opens an article by E.M. Badley, "The Genesis of Handicap: Definition, Models of Disablement, and Role of External Factors" in *Disability and Rehabilitation*, 1995, Vol.17, no.2, 53–62.

[8] In Britain "learning disability" has generally replaced "mental handicap". Other synonyms include "retardation".

society. Both of these characteristics, not just one or the other, must be present before a person can be said to have a learning disability. Scottish Executive has defined learning disability as: "a significant, lifelong condition which has three facets: reduced ability to understand new or complex information or to learn new skills; reduced ability to cope independently; and a condition which started before adulthood (before the age of 18) with a lasting effect on the individual's development".[9] The age limit is unusually high, but the boundaries between different potential causes of incapacity are not generally of significance in incapacity law.[10] The Millan Committee recommended that autistic spectrum disorders be included within the definition of learning disability.[11] Learning disability is not an illness or disease. It may be caused by an illness such as meningitis, or associated with a genetic condition, such as Down's Syndrome. It may be caused by physical damage to the brain during pregnancy, during birth, or thereafter. There may be complex social and psychological causes. In many cases the specific cause is unknown. Common consequences of learning disability are poor concentration, poor short-term memory, learning difficulty, and difficulty in understanding complex or abstract ideas. There is great variation in degrees of intellectual disability, even among people with the same diagnosis. For example, people with Down's Syndrome range from those who are profoundly handicapped to those owning their own homes, perhaps with a job and a mortgage, and with leisure and social activities to which their disabilities are irrelevant. Learning disabilities cannot be "cured", but with suitable education and training and a helpful environment, capabilities can continue to develop well into adulthood and handicaps (including any legal incapacities) reduced. Approximately 20,000 people in Scotland currently have severe learning disabilities.[12]

Brain injuries may be sustained at any age. They may have effects **1–7** similar to those of some learning disabilities, and in such cases are included in some definitions of learning disability: the Scottish Executive definition of learning disability quoted in the preceding paragraph would categorise arbitrarily as to whether an injury with such effects is sustained before or after the victim's 18th birthday. The Millan Committee recommended that acquired brain injury be included in the definition of mental illness[13]: again, such questions of categorisation are not generally of significance in incapacity law. Each year approximately 6,000 Scots sustain serious head injuries, 1,500 with lasting consequences.

Mental illness is a general term covering a variety of disturbances **1–8** affecting emotional, social and cognitive functioning and behaviour. Understanding and communication may be distorted (rather than

---

[9] *The same as you? A review of services for people with learning disabilities*, Scottish Executive, 2000, App.3.

[10] Under the Incapacity Act, different provisions apply if incapacity results from inability to communicate because of physical disability rather than "mental disorder" as defined in s.87(1).

[11] *Millan Report*, recommendation 4.9.

[12] Figures quoted for this and other disabilities are based on estimates made by the Alliance (see Definitions, page xli), and referred to during the parliamentary passage of the Incapacity Act.

[13] *Millan Report*, recommendation 4.5

deficient, as in learning disability) and behaviour may be misdirected (rather than inept, as in learning disability). Emotional reactions may in various ways and degrees be inappropriate. A broad definition of mental illness would include all of the following categories: (a) psychotic conditions, such as schizophrenia and bi-polar disorder (manic depression); (b) disorders with organic causes, such as dementias and degenerative brain disorders; (c) psycho-neurotic disorders, such as anxiety states and obsessional disorders; and (d) disorders of conduct and personality.[14] The Millan Committee proposed that: "Mental illness should be taken to include psychotic conditions, and non-psychotic mental illnesses such as anorexia nervosa, obsessive compulsive disorders, and disorders of mood. It should also include dementia and acquired brain injury with associated mental symptoms".[15] A survey report published by National Statistics[16] contained the following helpful descriptions:

> "*Neurotic disorders*, or depression and anxiety disorders, are characterised by a variety of symptoms such as fatigue and sleep problems, forgetfulness and concentration difficulties, irritability, worry, panic, hopelessness, and obsessions and compulsions, which are present to such a degree that they cause problems with daily activities and distress; and
>
> "*Psychotic disorders*, such as schizophrenia and manic depression, are disorders that produce disturbances in thinking and perception that are severe enough to distort the person's perception of the world and the relationship of events within it."

1–9 *Personality disorder* was described in the National Statistics report[17] in the following terms: "An individual has a personality disorder when aspects of their character and behavioural tendencies are developed to such an extreme that they result in considerable personal and social disruption. Personality disorder tends to appear in adolescence and persist into adulthood and leads to distress and impairment." There is debate about the status of personality disorder. It is included as a mental illness in the definition of "mental disorder" in the Incapacity Act (s.87(1)), maintaining consistency with the definition in s.1(2) of the Mental Health (Scotland) Act 1984 as amended by the Mental Health (Public Safety and Appeals) (Scotland) Act 1999.[18] The Millan Committee carefully considered aspects of personality disorder which remain problematical, and wrote: "There are various sub-categories of personality disorder. Some, such as borderline personality disorder, are close to accepted forms of mental illness. These may involve bizarre and self-destructive behaviour and significant distress to the sufferer. Others, particularly anti-social personality disorder, have been criticised as being diagnosed largely

---

[14] On the status of personality disorder, see para.1–9 *infra*.
[15] *Millan Report*, recommendation 4.5.
[16] *Psychiatric morbidity among adults living in private households*, 2000, the Stationery Office, December 2001: the quotations used here are taken from the summary *Mental Health among Adults* issued by National Statistics on December 18, 2001.
[17] *op.cit.*
[18] asp 1, s.3(1)(a).

through anti-social behaviour, and so could be seen as simply describing violent or dangerous people, rather than mental disorder."[19]

There are some 30,000 psychiatric admissions to Scottish hospitals **1–10** each year. National Statistics reported[20] that "About one in six adults aged 16 to 74 years living in private households in Great Britain have a neurotic disorder (or common mental disorder), such as depression, anxiety or phobias".

Conditions associated with ageing are of particular significance in **1–11** relation to issues of legal capacity. There are currently over 60,000 people in Scotland with moderate to severe dementia, and the number is projected to rise substantially as the population ages. The main characteristics of dementia are memory loss, personality changes, impaired ability to reason, poor personal care and disorientation. Often, the level of intellectual capability fluctuates. At time of writing dementia cannot be cured, but modern treatments can slow down the progress of the condition for some sufferers. This, coupled with a trend to early diagnosis, means that issues will frequently arise as to appropriate steps to be taken in anticipation of deteriorating capacity, while the person still has capacity to take those steps. Learning disabilities and existing mental illness may be exacerbated with old age. With some forms of learning disability, including Down's Syndrome, there is an increased risk of dementia, and of early onset.

Over 10,000 Scots annually sustain *strokes*. The effects of a stroke **1–12** may include communication difficulties of such severity that capacity is impaired, at least for a time. Severe communication difficulties, which may impair capacity, can also be caused by *multiple sensory handicap* (for example when both hearing and sight are seriously impaired) and by *serious physical illness*.

Temporary, acute and induced conditions may cause complete inca- **1–13** pacity, of short or long duration, as in coma or unconsciousness. Severe pain or shock, or treatment with opiates to control severe pain, or other forms of medical treatment, may impair capacity. Misuse of alcohol or drugs may also do so.[21]

Communication difficulties

Sensory impairment and/or *inability to communicate*, even in the **1–14** absence of any mental disorder, may impair capacity to the extent that they present a barrier, which cannot be overcome by any means,[22] to the receipt of information needed to make a decision, or the communication of a response to information which has been received. Multiple sensory impairment may present such a barrier, but in the absence of any intellectual impairment may be overcome to a remarkable degree even where the multiple sensory impairment is severe.

---

[19] *Millan Report*, para.77.
[20] *op.cit.*
[21] On intoxication in relation to contractual capacity, see McBryde, *op.cit.*, paras 3–48 *et seq.* and the cases there cited, including *Taylor v Provan* (1864) 2 M. 1226; *Pollock v Burns* (1875) 2 R. 497; and *Laing v Taylor*, 1978 S.L.T. (Sh. Ct) 59.
[22] On the importance, under the Incapacity Act, of overcoming communication difficulties, see paras 4–17 and 4–25 *infra*.

Illnesses, injuries or their treatment may temporarily impair the ability to receive information or to communicate.

Effects on legal capacity

1–15 As has already been stressed, diseases, injuries and disorders such as those described above are infinitely variable in the nature, degree and duration of the disabilities which they cause. Not all of them will necessarily cause an impairment of legal capacity, and none by reason of their diagnosis alone reverse the onus upon anyone seeking to establish incapacity.[23] It has nevertheless been estimated that at any one time some 100,000 adults in Scotland do have significant impairments of legal capacity.[24] Some legal incapacities are temporary, some lifelong, and some variable or progressive. Variations may sometimes be huge within short periods. Legal incapacities may reflect strengths and weaknesses in different skills, such as long-term memory, short-term memory, arithmetical competence, various areas of conceptual and cognitive functioning, communication abilities, and so on. For the same individual, such variations and diversities may affect particular legal capacities for particular purposes.

Minimising impairment of legal capacity

1–16 It is a fundamental principle of good practice, enshrined in statute in the Incapacity Act, that formal legal intervention should be the minimum necessary.[25] One consequence of that principle is that all reasonable measures should be taken to enhance capacity and to remove obstructions to the exercise of capacity.[26] Some potential causes of legal incapacity can be remedied altogether by appropriate treatment, or the person may in time recover. In other cases, while the underlying condition cannot be cured, appropriate treatment may restore full or substantial legal capacity. Some potential causes of legal incapacity which are irremediable may present in combination with elements which can be remedied, and the remedying of which will substantially enhance effective capacity. For example, an underlying condition may have resulted in self-neglect, leading to dehydration and inadequate diet and care, causing some temporary loss of capacity which can be substantially, and often quickly, remedied by appropriate treatment and care. Irremediable dementia or learning disability may be combined with depression or other disorders which can be addressed so as substantially to enhance effective capacity.

1–17 People who are vulnerable because of disabilities may be at a loss if brusquely presented with questions and asked for decisions. They may be able to formulate valid decisions if someone takes time to explain and to help them understand, analyse and decide. An apparent lack of capacity may be caused by communication difficulties which can be overcome by formulating questions requiring "yes/no" answers, or by using interpretative help.

---

[23] *In re W, supra.*
[24] See n.12 *supra* as to the source of this and other figures quoted in this chapter.
[25] Incapacity Act, ss.1(2) and (3).
[26] On "the duty to enhance mental capacity", see para.12:7 of *Assessment of Mental Capacity*, The Law Society and BMA, 1995, giving full and helpful guidance as to how this may be achieved.

People with a disability may have been "institutionalised". That is **1–18** to say, regardless of the physical setting in which they live, they may have been the passive recipients of care, conditioned to meekly following the wishes of others (or what they believe to be the wishes of others), and with unused or under-developed potential to formulate, express and assert their own views and decisions. With appropriate facilitation, they may be able to develop significantly enhanced effective capacity.

Distortions

People may try to mask or deny their own disabilities. For example, **1–19** an elderly person may maintain a charming and delightful manner, and may skilfully turn every conversation from the particular to the general, all concealing desperate efforts to mask, even to themselves, the true degree of their forgetfulness and disability. People with some forms of mental illness may totally reject the possibility that they are mentally unwell. Their denial ("lack of insight") may be firmly rooted in a belief in persecution. Even to suggest a mental problem may be seen as part of a conspiracy to persecute. People may on the contrary exaggerate their own disabilities. They may do so, for example, to try to evade criminal or civil responsibility, or in order to obtain perceived advantages. There is also a risk that people other than the sufferer may understate or overstate the degree of disability, either innocently or for their own ends. Motives may include over-protectiveness on the one hand, or unrealistic zeal to emphasise capabilities rather than incapacities on the other, or even both in incongruous combination.

Legal significance

Intellectual disabilities only have legal significance if legal capacity is **1–20** affected by them, or if they cause some special treatment under some rule of law to be applied, or if they at least cause such special treatment to become competent. In the broadest sense, such special treatment may comprise *special mechanisms* to make decisions, to safeguard welfare or assets, to carry out legally valid acts, or to enter legally valid transactions; *special exceptions* from civil liability, from criminal punishment, or from the consequences of disadvantageous transactions; *special protections* from financial exploitation, or from unfair discrimination, or from personal deprivation, exploitation or abuse; and *special benefits*, including financial benefits and benefits in kind. Where intellectual disabilities have potential legal significance, the contexts in which lawyers may require to address them include the following broad categories of issues:

- whether purported acts or transactions are voidable through *undue influence* or *facility and circumvention*;

- whether purported acts or transactions are void through lack of capacity, or proposed acts or transactions would be void (*validity*);

- what is the effect of loss of relevant capacity upon a contract already entered but not yet fully performed, a role already undertaken, or a relationship already established (*supervening incapacity*);

- whether there should be exemption from, or mitigation of, the civil and/or criminal consequences of wrongful conduct (*modified liability*);

- what *special benefits*, as defined above, are available;

- what *special protections*, as defined above, are available;

- what *anticipatory measures* may be taken in relation to possible future loss of capacity;

- what *responsive measures* may be taken in consequence of impairment of capacity which already exists;

- what measures may be taken by third parties to provide for existing or future incapacity (*third party measures*).

The Incapacity Act is concerned principally with responsive and anticipatory measures. These and third party measures are the main subject-matter of this book. While these categorisations help to make the subject manageable, not all of the boundaries are clearcut. In particular, there is overlap between responsive measures and third party measures. All of the categories described above are expanded upon in the following paragraphs. Those of particular relevance to the main subject-matter of this book are thereafter addressed in more detail.

Facility and circumvention; undue influence

1–21 An intellectual disability producing vulnerability which is exploited to an adult's detriment, or an intellectual disability combined with undue influence, may result in a purported act or transaction being set aside. The adult had sufficient capacity (otherwise the act or transaction would in any event have been void) but the undue influence renders it voidable. The topics of facility and circumvention, and of undue influence, are addressed in paras 1–36 to 1–40 below, as is their relevance to issues of capacity.

Validity

1–22 At a specific point in time an adult may or may not have had adequate capacity for a purported act or transaction. If the adult lacked adequate capacity for that particular act or transaction, it will be void. With a few exceptions such as purchase of "necessaries", the position in law will be the same as if the purported act or transaction had not taken place. Such issues may arise retrospectively, and sometimes—for example as to validity of a purported Will—posthumously. They may also arise prospectively, as to whether a proposed act or transaction would be valid. Further on validity, see paras 1–28 *et seq.* below.

Supervening incapacity

In some cases, the supervening inability of one party to a contract to perform his part of it, where he has not yet fully done so, has been held on the principle of mutuality to relieve the other party of his obligation to perform.[27] However, the implement of anticipatory measures or application of responsive measures may reactivate the parties' obligations. Supervening incapacity may *ipso facto* terminate a role or relationship, as where the articles of association of a company so provide in relation to directorships; or may warrant procedure to terminate, such as an application for termination of a partnership under the Partnership Act 1890, ss.32 and 35(a), or removal of a trustee under the Trusts (Scotland) Act 1921, s.23[28]; or may neither terminate the role or relationship, nor of itself render it terminable, as in the case of marriage.

1–23

Modified liability, special benefits and special protections

Modified liability and special benefits, as defined above, are largely outwith the scope of this book, but are referred to where they touch upon its principal subject-matter. Provisions for modified liability include the alternative disposals in criminal proceedings described in Chapters 10,[29] 11[30] and 12.[31] Some special benefits are referred to in Chapter 13, where—in the context of trusts—some special taxation provisions are considered in paras 13–19 *et seq.*, and various state and other benefits are considered in relation to means-testing in paras 13–31 *et seq.* Particular arrangements for the management of certain benefits are described in Chapter 12, paras 12–4 *et seq.* Special protections are a broad category: all of the measures and techniques described in this book have protective functions and include particular protective features directed to the various vulnerabilities which may result from intellectual disabilities. Other special protections, including those in criminal law,[32] are outwith the scope of this book, but aspects of the Disability Discrimination Act 1995 are relevant and are described briefly in paras 1–41 *et seq.* below.

1–24

Anticipatory measures

A person may wish to make future provision in relation to increasing intellectual disability in consequence of a condition which has already been diagnosed; or a person with no such condition or disability may nevertheless wish to make provision for the possibility of their own future incapacity, at some as yet unknown time and from some as yet unknown cause. On the basis that at any one time legally

1–25

---

[27] See *Eadie v MacBean's Curator Bonis* (1885) 12 R. 660, at 665 *per* L.P. Inglis.
[28] Though it must generally be shown that the impact of the incapacity upon the particular requirements and circumstances justifies the remedy—see *e.g. Eadie v MacBean's Curator Bonis*, where termination of a partnership was refused because the partner who had lost capacity had only contributed capital and had a curator bonis who wished the partnership to continue.
[29] Intervention orders under the Criminal Procedure (Scotland) Act 1995, see paras 10–77 and 10–78 *infra*.
[30] Guardianship under the 1995 Act, see paras 11–84 *et seq. infra*.
[31] Other disposals under the 1995 Act, see para.12–32 *infra*.
[32] *e.g.* under MHSA 1984, ss.106 and 107.

significant incapacity affects at least 100,000 Scots,[33] and that issues of legal incapacity are likely to affect every family sooner or later, it is increasingly considered as much best practice to make such provision, for example by granting a power of attorney, as it is to make a Will. Because such measures, like Wills, cannot be replicated when they are intended to take effect, particular care should be taken to establish capacity, if appropriate to enhance capacity, and to eliminate undue influence and the possibility that it may be suspected or alleged.

Responsive measures

1–26 An existing intellectual disability may require to be considered prospectively in relation either to a specific contemplated act or transaction, or to anticipated ongoing requirements for decisions to be validly made and communicated by or on behalf of the adult. It may be possible to ameliorate the intellectual disability sufficiently to restore capacity for at least some of the contemplated acts, transactions and decisions. It may be sensible (and possible) to postpone, to allow time for possible amelioration and improvement. Potential causes of actual or alleged undue influences can and should be removed. Where capacity is lacking and there is no reasonable prospect of it being restored (or being restored sufficiently soon), it may be necessary to put in place a legal technique to allow one or more decisions to be taken, or acts or transactions carried out, on behalf of the adult, rather than by the adult. A significant difference between child law and adult incapacity law is that for adults there is no equivalent of the parental role under which someone has (by reason of relationship or otherwise) automatic authority to act on behalf of those who lack capacity to act for themselves. In all cases, some specific procedure to confer such authority requires to be followed, or some legal technique[34] activated, before anyone can act for the incapacitated adult. It is frequently assumed, incorrectly, that a spouse or other relative can—by reason of close relationship—give valid medical consent; or that parents can—by reason of parentage, and without further formality—make valid decisions about personal welfare or other matters on behalf of an adult son or daughter with serious intellectual disabilities.

Third party measures

1–27 A donor, testator or other third party may make special provision—such as establishing a trust—either in consequence of an existing intellectual disability, or as a precaution in relation either to deterioration of an existing condition or the possibility of intellectual disability where none at present exists.

Tests of capacity

1–28 Legal criteria for establishing capacity are relevant to questions of past validity, prospective validity, the appropriateness of responsive measures, and the activation of anticipatory measures. The criteria for

---

[33] See n.12 *supra*.
[34] Such as *negotiorum gestio*—see paras 12–18 *et seq. infra*.

capacity are specific to the particular purpose, so that a person may at the same time lack capacity for some purposes but have it for others.[35] Thus some people deemed incapable under pre-Act law of managing their affairs or giving instructions for their management, and to whom curators bonis have been appointed, have nevertheless made valid Wills or have validly married. Examples of the diversity of purposes for which tests of legal capacity are relevant include: granting a power of attorney, making a Will,[36] revoking a Will,[37] instructing a solicitor, entering a particular contract,[38] operating a bank account, claiming and handling social security benefits, managing assets and affairs generally, making a gift,[39] litigating, giving evidence, voting, marrying,[40] consenting to or refusing health-care treatment,[41] consenting to research or innovative treatment,[42] and deciding personal matters. Capacity in all of these examples depends upon context, and may subdivide. Capacity to manage assets and affairs depends upon their nature and extent, and the decisions necessary—or likely to be necessary—to manage them, so that management capacity may subdivide into issues specific to different matters and decisions. Capacity to decide personal matters sub-divides into *inter alia* the various matters listed in para.3–7 below.

The Incapacity Act contains definitions of incapable and incapacity[43] for the purposes (only) of those responsive and anticipatory measures addressed in the Act. While the definition of incapacity is particularised in relation to the individual provisions of the Act, the definition itself is in generalised terms and (in respect that it sets out alternatives, including "incapable of acting" and "incapable of making decisions", without further definition) virtually circular.

1–29

This book does not attempt to define the criteria for capacity for each individual matter to which a test of capacity might be relevant. In generalised terms, capacity will normally depend upon some or all of the following factors:

1–30

(a) understanding of the nature of the decision, act or transaction;

(b) where a series of linked decisions is required, understanding of each and of their inter-relationship;

(c) where there are choices, understanding of those choices and ability to evaluate them;

---

[35] See McBryde, *op.cit.*, paras 3–45 and 3–46 and authorities there cited; and see paras 4–23 *et seq. infra* on the definition of "incapable" in the Incapacity Act.
[36] *Graham v Mauchen's Exrx*, 1995 G.W.D. 15–874; *Boyle v Boyle's Exr*, 1999 G.W.D. 12–584.
[37] *Sabatini, Re*.
[38] See McBryde, *op.cit.*, paras 3–38 *et seq.*
[39] *Beaney (deceased), Re* [1978] 1 W.L.R. 770.
[40] See *Park v Park*, 1914 S.L.T. 88; *Calder v Calder*, 1942 S.N. 40; *Durham v Durham* (1885) 10 P.D. 80; *Bennett v Bennett* [1969] 1 W.L.R. 430.
[41] See Ch.14.
[42] See Ch.14.
[43] s.1(6)—see paras 4–23 *et seq. infra*.

(d) where choices have been presented, ability to add further relevant options which have not been presented;

(e) knowledge of relevant circumstances, and understanding of their relevance;

(f) ability to retain the foregoing long enough to make a decision (or coherent series of decisions);

(g) where a decision has been requested, ability to recognise when such a decision may not be necessary (or immediately necessary), and ability to decline to make it (or to defer it) in such circumstances;

(h) ability actually to make, and commit to, a decision;

(i) ability to communicate the decision;

(j) ability to retain memory of the decision for an appropriate period.[44]

Not all of these elements will be relevant in all cases and situations. Inability in relation to (d) is unlikely to be held to invalidate a decision where other relevant criteria are met and the choices have been fairly and fully presented, but would almost certainly invalidate the decision where one or more potentially relevant options have not been presented. Similar considerations may apply to (g). In the Incapacity Act,[45] (j) is presented in absolute terms ("incapable of retaining the memory of decisions") as one of the alternative causes of incapacity for the purposes of the Act, yet for other purposes it may be irrelevant. For example, a testator may satisfy all of the other criteria to the extent that they are relevant, may repeatedly come to the same decision as to testamentary disposition, but may suffer from severe short-term memory loss so that—each time—the testator does not remember having already made precisely the same decision. There is no authority for suggesting that a Will made in such circumstances would be invalid. The position could be quite different if decisions made were inconsistent, or if (c), (d) or (e) were not met because the short-term memory loss had obliterated significant recent changes.

1–31 Whether acknowledged or not, there are proper aspects of public policy in balancing the elements of empowerment and respect for autonomy and self-determination, which in marginal cases would favour validity, against elements of protection which might favour invalidity. The courts have shown themselves reluctant (in marginal cases) to declare a Will invalid,[46] or (at least in the absence of indications of exploitation) to declare someone incapable of marrying, and would be likely to be similarly reluctant to hold that someone who chose to do so lacked capacity to instruct a solicitor. They might

---

[44] For suggested elements relevant to decision-making in health-care matters see para.14–10 *infra*.
[45] s.1(6).
[46] See *McDougal v McDougal's Trs*, 1931 S.C. 102 in relation to facility and circumvention, and paras 1–38 *et seq. infra* in relation to undue influence.

more readily be persuaded that there was lack of sufficient capacity in relation to, for example, transactions involving significant obligations, or exposure to financial risk, or unfavourable imbalance of benefit (in the broadest sense).

Assessment of capacity

Capacity is a question of law. It is a question of law, to be decided if necessary by a court, whether someone had sufficient capacity for an act or transaction to be valid,[47] or has enough capacity for a proposed one; whether they require special arrangements to make a decision or manage their affairs; whether special protective or restrictive measures should apply to them; whether they should be excused civil liability; and so on. However, the determination of such matters requires evidence, and the principal evidence will normally be medical evidence, or sometimes psychological or other evidence, though the courts may reach a conclusion inconsistent with the medical evidence, and have done so in cases such as *Rennie v Steven*[48] and *Brogan v Rennie*.[49] **1–32**

Partnership, understanding and effective communication between lawyer and assessor (doctor, psychologist or other) is essential to achieving accurate and relevant assessment which leads to an appropriate legal outcome. Although lawyers are not professionally qualified in the medical and psychological aspects of assessment of capacity, nevertheless it is an essential part of their professional competence to identify situations where capacity may be an issue, and where further enquiry or medical or psychological evidence may be necessary; to be able to explain fully and clearly to the assessor the factual circumstances in which need for assessment arises, the purpose of the assessment, and the relevant legal criteria; to give guidance as to the form of the assessor's report or certificate and the matters which should be addressed in it; and thereafter to understand an assessment expressed in terms relevant to the assessor's professional expertise, and to translate that assessment into an appropriate legal outcome. Excellent practical guidance on assessment of capacity by doctors has been published in England and is equally helpful in Scotland.[50] **1–33**

Criticisms by the present author a decade ago of inadequate assessment and certification remain relevant.[51] Doctors still complain that lawyers ask them to provide certificates in terms which they consider to be medically meaningless. "It seems that doctors give too much deference to lawyers, and lawyers give too much deference to doctors. Doctors either sign, or decline to sign, the certificate submitted by the lawyers, without challenging form and content. Lawyers accept whatever the doctor's certificate contains, without further **1–34**

---

[47] *Richmond v Richmond* (1914) 111 L.T. 273.
[48] 1991 G.W.D. 26–1559.
[49] 1991 G.W.D. 31–1885. See also the English case of *Birkin v Wing* (1890) 63 L.T. 80, where evidence of a solicitor supporting capacity was preferred to a doctor's evidence suggesting incapacity.
[50] Chapter 12 of *Assessment of Mental Capacity*, The Law Society and BMA, 1995: on legal aspects, only English law is described, and the legal content is of limited assistance in Scotland.
[51] See Ward, *The Power to Act* (1990), pp.98–101 and the criticisms in *Fraser v Paterson*, 1987 S.L.T. 562 of the certificates in that case.

enquiry, provided that it will enable them to obtain the outcome which they have been instructed to achieve."[52]

1-35 Assessors for their part, as matters of professional duty to the patient assessed and (when the certificate is to be put in evidence) of duty to the court, require to ensure that they understand and take account of the context and purpose of the assessment which they have been requested to carry out; to enter dialogue with the instructor when they believe that they should address questions other than, or in addition to, those which have initially been put; while taking due account of requirements as to the form of the certificate and the matters covered in it, to be robust in ensuring that the certificate fully and accurately states their professional opinion and that they have no unexpressed reservations; and to ensure that their certificate is worded so as to be fully and accurately understood by lawyers and laymen reading it in isolation from their own or other expert guidance and explanation. It is often helpful for the assessor to submit a draft of the proposed certificate to the instructing lawyer to ensure that relevant issues have been addressed, and that the certificate is clear and contains sufficient explanation. Relevant elements are demanded by the various prescribed forms of certificate under the Incapacity Act. These should be contrasted with the brief certificates hitherto frequently submitted with curatory petitions, giving no more information than the opinion that the person is "of unsound mind and incapable of managing her own affairs or giving instructions for their management".[53] Such brief and uninformative certification is unlikely to be acceptable for any purpose under the Incapacity Act.

Facility and circumvention; undue influence

1-36 As indicated in para.1-21 above, intellectual disability may be a relevant element in a finding that an act or transaction should be set aside on grounds of facility and circumvention, or on grounds of undue influence. As McBryde[54] points out: "The issues of circumvention and facility assume the presence of capacity".[55] The same applies where an issue of undue influence arises. McBryde concludes, surely correctly, that in both cases the act or transaction in question is voidable, not void,[56] with the consequence that a deed may only be reduced on such grounds if *restitutio in integrum* is possible.[57] These topics nevertheless remain relevant to a consideration of modern incapacity law, because of the particularity of the concept of incapacity emphasised above. Where an adult has been the victim of facility and

---

[52] *The Power to Act*, p.98.
[53] For circumstances in which such certification was severely criticised, see the Opinion of Lord Jauncey in *Fraser v Paterson*, above.
[54] *The Law of Contract in Scotland* (2nd ed.) paras 16-15 *et seq.*, citing *inter alia Spring v Martin's Trs*, 1910 S.C. 1087 (in which earlier authorities are reviewed); *Gibson's Exr v Anderson*, 1925 S.C. 774 at 786, *per* Lord Blackburn; *Bremner v Bremner*, 1939 S.L.T. 448 at 449, *per* Lord Russell; *Fraser v Irvine's Exr*, 1924 S.L.T. 114. In *op.cit.* Ch.16, McBryde provides a full account of both doctrines, not restricted to his context of contracts.
[55] But in *Boyle v Boyle's Exr*, 1999 G.W.D. 12-584, a will was reduced on grounds of both incapacity and undue influence.
[56] *The Law of Contract in Scotland* (2nd ed.) paras 16-26, citing *Gall v Bird* (1855) 17 D. 1027, and 16-40.
[57] *ibid.* para.16-47, citing *Forbes v Knox*, 1957 S.L.T. 102; 1957 S.C. 325.

circumvention, or of undue influence, and where the adult's vulnerability was caused or contributed to by intellectual disability, then a finding that the act or transaction should be set aside on such grounds presupposes capacity for the purpose of carrying out the act or entering the transaction, but may at the same time be tantamount to a finding that the adult lacked the capacity to resist the circumvention or undue influence. Incapacity of the latter type may justify responsive measures, as is explicitly recognised by the Incapacity Act: authority to intromit with funds, management by an establishment, and appointment of a guardian are all competent not only where adults are incapable of making relevant decisions, but also where they are incapable of safeguarding their interests in relation to relevant matters.[58] The requirements for a finding of facility and circumvention, or of undue influence, are summarised in the next two paragraphs respectively.

Facility and circumvention

Three elements must be present.[59] Provided that each is present in some degree, the court proceeds to assess the whole picture, so that in one case one of the elements might be dominant, while in another that same element might be relatively minor, and so on.[60] Firstly, there must be facility, rendering the adult liable to be intimidated, misled or imposed upon, and significantly impairing the adult's ability to resist such tactics. As will be clear from the discussion in the preceding paragraph, as regards validity the law draws a clear line between facility and incapacity. Secondly, someone must have taken unfair advantage of the facility by means such as "solicitation, pressure, importunity, even in some cases, suggestion"[61]; and must thus have caused or induced the act or transaction: there must have been circumvention. Thirdly, the resulting act or transaction must have been to the detriment of the adult: there must have been lesion. It is the detriment to the adult which is relevant, rather than the advantage secured by another party. However, in the case of an onerous contract or transaction, the benefit must have accrued to the person guilty of the circumvention,[62] but that is not necessary in the case of a gratuitous act or transaction.[63]

1–37

Undue influence

The criteria for reduction on grounds of undue influence differ from those for reduction on grounds of facility and circumvention, and may vary between a contract and a unilateral act or deed such as a Will.

1–38

---

[58] Incapacity Act, ss.25(1), 37(2) and 58(1)(a).
[59] *Morrison v Maclean's Trs* (1862) 24 D. 625; *Liston v Cowan* (1865) 3 M. 1041; *McDougal v McDougal's Trs*, 1931 S.C. 102.
[60] *Mackay v Campbell*, 1967 S.C. (HL) 53 at 61–62 (indicating that where there is clear proof of facility, circumvention may be inferred); *Munro v Strain* (1874) 1 R. 1039; *Bremner v Bremner*, 1939 S.L.T. 448.
[61] Lord Kyllachy in *Parnie v MacLean*, unreported, quoted by Lord Blackburn in *Gibson's Exr v Anderson*, 1925 S.C. 774 at 788, and in turn by McBryde *op.cit.* para.16–19.
[62] *Smith v Bank of Scotland*, 1997 S.C. (HL) 111, at 114 *per* Lord Jauncey, at 117 *per* Lord Clyde.
[63] *Clunie v Stirling* (1854) 17 D. 15; *Taylor v Tweedie* (1865) 3 M. 928; *Wheelans v Wheelans*, 1986 S.L.T. 164 (defender's wife held to have circumvented).

Firstly, there need not be facility, but there must be proof of a special relationship between the parties, described by Lord Guthrie as "a fiduciary or quasi-fiduciary relationship",[64] enabling one to exert a dominant influence over the other. Whether such a relationship exists depends on the facts of each case. The list of potential such relationships is not closed, and the authorities should be seen as providing examples of what was, or was not, such a relationship in the circumstances of each case.[65] In some cases, particular relationships and/or types of contract may create presumptions about the risk of undue influence, and/or about duties to ensure that independent advice is given.[66] Secondly, influence must have been exercised, and it must have been "undue". It would appear that in relation to Wills the influence must have amounted to coercion or fraud,[67] but that in relation to contracts there need not be proof of "corrupt motive, or deceit or fraudulent conduct",[68] and the influence requires to have been exercised by the other party to the contract, or on that party's behalf, in the case of an onerous contract.[69] Thirdly, as with facility and circumvention, there must have been detriment to the party influenced.[70]

1–39 That facility is not a necessary element may be seen as distancing the doctrine of undue influence further from incapacity law than facility and circumvention. Nevertheless, "facility" may be an element, and where an intellectual disability has impaired an adult's capacity to resist undue influence, then as suggested in para.1–36 above responsive measures may be appropriate. In addition, certifiers providing certificates to be incorporated in powers of attorney in terms of ss.15(3)(c) and 16(3)(c) of the Incapacity Act are specifically required to certify that they have no reason to believe that the grantor is acting under undue influence. As aspects of the criteria for a finding of undue influence seem to vary depending upon the nature of the deed or document, and as there is a dearth of authority in relation to the particular case of powers of attorney, certifiers would be prudent to apply the broader test of "undue influence" applicable to contracts generally. On the other hand, there may be cases where the proposed attorney has a special relationship with the grantor and has urged the grantor to grant the power of attorney. Strong influence must be distinguished from undue influence. "There is no case in Scotland where a contract has been held voidable on the ground of undue influence, where the influence has been exerted in genuine devotion to the interests of the person influenced".[71] Where the certifier is the solicitor taking instructions to prepare the power of attorney, the influencer has withdrawn at point of first contact between grantor and solicitor, and there is no evidence of persisting effects of influence

---

[64] *Forbes v Forbes' Trs*, 1957 S.C. 325 at 333, citing *Gloag on Contract* (2nd ed.) p.526.
[65] See *Honeyman's Executors v Sharp*, 1978 S.C. 223 and the other cases reviewed by McBryde *op.cit.*, paras 16–34 *et seq*.
[66] *Smith v Bank of Scotland*, 1997 S.C. (HL) 111.
[67] *Weir v Grace* (1899) 2 F. (HL) 30; *Forbes v Forbes' Trs* at 331. On reduction of Wills on grounds of undue influence, see also *Brogan v Rennie*, 1991 G.W.D. 31–1885 (reduction refused) and *Boyle v Boyle's Exr* (see above).
[68] McBryde *op.cit.*, para.16–39, citing *Gray v Binny* (1879) 7 R. 332; see also para.16–33.
[69] *Forbes v Forbes' Trs* at 333; *Smith v Bank of Scotland* at 114 and 117.
[70] *Forbes v Forbes' Trs* at 333.
[71] *Forbes v Forbes' Trs* at 333.

Personal welfare matters

Authorities and discussion as to both doctrines have generally addressed financial and management matters, rather than matters of personal welfare, but there is no reason in principle why the doctrines should not apply to both categories, and s.16(3)(c) of the Incapacity Act, referred to in the preceding paragraph, proceeds on the basis that a welfare power of attorney could be rendered voidable on grounds of undue influence or vitiated by "any other factor". One can envisage that one or other doctrine might be invoked in relation to welfare decisions by an adult, such as a decision to reside in a particular place (where the decision suited a relative alleged to have used circumvention or exerted undue influence, rather than being in the best interests of the adult), or to accept a particular package of care and treatment (where this suited the authority responsible for providing care and treatment, rather than the best interests of the adult, and circumvention or undue influence is similarly alleged). Such circumstances might warrant reversal of the decision in question, and might also warrant appointment of a guardian with welfare powers on grounds of the adult's incapacity in relation to acting to safeguard or promote his own personal welfare.[72]

1-40

Disability discrimination

The purpose of the Disability Discrimination Act 1995 ("DDA"), and regulations and guidance under it, is to protect people with disabilities from discrimination in relation to employment, the provision of goods, facilities and services, and the disposal or management of premises. Briefly described here are some of the principal provisions relevant to the main subject-matter of this book. Several of the relevant provisions of DDA are in broad terms and provide for more detailed provision to be contained in regulations. The Disability Rights Commission was established under the Disability Rights Commission Act 1999 (c.17) with functions including *inter alia* working towards elimination of discrimination against disabled persons, promoting the equalisation of opportunities for disabled persons, promoting good practice, and providing advice or information (or arranging for or supporting such provision).[73]

1-41

Disabled person

The definitions of "disability" and "disabled person" for the purposes of DDA include mental as well as physical impairments, if (in both cases) the impairment has a substantial and long-term adverse effect on the person's ability to carry out normal day-to-day activities,[74] if it qualifies in terms of the more detailed provisions of DDA, Schedule 1, and if it qualifies in terms of the further provisions

1-42

---

[72] See Incapacity Act, s.58(1)(a) and para.1–36 *supra*.
[73] Disability Rights Commission Act 1999, s.2. See also other provisions of s.2.
[74] DDA, s.1.

of regulations made under DDA, Schedule 1.[75] A mental impairment for these purposes includes an impairment resulting from or consisting of a mental illness "only if the illness is a clinically well-recognised illness".[76] The effect of an impairment is long-term if it has lasted or is likely to last for at least 12 months, or is likely to last for the rest of the person's life.[77] An impairment affects the ability to carry out normal day-to-day activities *inter alia* if it affects speech, hearing or eyesight; memory or ability to concentrate, learn or understand; or perception of the risk of physical danger.[78] Substantial adverse effects are deemed to continue if they have ceased but are likely to recur,[79] or if they are prevented only by measures such as medical treatment or use of aids,[80] and they are deemed to exist if the person has a progressive condition which has (or has had) an effect on the ability to carry out normal day-to-day activities which has not yet been substantial but is likely to become so.[81] In certain circumstances, persons registered as disabled in accordance with s.6 of the Disabled Persons (Employment) Act 1944 are deemed to be disabled for DDA purposes. A person who has had a disability, as defined, is protected by DDA in accordance with the provisions of DDA, s.2 and Schedule 2.

Provision of goods, facilities and services

1–43 Particularly relevant in the context of this book are the provisions of DDA concerning provision of goods, facilities and services.[82] The broad effects of those provisions include making it unlawful for a provider[83] to discriminate against a disabled person who has an intellectual disability but is nevertheless capable of the transaction in question, or in a discriminatory way to refuse to reasonably assist in facilitating or operating appropriate anticipatory or responsive measures where the disabled person is not himself or herself capable of the transaction in question. Under DDA, s.19(1), it is unlawful for the provider to discriminate (a) by refusing to provide (or deliberately not providing) services which he provides or is prepared to provide to members of the public, or (b) making it impossible or unreasonably difficult to make use of a service through failure in the duty to make reasonable adjustments, or (c) in the standard or manner of provision of service, or (d) in the terms on which the service is provided. Excepted from these provisions are various education services, transport services and other prescribed services.[84] "Discriminate" is defined

---

[75] See the Disability Discrimination (Meaning of Disability) Regulations 1996 (SI 1996/1455).
[76] DDA, Sch.1, para.1(1).
[77] DDA, Sch.1, para.2.
[78] DDA, Sch.1, para.4(1)(f), (g) and (h).
[79] DDA, Sch.1, para.2(2).
[80] DDA, Sch.1, para.6.
[81] DDA, Sch.1, para.8.
[82] DDA, ss.19, 20 and 21.
[83] Termed "the provider of services" in DDA, which expression includes the provision of any goods or facilities (DDA, s.19(2)(a)). DDA applies to provision in the United Kingdom (DDA, s.19(2)(b)).
[84] DDA, s.19(5). Education is dealt with in Part IV of DDA, and public transport in Part V. On education, see amendments to DDA in the Special Educational Needs and Disability Act 2001 (c.10), and see also the Standards in Scotland's Schools etc. (Scotland) Act 2000 (asp 6).

for these purposes as treating a disabled person less favourably for a reason which relates to his disability than the provider would treat others to whom that reason does not apply, if the provider cannot show that the treatment in question is justified,[85] or if the provider fails in the duty to make reasonable adjustments and cannot show that the failure is justified.[86] These provisions are specific to the disability, so that it would be unlawful to discriminate unjustifiably against people with mental disabilities compared with those with physical disabilities, or against a person with one particular mental disability compared with people with other kinds of mental disability.

Less favourable treatment is only justified if in the provider's opinion it falls within specified categories of justification, and if the opinion is reasonable in all the circumstances.[87] Among the specified categories of justification is that "in any case, the disabled person is incapable of entering into an enforceable agreement, or of giving an informed consent, and for that reason the treatment is reasonable in that case".[88] For the purposes of this provision, the incapacity must be specific to the particular transaction. It would not be reasonable to found on this ground where the incapacity does not prevent the provision in question because appropriate anticipatory or responsive measures are in place under which any necessary contracts can be entered or consents given on behalf of the disabled person; nor where the provider insists upon entering a contract or obtaining a consent not essential for the particular provision, or in terms more complex than necessary for it, and the disabled person is capable of anything reasonably required to secure the provision. The specified categories of justification also include that the treatment is necessary to avoid endangering the health or safety of the disabled person or others, or that but for it the service could not be provided to other members of the public, or that it is necessary to enable the provision of the service to the disabled person or to others, or that it reflects the greater cost to the provider of provision to the disabled person.[89]

1–44

Reasonable adjustments

The duty to make reasonable adjustments arises where a provider has a practice, policy or procedure which makes it impossible or unreasonably difficult for disabled persons to make use of a service which the provider provides, or is prepared to provide, to other members of the public. The provider's duty is to take such steps as are reasonable, in all the circumstances, to change that practice, policy or procedure so that it no longer has that effect.[90] It is also the duty of the provider to take such steps as are reasonable, in all the circumstances, to provide any auxiliary aid or service to enable or facilitate the use by a disabled person of services which the provider provides, or is prepared to provide, to the public.[91] The examples of provision of

1–45

---

[85] DDA, s.20(1).
[86] DDA, s.20(2).
[87] DDA, s.20(3).
[88] DDA, s.20(4)(b).
[89] DDA, s.20(4)—see also the ensuing sub-sections of DDA, s.20.
[90] DDA, s.21(1).
[91] DDA, s.21(4).

information on audio tape or of a sign-language interpreter are given, but the duty is not limited to those examples, though in case of doubt the court may consider the extent to which what is said to be required is *ejusdem generis*. In relation to the above duties, the provider is not required to take steps which would fundamentally alter the nature of the service in question or the nature of the provider's trade, profession or business,[92] or to incur expense above the prescribed maximum.[93] Here, as elsewhere, various matters may be prescribed by regulation. A breach of the duty to make reasonable adjustments is not civilly actionable as a breach of duty.[94] Within the parameters of DDA, s.21, the duty to make reasonable adjustments includes duties to accommodate intellectual disabilities and to facilitate the establishment and operation of appropriate anticipatory and responsive measures, in relation to people who qualify as disabled persons in terms of DDA.

Other provisions

1–46 Points identified above in relation to provision of goods, facilities and services are relevant also to the application to matters of intellectual disability of other areas of provision under DDA and regulations under that Act. The principal other areas are employment,[95] disposing of and managing premises,[96] education[97] and public transport.[98] In general terms, across DDA provision, discrimination includes discrimination against people with intellectual disabilities compared with those with physical disabilities and the general public, and discrimination against people with particular intellectual disabilities compared with those with other disabilities and the general public; for less favourable treatment to be justifiable, it must be justified not by reference to the existence of the intellectual disability but by its specific relevance to the matter in question; impairment of capacity to contract or consent is irrelevant unless capacity is impaired in relation to something essential to the particular matter in question, and is irrelevant unless reasonable adjustment to those requirements will not bring them within the person's capacity; it will be unreasonable to found on impairment of capacity where this could reasonably be overcome by facilitating or operating appropriate anticipatory or responsive measures; and it is likely to be unlawful to fail to make reasonable adjustments to allow appropriate anticipatory or responsive measures to be put in place and/or operated.

European Convention on Human Rights

1–47 Most of the provisions of ECHR are incorporated into Scots law by both the Human Rights Act 1998[99] and by the Scotland Act 1998.[1] While ECHR applies to everyone, including people with intellectual

---

[92] DDA, s.21(6).
[93] DDA, s.21(7).
[94] DDA, s.21(10).
[95] DDA, Part II.
[96] DDA, ss.22–28.
[97] DDA, Part IV. See n.84 to para.1–43 *supra*.
[98] DDA, Part V.
[99] c.42. See Sch.1 for relevant provisions of ECHR.
[1] c.46, s.57(2), see also s.100.

disabilities, some provisions are particularly relevant to the subject-matter of this book. Most notable is the provision of ECHR Article 6 that in the determination of his civil rights and obligations, everyone is entitled to a fair and public hearing within a reasonable time by an independent and impartial tribunal established by law. That right is unqualified except for strictly defined limitations on the requirement for judgements to be given publicly. The right to act for oneself and make one's own decisions in matters of one's own personal welfare, or about one's own property and financial affairs, is a fundamental civil right. A determination that one is incapable of acting and deciding, and that someone else should take over, is a matter which one is entitled to have determined by a fair and (except for the qualifications) public hearing by an independent and impartial tribunal established by law. As is pointed out at various places in this book, the imposition of such a determination *de facto*, or by a court or tribunal without a fair hearing, breaches Article 6.

Also of particular relevance are the rights, subject to qualifications, to respect for private and family life, home and correspondence[2] and to the peaceable enjoyment of possessions.[3] Under Article 5, the right to security of person is unqualified. The right to liberty is subject to qualifications, including "the lawful detention . . . of persons of unsound mind",[4] anyone deprived of liberty by arrest or detention being entitled to take proceedings by which the lawfulness of his detention shall be decided speedily by a court, and his release ordered if the detention is not lawful.[5] Article 14 provides that: "The enjoyment of the rights and freedoms set forth in this Convention shall be secured without discrimination on any grounds such as sex, race, colour, language, religion, political or other opinion, national or social origin, association with a national minority, property, birth or other status". Upon a reasonable construction, and given that disability discrimination is generally addressed by legislatures in broadly similar ways to discrimination on some or all of the grounds specified, it would appear reasonable to construe disability discrimination as *ejusdem generis* with the forms of discrimination specified, and thus included within "discrimination on any ground" and "other status". **1–48**

---

[2] ECHR, Art.8. See para.5–23 *infra*.
[3] ECHR, First Protocol, Art.1.
[4] ECHR, Art.5.1(e).
[5] ECHR, Art.5.4

CHAPTER 2

PROFESSIONAL AND PRACTICAL ISSUES

"It is indeed a paradox that in former times those who were often by reason of their handicap in most need of the law's protection were sometimes the last to receive it. Happily times change and both those who suffer from a disability and, as importantly, those who care for them are now more conscious that the law is available for their use and benefit"

(The Rt Hon. Lord Mackay of Clashfern, Foreword to "Mental Handicap and the Law", 1992)

Introduction

This chapter is directed specifically to practising solicitors, but contains points likely to be of interest to other readers. 2–1

In any society, the needs and vulnerabilities of citizens with disabilities and impairments of capacity present the most direct challenge to the professionalism of lawyers and the effectiveness of legal systems in meeting legitimate needs, safeguarding legitimate interests, and protecting and promoting fundamental rights and freedoms of all citizens.[1] The practising solicitor's two areas of professional responsibility, to individual clients and to society, are reflected in two questions. Who is my client? What is my professional duty to an unrepresented person who has, or may have, impaired capacity? In specific terms, these questions are addressed later. Several duties are relevant under both the first area of responsibilities to clients and the second as to people who are not clients. 2–2

Identification of potential incapacity

If potential incapacity is not identified and addressed, injustice may result. A solicitor will often be the person best placed to identify potential incapacity and to take or suggest appropriate measures, and in general terms will usually have a duty to do so: a direct duty when the person is a client, or is someone about whom others have consulted the solicitor; and also as part of the solicitor's general duty to society and to serve the interests of justice where a case of potential incapacity comes to the solicitor's notice within the scope of the solicitor's professional work and no-one else appears to be responding appropriately. In some cases the solicitor may be able only to advise and suggest; but should not neglect to do so. In others the solicitor may well be "a person claiming an interest"[2] or even "a person 2–3

---

[1] Internationally, this is one of the "litmus tests" of legal systems and of protection of human rights, especially in relation to emerging and re-emerging democracies. See Ward, *A New View* (1993).
[2] See Incapacity Act, ss.3(3), 14, 20(1), 53(1), 57(1), 69, 71(1), 73(1) and 74(1).

having an interest,[3] and thus able to proceed more proactively. The first step will often be to instruct assessment,[4] or to seek authority to do so: it will normally be the solicitor's duty to obtain an appropriate professional assessment where capacity is in doubt.[5]

2–4 There is a wide range of possible starting-points for the solicitor. A client may seem to be losing capacity, or to be mentally disordered, or may even himself express worries to such effect. The solicitor may have cause to believe that capacity may be doubtful or may be challenged. Family or others may express concerns that the person is losing capacity, or is mentally disordered; or family may assert that the person has capacity, but the solicitor may doubt it. MHSA procedures may have been proposed or taken. The solicitor may have been contacted by a doctor or social worker. Someone may have questioned the validity of a transaction or Will, or an intended act such as marriage. The suitability of the person's choice of accommodation (including, for example, a desire to leave a hospital or a nursing home) may be questioned. The person's ability to give medical consent, or to manage assets and finances, may be in doubt.

2–5 Situations to which solicitors should be particularly alert are where apparently vulnerable people appear to be passively under the domination of those holding substantial concentration of power and *de facto* exercising it, whether they be carers, family, or hospital or social work authorities. Such situations are particular cause for concern where no legal procedure has been followed to confer the powers which are *de facto* exercised and/or there has been no competent and independent (and, in the case of authorities, external) assessment of capacity. Such exercise of power, without lawful authority, in relation to adults with impaired capacity to decide matters for themselves and implement such decisions, is *prima facie* an infringement of the adults' fundamental rights and freedoms. It may well be the duty of the solicitor to point this out, notwithstanding that those exercising such *de facto* powers may genuinely believe that what they are doing accords with the adult's wishes and best interests—they themselves may be too close to the situation to recognise the extent to which they are influenced by their own needs and convenience. Those who claim always to respect the adult's wishes may nevertheless set the agenda of choices which are presented, and when. Internal assessments may be inconsistent in relation to capacity and consistent in preserving concentrations of power.[6] The underlying point in all such cases is that where an adult's life is controlled by others, and others make decisions *de facto* and without lawful authority, then *prima facie* the adult's rights and freedoms are infringed: see para.1–47 above. Whether responsive measures should be taken may raise questions of balance (as to whether they are necessary and would represent a lesser restriction of the adult's freedom[7]) and proportionality.

---

[3] Incapacity Act, ss.37(7)(a), 50 and 52: see para.14–59 *infra*.
[4] See paras 1–32 to 1–35 *supra*.
[5] 1995 J.L.S.S. 1074.
[6] An example in the author's experience is where hospital authorities certified incapacity in relation to management of funds, and in consequence assumed such management themselves, but denied any degree of incapacity in relation to decisions about personal health and welfare, where incapacity might have resulted in introduction of an independent element into such decision-making.
[7] Incapacity Act, ss.1(2) and (3).

Non-discrimination and communication

The provisions of the Disability Discrimination Act 1995 of course 2–6
apply to solicitors, in the provision of their services, in relation to
people with intellectual disabilities: relevant provisions include those
described in paras 1–41 *et seq.* above. Moreover, solicitors are under an
express professional obligation "to observe not only the letter but also
the spirit of the anti-discrimination legislation in dealings with clients,
employees and others".[8] A solicitor is entitled to accept or decline
instructions, and indeed a solicitor should decline to act if he believes
that he lacks the expertise or resources for the matter in question.[9]
However, a solicitor should not decline to act on grounds of a
prospective client's disability, physical or intellectual, itself. A solicitor
is also obliged to make reasonable adaptations to accommodate the
client's disability. In the case of intellectual and communication
disabilities, this includes in particular an obligation to take reasonable
steps to facilitate full exercise of such capacity as the person may have,
and to facilitate communication. An initial impression of incapacity, or
of greater incapacity than in fact exists, may be given by speech
impediment, hearing loss or nervousness. Simple and obvious steps
may include seeing the person in a location and circumstances where
the person is most likely to feel comfortable, confident and relaxed;
taking time, speaking in clear and simple language, and checking that
the person can hear; avoiding unnecessary distractions; avoiding
unnecessary use of abstract language and relating necessary abstract
concepts to the person's own experience; and (when there are
communication difficulties) eliciting information by a series of questions formulated to require only simple affirmatives or negatives, by
word or gesture, in reply.

Clients have the right to be accompanied by a relative or friend if 2–7
they wish. This may assist considerably, but may also raise questions
of confidentiality, inhibitedness or undue influence. One solution can
be for the companion to withdraw part-way through the interview:
companions will often volunteer to do so, and reluctance might
indicate cause for concern.

Similar issues arise when the companion provides interpretative 2–8
help. When the interpreter is a companion, it may be necessary to
establish clearly that the interpreter is acting as such and not, in some
degree, conveying the interpreter's own views. Use of a professional
interpreter may raise issues of cost: for example, Scottish Legal Aid
Board may require to be satisfied as to the necessity of such
expenditure.

Principles

In advising and acting for or in relation to people with intellectual 2–9
disabilities, solicitors should themselves follow the principles
described in paras 1–11 and 1–12. On the principle that disadvantages
and handicaps, including legal incapacities, are a product of disabilities, which may be irremediable, and environment (which almost
always can be influenced and improved) solicitors have a general

---

[8] Code of Conduct, para.11.
[9] Code of Conduct, para.5(b).

professional obligation to help people to minimise the consequences of their disabilities; to act for themselves and make their own decisions as far as possible; and to be protected from injustice or avoidable disadvantage. Where responsive measures are contemplated, whether or not within the scope of the Incapacity Act, solicitors should follow the principles of good practice (now formulated in s.1 of the Act in relation to its provisions) that any intervention by way of responsive measures or use of powers thereunder should (put simply) produce a benefit for the adult; represent the minimum necessary restriction of the adult's freedom; take account of present and past wishes of the adult; where reasonable and practicable take account of views of family, carers and others as may be appropriate; and encourage the development and use of skills wherever possible.[10]

Responsive measures inappropriate

2–10   From time to time solicitors are asked to assist in pursuing some form of legal intervention when it is not in fact appropriate, or in taking action which presumes a greater degree of intellectual disability than is in fact the case. Sometimes what people considered to have some degree of intellectual disability in fact require is help, training and encouragement to make their own decisions; or help in communication; or provision of other forms of help, or of services. Sometimes appropriate care and medical help can achieve a virtual transformation, often speedily, in people who have become caught in a downward spiral of self-neglect caused by and causing confusion and disorientation. Solicitors should never assume without good reason that they cannot obtain appropriate instructions direct from people, and assist them to make their own decisions, rather than initiating procedures to have decisions made for them, or deciding that nothing can be done about the situation. Competent instructions may include an element of delegation. An adult lacking the interest and energy, or perhaps even the competence, to manage all of the details of finances and affairs may nevertheless be able competently to select and appoint an attorney to do so.[11]

Who is my client?

2–11   In matters of incapacity, it is fundamental that there be clarity as to who is the solicitor's client with whom the solicitor-client relationship exists and to whom the solicitor's duties under that relationship are owed. There are three possibilities.

Adult is client

2–12   Firstly, the client has or may have an intellectual disability. The solicitor's obligation is of course to act in the client's legitimate best interests. The solicitor should consider the client's capacity to give instructions, and if necessary should have that capacity assessed. The

---

[10] See Ch.4.
[11] See para.6–19 *infra* and the case of *Re K, re F* [1988] 1 All E.R. 358 there cited.

solicitor should help the client to understand, communicate and give competent instructions. Once the solicitor-client relationship has been established, the obligation to act in the client's best interests does not simply disappear, if developing mental disability makes it progressively more difficult to take instructions. The solicitor must at the very least institute appropriate procedure for capacity to be assessed and any necessary steps taken to safeguard the client's position. Moreover, solicitors are under an explicit professional obligation not unreasonably to withdraw from acting.[12] It would be a breach of that obligation simply to abandon clients to their own fate in circumstances of deteriorating capacity. While there may not be a responsibility to do large amounts of work without prospect of remuneration, there is a clear responsibility to ensure that the client's interests are safeguarded, even if (for example) the solicitor does no more than report the circumstances to the local social work department, by reference to their responsibilities under ss.53(3) and 57(2) of the Incapacity Act. The contractual relationship between agent and client is not ended by incapacity, at least where the incapacity is temporary.[13]

Where it is proposed that an adult take anticipatory measures, then regardless of who made first contact with the solicitor, that adult—and only that adult—is the client. The Law Society of Scotland has found it necessary to give explicit warnings that in such situations solicitors must take instructions direct from the client and if necessary take steps to establish capacity, failure to do these things having resulted in findings of professional misconduct.[14]

2–13

Adult is not client

The second situation is where the client is someone other than the person who has (or may have) a mental disability. Such clients may be relatives, friends, people involved in professional or voluntary contact, service providers, and so on. They may for various reasons, and in good or bad faith, assert a greater or lesser degree of mental disability than is in fact the case.[15] The solicitor must balance his duty to his clients with his wider professional duty.[16] Should the mentally disabled person be separately represented, or independently safeguarded? It is reasonable to suggest that it would only be ethically acceptable for the solicitor to proceed without such measures, even where there is no specific requirement for them, if the solicitor is satisfied that the proposed course of action is reasonable and proper, and in the best interests of the mentally disabled person. It may well be impossible to decide such matters without medical or other assessment.

2–14

---

[12] Code of Conduct, paras 5(a) (last paragraph) and 5(f).
[13] *Wink v Mortimer* (1849) 11 D. 995.
[14] See 1995 J.L.S.S. 284 and 1996 J.L.S.S. 158.
[15] See para.1.14.
[16] In the Code of Conduct this is referred to in general terms, including (in the Introduction) by reference to duties to the public and to safeguarding human rights, and (in para.2) to the obligation to serve clients' best interests being qualified *inter alia* by the obligation to adhere to the principles of good professional conduct.

Hybrid situations

2–15 Thirdly, there are hybrid situations where the solicitor is consulted by a third party who requests the solicitor to safeguard the best interests of a person who has or may have an intellectual disability. If the third party has a role recognised by law in relation to the person (such as attorney, guardian, appointee under an intervention order, social security appointee, withdrawer, safeguarder or other) then the third party will often be the solicitor's client, albeit in the relevant capacity rather than as an individual, so that the second category above will apply, though the adult's interests and the obligations of the person to the adult will normally be a central consideration in the advice given. However, the third party may have power to instruct the solicitor to act for the person in the matter in question, and may do so. An attorney, an appointee under an intervention order, or a guardian may have express powers to do so.[17] A guardian has automatic power (subject to any express prohibition, condition or restriction by the sheriff) to act as an adult's legal representative in relation to any matter within the scope of the guardianship order,[18] and this power is understood to include power to instruct a solicitor. In such cases the adult is the client to whom the solicitor's professional obligations are owed, even although the third party provides the source of the solicitor's instructions and will normally (in the relevant capacity) be responsible for the solicitor's remuneration. In such a situation the solicitor should continuously monitor that he is both discharging his professional responsibilities to the adult and acting with (and within) the third party's instructions: unresolvable inconsistency between those two requirements would necessitate withdrawal from acting, but it is suggested that in an extreme situation the solicitor's obligations to the adult would include a responsibility to ensure that the adult's interests are safeguarded, in the same way as described in para.2–12 above, even in the face of objection by the third party. A variant of this situation is where the third party instructs the solicitor to provide independent advice in the adult's interests where the third party has, or could be said to have, personal interest or potential conflict of interest[19]: the principles described above also apply to this situation.

2–16 Where the third party is not acting in a role such as is described in the preceding paragraph, the first requirement is to ascertain whether the person can give instructions, and whether the person's best interests will be adequately safeguarded by acting on the person's own instructions. If so, it is then necessary to ascertain whether the person wishes to consult a solicitor, and to consult the same solicitor. It is almost always best to act on the person's instructions, if possible, and in this case the first category—the adult as client—applies, the role of the third party having simply been to make the introduction. Otherwise, it is necessary to advise the third party about what steps can or should be taken. The third party thus becomes the client, for the purposes of the advice given, and the second category applies.

---

[17] The Code of Conduct, para.3 refers to "recognised agents authorised to give instructions on behalf of the client; for example, persons authorised by a power of attorney...".
[18] Incapacity Act, s.64(3). See para.10–42 *infra*.
[19] See para.4–37 *infra*.

Hard cases

In all cases, the adult in question either is or is not the solicitor's **2–17** client. The type of "hybrid situation" described in para.2–16 above can exist only long enough for that to be established, one way or the other. If the adult lacks sufficient capacity validly to instruct the solicitor in the matter in question, the solicitor cannot act upon purported instructions. That is to state the obvious, but can produce hard situations when the solicitor may be under pressure to act improperly. Intestacy would cause injustice, a power of attorney would save great inconvenience, and so on; and in each case it is urged that the desired outcome is undoubtedly what the person "would have wanted". In this as in every other situation, the solicitor's absolute obligation is neither to commit nor countenance fraud or anything akin to fraud. The solicitor should instead identify and advise legitimate ways to achieve an appropriate outcome, which the Incapacity Act is designed to facilitate. See para.10–33 *et seq.* below as to the almost unlimited potential scope of intervention orders (and suggested circumstances in which it might be appropriate for an intervention order to authorise execution of a Will); guardians may be granted the specific powers which might otherwise have been considered appropriate for an attorney; and in all interventions under the Act it is not only appropriate but mandatory to take account of the adult's "present and past wishes and feelings" where ascertainable.[20]

In considering whether a client, or potential client, is competent to **2–18** give instructions in a particular matter, the solicitor should give careful consideration to each of the elements described in para.1–23 above which may be relevant, and should be careful not to omit any which might be relevant. For example, a client otherwise meeting all relevant criteria might nevertheless be unable actually to commit to a decision. There can be a fine line between advising and deciding. There may be a duty to point out the options and it may even be reasonable, especially if asked, to express an opinion—with reasons—as to which might be best, but the solicitor should be careful not to be manoeuvred into actually making the decision where a client's indecisiveness indicates an incapacity to commit to a decision.

Anticipatory measures—taking instructions

Anticipatory measures, such as granting powers of attorney, like **2–19** Wills require capacity at time of granting but are expected to operate when the grantor can no longer add, amend or clarify. Particular care is accordingly demanded of the solicitor in taking instructions and in reflecting those instructions in the document which is prepared. The need thus to state the obvious is demonstrated by the frequent incidence of problems caused by inadequately drawn powers of attorney. It appears that in some cases practice has not yet responded to the 1990 reforms[21] or subsequent developments,[22] and requires

---

[20] s.1(4)(a).

[21] Under the Law Reform (Miscellaneous Provisions) (Scotland) Act 1990, s.71, powers of attorney granted on or after January 1, 1991 automatically remained in force in the event of subsequent incapacity of the grantor, unless the power explicitly provided otherwise. Section 71 is repealed by the Incapacity Act and superseded by Part 2 of that Act for powers of attorney granted on or after April 2, 2001.

[22] See *e.g.* discussion of powers to make gifts and to take tax-planning measures in para.6–31 *infra*.

urgently to be updated. It seems unlikely that large numbers of adults should have granted powers of attorney containing extensive management powers but should deliberately have omitted to confer power to deal with pensions and social security benefits, or that spouses simultaneously granting powers of attorney—and perhaps simultaneously executing Wills—should have deliberately chosen to omit any powers or directions about claiming or discharging legal rights entitlements, or that so few grantors should have deliberately chosen to omit provisions regarding making gifts, taking tax-planning or similar measures, or providing for substitute attorneys. In relation to all anticipatory measures, it is imperative that full and careful instructions be taken. Pressure to minimise time spent, and thus costs, should be firmly resisted if that would result in provision of an inadequate service.

Gifts

2–20 The use of gifts is identified as a possible anticipatory measure in paras 3–9 and 7–4. A solicitor should never accept without careful enquiry instructions from a client—particularly a frail or elderly client—who wishes to make a gift of significant value. Frequently, the underlying purpose may be one which could be better achieved in some other way, or which would not in fact be achieved by the gift; or there might be assumptions and implied conditions which at the very least must be made explicit; or consequences and potential consequences may not have been addressed. It is not unknown for people to wish to give away assets because managing them has become too bothersome and burdensome: it may be better to grant a power of attorney, or to create a trust. The client may have made assumptions about means-testing or taxation advantages which are ill-founded, so that proceeding with the gift will deprive the client of the asset, fail to achieve the desired advantage, and perhaps create disadvantages which would not otherwise have arisen. There may be various unspoken assumptions. There may be an assumption that the donee will continue to provide care, help and support. That may be a very good reason for a legacy, which can be revoked if circumstances change; the difference between that and an irrevocable gift *inter vivos* must be spelled out. The intended arrangement may be akin to a trust, but quite apart from questions of the trustworthiness of the donee, it must be made very clear that separate patrimonies only exist where a trust is explicitly created. Except with a trust (in the legal sense) intentions can be defeated by the donee's financial or marital difficulties, by the unexpected death of the donee, and so on. Moreover, the donee's personal circumstances, and thus priorities, may change—not necessarily in ways which reflect any discredit upon the character of the donee. The donor may risk creating taxation or means-testing disadvantages in relation to the donee.

CHAPTER 3

THE INCAPACITY ACT—INTRODUCTION AND BACKGROUND

"In recent years there has been . . . a general trend towards developing the full individual potential of the mentally handicapped, enhancing their human dignity, integrating them into the community, giving them as normal and independent a lifestyle as possible . . . Against this background the law is the laggard. As it relates to the ordinary everyday lives of the mentally handicapped and their families, the law has stood still for generations, and it does not cope adequately with the modern situation."
("Scots Law and the Mentally Handicapped" (1984), p.108)

"We are in the early stages of a quiet revolution. The law shows signs of evolving, as never before, towards a responsiveness to the needs of people with mental handicaps. Exciting developments have occurred, yet at the same time there is far greater awareness of the inadequacies and backwardness of existing provision for mentally handicapped people in our law. A few bright lights perhaps emphasise the blackness of the rest of the picture, but it is this awareness which is generating a great groundswell of demand for wider-reaching improvements."
("The Power to Act" (1990), p.1)

"The law we have inherited looks like an archaeological site with an assortment of buildings from various eras in various states of disrepair, in various degrees unsuitable for modern living, totally unco-ordinated in layout and unstandardised in design, with many complete gaps, and dodgy areas where one can tread only with uncertainty and trepidation. But here in Scotland that is all that we have to live in, so people make the best of it, patching up here and there, building on an occasional new bit, but often suffering inconvenience or disadvantage, coming to grief, getting left out in the cold, or simply getting lost in the labyrinth.
"Increasingly in other jurisdictions the site has been cleared and a new structure erected, designed to meet modern needs in ways which accord with modern circumstances, perceptions and values. The best of these new structures are designed to be effective, efficient, accessible and user-friendly; clearly laid out and based on consistent application of clear and important basic principles.
"In Scotland over the last decade or more we have collectively looked at our own needs and experience, and at the best features of modern systems elsewhere, and have achieved a wide range of consensus as to what is required here."
(The author, speaking at seminar January 21, 1998, organised by the Alliance for the Promotion of the Incapable Adults Bill)

"An Act of the Scottish Parliament to make provision as to the property, financial affairs and personal welfare of adults who are incapable by reason of mental disorder or inability to communicate, and for connected purposes."
(Long title of Adults with Incapacity (Scotland) Act 2000 (asp 4))

"Old law" and "new law"

3–1 The Incapacity Act is part of a general trend, in many countries and in many areas of law, to shift from what may be termed "old law" to "new law". "Old law" was typified by a "black and white" approach under which people were simplistically classed as sane or insane, educable or ineducable, fully capable and responsible or lacking all capability and responsibility, and so on. Procedures were equally simplistic: an assessment amounting to little more than a diagnosis resulted in a standardised outcome, often complete loss of legal capacity, and frequently of indefinite duration. "New law" recognises the great variety of intellectual disabilities and resulting impairments of capacity. In each case, such capacity as a person in fact has should be respected, safeguarded and if possible encouraged; and there requires to be a balance between providing special measures where they are needed, but on the other hand not restricting, discriminating or disqualifying any more than necessary.

3–2 In Scots law, the pioneering transition from "old law" to "new law" was in the Education (Scotland) Act 1981, providing for the identification and assessment of the individual needs of pupils with special educational needs, and for the opening of an individual Record of Needs including *inter alia* a "package" of individualised provision to meet those needs. Procedurally, the characteristics of "new law" in its fully developed form are these. Firstly, a widely-drawn "gateway definition" ensures that procedures can be accessed by all who might benefit from them. Secondly, a coherent but flexible range of possible outcomes allows for appropriate measures to be taken in each individual case. Thirdly, there are governing principles to guide which special measures, if any, should be chosen and applied in each individual case. Fourthly, a process of assessment identifies the individual's circumstances, abilities, disabilities and needs, so that an appropriate individualised package of provision can be selected. Fifthly, similar principles to those governing the choice of provision are also applied to appointees in the exercise of the powers conferred, who are monitored. Sixthly, adaptation of the package of provision to changes in needs and circumstances is ensured by time-limiting of appointments and requirements for ongoing review.

History

3–3 In the period 1984–1990 attention was drawn to the deficiencies of existing law and suggestions were made for improvement.[1] In the same period tutors to adults were re-introduced in their modern form, the first such appointment being in 1986, initially to make good the lack of any true personal guardianship in Scots law (which role is taken over by welfare guardianship under the Incapacity Act), and thereafter also on occasions to deal with single issues (now covered by intervention orders). Internationally, the trend to reform accelerated during the same period. The Dependent Adults Acts of Alberta had already influenced the concept of revived tutors-dative. Proposals for

---

[1] See, for example, *Dementia and the Law: The Challenge Ahead* (Scottish Action on Dementia, 1988) and A.D. Ward, *Scots Law and the Mentally Handicapped* (1984) and *The Power to Act* (1990).

reform in Scotland were particularly influenced by the Protection of Personal and Property Rights Act 1988 of New Zealand and the Betreuungsgesetz 1990[2] of Germany. There have been similar reforms in many other jurisdictions. All have shared similar basic principles, and have effected similar transitions from "old law" to "new law". Historical and comparative material relevant to the new régime of intervention orders and guardianship is reviewed more extensively in Chapter 10.[3]

3–4 Formally, the process of reform commenced in Scotland with the Scottish Law Commission's Discussion Paper No.94, *Mentally Disabled Adults: Legal Arrangements for Managing their Welfare and Finances* (September 1991, "SLC Discussion Paper"). Consultation was wide-ranging, with considerable input from relevant organisations and interested individuals, including representatives of the whole range of relevant disabilities. The Commission published its *Report on Incapable Adults* (Report No.151, "SLC Report") in September 1995. Government published its own Consultation Paper *Managing the Finances and Welfare of Incapable Adults* in February 1997. There was increasing anxiety that the pace of deliberation did not match the urgency of the need for law reform. In December 1997 a number of concerned organisations formed the "Alliance for the Promotion of the Incapable Adults Bill" ("the Alliance"). Membership rapidly grew to over 70 voluntary, professional and other organisations, including over 30 national organisations. Active campaigning publicised examples of both the inappropriate and harmful outcomes under existing law and the numbers of adults in Scotland at any one time affected by some form of incapacity.[4]

3–5 The Alliance was unsuccessful in its initial aim of achieving legislation by Westminster in 1998/1999. Lobbying of all of the main Scottish political parties resulted in commitments by all to support legislation in the first session of the Scottish Parliament. Those commitments were honoured. The Scottish Executive published its proposals in *Making the right moves: Rights and protection for adults with incapacity* in August 1999. The Act followed as "the first large Bill on a major policy area to be passed by the Scottish Parliament".[5] The Act provided vindication and commendation of Scotland's new legislative arrangements. First and foremost, where Westminster could not find time for such essential law reform, the Scottish Parliament delivered in its first session. Secondly, there was unprecedented openness, involvement of affected citizens, and responsiveness to their views, on the part of Scottish Executive Ministers and officials, the key Parliamentary Committees (principally the Justice and Home Affairs Committee, and also the Health and Community Care Committee), and the Parliament itself. Rapid publication of papers and proceedings on the

---

[2] The régime introduced by the Betreuungsgesetz has now been in force for well over a decade. Around a million applications have been dealt with, providing a source of potentially helpful comparative precedents: see the cases described in para.5–15 *infra*. See also para.14–50 *infra* on the criteria under the Betreuungsgesetz for authorising sterilisation.
[3] paras 10–2 *et seq*.
[4] See para.1–6, n.12.
[5] Per Mr Iain Gray, Deputy Minister for Community Care, March 29, 2000, SP OR Vol.5, No.11, col.1120.

Parliament's website encouraged this process. Considerable demands were placed upon MSP's both by this openness and by the stringencies of unicameral legislation.[6]

3–6 The Bill was introduced on October 8, 1999, accompanied by Explanatory Notes SP Bill 5-EN and Policy Memorandum SP Bill 5-PM. It was preceded by informal consideration by the Justice and Home Affairs Committee. That Committee then heard oral evidence on November 3, 9 and 17, 1999, also considered written evidence, and agreed its Stage 1 Report on December 1, 1999. The stage 1 debate took place on December 9, 1999. The Health and Community Care Committee also considered the Bill at stage 1, at meetings on November 16 and 17, 1999. Its report appears as Appendix 1 to the Stage 1 Report. The Justice and Home Affairs Committee concluded stage 2 proceedings on March 1, 2000. Finally, the stage 3 debate took place on March 29, 2000, and after further amendment the Bill for the Act was passed on that date. A total of 327 amendments were tabled at stage 2, and 158 at stage 3. The Act takes account of *Principles Concerning the Legal Protection of Incapable Adults* (Council of Europe Recommendation No. R (99) 4 and explanatory memorandum), which might on occasion assist interpretation. The Act has been amended by the Regulation of Care (Scotland) Act 2001 (asp 8) ("ROCSA"), and this book takes account of those amendments. Possible further amendments in the proposed new MHSA described in para.3–31 below are mentioned at various points in this book.

Overview

3–7 The Act is concerned with decision-making about the personal welfare of adults with incapacity, and the management of their property and financial affairs. These two areas of personal decision-making and management have generally been dealt with separately in Scots law. Personal decision-making includes decisions about where to reside; with whom one lives and consorts, and social activities; work, education and training; applying for licences, permits and so on; taking legal proceedings in personal matters; health-care and welfare matters; opening and dealing with correspondence; and diet, dress and other routine daily matters. Management includes making decisions and exercising rights regarding property, money and other assets, including financial management generally and all acts of administration of money and property; entering contracts of any kind, from simple purchases to more complex transactions; and all other acts or transactions affecting finances, property or similar rights. Prior to the Act, provision in both areas was fragmented, outdated and often harmful. The Act introduced a coherent modern code of provision for both areas, integrating them more closely, but still preserving the distinction for many purposes.[7] In a number of its

---

[6] Leaving some errors and blemishes mentioned in this text where relevant (though some others, also mentioned where relevant, have arisen in the course of implementation—*e.g.* see n.53 to para.14–16 *infra*). It had been hoped that at least the more obvious apparent errors would be rectified in the proposed new MHSA—see para.3–31 *infra*— but at time of going to press this now seems unlikely.

[7] Such as the differentiation regarding powers of attorney (see Ch.6) and intervention and guardianship orders (see Ch.10), and the respective supervisory and investigatory roles of local authorities and the Public Guardian (see Ch.5).

provisions, it also distinguishes between incapacity caused solely by inability to communicate, on the one hand, and all other incapacities on the other. The Act is not however comprehensive. With reference to the broad categories identified in para.1–20 above, it does not address matters of past or prospective validity, or of third party measures, except indirectly but by necessary implication in relation to when and in what form responsive measures might be appropriate. Undue influence is mentioned only in relation to safeguards when powers of attorney are granted. Some previous responsive measures are abolished by the Act, and important new ones are introduced. Other responsive measures, and some anticipatory measures, are altered, and other measures in both categories are not directly affected. The SLC Report[8] recommended legislation on some topics which were deliberately omitted from the Act: see paras 3–28 and 3–29 below.

The full range of anticipatory, responsive and third party measures are relevant to the Act, and the Act is relevant to them, in two broad ways. Firstly, the Act requires that there should be no intervention under the Act unless the desired benefit cannot be achieved without such intervention[9] and that any intervention under the Act should represent the least restrictive option.[10] To meet these requirements, it is necessary to have regard to any measures already in place and any which could be put in place, whether or not within the scope of the Act. Secondly, the Act's s.1 principles[11] set out in statutory form, and apply to the Act's provisions, principles which represent good practice in relation to the application and operation of all measures concerning adults with incapacity. Breach of those principles, as now enacted, will accordingly be a *prima facie* indication for remedial action. Thus, breach of those principles by a social security nominee might justify application to appoint a new nominee, or application for an intervention order or guardianship order; and breach by the trustees of a private trust might justify an intervention order or guardianship order to enable the actings of the trustees to be challenged, or the position of the adult in relation to the trust to be effectively represented. **3–8**

Against the foregoing background, the following is a brief survey of the full range of measures, including those abolished by the Act. **3–9**

Personal welfare

Anticipatory measures

Created: statement of wishes and feelings (persuasive effect).
Amended: welfare powers of attorney.
Unaltered: advance directives.

Responsive measures

Abolished: tutors-at-law;
tutors-dative;
Mental Health Act guardians.

---

[8] See para.3–4 *supra*.
[9] s.1(2).
[10] s.1(3).
[11] See paras 4–2 *et seq. infra*.

Created: intervention orders;
guardianship orders;
authority to treat;
authority for medical research.

Unaltered: *parens patriae*;
medical treatment on grounds of necessity;
MHSA and Criminal Procedure Act provisions (except as regards guardianship)[12];
removal under National Assistance Act 1948, s.47 (as amended);
curators ad litem.

Management

Anticipatory measures

Created: statement of wishes and feelings (persuasive effect).

Amended: continuing powers of attorney;
joint bank accounts.

Unaltered: trusts (including trusts for administration);
gifts.[13]

Responsive measures

Abolished: tutors-at-law;
tutors-dative;
curatory;
hospital management.

Created: guardianship;
intervention orders;
authority to intromit;
management of residents' finances.

Unaltered: provisions for management of particular types of asset:
— social security benefits;
— vaccine damage payments;
— sheriff court management;
— criminal injuries compensation;
— miscellaneous statutory methods.
informal techniques:
— *negotiorum gestio*;
— informal voluntary arrangements;
— bare trusts.
judicial factors;
curators ad litem.

---

[12] See para.3–31 *infra* on reform of mental health law.
[13] See paras 2–20 *supra* and 7–4 *infra*.

Third party measures

Unaltered: *mortis causa* trusts;
 inter vivos trusts;
 nominations;
 gifts and bequests;
 provisions for management of particular assets and informal techniques as for responsive measures.

The categorisations adopted above are designed to assist understanding and use of the range of measures, and to facilitate structured presentation. These categorisations are broadly valid but not in all cases necessarily rigidly exclusive.[14]

Layout

The Act comprises seven Parts and six Schedules. Part 1 defines "adults" and contains the "gateway" definition of incapacity (s.1(6)). The general principles which determine whether to intervene, and if so in what manner, are set out in ss.1(2)–(4). These, and the further principle in s.1(5), apply to the actions of guardians, continuing and welfare attorneys, and managers of establishments. The importance of these general principles cannot be over-emphasised. They should be referred to in conjunction with almost every other provision of the Act. An example of their importance is that the limitation of liability in terms of s.82 is not available unless the principles have been complied with. Part 1 also contains general provisions regarding proceedings (including matters of intimation and expenses), appeals, and powers of the sheriff and of the Court of Session; general provisions regarding the Public Guardian, Mental Welfare Commission and local authorities; and provisions regarding investigations, codes of practice and appeals against decisions as to incapacity. The layout of Part 1 appears somewhat haphazard on first reading. Part 2 provides a new code of continuing powers of attorney and welfare powers of attorney. Part 3 contains relatively simple procedures to permit intromissions during incapacity with funds held by a "fundholder" (intended to include banks, building societies, and any other holders of funds). It also permits one holder of an account which is in joint names and operable by either to continue to intromit during incapacity of the other, unless the terms of the account or a court order provide otherwise. Part 4, amended by ROCSA, creates a new scheme of management by "authorised establishments", including a procedure to withdraw funds from a fundholder. Part 5 creates a new authority to give medical treatment; deals with medical treatment when relevant powers have been sought or are in force under guardianship or intervention orders, or where a welfare attorney has relevant powers; contains provisions about research; and provides for appeal on medical matters to the sheriff, and with leave of the sheriff to the Court of Session, by anyone having an interest. Part 6 contains the new scheme of intervention and guardianship orders, which may be

3–10

---

[14] See, for example, para.12–2 *infra* and footnote thereto.

granted by the sheriff. Orders may cover welfare matters, or financial and property matters, or both, and may be limited or plenary in the scope of powers conferred. Where guardianship is sought the court may grant an intervention order if that will suffice. Part 7 is headed "Miscellaneous", and as well as containing usual supplementary provisions creates the new offence of ill-treatment and wilful neglect described in para.3–27 below; provides that persons with powers under the Act who use funds improperly are liable to repay them with interest, but have a general exemption from liability for breach of duty of care or fiduciary duty where their actions or failure to act was reasonable and in good faith, and in accordance with the general principles in s.1; and substitutes the new form of guardianship created by the Act for MHSA guardianship under the Criminal Procedure (Scotland) Act 1995.

3–11 Schedule 1 is concerned solely with defining who are the managers of different categories of establishment for the new scheme of management of residents' finances under Part 4, and has been amended by ROCSA. Schedule 2 sets out the main management provisions applicable to guardians with property and financial powers, and should be read in conjunction with Part 6, because there is not always any obvious logic in the allocation of provisions to Part 6 or to Schedule 2. Schedule 3 deals with matters of jurisdiction and private international law, including those matters described in paras 3–20 to 3–26 below. Schedule 4 contains the transitional provisions in respect of existing curators, tutors, MHSA guardians and attorneys. Schedules 5 and 6 deal respectively with statutory amendments and statutory repeals.[15]

Regulations

3–12 The Subordinate Legislation Committee of the Scottish Parliament has on a number of occasions raised concerns that there is in its view an apparent error in the Act, in that while it provides that regulations may be made, it is not always explicit as to who may make them.[16] The response of Scottish Executive has been that the necessary inference to be drawn from the relevant provisions of the Act is that regulations are to be made by the Scottish Ministers, and that in each case where the issue has arisen there is no other inference to be drawn that any other person has power to make regulations of the kind in question.[17] The draftsmanship of the Act indeed appears to be deficient, but the Executive's view seems to be correct.[18] At relevant

---

[15] The repeals commence with the Curators Act 1585 and, taken with the Act itself, include all of the various successive methods of citing and naming primary legislation applicable to Scotland (as well as referring to one provision of an English Act).

[16] See the Scottish Legislation Committee's 14th Report 2001 (concerning SSI 2001/75), 18th Report 2002 (concerning SSI 2002/131) and 25th Report 2002 (concerning SSI 2002/208).

[17] ibid.

[18] It is perhaps surprising that a committee of the Parliament should consider it appropriate to question officials representing the Executive as to the interpretation of provisions unanimously passed in legislation enacted by the Parliament. The principle of statutory interpretation, in case of doubt, is to ascertain the intention of the legislature, in this case the Parliament of which the members of the committee are a part.

points, the Act uses the terms "prescribe" and "prescribed", defined in s.87(1) as meaning prescribed by regulations, except "for the purposes of anything which may be or is to be prescribed by the Public Guardian". Some provisions specify that the Scottish Ministers may prescribe certain matters, whereas others use "prescribed" without stating by whom.[19] However, the only provision about how regulations should be made is s.86(1) which refers to "Any power of the Scottish Ministers to make regulations under this Act". It provides that the powers of Scottish Ministers to make regulations shall be exerciseable by statutory instrument subject to annulment in pursuance of a resolution of the Scottish Parliament, the procedure which has in fact been followed in making regulations. No mechanism is provided for anyone other than the Scottish Ministers to make regulations. It would seem reasonable to infer that regulations may only be made either by the Public Guardian or the Scottish Ministers. If there is doubt, that doubt would seem to relate to the words "anything which may be . . . prescribed by the Public Guardian". "May" could refer to a provision of the Act that a particular matter "may be prescribed by the Public Guardian", or words to that effect, but there appear to be such provisions only in Schedule 2 to the Act, in relation to prescribed forms and their content[20]; or "may" could refer to a situation where the Act provides that something should be "prescribed" and the Public Guardian has in fact specified what is required. That has occurred, and no regulations have been made by Scottish Ministers, in relation (for example) to "specified particulars" in the many registration provisions of the Act, to the form and content of certificates issued by the Public Guardian, and to the forms and procedure for applications to the Public Guardian, notwithstanding the provisions of s.7(1)(a), (b) and (c) that the Scottish Ministers "may prescribe" such matters. The doubt, accordingly, concerns the extent to which forms and procedures adopted and promulgated by the Public Guardian have prescriptive force in terms of the Act.[21]

Section 86(2) provides that the regulatory powers of the Scottish Ministers may be exercised to make different provision for different cases or classes of case; and that those powers include power to make such incidental, supplemental, consequential or transitional provisions, or savings, as appear to the Scottish Ministers to be appropriate. Regulations made by the Scottish Ministers and in force at July 1, 2002 are listed in the Table of Statutory Instruments and reproduced in Appendix 2. Where they have been amended, they are reproduced as amended and where appropriate their generally cumbersome titles are reduced to abbreviated form, so that (for example) the Regulations SSI 2002/275, amended by SSI 2002/302, are reproduced as amended in the Appendix and are generally referred to as the Specified Treatments Regulations. See also "Abbreviations" on page xli.

3–13

---

[19] In close proximity, s.7(1) is an example of the first and s.7(2) of the second. Other terms are used elsewhere: *e.g.* under s.48(2) the Scottish Ministers may "specify" certain matters.

[20] Sch.2, para.3(2) regarding form and content of the inventory of the adult's estate, para.7(5) as to the form of a financial guardian's accounts, and para.7(6) as to form of audit certificate.

[21] For an example of where this doubt could become contentious, see para.11–77 *infra* on the procedure for application to the Public Guardian for recall of a guardian's financial powers.

Codes of Practice

3–14   Section 13 requires the Scottish Ministers to issue Codes of Practice in relation to certain specified matters, and authorises them to make Codes of Practice as to such other matters arising out of, or connected with, the Act as they consider appropriate. The Scottish Ministers are required to prepare Codes, or cause them to be prepared for their approval, after first consulting such bodies as appear to them to be concerned. The Scottish Ministers are required to lay copies of such Codes before the Parliament and to publish "every Code of Practice made under this Act and for the time being in force". The Scottish Ministers are also required to revise the Codes from time to time, or cause the Codes to be revised for their approval, and similar provisions regarding consultation, laying before Parliament and publication apply to revised Codes.

3–15   The Codes which the Scottish Ministers are required to prepare are Codes containing guidance as to the exercise of functions under the Act of various specified bodies and individuals. Referring to the lettering in s.13(1), and with the titles by which they are referred to in this book, the mandatory Codes published as at July 1, 2002 are those for: (a) local authorities and their chief social work officers and mental health officers ("the Local Authority Code"), (b) continuing and welfare attorneys ("the Part 2 Code"), (c) persons authorised under intervention orders and (d) guardians (published as a combined Code—the "Part 6 Code") , (e) withdrawers (the "Part 3 Code"), and (h) persons authorised to carry out medical treatment or research under Part 5 (the "Part 5 Code"). Part 4 of the Act is not expected to be brought into force until April 2003 and the Codes for managers of authorised establishments and for supervisory bodies have not yet been finalised or issued: they are referred to together as the "Part 4 Codes". No other Codes have been prepared or are contemplated. In this book, abbreviated references to "Code" or "Code of Practice" mean the Code relevant to the topic in question, where that is clear from the context.[22]

3–16   As the various Codes themselves point out,[23] the Act imposes no duty to comply with the Codes but they are statutory documents and failure to observe them could have legal consequences. The Codes give the example that failure to comply, if it caused harm or loss, could be founded upon in an action on grounds of negligence. More generally, the Part 5 Code points out that the courts are likely to have regard to the Codes in considering matters brought before them under the Act. One would add that it would be reasonable to expect the Public Guardian, Mental Welfare Commission, local authorities and supervisory bodies to have regard to the Codes in exercising their various supervisory and investigatory roles, in relation to recall of powers, and generally in relation to their functions.

3–17   The Part 5 Code[24] points out that Codes cannot foresee all the circumstances that might arise in practice, and the Act's general principles rather than a detailed requirement of a Code should be

---

[22] Not to be confused with those Codes is the *Code of Conduct for Scottish Solicitors*, published by the Law Society of Scotland and referred to as the "Code of Conduct".
[23] *e.g.* Part 6 Code, para.1.41.
[24] para.1.26.

followed in the event of conflict between them in a particular real-life situation. It recommends that any departure from the Code should be recorded, with reasons and the circumstances. That advice is directed to medical practitioners, but it would be sensible for that advice to be observed by anyone exercising functions to which any of the Codes applies. One would add that the Codes might assist the courts in interpreting the law, but cannot fetter them.

Much thought went into the preparation of the Codes. The first editions as promulgated sought to address concerns that earlier drafts were too legalistic in their language; read as commentaries on the Act's provisions rather than recommendations as to good practice under them; made some doubtful or incorrect assertions as to the law; and were lengthy and cumbersome. The last point has been addressed by dividing some of the Codes into self-contained Parts which stand alone, and issuing some Parts separately as well as in the full version. Some concerns as to the accuracy in law of the Codes remain.[25] 3–18

Commencement

The Act received Royal Assent on May 9, 2000. Its provisions have (and will have) effect from such dates as the Scottish Ministers have appointed and may appoint by statutory instrument, which may contain further transitional provisions and savings.[26] As at July 1, 2002 there had been three orders, the Commencement No.1 Order 2001,[27] the Commencement No.1 (Amendment) Order 2002,[28] and the Commencement No.2 Order 2002.[29] The combined effect of these and of ROCSA[30] is that the Act was in force on and from July 1, 2002 except that ss.81 and 82 were not yet in force insofar as relating to managers of authorised establishments, and except as regards the following provisions: 3–19

- Part 4 (ss.35–46) (as amended by ROCSA), para.2 of Schedule 1, para.5 of Schedule 4, and in Schedule 6 the repeal of MHSA 1984, s.94—all expected to be brought into force on April 1, 2003 but no Commencement Order yet made;

- para.1 of Schedule 1, and paras 10 and 11 of Schedule 2 (amending Social Work (Scotland) Act 1968 (c.49))—all deleted by ROCSA;

- para.7(d) of Schedule 4—not required because of the sequence of the implementation;

- in Schedule 3, paras 1(2)–(4), 2(2), 7(2)(b), 7(2)(e), 11 and 12— all awaiting ratification of the Hague Convention of January 13, 2000 on the International Protection of Adults;

---

[25] *e.g.* see para.14–16 *infra*.
[26] s.89.
[27] SSI 2001/81 (C.2).
[28] SSI 2002/172 (C.11).
[29] SSI 2002/189 (C.14).
[30] The Regulation of Care (Scotland) Act 2001 (asp 8)—see "Abbreviations".

- in Schedule 5, paras 17(22) and (23), respectively amending ss.55(3) and 95 of MHSA 1984; and

- para.4 of Schedule 5, relating to the Improvement of Land Act 1864 (27 & 28 Vict. c.114) and the references to that Act in Schedule 6.

Jurisdiction, applicable law and private international law

3–20 Schedule 3 of the Act, introduced by s.85, deals with matters of jurisdiction and private international law under the Act. The provisions of Schedule 3 noted in para.3–19 above are dependent upon ratification of the Hague Convention of January 13, 2000 on the International Protection of Adults, and have not yet been brought into force. They should be referred to for their terms. This and the following paragraphs describe the law as it is currently in force. Schedule 3 refers frequently to "judicial and administrative authorities": the following text uses, with that meaning, "courts and authorities".

Jurisdiction

3–21 Scottish courts and authorities have jurisdiction if one of the following criteria applies.[31] Firstly, the adult is habitually resident in Scotland or is deemed to be. An adult who is in Scotland is deemed to be habitually resident there if his habitual residence cannot be ascertained, or if he is a refugee, or if he has been internationally displaced by disturbance in the country of his habitual residence. Secondly, relevant property is located in Scotland, relevant property being property which is the subject of the application or proceedings, or in respect of which functions are carried out under the Act. Thirdly, where the matter is urgent and the adult is not habitually resident in Scotland, the adult or property belonging to the adult is present in Scotland and (in either case) it is a matter of urgency that the application or proceedings should be dealt with. Fourthly, the adult is present in Scotland and the intervention sought in the application or proceedings is of a temporary nature and its effect is limited to Scotland.

Applicable law

3–22 Scots law is the law applicable to anything done under the Act by a Scottish court or authority, but the court or authority may apply the law of another country if (a) the circumstances demonstrate a substantial connection with that other country, and (b) it appears appropriate to apply the law of that country, having regard to the adult's interests.[32] Where a measure for the protection of an adult has been taken in one state and is implemented in another, the conditions of its implementation are governed by the law of that other state.[33] Questions as to whether a person has authority to represent an adult are

---

[31] Sch.3, para.1.
[32] Sch.3, para.3(1) and (2). In determining element (b), the court should have regard *inter alia* to the Act's general principles (see Ch.4).
[33] Sch.3, para.3(4).

governed by the law of the country of the adult's habitual residence, except that they are governed by Scots law where such representation is for the purposes of the immediate personal welfare of the adult and the adult is in Scotland.[34]

Schedule 3, paras 4(6)–(8), apply where a representative, acting or purporting to act as such for an adult, enters a contract or transaction with another party, and both (or all) of the parties to the contract or transaction enter into it in the same country. It is not an objection to the validity of the contract or transaction that the representative was not entitled to act under the law of a country other than the country where the contract or transaction was concluded, unless the other party knew or ought to have known that the representative's entitlement to act was governed by the law of that other country. **3–23**

Schedule 3, paras 3(3) and 4(1)–(5), apply to powers of attorney and are described in para.6–53 below. **3–24**

The provisions of Schedule 3, paras 3 and 4, described and referred to in paras 3–22 to 3–24 above, are subject to the following provisos. Nothing in Schedule 3 displaces any enactment or rule of law which has mandatory effect for the protection of an adult with incapacity in Scotland, whatever law would otherwise be applicable, and nothing in Schedule 3 requires or enables the application in Scotland of any provision of the law of a country other than Scotland so as to produce a result which would be manifestly contrary to public policy.[35] **3–25**

Recognition and enforcement

Paragraphs 7–10 of Schedule 3 apply to measures taken under the law of a country other than Scotland for the personal welfare or the protection of property of an adult with incapacity. Such measures are recognised by the law of Scotland if the jurisdiction of the court or authority of the other country was based on the adult's habitual residence there, but recognition of such a measure may be refused in the following circumstances. Except in emergency, recognition may be refused if the court or authority which took the measure did so without the adult to whom it related being given an opportunity to be heard, and if those circumstances constituted a breach of natural justice. Recognition may also be refused if it would be manifestly contrary to public policy to recognise it; or if the measure conflicts with any enactment or rule of law of Scotland which is mandatory, whatever law would otherwise be applicable; or if the measure is incompatible with a later measure taken in Scotland or recognised by the law of Scotland. A measure which is enforceable in the country of origin and which is recognised by the law of Scotland in accordance with the provisions described above may be registered in accordance with rules of court. A measure so registered is as enforceable as a measure having the like effect granted by a court in Scotland. For the purposes of recognition or enforcement of a measure taken outside Scotland in relation to an adult, findings of fact going to jurisdiction made by the court or authority taking the measure are conclusive of the facts found. The validity or merits of a measure recognised by **3–26**

---

[34] Sch.3, para.3(5).
[35] Sch.3, paras 5 and 6.

Scots law by virtue of the provisions of Schedule 3 may not be questioned in any proceedings, except for the purposes of ascertaining its compliance with provisions of Schedule 3. Subject to limitations, Scottish Ministers may by order provide for the recognition and enforcement of orders made and measures taken by courts and authorities in other parts of the United Kingdom.

Criminal offence

3–27 The Act creates one offence. Under s.83 it is an offence for any person exercising powers under the Act relating to an adult's personal welfare to ill-treat or wilfully neglect that adult.[36] On summary conviction, the maximum sentence is imprisonment for six months or a fine of the statutory maximum, or both. On conviction on an indictment, the maximum penalty is imprisonment for two years, or a fine, or both. On an apparent limitation of this offence, see para.6–52 below.

Matters excluded from the Act

3–28 Some topics addressed in the law reform process and included in the Scottish Law Commission's proposals were excluded from the Bill as introduced, and from the Act. The Commission identified a need for a scheme of public management, particularly for the administration of small or modest estates. After considering various options, they proposed that this service could be provided by the Public Guardian, who could for the purpose be appointed as financial guardian.[37] No such scheme of public management is included in the Act. Early indications of experience in practice are that the Commission was correct to identify the need for such a scheme.

3–29 The SLC Report recommended legislation on the withholding and withdrawal of life-preserving treatment, and on advance directives. On the first topic, the Commission's Report was published prior to the decision in *Law Hospital NHS Trust v Lord Advocate*.[38] The Scottish Executive decided to exclude both topics from the Act, on the basis that it was preferable that the courts should continue to develop the law, rather than that it should yet be fixed in statute. This did not prevent considerable debate of the first topic during the Parliamentary proceedings. The current law on withholding and withdrawal of treatment may be found in *Law Hospital* (above) and is described in paras 14–25 *et seq.* below. There is no equivalent statement of current Scots law in relation to advance directives, but the position is reviewed in the SLC Report.[39] In England, the Lord Chancellor provided a useful survey of the law in *Making Decisions*, October, 1999. This topic is discussed in paras 7–5 *et seq.* below. Other points which arose in the law reform process but not taken up in the Act, including the proposal for "designated sheriffs",[40] are mentioned where appropriate in the course of this text.

---

[36] *cf.* MHSA 1984, s.105.
[37] See SLC Report, paras 6.52–6.60 and annexed draft Bill, clauses 4(2)(a) and 45(1)(b).
[38] 1996 S.L.T. 848.
[39] paras 5.41–5.46.
[40] See para.5–21 *infra*.

Legal Aid

In the financial memorandum (paras 415–418) which accompanied **3–30** the Bill as introduced on October 8, 1999, Scottish Executive confirmed that civil legal aid would be available for proceedings under the Act, including appeals to the sheriff on decisions taken by the Public Guardian. Eligibility would be assessed in the normal way. As with former tutor-dative proceedings, financial eligibility would take account of the adult's resources, not those of the applicant. Eligibility for legal advice and assistance on "the new measures under the legislation" would be assessed on the means of the applicant, rather than those of the adult. People becoming involved in proceedings, such as relatives contesting an application for an intervention or guardianship order, would be eligible for assistance by way of representation, assessed on the resources of the applicant. Legal aid would also be available to meet the costs of safeguarders (see s.3(4) and (5) and s.5), assessed by reference to the adult's resources. As regards financial assessment of applicants for civil legal aid, effect has been given to the terms of the financial memorandum by the insertion of regulation 14A in the Civil Legal Aid (Scotland) Regulations 1996.[41] Regulation 14A, which is reproduced in Appendix 2, refers to the proceedings listed in regulation 14A(2). Regulation 14A(1) provides that the adult's resources shall be assessed, and the applicant's personal resources disregarded, where the applicant is concerned in any of the listed proceedings "only as claiming or having an interest in the property, financial affairs or personal welfare of an incapable adult" under the Incapacity Act. The inclusion of "incapable" is inappropriate. The Act consistently, and correctly, refers to "the adult", and this must be the meaning of the Regulations: for example, item (b) of regulation 14A(2) specifically relates to proceedings where the question of incapacity is in dispute. The general question of financial assessment for legal advice and assistance has given rise to concern, and may be reviewed. Where the person with impaired capacity is the solicitor's client, then that person's means should be assessed, even though someone else may assist that person and sign the application form on that person's behalf. In this context, see the discussion of "who is my client?" in Chapter 2, paras 2–11 *et seq*. Under former MHSA guardianship, there was originally a discrepancy between England and Scotland in that non means-tested assistance by way of representation ("ABWOR") was available to persons subject to such applications in England, but not in Scotland. Following representations, non means-tested ABWOR became available in Scotland, but that has now been reversed in relation to welfare guardianship applications. There is an argument that non means-tested ABWOR should be available to the adult and to parties claiming an interest in any proceedings concerning welfare powers over an adult. There also appears to be a need for the status of appointees to be clarified where

---

[41] SI 1996/2444, as already previously amended by SI 1997/727, SI 1998/725, SI 1999/1042 and SSI 2000/182. Regulation 14A was first inserted with items (a)–(g) of reg.14A(2) by the Civil Legal Aid (Scotland) Amendment Regulations 2001 (SSI 2001/82). Items (h)–(k) were added by the Civil Legal Aid (Scotland) Amendment Regulations 2001 (SSI 2002/88), and items (l)–(n) by the Civil Legal Aid (Scotland) Amendment (No.2) Regulations 2002 (SSI 2002/254).

they seek Legal Advice and Assistance for the benefit of the adult. A further cause for concern is that legal aid assessed on the adult's means is currently available to safeguarders only if they are solicitors. It is possible that the opportunity of the Mental Health Bill may be taken to review generally the Legal Aid position in both adult incapacity and mental health matters.

Reform of mental health law

3–31 Although some initial recommendations to the Scottish Law Commission suggested that adult incapacity law and mental health law should be reviewed together, at the time when the Incapacity Bill was before the Parliament mental health law was under review by the Millan Committee,[42] and in the Incapacity Act the only substantial amendments to MHSA are those to guardianship[43] and hospital management.[44] The Millan Committee's Report *New Directions*, containing over 400 recommendations, was published in January 2001. The Scottish Executive's Policy Statement on Mental Health Legislation *Renewing Mental Health Law* was published in October 2001, followed by a draft Mental Health Bill (neither finalised nor complete) on June 27, 2002. While that draft contained no proposed amendments to the Incapacity Act, Scottish Executive indicated its intention to introduce at stage 2 of the Bill amendments to alter the provisions of the Incapacity Act concerning nearest relatives, including in particular the introduction of a provision to allow a person having an interest to apply to the sheriff to displace the nearest relative. It was understood that the Executive might also seek to amend the Incapacity Act to ensure consistency between the Incapacity Act and the new MHSA regarding definitions of mental disorder and nearest relative,[45] and to clarify the rights to be involved in proceedings under the Incapacity Act of the proposed "named person"[46] to be introduced in the new MHSA. It was also possible that the new MHSA might be used to rectify at least some of the apparent errors in the Incapacity Act mentioned in n.6 to para.3–5 above, and noted at various points in this book. The full Mental Health (Scotland) Bill was introduced in the Scottish Parliament on September 16, 2002. The only specific proposed amendment to the Incapacity Act was the transfer from the Incapacity Act to a new MHSA, and alteration of, some of the powers of the Mental Welfare Commission. The proposed changes are described in para.5–32 below, which is referred to where relevant provisions of the Incapacity Act are cited elsewhere. Other provisions of a new MHSA likely to be of significance, sooner or later, to incapacity law may include the transfer of jurisdiction in mental health matters from the sheriff to a tribunal.

---

[42] A committee chaired by the Rt Hon. Bruce Millan which commenced its review of MHSA 1984 in January 1999.
[43] MHSA, ss.36–52 and Part 6 of the Incapacity Act.
[44] MHSA, s.94 and Part 3 of the Incapacity Act.
[45] s.87(1) of the Incapacity Act.
[46] Not to be confused with the named person in education law: see Education (Record of Needs) (Scotland) Regulations 1982 (SI 1982/1222), reg.2(1), referring to Education (Scotland) Act 1980 (c.44) (as amended) s.62(2)(c).

England

Adult incapacity law in England, though in many respects substantially different from Scots law and less neglected by Westminster, is nevertheless in need of reform. There has been a parallel process of reform in England, but (at least until recently) no equivalent of the Alliance's campaign,[47] and Westminster has not yet found legislative time to address the English proposals. In England, management provisions meeting broadly the same needs as were formerly met by curatory (and are now met by guardianship and intervention orders) are contained within mental health legislation.[48] A separate Court of Protection has jurisdiction. There is provision for making statutory Wills on behalf of people with incapacity.[49] Differences in the English approach to reform go beyond differences in existing provision. At no time has there been any support in Scotland for any provision, such as has been proposed in England (see *Making Decisions*, October 1999), that there should be general authority to anyone to do what they think reasonable in relation to the personal welfare or healthcare of adults with incapacity. The Scottish view has been that such a provision would be inappropriately paternalistic, and contrary to the best interests and human rights of such adults. Generally, the difference in emphasis of English proposals is characterised by the use of "manager", even for personal welfare matters, where the Scottish Act uses "guardian".

3–32

---

[47] The Law Society (of England and Wales), British Medical Association and Mencap, as representatives of an alliance of organisations called the Making Decisions Alliance, launched a campaign for legislation in England in July 2002.
[48] Mental Health Act 1983 (c.20), Part VII.
[49] Mental Health Act 1983, ss.96 and 97.

CHAPTER 4

THE INCAPACITY ACT—GENERAL PRINCIPLES AND DEFINITION OF INCAPACITY

"What the law is—or should be—trying to do is to give to people with mental disabilities the same rights, status or protections as other citizens. This has to be a matter of balance. Special provisions all seek to reduce deficits in legal status by addressing deficits in legal capacity; but by the very fact of dealing differently with some categories of people, these special provisions create a deficit by being discriminatory. To protect usually means also to restrict; to provide a mechanism to make decisions for or about me reduces my right to make my own decisions; and so on.
"In consequence, we expect the law to apply the same principles as are applied in other areas of provision for people with mental disabilities. The legal environment should be as normal as capabilities, needs and circumstances permit. There should be no special provision, no intervention, no differentiation, unless it is shown to be necessary. By necessary we mean that the desired outcome cannot be achieved by some less restrictive means, and that there will be positive advantage in applying it. The intervention or differentiation should be as much as is needed to achieve that advantage, but no more. Where however some special provision is needed, it should be provided; it should contain necessary safeguards and protections; and it should impose no unnecessary or inappropriate limitations, disqualifications or other disadvantages. Procedures should be no more complex or difficult than necessary. They should be workable, accessible and fair."

(The author, speaking at seminar January 21, 1998, organised by the Alliance for the Promotion of the Incapable Adults Bill)

Introduction

The Act is a code of law in that it sets out a coherent range of provision for the matters which it addresses, based upon general principles designed to ensure that in all its applications the Act achieves its fundamental purpose. In addition to the statutory general principles described in the immediately following paragraphs, also important are the existing common law principles of fiduciary duty and duty of care, described later in this chapter. The Act's definitions of "incapable" and "incapacity" determine access to the Act's régime and the applicability of its particular provisions. **4–1**

Application of general principles

There are five general principles.[1] The first four have comprehensive application. Effect must be given to them "in relation to any intervention in the affairs of an adult under or in pursuance of this Act".[2] The fifth (in addition to the first four) must be complied with by **4–2**

---

[1] Earlier commentaries referred to four. The Codes of Practice describe s.1(4) as containing two, and refer in total to five. That approach is adopted here.
[2] s.1(1).

guardians, attorneys and managers of establishments. The prescriptive words that the principles "shall be given effect to" would suggest that the principles, such as those of benefit to the adult in the first and of the option least restrictive of the adult's freedom in the second, should prevail in circumstances where apparent conflict with other provisions of the Act raises issues of interpretation. More generally, reference to the principles will usually assist—often decisively—in resolving points of difficulty in the application of the Act's provisions to particular circumstances, or of interpretation.

Intervention

4–3   "Intervention" includes "any order made in or for the purpose of any proceedings under the Act for or in connection with an adult".[3] The term is not further defined,[4] but it is clear from their debates that the Parliament intended that it should mean not only the various procedures under the Act, but also the acts and decisions of relevant appointees and others. Also, "an intervention can encompass a positive and a negative act" (*e.g.* a decision to do something or a decision not to do it).[5] The multiplicity of circumstances and issues which can arise in relation to adults with incapacity may in time necessitate judicial interpretation, but in most situations difficulty will be avoided if it is remembered that a broad interpretation was clearly intended, encompassing (it is suggested) any decision, act or deliberate omission within the broad scope of the Act's provisions in any way affecting (or intended or having the potential to affect) the welfare, affairs, interests or status of an adult with incapacity.

Consequences of non-compliance

4–4   Failure to comply with the general principles will justify invocation of any appropriate remedies and supervisory provisions of the Act, including by application to the court, the Public Guardian, Mental Welfare Commission, local authorities and supervisory bodies. Contravention of the principles to the disadvantage of an adult to whom no measures under the Act currently apply might justify intervention by means of measures under the Act. Contravention by an official or official body would justify judicial remedies, and contravention by a court would open the court's decision to any competent mode of appeal.

4–5   Section 82 of the Act exempts appointees from liability for breach of duties of care and fiduciary duties in respect of acts and omissions which are reasonable and in good faith, but even when they are reasonable and in good faith the exemption does not apply if the appointee has failed to comply with the general principles. Under s.67(4), a guardian is personally liable under any transaction where he fails to disclose that he acts as guardian, but may be reimbursed from

---

[3] s.1(1).

[4] In resisting attempts to introduce a definition, the Scottish Parliament appeared to concentrate almost exclusively on perceived difficulties in relation to the medical provisions of Part 5, *e.g.* see SP OR Vol.5, No.11, cols 1047–1058, and not to have weighed them against possible advantages of a definition for the broader provisions of the Act.

[5] Mr Angus MacKay, Deputy Minister for Justice, SP OR Vol.5, No.11, col.1047.

the adult's estate for any loss consequently suffered provided that he is "not otherwise in breach of any requirement of the Act relating to such guardians": contravention of the general principles accordingly removes this right of relief.

The first principle (section 1(2))

There must be no intervention in the affairs of an adult unless the intervention will benefit the adult and such benefit cannot reasonably be achieved without that intervention. The "person responsible for authorising or effecting the intervention" must be satisfied that both requirements will be met, and otherwise must not authorise or effect the proposed intervention. 4–6

"The person responsible for authorising or effecting the intervention"

This includes (but is not limited to) the courts, the Public Guardian, managers of establishments both when deciding to seek certification under s.37(2) and when acting thereafter, medical practitioners when certifying for purposes of Parts 4 or 5, supervisory bodies when exercising powers in relation to individual adults, persons acting under any authority conferred by Part 5, and appointees of all kinds. 4–7

"Benefit"

There should be no intervention merely because of incapacity,[6] however severe. There must be both incapacity and need, and the intervention must meet that need. "Benefit" is not defined in the Act, but the courts can be expected to adopt a broad definition. For example, there is nothing in the proceedings of the Scottish Parliament to suggest that it intended to curtail the developing trend of authorising curators bonis to make gifts or adopt Inheritance Tax saving measures where appropriate.[7] With due caution, "benefit" can reasonably be interpreted as encompassing overcoming the limitations created by incapacity, so as to permit something which the adult could reasonably be expected to have chosen to do if capable, even though of a gratuitous or unselfish nature. This interpretation is supported, for example, by the provisions of s.66 regarding gifts from the estate of an adult under guardianship, and of s.51(4) regarding research which may achieve "real and direct benefit" to others having the same incapacity as the adult but not to the adult himself.[8] The requirements of s.1(4) to ascertain the adult's own present or past wishes and feelings, and to consult, may assist in determining what could reasonably be regarded as "benefit" in difficult cases. 4–8

---

[6] See paras 4–23 *et seq. infra.*
[7] See, for example, *B's Curator Bonis* (Sh. Ct), 1995 S.C.L.R. 671 and *D's Curator Bonis* (Noter), 1997 G.W.D. 13–538 and 1998 S.L.T. 2, referred to in the context of powers of attorney in para.6–31 *infra*.
[8] See also the commentary on s.28(2) in the official Explanatory Notes—but see para.8–11 *infra*.

"Such benefit cannot reasonably be achieved without the intervention"

4–9 Even where there is both incapacity and need, and the intervention would meet that need, there must still be no intervention, in the legal sense, if the need can to a reasonable extent be met in some other way, or if there are prospects for recovery of capacity and decisions or action can reasonably be deferred. Provision of treatment or care may allow the adult to regain sufficient capacity to make a decision. Patient explanation in relaxed and helpful surroundings, or re-writing legalese in plain English, or assistance with communication, may all enable the adult to act without formal intervention. It may be possible to remove the problem rather than impose intervention upon the adult.[9] Provision of appropriate facilities and services may suffice. The effect of s.1(2) is to create a positive obligation to take appropriate informal steps, if feasible and reasonable, where intervention would otherwise be necessary. However, neither s.1(2) nor any other provision of the Act sanctions the imposition *de facto* of intervention of a kind which could have been obtained under the Act, without following the Act's procedures, upon an adult who appears to be compliant but cannot validly consent. To impose *de facto* provisions, such as guardianship powers, without the appropriate procedure to obtain those powers, and thus without the resulting monitoring and safeguards, would contravene ECHR Article 6[10] and would breach the second principle (below). Accordingly, in such situations not only is intervention under the Act not blocked by s.1(2), but continuation of *de facto* arrangements without such intervention might be wrongful.

Wider application

4–10 The requirements of s.1(2), and the above considerations, also apply to further intervention where other formal measures are already in place. Such measures may be within or outwith the scope of the Act. There should be no further intervention if the desired benefit can reasonably be achieved by more appropriate use of measures already in place in relation to the adult.

4–11 Finally and importantly, s.1(2) read in conjunction with s.1(3) requires consideration to be given to the suitability of taking formal measures outwith the scope of the Act. It is reasonable to read ss.1(2) and 1(3) in conjunction, because nowhere in the Act is one of them disapplied where the other applies. Section 1(3), described next, requires any intervention to be the option which is least restrictive in relation to the adult's freedom. To contravene that principle cannot be reasonable in terms of s.1(2). Section 1(2) prohibits an intervention under or in pursuance of the Act if the desired benefit could "reasonably be achieved" without that intervention, by using instead a less restrictive measure from outwith the scope of the Act. The full range of potentially relevant measures within and outwith the Act is summarised in para.3–9 above.

The second principle (section 1(3))

4–12 The second principle applies where it has been determined that an intervention is to be made. Under the second principle the intervention must be the least restrictive option in relation to the freedom of

---

[9] See paras 1–16 and 2–6 to 2–8 *supra*.
[10] See para.1–47 *supra*.

the adult, consistent with the purpose of the intervention. Thus where there is incapacity and need, and need cannot be met without intervention, the principle of minimum necessary intervention applies. This principle operates at three levels: the choice of procedure; where the chosen procedure offers such flexibility, the choice of powers conferred; and the decisions and actions, on an ongoing basis, of appointees and others acting under the Act's provisions. The reference to "freedom" raises an important point also relevant to the first principle: the exercise *de facto* of powers such as guardianship powers without legal authority, without any procedure to determine whether and to what extent such powers are needed and upon whom they should properly be conferred, and without the attendant régime of supervision and accountability, is by far the greatest restriction of the adult's freedom, and will often be wrongful and a contravention of ECHR Article 6.[11]

Choice of procedure

4–13 At the level of choice of procedure, there is room for debate whether the options referred to in s.1(3) are limited to those within the Act's scheme of provision. However, that debate would have no practical significance. If a measure outwith the Act would achieve the desired purpose with less restriction of the adult's freedom than a measure within the Act, then even if that is not a consideration for the purposes of s.1(3), it would nevertheless cause the measure within the Act to be prohibited by s.1(2), as described in para.4–11 above; and, as pointed out there, ss.1(2) and 1(3) always apply together. Of the measures within the Act's scheme of provision, the operation of a power of attorney will generally be the least restrictive of the options under the Act, because that measure will have been created by the adult, rather than imposed upon the adult. Section 58 effectively places guardianship as the most restrictive of the options under the Act. Section 58(1) permits the sheriff to grant a guardianship application if the adult is incapable as defined in s.58(1)(a) and only if "no other means provided by or under this Act" would suffice. However, that limitation to measures under the Act does not apply to the recall and termination provisions of s.71(1)(c), provision (ii) of which refers to the adult's interests being "satisfactorily safeguarded or promoted otherwise than by guardianship". It is reasonable to presume that the legislature would not have permitted this apparent inconsistency if it would have had practical significance: on the view that ss.1(2) and 1(3) always apply together and that, taken together, they require measures both within and outwith the Act to be considered, the apparent inconsistency is of no significance. Although s.58 places guardianship as the most restrictive of the options under the Act, in balancing the Act's other procedures it is not possible to create a hierarchy unrelated to circumstances in individual cases, because s.1(3) refers to the degree of restriction of freedom, not (for example) the simplicity of the procedure, and there may be situations (again by way of example) where the protections afforded by a more formal procedure may represent a lesser restriction of the adult's freedom

---

[11] See para.1–47 *supra*.

than a simpler alternative. This matter must be carefully addressed by anyone empowered to put in place any of the interventions under the Act. For example, if the managers of an establishment take Part 4 powers in circumstances where this does not in fact represent the option least restrictive of the adult's freedoms, then such contravention of s.1 disqualifies them from the limitation of liability under s.82.

Choice of powers

4–14 Several of the Act's procedures offer flexibility in choice of powers conferred. In each individual case, under the second principle the choice must be the least restrictive of the adult's freedom consistent with the purpose of the intervention. This applies, for example, to the choice of powers under a guardianship order; to the extent of powers granted under an intervention order or the authority to intromit; and to the extent of exercise of the provisions for authority to treat in Part 5 of the Act.

Exercise of powers

4–15 The third level at which the second principle applies is that individual acts and decisions—individual "interventions", including decisions to refrain from acting—must also comply with this principle. This requirement applies to attorneys, guardians, appointees under intervention orders, people authorised to intromit with funds, people accessing joint accounts, managers of residents' finances, anyone acting by virtue of the authority to give medical treatment; and also to the sheriff exercising his various jurisdictions under the Act, to the Public Guardian, local authorities and Mental Welfare Commission discharging responsibilities and exercising functions under the Act, and so on.

The third principle (section 1(4)(a))

4–16 Account must be taken of the present and past wishes and feelings of the adult in determining whether to intervene, and if so what intervention should be made. This principle therefore applies at the several levels identified above of whether to intervene at all; what procedure should be applied; the selection of powers or scope within the chosen procedure; and individual acts and decisions by appointees and others (including decisions to do nothing). This requirement will clearly have been contravened if wishes and feelings of the adult could have been ascertained but were not. Where they have been ascertained, issues may still arise as to whether account has been properly taken of them. While relative weight will always be a matter of balance in particular circumstances, and the elements of the third and fourth principles in s.1(4) are not stated to be in order of priority, one would generally expect clear present wishes and feelings of the adult to take priority over those expressed in the past,[12] and the adult's own wishes and feelings to take priority over the views of others. See also the discussion in Chapter 15.

---

[12] An example of an exception might be an adult with fluctuating mental illness who has expressed clear wishes when relatively well, and has asked that those wishes be followed even though contradicted by the adult when unwell.

The obligation to take account of the adult's present and past 4–17 wishes and feelings, if ascertainable, is absolute. The qualification "insofar as it is reasonable and practicable to do so" applies to the fourth principle but not to the third. The adult's own wishes and feelings must be taken into account "so far as they can be ascertained by any means of communication, whether human or by mechanical aid (whether of an interpretative nature or otherwise) appropriate to the adult". As regards present wishes and feelings, research shows that advanced modern psychological techniques may allow the wishes and feelings of severely incapacitated people to be accessed, that their wishes and feelings when in such a situation may be very different from those expressed when contemplating such circumstances hypothetically in the past, and that the incapacitating event may have caused a change of character rendering past wishes and feelings no longer relevant to the present adult.[13] It is reasonable to suggest that where wishes and feelings have altered radically when confronted with the reality of an incapacitating condition, or have been altered by it, then the present adult should not be treated as irrevocably "owned" by the past adult, and (as suggested above) those present wishes and feelings should normally prevail.

Best interests, or words to similar effect, are not explicitly mentioned in s.1. In the case of adults, however disabled, the adult's own wishes and feelings, present or past, should normally carry substantial weight, even when the views of other people as to what they consider to be in the adult's best interests may differ. Precedents from child law are unlikely to be relevant, appropriate or helpful. Of the freedoms referred to in s.1(3), the freedom of self-determination will be the most important in many cases. 4–18

Past wishes and feelings, which should be taken into account, 4–19 should be distinguished from valid and unrevoked advance directives and the like, which may be legally binding (see paras 7–5 et seq. below). However, the obligation to take account of wishes and feelings has the consequence that a statement of wishes and feelings is now a useful persuasive anticipatory technique: see para.7–13 below. Wishes and feelings may be combined with, but should be distinguished from, opposition, resistance or unwillingness which has mandatory rather than advisory effect in some provisions of the Act. Notwithstanding incapacity, an adult may not be placed in hospital for treatment of mental disorder "against his will" by an attorney[14] or guardian[15] or under s.47(2) authority.[16] Treatments specified in Schedule 1, Part 1 to the Specified Treatments Regulations may not be given if the adult opposes or resists.[17] Research may not be carried out on an adult who indicates unwillingness.[18]

---

[13] See, for example, *Neuropsychological assessment after extremely severe head injury in a case of life or death* (T.M. McMillan, "Brain Injury", 1997, Vol.11, No.7, 483–490) and *Neuropsychological assessment of a potential "euthanasia" case: a 5 year follow up* (T.M. McMillan and C.M. Herbert, "Brain Injury", 2000, Vol.14, No.2, 197–203), both of which articles relate to the same young woman who had been severely brain-damaged, following a road accident, and in respect of whom permission had been sought to terminate involuntary feeding.
[14] s.16(6)(b)—see para.14–17 *infra*.
[15] s.64(2)(a)—see para.14–17 *infra*.
[16] s.47(7)(a)—see para.14–45 *infra*.
[17] SSI 2002/275 as amended by SSI 2002/302, reg.3—see para.14–49 *infra*.
[18] s.51(3)(b)—see para.14–65 *infra*.

The fourth principle (section 1(4)(b)–(d))

4–20 In determining whether to intervene, and if so what intervention should be made, account should be taken of the views of various specified categories of persons insofar as it is reasonable and practicable to do so. This applies at the same several levels as the third principle (see para.4–16 above), but subject to the qualifications of reasonability and practicability. The categories are:

— the nearest relative[19] and the primary carer,[20] under s.1(4)(b);

— any guardian, continuing attorney or welfare attorney of the adult who has powers relating to the proposed intervention, under s.1(4)(c)(i);

— any person whom the sheriff has directed to be consulted, under s.1(4)(c)(i) (which direction may have been made, for example, in a guardianship or intervention order, or upon an application under s.3(3)[21]);

— any other person appearing, to the person responsible for authorising or effecting the intervention, to have an interest in the welfare of the adult or in the proposed intervention, where these views have been made known to the person responsible, under s.1(4)(d).

4–21 Persons consulted under the fourth principle may also be able to assist in ascertaining the adult's own wishes and feelings, present or past, for the purposes of the third principle. They may require to be reassured that their own views are important, and will be properly taken into account, but requested to make a clear distinction between that and providing evidence of the adult's own wishes and feelings. The value of their evidence for the latter purpose may be impaired if, even with appropriate guidance, they do not appear clearly to understand and make the distinction. It may be necessary to apply the same distinction when asking the sheriff to direct that a person be consulted under s.1(4)(c)(ii): that provision would not appear to be appropriate for identifying a person with skills in facilitating the ascertainment of the adult's wishes and feelings, for which purpose it is of course vital that such person's own views should in no way intrude.[22]

The fifth principle (section 1(5))

4–22 Specified categories of appointees are required, in addition to observing the first four principles, to encourage the adult to exercise whatever skills the adult has concerning his property, financial affairs

---

[19] See paras 5–38 and 5–39 *infra*.
[20] See para.5–40 *infra*.
[21] On s.3(3), see paras 5–14 and 5–15 *infra*.
[22] A non-legal advocate may of course have developed rapport and understanding with the adult enabling the advocate both to assist in identifying the adult's own wishes and feelings and also to express views, formed on the basis of that rapport and understanding and excluding the advocate's personal pre-conceptions, which views may be relevant and valuable.

or personal welfare, as the case may be, and to develop new such skills. They are required to do so insofar as it is reasonable and practicable. The appointees to whom this principle applies are guardians, continuing attorneys, welfare attorneys and managers of establishments exercising functions under the Act or under any order of the sheriff in relation to an adult. Instead of appointments imposing artificial incapacity which might exceed actual incapacity, there is instead now an obligation to encourage the exercise and development of skills. In the case of guardianship, this should be read in conjunction with s.64(1)(e), under which guardians may be empowered to authorise the adult to carry out transactions, and s.67(1), which limits the extent to which the guardianship order results in legal incapacity.[23]

Definition of incapacity (section 1(6))

For the purposes of the Act, incapacity may be caused either by "mental disorder" or by inability to communicate because of physical disability. In relation to any particular provision of the Act, a person is incapable if by reason of either or both of those causes the person is incapable of (a) acting, or (b) making decisions, or (c) communicating decisions, or (d) understanding decisions, or (e) retaining the memory of decisions. This definition accordingly requires to be considered at two levels: firstly, the two broad potential gateways to the Act's régime, those of mental disorder and inability to communicate; and secondly, the five alternative criteria by which an adult who passes through one of those gateways may be deemed incapable "as mentioned in any provision of this Act". 4–23

First gateway: "mental disorder"

Not without some criticism and debate, the Parliament adopted for this, the broader of the Act's two gateway definitions, the same definition of "mental disorder" as currently appears in MHSA 1984: "mental illness (including personality disorder) or mental handicap[24] however caused or manifested; but an adult shall not be treated as suffering from mental disorder by reason only of promiscuity or other immoral conduct, sexual deviancy, dependence on alcohol or drugs, or acting as no prudent person would act".[25] Even for MHSA purposes, that definition has been criticised as unsatisfactory. The draft Mental Health (Scotland) Bill published on July 27, 2002[26] proposed a simple definition that mental disorder should mean "any (a) mental illness, (b) personality disorder, or (c) learning disability, however caused or manifested". The Millan Committee recommended retention, in updated form, of specific exclusions relating to 4–24

---

[23] See para.11–32 *infra*.
[24] *i.e.* learning disability. See para.1–6 *supra*.
[25] Incapacity Act, s.87(1); see also MHSA 1984, s.1(2), as amended with effect from September 1, 1999 by the Mental Health (Public Safety and Appeals) (Scotland) Act 1999 (asp 1), s.3(1)(a). On various elements of the definition, see paras 1–6 *et seq. supra*. It is doubtful whether the Scottish courts would be tempted to adopt the simplistic approach in the English case of *W v L* (1974) Q.B. 711 that "mental illness" has no particular medical or legal significance and should be interpreted "in the way that any ordinary, sensible person would interpret" those words.
[26] s.98: on MHSA reform see para.3–31 *supra*.

substance misuse, sexual orientation or behaviour, and anti-social or imprudent behaviour, but the circular accompanying the draft Bill questioned whether specifying such exclusions might create confusion about whether other conditions are included, and about situations where a mental disorder is complicated by excepted factors. It was indicated that the Executive had not reached a final view, but the Mental Health (Scotland) Bill as introduced on September 16, 2002 contained the same definition as the draft Bill, as quoted above. It is likely that any new definition adopted in reformed mental health legislation will be reflected in an amendment to the Incapacity Act definition. However, there was also concern about adopting the same definition for both Incapacity Act and MHSA purposes: it could be argued that MHSA is primarily concerned with imposition of compulsory measures and thus requires strict definitions, whereas the Incapacity Act requires a broad gateway to possible use of enabling and empowering provisions. In relation to an amendment prompted by concerns as to whether the definition covered all of the causes of incapacity to which the Incapacity Act was intended to apply, Mr Iain Gray, Deputy Minister for Community Care, said[27]: "If ... the amendment has been prompted by lingering concerns about whether the definition of mental disorder covers all the underlying conditions that should be included, specifically the effects of head injuries or a stroke, our medical and legal advice is that those conditions fall within the definition. That ties in with well-known international medical terminology. The definition already spells it out that mental disorder is however caused or manifested. However caused is intended to cover whatever physical accident or illness led to the condition causing incapacity. The Executive acknowledges that the current definition of mental disorder in [MHSA] needs to be reviewed and updated. That is why the Committee chaired by Bruce Millan was set up to undertake that work. When it reports, we will have the advantage of the Millan Committee's wide public consultation and expertise. We will then be able to maintain the advantages of consistency between incapacity law and mental health law. We will also avoid the likelihood of two changes to the existing definition in quick succession, which would be difficult for both professionals and the public to follow."

Second gateway: physical inability to communicate

4–25 In relation to the second gateway, there is a similar obligation to facilitate communication as applies to the third principle. The language of s.1(6) is in this respect similar to s.1(4)(a). A person is not to be deemed unable to communicate because of physical disability "by reason only of a lack or deficiency in a faculty of communication if that lack or deficiency can be made good by human or mechanical aid (whether of an interpretative nature or otherwise)". The considerations discussed in para.4–17 accordingly apply also to this gateway definition.

4–26 This is the narrower of the two gateways. It admits only those whose inability to communicate is a complete bar to exercise of capacity in a matter in which a decision cannot reasonably be

---

[27] SP OR Vol.5, No.11, cols 1043–1044.

deferred, and whose inability to communicate results from physical disability. If the inability to communicate is the result of a mental rather than a physical disability, the first rather than the second gateway applies. The distinction is important because there is differentiation in some provisions of the Act between incapacity caused (wholly or partly) by mental disorder, and incapacity caused solely by inability to communicate due to physical disability. In relation to the latter, the Mental Welfare Commission generally does not have a role[28]; the report under s.57(3)(b) for guardianship and intervention order applications is provided by the chief social work officer rather than the mental health officer; and certification by an approved psychiatrist is not mandatory.[29] The differentiation may present difficulties of interpretation in individual cases. In *Fraser v Paterson*,[30] Lord Jauncey said of the victim of a stroke that while she "has very severe difficulties of communication she is very far from being of unsound mind in the sense in which that term is normally accepted by doctors and lawyers". Upon that description, one suspects that under the Act her incapacity might have been classed as arising from an inability to communicate through physical disability, rather than from mental disorder, notwithstanding Mr Gray's apparent inclusion within the latter of all incapacity caused by strokes.[31] The Scottish Law Commission classed persons in a coma or unconscious as physically unable to communicate.[32] See also paras 1–13 and 1–14 above. While dependency on alcohol or drugs is excluded from the definition of mental disorder, an inability meaningfully to communicate a decision through misuse of alcohol or drugs would seem, for the duration of that inability, to be incapacity for the purposes of the Act on grounds of physical inability to communicate.

The criteria for incapacity

The Act's five alternative criteria for incapacity[33] are only relevant **4–27** when caused by mental disability or physical inability to communicate, that is to say, only to adults who have passed through one of the two gateways. Moreover, the Act's definitions of "incapable" and "incapacity", as with its other definitions, are only "for the purposes of this Act". They will not necessarily be interpreted as coinciding with the tests of capacity for other purposes, such as determining whether a purported act or transaction is void. For example, the courts are unlikely to depart from their policy of reluctance to declare a person incapable of testamentary capacity, and might decline to apply—for that purpose—the element of "retaining the memory of decisions" in the case of someone who is incapable of retaining memory of the decision as to appropriate testamentary provision, yet who consistently and repeatedly reaches the same decision in a manner otherwise satisfying all relevant tests of capacity.[34] The Act's

---

[28] See *inter alia* s.9.
[29] See *e.g.* s.57(3)(a) and the Adults with Incapacity (Evidence in Relation to Dispensing with Intimation or Notification) (Scotland) Regulations 2001 (SSI 2001/79), reg.2(3).
[30] 1987 S.L.T. 562.
[31] See para.4–24 *supra*.
[32] SLC Report, para.5.2.
[33] Elements (a)–(e) in s.1(6) quoted in para.4–23 *supra*.
[34] See paras 1–28 *et seq. supra*.

criterion of "retaining the memory of decisions" is in any event likely to be interpreted as referring to retention of memory to a degree, and for a duration, appropriate to the matter in question. No-one retains total and indefinite memory of all competent decisions. An element of proportionality is also likely to be applied to "understanding decisions".

4–28 There is an important element of particularity in "as mentioned in any provision of this Act". The Act does not create any general category of people who are incapable. Incapacity is specific to a particular matter and to the particular provisions of the Act referring to that matter; in any event, that would appear to be the appropriate understanding of this phrase in the Act in its final form, and a reasonable one. When the Bill was first introduced, the phrase served a somewhat different purpose, because some or all of the five elements (a)–(e) in s.1(6) were quoted in relation to each relevant mention of "incapable" throughout the Act, but almost all of those references to individual elements were removed by Scottish Executive amendments during stage 2. The Act does however retain references to element (a), "acting", and at several points combines elements (b)–(e) in references to an adult being or becoming "incapable in relation to decisions" about specified matters. Thus the criteria for guardianship in s.58(1)(a) refer to an adult being either incapable "in relation to decisions" about his property, financial affairs or personal welfare, or being incapable of "acting to safeguard or promote his interests in" any such matters. The same alternatives appear in relation to funds in the criteria for authority to intromit in s.25(1), and in relation to affairs in the criteria for management by an establishment in s.37(2). Section 53(1), on the criteria for an intervention order, makes a similar distinction when referring to the adult being "incapable of taking the action" to which the application relates, or being "incapable in relation to the decision about his property, financial affairs or personal welfare" to which it relates. Provisions about continuing and welfare powers of attorney, authority to treat, and participation in research refer only to the adult being incapable of making decisions about relevant matters.[35]

Appeals

4–29 Decisions as to the incapacity of an adult made by anyone other than the sheriff may be appealed to the sheriff under s.14, which also provides for appeal to the sheriff principal against decisions by the sheriff as to incapacity, with further appeal to the Court of Session. On proceedings before those courts, see Chapter 5.

Good practice—the six levels

4–30 There are six broad levels at which the Act engages with an individual's disabilities, incapacities and abilities. It can be helpful to retain a clear overview of them, and to proceed stepwise through them to the extent appropriate in individual cases. Firstly there are the gateways designed to ensure that no-one who might reasonably and properly benefit from the Act's provisions will be excluded from them.

---

[35] ss.15(1), 16(5)(b)(i), 47(1)(a) and 51(1) respectively.

Only if the adult has a mental disorder, as defined, or a physical inability to communicate, is the Act's régime potentially relevant to that adult. Secondly, however, an adult who has entered the gateway will only be deemed incapable if one or more of the particular criteria (a)–(e) in s.1(6) is shown to apply, and then only for the purpose and to the extent so shown to apply. Thirdly, having entered the gateway and having also established relevant incapacity, the first and second general principles apply the stringent requirements, before we go any further, that there should be no intervention under the Act unless it can be shown that the intervention will achieve benefit, that the benefit cannot reasonably be achieved without the intervention, and that the least restrictive option has been selected. Fourthly, if we have entered the gateway, established relevant incapacity and satisfied the first and second principles, any of the appointees mentioned in the fifth principle must nevertheless encourage the exercise and development of skills, and this principle is linked to provisions which can give validity to resulting acts and transactions. Fifthly, where there is relevant incapacity, then however severe that incapacity may be there is the absolute obligation under the third principle to ascertain present and past wishes and feelings of the adult, if that can be done by any means. Sixthly, where there is relevant incapacity, opposition, resistance or unwillingness has decisive effect in the particular circumstances mentioned in para.4–19 above.

Duty of care and fiduciary duty

A competent person acting for himself is free, within the boundaries **4–31** of what is permissible in law, to act in ways which might be deemed by others to deviate from normal prudence as far as he wishes in the directions of excessive caution or great folly. It is sufficient sanction that he himself must bear the consequences of his own decisions and actions. The position is quite different when one person, here termed "the fiduciary", has accepted an appointment to act for another, here termed "the adult". The consequences of any folly by the fiduciary will be suffered by the adult. Additionally, there is the potential for conflict of interest between the fiduciary's responsibilities and duties as fiduciary, and his own personal interests. In the case of incapacity, the fiduciary will normally have been appointed precisely because the adult is unable to safeguard his own interests. The common law has always sought to provide safeguards in such situations. In particular, in the context of this book, common law duties of care and fiduciary duties are owed to adults by those empowered to act for those adults in relation to their property, financial affairs or personal welfare. Fiduciaries governed by the Incapacity Act who owe such duties include guardians, attorneys, appointees under intervention orders, withdrawers, managers of establishments, equivalents of guardians under the law of other countries if such guardianship is recognised by Scots law, and equivalents of attorneys under the law of other countries. Such duties are also owed by fiduciaries exercising such functions under measures outwith the scope of the Act. In particular, they are owed by trustees under all types of trust, including *inter vivos* and *mortis causa* trusts and trusts for administration. Trustees owe those duties to all those with an interest in the trust, which adds to their duties a requirement for balance and fairness among different interests which may conflict with each other.

4–32 Because the relevant common law principles are well-developed and well-established, it would have been inappropriate to attempt to re-state them in the Incapacity Act, and that has not been attempted. The core principles are encapsulated within the terms themselves, "duty of care" and "fiduciary duty". Precedents, established mainly in relation to trustees and judicial factors but applicable to all fiduciaries,[36] amplify and develop the core principles, rather than placing them within rigid rules,[37] and it is right that the courts be free to apply existing principles in ways appropriate to the particular circumstances brought before them, and appropriate to the characteristics of the new categories of fiduciaries created by the Act. The Scottish Law Commission pointed out[38] that professional fiduciaries would be familiar with such duties but lay fiduciaries might not, and they particularly recommended that the Codes of Practice should deal with the matter: it is thus particularly appropriate to have regard to the Codes in considering the applicability of the principles to relationships created by the Act.

4–33 While the Act does not attempt to re-state the principles, it contains provisions relevant to them. Section 82 exempts appointees under the Act from liability for any breach of any duty of care or fiduciary duty owed to the adult if they have acted reasonably, in good faith, and in accordance with the general principles in s.1. It likewise exempts them from such liability for failure to act if the failure was reasonable, in good faith, and in accordance with the general principles in s.1. Section 82 implements recommendations by the Scottish Law Commission arising from concerns that full application of existing principles would be inappropriate where, for example, an attorney or guardian was a spouse or other close relative, perhaps living with the adult, and where the adult's incapacity would prevent the adult from authorising or acceding to everything which might otherwise be regarded as a breach of duty.[39] The Commission took the view that it would not be possible to set out all the circumstances where a breach of fiduciary duty should be overlooked, nor would it be practicable to require applications to court for dispensations in respect of every breach. The Commission concluded that "the solution lies in the requirements of reasonableness, good faith and adherence to the general principles".[40]

4–34 The following description of the main characteristics of the common law duty of care and fiduciary duty should be read subject to the points that (a) in relation to fiduciaries under the Incapacity Act they are qualified by s.82, (b) in the case of all attorneys, they may be qualified by the power of attorney, (c) in the case of fiduciaries appointed under any other document, such as a Deed of Trust, they may also be qualified by that document, (d) except as above, they apply fully, and (e) they apply to fiduciaries with welfare functions as well as to those with management functions.

---

[36] See *e.g. dicta* of Lord Normand in *Dale v I.R.C.* [1954] A.C. 11 at 26.
[37] See *e.g. dicta* of Lord Dunedin in *Wright v Morgan* [1926] A.C. 788 at 797.
[38] SLC Report, para.2.76.
[39] *cf.* the provision of s.59(5) that, in relation to suitability for appointment as guardian, likely conflict of interest should not be regarded as arising only through close relationship to, or residing with, the adult.
[40] SLC Report, para.2.79.

Duty of care

The basic rule is that a fiduciary must exercise the same level of **4–35**
diligence and care as a person of ordinary prudence would reasonably
be expected to exercise in relation to that person's own affairs.[41] The
standard expected is higher where the fiduciary is remunerated,[42] and
where the fiduciary has relevant professional skills the fiduciary must
exercise the standard of skill and care of a reasonably competent
member of that profession.[43]

Fiduciary duty

Within the scope of the role conferred upon him and the powers **4–36**
entrusted to him, the fiduciary must be faithful to his responsibilities
and to the adult's interests. He must not only act properly, but must
be clearly seen to be doing so. Precedents arise where the fiduciary's
conduct has been challenged, and accordingly delineate the negative
counterparts of those principles. Under common law principles,
unqualified by s.82, the fiduciary must not enter transactions or make
decisions in which he has a personal interest which conflicts with the
adult's interests or with the fiduciary's responsibilities to the adult,[44]
or which could so conflict, regardless of whether the fiduciary in fact
allows such conflict to occur or in fact allows himself to be influenced
by such conflict.[45] A fiduciary who acts so that his personal interest is
brought into conflict with his duties is said to act as *auctor in rem suam*.
The fiduciary must act gratuitously and make no personal profit from
his appointment, except only to the extent expressly authorised in
terms of his appointment.[46] Not only must he avoid conflict between
his duty and his interest, but he must also maintain confidentiality,
both as a duty in its own right[47] and also to avoid unfairness in
dealings with third parties, such as potential purchasers of an asset
belonging to the adult.[48] Potential conflict, and the risk of misuse of
confidential information, may extend beyond the fiduciary himself to
persons or entities connected with the fiduciary. Here there are no
absolute rules forbidding transactions with persons connected in
specified ways, but where there is a connection the courts will
scrutinise the transaction and may set it aside.[49] Where the third party
is a relative of the fiduciary and there is "any other fact" to confirm
the suspicion which that relationship arouses, it would "require a very
strong case to remove" that suspicion.[50] Also potentially reducible on

---

[41] *Kennedy v Kennedy* (1884) 12 R. 275; *Knox v Mackinnon* (1888) 15 R. (HL) 83; *Crabbe v Whyte* (1891) 18 R. 1065; *Buchanan v Eaton*, 1911 S.C. (HL) 40; *Tibbert v McColl*, 1994 S.L.T. 1227.
[42] *Re Waterman's Will Trusts* [1952] 2 All E.R. 1054.
[43] See *e.g.* the Part 6 Code, paras 2.42 and 4.1.
[44] *York Buildings Co. v Mackenzie* (1795) 3 Pat. App. 378; *Aberdeen Ry v Blaikie Bros.* (1854) 1 Macq. 461; *Aitken v Hunter* (1871) 9 M. 756; *Mags of Aberdeen v University of Aberdeen* (1877) 4 R. (HL) 48.
[45] See *Aberdeen Ry v Blaikie Bros* (1853) 1 Macq. 461; *Laird v Laird* (1855) 17 D. 984; *Hamilton v Wright* (1842) 1 Bell's App. Cas. 574; *Elias v Black* (1856) 18 D. 1225; *Wright v Morgan* [1926] A.C. 788.
[46] *Regal (Hastings) Ltd v Gulliver* [1942] 1 All E.R. 378 at 391.
[47] *e.g.* see Part 6 Code, para.5.62.3.
[48] *Hall's Trs v McArthur*, 1918 S.C. 646.
[49] See Wilson and Duncan, *Trusts, Trustees and Executors*, paras 26–08 and 26–09.
[50] *Ferraby v Hobson* (1847) 2 Phillips 255, at 261.

such grounds are transactions with other connected persons, including a firm of which the fiduciary is a partner[51] and a company of which he is a director.[52] A transaction with a company of which the fiduciary is merely a member, even with a substantial interest, may be scrutinised but is less likely to be set aside.[53] While it has been held that it is not a breach of fiduciary duty for a person who holds two fiduciary roles to enter a transaction with himself in those two capacities, the transaction may be set aside if in fact prejudicial to one or the other.[54] Wilson and Duncan[55] list particular types of contract which a fiduciary should not enter, prefaced with the principle that the prohibition arises not from the subject-matter of the contract but from the fiduciary character of the contracting party.[56] After termination of the fiduciary's appointment, there is a continuing obligation not to use or divulge inappropriately knowledge or information "belonging" to the adult and obtained in the fiduciary role during its currency.[57]

The Codes—conflict of interest

4–37   In cases where s.82 modifies the common law prohibition against acting where there is actual or potential conflict of interest, the Codes give guidance on how the fiduciary should deal with potential conflict of interest. The relevant sections are headed "Dealing with conflict of interest", and should be referred to.[58] The Act's s.1 principles must always be adhered to, because s.82 provides no relief where they are contravened. However, it will often be in the adult's interests for the fiduciary to be someone close to the adult, where there may be significant areas of potential conflict of interest, often requiring careful judgements balancing different benefits. Courses open to the fiduciary and mentioned in the Codes include engaging a solicitor to act independently in investigating, considering and representing the adult's interests[59]; in welfare matters, seeking advice from the local authority or Mental Welfare Commission[60]; in management matters, seeking advice from the Public Guardian[61]; or applying to the sheriff for directions under the Incapacity Act s.3(3), or for consequential or ancillary orders, provisions or directions under s.3(1).[62]

The Codes—confidentiality

4–38   The Codes identify three issues concerning confidentiality: the ability and entitlement of fiduciaries to have access to confidential information about the adult; the use and proper disclosure of such

---

[51] *Ex p. Moore* (1881) 51 L.J. Ch.72.
[52] *Dunn v Chambers* (1897) 25 R. 247.
[53] *Farrar v Farrars Ltd* (1888) 40 Ch.D. 395.
[54] See *Templeton v Burgh of Ayr*, 1912 1 S.L.T. 421, and Wilson and Duncan *op.cit.* para.26–09.
[55] *op.cit.*, paras 26–12 *et seq.*
[56] Citing *Aberdeen Ry v Blaikie Bros.* (1853) 1 Macq. 461 at 472.
[57] *CMS Dolphin Ltd v Simonet* [2002] B.C.C. 600.
[58] See *e.g.* Part 2 Code, paras 5.92 *et seq.* and 6.89 *et seq.*; Part 6 Code, paras 2.42 *et seq.*, 3.59 *et seq.* and 5.79 *et seq.*; Local Authority Code paras 5.41 *et seq.* and 6.62 *et seq.*
[59] See para.2–15 *supra*.
[60] See Incapacity Act, ss.9(1)(g) and 10(1)(e).
[61] s.6(1)(e).
[62] See paras 5–14 and 5–6 respectively *infra*.

confidential information; and the fiduciary duty to maintain the adult's confidentiality. Questions of access to and disclosure of confidential information are best addressed in the terms of the fiduciary's appointment,[63] though duties of the fiduciary and others not to disclose confidential information are not absolute and may be displaced by other duties to serve the adult's best interests, in circumstances where disclosure has been properly requested with a view to acting properly in the adult's best interests. For the fiduciary, the duty to maintain confidentiality should be the starting-point, but may be overridden by another specific duty or the duty of care. Likewise, for example, the duty to maintain confidentiality of a solicitor holding the adult's Will may be overridden in the adult's interests where the fiduciary proposes to dispose of certain assets but wishes to ascertain whether any such asset has been specifically bequeathed to anyone: such bequest would be a clear indication of the adult's wishes and feelings of which the fiduciary ought properly to take account (and would thus be properly entitled to ascertain) in terms of s.1(4)(a) of the Act. In case of difficulty in obtaining access to confidential information, the Codes recommend seeking the advice of relevant authorities, taking legal advice, or seeking an intervention order in relation to the information in question.[64]

---

[63] *e.g.* see *Style* Power of Attorney, Appendix 5, power 3.3.
[64] *e.g.* see Part 6 Code, para.5.65.

CHAPTER 5

KEY ROLES AND FUNCTIONS UNDER THE ACT

Introduction

At the centre of the scheme of provision of the Incapacity Act stands **5–1** the adult whose capacity is, or may be, impaired. Within the scope of that scheme of provision, the Act seeks to recognise, to respect and where appropriate to foster such capacity as the adult may have; to minimise the disadvantages and discrimination which might result from impairment of capacity; and to provide protection against the particular vulnerabilities of adults whose capacity is impaired. In seeking to achieve that purpose, the Act creates new roles and adds new functions and responsibilities to existing roles. This chapter describes the principal functions, powers and responsibilities under the Act of the sheriff (paras 5–2 to 5–21), the Court of Session (para.5–22), the Public Guardian (paras 5–23 to 5–27), the Mental Welfare Commission (paras 5–28 to 5–31) and local authorities (paras 5–33 and 5–34), and thereafter in alphabetical order certain others who have key roles and functions. This is not however a directory of all those with significant roles and functions: where roles and functions relate substantially to one Part of the Act, they are generally defined and described in the following particular chapters, rather than in this general chapter. In this chapter, provisions applicable to both the sheriff and the Court of Session are described principally in relation to the sheriff, with cross-references as regards the Court of Session. The other descriptions are each designed to be substantially self-contained. This chapter concludes by bringing together powers and procedures under the Act which may be exercised or invoked in relation to techniques and measures outwith the scope of the Act.

The sheriff

General

A criticism of former law was that if one procedure had been **5–2** initiated and found to be inappropriate, it was generally necessary to re-commence *ab initio* with another. Experience of proceedings concerning adults with impaired capacity indicates that not infrequently it will be found appropriate to grant an order differing from that sought at the outset. Thus, for example, an unreported MHSA guardianship application in Glasgow Sheriff Court in 2000 was continued (and then dismissed) to allow the Court of Session to be petitioned for appointment of tutors-dative, on the basis that such an appointment was more appropriate to meet the needs of the case, allowing an elderly lady to return home with suitable powers in place to facilitate a prompt response if her physical health deteriorated.[1] Moreover, as that example illustrates, the historical allocation of jurisdiction between the sheriff and Court of Session had become illogical and inconvenient. The Act proceeded upon a consensus that the principal jurisdiction under the Act should rest with a single forum, and that so far as appropriate there should be a "one-door" approach, under which (for example) personal and/or property powers, and anything from an intervention order through guardianship with limited powers to guardianship with extensive powers, might be granted following upon the same application.[2]

5–3 The chosen forum is the sheriff court. The sheriff has jurisdiction to grant intervention and guardianship orders[3] and has jurisdiction in the various matters in paras 5–14 to 5–20 below. The sheriff has the broad discretionary and ancillary powers described in paras 5–6 *et seq.* below. Matters reserved to the Court of Session are described in para.5–22. Paragraphs 5–7 to 5–10 and 5–16 to 5–17 below apply also in general terms to the Court of Session.

Jurisdiction

5–4 The sheriff who has jurisdiction is the sheriff in relation to whose sheriffdom one of the following criteria applies.[4] Firstly, the adult is habitually resident in the sheriffdom.[5] Secondly, relevant property is located within the sheriffdom, relevant property being property which is the subject of the application or proceedings, or in respect of which functions are carried out under the Act. Thirdly, where the matter is urgent and the adult is not habitually resident in Scotland, the adult or property belonging to the adult is present in the sheriffdom. Fourthly, the adult is present in the sheriffdom and the intervention sought in the application or proceedings is of a temporary nature and its effect is limited to Scotland. Fifthly, the sheriff will also have jurisdiction to vary or recall any intervention or guardianship order made by him if no contracting state, outside the United Kingdom, under the Hague Convention of January 13, 2000 on the International Protection of Adults has jurisdiction, and if either no other court or authority has jurisdiction, or another court or authority has jurisdiction but it would be unreasonable to expect the applicant to invoke that jurisdiction, or that other court or authority has declined to exercise jurisdiction[6]: jurisdiction will thus normally follow that adult or the adults' property, rather than remaining with the court which made the original order. Finally, even though another judicial or administrative authority has jurisdiction, the sheriff has jurisdiction to take measures considered by the sheriff to be immediately necessary in the interests of the adult if the adult is present in the sheriffdom, except that if none of the preceding grounds applies then the relevant sheriff under this last ground is the sheriff of the Lothians and

---

[1] *Millborrow, Applicant (for appointment of guardian to D)*, unreported, 2000.
[2] See ss.58(3) and 64(1).
[3] Under Part 6 of the Act. See Ch.10.
[4] Sch.3, paras 1(1) and 2.
[5] The adult's place of residence also determines which is the relevant local authority, s.87(1).
[6] Under Sch.3, para.2(2), in respect of which no Commencement Order has yet been made—see para.3–20 *supra*.

Borders at Edinburgh. On jurisdiction generally and matters of private international law, see paras 3–20 *et seq.* above.

Procedure

Procedure before the sheriff under the Act is by way of Summary Application,[7] and is accordingly governed by the Act of Sederunt (Summary Applications, Statutory Applications and Appeals etc. Rules) 1999 ("the Rules"), particularly Chapter 3, Part XVI thereof[8] and, in the Schedule,[9] Forms 20–24. Procedural powers and provisions specific to intervention and guardianship orders are described in Chapters 10 and 11. Under the Rules there are prescribed forms for applications to the sheriff (Form 23), appeals to the sheriff (Form 24), notice of application (Form 20), notice to managers (Form 21) and certificates of delivery by managers (Form 22). Upon submission of the application (or other proceedings) the sheriff fixes a hearing; where he considers it appropriate, orders answers within a specified period; and orders service and intimation.[10] Unless any person upon whom the application is to be served is outside Europe, the hearing must be fixed to take place within 28 days of the first order.[11] It may take place "in a hospital or other place" where the sheriff considers that appropriate in all the circumstances and so orders.[12] Where the applicant is an individual without legal representation, service is effected by the sheriff clerk.[13] The application requires to be served on the adult[14] unless under s.11 the sheriff dispenses with such service as likely to pose serious risk to the adult's health (see para.5–9 below). If the adult is in an "authorised establishment",[15] then instead of service of Form 20 direct on the adult, Forms 20, 21 and 22 require to be served on the managers, whether or not an order under s.11 has been made. Unless such an order has been made, the managers must deliver the Form 20 to the adult and return completed Form 22 to the sheriff clerk.[16] The application must also be served on the nearest relative (subject to any order under s.4—see paras 5–16 and 5–17 below); the adult's primary carer,[17] if there is one; any guardian, or continuing or welfare attorney, with relevant powers; the Public Guardian; any other person directed by the sheriff[18]; and, where the application has been remitted to the sheriff under Rule 3.16.9 (which

5–5

---

[7] s.2(2).
[8] Added by para.3(2) of the Act of Sederunt (Summary Applications, Statutory Applications and Appeals etc. Rules) Amendment (Adults with Incapacity) 2001 (SSI 2001/142) issued March 30, 2001 and amended by Act of Sederunt (Summary Applications, Statutory Applications and Appeals etc. Rules) Amendment (No.3) (Adults with Incapacity) 2002 (SSI 2002/146) issued March 15, 2002.
[9] *ibid.* para.3(3).
[10] Rule 3.16.2.
[11] Rule 3.16.6.
[12] Rule 3.16.3.
[13] Rule 3.16.4(2).
[14] Rule 3.16.4(1)(a).
[15] As defined in s.35(2) (Rule 3.16.1), the managers being as defined in Sch.1 to the Act—see para.9–3 *infra.*
[16] Rule 3.16.4(3) and (4). Rule 3.16.4(3) specifies the method of service on the managers.
[17] See para.5–40 *infra.*
[18] All under Rule 3.16.4(1).

provides that the Public Guardian, or other party authorised under the Act to remit an application to the sheriff, must transmit the relevant papers to the appropriate sheriff clerk within four days of the decision to remit[19]), on the party who so remitted it.[20] The application must be served on the Mental Welfare Commission and/or the local authority "where appropriate", presumably meaning (but not always limited to) applications addressing personal welfare, with the Commission limited to mental disorder cases.[21] At the hearing the sheriff may determine the application or order such further procedure as he thinks fit.[22] Subsequent applications or proceedings (including those for renewal) take the form of minute lodged in process, unless the Act or the Rules prescribe otherwise.[23] Except where the sheriff directs otherwise, the minute requires to be lodged in accordance with, and is governed by, Chapter 14 of the Ordinary Cause Rules.[24] Where a subsequent application is made in a different sheriffdom, the court process must be transmitted there within four days of the sheriff clerk there so requesting.[25]

General discretionary and ancillary powers

5–6 In any application or other proceedings under the Act, the sheriff may make such consequential or ancillary order, provision or direction as he considers appropriate.[26] The sheriff may attach to any order made by him such conditions or restrictions as appear to him to be appropriate,[27] which conditions and restrictions may be varied upon application by the person authorised under the relevant order, by the adult, or by any person entitled to apply for the relevant order.[28] In relation to the adult who is the subject of the application or proceedings, the sheriff may order that any reports be lodged with the court, or that the adult be assessed or interviewed and that a report of such assessment or interview be lodged.[29] The sheriff may make such further enquiries or call for such further information as appears to the sheriff to be appropriate.[30] The sheriff may make such interim order as appears to the sheriff to be appropriate, pending the disposal of the application or proceedings.[31] These broad discretionary powers enable applicants and other parties to proceedings to seek the court's assistance where there is difficulty in obtaining information likely to be necessary to enable the court to make an appropriate disposal. They can be invoked by the court *ex proprio motu* for such purposes, and they provide the flexibility to match interim orders and final disposals to the infinite diversity of needs and circumstances likely to

---

[19] See para.5–20 *infra* for various provisions under which such remits are competent.
[20] Rule 3.16.4(5).
[21] Rule 3.16.4(1)(ea) and (eb).
[22] Rule 3.16.6(2)—see the general powers of the sheriff described in para.5–6 *infra*.
[23] Rule 3.16.8(1).
[24] Rule 3.16.8(1A).
[25] Rule 3.16.8(2) and (3).
[26] s.3(1).
[27] s.3(2)(a).
[28] s.3(6).
[29] s.3(2)(b).
[30] s.3(2)(c).
[31] s.3(2)(d).

Safeguarders

5–7 In all applications and other proceedings under the Act the sheriff is required to consider whether it is necessary to appoint a safeguarder. The power to appoint a safeguarder is in addition to, and does not replace, any existing powers to appoint someone to represent the interests of the adult, such as a curator ad litem. The safeguarder has a general function to safeguard the interests of the person who is the subject of the proceedings, including conveying that person's views to the sheriff "so far as they are ascertainable". However, where the sheriff considers it inappropriate for the safeguarder to convey the person's views, the sheriff may appoint someone else to do so.[32] Similar provisions apply to the Court of Session in appeals and other proceedings under the Act.[33] On curators ad litem, see also paras 12–26 and 12–35 below.

General principles

5–8 In relation to any intervention under the Act the sheriff is required to apply the general principles.[34] These include the absolute obligation to take account of the adult's present and past wishes and feelings so far as ascertainable by any means. In discharging that responsibility, the sheriff may be assisted by a safeguarder or by someone else appointed specifically to convey the adult's views.[35] The latter is described in official guidance[36] as a curator ad litem. Where there is doubt about whether relevant views are ascertainable, or specialist skills may be required to ascertain them, the sheriff's powers under s.3(1) and (2) may also be of assistance. By whomever the adult's views are ascertained and conveyed, there must be a clear distinction between that function, on the one hand, and any wider assistance to the court in seeking to arrive at an appropriate decision, on the other. Note that s.3(5) refers to the "views" of the person who is the subject of the application or proceedings, whereas s.1(4)(a) setting out the third principle refers to the adult's "wishes and feelings". It is suggested that "views" encompass both competent views and also "wishes and feelings", whatever the degree of any impairment of relevant capacity.

Intimation to the adult

5–9 It is central to the philosophy and principles of the Act that intimation of applications and other proceedings, and notification of relevant interlocutors, be given to the adult. On occasions such

---

[32] ss.3(4) and (5). As to ascertaining and conveying the person's views, see paras 4–16 et seq. supra and para.5–8 infra.
[33] Under s.5. See para.5–22 infra.
[34] ss.1(1)–(4). See Ch.4.
[35] s.3(4) and (5). See para.5–7 supra.
[36] Explanatory Notes to the Act, para.26.

intimation or notification would be likely to pose a serious risk to the adult's health. Under s.11(1), the court may dispense with intimation or notification if it considers that there is such a risk. The Rules permit the sheriff to do so upon production of two medical certificates stating that intimation or notification would be likely to pose such a risk.[37] The certificates must be prepared by medical practitioners independently of each other, and where the incapacity is caused by mental disorder one of the certifiers must be an approved psychiatrist.[38] There have been criticisms that under curatory procedure applications to dispense with service have been made lightly, and may on occasions have been related to convenience rather than to serious risk to health. The fact that the adult may be seriously upset by, and seek to oppose, an application is *prima facie* a reason to ensure that the adult hears about and fully understands the application, and is afforded an opportunity to oppose. Having regard to ECHR and s.1 principles, it is to be anticipated that the courts will require clear, reasoned and robust evidence before exercising discretion to dispense with intimation or notification, and may not necessarily accept without question medical certification which lacks those qualities. The chief social work officer must not notify under s.64(9) when the sheriff has given a direction under s.11(1)—see s.64(10), and see also s.76(4). In case of similar risk to the adult's health, the Public Guardian must not give intimation or notification otherwise required under the Act,[39] and managers of establishments may under s.37(8) seek a direction from their supervisory body that they need not notify the adult under ss.37(3) and (4).[40]

Expenses

5–10　The only specific provisions in the Act regarding expenses appear in ss.8 and 68(3). Section 8 concerns expenses incurred by the Public Guardian, Mental Welfare Commission or (except where s.68 applies) the local authority. Under s.8(1), where any such body is a party to proceedings for the purpose of protecting the interests of the adult, the court may make an award of expenses against the adult or any person whose actings have resulted in the proceedings. Under s.8(2), where the purpose is to represent the public interest, the court may make an award of expenses against any person whose actings have resulted in the proceedings or on whose part there has been unreasonable conduct in relation to the proceedings. As introduced, s.8 would have empowered the court to award against the adult's estate expenses incurred by the above bodies both for protecting the adult's interests and also for representing the public interest. The Scottish Parliament unanimously supported the view that the adult's estate should not bear the cost of representing the public interest, except in (rare but possible) cases where the conduct of the adult has resulted in the proceedings or has been unreasonable in relation to the proceedings. However, the inclusion of reference to the adult in s.8(1) but not

---

[37] Rule 3.16.5(1).
[38] Rule 3.16.5(2) and (3). As regards "mental disorder", see para.4–24 *supra*. As regards approved psychiatrists, see para.5–36 *infra*.
[39] See s.11(2) and para.5–25 *infra*.
[40] See para.9–7 *infra*.

in s.8(2) might open an argument that no award should be made under s.8(2) against the adult.

Section 68(3) applies to the cost of any application by a local authority for appointment of the chief social work officer as guardian and to any subsequent application by the chief social work officer while acting as guardian. It is provided that the local authority shall meet the cost of applications relating to the adult's personal welfare, but may recover from the adult's estate the cost of applications relating to the adult's property or financial affairs. Where the application relates both to personal welfare and to property and financial affairs, the sheriff shall, in determining the application, apportion the cost as he thinks fit. These provisions present difficulties because it is clear from s.59 that only personal welfare powers, and not property or financial powers, may be conferred on the chief social work officer. Section 59(2) provides that where the guardianship order confers both welfare and financial powers and the chief social work officer is one of the guardians, he may have only welfare powers, and accordingly a joint guardian would be required to exercise the property and financial powers. That can be the only situation in which the provisions regarding applications relating to the adult's property or financial affairs can apply. Because s.68(3) is mandatory as to the cost of personal welfare applications and s.8 is excluded, the local authority must meet "the cost" however much the cost may have been inflated by the intervention or conduct of other parties or of the adult, and there could be room for argument as to whether "the cost" is limited to the local authority's own costs. On s.68(3) see also para.11–34 below. 5–11

There are no other express provisions in the Act regarding the expenses of court proceedings under the Act. Expenses would accordingly appear to be within the sheriff's discretion, either under the sheriff's general powers in s.3 or (as all applications under the Act are to be made by summary application[41]) under the sheriff's inherent power to dispose of questions of expenses in summary applications.[42] While expenses are not normally awarded in applications to the sheriff in his administrative, rather than judicial, capacity,[43] the purposes of most, if not all, of the provisions of the Act for application, remit or appeal to the sheriff include ensuring compliance with ECHR Article 6, therefore it seems unlikely that any procedure before the sheriff under the Act would be held to be administrative rather than judicial.[44] 5–12

Appeals

Except where the Act expressly provides otherwise, appeal lies to the sheriff principal and thence (with leave of the sheriff principal) to the Court of Session against any decision of the sheriff at first instance 5–13

---

[41] s.2(2).
[42] See Macphail, *Sheriff Court Practice* (Nicholson and Stewart, 2nd ed., 1998), Vol.I, para.25.46.
[43] *ibid.* para.25.47.
[44] But see *ibid.* para.25.38 for cases where, for purposes of right to appeal, decisions by the sheriff under MHSA 1984, s.29(4) have been held to be administrative. The Incapacity Act is explicit (see para.5–13 *infra*) that the sheriff's decisions under that Act are appealable except where the Act stipulates otherwise, but such stipulation does not *ipso facto* render proceedings administrative rather than judicial.

in any application to the sheriff or any other proceedings before the sheriff under the Act.[45] Appeals against a decision of a sheriff regarding medical treatment under s.52 lie (with the leave of the sheriff) direct to the Court of Session. Matters in which the sheriff's decision is final include various applications, remits and appeals described in para.5–20 below.

Giving directions

5–14 Apart from jurisdiction in relation to intervention orders and guardianship under Part 6 of the Act[46] and the discretionary and ancillary powers described in para.5–6 above, the sheriff has jurisdiction under the Act in the matters described in this and the following paragraphs. Under s.3(3) the adult, or anyone else claiming an interest in the property, financial affairs or personal welfare of the adult, may apply to the sheriff to make an order giving directions to any persons exercising functions under the Act, or exercising similar functions under the law of any country.[47] Directions could thus be given to appointees, the Public Guardian, local authorities, supervisory bodies and others. Upon such application, the sheriff may give such directions as appear to the sheriff to be appropriate as to the exercise of functions under the Act, or the taking of decisions or action, in relation to an adult. This is a broad and potentially very useful power for resolving not only disputes but also doubts and difficulties where there is no dispute. For example, an appointee (including an attorney) could seek directions as to whether a proposed course of action was *intra vires* and/or appropriate, where the degree of doubt and/or the significance of the matter justified seeking judicial authority. That could be appropriate not only in the interests of the adult, but perhaps also having regard to other and potentially conflicting interests, or for the protection of the appointee from future criticism. Likewise, for example, a medical practitioner concerned about the proper exercise of functions under Part 5 or other provisions of the Act could, where the circumstances justified it, seek directions as to how he should proceed.[48] Section 62(8) specifically authorises one or more joint guardians to apply to the sheriff for directions under s.3 if they are in disagreement, but that explicit provision is probably unnecessary and there appears to be no reason why one or more concurrent guardians or joint or concurrent attorneys should not make similar application.[49]

5–15 While sheriffs may be asked by persons exercising functions to give them directions, or to resolve differences between joint appointees, the jurisdiction to give directions is likely otherwise to be invoked by the adult or someone else who disagrees with a decision or course of action taken or proposed by a person exercising functions. As to principles which the Scottish courts might find it appropriate to follow in such situations, assistance may be provided by some of the decisions of the German courts under the régime introduced by the

---

[45] s.2(3).
[46] See Chs 10 and 11.
[47] See paras 3–20 *et seq. supra* as to jurisdiction.
[48] See, for example, the "circular dilemma" referred to in para.10–48 *infra*.
[49] See paras 6–20 and 11–7 *infra*.

Betreuungsgesetz of 1990.[50] The overall approach of the German courts can reasonably be summarised as refusing to interfere with an appointee's decision or proposed action where there is no prejudice to the adult's welfare or interests and there are no grounds for terminating the appointment. Put another way and in a Scottish context, if more than one course of action would be consistent with serving the adult's welfare and/or interests and would be in accordance with the general principles, and if there are no grounds for revoking the appointee's appointment or removing relevant powers, then the court would not at the urging of an applicant substitute the court's choice for that of the appointee. Where there was a choice between approving the use of restraints in an open home for the elderly, or placement in a closed institution, the betreuer (guardian) had chosen the former, but the guardianship court had directed the betreuer to choose the latter, LG Köln (the County Court of Cologne) on appeal set aside the decision of the guardianship court and held that the court had no power to overrule the reasonable decisions of the betreuer: it also held that the betreuer's choice represented the less restrictive option[51] (on the latter point, *cf.* the second principle of the Incapacity Act described in paras 4–13 *et seq.* above). Where a woman's husband sought an order that his wife should be moved to a different residential care facility from that in which her guardian had placed her, the courts at first instance and on appeal, and OLG Schleswig (the High Court of the State of Schleswig-Holstein) on further appeal, all held that the guardian's decision was reasonable and therefore should not be interfered with: OLG Schleswig also noted and stressed that while the lady could no longer express views on the matter, when interviewed in the past she had expressed herself content with her existing residence and care[52] (on the latter point, *cf.* the third principle of the Incapacity Act described in paras 4–16 *et seq.* above). That case followed an earlier decision at the second level of appeal in 1991 after introduction of the Betreuungsgesetz, but concerning the decision of a guardian ("pfleger") under the previous law. The guardian had placed an elderly lady in a care home, the lady's daughter desired that the lady be placed in the daughter's home to be cared for by the daughter, and the guardian had concerns about the daughter's ability to provide the 24-hour care needed by the lady: the courts at all levels refused to interfere with the guardian's decision.[53] In a decision on appeal by LG Chemnitz (County Court of Chemnitz, State of Saxony),[54] the dispute was between a mentally ill man and his own guardian. The man had previously been ejected from his flat in Leipzig and the guardian had found a placement for him in a residential facility for people with mental illness in Chemnitz. After four years there, he complained to the guardianship court that he wanted to move back to a flat in Leipzig, was critical of his guardian, but was inconsistent about whether he wanted a change of guardian.

---

[50] See para.3–3 *supra*. The author is indebted to Ulrich Hellmann, Legal Adviser, Lebenshilfe for identifying relevant precedents, including those referred to in this paragraph, and assisting with translation.
[51] LG Köln, Beschluss v. 27.4.1992–1 T 117/92.
[52] OLG Schleswig (2. ZS Beschluss v. 2.5.1996–2 W 106/95).
[53] OLG Bayern (High Court of Bavaria) (3. ZS, Beschluss v. 27.6.1991—BReg. 3 Z 52/91).
[54] LG Chemnitz (11. ZK, Beschluss v. 9.5.2000–11 T 1270/00).

The guardian was concerned that the man had become well settled in his existing placement and that an abrupt change could be damaging, and he was also concerned about a report from the residential facility that the man would not be able to live on his own. The guardianship court renewed the appointment of the same guardian but additionally ordered the guardian to arrange a change of residence within four months and to refrain from "influencing the wishes" of the man. On appeal, the additional orders were set aside as inappropriate.

Orders regarding functions of nearest relative

5–16 Under the Act, the nearest relative of the adult has the functions described in para.5–39 below. Subject to the modifications mentioned in that paragraph, the definition of "nearest relative" in MHSA 1984 is imported into the Incapacity Act. However, a serious criticism of MHSA is that it confers no power to disqualify an unsuitable nearest relative, even if (for example) the nearest relative has abused the patient or is otherwise unsuitable to receive information or play any role. Section 4 addresses that deficiency, for the purposes of the Incapacity Act only. Under s.4(1)(a) the court may order that neither information nor intimation be given to the nearest relative. The court may order under s.4(1)(b) that someone else should exercise the functions of nearest relative, or under s.4(1)(c) that no-one should do so, in both cases for the duration of the order. The substitute nearest relative must be a person who would "otherwise" be entitled to be a nearest relative in terms of the Act, who in the court's opinion is a proper person to act as such, and who is willing to do so. "Otherwise" presumably means but for the existence as nearest relative of the person superseded in that role in terms of the order. Unnecessarily, but presumably for emphasis, the court is specifically enjoined in proceedings under s.4 to have regard to s.1 of the Act. The court may only make a s.4 order if satisfied that to do so will benefit the adult. The Court of Session has concurrent jurisdiction under s.4.

5–17 Applications for orders under s.4(1) and for variation of such orders under s.4(3) may in terms of s.4(4) only be made by an adult who is incapable at the time of the application. Accordingly, such application may not be made by a capable adult in anticipation of that adult's own incapacity, or by anyone other than the incapable adult. It will be interesting to follow how the courts give meaning to a procedure which may only be used by a person who, by definition, might be incapable of it. Indeed, if "incapable" in the Act is to be construed as meaning incapable of the particular matter referred to (see para.4–28 above) then this is a procedure which may only be used by a person who, by definition, *is* incapable of using it. It may be that the Scottish Parliament intended that s.4(4) should prevent persons on their own behalf making such application in respect of an incapable adult, but should not prevent such application by someone with authority to bring it in name of and on behalf of the incapable adult (such as someone empowered to do so by an intervention order under Part 6). It was understood that Scottish Executive intended to amend the Mental Health (Scotland) Bill to allow persons having an interest to make applications under s.4.[55]

---

[55] But the Executive did not. See para.3–31 *supra*.

Appeal against decisions as to incapacity

Section 14 contains general rights to appeal against decisions under the Act as to incapacity of an adult. Appeals may be brought by that adult or by anyone claiming an interest in the adult's property, financial affairs or personal welfare relating to the purpose for which the decision was taken. Where the decision was made by anyone other than the sheriff, appeal lies to the sheriff. Where the decision was made by the sheriff, appeal lies to the sheriff principal and thence, with leave of the sheriff principal, to the Court of Session.

5–18

Appeal against decisions as to medical treatment

Any decision taken for the purposes of Part 5 of the Act[56] as to the medical treatment of an adult, other than a decision by a medical practitioner under s.50,[57] may be appealed under s.52. Such an appeal may be brought by any person *having* an interest (not merely claiming an interest)—see para.14–59 below. Appeal lies to the sheriff and thence, as noted in para.5–13 above, with the leave of the sheriff direct to the Court of Session. In relation to certification under s.47(1) for the purpose of the new authority to treat, issues may arise as to whether an appeal to the sheriff is an appeal against a decision as to incapacity in terms of s.14 or as to medical treatment in terms of s.52. In the former case, appeal may be brought by the adult or "any person claiming an interest"; in the latter, as noted above, only by "any person having an interest". In the former case, further appeal lies next to the sheriff principal; in the latter, to the Court of Session.

5–19

Miscellaneous applications, remits and appeals

Remits and appeals to the sheriff, under which the sheriff's decision is final, include the following: in relation to attorneys, appeals under s.19(6) against decisions of the Public Guardian as to whether a person is prepared to act or a specified event has occurred, and applications for orders in terms of s.20(2)(a)–(d) placing attorneys under supervision or ordaining them to submit accounts or to report; in relation to authority to intromit with funds, remits of applications under s.26(8), and appeals against decisions of the Public Guardian under ss.26(9), 29(4), 31(6) and 33(3); in relation to management of residents' finances, appeals under s.45(6) against decisions of a supervisory body; and in relation to guardians, orders under s.64(7) giving effect to the orders or demands of the Public Guardian, remits under s.66(7) and appeals under s.66(8) in relation to applications to authorise gifts, appeals under s.68(8) concerning remuneration, remits under s.72(5) and appeals under s.72(6) concerning discharge, remits under s.73(8) and appeals under s.73(9) concerning recall, various applications under Schedule 2 regarding management, and appeals under para.6(7) of Schedule 4 against determinations by the Public Guardian about the application of Schedule 2 to guardians under the transitional provisions of Schedule 4. In relation to attorneys, the sheriff also has

5–20

---

[56] See Ch.14.
[57] See paras 14–60 and 14–61 *infra*. Appeals under s.50 lie direct to the Court of Session.

powers under s.20(2)(e) to revoke particular powers granted or the appointment, to which powers the normal appeal provisions described in the first sentence of para.5–13 above apply. See para.9–16 below on the sheriff's power under ROCSA s.18 to cancel registration of an establishment upon summary application by the Scottish Commission for the Regulation of Care.

Comment

5–21 The draft Bill annexed to the Scottish Law Commission Report contained, in clause 2(5), a suggested provision that: "All applications and proceedings under this Act shall be disposed of by a sheriff nominated for the time being for that purpose by the sheriff principal, unless no such sheriff is available to do so." The Scottish Law Commission discussed choice of forum in paras 2.18–2.31 of its Report. Although the option of using the courts had attracted most support, there was considerable support for the alternatives of tribunals or hearings, and considerable disquiet about the suitability of the courts, perceived disadvantages including that the courts would be "intimidating, legalistic, adversarial and only willing to look at the issues put in front of them, lacking in understanding of the needs of the mentally incapable, slow, expensive and associated with criminal proceedings". The Scottish Law Commission took the view that some (and therefore, by implication, not all) of the criticisms were unfounded; and also adopted, and described as "excellent", a suggestion by the Law Society of Scotland that proceedings under the Act should be conducted by specially selected "designated sheriffs". Not even the modest proposal in the draft Bill annexed to the Scottish Law Commission Report was adopted in the Act, nor is it reflected in the Rules. The need to address the issues giving rise to that proposal, in the conduct of proceedings by the courts, will be sharpened by the need to comply with the requirement of ECHR Article 6 for a "fair" hearing in an area where most, if not all, other modern jurisdictions rest with specialised courts or tribunals because of the essential requirement for an informed and proactive, rather than traditionally reactive, judicial role. The Mental Health (Scotland) Bill introduced on September 16, 2002,[58] following the recommendations of the Millan Committee, proposes establishment of a Mental Health Tribunal for Scotland: concurrent experience of such a tribunal in mental health matters and sheriff courts in incapacity matters could lead at some future date to one or the other taking over both jurisdictions, following comparative assessment of performance.

Court of Session

5–22 Whereas the Court of Session previously had exclusive jurisdiction to appoint tutors to adults[59] and concurrent jurisdiction to appoint curators bonis,[60] the equivalent jurisdiction at first instance under the Act is exclusively with the sheriff. The Court of Session retains an

---

[58] See para.3–31 *supra*.
[59] See "Revival of Tutors-Dative", 1987 S.L.T. (News) 69.
[60] The Court of Session's jurisdiction was originally exclusive, but extended to the sheriff by the Judicial Factors (Scotland) Act 1880.

appellate role and also a particular role in relation to medical matters.[61] Where appeal is competent,[62] it lies first to the sheriff principal and thence, with leave of the sheriff principal, to the Court of Session,[63] except that appeals concerning medical treatment under s.52 lie first to the sheriff and thence, with leave of the sheriff, to the Court of Session. Under s.50, appeals lie direct to the Court of Session, bypassing both the sheriff and the sheriff principal. Section 50 deals with decisions about medical treatment where an appointee has relevant powers. If appointee and medical practitioner are in agreement, anyone *having* an interest may appeal to the Court of Session. Appeals against the decision of a nominated medical practitioner under s.50 also lie direct to the Court of Session. Under the Specified Treatments Regulations[64] certain treatments require the approval of the Court of Session. The role accorded to the Court of Session by ss.50 and 52 and by the Regulations allows that court, with authority and consistency, to develop the law in relation to matters which may arise from Part 5 of the Act, in like manner as it has been left to that court to deal with any further issues which may arise in relation to withholding and withdrawal of life-preserving treatment following upon *Law Hospital NHS Trust v Lord Advocate*.[65] The *parens patriae* jurisdiction, discussed in that case, is unaffected by the Act (except as regards appointment of tutors-dative, which is no longer competent). The Court of Session has the same powers as the sheriff in relation to the nearest relative[66] and similar provisions apply regarding safeguarders and appointment of another person to convey the adult's views.[67] The provisions of s.8 regarding expenses and s.11 regarding intimation to the adult apply to the Court of Session as well as to the sheriff.[68] On jurisdiction of the Scottish courts and matters of private international law, see paras 3–20 *et seq.* above.

Public Guardian

On April 2, 2001 the Accountant of Court became the Public Guardian.[69] The Public Guardian's office is at Hadrian House, Callendar Business Park, Callendar Road, Falkirk FK1 1XR, Tel. 01324 678 300, e-mail: opg@scotcourts.gov.uk. Section 6 helpfully brings together various general functions conferred upon the Public Guardian. Several of the provisions of s.6 must be read with the more detailed provisions appearing subsequently throughout the Act. The Public Guardian's functions, except for the functions of registration under s.6(2)(b) and consultation under s.6(2)(f), relate to property and financial affairs, and do not extend to personal welfare. The Public Guardian has a general function of supervising guardians and

5–23

---

[61] See Ch.14.
[62] See paras 5–13 and 5–20 *supra*.
[63] s.2(3).
[64] The Adults with Incapacity (Specified Medical Treatments) (Scotland) Regulations 2002 (SSI 2002/275) as amended by SSI 2002/302 made under s.48: see paras 14–48 *et seq. infra*.
[65] 1996 S.L.T. 848, 1996 S.C.L.R. 491, 1996 S.C. 301. See paras 14–25 *et seq. infra*.
[66] s.4 (see paras 5–16 and 5–17).
[67] Under s.5. *Cf.* s.3(4) and (5), and see paras 5–7 and 5–8.
[68] See paras 5–10 and 5–9 *supra*, respectively.
[69] s.6(1) and No.1 Commencement Order.

appointees under intervention orders in property and financial matters.[70] He is required to establish and maintain various separate registers, and to make them available for inspection by members of the public during normal office hours on payment of a prescribed fee.[71] He is required to enter in each register any matter which he is required to enter under the relevant provisions of the Act and also "any other matter of which he becomes aware relating to the existence or scope of the power, authorisation or order as the case may be". The Act contains no provisions to protect confidentiality in relation to this last requirement and the public right of inspection, which could raise issues in relation to ECHR Article 8[72] and the disclosure by appointees to the Public Guardian of confidential information received by them concerning the adult. It is understood that the Public Guardian's current policy is that the public registers disclose standard particulars[73] and can be viewed by anyone on demand, but that further disclosure and provision of copies would be on cause shown and subject to the Public Guardian's discretion.[74] The registers kept by the Public Guardian relate to continuing powers of attorney governed by Scots law[75]; welfare powers of attorney governed by Scots law[76]; authorisations to intromit with funds[77]; guardianship orders[78]; and intervention orders.[79] As with all others exercising functions under the Act, the Public Guardian must comply with the general principles[80] and may be given directions by the sheriff under s.3(3).[81]

5–24 In relation to the property and financial affairs of adults, the Public Guardian is required to receive and investigate complaints concerning continuing attorneys, intromissions with funds under Part 3,[82] guardians, and appointees under intervention orders,[83] and also to investigate any circumstances made known to the Public Guardian in which the property or financial affairs of an adult seem to him to be at risk.[84] The latter is an important function which, in the context of the Act, is likely to be interpreted as meaning risk containing an element of incapacity or apparent incapacity on the part of the adult. In consequence of any investigation described in this paragraph, the Public Guardian may take such steps (including making an application to the sheriff[85]) as seem to him to be necessary to safeguard the property or

---

[70] s.6(2)(a), and see generally the provisions of Part 6 and Sch.2.
[71] See the Adults with Incapacity (Public Guardian's Fees) (Scotland) Regulations 2001 (SSI 2001/75) as amended by SSI 2002/131, which also prescribe fees for supplying copies.
[72] See para.1–48 *supra*.
[73] Date of registration, Public Guardian's reference, name of adult, name of appointee, type of appointment, whether appointment is terminated.
[74] For example, in the case of powers of attorney, as to the terms of the document itself (letter to the author July 16, 2001, by which date some duplicate or replacement certificates had already been requested).
[75] s.6(2)(b)(i), and see Part 2.
[76] s.6(2)(b)(ii), and see Part 2.
[77] s.6(2)(b)(iii), and see Part 3.
[78] s.6(2)(b)(iv), and see Part 6 and Sch.2.
[79] s.6(2)(b)(v), and see Part 6.
[80] ss.1(1)–(4). See Ch.4.
[81] See para.5–14 *supra*.
[82] For the Public Guardian's further powers under Part 3, see para.8–14 *infra*.
[83] s.6(2)(c). Complaints against equivalent appointees to guardians and continuing attorneys under other jurisdictions are included by s.6(3).
[84] s.6(2)(d).
[85] See paras 5–14 to 5–20 *supra*.

financial affairs of the adult.[86] In relation to their respective investigatory powers, the Public Guardian, Mental Welfare Commission and local authority are required to provide each other with such information and assistance as may be necessary to facilitate the investigation.[87] They are also required to consult among each other on cases or matters relating to the exercise of functions under the Act in which there is, or appears to be, a common interest.[88] It is relevant to note in this context the duties of local authorities to apply for intervention orders (s.53(3)) and guardianship orders (s.57(2)), and the investigatory duties under s.40(2) and (3) of supervisory bodies in relation to management by authorised establishments under Part 4. In his first year from April 2, 2001 the Public Guardian commenced 64 investigations, 16 at the instance of the Mental Welfare Commission or a local authority, and 2 of them joint investigations with a local authority where there were both financial and welfare concerns. The Accountant of Court increasingly saw it as his function to provide curators bonis (and other judicial factors) with information and advice, and s.6(2)(e) provides for performance of that function by the Public Guardian in relation to guardians, continuing attorneys, withdrawers and appointees under intervention orders in relation to performance of functions under the Act concerning property and financial affairs.

Where the Public Guardian considers that an intimation or notification otherwise required to be given to the adult would be likely to pose a serious risk to the adult's health, he must not give it.[89] In deciding the matter, the Public Guardian is required to take into account two medical certificates stating that intimation or notification to the adult could be likely to pose such a risk. The certificates must be prepared by medical practitioners independently of each other, and where the incapacity is caused by mental disorder one of the certifiers must be an approved psychiatrist.[90] A decision by the sheriff under the sheriff's equivalent powers is binding on the Public Guardian for the purposes of s.76.[91] 5-25

The fees payable to the Public Guardian are prescribed by regulations and the Public Guardian is not obliged to act until the fee is paid.[92] Certificates issued by the Public Guardian under the Act are conclusive evidence of the matters in them for the purposes of any proceedings.[93] At time of writing the Scottish Ministers have not 5-26

---

[86] s.12(1), the wording of which probably also authorises him to take steps in relation to personal welfare concerns coming to his notice, though this would normally be done by referring the matter to the local authority or Mental Welfare Commission for them to exercise their equivalent powers.
[87] s.12(2).
[88] ss.6(2)(f), 9(1)(c) and 10(1)(b).
[89] s.11(2). Unlike the sheriff under s.11(1) (see para.5–9 *supra*) the Public Guardian has no discretion once he has concluded that there is a serious health risk.
[90] The Adults with Incapacity (Evidence in Relation to Dispensing with Intimation or Notification) (Scotland) Regulations 2001 (SSI 2001/79). As regards "mental disorder", see para.4–24 *supra*. As regards approved psychiatrists, see para.5–36 *infra*.
[91] See para.5–9 *supra* and s.76(4).
[92] The Adults with Incapacity (Public Guardian's Fees) (Scotland) Regulations 2001 (SSI 2001/75) and s.7(2). The 2001 Regulations were amended by the Adults with Incapacity (Public Guardian's Fees) (Scotland) Amendment Regulations 2002 (SSI 2002/131).
[93] s.7(3).

5-27 exercised their powers to make regulations under s.7(1)(a), (b) and (c). See para.3–12 above.

The Public Guardian has prescribed and promulgated various matters[94] and has published a wide and useful range of forms, styles and guidance notes written with commendable clarity, all available on his website www.scotcourts.gov.uk. Several are referred to where appropriate in the course of this book.

Mental Welfare Commission

5-28 The Mental Welfare Commission for Scotland was established by MHSA 1960[95] and continued in being by MHSA 1984, under which the Commission plays a major role in protecting the persons and interests of people with mental disorders.[96] It deals with both individual cases and issues of general concern. It has a wide range of powers and functions.[97] It is proposed that the new MHSA[98] will, in accordance with the recommendations of the Millan Committee, facilitate "a more strategic approach to performing its role of protecting individual patients" and give it the role of monitoring and promoting best practice in the operation of the new MHSA.[99] The Commission's address is: K Floor, Argyle House, 3 Lady Lawson Street, Edinburgh EH3 9SH, Tel. 0131 222 6111.

5-29 The Commission now has additional functions under the Incapacity Act in relation to adults to whom the Act applies because of mental disorder, or for reasons which include mental disorder, but not (except under s.50[1]) to those to whom it applies only by reason of inability to communicate because of physical disability,[2] in relation to whom the Public Guardian (see paras 5–23 *et seq.* above) and the local authority (see para.5–33 below) do have protective and other functions. Subject to the above limitation, the Commission has a general duty to exercise protective functions in respect of adults subject to guardianship and intervention orders, insofar as relating to personal welfare.[3]

5-30 With the supersession of MHSA guardianship, the visiting and investigative functions of the Commission under MHSA 1984, s.3(2) are now limited to detained patients, deleting the previous references to MHSA guardianship. Sections 9(1)(b), (e) and (f) of the Incapacity Act substantially broaden the Commission's visiting and investigative functions by applying them to any adult to whom the Act applies by reasons of, or including, mental disorder—not limited to those subject to orders under Part 6 or in relation to whom any measures under the Act have been taken. The specific functions are to visit any such adult as often as they think appropriate and, if they consider that any personal welfare matters ought to be brought to the attention of the relevant Health Board or local authority, or any other body, to report

---

[94] See para.3–12 *supra*.
[95] 8 & 9 Eliz. 2 c.61, s.2.
[96] See para.4–24 *supra*.
[97] See MHSA 1984, ss.2–6.
[98] See paras 5–32 *infra* and 3–31 *supra*.
[99] Mental Health (Scotland) Bill, Policy Memorandum, paras 15 and 16.
[1] See para.5–31 *infra*.
[2] s.9(1). See paras 4–25 and 4–26 *supra*.
[3] s.9(1)(a): but see para.5–32 *infra*.

them accordingly[4]; to investigate any circumstances made known to them in which the personal welfare of such an adult seems to them to be at risk[5]; and to investigate any circumstances made known to them in which there may be risk of loss or damage to such an adult's property because of the adult's mental disorder.[6] While the Commission's functions under the Act are for the most part concerned with personal welfare, this last-mentioned important function concerns the adult's property. The Commission have an additional function to receive and investigate certain complaints where the Commission are not satisfied with any investigations or failure to investigate by a local authority in relation to a complaint concerning the exercise of personal welfare functions in relation to welfare attorneys, guardians or appointees under intervention orders[7] or similar appointees under other jurisdictions.[8] In consequence of any investigation described in this paragraph, the Commission may take such steps (including making an application to the sheriff[9]) as seem to them to be necessary to safeguard the property, financial affairs or personal welfare of such an adult.[10] In relation to their respective investigatory powers, the Commission, the Public Guardian and the local authority are required to provide each other with such information and assistance as may be necessary to facilitate the investigation.[11] They are also required to consult among each other on cases or matters relating to the exercise of functions under the Act in which there is, or appears to be, a common interest.[12]

The Commission also has the functions of providing information **5-31** and advice to welfare attorneys, guardians and appointees under intervention orders in relation to performance of personal welfare functions[13] as regards such adults[14]; and establishing and maintaining lists of nominated medical practitioners, and appointing them in particular cases, under the medical provisions of s.50[15] in relation to all adults with relevant incapacity, including those with physical inability to communicate and no mental disorder. Guardians, welfare attorneys and appointees under intervention orders, or the local authority, must afford the Commission all facilities necessary to enable the Commission to carry out their functions in respect of adults with incapacity resulting from mental disorder.[16] Copies of welfare powers of attorney are sent to the Commission by the Public Guardian upon registration.[17]

---

[4] s.9(1)(b), which could be interpreted as an obligation to visit (or at least to determine when to visit) every adult with incapacity as defined in s.1(6). Even to identify all such adults would be a practical impossibility. This difficulty is likely to be remedied under the proposed new MHSA—see para.5–32 *infra*.
[5] s.9(1)(e): but see para.5–32 *infra*.
[6] s.9(1)(f): but see para.5–32 *infra*.
[7] s.9(1)(d).
[8] s.9(3).
[9] See paras 5–14 to 5–20 *supra*.
[10] s.12(1).
[11] s.12(2).
[12] ss.9(1)(c), 6(2)(f) and 10(1)(b).
[13] s.9(1)(g). This duplicates the function of local authorities under s.10(1)(e).
[14] See first sentence of para.5–29 *supra*.
[15] s.50(9). See para.14–2 *infra*.
[16] s.9(2).
[17] s.19(2)(c). See para.6–17 *infra*.

Changes in Mental Health (Scotland) Bill

5–32 The Mental Health (Scotland) Bill, introduced on September 16, 2002,[18] proposed that some of the Commission's functions described above be transferred to a new MHSA, and altered. It proposed that paras (a), (b), (e) and (f) of s.9(1) of the Incapacity Act be deleted. Paragraph (a) (protective functions regarding adults subject to intervention and guardianship orders) has no direct equivalent in the Bill. Paragraph (b) (visiting adults) is proposed to be replaced by MHSA functions limited, as regards Incapacity Act matters, to adults subject to intervention and guardianship orders and who have granted welfare powers of attorney which have been copied to the Commission upon registration.[19] Paragraphs (e) and (f) (investigations) are proposed to be replaced by more detailed investigative provisions in a new MHSA. Where paras (a), (b), (e) and (f) of s.9(1) are referred to in this book, it is likely to be necessary to refer instead to provisions of the new MHSA, once they have been enacted and brought into force.

Local authorities

5–33 References in the Act to the local authority mean the local authority for the area in which the adult resides[20] or, where an adult's personal welfare seems to be at risk, the area in which the adult is present.[21] Chief social work officers and mental health officers have the functions under the Act described in paras 5–35 and 5–37 respectively below. The general functions of local authorities under the Act are brought together in s.10. Except for the consultation provisions of s.10(1)(b), their functions under this section are limited to personal welfare matters. However, their duties to apply for intervention orders under s.53(3) and guardianship orders under s.57(2) relate to protection of the property or financial affairs of the adult, as well as personal welfare[22]; and under s.44(4)(b) managers who have been managing a resident's affairs under Part 4 must, if the resident leaves and remains incapable, notify the local authority for the area in which they expect him to reside (unless he has moved to another "authorised establishment"[23] or into local authority care).

5–34 The local authority have a general function of supervising guardians with personal welfare functions.[24] Appointees under intervention orders may be placed under the supervision of the local authority by the sheriff either in terms of the intervention order itself, or by variation thereof,[25] or perhaps upon an application under s.3(3).[26] On supervision by the local authority of welfare guardians and appointees under intervention orders, see paras 10–66 and 10–67 below. See also

---

[18] See para.3–31 *supra*.
[19] Under s.19(2)(c) of the Incapacity Act. For all of the foregoing categories, the Bill as published refers to "patients" rather than to adults. The proposed definition of "patients" would exclude people physically unable to communicate.
[20] s.87(1), in terms of which "local authority" means a council established in accordance with s.2 of the Local Government etc. (Scotland) Act 1994 (c.39).
[21] For the purposes of s.10(1)(d), see s.10(2).
[22] See para.10–47 *infra*.
[23] See para.9–2.
[24] s.10(1)(a).
[25] s.53(8).
[26] See paras 5–14 and 5–15 *supra*.

the relevant regulations.[27] In relation to personal welfare matters, the local authority are required to receive and investigate complaints concerning welfare attorneys, guardians and appointees under intervention orders,[28] and also to investigate any circumstances made known to them in which the personal welfare of an adult seems to them to be at risk.[29] In the context of the Act, the latter function is likely to be interpreted as meaning risk containing an element of incapacity or apparent incapacity on the part of the adult. In consequence of any investigation described in this paragraph, the local authority may take such steps (including making an application to the sheriff[30]) as seem to them to be necessary to safeguard the personal welfare of the adult.[31] In relation to their respective investigatory powers, the local authority, Public Guardian and Mental Welfare Commission are required to provide each other with such information and assistance as may be necessary to facilitate the investigation.[32] They are also required to consult among each other on cases or matters relating to the exercise of functions under the Act in which there is, or appears to be, a common interest.[33] Local authorities have an additional duty to afford to the Mental Welfare Commission all facilities necessary to enable the Commission to carry out their functions in respect of adults with mental disorder.[34] The sheriff may place welfare attorneys under the supervision of the local authority to such extent as may be specified in the sheriff's order.[35] An attorney under such supervision must notify the local authority in writing of intention to resign.[36]

Other roles and responsibilities

Chief social work officers

The chief social work officer ("chief officer") is referred to in the Act, **5–35** but not defined; but clearly must be the chief social work officer as defined in the Social Work (Scotland) Act 1968 ("the 1968 Act") (c.49), s.3.[37] The social work functions of local authorities are contained in the 1968 Act itself and in the several enactments and provisions listed in s.5(1B) of the 1968 Act. For the purposes of those functions, local authorities are required by s.3 of the 1968 Act to appoint chief social

---

[27] The Adults with Incapacity (Supervision of Welfare Guardians etc. by Local Authorities) (Scotland) Regulations 2002 (SSI 2002/95) made under s.10(3)(a) and (b)(i).
[28] s.10(1)(c). Complaints against equivalent appointees to guardians and welfare attorneys under other jurisdictions are included by s.10(4).
[29] s.10(1)(d).
[30] See paras 5–14 to 5–20 *supra*.
[31] s.12(1), which also authorises them to take steps in relation to property and financial concerns coming to their notice, though this would normally be done by referring the matter to the Public Guardian for him to exercise his equivalent powers, except where ss.53(3) or 57(2) apply (see para.5–33 *supra*).
[32] s.12(2).
[33] ss.10(1)(b), 6(2)(f) and 9(1)(c).
[34] s.9(2).
[35] s.20(2)(c), and see the Adults with Incapacity (Supervision of Welfare Attorneys by Local Authorities) (Scotland) Regulations 2001 (SSI 2001/77), made under s.10(3)(b)(ii).
[36] s.23(1).
[37] As substituted by the Local Government etc. (Scotland) Act 1994 (c.39), s.45.

work officers, whose qualifications are such as may be prescribed by the Secretary of State.[38] Under the Incapacity Act, notification must be given to the chief officer of intention to apply for guardianship or intervention orders with welfare powers.[39] The chief officer provides the "third report" where, in such applications, incapacity is caused solely by inability to communicate.[40] The chief officer may be appointed welfare guardian, in which case he must appoint a responsible officer: provisions relating to the chief officer as welfare guardian are described in paras 11–3 to 11–8, 11–14, 11–17, 11–27 and 11–34 below. When exercising functions under the Act, the chief officer must comply with the Act's general principles, and may be given directions by the sheriff under s.3(3).[41] Guidance is given to chief officers in the Local Authority Code.

Medical practitioners (including approved psychiatrists)

5–36   Doctors have important functions throughout the Act. They have particular roles under Part 5 and regulations thereunder, as described in Chapter 14: guidance is given in the Part 5 Code. In Part 5 and elsewhere the Act confers particular functions on doctors with particular qualifications, as described in para.14–2 below. Notable across the Act's provisions generally is the role of doctors "approved ... by a health board as having special experience in the diagnosis or treatment of mental disorder",[42] in this book called "approved psychiatrists". Outwith Part 5, doctors have the function of providing medical certificates under Part 3 (see para.8–8 below), providing and reviewing medical certificates under Part 4 (see paras 9–8 and 9–19 below), and providing medical certificates under Part 6 and under the equivalent provisions of the Criminal Procedure (Scotland) Act 1995 (see paras 10–48 and 11–86 below). They have the function of providing certificates that intimations or notifications should not be given to the adult because of serious risk to the adult's health (see paras 5–9 and 5–25 above). As a general rule, where two certificates are required and the adult's incapacity results from mental disorder (or reasons including mental disorder), then one of the certificates must be provided by an approved psychiatrist: this applies to certification under Part 6 and under the equivalent provisions of the Criminal Procedure (Scotland) Act 1995, and certification that intimations or notifications should not be given to the adult. Approved psychiatrists may also provide the other certificate, or do anything else which may be done by any medical practitioner. British Medical Association has suggested that it be made competent for certification under the Act to be provided by other health-care professionals such as appropriately trained specialist nurses and clinical psychologists.[43] As to functions which are not specifically medical, doctors may grant the certificates which require to be incorporated in CPA's and WPA's (see para.6–12 below), and may

---

[38] See the Qualifications of Chief Social Work Officers (Scotland) Regulations 1996 (SI 1996/515).
[39] ss.57(4) and 53(4)—see para.10–47 *infra*.
[40] s.57(3)(b)—see para.10–49 *infra*.
[41] See paras 5–14 and 5–15 *supra*.
[42] MHSA 1984, s.20(1)(b).
[43] See also paras 10–48 and 14–43 *infra*.

countersign applications for authority to intromit (see para.8–6 below) unless they have also granted the medical certificate for the same application. When exercising any of their functions under the Act, all doctors must comply with the Act's general principles, and may be given directions by the sheriff under s.3(3) (see para.5–14 above). Their decisions as to incapacity may be appealed under s.14,[44] and Part 5 also contains various provisions for recourse to the courts.

Mental health officers

"Mental health officer" is defined in MHSA 1984, s.125(1) as being "an officer of a local authority appointed to act as a mental health officer for the purposes of this Act", but is not defined in the Incapacity Act. Although the limitation to "for the purposes of this Act" in the MHSA definition could be said to present a difficulty, in the absence of any alternatives the mental health officer under the Incapacity Act must clearly be the same as under MHSA.[45] Mental health officers have various important functions under MHSA 1984, including functions of initiating applications, consenting to certain steps and making reports. Other MHSA functions include the right to demand admission to premises described in para.12–31 below. Local authorities have a duty to appoint sufficient mental health officers to discharge relevant MHSA functions.[46] Candidates for appointment as mental health officers require to have a professional qualification in social work and normally require to have had at least two years' post-qualifying experience, following which they must complete an approved training course.[47] If then approved by the local authority as having competence in dealing with persons who are suffering from mental disorder, they may be appointed by the local authority.[48] Under the Incapacity Act, mental health officers now have the additional function of providing the third report in applications for intervention or guardianship orders seeking welfare powers (see paras 10–49 to 10–50 below) and in relation to equivalent appointments under the Criminal Procedure (Scotland) Act 1995 (see para.11–86 below). They may countersign applications for authority to intromit (see para.8–6 below). When exercising functions under the Incapacity Act, the mental health officer must comply with the Act's general principles, and may be given directions by the sheriff under s.3(3) (see para.5–14). Guidance is provided to mental health officers by the Local Authority Code.

5–37

Nearest relative

Subject to two modifications, the nearest relative under the Incapacity Act is the same person as under MHSA.[49] The first modification is that for the purposes of the Incapacity Act the Court of Session or

5–38

---

[44] See para.5–18 *supra*.
[45] In the Countersignatories of Applications for Authority to Intromit Regulations, "mental health officer" is defined by reference to the MHSA definition—see para.8–6 *infra*.
[46] MHSA 1984, s.9(1).
[47] See Scottish Office Circular SWSG 19/96.
[48] MHSA 1984, s.9: see also the Mental Health (Scotland) Act 1984 (Appointed Day) Order 1986 (SI 1986/374) under which the relevant provisions came into effect on April 1, 1986.
[49] Incapacity Act, s.87(1), MHSA, ss.53–57.

the sheriff may, under s.4, upon application by an incapable adult order that information and intimations should be withheld from the nearest relative, or that an alternative nearest relative be appointed, or that no-one should exercise the functions of nearest relative, all as more particularly described in paras 5–16 and 5–17 above. The second modification is that a same-sex partner shall be nearest relative if that partner has lived with the adult "in a relationship which has the characteristics, other than that the persons are of the opposite sex, of the relationship between husband and wife" for the last six months (or if the adult is a hospital in-patient, for six months prior to admission) and if the adult is either unmarried, or separated either by agreement or court order, or if either party to the adult's marriage has been in desertion for a period and the desertion persists.[50] Apart from this modification, the nearest relative should be identified in accordance with MHSA 1984, ss.53–57, the provisions of which are complex and not fully described here.[51] In summary, the nearest relative is the first person on the following list who cares for the adult, or (if none of them cares for the adult) simply the first person on the list. The list comprises: spouse (if there is no continuing separation or desertion) or person living with the adult as husband or wife; child; parent; sibling; grandparent; grandchild; uncle or aunt; nephew or niece. Except for spouses, the nearest relative must be aged over 18 (a similar exception for parents is not relevant to the Incapacity Act). The nearest relative may be the same person as the primary carer.[52] Provisions regarding the nearest relative may be amended by the new MHSA: see para.3–31 above.

5–39   Under the fourth principle, the views of the nearest relative must be taken into account insofar as it is reasonable and practicable to do so.[53] An application for authority to intromit must give particulars of the nearest relative, to whom the application must be intimated by the Public Guardian.[54] Managers of establishments must intimate to the nearest relative their intention to have a resident medically examined with a view to managing that resident's affairs under Part 4,[55] and must produce relevant records when requested by the nearest relative.[56] The nearest relative may consent to research for the purposes of s.51 where there is no guardian or welfare attorney with relevant powers.[57] The Public Guardian must intimate to the nearest relative an application made to the Public Guardian for discharge of a financial guardian and the nearest relative is entitled to make objection and to be heard.[58] Similarly, application to the Public Guardian, Mental Welfare Commission or local authority for recall of a guardian's powers, or the intention of one of those authorities at its own instance to recall such powers, must be intimated to the nearest relative, who is entitled to object and to be heard.[59] An application by a guardian to

---

[50] ss.87(2) and (3).
[51] A helpful explanation is given in Blackie & Patrick, *Mental Health: A Guide to the Law in Scotland*, pp.13–14.
[52] See para.5–40 *infra*.
[53] s.1(4)(b), see paras 4–20 and 4–21 *supra*.
[54] s.26(1)(d) and (3).
[55] s.37(3).
[56] s.41(f).
[57] s.51(3)(f).
[58] s.72(2).
[59] s.73(5).

the Public Guardian for consent to dispose of accommodation must be intimated by the Public Guardian to the nearest relative.[60]

Primary carer

An adult's primary carer is the person or organisation primarily engaged in caring for the adult.[61] The primary carer may be the same person as the nearest relative.[62] Under the fourth principle the views of the primary carer must be taken into account insofar as it is reasonable and practicable to do so.[63] An application for authority to intromit must give particulars of the primary carer, to whom the application must be intimated by the Public Guardian.[64] The Public Guardian must intimate to the primary carer an application made to the Public Guardian for discharge of a financial guardian and the primary carer is entitled to make objection and be heard.[65] Similarly, application to the Public Guardian, Mental Welfare Commission or local authority for recall of a guardian's powers, or the intention of one of those authorities at its own instance to recall such powers, must be intimated to the primary carer, who is entitled to object and be heard.[66] An application by a guardian to the Public Guardian for consent to dispose of accommodation must be intimated by the Public Guardian to the primary carer.[67] A continuing or welfare attorney wishing to resign must notify the primary carer in writing of that intention, unless the grantor of the power of attorney has a guardian.[68]

Powers applicable to non-Act measures

Some powers and procedures under the Incapacity Act which have been described in this chapter may be exercised or invoked in relation to techniques and measures outwith the scope of the Act. Such powers and procedures include the following: investigation by the Public Guardian of any circumstances made known to him in which an adult's property or financial affairs seem to him to be at risk,[69] and by the local authority of any circumstances made known to them in which the adult's personal welfare seems to them to be at risk[70]; the similar investigatory functions of the Mental Welfare Commission where personal welfare or (by reason of mental disorder) the adult's property seems to be at risk,[71] though these functions are likely to be transferred to a new MHSA in amended form as described in para.5–32 above; visiting by the Mental Welfare Commission of any adult to whom the Act applies by reason of mental disorder, or by reasons including mental disorder,[72] though as described in para.5–32 that

5–40

5–41

---

[60] Sch.2, para.6(2).
[61] s.87(1).
[62] See paras 5–38 and 5–39 *supra*.
[63] s.1(4)(b), see paras 4–20 and 4–21.
[64] ss.26(1)(d) and (3).
[65] s.72(2).
[66] s.73(5).
[67] Sch.2, para.6(2).
[68] s.23(1)(c).
[69] s.6(2)(d).
[70] s.10(1)(d).
[71] ss.9(1)(e) and (f).
[72] s.9(1)(b).

provision is likely to be restricted in its scope and also transferred to a new MHSA; the provisions for consultation and co-operation among the Public Guardian, Mental Welfare Commission and local authorities[73] and the powers of each to take necessary steps in consequence of investigations, including making an application to the sheriff.[74] Such applications could include applications for intervention or guardianship orders, and any other person claiming an interest could apply for such an order in consequence of concerns about the operation or effect of techniques and measures outwith the scope of the Act. See ss.53(3) and 57(2) regarding circumstances in which the local authority has a duty to apply for intervention or guardianship orders respectively.[75]

---

[73] ss.6(2)(f), 9(1)(c), 10(1)(b) and 12(2).
[74] s.12(1).
[75] All of the powers and procedures specified in this paragraph are described, with cross-references as appropriate, in paras 5–23 to 5–34 of this chapter.

CHAPTER 6

POWERS OF ATTORNEY

Note: This chapter refers to the Style which forms Appendix 5, any use of which should be selective and subject to the terms of this chapter and in particular para.6–29. Other styles appear in the course of this chapter. As noted in Abbreviations (page xli) continuing and welfare powers of attorney are referred to respectively as CPA's and WPA's. Except where otherwise indicated, references to powers and to attorneys mean those under CPA's and WPA's, and the law is described as it applies to such powers of attorney granted on or after April 2, 2001.

Introduction

By power of attorney the grantor may appoint an attorney to act for the grantor. The term describes both the authority conferred and the document by which it is granted. While the technique has been well established in Scots law for centuries,[1] the term itself was for long treated by lawyers with disdain[2] and "factory" or "factory and commission" preferred. Halliday uses the latter for the relevant chapter heading[3] and the *Encyclopaedia* deals with powers of attorney under "agency and mandate", the former when the appointment is remunerated and the latter when it is gratuitous.[4] However, "power of attorney" was described and used by Scottish Law Commission as the "modern term"[5] and the Act uses older terminology only in its transitional provisions, which refer to "an attorney under a contract of mandate or agency".[6] The Act refers to equivalent foreign powers as being conferred by "contract, grant or appointment".[7] The classical Scottish position is described by Erskine as follows: "As the bare granting of a power to act, can infer no obligation on the person empowered, who is at liberty to refuse office, this contract cannot be perfected till the mandatory has undertaken to execute the mandate; which he may do, either by word, by writing or by any deed which sufficiently discovers his resolution."[8] That formulation assists consideration of the issue of interpretation discussed in paras 6–6 to 6–8 below.

6–1

---

[1] *e.g.* Stair's *The Institutions of the Law of Scotland*, Book I, Title 12 (1693).
[2] *e.g.* "The appointment is also styled a power or letter of attorney; but these terms are more familiarly applied to authorities to be executed in England or other foreign countries": Professor Menzies's *Lectures on Conveyancing* (2nd ed., 1900).
[3] Halliday, *Conveyancing Law and Practice* (2nd ed.), Ch.13.
[4] *Stair Memorial Encyclopaedia*, Vol.1, paras 604 and 665–700.
[5] Scottish Law Commission Discussion Paper No.94, *Mentally Disabled Adults* (September 1991) para.5.1.
[6] Sch.4, para.4. Rule 3.16.1 of the Act of Sederunt (Summary Applications, Statutory Applications and Appeals etc. Rules) 1999 (see para.5–5 *supra*) defines "power of attorney" as including a factory and commission.
[7] See *e.g.* ss.1(7), 16(8) and 20(5).
[8] Erskine's *Institute*, 3.3.31.

6–2　As "power of attorney" is not a well-established term of art with clear boundaries to its definition, issues may arise as to whether or not a particular arrangement (regardless of the terminology employed) is a power of attorney and subject to the Act's provisions. Powers may be special, authorising one particular matter or transaction only, or general, authorising routine general management, but under general powers various matters are not authorised unless specifically included[9] and there may be doubt about others, so that modern general powers typically commence with general wording but then proceed to define precisely and often at length the powers which the grantor seeks to confer. There are some things which an attorney cannot be authorised to do.[10] Powers may be granted for commercial or administrative purposes, for which special powers are more common, or by private individuals. They may be granted for use abroad, or during the grantor's own absence, or when the grantor is physically unwell, or wishes to concentrate on other matters, or (in the case of special powers) prefers to avoid direct personal involvement or wishes to place conduct of a matter entirely in the hands of someone with special skills. They also may be granted in anticipation of incapacity, which is the only category relevant to this book and to the Act. Works such as Halliday and the *Encyclopaedia* (above) should be referred to not only as to all categories other than the last, but also in relation to the last category insofar as the law has not been altered by the Act: Part 2 of the Act is unique in that it amends an existing well-established body of law, whereas Parts 3–6 introduce new techniques (with the one exception of s.32[11]).

6–3　There is unresolved doubt as to whether powers granted before January 1, 1991 are operable following the grantor's loss of capacity.[12] Halliday's view is that they are not, and he admits to doubt only in relation to "temporary insanity",[13] but this author doubts whether a court would feel impelled by such authority as exists to deny the explicit direction in a pre-1991 power of attorney that it be operated, and only operated, following the grantor's loss of capacity.[14] Powers granted from January 1, 1991 to April 1, 2001 automatically survive incapacity unless the contrary is stated in them.[15] Powers granted from April 2, 2001 may only be operated following the grantor's loss of capacity if the Act's requirements have been complied with.[16] Some but not all of the Act's provisions apply where, under a contract of mandate or agency executed before April 2, 2001, the attorney was on that date already acting for a grantor who has lost capacity, or after that date commences to do so.[17]

---

[9] This was the traditional pre-Act view, but see the discussion in para.6–25. See para.6–26 for powers which have been held not to be authorised unless specifically granted.

[10] See paras 6–23 and 6–24.

[11] See paras 7–1, 7–2 and 8–18 *infra*.

[12] This point was debated as long ago as *Pollock v Paterson*, December 10, 1811, F.C., and was still described by Scottish Law Commission in 1991 as "a matter of doubt" (Discussion Paper No.94, above, para.5.5).

[13] Halliday *op. cit.* para.13–11, referring to *Wink v Mortimer* (1849) 11 D. 995. In practice, Halliday's view is best respected by prudent conveyancers.

[14] A pre-1991 power in such terms was referred to the author in 2001.

[15] Law Reform (Miscellaneous Provisions) (Scotland) Act 1990, s.71.

[16] s.18 and the Adults with Incapacity (Scotland) Act 2000 (Commencement No.1) Order 2001 (SSI 2001/81).

[17] Sch.4, para.4. See paras 6–54 *et seq. infra*.

The Act differentiates between CPA's, which deal with property or **6-4** financial affairs, and WPA's, which deal with personal welfare matters. The two categories are not defined in the Act, but are described in para.3–7 above. The Part 2 Code[18] describes examples of continuing powers in para.2.18 and of welfare powers in para.3.20. The *Style* contains examples of specific powers which the author would consider to be continuing powers in Schedule Part 1, welfare powers in Schedule Part 2, and powers which may be either in Schedule Part 3. The Public Guardian's Office have suggested that power 1.5, out of context, might be considered to be also a welfare power. If it is intended that a power of attorney should be a CPA or WPA only, safe practice is to include a declaration that all specific powers in the document are to be construed subject to the limitation that they are continuing or welfare powers (as the case may be) only. The Public Guardian will not register a power which in his view includes welfare powers if only a certificate for a CPA is incorporated (and vice versa), which will defeat the grantor's intention altogether if the grantor has by then lost capacity.

Attorneys are subject to the fiduciary duty and duty of care **6-5** described in Chapter 4, and also to all five general principles there described if the grantor has lost capacity, in which case the first four principles also apply to anyone else exercising functions under the Act in relation to powers of attorney, including the sheriff and the Public Guardian. It is suggested that, in any doubtful case, there should be a strong presumption in favour of giving effect to a grantor's directions and wishes as expressed in a power of attorney on the basis, firstly, that of available techniques, a power of attorney is generally the least restrictive of the adult's freedom (second principle) because it represents the adult's own choice of who should be empowered to do what, rather than an imposed solution; secondly, that giving full effect to the terms of such an explicit appointment clearly complies with the third principle; and thirdly, to avoid triggering some other intervention which otherwise would be unnecessary (referring consequentially to the first principle). Advice on good practice is given in the Part 2 Code.[19]

Contract or grant?

Paragraph 6–1 above describes the classic Scots law position that the **6-6** authority conferred by what is nowadays called a power of attorney comes into effect upon a contract being entered between grantor and attorney. When the grantor grants (*i.e.* executes[20]) the power of attorney document, he has taken the first step. The document requires to be intimated to the attorney, and the attorney requires to accept (by explicit written or verbal acceptance, or impliedly by commencing to act) to establish the contract. Some commentators have assumed that "power of attorney" in the Act always means the completed contract: the "contract" interpretation. However, as pointed out at the beginning of this chapter, the term "power of attorney" can also mean the

---

[18] *Code of Practice for Continuing and Welfare Attorneys*, SE/2001/90, issued March 2001 pursuant to s.13(3) of the Act.
[19] See n.18 *supra*.
[20] See *Erskine*, passage quoted in para.6–1 *supra*.

document. If that is the meaning in ss.15, 16 and 18 of the Act, the power of attorney has been granted by the grantor (and effectively granted, if the Act's requirements have been complied with) as soon as it has been executed by the grantor: this is the "grant" interpretation. The difference between the two interpretations has significant consequences as to the effect of the Act's provisions in relation to the period between grant and acceptance. However, neither interpretation resolves the further difficulty addressed in para.6–57 below.

The contract interpretation

6–7   Under the contract interpretation, no power of attorney has come into effect until the attorney has accepted. Some of the consequences have been spelled out by Swinton.[21] Section 18[22] provides that powers granted on or after April 2, 2001 will only survive the grantor's incapacity if granted in accordance with ss.15 or 16, and s.15 provides in relation to CPA's that they shall "continue" to have effect if granted in accordance with the provisions of that section. If one assumes that the "contract" interpretation applies, as Swinton does, the CPA can only "continue" to have effect if it has already taken effect, so that the attorney requires to have accepted the appointment before the grantor loses capacity; yet nothing in the Act's provisions limits registration to powers which are effective in accordance with that interpretation, or identifies in any way powers which are ineffective on that basis. Though not mentioned by Swinton, there would be potentially greater difficulties in relation to a substitute attorney taking over perhaps years after the grantor's incapacity,[23] and probably insuperable difficulties if the substitute is appointed by a substitute mechanism such as is described in para.6–21 below.

The grant model

6–8   The above difficulties do not arise under the "grant" interpretation. Under that interpretation, the references to the "granting" of a power of attorney in ss.15, 16 and 18 all use "granting" as *Erskine* did[24] to mean the initial step of execution by the grantor. If the grantor executes on or after April 2, 2001, then under s.18 the Act's requirements apply[25]; and if the relevant provisions of ss.15 and/or 16 have been complied with, the grantor can relax in the knowledge that the document which he has executed is thereupon effective in terms of the Act, and will continue to be effective whether or not he loses capacity before any subsequent step occurs. Using the basic formula that offer plus acceptance creates contract, under the "contract" interpretation the power of attorney which survives the grantor's incapacity is the completed contract, whereas under the "grant" interpretation the power of attorney which survives the grantor's incapacity is the offer, in the form of the power of attorney document. Whether an attorney or substitute attorney accepts office before or

---

[21] "Effective Continuing Powers of Attorney", 2002 S.L.T. (News) 215.
[22] Together with the No.1 Commencement Order.
[23] See s.23(4)(b).
[24] See para.6–1 *supra*.
[25] This is the interpretation adopted by the Public Guardian.

after the grantor's incapacity is irrelevant. This "grant" interpretation fits the terminology and provisions of the Act so well that, in this author's view, it must surely be correct.[26] As noted in para.6–1 above, equivalent foreign powers are referred to in the Act as being conferred by "contract, grant or appointment". Having established the use of those terms in that context, the Act refers to attorneys "under a contract of mandate or agency" only in relation to pre-Act powers under para.4 of Schedule 4. For post-Act powers, the emphasis is placed upon the power of attorney document. Under the "grant" interpretation, all the references to granting the power of attorney in ss.15 and 16 means its execution by the grantor, and because the document is then effective, the registration provisions of s.19(2) and the substitute provisions of s.23(4)(b) are concerned only with evidence that the attorney or substitute attorney is willing to act. If the attorney was unaware of the existence of the power of attorney document until after the grantor lost capacity, that would be contrary to the recommendations of the Part 2 Code, but that would not prevent the attorney deciding to accept appointment, signing the registration application to confirm his willingness to act, and obtaining a certificate of registration and authenticated copy of the power of attorney which—by the clear implication of s.19(4)—is all that he requires as evidence of his authority to act (subject always, of course, to the terms of the document itself and the limitations described in paras 6–23 to 6–26 below). The same applies to a substitute attorney. If substitute mechanisms are competent, the same also applies to a substitute attorney not even identified until long after the grantor's loss of capacity. Upon execution, the power of attorney document became effective for the purposes of appointment, and acceptance of such appointment, at any subsequent time during the grantor's lifetime if those steps occur in accordance with competent provisions contained within the document.

Creation and Registration

A CPA granted by an individual will continue to have effect if the grantor becomes incapable in relation to matters covered by the power of attorney if, but only if, it complies with s.15,[27] but may only be operated following registration in accordance with s.19. The grantor may provide that the CPA may be operable before as well as after loss of capacity, but even though the grantor remains capable the power must still be registered before it can be operated.[28] Alternatively, the grantor may stipulate that the CPA may only be operated following loss of relevant capacity or occurrence of some other

6–9

---

[26] The author himself raised concerns about "granted" at J.L.S.S. Vol.46, No.5, p.22 (May 2001). The author thanks Mr Ken Young, Director of Legal Services, the Registers of Scotland, for drawing his attention—in this context—to *Erskine's* use of "granting", as quoted in para.6–1 *supra*.

[27] s.18. Except in paras 6–54 *et seq.* below, the law is described as it applies to powers granted (*i.e.* executed—see para.6–8 *supra*) on or after April 2, 2001; but, except as regards provisions introduced by the Incapacity Act, the law described generally applies to both pre-Act and post-Act powers.

[28] On the basis of s.19(1) and the definition of CPA in s.15(1) and (2). Of course, unless the power is expressly intended to be operable after loss of capacity, it is not a CPA at all and the Act's provisions do not apply.

specified event, and as a separate matter may or may not specify that it may be registered only upon loss of capacity or occurrence of some other specified event.[29] The advantage of early registration is that the grantor can still re-consider and re-execute if for any reason the Public Guardian declines to register. Deferred registration, on the other hand, helps to ensure that the power will not be exercised prematurely. Third parties dealing with attorneys must remember that while an unregistered CPA is never operable, a registered one may also not yet be operable, and the terms of the document should be checked. Whether a registered CPA is operable after the grantor has lost, then regained, relevant capacity depends upon construction of the document. It is accordingly good practice for the document to be explicit in that regard.[30]

6–10 A WPA may not be operated unless it complies with s.16,[31] has been registered in accordance with s.19, and either the grantor is in fact incapable in relation to the matters covered by the WPA, or the attorney reasonably believes the grantor to be so incapable.[32] If the grantor regains such capacity, or if the attorney no longer reasonably believes that the grantor is incapable, the WPA may no longer be operated.[33] The grantor of a WPA still has the option to stipulate that registration be deferred until there is evidence of loss of capacity, with the same advantages, disadvantages and consequences as for CPA's (para.6–9 above).

Creation

6–11 The following requirements apply to both CPA's and WPA's. The power must be in writing and subscribed by the grantor, but need not be self-proving (though in practice powers usually are, and must be if they are to be registered in the Books of Council and Session).[34] The power must clearly state that the grantor intends it to be a CPA and/or a WPA,[35] and it must "incorporate" a certificate in the prescribed form.[36] There are separate forms of certificate for CPA's and WPA's, and both certificates are required for powers which are both (in which case absence of one will render the power unregistrable and thus inoperable—see para.6–9 above).

Certifiers and certificates

6–12 The certifier must be a solicitor, practising member of the Faculty of Advocates, or registered medical practitioner.[37] "Solicitor" is not defined, and accordingly may not be limited to a practising Scottish

---

[29] s.19(3).
[30] See *Style* clauses Three and Four.
[31] s.18. See n.27 *supra*.
[32] s.16(5)(b).
[33] *ibid.*, which provides that a WPA "shall not be exerciseable unless . . . the grantor is incapable . . . ", which clearly means incapable at time of such exercise.
[34] ss.15(3), 15(3)(a), 16(3) and 16(3)(a).
[35] ss.15(3)(b) and 16(3)(b).
[36] ss.15(3)(c) and 16(3)(c), and the Adults with Incapacity (Certificates in Relation to Powers of Attorney) (Scotland) Regulations 2001 (SSI 2001/80), reg.2 and Sch.1 for CPA's, reg.3 and Sch.2 for WPA's: see Appendix 2.
[37] ss.15(3)(c) and 16(3)(c) and the Adults with Incapacity (Certificates in Relation to Powers of Attorney) (Scotland) Regulations 2001 (SSI 2001/80), reg.4.

solicitor,[38] though the Public Guardian has indicated that he will not accept certificates by other solicitors unless and until it is judicially determined that for this purpose "solicitor" is not so limited. The certifier must not be the attorney (or a joint or substitute attorney),[39] but may be the person who drew the power, or the partner of an attorney, and may witness the grantor's signature (if it be witnessed). The certifier must interview the grantor immediately before the grantor subscribes, and must confirm in the certificate that the certifier has done so.[40] Having regard to the requirement to "incorporate" the certificate (see below) the safe procedure is for interview, subscription and certification to take place immediately one after the other, *unico contextu*.

The certifier must be satisfied that "at the time" (of interview, **6–13** subscription and certification, it is suggested) the grantor understood the nature and content of the document, and must so certify. The certifier must specify that he is so satisfied either from his own knowledge of the grantor or because he has consulted "other persons" named in the certificate.[41] The form of certificate allows the certifier to enter both grounds. Note the plural "other persons": there must be at least two, who might be (for example) a medical practitioner and a relative or friend; or a doctor who states that the grantor is sometimes but not always capable and a nurse whom the doctor confirms will be able to advise when the grantor is capable. A prudent certifier will seek, and specify, suitably qualified assistance whenever the certifier has any doubt, or others could be in doubt, or there is a possibility of someone alleging incapacity at time of granting. A certifier who consults others must still interview the grantor. A prudent certifier will keep notes of the basis of his own knowledge, of the interview and of what any "other persons" said to him; and will preserve relevant written communications from "other persons".

Also, the certifier may only issue the certificate if the certifier has no **6–14** reason to believe that the grantor is acting under undue influence, and no reason to believe that any other factor vitiates the granting of the power; and the certifier must so certify.[42] A prudent certifier will also keep notes of these aspects. On undue influence, both generally and in the context of such certification, see paras 1–38 and 1–39 above. Other potential vitiating factors include facility and circumvention,[43] force and fear, fraud and essential error. Note that where the contract between grantor and attorney is gratuitous, as many are, unilateral error may vitiate it.[44]

The requirement to "incorporate" the certificates[45] caused debate **6–15** following passing of the Act. The novelty is that an annexation incorporated in a document will normally exist at time of execution, but the certificate certifies the situation at time of granting, and

---

[38] Contrast the definition by reference to s.65(1) of the Solicitors (Scotland) Act 1980 (c.46) (as amended) for countersignatories of applications for authority to intromit: see para.8–6 *infra*. and regulations there referred to.
[39] ss.15(4) and 16(4).
[40] ss.15(3)(c)(i) and 16(3)(c)(i).
[41] ss.15(3)(c)(ii) and 16(3)(c)(ii).
[42] ss.15(3)(c)(iii) and 16(3)(c)(iii).
[43] See paras 1–36 and 1–37 *supra*.
[44] *Hunter v Bradford Property Trust Ltd*, 1970 S.L.T. (HL) 173.
[45] ss.15(3)(c) and 16(3)(c).

therefore on any interpretation of "granting"[46] cannot be signed until after execution of the power. The question is whether the Parliament has created a new category of incorporation, or intended that the requirements of the Incapacity Act be fitted within the scheme of s.8 of the Requirements of Writing (Scotland) Act 1995.[47] On basic principles of statutory interpretation, ss.15(3) and 16(3) of the Incapacity Act must be interpreted so as to give effect to their evident intention, and cannot be nullified by an earlier statute. The Public Guardian has intimated that: "The Public Guardian will accept certificates that are simply attached to the power of attorney document in the same manner as all other pages of the document itself. This is likely to mean 'stapled' in the vast majority of instances. However, no case will simply be rejected without consideration and it should in any event be remembered that upon registration the 'default procedure' will be to send a copy of the document to the grantor and possibly two nominated persons."[48] After considering the point, the Keeper of the Registers has indicated that he will accept powers of attorney and their certificates under ss.15(3) and 16(3) for registration in the Books of Council and Session.[49] A cautious approach would be to have regard to the provisions of s.8(1) of the 1995 Act that an annexation does not require to be signed or subscribed by the grantor of a document provided that it is referred to in the document, and identified on its face as being the annexation referred to in the document; to include reference in the document such as appears at the beginning of *Style* clause Ten; to rely on the prescribed terms of the certificate as regards identification on the face of the annexation; and to bind the certificates into the document in the same manner as all other pages as advised by the Public Guardian.

Registration with Public Guardian

6–16 The attorney has no authority to act until the power has been registered with the Public Guardian.[50] The Scottish Ministers have not exercised their power under s.7(1)(c) to prescribe forms and procedures,[51] but the Public Guardian (address etc. para.5–23) issues a user-friendly information pack containing *inter alia* a registration form, guidance notes for registration, and guidance for solicitors and advisers.[52] The registration application form provides for signature by the attorney(s) confirming willingness to act. Details of any substitute attorneys require to be inserted, but they do not require to sign. The power, with appropriate certificate(s) "incorporated" (see para.6–15 above), requires to be submitted to the Public Guardian with the completed application form and remittance for the registration fee.[53] The Public Guardian is required to register the power in the appropriate register[54] if he is satisfied with the validity of the power (including

---

[46] ss.15(3)(b) and (c) and 16(3)(b) and (c). See paras 6–6 to 6–8 *supra*.
[47] 1995 c.7.
[48] J.L.S.S. Vol.46, No.3, p.11 (March 2001).
[49] Correspondence with the author. See also para.6–18 *infra*.
[50] s.19(1). See paras 6–9 and 6–10 *supra*.
[51] Nor have they prescribed the form of certificate (see para.6–17 *infra*) under s.7(1)(b). See para.3–12 *supra*.
[52] The Public Guardian has also devised a form of certificate of registration.
[53] Currently £35: the Adults with Incapacity (Public Guardian's Fees) (Scotland) Regulations 2001 (SSI 2001/75).
[54] s.6(2)(b)(i) and (ii). See paras 3–12 and 5–23 *supra*.

the certificate(s)), as to the willingness of the attorney(s) to act,[55] and that any pre-condition for registration has been satisfied. The pre-condition is a stipulation in the power that the Public Guardian shall not register it until the occurrence of a specified event. If the power contains such a pre-condition, the Public Guardian may not register it (and thus it may not be operated[56]) until the Public Guardian has been satisfied that the specified event has occurred.[57] As explained in paras 6–9 and 6–10 above, provisions deferring registration are a separate matter from provisions deferring operability. The *Style* contains in paragraphs Three and Four provisions deferring operability. Similar wording could be used to defer registration, if desired, and risk of difficulty or delay at time of registration is likely to be minimised with a reasonably precise requirement, such as for one or more medical certificates in specified terms, rather than—for example—a reference simply to "my loss of capacity". A decision of the Public Guardian as to whether a person is prepared to act as attorney or as to whether a pre-condition for registration has been satisfied may be appealed to the sheriff, whose decision is final.[58] If the pre-condition entails a decision as to incapacity, an alternative would appear to be to appeal that decision under s.14, under which further appeal is competent.[59] It is understood that in the first year from April 2, 2001 the Public Guardian registered 5,518 powers of attorney, of which 3,890 were CPA's, 189 were WPA's and 1,439 were combined powers.

Certificate of registration and copies of power

Upon registration the Public Guardian is required to send a certificate of registration and copy power to the sender of the registration application,[60] who may or may not be the attorney. The Public Guardian is also required to send copies of the power (but not the certificate) to the grantor[61]; if the power so specifies, to one or two (but no more) individuals or holders of specified offices or positions[62]; and if the power is a WPA or combined CPA and WPA, to the Mental Welfare Commission.[63] Section 19(4) provides that copies authenticated by the Public Guardian "shall be accepted for all purposes as sufficient evidence of the contents of the original and of any matter relating thereto appearing in the copy", thus providing another alternative in addition to the existing options of exhibiting a registered extract from the Books of Council and Session or a copy certified in accordance with the rather cumbersome requirements of Powers of

6–17

---

[55] s.19(2).
[56] s.19(1).
[57] s.19(3).
[58] s.19(6). See para.5–20 *supra*.
[59] See para.5–18 *supra*.
[60] s.19(2)(b). The Public Guardian issues the certificate and copy power, with embossed stamp on every page, heat sealed together in a protective binder; duplicates or replacements of this "package" may be obtained from the Public Guardian (upon payment of his fee) by the sender, attorney or grantor (note issued by the Public Guardian on October 26, 2001). The principal power is retained by the Public Guardian.
[61] s.19(5)(a).
[62] s.19(5)(b).
[63] s.19(2)(c).

Attorney Act 1971.[64] An advantage of authenticated copies under s.19(4) is that it is obvious that they are CPA's or WPA's and that they have been registered.[65] As the Public Guardian retains the original, exhibition of the original is not an option for CPA's and WPA's (unless they have been executed in duplicate). The 1971 Act provides that the terms of any power of attorney may be proved by a copy authenticated on each page and at the end by the grantor, or by a solicitor or stockbroker. The certificate at the end of each page reads "I certify this page to be a true and complete copy of the corresponding page of the original instrument", and the certificate at the end of the copy document reads "I certify the foregoing reproduction to be a true and complete copy of the original instrument".

Registration in Books of Council and Session

6–18   The Public Guardian has indicated that he will accept for registration under s.19 of the Act a registered extract from the Books of Council and Session. It is understood that the Keeper of the Registers will accept for registration in the Books of Council and Session a copy issued by the Public Guardian. Accordingly, such dual registration would appear to be competent in either order. Registration in the Books of Council and Session will ensure preservation in the event of proposed or required[66] deferral of registration with the Public Guardian, and ensures availability of extracts at any time. A power to be registered in the Books of Council and Session should be self-proving, though this is not a requirement for validity under the Incapacity Act.[67]

Grantor

6–19   The grantor of a power of attorney should have attained the age of 16.[68] While powers of attorney by more than one grantor are not uncommon, the references in ss.15(1) and 16(1) to grant by "an individual", coupled with the whole scheme of Part 2 of the Act, indicate that a CPA or WPA should be granted by a single individual only. In respect that s.16(7) provides *inter alia* that a WPA shall not come to an end in the event of the grantor's bankruptcy, there would appear to be no reason why a bankrupt should not grant a WPA. It could be argued that a bankrupt is not disqualified from granting a CPA to provide for the grantor's possible future incapacity if the CPA is declared to be not operable prior to the grantor's discharge. The grantor must have adequate capacity to grant the power (see

---

[64] 1971 c.27, s.3.

[65] In the absence of regulations prescribing the method of authentication by the Public Guardian (see para.6–12 *supra*), he impresses an embossed stamp on all copies of the power which he issues (note issued by the Public Guardian on October 26, 2001). Up to time of writing the stamp is frequently so faint as to be barely detectable. Persons to whom such copies are exhibited should check carefully before rejecting them as unauthenticated. The Public Guardian is understood to be aware of this problem and to be seeking a solution.

[66] s.19(3). See para.6–16 *supra*.

[67] See ss.15(3)(a) and 16(3)(a), and para.6–11 *supra*. See para.6–15 *supra* on registration of certificates under ss.15(3) and 16(3).

[68] On the basis that powers are not commonly granted by younger persons in any circumstances, Age of Legal Capacity (Scotland) Act 1991 (c.50), ss.1 and 2.

paras 1–28 *et seq.* above), but a distinction can be made between capacity to grant the power and capacity fully to exercise all of the powers granted. In England it has been recognised that a grantor may at time of execution understand the nature and effect of the power, so that it will be valid, even though not necessarily capable of himself or herself in fact managing his or her property and affairs.[69] Law and practice in Scotland differs from England in that Scottish powers generally express specifically all of the powers which are to be exercised, and at least in some respects may require to do so.[70] However, the distinction is still valid in Scotland. Validity depends upon the grantor's capacity in relation to the document executed, not the grantor's own capacity to do everything authorised. This can be significant, for example, where the grantor has a relatively mild learning disability or is in the early stages of a degenerative condition. Trends towards early detection of such conditions, and new treatments to halt or at least slow their progress,[71] render this question increasingly important. To ensure adequate understanding, the draftsman may require to reflect clear and simple instructions in the language of the power (and large print may help some grantors). The *Style*, or anything approaching its length, language and complexity, might be quite inappropriate, and something along the following lines might be adequate. This is still a fairly wide-ranging combined CPA and WPA, with a substitute appointment, and many grantors may require or desire only some of the elements offered in it.[72] Moreover, if this text is too long for the grantor's attention span, the alternatives are to shorten it, if necessary to bare essentials, or dispense with a power of attorney altogether.

1 *I [A] appoint my son [B] to be my attorney. I give him full power to manage my property and financial affairs for me from now on. I wish him to continue doing so if I lose capacity. In addition to general management of my affairs, I authorise him to do the following. In each case, he may decide whether or not to do them. He may also decide when, and on what terms.*

  (a) *Operate my bank and building society accounts. Close them. Open new accounts for my money.*
  (b) *Deal with my investments, sell them, make new investments.*
  (c) *Deal with my tax and pension.*
  (d) *Claim and deal with benefits.*
  (e) *Pay my costs and expenses.*
  (f) *Pay for holidays, outings, care, services and so on.*
  (g) *Open and deal with business correspondence.*
  (h) *Make gifts to my grandchildren at Christmas, birthdays and any other suitable times.*

---

[69] *Re K, re F* [1988] 1 All E.R. 358.
[70] See paras 6–25 and 6–26 *infra*.
[71] Such as Donepazil (Aricept), a treatment for cognitive symptoms of dementia, which in some patients has been demonstrated to achieve substantial slowing of the progress of dementia.
[72] One registered CPA comprised the following elements from this style: clause 1 with sub-paragraphs (a), (c), (d), (e), (g) and (i) only, adapting (i) to refer to giving up a tenancy, clause 3, the first sentence of clause 5, and clause 6 adapted to refer to one attorney only.

(i) *If I have to leave my home and will not be able to return, to sell it, deal with all matters arising, and sign everything for me. Also to sell or give away anything in my house which is not required or cannot easily be kept. However, I have given my son a copy of my Will, and items left to anyone should be offered to that person, rather than to anyone else or sold.*

2 *I also appoint my son [B] to make welfare decisions for me at any time when I am not capable. In particular he may do the following if I cannot. He may make decisions about my accommodation, medical treatment, care, diet and dress. He may take or send me on holidays or outings. He may have any confidential information about me and decide who else may have it. He may open and deal with any personal correspondence.*

3 *I also appoint my son to take any court action, or other steps, to safeguard my interests or welfare. He may defend any proceedings. He may agree any solution to any dispute.*

4 *If my son [B] stops acting as my attorney for any reason, I appoint my daughter [C] to take over as my substitute attorney, with all of the powers given above to my son [B].*

5 *In anything of importance, my son [B] as attorney should consult me unless I am unable to comment in any way. He should also consult my other children, if reasonably possible. In particular, he should do these things before selling my house, selling or giving away anything else, deciding where I should live, or making any medical decisions other than minor and routine ones. My daughter [C] should do all of the above if she is acting as my attorney.*

6 *Everything done and decided by my son [B] and/or my daughter [C] as my attorney shall be as effective as if competently done or decided by me myself.*

Neither certification nor registration with the Public Guardian are conclusive evidence of validity. Challenge remains competent on grounds of lack of capacity, undue influence or other vitiating factors.

Attorneys

6–20 A welfare attorney must be an individual, and may not be an individual acting in the capacity of an officer of a local authority or an officer of any other statutory body. It would appear that a welfare attorney could be an officer of a voluntary organisation or other body not "established by or under an enactment".[73] This is the only explicit restriction in the Act. It remains competent to appoint as continuing attorney either an individual or any other competent entity,[74] and under both CPA's and WPA's to appoint joint and/or substitute

---

[73] s.16(5)(a).
[74] The competence of the proposed attorney should be checked, for example in the case of a company by referring to the Memorandum and Articles of Association.

attorneys.[75] Joint appointments may be of two kinds: "true" joint appointments under which two or more attorneys act jointly with the same powers, and concurrent[76] appointments where attorneys act concurrently with different powers. Under a concurrent appointment, for example, one attorney may have continuing powers and the other welfare powers, in which case an alternative might be to grant separately a CPA and a WPA, but that may be less convenient where there is a single initial appointment and concurrent substitute appointment. Where there is concurrency, the division is not always a simple division between continuing and welfare powers: the author has seen various other arrangements.[77]

The Public Guardian has indicated that he does not consider it **6–21** competent under either WPA's or CPA's to provide for appointment of under-attorneys, or for a "substitute mechanism". Provision for appointment of under-attorneys was common in pre-Act practice,[78] though not so frequently used. A "substitute mechanism" is an alternative to a named substitute, under which the power contains a mechanism by which a substitute may be appointed if the original attorney ceases to act. The basis of the Public Guardian's view is not self-evident from the Act, particularly on the view that the Act does not alter existing law and practice except to the extent that it does so explicitly or by necessary implication, and particularly in relation to CPA's, for which the Act introduces no new restrictions upon whom may be appointed. The Public Guardian has indicated that he will adhere to his view unless and until directed otherwise by a court.[79] Pending authoritative clarification, grantors and their advisers will generally avoid the difficulty by not including such powers,[80] thus (as always in such situations) reducing the likelihood of early clarification. If and when it becomes generally accepted that such powers remain competent, the certifier[81] should not accept appointment as under-attorney and should not be within the class of persons who could be appointed substitute attorney. A possible example of a substitute mechanism would be as follows:

In the event of [the first attorney] for any reason not taking up office as my attorney or at any time and for any reason ceasing to act as my attorney, I nominate and appoint as my substitute attorney any solicitor who is at the time a consultant, partner or associate of the firm of Messrs X and Y, or any successor firm thereof, and who is nominated by the senior partner at the time of that firm, provided that it has been shown to the reasonable satisfaction of such senior partner (a) that I am no longer capable of validly appointing a fresh attorney myself, (b) that all possible

---

[75] This is confirmed by the references to both in s.23. The Public Guardian's registration forms provide for both. But for the clear terms of s.23, "only to an individual" in s.16(5)(a) could well have been interpreted as excluding joint, and perhaps also substitute, appointments of welfare attorneys.

[76] "Concurrent" is adopted in this book in relation both to attorneys and to guardians (see para.11–6 *infra*), in order to make the distinction, but is not used in the Act.

[77] *e.g.* where medical decisions were dealt with differently from other welfare powers.

[78] See for example power (15) in the much-used style offered by Halliday *op.cit.*, para.13–12.

[79] An appropriate procedure would be under s.3(3), see para.5–14.

[80] Thus the *Style* excludes them.

[81] See para.6–12.

steps have been taken to ascertain any views which I may be able to express, and reasonable steps have been taken to ascertain any views which I may in the past have expressed, as to who might be a suitable or unsuitable appointee and any such views have been taken into account by such senior partner, and (c) that the person nominated is a proper and suitable person to act as my attorney hereunder, and is able and willing to do so.

6–22 An attorney who is an individual must have attained the age of 16[82] and must be capable of validly accepting the appointment at time of acceptance. A bankrupt cannot accept an appointment containing continuing powers, but can now probably accept an appointment containing welfare powers only.[83]

Powers

Powers which cannot be conferred

6–23 As noted in para.6–2, there are some things which an attorney cannot be authorised to do. The Act introduces some restrictions in relation to WPA's, expressed as things which a welfare attorney may not do, rather than as powers which must not be included, but in relation both to matters excluded by the Act and those, dealt with in para.6–24 below, excluded by existing law, it would probably be unwise as well as pointless purportedly to include specifically powers which cannot be exercised, perhaps risking difficulty over registration. Under s.16(6)(a), a welfare attorney may not "place the granter in a hospital for the treatment of mental disorder against his will". It would appear that "against his will" should be interpreted as referring to an expression of disagreement or resistance by any means, verbal or non-verbal, by a grantor incapable of valid consent. If the grantor were (or were believed to be) capable of validly giving or refusing consent to such hospital admission, then under s.16(5)(b) the relevant power is not exerciseable at all. Accordingly, "against his will" cannot be synonymous with "except with his (valid) consent", because if that were the intention the prohibition would simply be against placing the grantor in a hospital for the treatment of mental disorder, without the words "against his will". On this interpretation, it would appear that a welfare attorney with relevant powers could place in hospital for treatment of a mental disorder a grantor incapable of validly consenting but giving no indication of unwillingness. It is suggested that relevant powers would require to be precise and clear, explicitly excluding use of MHSA procedures, and expressing or at least implying aversion to use of such procedures[84]; and that in any other case it would be better and safer practice to use MHSA procedures. Under s.16(6)(b), referring to s.48(1) (which in turn refers to MHSA Part X), a welfare attorney may not consent to any treatment to which

---

[82] Age of Legal Capacity (Scotland) Act 1991, s.1.
[83] Under s.16(7) a WPA does not end upon the attorney's bankruptcy, from which it may be inferred that the Parliament did not intend that an otherwise suitable bankrupt should be disqualified from appointment.
[84] It will be wise to ensure, at time of instructions, that the grantor is aware of the protections provided to detained patients under MHSA, and weighs these against any perceived stigma.

Part X applies[85] to a grantor detained under MHSA. Also under s.16(6)(b), a welfare attorney may not consent to any medical treatment, or medical treatment of any class, specified in regulations under s.48(2).[86] The qualification "against his will" does not appear in s.16(6)(b) (or in s.48).

Apart from the specific prohibitions introduced by the Act and **6–24** described in para.6–23 above, there is little direct authority as to powers which cannot competently be conferred on attorneys (or which, put another way, cannot competently be exercised even though they purport to be granted explicitly). Such incompetent powers can however be identified in three broad groupings, which sometimes overlap. Firstly, there are matters personal to the grantor which the grantor has no authority to delegate, either because they relate to a role or appointment in which the grantor is *delectus persona*, or on the principle *delegatus non potest delegare*, or for similar reasons. Thus a grantor cannot appoint an attorney to carry out functions as an employee, or of a position to which the grantor has been appointed or elected. The discretionary functions of a trustee (or executor)[87] or company director[88] cannot be delegated to an attorney, nor can other forms of appointment under the Act. Secondly, there are matters where a proxy or substitute may be appointed only by a specified procedure. Examples include the appointment of a proxy to vote in an election,[89] and procedures to appoint alternate directors of companies. Thirdly, some things may be done only by an individual acting personally, such as marrying[90] or giving evidence, including evidence in the form of a sworn affidavit. This has an impact on conveyancing practice when a house is being sold on behalf of someone lacking capacity, and evidence is required that there is no non-entitled spouse. Neither an attorney nor anyone else can swear an affidavit on behalf of the seller.[91] It is generally believed that an attorney cannot be authorised to make a Will.[92] A variant of this third category comprises continuing powers only exerciseable upon proof that the grantor has lost capacity, an example being applying for forms of investment with taxation advantages.

Powers which require to be express

A general power of attorney (see para.6–2) authorises routine **6–25** general management only, and the traditional view is that various matters—including those noted in para.6–26 below—will not be authorised unless specifically included. There is no clear modern authority as to what is the scope of such routine general management.

---

[85] Certain treatments for mental disorder.
[86] Currently the Specified Treatments Regulations. See paras 14–17 *et seq.* and 14–48 *et seq. infra.*
[87] *Freen v Beveridge* (1832) 10 S. 727. As to executors, see *Currie on Confirmation of Executors* (8th ed.), para.8.39 and the case there described of *Leishman*, December 17, 1980, unreported.
[88] See *The Conveyancing Opinions of Professor J.M. Halliday*, Opinion 61, p.263.
[89] See Representation of the People Act 2000 (c.2), s.12 and Sch.4.
[90] Marriage (Scotland) Act 1977 (c.15), ss.13(1)(b) and 19(2)(b).
[91] See *Registration of Title Practice Book* (2nd ed.), para.6.42 for the appropriate procedure in such cases. See also the recommendations in para.6–32 *infra.*
[92] *cf.* para.10–34 *infra.*

A century ago Menzies[93] wrote: "A general factory or mandate confers only powers of general management, such as the collection of rents, interests, and such acts of ordinary administration as are necessary to preserve an estate and render it productive". The traditional rule, however, is that powers of attorney are strictly construed,[94] so that despite the general and often comprehensive wording with which general powers commence, in the absence of law reform or judicial authority indicating otherwise, Halliday's advice remains sound: "The safe practice therefore is to express specifically all powers that may be required since nothing more will be implied",[95] notwithstanding that the initial paragraph of Halliday's own style[96] confers "full power to do everything regarding my estate and affairs which I could have done myself without limitation by reason of anything herein contained"[97] and declares the following specific powers to be "without prejudice to the foregoing generality". Safe practice is not necessarily the law, however, particularly when most of the authorities still guiding safe practice are from a distant era. Broadly, there are at least four possible interpretations of Halliday's style: firstly, that the initial paragraph is fully effective and the specific powers which follow it unnecessary; secondly, that the initial paragraph is quite ineffective as regards powers granted, and that only the specific powers in the following paragraphs are conferred; thirdly, that the initial paragraph is only partially effective and that some but not all of the ensuing powers would not have been conferred if not expressly included; and fourthly, that the initial paragraph is limited only by the rule *posteriora derogant prioribus* under which the authority in the initial paragraph is restricted to acts and decisions of the same kind as those listed in specific terms (so that, for example, the Halliday style would be held not to confer power to make gifts). The old authorities appear to apply both the third and fourth interpretations, and matters which require to be expressly included in terms of those authorities are listed in para.6–26 below. However, in the case there cited as authority for requiring express power to sell or dispose of heritage, the power in question was in fact held to be ambiguous, and the prior conduct of the parties to resolve that ambiguity in favour of holding that the attorney did have such power.[98] If the old authorities are nevertheless to be interpreted as requiring express authority in terms, and if in a particular case those authorities were to be in conflict with the intention of the grantor, evident from general words though not expressed in specific terms, it would not be surprising if a modern court were to prefer the latter. In the case of CPA's and WPA's, the court might consider itself obliged to do so on the basis suggested in para.6–5 above. The discussion in the SLC Report on this topic was limited to gifts, attorney's remuneration and seeing the grantor's Will, concluding on each that power should not be implied but could be expressly conferred (in the case of remuneration, the Report says "expressly" in para.3.43 and "expressly or by clear implication" in

---

[93] *op.cit.* p.413.
[94] *Goodall v Bilsland*, 1909 S.C. 1152; *Park v Mood*, 1919 1 S.L.T. 170.
[95] Halliday, *Conveyancing Law and Practice* (2nd ed.), para.13–03.
[96] *op.cit.* para.13–12.
[97] *cf.* the initial words of *Style* clauses 3 and 4.
[98] *Thomas v Walker's Trustees* (1829) 7 S. 828.

para.3.44), and that accordingly no reform was necessary "as the existing law on powers of attorney will apply to continuing attorneys".[99] Acknowledging the uncertainties, this author would suggest that a power such as the *Style* should be construed subject to the limitation *posteriora derogant prioribus*, and that the old cases should be seen not as a closed and rigid list of matters excluded if not specifically expressed in terms, but as guidance in construing any particular deed as to the criteria of importance and distinctiveness in determining whether a particular unexpressed matter falls *ejusdem generis* with those specifically conferred and within the grantor's broad intention. That leaves the case of the grantor so brave or short of time as to specify no particular powers at all and simply to confer "the whole powers in relation to my affairs, including my property and financial affairs, which can competently be granted upon a continuing attorney without limitation", or similar. Tentatively, in the context of modern practice and the common experience of contemporary society, this author would suggest that such a power could reasonably be construed as excluding only (one) actions which would put the attorney in breach of fiduciary duty unless specifically authorised by the grantor (thus excluding, for example, power such as is conferred by declaration (b) at the end of *Style* Schedule power 1.24), (two) actions which would change the character of the administration to something different from and/or potentially of longer duration than administration by the attorney (such as is provided for in *Style* Schedule power 1.23), and (three) powers quite beyond the scope of any likely to be considered by a conscientious and well-advised modern day grantor seeking to confer the widest possible powers upon a trusted attorney in the category actually chosen (so that there would be some differences, for example, between grants in such terms in favour of a close relative and such grants in favour of an independent professional). Otherwise, it is suggested, such a power should not be construed as excluding the remaining matters listed in para.6–26 below, and that it should be construed as conferring *inter alia* all the remaining powers in *Style* Schedule Part 1. That, it is tentatively suggested, is how the underlying principle of the old cases should be applied in the interpretation of deeds granted in the twenty-first century.

6–26 Subject to the foregoing discussion, the powers traditionally required to be specifically expressed in order to be conferred at all, so far as still relevant, include power to sell heritage[1] or otherwise dispose of heritage, or sell or dispose of moveables "of great value"; to purchase heritage or valuable moveables[2]; to grant a lease,[3] or servitude or similar rights[4]; to compromise claims,[5] agree postponement of a security,[6] or allow payment to be postponed,[7] or submit a

---

[99] Scottish Law Commission, *Report on Incapable Adults* (No.151, September 1995) paras 3.43–3.46.
[1] *Thomas v Walker's Trustees*, *supra*, but see comment thereon in para.6–21.
[2] *Stewart v Johnston* (1857) 19 D. 1071.
[3] *Danish Dairy Co. Limited v Gillespie*, 1922 S.C. 656.
[4] *Macgregor v Balfour* (1899) 2 F. 345.
[5] *Hollinworth v Dunbar*, January 21, 1813, FC.
[6] *Bridges v Willison's Trustees* (1831) 10 S. 43.
[7] *Ainslie v Arbuthnot and Co.*, February 7, 1743, 1 Cr. & St. App. 340.

claim to arbitration[8]; to borrow money or grant security,[9] except where necessary to protect the grantor's property[10]; to delegate the attorney's powers[11]; to remunerate the attorney[12] or do anything which (unless authorised) would breach the attorney's fiduciary duty; or to make gifts or allow the grantor's property to be used gratuitously for third party benefit.[13]

"Statutory powers?"

6–27   Conversely, the attorney is authorised by statute to deal with certain tax matters and (if the grantor is incapacitated) to retain funds to cover tax liabilities as described in para.6–48 below, whether or not such powers are granted in the deed. Continuing and welfare attorneys are also authorised by statute to attend private interviews (without compromising their status as private) between a person authorised by the Scottish Commission for the Regulation of Care and a grantor in receipt of care, in pursuance of the Commission's powers of inspection under the Regulation of Care (Scotland) Act 2001.[14] Subject to the approval of the Director of Savings, an attorney may purchase premium bonds on behalf of any adult, including an adult who is "mentally disordered".[15] Any continuing trend of conferring powers and/or duties by statute upon attorneys will potentially have at least two consequences. Firstly, it may add a further element to the discussion in para.6–25 above. Secondly, it will raise—indeed, by virtue of the examples quoted above, has already raised—issues about the status of such "statutory powers" and their inter-relationship with the terms of the power of attorney document. To what extent are such statutory powers deemed to be granted even though not conferred by the document, as appears to be the case in relation to the tax provisions referred to? To what extent can they be expressly excluded by the document? Is participation of attorneys under provisions such as those under regulation of care legislation limited to matters within the powers conferred by the document upon the attorney in question? It will only be possible to suggest guiding principles in such matters if such use of "statutory powers" develops beyond the examples given.

Good practice, the Style

6–28   As is emphasised in para.2–13 above, the grantor is the draftsman's client from whom instructions must be taken direct. Good practice in advising and drafting is governed by three considerations. Firstly, with the few limitations mentioned in paras 6–23 and 6–24, the grantor has almost complete flexibility to choose the powers to be

---

[8] *Livingston v Johnston* (1830) 8 S. 594.
[9] *Sinclair, Moorhead & Co. v Wallace & Co.* (1880) 7 R. 874.
[10] *Thomson v Fullarton* (1842) 5 D. 379.
[11] *Dempster v Potts* (1836) 14 S. 521. Unless the power specifies otherwise (*e.g.* see *Style* clause Eighth), the attorney is liable to the grantor for any negligence or lack of skill of anyone to whom the attorney has delegated, *McNeil, Rowan & Co. v Dawling* (1696) Mor. 10085.
[12] *Orbiston v Hamilton* (1736) Mor. 4063. As to indemnification, see para.6–33 *infra*.
[13] SLC Report, para.3.43. On the foregoing generally, see also Montgomerie Bell, *Lectures*, p.448 and Menzies *op.cit.* pp.413–414.
[14] asp 8, s.25(6) and (7).
[15] Premium Savings Bonds Regulations 1972, reg.4(3).

granted. Secondly, the consequence for good practice of the discussion in para.6–25 above is that for the avoidance of uncertainty all necessary and desired powers should be expressed specifically in the deed. Thirdly, once the grantor has lost capacity, there is no mechanism for varying the deed or granting additional powers (unless it were to be held appropriate to do so by intervention order, though it would seem better for such an order to confer necessary powers direct, under the order, rather than by varying the power of attorney). In consequence, in every case full and careful instructions should be taken and should be reflected in the drafting of the power.

The *Style* is a lengthy and detailed document. It is suitable for a **6–29** grantor able to understand and consider a first draft in such form, and give further instructions on it. Paragraph 6–19 above offers a simpler form, which can in turn be further simplified. The *Style* is not intended for use unamended. On registration and commencement (see paras 6–9, 6–10 and 6–16 above), the *Style* addresses the complex alternative of immediate registration and deferred operability. Many grantors will prefer either deferred registration or, as regards continuing powers, immediate operability, sometimes combined with a separate arrangement with the attorney as to the circumstances in which the attorney will in fact act.[16] Both of these reduce the potential difficulties of dealing with third parties which *Style* clause Six seeks to address. The *Style* proceeds in favour of one first attorney and joint substitutes with wide-ranging continuing and welfare powers. It can be adjusted for joint first attorneys, single or no substitutes, concurrent as opposed to joint appointment,[17] and continuing or welfare powers only. In these matters, and in relation to the specific powers in the Schedule Parts 1–3, the starting-point should be the grantor's own unprompted wishes and proposals; then a review of the grantor's assets, circumstances, expectations and future plans; and finally a review of this or any other style as a checklist as to what the grantor may wish to include, omit or expressly exclude. *Style* provisions included may well require adaptation. The *Style* provisions are anonymous in that they do not contain specific directions which an individual grantor may well wish to give as to how particular powers should be exercised or what steps should be taken if particular circumstances should arise (though the risk of creating undue inflexibility can be avoided by the alternative of recording wishes in Schedule Part 5—see paras 6–30 and 7–13 below). *Style* Schedule Part 4 affords an opportunity expressly to exclude particular matters, which may necessitate the transfer of particular provisions from the preceding parts: to reduce the risk of any misunderstanding, it is good practice to identify each excluded power expressly as such, as in the *Style*. Powers the absence of which appear to cause frequent problems are addressed in *Style* Schedule paras 1.20, 1.24, 1.26, 2.6 and 3.3. Powers similar to 1.23 have on occasions helped overcome otherwise difficult problems, such as where a professional attorney is about to retire and there is no substitute attorney. Where the grantor has had a previous period of incapacity and one or more other management

---

[16] Such arrangements can probably only be non-binding. If binding, it would be at least arguable that they too would require to be in writing, certified and registered.

[17] See para.6–9 *supra*.

techniques have been operated, it will usually be wise to include a power such as this:

> *Without prejudice to the generality of any of the other provisions hereof, to examine and investigate all intromissions by my guardian and by hospital authorities/registered establishments or any withdrawer or any other body, person or persons with my funds and assets or any of them and all acts or purported acts of management by them or any of them in relation to my affairs, and to take such action in relation thereto or in consequence thereof as my Attorney may consider appropriate, including action to obtain accountings, access to records or production of other information and explanations, to retrieve any funds or property, to obtain payment of any interest lost or not accounted for, or otherwise.*

Halliday and Burns offer styles for other particular circumstances.[18] In this book, as well as the simpler style offered in para.6–19 above, further style clauses appear in para.6–21 and this paragraph. The use of WPA's in conjunction with advance directives is addressed in para.7–9 below, where styles of linking clauses are offered.

6–30   As noted in para.6–9, it is good practice in CPA's to be explicit on whether powers continue following full or partial regaining of capacity. The *Style* provision Three provides for powers to commence upon either request by the grantor, or medical certification or confirmation of loss of capacity; for all of the continuing powers to come into force when thus triggered; and for them to remain in force notwithstanding any regaining of relevant capacity. A simpler variation, if desired, is for all continuing powers to come into force immediately upon granting and to remain in force regardless of subsequent variations in capacity. WPA's may only be exercised during relevant incapacity (see para.6–10 above), but to help ensure compliance *Style* provision Four is explicit. A variation in relation to a fully trusted attorney would be to dispense with medical certification or confirmation in relation to welfare powers and to rely on the attorney's "reasonable belief" as to incapacity.[19] The *Style* is explicit on other matters which are in any event requirements of the Act, including compliance with s.1 principles.[20] With reference to the third principle,[21] *Style* Schedule offers an opportunity to record wishes and feelings[22] in Part 5, and on the fourth principle[23] to name persons to be consulted in Part 6. Either or both of these may of course be dispensed with. Powers may include a clause of acceptance, or endorsed acceptance, by the attorney, which both records acceptance of the appointment and also provides on the face of the deed (and any copies) a specimen of the attorney's signature. If the attorney is the grantor's spouse and the grantor would wish the attorney to be empowered to continue to act following any decree of separation or

---

[18] *Halliday op.cit.* paras 13–13, 13–14, 13–20 and 13–21; Burns, *Conveyancing Practice* (4th ed.), pp.61–63.
[19] See s.16(5)(b)(ii).
[20] *Style* provision Nine.
[21] paras 4–16 to 4–19 *supra*.
[22] Those in the *Style* relate to medical decisions (see Ch.14), but of course any relevant wishes and feelings may be recorded here.
[23] paras 4–20 and 4–21 *supra*.

divorce or declarator of nullity (or any one of those events), that must be explicitly specified in the document.[24] Although the purpose of the Part 2 Code[25] is to offer guidance to attorneys, it sensibly extends to matters of good practice prior to appointments coming into effect, and should be referred to in relation to the granting of powers of attorney, as should the Information Pack (including Guidance Notes) issued by the Public Guardian.[26]

Gifts and tax planning

During the 1990's it became accepted practice that there were circumstances where it could be appropriate for curators bonis to make gifts, execute Deeds of Arrangement, or take other such steps, for tax-planning or other reasons. Special powers to agree to variation of a Will were conferred in *B's Curator Bonis*,[27] and powers to make gifts for inheritance tax planning purposes were conferred in *D's Curator Bonis, Noter*.[28] The latter decision proceeded upon the principle that a curator was for such purposes in the same category as an agent or factor, and not subject to the same constraints as a trustee. As such, a curator was, in the words of Lord Nimmo Smith: "entitled to form his own view as to what the ward would have been likely to decide if she had retained her mental capacity and had, for example, been advised of the consequences in terms of inheritance tax if her estate was retained until her death: see *B's Curator Bonis, Noter*. This does not, however, appear to me to be exhaustive. In my opinion it would, in addition, be necessary to ask what a reasonable and prudent person would decide, having regard to all the relevant circumstances and to appropriate professional advice." If in modern practice a curator could have done these things on the basis that for such purposes a curator was akin to an agent or factor, then in preparing powers of attorney it is clearly good practice in appropriate cases to take instructions on inclusion of powers to do such things. While a possible style is offered in *Style* Schedule paras 1.24 and 1.25, the grantor may well wish to apply a range of limitations as to amounts, beneficiaries, assets disposable or to be retained, need for professional advice, circumstances in which powers may or may not be exercised, and so on. A particular issue is whether the attorney may make a gift to himself. There are circumstances where a grantor may insist on including such power, subject to safeguards: for example, where the attorney is one of several children, providing that they should all benefit equally from any such exercise, and requiring independent professional advice including as to a reasonable amount of estate to retain for the grantor's needs. A better option might be to appoint a professional attorney, perhaps only for the purpose of this and immediately related powers (see the reference to "concurrent powers" in para.6–9).

6–31

---

[24] s.24(1).
[25] See para.6–4.
[26] See para.6–16 *supra*.
[27] (Sh. Ct) 1995 S.C.L.R. 671.
[28] 1997 G.W.D. 13–538 and 1998 S.L.T. 2.

Good practice—extraneous matters

6–32 Usually, grantors of continuing and welfare powers seek to make overall provision for the eventuality of loss of capacity. It is therefore good practice to review the circumstances broadly, both to identify matters to be addressed in the power of attorney and also to identify other steps which should be taken, particularly with reference to excluded powers discussed in paras 6–23 and 6–24. Where spouses or partners both grant powers, a further dimension is added. It is wise to review Wills and any tax-planning arrangements to ensure consistency. Should any renunciations be executed, for example of legal rights entitlements or under the Matrimonial Homes (Family Protection) (Scotland) Act 1981? Any trusteeships, directorships or the like should be identified. If the grantor has a controlling interest in a family company, he may wish to introduce provisions for alternate directors in the Articles, and/or make additional or alternate appointments, and/or instruct the attorney how to exercise the grantor's voting rights as shareholder in the matter of appointment of directors, and/or specifically authorise the attorney to exercise those rights so as to appoint himself as director. If the grantor is sole proprietor of a house and there is no non-entitled spouse, it may well be helpful for the grantor to swear an affidavit to that effect, particularly if the grantor has never been married or has been unmarried for a lengthy period. Upon a future sale, further evidence for the purposes of the Matrimonial Homes (Family Protection) (Scotland) Act 1981 will only be required from the date of the grantor's affidavit (and may be provided *inter alia* by the attorney, as an individual rather than as attorney), instead of for a much longer period for which it might be difficult to find appropriate evidence.[29] The grantor may wish to execute an advance directive in conjunction with the power of attorney, rather than recording wishes and feelings in such matters as in *Style* Schedule Part 5.[30] Rarely, a trust for administration[31] may be preferable to a power of attorney.

Attorneys' actings and duties

6–33 Attorneys are obliged to comply with all of the general principles (see paras 4–2 *et seq.* above). They have the fiduciary duties and duty of care described in paras 4–31 *et seq.* above. They must not purport to act outwith the powers conferred: in practice, problems and issues arise with surprising frequency because attorneys (and those dealing with them, and even those advising them and taking instructions from them) have failed to consider the limitations of the powers conferred and the constraints of the terms in which they are conferred. In this context, see paras 6–26 and 6–29 above. Attorneys must not act after receiving intimation of the termination or suspension of their authority or power to act. An attorney must repay, with interest at the rate applicable to sheriff court decrees, any funds of the grantor

---

[29] To appreciate the potential difficulties, it is necessary only to envisage the sale of a former home of a centenarian, believed never to have married, who has lost all memory and capacity and has no surviving near relatives, in relation to the registration requirements referred to in para.6–24 *supra*, n.91.
[30] On advance directives, see paras 7–5 *et seq. infra*.
[31] See para.7–3 *infra*.

used in breach of fiduciary duty, outwith the powers conferred or after receiving intimation of termination or suspension.[32] On the converse question of whether within his powers the attorney has a duty to act, at common law this depends on the terms of the document. By accepting the appointment, the attorney comes under obligation to carry out any specific purpose for which it is granted (such as a special power to carry through a particular transaction), but under a general power which empowers rather than directs, the attorney is not under specific obligation to act but is required to exercise the diligence and skill of a prudent person in the management of his own affairs.[33] An attorney appointed in his professional capacity must exercise a professional standard of care. In their Discussion Paper, Scottish Law Commission suggested that continuing attorneys should be under a statutory duty to carry out the functions specified in the CPA, and they sought views as regards welfare attorneys,[34] but in their Report recommended against creating a duty to act.[35] The Act creates no statutory duty to act, and provides that attorneys under CPA's and WPA's are not obliged to do anything within their powers if doing it would be unduly burdensome or expensive in relation to its value or utility.[36] Also, in s.82 the Act exempts attorneys from liability for acts or omissions which are in breach of fiduciary duties or duties of care, if the act or omission is reasonable, in good faith and in accordance with the general principles. Nevertheless, the terms of the document may, upon acceptance of appointment by the attorney, create obligations to act in particular circumstances and matters; the duty of care may require that an attorney (and in particular a professional attorney) should act; and in respect that a decision not to act can be an "intervention",[37] the general principles may require the attorney to act.[38] A welfare attorney is obliged, with criminal sanctions,[39] to act when failure to do so would amount to wilful neglect of the grantor. Attorneys under CPA's have the tax obligations described in para.6–48 below. Attorneys are required to keep records of the exercise of their powers[40]: the Part 2 Code contains guidance as to the records to be kept.[41] The obligation to keep records should be read in conjunction with the sheriff's powers to order attorneys to submit accounts (in the case of CPA's) or reports (in the case of WPA's) in respect of "any period".[42] While in this and other matters the function of the Code is to provide guidance as to the exercise of functions by attorneys and related matters,[43] and

---

[32] s.81, but subject to the provisions of s.82 described below in this paragraph.
[33] Stair's *Institutions* I.12.10; *Stiven v Watson* (1874) 1 R. 412; *Copland v Brogan*, 1916 S.C. 277, 1916 1 S.L.T. 13; see also *Stair Memorial Encyclopaedia*, Vol.1 "Agency and Mandate", paras 665–700. On the point that failure to exercise powers does not necessarily give rise to liability merely because they have been conferred, see *Murphy v Brentwood District Council* [1990] 3 W.L.R. 414.
[34] SLC Discussion Paper No.94, paras 5.70–5.74 and 5.122.
[35] SLC Report, paras 3.49–3.52.
[36] s.17.
[37] See para.4–3 *supra*.
[38] While s.82 may be available in the first and second cases, it cannot apply to the third (breach of general principles).
[39] Under s.83. See paras 3–27 *supra* and 6–35 *infra*.
[40] s.21.
[41] Part 2 Code, paras 5.70–5.72 and 6.66.
[42] s.20(2)(b) and (d)—see para.6–38 *infra*.
[43] s.13.

while such guidance as to good practice is not binding, nevertheless a failure without good and proper reason to follow good practice as described in the Code could justify the sanctions described in paras 6–38 *et seq.* below. Continuing attorneys may seek information and advice from the Public Guardian,[44] welfare attorneys from the Mental Welfare Commission[45] or local authority.[46]

6–34 Attorneys have a duty to advise various matters to the Public Guardian.[47] The duty to do so arises once the power has been registered, and must accordingly be complied with even though the power has not yet become operational. The matters which must be notified are any change in the grantor's or attorney's address and any other event resulting in termination of the power.[48] The Public Guardian is required to enter relevant particulars[49] in the appropriate register; to notify the grantor (except in the case of the grantor's own change of address or death) subject to s.11(2)[50]; and in the case of a WPA to notify the local authority and (except where incapacity results solely from physical inability to communicate) Mental Welfare Commission. On notification of termination, the Act is not clear as to whether termination as regards one attorney should be notified where a joint attorney continues or a substitute takes over. This author suggests that the scheme of the Act indicates that notification of such termination should be given under s.22(1)(d), even though that provision could in isolation be interpreted as referring only to final termination of all authority under the document.[51]

6–35 An attorney exercising welfare powers who ill-treats or wilfully neglects the grantor is guilty of an offence and liable on summary conviction to imprisonment for a maximum of six months or a fine not exceeding the statutory maximum, or both; and upon conviction on indictment, to imprisonment for a maximum of two years or a fine, or both.[52]

Solicitor attorneys

6–36 There are additional safeguards and requirements where the attorney is a solicitor. There are the protections of the Guarantee Fund and Indemnity Insurance, and solicitors must comply with Rule 23 of the Solicitors (Scotland) Accounts, Accountants Certificate, Professional Practice and Guarantee Fund Rules 2001, which provides as follows:

> "23 (1) This Rule shall, subject to paragraph (2) below, apply to monies received or payments made by a solicitor by virtue

---

[44] s.6(2)(e).
[45] s.9(1)(g).
[46] s.10(1)(e).
[47] s.22(1).
[48] On termination, see paras 6–43 *et seq. infra*.
[49] "Prescribed particulars" in s.22(1), but relevant regulations have not been made—see para.3–12 *supra*.
[50] See para.5–25 *supra*.
[51] "Power of attorney" describes both the authority conferred and the document by which it is granted (see para.6–1 *supra*) and the former, it is suggested, can be particularised to one appointee.
[52] s.83.

of any power of attorney in his favour.

(2) In the event of any power of attorney granted in favour of a solicitor continuing to have effect by virtue of ss.15 or 88 of the Adults with Incapacity (Scotland) Act 2001 any money of the granter held or received by the solicitor shall become clients' money.

(3) Every solicitor shall deliver to the Council a list of any powers of attorney in the solicitor's favour held or granted during an accounting period, the list to be as set out in the Certificate."

These provisions (which except for the references to the Act repeat the equivalent previous Rule) do not appear to be very well thought out, and require revision. Rule 23(1) seems to be meaningless. Rule 23(2) is triggered by the grantor's loss of capacity, but there is no mechanism for enquiring into, assessing or recording such loss of capacity. The reference to s.88 is meaningless, because where pre-Act powers continue to have effect during incapacity they do so by virtue of the law applicable when they were granted, not by virtue of s.88 or the schedule which it introduces. This appears to produce the curious result that the provisions of Rule 23(2) apply only to post-Act powers, and no longer to pre-Act powers. Rule 23(3) (which applies to all powers of attorney) does not require separate identification of grantors to which Rule 23(2) applies. Some solicitors would in any event normally treat all funds held or received under powers of attorney as clients' funds, whether or not the grantors had lost capacity. Others have expressed concerns that this could be too restrictive, for example in hindering continued operation of existing bank accounts—which would obviously be undesirable in many cases—but that seems to go beyond a reasonable interpretation of "money of the grantor held or received". The interpretation of Rule 23(2) can present difficulties where there are joint attorneys of whom only one is a solicitor. The best practical answer is to recommend that it is generally unwise for a solicitor to accept a joint appointment with a non-solicitor at all, at least in cases where Rule 23(2) is likely to be triggered. A further control on solicitors acting under powers of attorney is that the general accounting requirements of Rule 8 specifically apply to money received or payments made by a solicitor by virtue of any power of attorney in his favour. So, while funds held or received are only "clients' funds" if the grantor has lost capacity and the power was granted on or after April 2, 2001, the accounting provisions of Rule 8 apply to intromissions under all powers of attorney, whether the grantor has lost capacity or not. Rule 8 is in practical application hardly less unclear than Rule 23. In the context of arrangements such as mandates and direct debits, it is not self-evident where, precisely, lie the boundaries of the definition of "money received or payments made by a solicitor".

Remuneration and indemnification

6–37 An attorney is not entitled to remuneration unless remuneration is expressly authorised by the grantor.[53] The common law rule, not

---

[53] *Orbiston v Hamilton* above, see para.6–26 *supra*.

modified by the Act, is that the attorney is entitled to be indemnified by the grantor in respect of liabilities and expenses properly incurred, and losses sustained in the proper discharge of the attorney's duties,[54] though if the attorney is to reimburse himself for any of the foregoing, express power to do so is probably required.[55]

Powers of the sheriff and others

The sheriff

6–38 Application may be made to the sheriff by the grantor, the attorney or anyone else claiming an interest to give directions under s.3(3) to the attorney as to exercise of the attorney's functions and the taking of decisions or action in relation to the grantor by the attorney.[56] It is suggested that one or more attorneys with joint or concurrent powers could seek directions under s.3(3) in the event of disagreement between such attorneys. Application may also be made to the sheriff by anyone claiming a relevant interest for an order under s.20. The sheriff may make such an order if satisfied, firstly, that the grantor is incapable, in relation to relevant powers, of making decisions or safeguarding his affairs or welfare, or promoting his interests in his affairs or welfare; and, secondly, the order is necessary to safeguard or promote those interests. The sheriff may place a continuing attorney under the Public Guardian's supervision to such extent as the sheriff may specify and/or ordain the continuing attorney to submit accounts in respect of "any period" specified to the Public Guardian for audit. The sheriff may place a welfare attorney under the local authority's supervision to such extent as the sheriff may specify and/or ordain the welfare attorney to give to the sheriff a report as to the manner in which the attorney has exercised his powers during "any period" specified. Although this procedure is only available when the grantor has lost capacity, "any period" could under a CPA include a period prior to loss of capacity, if the attorney had acted then, and under a CPA or WPA could mean a period prior to April 2, 2001 (when Part 2 of the Act came into force). Where a welfare attorney is placed under the supervision of the local authority, regulations made under s.10(3)(b) apply.[57] Also under s.20 procedure, the sheriff may under s.20(2)(e) revoke any of the "powers granted" or revoke the appointment of "an attorney". Accordingly, under a joint appointment he could not remove selected powers from one attorney only, but he could revoke one appointment and leave the other in force; and where there is a substitute, revocation of the appointment of the existing attorney(s) only would trigger the substitution. The sheriff clerk is required to send the copy interlocutor making any order under s.20 to the Public Guardian, who is required to enter relevant particulars in the appropriate register and to notify the attorney; subject to s.11(2),[58] the adult; and in the case of an order concerning a

---

[54] *Smith v Harding* (1877) 5 R. 147.
[55] *Style* power 3.4 is limited to out-of-pocket costs.
[56] See paras 5–14 and 5–15 *supra*.
[57] The Adults with Incapacity (Supervision of Welfare Attorneys by Local Authorities) (Scotland) Regulations 2001 (SSI 2001/77). The Local Authority Code gives guidance.
[58] See para.5–25 *supra*.

welfare attorney, the local authority and (except where incapacity is solely the result of physical inability to communicate) the Mental Welfare Commission.

In procedure under ss.3(3) and 20, the sheriff is required to apply the first four general principles, and the other provisions described in paras 5–5 *et seq.* above apply. Decisions under ss.3(3) and 20(2)(e) are appealable; those under other paragraphs of s.20(2) are not. In relation to s.20, see also para.6–53 below. 6–39

The sheriff's powers under the Act do not displace other remedies. The grantor if competent to do so, an appointee under an intervention or guardianship order empowered to do so, the grantor's executor, and anyone else with an interest to do so may call upon the attorney to account for his intromissions, if necessary by action of count, reckoning and payment,[59] and may seek damages for loss, injury or damage sustained if the attorney has acted in excess of his powers, or contrary to express direction in the document, or in breach of duty of care.[60] In the case of unauthorised actings causing loss to a third party with whom the attorney has purported to transact, the attorney is liable to the third party.[61] It would appear that loss, injury or damage caused by the attorney through failure to comply with the general principles would be actionable. 6–40

Other authorities

Continuing attorneys are subject to investigation of complaints by the Public Guardian,[62] welfare attorneys by the Mental Welfare Commission[63] or local authority.[64] Attorneys may also be subject to investigation by any of those authorities where the grantor's affairs or welfare seem to the authority in question to be at risk.[65] Following any such investigation, the relevant authority may make appropriate application to the sheriff,[66] which could be under ss.3(3) or 20. They, or anyone else claiming an interest, could also apply for an intervention or guardianship order, though only a guardianship order ends the authority of an attorney in relation to matters covered by the guardianship order.[67] See also Chapter 5. 6–41

Inter-relationship with other techniques

Where there is an attorney with relevant powers, the provisions of Part 3 of the Act (regarding authority to intromit and joint accounts) do not apply,[68] nor do the provisions of Part 4 (regarding management of residents' finances),[69] nor does the new authority to treat 6–42

---

[59] *Tyler v Logan* (1904) 7 F. 123; 12 S.L.T. 466; see also *Reid v Reid Bros* (1887) 14 R. 789; though see *Russell v Cleland* (1885) 23 S.L.R. 211.
[60] *Stiven v Watson* (1874) 1 R. 412; *Copland v Brogan*, 1916 S.C. 277; 1916 1 S.L.T. 13.
[61] *Anderson v Croall & Sons Ltd* (1903) 6 F. 153; 11 S.L.T. 453.
[62] s.6(2)(c).
[63] s.9(1)(d). Section 9(1)(e) could also be relevant, as could s.9(1)(f) in relation to continuing powers: but see para.5–32 *supra*. The Commission only has a role where the grantor has a mental disorder—see s.9(1) and para.5–29 *supra*.
[64] s.10(1)(c).
[65] ss.6(2)(d), 9(1)(e) (but see para.5–32 *supra*), and 10(1)(d).
[66] s.12(1).
[67] s.24(2).
[68] s.34.
[69] s.46.

under s.47 unless the medical practitioner primarily responsible for treating the grantor is unaware of the attorney's appointment or it would be unreasonable or impracticable for the medical practitioner to obtain the attorney's consent.[70] As noted below,[71] a guardianship order ends the authority of an attorney in relation to matters within the guardian's powers,[72] but there is no equivalent provision in relation to intervention orders.

Termination

6-43 Events which terminate a CPA or WPA include express revocation by the grantor[73]; resignation of the attorney (but see para.6–45 below); death of the grantor[74] or attorney; the incapacity of the attorney; revocation of the attorney's appointment by the court[75]; and where the grantor and attorney are married, decrees of separation or divorce granted to either party or decree of nullity, unless the document provides otherwise.[76] Where such an event relates to one attorney and there is a joint or substitute attorney, only the authority of the attorney to which the event relates is terminated. An attorney's authority will terminate by any provision of the document which has that effect, including any provision triggering substitution (which may be something other than one of the events listed above). A CPA is terminated by the bankruptcy of the grantor,[77] but a WPA is not terminated by the bankruptcy of the grantor or attorney.[78] The authority of an attorney in relation to any matter ends upon revocation by the court of the relevant powers[79] or appointment of a guardian with relevant powers[80] (just as appointment of a curator bonis under previous law terminated the authority of an attorney[81]). Where a power is granted for a specific duration or a particular purpose, it terminates when the duration expires or achievement of its purpose is fully completed.[82] A power granted on or after April 2, 2001 which does not comply with the requirements of ss.15 or 16 ceases to have effect during relevant incapacity of the grantor.[83]

6-44 Issues may arise as to the effect of subsequent grant to a different attorney of powers previously conferred under an earlier document, without express revocation of the earlier appointment. Such situations have been experienced in pre-Act practice. It is suggested that the later grant, if valid, impliedly revokes the earlier, but in practice questions are likely to arise as to the grantor's capacity,[84] and it would

---

[70] s.50(2)—see para.14–46 *infra*.
[71] para.6–43 *infra*.
[72] s.24(2).
[73] *Walker v Somerville* (1837) 16 S. 217.
[74] *Life Association of Scotland v Douglas* (1886) 13 R. 910.
[75] s.20(2)(e)(ii).
[76] s.24(1).
[77] *McKenzie v Campbell* (1894) 21 R. 904.
[78] s.16(7): see s.87(4) for the definition of bankruptcy.
[79] s.20(2)(e)(i)—see para.6–38 *supra*.
[80] s.24(2).
[81] *Fraser v Paterson*, 1987 S.L.T. 562.
[82] *Black v Cullen* (1853) 15 D. 646; *Gillow v Lord Aberdare* (1892) 9 T.L.R. 12, CA; *Brenan v Campbell's Trs* (1898) 25 R. 423.
[83] s.18.
[84] Inability to remember the earlier grant might indicate incapacity—*cf.* s.1(6)(e).

appear that the Public Guardian would require either to register termination of the earlier power or to refuse to register the later power. There would be further difficulty where some but not all of the powers conferred in the earlier document are duplicated in the later. An application to the sheriff under s.3(3) to give directions to the Public Guardian, or under s.20(2)(e) to revoke powers or appointment under one or other document,[85] might be necessary.

Once a power of attorney has been registered with the Public Guardian, and whether or not it has yet become operable, the requirements described in this paragraph apply upon events of termination. Firstly, upon any event of termination, the attorney if surviving (or any surviving attorney in the case of a joint or substitute appointment) must notify the Public Guardian in accordance with para.6–30 above. Secondly, if the attorney dies and his personal representatives are aware of the existence of the power, they must notify the Public Guardian, and the Public Guardian is required to enter relevant particulars[86] in the appropriate register; subject to s.11(2),[87] to notify the grantor; and in the case of a WPA to notify the local authority and (except where incapacity results solely from physical inability to communicate) Mental Welfare Commission.[88] Thirdly, s.23 makes provision regarding resignation of the attorney. The attorney must give written notice of intention to resign to the grantor; the Public Guardian; any guardian; if there is no guardian, the grantor's primary carer; and the local authority if they are supervising the attorney.[89] As regards notice to the grantor, s.11 does not apply, so that notice must be given to the grantor even if that would pose serious risk to the grantor's health. This may be an unintentional omission, given the extent to which other provisions of the Act permit or require notice not to be given in such circumstances: s.11 permits the sheriff and requires the Public Guardian to dispense with any notice to the adult under the Act in such circumstances, so that (for example) the resignation of a guardian will not be notified in such circumstances[90]; a direction by the sheriff under s.11(1) is extended to subsequent notifications by the chief social work officer under s.64(9) and (10) (or by him or the Public Guardian under s.76); and a similar direction may be given by supervisory bodies under s.37(8) as to intimations by managers of establishments to residents.[91] The solution for an attorney desiring for good reason to resign, and fearing such serious risk to the grantor's health, would be to apply to the sheriff to revoke his own appointment under s.20 and to direct in terms of s.11(1) that intimation should not be given to the grantor.[92] Where the Public Guardian receives intimation of intention to resign from a welfare attorney, the Public Guardian must notify the local

6–45

---

[85] Which would presumably be refused as incompetent and unnecessary in relation to a document held to be invalid.
[86] "Prescribed particulars" in s.22(2) but relevant regulations have not been made—see para.3–12 *supra*.
[87] See para.5–25 *supra*.
[88] s.22(2).
[89] s.23(1).
[90] See s.75(3) and (4), in conjunction with s.11(2).
[91] For a similar omission, see s.73 and para.11–77 *infra*.
[92] There should be no doubts about the competence of this: for example, s.75 envisages applications by guardians for their own removal.

authority; and the Public Guardian must notify Mental Welfare Commission "in a case where the incapacity of the adult is by reason of, or reasons which include, mental disorder", but it is not clear how the Public Guardian is to know whether the grantor has lost capacity or, if he has, whether the causes include mental disorder.[93] Resignation is delayed unless there is a joint or substitute attorney and the notice to the Public Guardian is accompanied by evidence of the willingness of the joint attorney to continue to act, or of the substitute attorney to take over acting, in which case the resignation takes effect when the Public Guardian receives the notice and accompanying evidence.[94] Except in such cases, resignation does not take effect until expiry of a period of 28 days from the date when the Public Guardian receives the notice.[95] Whether resignation takes effect immediately or after 28 days, when it becomes effective the Public Guardian is required to enter relevant particulars in the appropriate register.[96]

Effect of termination—third parties

6–46 The common law rule is that a transaction entered after an event of termination is valid if entered by the attorney in good faith and without knowledge of the termination,[97] and the third party with whom the attorney has transacted can hold the grantor bound by the transaction provided that the third party was unaware of the termination.[98] Scottish Law Commission commented: "The existing Scottish law on the effects of termination of powers of attorney seems sensible and should be adopted for CPA's. Third parties transacting with an attorney should not be expected to make independent enquiries as to whether the attorney's authority has been terminated by some event. Similarly, attorneys should not have to run the risk of personal liability by continuing to act when their authority has been terminated by some event unknown to them."[99] These principles are extended by s.24 to the statutory grounds of termination under s.24(1) (decree of separation, divorce or nullity where the attorney is spouse of the grantor) and s.24(2) (appointment of guardian with relevant powers). No liability is incurred by any person who acts in good faith and in ignorance of such termination. Title to heritage acquired by anyone so acting is not challengeable on grounds of such termination alone.[1]

Attorneys as agents

6–47 Powers of attorney are a type of agency agreement. Subject to the specialities described in this chapter, relevant principles of the law of agency apply. They apply, for example, to matters of disclosure and

---

[93] s.23(4).
[94] s.23(4).
[95] s.23(3).
[96] s.23(2), which refers to "prescribed particulars", but relevant regulations have not been made—see para.6–12 *supra*.
[97] *Campbell v Anderson* (1829) 3 W & S 384; *Pollock v Paterson*, December 10, 1811 FC.
[98] *North of Scotland Banking Company v Behn, Moller & Co.* (1881) 8 R. 423.
[99] SLC Discussion Paper No. 94, para.5.90.
[1] s.24(4).

non-disclosure of the agency,[2] and generally to rights, duties and liabilities in the three related relationships among grantor as principal, attorney as agent, and third party. The general law of agency in these matters is not described here in detail. Lawyers should refer to texts such as the *Encyclopaedia*.[3] Put briefly for other readers, the main principles (to which there are some exceptions) are as follows. If the attorney discloses that he is acting as attorney on behalf of the grantor in dealings with a third party, and provided that the attorney acts within his authority, the resulting transaction is in law a transaction between grantor and third party; the attorney has no personal liability; and the attorney has no personal rights against the third party except to recover any losses wrongfully caused by the third party to the attorney arising from those dealings. If the attorney fails to disclose that he is acting as attorney, and the third party is unaware that he is doing so, the attorney bears personal liability to the third party under any transaction entered. If the attorney purportedly acts as such but acts outwith his authority, he is liable to the third party for breach of an implied warranty that he is acting within his authority, unless the grantor (being capable of doing so) ratifies what the attorney has done or has acted so as to lead the third party reasonably to believe that the attorney has relevant authority, or unless the act in question is by law beyond the attorney's authority.[4] If the grantor has lost capacity and the power of attorney document has been shown to the third party, questions of what the attorney is empowered to do become questions of law.[5]

Income tax

As an agent for the grantor, an attorney under a CPA must, if required by the Inspector of Taxes to do so, make a return to the Inspector of all money, profits and gains chargeable to income tax which are received by the attorney and belong to the grantor. The attorney must provide a declaration as to whether the grantor is of full age, a married woman, resident in the United Kingdom, or incapacitated. If the grantor is incapacitated, the attorney is authorised to retain funds to meet the grantor's tax liabilities, but must meet those liabilities whether he has retained sufficient funds or not.[6] Further tax obligations fall upon attorneys as agents in certain circumstances, including when the grantor is not resident in the United Kingdom.[7] 6–48

English and foreign powers

English powers of attorney, including English enduring powers of attorney (EPA's) are frequently operated in Scotland. Other non-Scottish powers of attorney are also operated here. The general rule of 6–49

---

[2] See para.6–42 *supra* for the significance of advising, or failing to advise, a responsible medical practitioner of the existence of a WPA with medical powers.
[3] *Stair Memorial Encyclopaedia*, Vol.1 "Agency and Mandate".
[4] *Beattie v Lord Ebury* (1874–75) L.R. 7 HL 102.
[5] Because in such circumstances the powers conferred require to be in writing (ss.15(3) and 16(3)); the possibilities of additional powers, ratification or ostensible authority are precluded; and the proper interpretation of the document is a question of law.
[6] Taxes Management Act 1970 (c.9), ss.13(1), 72, and 76(2): on penalties, see s.98. An "incapacitated person" includes any "person of unsound mind, lunatic, idiot or insane person" (s.118(1), the antiquated and inappropriate terminology of which is in need of reform).
[7] *e.g.* see *ibid.* ss.19 *et seq.*, 78, 83 and 98.

private international law applies: the proper law of a contract or document governs its legal effect.[8] While a contract entered by an attorney in Scotland will normally be governed by Scots law, the construction of the power of attorney itself is a matter for the proper law of the power of attorney.

English powers

6–50   In England, the grantor and attorney are termed donor and donee respectively. There are substantial differences between English and Scots law regarding powers of attorney. For example, in England a power of attorney can be used to create a security by grantor in favour of attorney, and such powers can remain in force beyond the death, incapacity, winding-up or dissolution of the grantor.[9] In relation to incapacity, the English régime of enduring powers of attorney (EPA's) is quite different. An English EPA goes substantially into abeyance upon the grantor's loss of capacity, and is revived upon subsequent registration with the Court of Protection.[10] English EPA's are typically very brief, at the opposite extreme from Scottish documents such as the *Style*. They usually appoint the attorney "to be my attorney for the purpose of the Enduring Powers of Attorney Act 1985 with general authority to act on my behalf in relation to all my property and affairs". Section 3(2) of the 1985 Act provides that such a power confers authority "to do on behalf of the donor anything which the donor can lawfully do by an attorney" subject to the restrictions in s.3(5). Examples of the powers thus conferred include selling or mortgaging the donor's house, operating bank and building society accounts, and buying and selling shares.[11] Accordingly, an English attorney under a duly registered EPA will normally be able to convey Scottish heritage held in name of the grantor, notwithstanding that the EPA contains no express authority to do so. However, an English or other non-Scottish power cannot authorise an attorney to do in Scotland something which no attorney can be empowered to do here.[12]

All non-Scottish powers

6–51   Various provisions of the Act apply to non-Scottish powers or to appointees acting under them. Generally, the Act refers to powers (or appointees having powers), however expressed, under a contract, grant or appointment governed by the law of any country. In relation to continuing powers, the Act refers to powers relating to the grantor's property or financial affairs which have continuing effect notwithstanding the grantor's incapacity. In relation to welfare powers, the

---

[8] See *Stair Memorial Encyclopaedia*, Vol.17 "Private International Law", paras 248, 271 and 272, and the authorities there cited.
[9] Powers of Attorney Act 1971, s.4.
[10] Enduring Powers of Attorney Act 1985, s.1(1)(b). While the power is in abeyance, the attorney (if he has applied for registration) may take action under s.1(2) and the court may take action under s.5.
[11] Thurston, *Powers of Attorney—A Practical Guide* (2nd ed.), p.76. Thurston is a clear and concise text, and includes the texts of the 1971 and 1985 Acts.
[12] For example, s.9(3) of the Conveyancing and Feudal Reform (Scotland) Act 1970 precludes in relation to Scottish heritage the use described above of an English power of attorney to create a form of security.

Act refers to powers relating to the grantor's personal welfare which have effect during the grantor's incapacity. The provisions thus applied to non-Scottish powers, and to appointments under them, are: those concerning taking account of the views of attorneys under the fourth general principle[13]; the receipt and investigation of complaints by the Public Guardian,[14] Mental Welfare Commission,[15] and local authorities[16]; where the grantor is habitually resident in Scotland, the restriction of exercise of welfare powers to periods when the grantor is incapable, or reasonably believed by the attorney to be incapable[17]; the medical powers excluded by s.16(6)[18]; the powers of the sheriff under s.20[19]; the supersession of an attorney by appointment of a guardian with relevant powers[20]; the disapplication, when there is a continuing attorney, of Part 3[21] and Part 4[22]; the provisions of s.50 regarding medical treatment where there is a welfare attorney with relevant powers[23]; and the limitation of liability provisions of s.82(1).[24]

The powers of the sheriff to give directions under s.3(3)[25] include **6–52** directions to persons exercising functions conferred by the law of any country of a like nature to any functions conferred by the Act.[26] Section 83, which creates the offence of ill-treatment and wilful neglect, rather surprisingly does not refer to appointees under non-Scottish powers, but could perhaps raise questions of interpretation of "any person exercising powers under this Act relating to the personal welfare of an adult". It is suggested that s.83 could apply to an appointee under a non-Scottish welfare power actively exercising functions in relation to medical matters under s.50.

Applicable law

In addition to the provisions regarding applicable law described in **6–53** paras 3–22 *et seq.* above, the following provisions of Schedule 3 apply specifically to powers of attorney. Under para.4 of that Schedule, the existence, extent, modification and extinction of CPA's and WPA's (including like powers, however described) is governed by the law of the state in which the grantor habitually resided when the powers were granted, except that where the grantor so provides in writing, the law applicable shall instead be the law of a state of which the grantor is a national, or in which the grantor was habitually resident before the grant, or in which the property of the grantor is located (but only as regards that property). The manner of exercise of a CPA or WPA is governed by the law of the state in which its exercise takes

---

[13] s.1(4)(c)(i), per s.1(7)(b) and (c).
[14] s.6 (2)(c), per s.6 (3).
[15] s.9(1)(d), per s.9(3).
[16] s.10(1)(c), per s.10(4).
[17] s.16(5)(b), per s.16(8)(a).
[18] Per s.16(8)(b).
[19] Per s.20(5). See also para.6–53 *infra*.
[20] s.24(2), per s.24(3).
[21] s.34(1), per s.34(2)(b).
[22] s.46(1), per s.46(2)(b).
[23] Per s.50(10)(b).
[24] Per s.82(2)(b) and (c).
[25] See paras 5–14 and 5–15 *supra*.
[26] Per s.3(3)(b).

place. However, nothing in the provisions described above prevents the sheriff from exercising powers under s.20 of the Act[27] so as to safeguard the welfare or property of the grantor. Paragraph 3(3) requires Scottish courts and authorities to take into consideration to the extent possible the law which governs the power of attorney in accordance with the provisions described above "in the exercise of the powers conferred by s.18". The reference to s.18 would appear to be erroneous. It seems likely that the Parliament intended to refer here also to the powers of the sheriff contained in s.20, and that this provision was not adjusted to follow alterations in the numbering of sections during the Act's parliamentary passage. The above provisions are subject to the provisos described in para.3–25 above.

Transitional provisions

6–54   The transitional provisions of para.4 of Schedule 4 are poorly drafted and give rise to the difficulties of interpretation discussed in paras 6–57 and 6–58. Paragraphs 6–55 and 6–56 offer a suggested interpretation. Paragraphs 6–57 and 6–58 explain how, on points of uncertainty, this interpretation has been arrived at. In the following paragraphs, "pre-Act powers" and "post-Act powers" mean powers of attorney executed by the grantor respectively before commencement of relevant provisions of the Act on April 2, 2001, or on or after that date; and "commencement" means such commencement.

6–55   Post-Act powers may only be operated following the grantor's loss of capacity if the Act's requirements have been complied with,[28] and the Act's régime applies fully to them. Attorneys to adults under pre-Act powers in office on April 2, 2001 became continuing attorneys on that date (if their powers related solely to the grantor's property or financial affairs), or welfare attorneys (if their powers related solely to the grantor's personal welfare), or both (if they had powers in both categories).[29] Attorneys to adults under pre-Act powers who take up office after that date become continuing attorneys, welfare attorneys or both (as the case may be) when they take up office.[30] The Act's régime applies only partially to attorneys under pre-Act powers who thus became or become continuing and/or welfare attorneys on or after April 2, 2001.[31] Disapplied in relation to continuing attorneys only are: s.6(2)(c)(i) (receipt and investigation of complaints by the Public Guardian) and s.15 (formalities for granting a CPA). Disapplied in relation to welfare attorneys only are: s.16(1)–(4) (formalities for granting a WPA) and s.16(7) (power not ended by bankruptcy of granter or attorney). Disapplied in relation to both continuing and welfare attorneys are ss.19 and 20(3)(a) (registration provisions), s.21 (requirement to keep records), s.22 (notification to Public Guardian) and s.23 (provisions regarding resignation of attorneys).

6–56   The provisions of the Act which apply to attorneys under pre-Act powers include the following: the general principles in s.1(1)–(5); the powers of the sheriff to give directions under s.3(3); the Public

---

[27] See paras 6–38 *et seq.* above.
[28] s.18.
[29] Sch.4, para.4(1).
[30] Sch.4, para.4(3).
[31] Sch.4, paras 4(4)–(7).

Guardian's functions under s.6(2)(d) to investigate where an adult's property or financial affairs seem to him to be at risk, and under s.6(2)(e) to provide advice; the functions, including investigatory powers, of Mental Welfare Commission and local authorities under ss.9 and 10 respectively; the provisions of s.16(5) that welfare attorneys must be individuals and may only act while the grantor is incapable or reasonably believed by the attorney to be so; the limitation on what a welfare attorney may do in s.16(6); the provision of s.17 that attorneys are not obliged to act when doing so would, in relation to value or utility, be unduly burdensome; the sheriff's powers under s.20, only the registration provisions of s.20(3)(a) being excluded—so although such attorneys are not required to keep records under s.21 they may be ordered to submit accounts or reports under s.20; where the attorney is spouse of the grantor, the provisions of s.24(1) that the power ceases on decree of separation or divorce, or declarator of nullity; the provision of s.24(2) that the power ends on appointment of a guardian with relevant powers; the obligation to repay funds under s.81; the limitation of liability under s.82; and the offence of ill-treatment or neglect under s.83.

The difficulties of interpretation fall into two groups. The first **6–57** concerns para.4(2)[32] of Schedule 4 and its inter-relationship with s.18. If, as suggested in paras 6–6 and 6–8 above, "granted" in s.18 means "executed by the grantor", then s.18 does not apply the full régime of the Act to powers executed by the grantor before commencement on April 2, 2001 but not accepted by the attorney till after that date; but in that situation there is clearly no contract between guardian and attorney until after that date; yet para.4(2) refers to attorneys under contracts executed before that date. Does that mean that such attorneys do not become continuing or welfare attorneys at all, and that none of the Act's provisions apply to them, thus (for example) providing them with a defence that any proceedings against them under any of the provisions referred to in para.6–56 above are incompetent? It is improbable that the Parliament intended that between the categories of pre-Act powers to which some of the Act's provisions apply and post-Act powers to which they all apply, there should be a small category, executed by the grantor before commencement and accepted by the attorney thereafter, to which none of the Act's provisions apply. The Parliament could have avoided this difficulty by adopting the same terminology in s.18 and para.4, referring in para.4 to a power of attorney granted before commencement. The difficulty could nevertheless be overcome by interpreting "a contract of mandate or agency executed before the relevant date" as meaning such a contract "executed by the grantor" before that date. This, it is suggested, is the only interpretation which would give effect to the apparent intention of the Parliament. It is an interpretation which perhaps mitigates the other significant difficulty in para.4(2), namely the question of how, if the contract is executed before commencement, the attorney could be "appointed" afterwards. Here again, a literal interpretation would open a gap in the Act's

---

[32] Originally this was para.4(3), there being no para.4(2). Only the erroneous numbering was addressed by the correction slip referred to in Appendix 1 *infra*, leaving the more significant difficulties discussed in this and the next paragraph.

coverage, on the basis that the only attorneys brought partially within the Act's régime by para.4(2) are those appointed at some time after commencement by a "substitute mechanism" such as is described in para.6–21 above. On the basis that such a literal interpretation would not give effect to the Parliament's evident intention, it is not adopted here.

6–58 Paragraphs 4(3) to 4(6) are plainly garbled. In para.4(3) the words "the following provisions shall have effect as modified or disapplied by sub-para.(3)" are meaningless. There are no "following provisions", and the cross-reference makes no sense in relation to sub-para.(3) itself or to any other sub-paragraph. The same problem arises in para.4(5). Paragraphs 4(4) and 4(6) do not tell us to whom, what or in what circumstances the provisions there listed "shall not apply", and the only available guidance is the assertion in s.88(1) that the provisions of Schedule 4, introduced by that section, relate to "the continuation of existing powers". It is suggested that courts would require to approach these provisions on the basis that the Parliament intended that they should have coherent meaning, and that the only interpretation which gives them coherent meaning is to take paras 4(3) and 4(4) together as meaning that the Act's provisions, except for those specified in para.4(4), apply to continuing attorneys acting after commencement under documents executed by the grantor before commencement; and to apply paras 4(5) and 4(6) similarly to welfare attorneys.[33]

---

[33] Also on the transitional provisions, para.7(a) of Sch.4 was necessary because Part 2 of the Act came into force before Part 6.

CHAPTER 7

OTHER ANTICIPATORY TECHNIQUES

Joint accounts

The technique of joint bank and other accounts, operable by either **7–1** account-holder, has frequently been adopted by couples and others not only for immediate ease of administration and in anticipation of the death of either, but also with the purpose of facilitating continued operation in the event of incapacity of either. In the past, this last intention was often frustrated when banks took the view that upon intimation of incapacity of one account-holder the mandate was terminated so that the account could not be operated by either holder—an outcome worse than the situation which the technique was expected to avert.[1] Section 32 of the Incapacity Act responded to the resulting outcry by providing that where an account with a fundholder[2] is held by any individual "along with one or more others" and the individual loses relevant capacity, the other(s) may continue to operate the account, unless otherwise provided by the terms of the account or by a court order. "One or more others" probably means other account-holders, rather than other individuals: though this point is debatable, it would arise only when the account is held jointly by an individual and an entity other than an individual. "Continue", coupled with the exclusion where the terms of the account provide otherwise, probably limits the provision to accounts operable by either (or each) account-holder, excluding accounts operable only upon the signature of both (or all), though that point is perhaps also debatable. What is clear is that where joint holders do not wish s.23 to apply (which may be the case in relation to some personal accounts as well as some commercial accounts) they should ensure that the effect of s.23 is specifically excluded by the terms of the account.

Where an account-holder continues to operate an account by virtue **7–2** of s.23, that is an intervention in terms of s.1 of the Act and the first four general principles apply to the initiation and operation of the technique. On the basis that the account-holder continuing to operate is exercising functions under the Act, the sheriff has jurisdiction under s.3(3) to give directions on the application of anyone claiming an interest.[3] The function of the Public Guardian under s.6(2)(c)[4] of

---

[1] Not all banks took this view. Enquiries by the Law Society of Scotland revealed a considerable diversity of practice. The view that the account should be frozen does not appear ever to have been judicially challenged.
[2] Defined in s.25(1) as a person or organisation holding funds.
[3] See paras 5–14 and 5–15 *supra*.
[4] See para.5–24 *supra*.

receiving and investigating complaints regarding exercise of functions "concerning intromissions with funds under Part 3" would appear to include intromissions in pursuance of s.23. If the funds of the accountholder who has lost relevant capacity seem to be at risk, the Public Guardian may investigate under s.6(2)(d),[5] as may the Mental Welfare Commission where the risk arises from mental disorder.[6] Section 23 does not apply where, in relation to the funds or account in question, a guardian or continuing attorney (or foreign equivalent) has powers or an intervention order has been granted; but no liability attaches to anyone acting under s.23 in good faith and in ignorance of such powers or order.[7] Guidance to those acting under s.23 is contained in s.6 of the *Code of Practice for Persons Authorised under Part 3 to Access Funds of an Adult*.[8]

Trusts for administration

7–3   Although trusts for administration were more common prior to 1991, situations still occasionally arise where this may represent the appropriate anticipatory technique. Under a trust for administration, the grantor places some or all assets in the hands of trustees, to administer for the grantor's benefit in accordance with the Deed of Trust. Prior to January 1, 1991, when s.71 of the Law Reform (Miscellaneous Provisions) (Scotland) Act 1990 took effect, prudent conveyancers generally advised a trust for administration rather than a power of attorney when an adult wished to provide for administration following any future loss of capacity.[9] Since 1991 the technique has still occasionally been employed, and continues to be relevant, as an alternative to a power of attorney, where an adult has a fluctuating illness with a history of episodes of unwise actings and uncontrolled spending when unwell, subsequently regretted. Trustees under a trust for administration, in whom the grantor's assets are vested as trustees, are likely to be better placed than an attorney to resist the grantor's attempts to defeat the arrangement during future episodes. The grantor may of course revoke such a trust at any time while competent to do so; but for so long as the arrangement represents the grantor's competent wishes, the grantor is only likely to attempt to revoke during episodes of illness when not competent to do so. The technique is not governed by the Act, but such a trust can be subject to investigation by the Public Guardian under s.6(2)(d),[10] and can be subject to the other Incapacity Act provisions applicable to non-Act measures described in para.5–41 above. The old remedy of interdiction is no longer available.[11] During incapacity of the grantor, such trustees are responsible, assessable and chargeable in respect of income tax matters,[12] and may claim reliefs.[13]

---

[5] See para.5–24 *supra*.
[6] s.9(1)(f)—see para.5–30 *supra*: but see also para.5–32 *supra*.
[7] s.34.
[8] SE/2001/89, March 2001, pursuant to s.13(3).
[9] The status of pre-1991 powers of attorney is discussed at para.6–3 *supra*.
[10] See para.5–24 *supra*. At least one such trust has already been subject to such investigation. The appropriateness of the arrangement, and of the manner in which it was being operated, were confirmed in that case.
[11] For a description, see Walker, *The Oxford Companion to Law*, p.629.
[12] Taxes Management Act 1970 (c.9), s.72. On "incapacitated" see para.6–48 *supra*.
[13] *ibid.* s.42(6).

Gifts

Gifts must be included in any discussion of techniques anticipatory **7–4** of possible future incapacity for no other or better reason than that when adults propose to make gifts, enquiry sometimes elicits the motive (or a motive) of avoiding the perceived difficulties of management in the event of impairment of capacity. Such use of gifts is mentioned in para.3–9 above and discussed in para.2–20 above, where some of the hazards are identified. Putting funds or assets in joint names[14] may entail an element of gift. The extent to which it is intended, or not intended, to make a gift should be clearly identified, and the arrangements structured and recorded accordingly.

Advance directives

Advance directives are also known as "living Wills", "advance **7–5** directions" and "advance statements", the last being adopted by the Scottish Law Commission[15] to cover both documents recording wishes and feelings ("advisory statements") and documents which seek to be binding. Only the latter is a decision-making technique, hence "advance directives" here, meaning a document which seeks in advance to give or refuse consent to future medical or other healthcare treatment.[16] Of course, all decisions to give or refuse such consent have future application. Unless explicitly time-limited, or unless the circumstances change materially, if the patient makes such a decision today it will hold good tomorrow. The question in law is when such a decision will cease to have effect. A patient cannot demand to be given treatment considered by doctors to be clinically or ethically inappropriate, but the question becomes critical where the patient has refused treatment which doctors consider to be clinically and ethically appropriate and which, but for the refusal, they would be justified in giving.[17] The dilemma for doctors is also critical: to give such treatment in the face of a competent and valid refusal of consent would potentially be wrongful and an assault; but if the purported refusal of consent is no longer valid or not applicable to the circumstances which have arisen, failure to give necessary treatment could be deemed negligent and professionally wrongful. As to the position in law, the available authorities are English, but there does not appear to be any basis for anticipating that the Scottish courts would take a

---

[14] As regards funds, see paras 7–1 and 7–2 *supra*.

[15] SLC Report, paras 5.41–5.59 and clause 40 of draft Bill. For other terms, and more importantly a helpful practical discussion of the subject, see A.R. Barr *et al.*, *Drafting Wills in Scotland* (Butterworths, 1994) paras 3.63–3.67. The most comprehensive modern treatment of the subject of which the present author is aware is that by Chris Docker in *Tolley's Finance and Law for the Older Client*, Society of Trust and Estate Practitioners (looseleaf, as updated to April 2002). Also recommended is a paper *Advance Directives—What is the Current Position?* and annexures given by Ann Sommerville of British Medical Association at a joint conference with the Law Society of Scotland and the British Medical Association on *Competency & Consent in Vulnerable Persons* on March 27, 2000 (course papers available from the Law Society of Scotland).

[16] A. Sommerville *op.cit.* defined advance directives as "a subset of more generalised advance statements".

[17] *e.g.* by the principle of necessity—see paras 14–30 *et seq. infra*. The relationship between advance directives and the statutory authority to treat is discussed in paras 7–9 and 7–10 *infra*.

different view, particularly on the basic proposition enunciated, albeit *obiter*, in the House of Lords by Lord Goff of Chievely in *Airedale NHS Trust v Bland*[18]: "It has been held that a patient of sound mind may, if properly informed, require that life support be discontinued. The same principle applies where the patient's refusal to give consent has been expressed at an earlier date before he became unconscious or otherwise incapable of communicating it." If the advance directive is not competently given, then it cannot have binding effect, even though for purposes of the Incapacity Act it may still be evidence of wishes and feelings. If the advance directive is competently given, it will not cease to have effect merely by effluxion of any particular period of time, but the English authorities identify two circumstances in which it will be ineffective. "If the factual situation falls outwith the scope of the [advance] refusal or if the assumption upon which it is based is falsified, the refusal ceases to be effective", *Re T (Adult: Refusal of Treatment)*.[19] In that case, an advance directive was held ineffective because it was made without proper appreciation of the consequences (that the refusal of a blood transfusion could result in death—though there were also suggestions of undue influence by a parent). The same principles produced the opposite result in *Re C (Adult: Refusal of Treatment)*,[20] where a man with a gangrenous leg obtained an injunction against its amputation: the court was satisfied that he sufficiently understood the nature, purpose and effect of the proposed treatment and the probable consequences of refusal. The Scottish Law Commission summarised the position as follows: "The current law in England and Wales that an advance refusal is binding is qualified by the further rules that the factual situation facing the doctors must be within the scope of the refusal, the assumptions upon which it is based must not be falsified, and the patient must have been capable at the time of making the refusal. This may well also be the law in Scotland although it is not possible to state this with certainty in the absence of any authoritative statements by the courts".[21] Legislative provision for Scotland was suggested by the Commission,[22] but not included in the Incapacity Act, on the basis that: "Attempts to legislate in this area will not adequately cover all situations which might arise, and could produce unintended and undesirable results in individual cases".[23] It is thus left to the courts to decide and develop the law in the light of the circumstances of such cases as may be brought before them, and the arguments then presented, though it is possible that powers under the Incapacity Act applicable to non-Act measures (as described in para.5–41 above) might be invoked in relation to issues concerning or arising from an advance directive. Earlier, the House of Lords Select Committee on Medical Ethics commended the use of advance statements but took the view that legislation was unnecessary, in particular on the point that it was already the law that a doctor acting in accordance with an advance directive would not be guilty of negligence or of any criminal offence.[24]

---

[18] [1993] A.C. 789.
[19] [1992] 4 All E.R. 649.
[20] [1994] 1 W.L.R. 290.
[21] SLC Report, para.5.46.
[22] SLC Report, draft Bill, clause 40.
[23] Scottish Executive Policy Statement, *Making the Right Moves: Rights and Protection for Adults with Incapacity*, August 1999, para.6.14.
[24] Report 1994, approved in government response Cmd. 2552.

BMA policy

In accordance with a recommendation of the Select Committee, the 7–6
British Medical Association published in 1995 a code of practice on
"Advance Statements about Medical Treatment", and in May 1995 a
short paper "BMA Views on Advance Statements" which concluded
with the following summary[25]:

"(1) The BMA strongly supports the principle of an advance statement. Through advance statements, patients have a legal right to decline specific treatment, including life-prolonging treatment. (2) Patients cannot use advance statements to insist on the provision of certain treatments but they may authorise or refuse treatments. (3) Drafting an advance statement is the patient's responsibility. It is recommended that this be done with medical advice and counselling as part of a continuing doctor-patient dialogue. (4) It is the responsibility of the patient to ensure that the existence of an advance statement is known to those who may be asked to comply with its provisions. (5) No person has a legal right to accept or decline treatment on behalf of another adult.[26] Nevertheless, in addition to advance statements, the BMA recognises that the nomination of a health care proxy by the patient may be another helpful development in communicating the patient's views when the individual is no longer capable of expressing these. (6) It is strongly recommended that patients review their advance statements at regular intervals and destroy rather than amend the advance statement if they feel dubious about any previously expressed choices. (7) The BMA urges its members to consider their own views and inform patients at the outset of any absolute objection the doctor has to the principle of an advance statement. Doctors with a conscientious objection to curtailing treatment are not obliged to comply with an advance statement but must be ready to step aside. They should ensure that at the time of drafting, the patient is aware of the situation and can make an informed choice. (8) The Association encourages doctors to raise the subject of an advance statement in a sensitive manner with patients who are anxious about the possible administration of unwanted treatments at a later stage. (9) Late discovery of an advance statement after life-prolonging treatment has been initiated is not sufficient grounds for ignoring it. (10) There is a significant ethical and legal difference between the concept of an advance statement and the issue of euthanasia. In supporting advance statements, the BMA confirms its commitment to the fundamental and legitimate right of patients to accept or reject treatment options. This is in contrast with euthanasia, where the primary purpose is to actively cause or hasten death. Euthanasia is illegal and the Association's conclusions should not be seen as supporting it."

---

[25] The author is grateful to British Medical Association for permission to reproduce the text quoted here.
[26] This is (and was when published) incorrect in Scotland. See Ch.14.

Taking instructions

7–7 As with powers of attorney, great care must be exercised when taking instructions to prepare an advance directive. That is particularly necessary where the grantor has indicated an intention to refuse treatments of certain kinds or in certain circumstances, even at risk of shortening life. The following suggestions are not intended to be prescriptive or comprehensive, but may be found helpful. Firstly, if the solicitor has conscientious or ethical objections to what is proposed, the client should be courteously advised of these at the outset, and advised to seek assistance elsewhere. Some solicitors will already have clear views as to their own stance; those who do not should, before commencing to take instructions, reflect as to whether they will be able properly and with clear conscience to give the professional standard of service to which the grantor will be entitled, if the solicitor proceeds. Secondly, with reference to the discussion in para.7–5 above, it should be explained that there is a degree of uncertainty about the precise status and enforceability of advance directives in Scots law. Thirdly, it should be stressed that there is no doubt about the illegality of euthanasia, and an explanation should be given of the clear distinction between (on the one hand) a patient's legitimate right to accept or reject treatment options and (on the other) the illegality of anything which has the primary purpose of actively causing or hastening death. Fourthly, the grantor should be taken through the points in the summary of BMA views quoted in para.7–6 above. Fifthly, at this point, and also at any subsequent point where it may appear appropriate to do so, the grantor should be offered the alternative of recording non-binding wishes and feelings. It should be explained that anyone exercising any intervention in terms of the Incapacity Act, including the medical authority to treat under s.47, will be under an absolute obligation to ascertain and take account of the grantor's wishes and feelings if the grantor then lacks capacity to make relevant decisions. Such wishes and feelings could be included in a welfare power of attorney (see the *Style* in Appendix 5, Schedule Part 5) or separately recorded. Sixthly, if after these preliminaries the grantor proceeds to instruct an advance directive, the task of the solicitor—as always—is to ascertain and accurately implement the wishes and instructions of the grantor, provided that they are lawful, but to ensure that relevant issues have been identified and properly considered by the grantor. Any styles create a particular danger that the draftsman's words intrude or constrain. Presented with care, a style can sometimes helpfully prompt a grantor to identify what he does not want, or to propose his own words. Styles such as those referred to in para.7–8 below raise issues which many grantors may require to address, not necessarily with the same outcome.

Styles

7–8 Styles of advance directive, one simple and the other more detailed, are offered by Docker.[27] A style similar to the more detailed one, though now somewhat outdated, is reproduced in *Drafting Wills in*

---

[27] *op.cit.*: see n.15 to para.7–5 *supra*, referring to *Tolley's Finance and Law for the Older Client*. The foreword to this work indicates that it is intended to address the UK position, but in the main it covers only English law. The exception is section G "Living Wills" in which Docker covers both Scotland and England, very fully. As with all styles, his should not be drawn upon without reference to his text.

Scotland.[28] The *Style* power of attorney in Appendix 5 contains in Schedule Part 5 a statement of wishes and feelings[29] (an advisory statement, not an advance directive) containing material drawn from Docker's simpler style, with his permission, and may in turn be of some assistance in drafting an advance directive. Styles should only be presented to a grantor in the context of the recommendations in para.7–7 above, and the terms and consequences of each clause should be discussed fully, with a view to amendment or to adopting the alternative of a statement of wishes and feelings.

Linking to power of attorney

An advance directive can be linked to a power of attorney. This overcomes concerns that it might be competent for the authority to treat under s.47 of the Incapacity Act to be operated so as to nullify an advance directive. That would be contrary to the primacy of a person's "basic human right" to make his or her own decisions, described in para.14–3 below, and the fundamental principle that the whole régime of responsive measures applies only if and to the extent that the person has not put in place his or her own competent and relevant anticipatory measures. Moreover, those operating s.47 are required to apply the general principles, including taking into account the adult's past and present wishes and feelings. Nevertheless, although s.47 is "without prejudice to any authority conferred by any other enactment or rule of law",[30] it is silent on the effect of advance directives.[31] However, the Act does stipulate that the authority to treat under s.47 does not apply where a welfare attorney has relevant powers, the doctor is aware of this, and it would be reasonable and practicable for the doctor to obtain the attorney's consent.[32] Linkage between an advance directive and a power of attorney could be achieved by the following adaptations to the *Style* power of attorney in Appendix 5.

7–9

Firstly, add to Part 2 of the Schedule: *[2.10] To do anything and everything authorised by the Advance Directive referred to in paragraph 3.3(c) of Part 3 of this Schedule and any other documents such as are therein referred to and to do anything and everything reasonably necessary or appropriate in order to ensure compliance therewith and the purpose and intention thereof (as my Attorney, acting reasonably and in accordance with his or her knowledge of me and my wishes and circumstances, may in his or her discretion consider such intention and purpose to be) notwithstanding that my life may be shortened by compliance, or ensuring compliance, with any valid and applicable refusals of treatment by me.*

Secondly, add to the items specified in Schedule Part 3, clause 3.3: *[(c)] an Advance Directive executed by me of even date herewith and any further Advance Directives or documents of similar nature (including documents amending, revoking or replacing the same) by me.*

If an adult whose capacity had become impaired was found to have executed both a Power of Attorney with relevant powers and an

---

[28] Barr *et al.*: see n.15 to para.7–5 *supra*.
[29] See para.7–13 *infra*.
[30] s.47(2).
[31] The equivalent provision in the SLC draft Bill was declared to be subject to the proposed clause on advance directives.
[32] s.50(1) and (2). In such cases the position is governed by the remainder of s.50.

Use of interdict

7–10 The most effective way of ensuring compliance with a refusal of treatment, including a refusal contained in an advance directive, would be to obtain an interdict prohibiting the treatment. That would appear to be one of the reasons for the specific references to interdicts in ss.47(10), 49(3) and 50(8) of the Incapacity Act, and in regulation 5(3) of the Specified Treatments Regulations.[33]

Mental health legislation

7–11 Subject to certain exceptions, treatment may be given without consent to a patient liable to be detained under MHSA 1984 if the treatment is given for the patient's mental disorder and if the treatment is given by or under the direction of the responsible medical officer.[34] Because such treatment may be given without consent, an advance directive refusing any particular category of treatment is in such circumstances ineffective. In some countries an advance directive has been held effective to prevent specified treatments under compulsory provisions.[35] Conversely, there may be provision to permit patients to bind themselves in advance to agreed treatments.[36] In Scotland, the Scottish Executive has accepted the recommendation of the Millan Report that advance statements should be encouraged, that those providing treatment should be required to take a valid advance statement into account, but that advance statements should not be legally binding in relation to treatment authorised by the proposed new MHSA.[37]

Guardianship and intervention orders

7–12 The Incapacity Act is not explicit on the inter-relationship between an existing advance directive and a subsequent guardianship or intervention order conferring relevant powers. Clearly, provided that the advance directive was known about when the order was made, the sheriff would be obliged to take account of it when making the order, as an expression of the adult's wishes and feelings in terms of the third principle.[38] Even if it only came to light subsequently, the appointee under the order would likewise be obliged to take account of it. But may the sheriff override it in his order, or may the appointee

---

[33] See paras 14–45 to 14–53 *infra*.
[34] MHSA 1984, s.103. See s.96(1) for the categories of patient excepted and ss.97 and 98 for the categories of treatment excepted.
[35] A "psychiatric will" was upheld by a decision of the Administrative Tribunal of the Canton of Geneva on March 7, 1995 in *K v Department de l'Action Sociale et de la Santé* A(702) 1992—ASAN.
[36] As in the provision of the Dutch Mental Health Act of 1994 that a patient may consent to compulsory detention for one period of six months.
[37] Scottish Executive Policy Statement, *Renewing Mental Health Law* (2001) paras 33 *et seq*. On the proposed new MHSA, see para.3–31 *supra*.
[38] s.1(4)(a).

make a decision contrary to its terms (in each case having duly taken account of its terms)? As explained in paras 11–31 and 14–9 below, it would appear that except in relation to "transactions" an adult competent to do so may make effective decisions notwithstanding a guardian's powers. It would be reasonable to argue that the same applies to a competent past decision which remains applicable to the circumstances; and more fundamentally that the whole régime of responsive measures applies only if and to the extent that the adult has not put in place his or her own competent and relevant anticipatory measures.

Statement of wishes and feelings

A statement of wishes and feelings does not have binding, directive effect upon anyone to whom it is addressed. Nevertheless, as discussed in paras 4–16 to 4–19 above, account must be taken of the past and present wishes and feelings of an adult whose relevant capacity is impaired in relation to any intervention under the Incapacity Act.[39] The obligation to ascertain and take account of the adult's wishes and feelings is not qualified by the words "in so far as it is reasonable and practicable to do so". The obligation is to that extent absolute. And to that extent, accordingly, for an adult to consider and record wishes and feelings is a useful persuasive anticipatory technique. The use of that technique in relation to medical matters is referred to in para.7–7 above. It is however a technique of general application, relevant to any matter upon which decisions might require to be made for the adult in the event of impairment of capacity. Wishes and feelings may be recorded in a power of attorney (as is provided for in the *Style* in Appendix 5, Schedule Part 5) or in a separate document. It is important that the existence and whereabouts of a written record of wishes and feelings be intimated as may be appropriate, particularly if contained in a separate document.

7–13

---

[39] s.1(4)(a).

CHAPTER 8

AUTHORITY TO INTROMIT AND TRANSFER

"Our investigations have revealed that there is an unmet need for simple inexpensive ways of managing the property or financial affairs of incapable adults with modest means" (SLC Report, para.4.1)

Introduction

Relatively simple procedures to permit intromissions with and transfers of funds held by "fundholders" on behalf of adults who have lost relevant capacity were introduced by Part 3 of the Incapacity Act and relevant regulations.[1] The Scottish Ministers have issued the Part 3 Code.[2] The Public Guardian (details in para.5–23 above, for website see para.5–27 above) issues Guidance Notes on Applications to Access Funds, an Application Form for Authority to Access Funds and an Application Form for Authority to Transfer Funds. Under the procedure for authority to intromit, a "withdrawer" may apply to the Public Guardian for a certificate authorising withdrawal of specified sums from a "specified account" for authorised purposes. Normally, the withdrawer will open a new account called the "designated account". The designated account may be used only for authorised purposes under the scheme. The specified account will be frozen except only for authorised transfers to the designated account, and any other methods of payment (such as by direct debit or standing order) which may be authorised by the Public Guardian. Under the procedure for authority to transfer, the Public Guardian may authorise transfers from a "specified account" to another account, and may by such transfer change the type of account in which the adult's funds are held. No specified account or designated account may be overdrawn. The Public Guardian's Guidance and forms proceed on the basis that the procedure for authority to transfer funds may be used to change the account-type of the account in which the funds are held (that is to say, the "specified account" in name of the adult) without transferring funds from one account to another. Only 91 applications to intromit were granted during the first year of operation from April 2, 2001, indicating that many informal arrangements[3] previously

8–1

---

[1] See the Adults with Incapacity (Public Guardian's Fees) (Scotland) Regulations 2001 (SSI 2001/75), the Adults with Incapacity (Certificates from Medical Practitioners) (Accounts and Funds) (Scotland) Regulations 2001 (SSI 2001/76) and the Adults with Incapacity (Countersignatories of Applications for Authority to Intromit) (Scotland) Regulations 2001 (SSI 2001/78).
[2] *Code of Practice for Persons Authorised under Part 3 to Access Funds of an Adult*, SE/2001/89, March 2001, issued pursuant to s.13(3).
[3] See paras 12–21 *et seq. infra*.

established may still be in operation, and also that there may still be insufficient awareness of the availability and applicability of Part 3 arrangements, with the consequence that (contrary to the second general principle[4]) unnecessarily complex and restrictive measures may sometimes be adopted instead. In particular, guardianship can often be avoided—which it must be, if reasonably possible[5]—by use of an intervention order and Part 3 procedures in combination.

Terminology

8–2 A fundholder is any person or organisation holding funds in sole name of an adult.[6] Accordingly, the provisions are not limited to funds held in bank, building society and similar accounts, even though most commonly used in relation to such accounts. They may also be used, for example, to access funds held by a solicitor or other agent. Under the procedure for authority to intromit, the specified account is the account in sole name of the adult with the fundholder[7] and the designated account is the account opened by the withdrawer solely for the purpose of receiving funds transferred from the specified account and intromitting with those funds.[8] Under the procedure for authority to transfer, the "specified account" from which funds are transferred is the same "specified account" as that to which a simultaneous or earlier application for authority to intromit has been made, though the transferee account is also specified, as also may be the new account-type.[9] The person authorised to operate the authority to intromit is the "withdrawer".[10]

Limitations

8–3 The procedures only apply to accounts in sole name of an adult who has lost relevant capacity.[11] They do not apply where powers relating to the funds or account in question are held by a guardian or attorney (or foreign equivalent) or have been granted under an intervention order; but no liability is incurred by anyone acting under Part 3 provisions in good faith and in ignorance of such powers.[12] The applicant and withdrawer must be an individual. Persons acting in the capacity of officers of a local authority or statutory body are specifically excluded.[13] Only one authority to intromit may be in force at the same time, and applications cannot be made if an existing authority is in force.[14] There is no procedure to vary or extend an existing authority, therefore if it is found to be inadequate in any respect, the only solution under Part 3 procedures is to ask the Public Guardian to

---

[4] See s.1(3) and paras 4–12 *et seq. supra*.
[5] See s.58(1)(b) and para.4–13 *supra*.
[6] s.25(1).
[7] s.25(2).
[8] s.26(1)(g).
[9] s.33(1) and (2).
[10] s.26(10).
[11] s.25(1). For provisions applicable on loss of capacity of one holder of a joint account under s.32, see paras 7–1 and 7–2 *supra*.
[12] s.34, see also s.31(7). Until Part 6 of the Act came into force, the transitional provisions of Sch.4, para.7(c) applied to these provisions.
[13] s.25(1).
[14] s.25(2).

recall the existing authority, and then to make fresh application. Section 25(2) permits application in respect of "a specified account", in the singular, so the procedure may be operated in relation to one account only. The authority to transfer cannot be used to transfer funds from any account other than the same specified account. Accordingly, an application to intromit, even with related application to transfer, cannot be used to access more than one account in name of the adult. The position when the adult has several accounts is not addressed in the Part 3 Code or the Public Guardian's Guidance. Theoretically, it would seem possible with the Public Guardian's agreement to obtain a series of short-lived consolidating authorities followed by one operating authority. A better solution, probably, would be to obtain an intervention order for the purposes of consolidation, followed by a normal application to intromit in respect of the consolidated account as specified account. The Part 3 scheme is intended to be a simple scheme, with relatively simple formalities and controls, for relatively simple and straightforward situations: where there are complications, the possibilities should be borne in mind of using an intervention order as a preliminary, in parallel or instead; or of using guardianship if necessary and justified.

Applications—authority to intromit

Applications for authority to intromit comprise three elements: Part A of the application form duly completed by the prospective withdrawer as applicant; Part B comprising a declaration by a countersignatory; and a medical certificate. These require to be submitted within 14 days of countersignature to the Public Guardian, to whom a fee is payable.[15]

Part A

Part A of the application form requires insertion of particulars of the applicant and the adult, and follows the Act in requiring a statement of the purposes of the proposed intromission, with specific sums relating to each purpose; the names and addresses of the nearest relative[16] and primary carer[17] of the adult, if known; particulars of the "specified account" in relation to which the authority is sought; an undertaking to open a "designated account" solely for the purpose of receiving the transferred funds and intromitting with them; and the signature of the applicant.[18] The form provides for a request that authority be granted for other than the standard period of three years[19]; an indication that the applicant believes that the adult should not be notified[20]; and particulars of any existing direct debits or standing orders on the specified account which the applicant wishes to continue under the Public Guardian's discretionary power to authorise payments by methods other than transfers to the designated

8-4

8-5

---

[15] ss.26(2), 7(2) and the Adults with Incapacity (Public Guardian's Fees) (Scotland) Regulations 2001 (SSI 2001/75).
[16] See paras 5–38 and 5–39 *supra*.
[17] See para.5–40 *supra*.
[18] s.26(1)(a), (d), (e), (g) and (b).
[19] See s.31(2) and para.8–15 *infra*.
[20] See s.11(2) and para.5–25 *supra*.

account.[21] As regards the specified purposes and amounts, as there is no procedure for subsequent variation (see para.8–3) particular care must be taken. The form helpfully lists items commonly required, but it is for the applicant to consider carefully what should be added at "Other".

Countersignature—Part B

8–6 The countersignatory is required to declare that he believes the information in Part A to be true and that he believes the applicant to be a fit and proper person to intromit with the funds. He also requires to declare that he knows the applicant and has known the applicant for at least two years prior to the date of the application; that he knows the adult (though he does not require to have known the adult for any minimum period); and that he is not one of those excluded from being countersignatory. Excluded are relatives of the applicant or adult, persons residing with the applicant or the adult, a director or employee of the fundholder, the signatory of the medical certificate, and a solicitor acting in relation to any matter under the Act for any of the foregoing or for the adult.[22] The classes of persons who may countersign are set out in the Schedule to the Adults with Incapacity (Countersignatories of Applications for Authority to Intromit) (Scotland) Regulations 2001 (SSI 2001/78), and are as follows: a practising member of the Faculty of Advocates, a constable of a police force, an established civil servant, an executry practitioner,[23] a justice of the peace, a councillor,[24] a member of parliament, a member of the European parliament, a member of the Scottish parliament, a mental health officer,[25] a minister of religion, a qualified conveyancer,[26] a registered European lawyer,[27] a registered medical practitioner, a registered nurse, a solicitor,[28] or a registered teacher.[29]

8–7 There can only be one countersignatory, who must know both the applicant and the adult. That may sometimes present difficulties, for example when the applicant is a relative living at a considerable distance from the adult; though it may be helpful that the countersignatory need only have "known" the adult for a very short period, which does not require to be specified. More applicants may have difficulty in finding a qualified countersignatory who has known the applicant for at least two years, and knows the applicant well enough to certify the applicant's suitability. However, there does not require

---

[21] s.29(3).

[22] s.26(1)(c).

[23] As defined in s.23 of the Law Reform (Miscellaneous Provisions) (Scotland) Act 1990 (c.40).

[24] A member of a Council constituted by s.2 of the Local Government Etc. (Scotland) Act 1994 (c.39), as amended by the Environment Act 1995 (c.25), Sch.22, para.232(1).

[25] As defined in s.125 of the Mental Health (Scotland) Act 1984 (c.36). See para.5–37 *supra*.

[26] As defined in s.23 of the Law Reform (Miscellaneous Provisions) (Scotland) Act 1990 (c.40).

[27] As defined in reg.2 of the European Communities (Lawyer's Practice) (Scotland) Regulations 2000 (SSI 2000/121).

[28] As defined in s.65(1) of the Solicitors (Scotland) Act 1980 (c.46) (as amended and partly repealed by the Law Reform (Miscellaneous Provisions) (Scotland) Act 1990 (c.40), Sch.8, para.29(15) and Sch.9).

[29] As defined in s.135 of the Education (Scotland) Act 1980 (c.44).

to have been continuous or even regular contact for the minimum two-year period, and it is a matter for countersignatories to consider precisely what they are being asked to certify and whether they can properly do so.[30]

Medical certificate

The certificate by a medical practitioner requires to certify that (in the practitioner's opinion) the adult is incapable in relation to decisions about the funds to which the application relates, or incapable of safeguarding his or her interests in those funds. The medical practitioner also certifies whether in his opinion such incapacity results from mental disorder or physical inability to communicate or both. The certificate includes a "brief description" of the mental disorder and/or inability to communicate.[31]

Procedure

Upon receipt of the application, properly completed and timeously submitted, the Public Guardian intimates it to the adult (subject to s.11(2)[32]); to the adult's nearest relative and primary carer[33]; and to anyone whom the Public Guardian considers has an interest in the application. In each case, the Public Guardian advises that they may object within 21 days. The Public Guardian must not grant the application without first giving any objector an opportunity to be heard.[34] After hearing any objections, the Public Guardian may grant the application, or intimate that he proposes to refuse it, or remit it to the sheriff. If he grants it, or if upon appeal (see below) the sheriff decides that he should do so, he enters prescribed particulars in the relevant register and issues the certificate of authority to the withdrawer.[35] If he proposes to refuse it, he must intimate that decision to the applicant and advise the applicant that he may object to the refusal within the "prescribed period". The Public Guardian must not refuse the application without affording an objecting applicant an opportunity of being heard.[36] Refusal does not bar a further application. The Public Guardian may remit the application to the sheriff either at the Public Guardian's own instance, or at the instance of the applicant or any objector to the application.[37] A decision of the Public Guardian to grant the application, refuse it, or refuse to remit it to the sheriff may all be appealed to the sheriff.[38] If the applicant has asked

---

[30] A similar issue arises in relation to the "third report" in applications for guardianship and intervention orders (and the renewal of guardianship)—see para.10–49 *infra*.
[31] s.26(1)(f) and the Adults with Incapacity (Certificates from Medical Practitioners) (Accounts and Funds) (Scotland) Regulations 2001 (SSI 2001/76)—see also paras 4–24 to 4–26 *supra*.
[32] See para.5–25 *supra*.
[33] See paras 5–38 to 5–40 *supra*.
[34] s.26(3). No regulations have been made to specify the "prescribed period". It is understood that the Public Guardian allows 21 days—see para.3–12 *supra*. The Public Guardian's guidance notes indicate willingness to hear objections by telephone.
[35] ss.26(4) and 6(2)(b)(iii).
[36] s.26(7). No regulations have been made to specify the "prescribed period". It is understood that the Public Guardian allows 21 days—see para.3–12 *supra*.
[37] s.26(8).
[38] s.26(9).

the Public Guardian to authorise payment other than by the normal method of transfer from specified account to designated account, the Public Guardian may grant or refuse that application.[39] Refusal may be appealed to the sheriff.[40] Decisions of the sheriff upon such remits and appeals are final.[41]

Certificate of authority

8–10 The certificate of authority must instruct the fundholder that the specified account must not be overdrawn, and the withdrawer that the designated account must not be overdrawn. If either is overdrawn, the fundholder of the overdrawn account has right of relief against the withdrawer.[42] The certificate of authority must instruct the fundholder of the specified account that all operations on that account are prohibited, except for operations by the withdrawer in accordance with the certificate.[43] The certificate accordingly requires to specify the authorised operations, and may in particular specify the extent to which a withdrawer resident with the adult may apply withdrawn funds towards household expenses.[44] The certificate requires to be presented to the fundholder of the specified account, in order to permit that fundholder to arrange transfers to the designated account as authorised by the Public Guardian and/or such other methods of payment as may have been so authorised.[45]

Purposes

8–11 The authorised purposes for which the adult's funds may be used include (a) payment of the adult's central and local government taxes, (b) provision of sustenance, accommodation, fuel, clothing and related goods and services for the adult, (c) provision of other services to look after or care for the adult, and (d) settlement of debts incurred by the adult or in respect of the adult (including the Public Guardian's prescribed fee in respect of the application).[46] The Public Guardian may (in any particular case) authorise payment for provision of other items.[47] A withdrawer resident with the adult may, as indicated in para.8–10 above, be authorised by the Public Guardian to apply withdrawn funds towards household expenses,[48] but otherwise funds may only be used "for the benefit of the adult". The official Explanatory Notes on the Act suggest that "small gifts to family members" could be authorised. If the interpretation of "benefit" offered in para.4–8 above is correct, then this would not be prohibited, but s.28(1) consistently refers to "provision ... for the adult", and it remains to be seen whether the Public Guardian would take the view that his discretion to authorise provision of "other items" includes, in

---

[39] s.29(3).
[40] s.29(4).
[41] ss.26(8) and (9) and 29(4).
[42] s.26(5).
[43] s.26(6).
[44] s.28(4).
[45] s.29(1) and (3).
[46] s.28(1).
[47] s.28(2).
[48] s.28(4).

the context of s.28 as a whole, provision to anyone other than the adult. The official Explanatory Notes also suggest that these provisions would not cover "the applicant's legal fees or any expenses incurred in relation to the application"; but it would seem that these, if properly incurred "in respect of the adult" would (like the Public Guardian's fees) be included within the explicit terms of s.28(1)(d).

Withdrawer's actings and duties

The general principles in s.1(2)–(4) of the Act apply to withdrawers and others intervening in the adult's affairs under or in pursuance of Part 3. Withdrawers have the fiduciary duties and duty of care described in paras 4–31 *et seq.* above. A withdrawer must repay, with interest at the rate applicable to sheriff court decrees, any funds of the adult used in breach of fiduciary duty, outwith the withdrawer's authority or after receiving intimation of termination or suspension.[49] Withdrawers are however exempted from liability for acts or omissions which are in breach of fiduciary duties or duties of care, if the act or omission is reasonable, in good faith and in accordance with the general principles.[50] Withdrawers may seek information and advice from the Public Guardian.[51]

8–12

Any change in the address of the withdrawer or the adult as registered with the Public Guardian must be notified by the withdrawer to the Public Guardian, who enters the change in the relevant register.[52]

8–13

Supervision

The Public Guardian may make inquiries from time to time as to the manner in which a withdrawer has exercised his functions under Part 3 of the Act, and may ask the withdrawer to produce any records which he has relating to his intromissions.[53] The Public Guardian may require fundholders of specified and designated accounts to make their records of those accounts available to the Public Guardian: the fundholder may charge against the account any reasonable fee for doing so.[54] The Public Guardian may receive and investigate any complaint concerning exercise of functions by anyone in relation to intromissions with funds under Part 3 of the Act.[55] Also relevant may be the Public Guardian's general power to investigate where an adult's property or financial affairs seem to be at risk,[56] and the Mental Welfare Commission's power to investigate when an adult's property may be exposed to risk by reason of mental disorder.[57] The sheriff has jurisdiction to give directions to anyone exercising functions under Part 3, including the Public Guardian, on the application of anyone claiming an interest, under s.3(3).[58]

8–14

---

[49] s.81.
[50] s.82.
[51] s.6(2)(e).
[52] s.27 and s.6(2)(b)(iii).
[53] s.30(2).
[54] s.30(3) and (4).
[55] s.6(2)(c). See also s.12, and see para.5–24 *supra*.
[56] s.6(2)(d), and see para.5–24 *supra*.
[57] s.9(1)(f)—see para.5–30 *supra*: but see also para.5–32 *supra*.
[58] See paras 5–14 and 5–15 *supra*.

Duration and termination

8–15 The normal duration of the authority to intromit is three years from the date of the certificate. The Public Guardian may reduce or extend the period, and may extend it without limit of time.[59] Any such decision may be appealed to the sheriff, whose decision is final.[60] A fresh application for authority to intromit may be made after expiry of a previous authority.[61]

8–16 The Public Guardian may suspend or terminate the withdrawer's authority, thus suspending or terminating all operations on the designated account. The Public Guardian must forthwith intimate the suspension or termination to the withdrawer and to the fundholder of the designated account.[62] The Public Guardian may however simultaneously issue a certificate of authority giving the withdrawer interim authority to continue to intromit for up to four weeks.[63] The Public Guardian's decision to suspend or terminate may be appealed to the sheriff, whose decision is final, and the suspension or termination remains in force until the appeal is determined.[64] The fundholder of the specified account is liable to the adult for any funds removed from that account when the fundholder is aware of termination or suspension, but has a right of relief against the withdrawer.[65] Suspension or termination does not prevent a fresh application.[66] The withdrawer's authority ends automatically upon granting of guardianship powers or an intervention order relating to the relevant funds or account, or upon a continuing attorney acquiring authority in relation to them. No liability is incurred by anyone acting in good faith under Part 3 in ignorance of such termination of the withdrawer's authority.[67]

Transfer of funds

8–17 Application for authority to transfer may be made to the Public Guardian simultaneously with an application for authority to intromit, or at any time thereafter. Funds may be transferred only from the "specified account" under the authority to intromit. The transferee account must be specified in the application, and the kind of account may be specified. The Public Guardian's decision on the application may be appealed to the sheriff, whose decision is final.[68] The form of application issued by the Public Guardian provides both for changing the type of account of the original "specified account", and for transfer to another new or existing account, in respect of which information on the type of account is sought. In all cases, an explanation of the reasons for the application is sought. There are no

---

[59] s.31(1) and (2).
[60] s.31(6).
[61] s.26(5).
[62] s.31(3).
[63] s.31(4). The registration provisions of s.26(4)(a) apply to such interim authority.
[64] s.31(6).
[65] s.29(2). The notification provisions of s.31(3) do not require intimation to the fundholder of the specified account.
[66] s.31(5).
[67] s.31(7). These provisions apply also where powers are acquired by foreign equivalents of guardians and attorneys—s.31(8). Until Part 6 of the Act came into force, the transitional provisions of Sch.4, para.7(b) applied to these provisions.
[68] s.35.

provisions for notification of the transfer application, or objection to it, but (as always) the general principles in s.1(2)–(4) apply, as do the sheriff's power to give directions under s.3(3) and the Public Guardian's general powers described in para.5–24 above.

Related provisions

Joint accounts

Joint accounts are treated in this book as an anticipatory technique, and the provisions of s.32 regarding such accounts are accordingly described in Chapter 7, paras 7–1 and 7–2. Those provisions may of course also be used in response to incapacity, rather than following planned anticipation. **8–18**

Managers of establishments

Under s.42, managers of an authorised establishment may apply to their supervisory body for a certificate permitting one or more "authorised persons" to make specified withdrawals from specified accounts or other funds of the resident. This provision is described in Chapter 9. See para.9–12 below. **8–19**

CHAPTER 9

MANAGEMENT OF RESIDENTS' FINANCES

Note: In this chapter "ROCSA" means the Regulation of Care (Scotland) Act 2001 (asp 8); "SCRC" means the Scottish Commission for the Regulation of Care; "the 1978 Act" means the National Health Service (Scotland) Act 1978 (c.29); and (as throughout this book) "MHSA 1984" means Mental Health (Scotland) Act 1984 (c.36).

Introduction

Part 4 of the Incapacity Act provides a procedure under which **9–1** "residents' affairs" may be managed on behalf of individual residents in authorised establishments by the managers of those establishments. Part 4 also includes a procedure under which a qualified nominee of the managers may be authorised to withdraw funds belonging to a resident. Managers have an obligation[1] to consider the options in relation to any resident lacking relevant capacity, and to initiate Part 4 procedure if they consider it to be the most appropriate choice. The principal supervisory body under Part 4 is SCRC or the Health Board, depending upon the category of establishment, rather than the Public Guardian as with other methods of management under the Act. These provisions replace hospital management under MHSA, s.94.[2] Several unsatisfactory aspects of that form of management were identified by the Scottish Law Commission.[3] Moreover, adults with incapacity increasingly live in a variety of establishments other than hospitals, creating pressures which could not await the Incapacity Act: the last pre-devolution Westminster legislation on a devolved subject was the Mental Health (Amendment) (Scotland) Act 1999[4] to permit unblocking of funds held for patients following discharge. As that was seen as a temporary measure pending reform, which alleviated immediate problems but did not solve them, it is unfortunate—and has caused much disappointment—that implementation of Part 4 did not receive the priority which it clearly deserved. At time of writing it was anticipated that Part 4 would not be implemented until April 1, 2003,

---

[1] On the basis of "they *shall* cause to be examined . . . *any* resident . . . " (author's italics) in s.37(2).
[2] See para.9–22 *infra* for a brief summary.
[3] SLC Report, paras 4.33–4.39. SLC also mentioned (*ibid.* para.4.35) possible breach of ECHR Art.6(1) in that this was a simple administrative procedure and that such determination of the civil right to manage one's own affairs was not decided by an independent and impartial tribunal established by law after a fair and public hearing: SLC did not mention that a more serious criticism, and a clearer breach of ECHR, was the lack of a mechanism under s.94 to challenge in court a decision to impose s.94 management.
[4] c.32, introduced as a Private Member's Bill by Eric Clarke, MP.

nine months after all remaining other Parts of the Incapacity Act came into force. With the passage on July 5, 2001 (well before the originally intended implementation date of Part 4 of April 1, 2002) of ROCSA, the original provisions of Part 4 of the Incapacity Act were amended, and ROCSA itself now also contains relevant provisions. It is anticipated that relevant regulations will be made under both the Incapacity Act and ROCSA and that Scottish Ministers will issue a *Code of Practice for Supervisory Bodies* and a *Code of Practice for Managers of Authorised Establishments*.[5] The latter will supersede Scottish Executive Circular No. CCD2, *Protection of the Finances and Other Property of People Incapable of Managing Their Own Affairs*,[6] which was recommended to be used in conjunction with the "Crosby Report"[7] pending implementation of Part 4 of the Incapacity Act. For transitional provisions concerning management under MHSA s.94, see paras 9–23 and 9–24 below.

Terminology

9–2   For the purposes of Part 4 of the Incapacity Act, a "resident" is an adult whose main residence is an authorised establishment, or an adult who is liable to be detained under MHSA in an authorised establishment.[8] "Authorised establishments" are divided into "registered establishments" and "unregistered establishments".[9] "Registered establishments" comprise independent hospitals,[10] private psychiatric hospitals,[11] care home services,[12] and limited registration services.[13] "Unregistered establishments" comprise health service hospitals[14] and the State Hospital.[15] The list of authorised establishments

---

[5] Drafts of both Codes were issued for consultation on September 6, 2002, as was a draft of the Adults with Incapacity (Management of Residents' Finances) (Scotland) Regulations 2003, referred to in this chapter as "the draft regulations", the terms of which are briefly described where relevant in footnotes to this chapter.

[6] Published October 1999.

[7] *Report of the Working Party on the Management of Incapax Service Users' Funds* (1985).

[8] s.35(5).

[9] s.35(2).

[10] A hospital (as defined in the 1978 Act, s.108(1)) which is not a Health Service hospital (as there defined) nor a private psychiatric hospital (see n.11 *infra*.), though a separate, detached unit of a Health Service hospital which does not provide treatment or nursing in pursuance of the 1978 Act is also an independent hospital for this purpose: Incapacity Act, s.35(1)(b), (2) and (6) and ROCSA, s.77(1) and (2).

[11] Premises used or intended to be used to receive and detain detained patients which are not (a) vested in Scottish Ministers or managed by an NHS Trust, or (b) a State Hospital, or (c) managed by a government department or provided by a local authority: per Incapacity Act, s.35(1)(b), (2) and (6), ROCSA, s.77(1), MHSA 1984, ss.12(2) (as amended) and 125(1).

[12] A service providing accommodation together with nursing, personal care or personal support for persons by reason of their vulnerability or need, but excluding (a) hospitals, (b) public, independent or grant-aided schools, (c) independent health care services (see ROCSA, s.2(5) and definitions there referred to), and (d) any services excepted by regulations: per Incapacity Act, s.35(1)(d), (2) and (6) and ROCSA, ss.2(3) and 77(1).

[13] A service providing accommodation which has opted into Part 4 of the Incapacity Act in accordance with ROCSA, s.8: per Incapacity Act, s.35(1)(e), (2) and (6) and ROCSA, ss.8(4) and 77(1): see para.9–4 *infra*.

[14] As defined in 1978 Act, s.108(1): per Incapacity Act, s.35(1)(a), (2) and (6) and ROCSA, s.77(1).

[15] As defined in 1978 Act, s.102: per Incapacity Act, s.35(1)(c) and (2) and s.87—"a State hospital" in the Act, but there is only one.

may be amended by regulation.[16] The "managers" of establishments are as defined in Schedule 1 of the Incapacity Act (except where a supervisory body become managers)—see para.9-3 below. The managers of a "registered establishment" (but not an "unregistered establishment") may opt out of Part 4 by notice in writing to SCRC, as may an applicant for registration as a care service under ROCSA, s.7(1).[17] "Limited registration services" are services which opt in—see para.9-4 below. The "supervisory bodies" are normally SCRC for registered establishments, and, for unregistered establishments, the Health Board of the area in which the establishment is situated,[18] but the Scottish Ministers may substitute a different supervisory body for any authorised establishment.[19] Part 4 management is limited to "residents' affairs", which are defined in s.39 and described in para.9-9 below. ROCSA generally refers to "service users" rather than "residents", and to "services" rather than "establishments". Health legislation refers to "patients" and "hospitals", and "patient" has a specialised definition in MHSA.[20] Such alternative terminology may be encountered in material relating to Part 4 of the Incapacity Act, and in particular it is understood that ROCSA terminology may be used in relevant codes of practice.

Managers

The "managers" of establishments for the purposes of Part 4 are: for an NHS (non-trust) hospital (a hospital vested in Scottish Ministers under the 1978 Act), the Health Board responsible for administering it; for an NHS trust hospital, the directors of that trust; for a state hospital, the State Hospital Management Committee (if appointed) or the entity or person appointed to manage it; and for all registered establishments[21] (a) the person identified as manager in the application for registration under ROCSA, s.7, (b) the local authority or the person appointed by the local authority to manage the service, in the case of a local authority service registered under ROCSA, s.33, or (c) the person specified as being the manager in any regulations under ROCSA, s.29(7)(j). The Scottish Ministers may amend the list of managers.[22] Where the relevant supervisory body has revoked a power to manage, that supervisory body itself initially becomes the manager of residents' affairs for the establishment in question.[23] **9-3**

---

[16] s.35(4).
[17] s.35(3).
[18] s.40(1), which in the case of the State Hospital is interpreted as meaning the State Hospital Board.
[19] s.40(4).
[20] s.125(1).
[21] Confusingly, Incapacity Act, Sch.1, para.1(d) refers to "care service or limited registration service", but by virtue of the definitions in ROCSA, s.2 this encompasses all "registered services" listed in Incapacity Act, s.35. Note in particular that independent hospitals and private psychiatric hospitals are included in the definition of "independent health care service" (per ROCSA, s.2(5)), in turn along with care home services included in the definition of "care service" (per ROCSA, s.2(1)).
[22] Incapacity Act, s.35(5) and Sch.1.
[23] s.45(3)—see para.9-15 *infra*.

Limited registration

9–4 The purpose of limited registration under ROCSA[24] is to enable Part 4 to be operated by the providers of a service which would not otherwise be an "authorised service" within the meaning of Part 4. Limited registration is only available to a service which provides accommodation, whether or not it also provides care.[25] Application is made to SCRC by naming the individual who is to be manager, and providing such information as may be prescribed by regulations and reasonably required by SCRC, and accompanied by the appropriate fee.[26] The same provisions concerning grant or refusal of registration by SCRC apply as for registration of care services.[27] The provisions of ROCSA briefly referred to in para.9–16 below apply to all registered services, including limited registration services.

Opting out

9–5 Procedurally, it is simple for managers and applicants to opt out of the provisions of Part 4 in relation to registered establishments. As indicated in para.9–2 above, they require only to give written notice to that effect to the relevant supervisory body (normally SCRC). In practice, managers of establishments which accommodate or may accommodate people with impaired capacity will require to consider very carefully before taking such a step. Residents and their families are entitled to expect that an appropriate service should cater for management needs just as it caters for physical and other needs. Refusal to provide such a service to residents with impaired capacity might in some circumstances be construed as discriminatory, contrary to the Disability Discrimination Act 1995[28] or to non-discrimination policies to which the provider has subscribed or become contractually committed. For no better reason than the lack of procedures, many care providers have become accustomed to operating what they term "informal arrangements", fudging the distinction between vulnerable but competent people able to give valid consent to such arrangements, on the one hand, and those lacking relevant capacity on the other. In relation to the latter group, "informal arrangements" operated without the competent and valid consent of the resident are no longer an option, and imposition of management arrangements without proper procedure would appear to contravene ECHR Article 6(1).[29] The Parliament has in Part 4 provided a procedure to enable managers, where appropriate and necessary, to provide the management service which residents are entitled to expect. It is probable that common law techniques such as *negotiorum gestio*[30] are no longer available to managers where Part 4 management would be appropriate and competent, applying the principle of *B v Forsey*[31] that where

---

[24] ROCSA, s.8.
[25] ROCSA, s.8(1).
[26] ROCSA, ss.7(2) and 8(2): ss.7(3)–(5) apply to multiple applications and s.24 to registration fees, per s.8(3).
[27] ROCSA, ss.7(3)–(5), 9, 24 and 28, per s.8(3).
[28] See paras 1–41 *et seq. supra*.
[29] See para.1–47 *supra*. See also SLC comments referred to in n.3 to para.9–1 *supra*.
[30] See paras 12–18 *et seq. infra*.
[31] 1988 S.L.T. 572, HL.

the legislature has provided specific powers and procedures, common law alternatives lacking suitable procedural and other safeguards are no longer available. See para.9–6 below on the consideration of alternatives.

Procedure

Procedure in relation to an individual resident is initiated by the managers. If they believe that a resident in their establishment is not capable[32] of making decisions or safeguarding his interests in relation to any of his affairs within the scope of s.39,[33] they must consider all appropriate options.[34] In doing so they must comply with the general principles in s.1(2)–(4).[35] On the basis of the discussion of the first principle in para.4–9 above, and having regard also to the discussion in para.9–5, it is not an option to impose an "informal arrangement" on a resident lacking relevant capacity, and accordingly unable to give competent consent to such an arrangement. Also, having regard to the Act's fundamental purpose of making appropriate provision for the management and decision-making needs of adults with incapacity, it seems unlikely that "other appropriate courses of action" would encompass alternatives which might be theoretically suitable but which the managers could not reasonably conclude would be likely to be put in place, so that the resident would be left without appropriate provision to meet identified needs. 9–6

If the resident has management needs which require to be provided for and, having considered the options as described in para.9–6, the managers decide that management under Part 4 is the most appropriate course of action, they require to take the following steps. Firstly, they should consider whether intimation of the intention to require a medical examination (see below) would be likely to cause a serious risk to the resident's health. If so, they may apply to the relevant supervisory body for a direction that they need not intimate to the resident.[36] Secondly, unless so directed, they intimate to the resident their intention to require such medical examination. They give similar intimation to the resident's nearest relative.[37] Thirdly, they have the resident examined by a medical practitioner.[38] 9–7

Medical examination and certificate

The medical practitioner who examines the resident must not be related to the resident or to any of the managers, and must not have a direct or indirect financial interest in the authorised establishment.[39] If the medical practitioner finds that the resident is incapable of making 9–8

---

[32] See s.1(6) and paras 4–23 *et seq. supra.*
[33] See para.9–9 *infra.*
[34] s.37(2).
[35] See paras 4–2 *et seq. supra.*
[36] s.37(3) and (8). The Scottish Ministers may prescribe by regulation the evidence which the supervisory body should take into account in deciding whether to give such a direction (s.37(9)). *Cf.* s.11 and the discussion thereof in paras 5–9 and 5–25 *supra.* The requirements proposed in the draft regulations (see n.5 to para.9–1 *supra*) are similar to those for s.11 as described in paras 5–9 and 5–25 *supra.*
[37] s.37(3). On the nearest relative, see paras 5–38 and 5–39 *supra.*
[38] s.37(2).
[39] s.37(6).

decisions or safeguarding his interests in relation to relevant affairs, the medical practitioner is required to issue a medical certificate to that effect.[40] Unless the managers consider that doing so would pose a serious risk to the resident's health and obtain a direction from the relevant supervisory body that they need not do so,[41] they send a copy of the certificate to the resident and notify the resident (a) of the other courses of action considered and why they were considered inappropriate, and (b) that they intend to manage his affairs. They also send a copy of the certificate, and give similar notification, to the relevant supervisory body.[42] The resident or anyone claiming an interest may appeal to the sheriff the decision as to the resident's incapacity,[43] and may also seek from the sheriff an order giving directions to anyone exercising functions under this procedure.[44] The certificate is the authority for the managers to manage the relevant affairs of the resident[45] and expires three years after it is issued.[46] On review of certificates, see para.9–19 below. Upon expiry, the full procedure may be followed again.[47]

Management

Scope

9–9 Management under Part 4 is limited to "residents' affairs" as defined in s.39.[48] The definition encompasses: firstly, claiming, receiving, holding and spending any pension, benefit, allowance or other payment, with the exception of any under the Social Security Contributions and Benefits Act 1992 (c.4); secondly, claiming, receiving, holding and spending any money to which the resident is entitled; thirdly, holding any other moveable property to which the resident is entitled; and fourthly, disposing of such moveable property.[49] Regulations will prescribe a maximum value of "any matter" which may be managed,[50] but in relation to an individual resident the relevant supervisory body may permit the managers to manage any matter above the prescribed maximum value.[51] Management under Part 4 is excluded where powers relating to the matter in question are held by a guardian or attorney (or foreign equivalent) or have been granted under an intervention order; but no liability is incurred by anyone

---

[40] s.37(2), under which the form of certificate will be prescribed by regulations. A form is proposed in Sch.1 to the draft regulations (see n.5 to para.9–1 *supra*).
[41] s.37(4) and (8), see n.36 *supra*.
[42] s.37(4) and (5).
[43] s.14, see para.5–18 *supra*.
[44] s.3(3), see para.5–14 *supra*.
[45] s.37(1)—as to the relevant affairs, see s.39 and para.9–9 *infra*.
[46] s.37(7)(b), unless the authority to manage terminates earlier—see para.9–19 *infra*.
[47] There is no express provision to this effect, but neither is there any prohibition or limitation on repeating the procedure, nor any simplified renewal procedure.
[48] Per s.37(1).
[49] s.39(1).
[50] s.39(3): the draft regulations (see n.5 to para.9–1 *supra*) propose an overall maximum amount under management for a resident at any one time of £5,000, and a maximum value for any disposal of moveable property of £250, in both cases except with the consent of the relevant supervisory body.
[51] s.39(4): the Mental Welfare Commission had a similar power under MHSA, s.94(2).

acting under Part 4 provisions in good faith and in ignorance of such powers.[52]

Duties and functions of managers

Under s.39(2), in managing "residents' affairs" the managers must **9–10** act only for the benefit of the resident, and they must have regard to the sentimental value that any item might have for the resident, or would have had but for the resident's incapacity.[53] It would seem appropriate to give "benefit", for this purpose, the same broad meaning as in the first principle.[54] Under s.41 the managers have the following duties. They must claim, receive and hold any pension, benefit, allowance or other payment to which the resident is entitled, other than any under the Social Security Contributions and Benefits Act 1992. They must keep residents' funds separate from the establishment's own funds, and must comply with any requirements of the relevant supervisory body as regards keeping the funds of each individual resident separate or distinguishable from the funds of other residents. Regulations may prescribe a maximum figure above which funds held for an individual resident must be placed so as to earn interest,[55] and the managers must comply with that requirement. They must keep records of all transactions in relation to funds held and managed for each resident. In particular, they must ensure that details of the balance held and any interest due to each resident can be ascertained at any time. They must produce these records when requested to do so by the resident, the resident's nearest relative[56] or the relevant supervisory body. They must spend an individual resident's funds only on items or services which are of benefit[57] to that resident. The managers must not spend a resident's money on items or services which, as part of the establishment's normal service, are provided by the establishment to or for such resident. Finally, the managers must make "proper provision" for indemnifying residents. The indemnity must cover any loss attributable to: firstly, any act or omission of the managers, or of others for whom the managers are responsible, in exercising the powers conferred by Part 4; secondly, any expenditure in breach of the requirement to spend money only on items or services which are of benefit to the resident; and thirdly, any breach of duty, misuse of funds or failure to act reasonably and in good faith on the part of the managers. Section 39(5) provides that for the purposes of s.39, "manage" denotes no greater responsibility than complying with the duties set out in that section, but there is no equivalent provision in relation to s.41. The managers have the duty regarding review of certificates described in para.9–19 below.[58]

The managers must comply with all five general principles in s.1 as **9–11** described in paras 4–2 *et seq.* above. In relation to the resident, their duties accordingly include the absolute duty to ascertain the resident's

---

[52] s.46. The transitional provisions of Sch.4, para.7(d) would only have been required if Part 4 had come into force before Part 6.
[53] s.39(2).
[54] See s.1(2) and para.4–8 *supra*.
[55] The draft regulations (see n.5 to para.9–1) propose £500.
[56] See paras 5–38 and 5–39 *supra*.
[57] Again, it is suggested that it would be appropriate to interpret "benefit" in the same way as is proposed in relation to the first principle—see s.1(2) and para.4–8 *supra*.
[58] Under s.37(7)(a).

wishes and feelings, if ascertainable by any means, and to take account of them; and the duty, insofar as reasonable and practicable, to encourage exercise and development of relevant skills. Specific provision to validate the resident's own acts and transactions is unnecessary, because procedure under Part 4 does not automatically remove capacity in relation to residents' affairs.[59] The managers have the fiduciary duties and duties of care described in paras 4–31 *et seq.* above. The managers must repay, with interest at the rate applicable to sheriff court decrees, any funds of the resident used in breach of fiduciary duty, outwith the manager's authority or after receiving intimation of termination or suspension of their authority to manage.[60] Managers are however exempted from liability for acts or omissions which are in breach of fiduciary duties or duties of care, if the act or omission is reasonable, in good faith and in accordance with the general principles.[61]

Withdrawal of funds

9–12   Under s.42, the managers may apply to the relevant supervisory body for a certificate authorising withdrawals from accounts or other funds of the resident. The application must be in writing[62] and must specify one or more nominees to exercise the authority. The nominees must be managers, officers or members of staff of the establishment.[63] The certificate of authority requires to be signed by an officer of the supervisory body authorised to do so. It specifies the accounts or other funds of the resident to which it relates and names the nominee or nominees, who become the "authorised persons". It also specifies the period of validity of the authority to withdraw, which must not exceed the period of validity of the certificate under s.37(2) described in para.9–8 above.[64] At any time after issuing the certificate, the supervisory body may revoke it. If it does so, it must notify the fundholder.[65] The certificate authorises the "authorised persons" to make withdrawals from the specified accounts or sources of funds, and it authorises the fundholder or fundholders to make payments accordingly.[66] "Fundholder" is not defined in Part 4, but clearly has the same meaning as in Part 3, namely the person or organisation holding the funds.[67] This procedure is not limited to a single account, as is the procedure for withdrawal of funds under Part 3. It lacks several of the safeguards and controls under the equivalent procedure in Part 3, including intimation provisions equivalent to those in Part 3 or in relation to the principal authority under Part 4, but as with any intervention the s.1 principles apply, including the requirement to take account of the present and past wishes of the resident, if ascertainable, under the third principle and to take account of the views of others in accordance with the fourth principle.

---

[59] Contrast the effect of guardianship under s.67(1).
[60] s.81.
[61] s.82.
[62] s.42(1).
[63] s.42(2).
[64] s.42(3).
[65] s.42(5).
[66] s.42(4).
[67] s.25(1).

Registered establishments—regulation under ROCSA

Registered establishments[68] are subject to the provisions of ROCSA, many of which are potentially relevant to management under Part 4 of the Incapacity Act. Scottish Ministers have wide powers under ROCSA, s.29 to make regulations, including regulations regarding management and training of care service staff[69]; facilities and particular services to be provided; keeping of accounts, documents and records; making returns to SCRC, with details of contents, intervals and periods covered; and notification of particular events.[70] Regulations on various topics, including those mentioned above, may provide that breach of those regulations is an offence.[71] On provisions of ROCSA of particular relevance, see also para.9–16 below.

9–13

Supervision

Supervisory bodies

As stated in para.9–2 above, the supervisory bodies are normally SCRC for registered establishments and the relevant Health Board for unregistered establishments.[72] The relevant supervisory body must from time to time make inquiry as to the manner in which the managers of an authorised establishment are carrying out the management of residents' affairs, and in particular the manner in which they are carrying out their functions under s.41.[73] The relevant supervisory body must investigate any complaint received as to the manner in which the managers of an authorised establishment are managing residents' affairs.[74]

9–14

The relevant supervisory body may under s.45 revoke the power to manage in relation to a particular establishment. They may do so if it appears to them (a) that the managers of that establishment are no longer operating as such, or (b) that the managers have failed to comply with any requirement of Part 4, or (c) that for any other reason it is no longer appropriate that the managers should continue to manage residents' affairs.[75] Within 14 days of revocation, the supervisory body must take over management of the residents' affairs, and in relation to that management become subject to all requirements imposed by Part 4 on managers.[76] Within three months of taking over management, they must cause management to be transferred to such other establishment, authority or person as they consider

9–15

---

[68] See para.9–2 *supra*.
[69] ROCSA, s.29(2)(h).
[70] ROCSA, s.29(7)(a)–(f).
[71] ROCSA, s.29(10) and (11): the penalty on summary conviction shall be a fine not exceeding 5 on the standard scale.
[72] s.35(2); unless the Scottish Ministers substitute a different supervisory body under s.40(4).
[73] s.40(2). On s.41 functions, see para.9–10 *supra*.
[74] s.40(3).
[75] s.45(1).
[76] s.45(3).

appropriate.[77] When the supervisory body is satisfied that the grounds of revocation no longer apply, they may annul the revocation of the power to manage (and where necessary may annul the revocation of the registration).[78] Any decision of the supervisory body may be appealed to the sheriff, whose decision is final.[79]

9–16   SCRC as the supervisory body for registered establishments has further extensive powers under ROCSA. These include powers to establish complaints procedures (under ROCSA, s.6); to give improvement notices (under ROCSA, ss.10 and 11); to propose cancellation of registration after expiry of the period specified in an improvement notice (under ROCSA, s.12); to attach conditions to a grant of registration (under ROCSA, s.9) and to vary such conditions or impose new conditions (under ROCSA, s.13)[80]; in urgent situations, to make summary application to the sheriff for cancellation of registration (under ROCSA, s.18); and to demand information and to inspect (under ROCSA, ss.25–27).[81] Regulations under ROCSA, s.28 may *inter alia* confer additional functions on SCRC and make further provision about registration. The provisions of ROCSA referred to in this paragraph and footnotes thereto, and in n.27 to para.9–4, apply to all registered establishments, including limited registration services.[82]

9–17   The supervisory bodies, in relation to any intervention in the affairs of an adult under or in pursuance of the Incapacity Act, must comply with the general principles in s.1(2)–(4) of that Act, and also—when themselves acting as managers as described in para.9–15 above—the fifth principle in s.1(5). SCRC in all its functions under ROCSA is required to comply with the general principles in ROCSA, s.59, which are: that the safety and welfare of all persons who use, or are eligible to use, care services are to be protected and enhanced; that the independence of those persons is to be promoted; and that diversity in the provision of care services is to be promoted with a view to those persons being afforded choice.[83]

9–18   The Public Guardian's general power to investigate where an adult's property or financial affairs seem to be at risk,[84] and the Mental Welfare Commission's power to investigate when an adult's property may be exposed to risk by mental disorder,[85] can be exercised in any situation, including where adults reside in registered or unregistered establishments, whether under Part 4 management or not. The sheriff has jurisdiction to give directions to anyone exercising functions under Part 4 on the application of anyone claiming an interest, under s.3(3).[86]

---

[77] s.45(4). A person to whom management is transferred could be the resident, from which it is clear that "management" in this subsection is not limited to management under Part 4.
[78] s.45(5).
[79] s.45(6).
[80] See ROCSA, ss.14–17, 19 and 20 for further powers.
[81] On the giving of notices under ROCSA, see ROCSA, s.32.
[82] Except that ROCSA, s.29(4) and (6) do not apply to limited registration services.
[83] ROCSA, s.29(2), (3) and (4) respectively. Under ROCSA, s.59(1), the principles also apply to the Scottish Ministers.
[84] s.6(2)(d), and see para.5–24 *supra*.
[85] s.9(1)(f)—see para.5–30 *supra*: but see also para.5–32 *supra*.
[86] See para.5–14 *supra*.

Changes in capacity or residence

Review of certificate

The certificate under s.37[87] must be reviewed if it appears to the managers, or to the medical practitioner who granted the certificate, or to anyone "having" an interest[88] in any of the resident's affairs,[89] that there has been any change in the condition or circumstances of the resident bearing on the resident's incapacity.[90]

9–19

Resident regains relevant capacity

Where the resident regains relevant capacity,[91] the managers must prepare a statement of the resident's affairs[92] as at the date when he regained capacity, and give him a copy.[93] The managers are obliged to continue managing the resident's affairs for up to three months after he regains capacity, notwithstanding that he has regained capacity, "while such other arrangements as are necessary for managing his affairs are being made".[94] At first sight, it might be difficult to reconcile this provision for ongoing management following regaining of capacity with the first and second general principles,[95] which would certainly oblige the managers to hand over to the (now capable) adult immediately upon demand, but the provision is presumably designed to stop the managers handing over prematurely when the adult needs or desires time to make his own arrangements. At the end of this period of continued interim management, the managers must prepare a further statement and give the adult a copy.[96] The foregoing provisions apply whether or not the resident leaves the establishment. Where the resident does leave the establishment, then the managers have an additional duty to transfer his affairs to him[97]; and they must also within 14 days of his leaving notify their supervisory body.[98]

9–20

Resident leaves, capacity not regained

The following provisions apply when a resident whose affairs are being managed under Part 4 leaves the establishment but has not regained relevant capacity. The managers must prepare a statement of that resident's affairs[99] as at the date when he moves. If he moves to another authorised establishment, they must send a copy to the managers of the new establishment.[1] Otherwise, they must give a copy to any person who appears to them to be the person who will

9–21

---

[87] See para.9–8 *supra*.
[88] See para.14–59 *infra*.
[89] As defined in s.39—see para.9–9 *supra*.
[90] s.37(7)(a).
[91] ss.43 and 44 say "ceases to be incapable of managing his affairs" and "ceases to be incapable", but see commentary in paras 4–23 *et seq. supra* on definition of "incapable".
[92] Defined in s.39—see para.9–9 *supra*.
[93] s.43(2).
[94] s.44(1).
[95] ss.1(2) and (3)—see paras 4–6 *et seq.* and 4–12 *et seq.* respectively *supra*.
[96] s.44(2).
[97] s.44(3).
[98] s.44(4)(a).
[99] Defined in s.39—see para.9–9 *supra*.
[1] s.43(3).

manage his affairs.[2] In either case, the managers of the establishment which he left must continue to manage for up to three months while such other arrangements as are necessary for managing his affairs are being made.[3] When this period for further management ends, they must prepare a further statement as at the date when it ends and give a copy to "any person who appears to them to be the person who will manage his affairs".[4] They must take such steps as are necessary to transfer the former resident's affairs to whichever establishment, authority or person is to manage them[5]; and they must also within 14 days of his leaving inform their supervisory body and (unless he has moved to another authorised establishment or into local authority care) inform the local authority of the area in which they expect him to reside.[6]

Transitional provisions—MHSA management

9–22   As mentioned in para.9–1 above, management under MHSA 1984, s.94 is superseded by Part 4 of the Incapacity Act. Under MHSA 1984, managers of hospitals were authorised to receive, hold and expend money and valuables for patients liable to be detained or receiving treatment for mental disorder, upon a certificate from the medical officer in charge of the patient's treatment.[7] The managers required the consent of the Mental Welfare Commission to receive or hold money or valuables in excess of a prescribed limit.[8] Under the 1999 amendments referred to in para.9–1 above, they could continue to hold and expend despite the person ceasing to be liable to be detained or ceasing to receive treatment for mental disorder as a hospital patient.[9] See MHSA 1984, s.94, as amended, for other relevant provisions.

9–23   Upon commencement of Part 4 of the Incapacity Act, hospital managers who have received and hold money and valuables for a patient may continue to do so for up to three years from commencement. After commencement, however, they do so under the provisions of Part 4, with only limited qualifications.[10] Firstly, they may do so upon the certificate previously issued under MHSA 1984, s.94(1), and they do not require a certificate under s.37 of the Incapacity Act[11] to continue managing the money and valuables held at commencement.[12] However, the other requirements of s.37 do apply, including the obligation to consider options in relation to any further management needs which may arise, and the obligation to review,[13] and it appears that they would require to follow s.37 procedure (including the certification requirements) to manage anything in addition to

---

[2] s.43(4).
[3] s.44(1).
[4] s.44(2).
[5] s.44(3).
[6] s.44(4).
[7] MHSA 1984, s.94(1) and (3).
[8] MHSA 1984, s.94(2).
[9] MHSA 1984, s.94(3A).
[10] Incapacity Act, Sch.4, para.5(1).
[11] See para.9–8 *supra*.
[12] Sch.4, para.5(2).
[13] See paras 9–6 and 9–19 *supra*.

money and valuables held at commencement. Secondly, if at commencement they held authority from Mental Welfare Commission to hold money and valuables to a value which exceeds the current maximum under regulations in terms of s.39(3) of the Incapacity Act,[14] they may continue to do so.[15] Thirdly, and rather puzzlingly, the whole of s.35 of the Incapacity Act is disapplied,[16] thus *inter alia* disapplying in relation to management by hospitals under these transitional provisions the definitions of "unregistered establishments" and "authorised establishments". Construing the transitional provisions as a whole, it seems clear that subject only to the specific qualifications described, hospitals in this role manage as if they were authorised establishments under Part 4, and the only area of possible doubt concerns the role of supervisory body, in that s.40(1) allocates supervisory bodies to registered and unregistered establishments respectively. At time of writing, the proposed treatment of this issue in the relevant codes of practice is not yet available.

By virtue of MHSA 1984, s.94(3A), some people who continue to have some of their affairs managed by hospitals during the period of three years from commencement of Part 4 may be resident in "registered establishments" or elsewhere, provided that s.94(3A) was triggered in relation to them before commencement. If however the patient or former patient regains capacity or leaves hospital after commencement, then it appears that the relevant provisions of the Incapacity Act described respectively in paras 9–20 and 9–21 above will apply.

9–24

---

[14] See para.9–9 *supra*.
[15] Sch.4, para.5(4).
[16] Per Sch.4, para.5(3); s.38, also disapplied, was repealed by ROCSA, Sch.4, as were s.36 and the amendments in Sch.5, paras 10 and 11 to Social Work (Scotland) Act 1968 (c.49).

Chapter 10

INTERVENTION ORDERS AND GUARDIANSHIP—GENERAL

"The mentally retarded person has a right to a qualified guardian when this is required to protect his personal wellbeing and interest"
(United Nations Declaration on the Rights of Mentally Retarded Persons, 1971 UN General Assembly 26th Session, Resolution 2856, Article 5)

"It cannot be stressed too strongly that modern use of tutor-dative procedure is no more than a useful stop-gap. Employed appropriately and responsibly, the procedure meets needs for which there is no other provision at all in our law. However, it is neither an ideal nor a comprehensive solution. It lacks sufficient checks and balances. We require an integrated statutory code designed to meet the various needs of adults who lack (or lose) full legal capacity."
(The author, "The Power to Act" (1990), p.54)

Introduction

10–1 Guardianship and intervention orders provide a comprehensive and flexible, but not exclusive, régime of responsive measures[1] to meet the needs of adults with impaired capacity to take action, safeguard or promote their interests, or make decisions in relation to their property, financial affairs or personal welfare.[2] This new régime is a statutory creation introduced by the Incapacity Act. The principal relevant provisions appear in Parts 1, 6 and 7 of that Act, and in Schedules 2 and 3. Regulations of particular relevance are the Supervision of Welfare Guardians etc by Local Authorities Regulations,[3] the Reports in Relation to Guardianship and Intervention Orders Regulations,[4] the Recall of Welfare Guardians' Powers Regulations,[5] the Non-compliance with Decisions of Welfare Guardians Regulations[6] and the Specified Treatments Regulations.[7] Relevant Codes of Practice are the Part 6 Code, the Local Authority Code (particularly sections 5, 6 and

---

[1] See para.1–19 *supra*.
[2] See Incapacity Act, ss.53(1), 58(1) and 64(1).
[3] The Adults with Incapacity (Supervision of Welfare Guardians etc by Local Authorities) (Scotland) Regulations 2002 (SSI 2002/95).
[4] The Adults with Incapacity (Reports in Relation to Guardianship and Intervention Orders) (Scotland) Regulations 2002 (SSI 2002/96).
[5] The Adults with Incapacity (Recall of Welfare Guardians' Powers) (Scotland) Regulations 2002 (SSI 2002/97).
[6] The Adults with Incapacity (Non-compliance with Decisions of Welfare Guardians) (Scotland) Regulations 2002 (SSI 2002/98).
[7] The Adults with Incapacity (Specified Medical Treatments) (Scotland) Regulations 2002 (SSI 2002/275) as amended by the Adults with Incapacity (Specified Medical Treatments) (Scotland) Amendment Regulations 2002 (SSI 2002/302).

7), and the Part 5 Code (particularly where it refers to "proxies"). The new régime came into force on April 1, 2002,[8] when it superseded (in ascending order of antiquity) MHSA guardians, curators bonis to adults, tutors-at-law and tutors-dative.[9] Experience of all four superseded techniques influenced the creation of the new régime. Remarkably, over the 16 years preceding commencement of the new régime the most ancient of all—tutors-dative—had the most fundamental influence. The influence of each is summarised in the following paragraphs. The historical and comparative themes touched on are among the most fascinating which the law has to offer; and in their potential to bring real benefit to some vulnerable and disadvantaged sections of society, the most rewarding.[10] In recent decades their disparate lessons have been drawn together to drive the transition described in Chapter 3 from "old law" to "new law". For ease of reference, those terms are used below with the meanings defined in paras 3–1 and 3–2. The following discussion seeks in particular to pick out the strands in those themes which can be carried forward as aids to achieving good practice under the new régime of guardianship and intervention orders. Precedents cited and styles quoted may also assist in individual cases under the new régime, if used with care. As well as replacing the four superseded techniques, the new régime is likely on occasions to provide solutions preferable to use of responsive techniques which remain available.[11]

THE SUPERSEDED TECHNIQUES—RELEVANT PRINCIPLES AND PRECEDENTS

Statutory (MHSA) guardians

10–2   Statutory guardians had plenary personal powers from 1913 to 1984, and thereafter limited but still fixed personal powers. They never had financial, property or management powers. Statutory guardianship was proposed by the Royal Commission on the Care and Control of the Feeble-Minded in 1908[12] and introduced by the Mental Deficiency and Lunacy (Scotland) Act 1913. The Lunacy (Scotland) Acts 1857 and 1862 had initiated a strong trend towards institutionalisation, so that within half a century the Royal Commission found "lunatic asylums crowded with patients who do not require the careful hospital management that well-equipped asylums now afford, and who might be treated in many other ways more economically and as efficiently". But they also found many people whom we would now describe as

---

[8] The Adults with Incapacity (Scotland) Act 2000 (Commencement No.1) Order 2001 (SSI 2001/81).
[9] See s.80 regarding curators bonis and tutors to adults, Sch.6 (repealing MHSA, ss.36–52) regarding MHSA guardians, and Sch.4 for transitional provisions (see also paras 10–2 et seq. and 11–92 et seq. infra).
[10] On his own explorations of those themes, the present author has written elsewhere. They form the principal subject-matter of *The Power to Act* (1990). See also "Revival of Tutors-Dative", 1987 S.L.T. (News) 69; "Tutors to Adults: Developments", 1992 S.L.T. (News) 325; Ashton & Ward, *Mental Handicap and the Law* (1992) especially pp.136–141 and 589–604; and *A New View* (1993), especially sections 3.9, 4.2 and postscript (p.198 in English-language edition).
[11] See summary of techniques in para.3–9 *supra*, and discussion of responsive measures outwith the Act in Ch.12.
[12] The Commission was appointed in 1904 and published its Report in 1908, Cd.4202.

having learning disabilities inappropriately imprisoned, and many more "at large in the population" who were considered to be "exposed to constant moral danger themselves, and become the source of lasting injury to the community". The 1913 Act implemented the Commission's suggested remedy, a dual régime under which patients were "placed" either in institutions or in guardianship. From 1913 to 1984 the guardian had the personal welfare and personal decision-making powers which he would have had "if he were the father of the patient and the patient were a pupil child".[13]

Use of guardianship dwindled, the numbers in guardianship falling from 2,440 in 1960 to around 300 by 1982, but it was suggested that "guardianship may continue to have value as a means of ensuring that some mentally disordered people living in the community receive the protection and support they require, provided the system is adapted to current circumstances"; and it was proposed that "guardianship powers should be limited to those which are considered essential, rather than, as at present, all the powers of the father of a child under 14; the aim being to achieve a reduction of detention and restriction and an emphasis on the protective function of guardianship".[14] It was proposed that guardians should have three specific "essential powers" and that the sheriff should be able to confer additional powers where necessary.[15] That flexibility, if adopted, would have represented a significant advance from the fixed provision of "old law" to the individualised provision of "new law",[16] a trend already well-established internationally and generally accepted—except by the UK parliament, which legislated for the fixed "essential powers" only, namely to decide place of residence; to require "the patient" to attend for medical treatment, occupation, education or training; and to require that doctors and others should have access to "the patient".[17] Guardianship may have advanced from "detention and restriction" to a "protective function", but was "based on the concept of official intervention to remedy unsatisfactory situations and is not true personal guardianship".[18] Moreover, although powers had been narrowed to a specifically interventionist function, they lacked the back-up powers to make them effective. They were designed only to be used when "the patient" was non-compliant, yet (for example) the power to determine residence could not be enforced, except for retrieving "the patient" after he had absconded; and although the guardian could require "the patient" to attend hospital or be seen by a doctor, the guardian could not consent to examination or treatment on behalf of "the patient".[19] Surprisingly for legislation as recent as the 1980's, the concept of impersonal, corporate guardianship by the local authority, without any named

10–3

---

[13] Mental Health (Scotland) Act 1960, s.29(4). Different wording with the same effect appeared in the Mental Deficiency and Lunacy (Scotland) Act 1913, s.11(2).
[14] Scottish Home and Health Department and Scottish Education Department, Social Work Services Group *Review of the Mental Health (Scotland) Act 1960*, April 1982, p.6.
[15] *ibid.*
[16] See paras 3–1 and 3–2 *supra*.
[17] Introduced by the Mental Health (Scotland) (Amendment) Act 1983 and consolidated in MHSA 1984, s.41(2).
[18] SLC Discussion Paper, para.2.22(c).
[19] Only a tutor-dative with appropriate powers could do so, if "the patient" lacked relevant capacity.

person designated to carry out the function, was retained and continued to be used.

10–4 MHSA guardianship nevertheless contained positive features which have been carried forward into the new régime. Ever since the introduction of statutory guardianship in 1913, the sheriff court has had jurisdiction. Unlike tutory, where only the Court of Session had jurisdiction, this provided locally available jurisdiction throughout Scotland, adopted under the Incapacity Act for all guardianship and intervention orders. MHSA procedures for guardianship, and also for detention, will probably have been the greatest source of practical experience relevant to the new régime for sheriffs and those who appear before them. Since its establishment in terms of the Mental Health (Scotland) Act 1960, the Mental Welfare Commission had an important supervisory role in relation to statutory guardianship which had no equivalent as regards tutory, but which for welfare guardianship under the Incapacity Act is reflected in the roles of local authorities and (except where incapacity results solely from physical inability to communicate) the Commission. The 1983/1984 reforms introduced for MHSA guardianship the role of the mental health officer and, for procedural purposes, the requirement for two medical certificates and a report from the mental health officer, so that applications proceeded not only upon diagnosis but also upon a professional social work assessment of whether guardianship was necessary in the interests of the welfare of "the patient".[20] That role has been carried forward to a wider remit under the new régime of the Incapacity Act.[21] Under the new régime, if an adult should require precisely the guardianship powers of MHSA guardians under the 1984 Act and nothing more, then of course those powers can still be conferred. It will be interesting to see how often, if at all, that occurs.

Curators bonis

10–5 Curators bonis were managers of property and finances. They had no personal welfare powers.[22] During the twentieth century, curatory was almost the only general management technique used for adults with impaired capacity. In both law and practice, it provided valuable experience—drawn on selectively for the Incapacity Act management régime—of the important elements of security, accountability and supervision. Latterly, best practice in using curatory powers proactively and if appropriate innovatively in the interests of wards, as described in para.10–7 below, provided experience and examples of potential benefit to good practice under the new régime. The severest criticisms of curatory were in the main truly criticisms firstly of entrenched bad practice, and secondly of the lack of suitable alternatives for adults with limited management needs, modest or little

---

[20] MHSA 1984, s.37(3), see also s.36(b); though in this form, even this aspect was criticised by SLC as giving the mental health officer an "effective veto" (SLC Report, para.6.3).

[21] See paras 10–48 *et seq. infra*.

[22] In one old case, *Christie's Curator* (1869) 7 M. 1130, a curator was authorised to have his ward transferred to an asylum, but the better modern practice, if personal powers were required, was to appoint a tutor-dative with personal powers only to hold office in parallel with the curator bonis: see *Dick v Douglas*, 1924 S.C. 287; 1924 S.L.T. 578. In *Usher's Curator, Petr*, 1989 (unreported) a curator was himself appointed tutor-dative to consent to a major operation.

wealth, or partial capacity. The worst problems and injustices arose because curatory was ill-suited to such situations but was used for want of alternatives, often rigidly and insensitively.

Curatory was a typical "old law" procedure. Curators had fixed and plenary financial, property and management powers. Their appointment deprived the adult of legal capacity in all such matters. Appointment was neither time-limited nor reviewed. Despite severe judicial criticism, appointment proceeded upon brief, standardised medical certificates.[23] Service of the petition was frequently, indeed sometimes almost routinely, dispensed with. In relation to smaller estates, curatory was expensive, sometimes to the extent of exhausting them: the system designed to protect assets became the major predator upon them. There was no obligation to observe the principles now contained in s.1(4) of the Incapacity Act.[24] Many curators disregarded them, and some never met the adults whose affairs they managed, even when those adults were well able to express relevant wishes and feelings. Indeed, curatory—in its statutory provisions and application in practice—frequently contravened all of the fundamental principles of good practice now contained in s.1 of the Incapacity Act.[25]

Historical development

Curators bonis were a judicial introduction: the Court of Session started appointing them around the beginning of the eighteenth century, for two reasons. Firstly, cognition procedure to appoint tutors-at-law was slow, cumbersome and expensive. Curators bonis could be appointed relatively quickly, and acted as managers pending appointment of a tutor-at-law. Secondly, tutors-at-law could only be appointed to people who came within the extreme definitions of "furious" or "fatuous",[26] whereas curators bonis could be appointed to people incapable of managing their own affairs, yet not with such severe illness or profound learning disability as to be classified as "furious" or "fatuous". After such appointments had become prevalent, they were first regulated by an Act of Sederunt of 1730. The only substantial updating was by the Judicial Factors Act 1849. Subsequent amendments to the régimes were relatively minor, the most significant being the extension of jurisdiction to the sheriff court, initially by the Judicial Factors (Scotland) Act 1880. The tone of the curatory régime, from 1849 until its demise in 2001, was set by the narrative in the 1849 Act itself that: "It has been found that the existing regulations and the present means of enforcing them are imperfect and insufficient for preventing in many instances the occurrence of great irregularity in the conduct of curators bonis and others, and in consequence thereof great loss has resulted to the funds and estates under their charge and to the parties interested therein." The narrative concluded that it was "expedient to make provision for the more

---

[23] "It would not be profitable to speculate upon the circumstances in which the two learned psychiatrists came to express their brief opinion": *Fraser v Paterson*, 1987 S.L.T. 562 *per* Lord Jauncey.
[24] See paras 4–16 *et seq. supra*.
[25] For discussion of the deficiencies of curatory, and examples of the serious injustices in consequence inflicted, see *The Power to Act*, Ch.X.
[26] Until the Court of Session Act 1868 extended appointment to anyone incapable of managing his affairs because of unsoundness of mind.

regular accounting and official management of persons who shall hereafter be served as curator to any insane person or idiot". The positive consequence of this approach was the régime of security, accountability and supervision, referred to in para.10–5 above, which stood the test of time, and which latterly was beneficially combined with encouragement from the Accountant of Court to curators to be proactive and inventive in cases where such was in the best interests of the ward,[27] and willingness of the courts to extend the scope of special powers granted where shown to be appropriate.[28] However, the approach of the 1849 Act also had a crushingly negative impact on the ethos of curatory, to the disadvantage of many people with impaired capacity and the dismay of their families. Notwithstanding the increasing readiness latterly of the Accountant of Court to discuss and where appropriate encourage more positive use of powers, and of the courts to be innovative in conferring special powers, in the case of many curatories that negative ethos persisted until abolition. It contributed to the "preservation" issue discussed in the following paragraphs, and in 1990 it moved this author to write: "So the problem [addressed by the 1849 Act] was that irregularities on the part of curators were resulting in losses to funds and estates, and the solution was the provision of more regular accounting and official administration. Thus was established the present-day régime— expensive to administer, cumbersome and rigid, insensitive and remote, heedless of the rights and status of the mentally disabled person, dominated by the requirements of 'regular accounting and official administration' ".[29]

The "preservation" issue

10–8 The discussion and argument which follows,[30] on the "preservation" issue mentioned above, retains more than historical significance notwithstanding the demise of curatory. It addresses the perpetual question of what principles should inform the approach of anyone charged with making decisions for those unable to make their own, the theme of the concluding chapter of this book. It serves as a warning of the potential of a misplaced ethos, of lack of rigour in confronting incongruities, and perhaps of the inertia of administrative convenience, to take a system ever further away from the needs which it ought to serve. The new régime will not achieve its purpose unless all those operating it, as a priority above all others, engage and remain engaged with the human reality of those whom it is intended to serve. And, over course of time, it will not continue to achieve its purpose if, like curatory, it becomes ossified in what may once have been perceived as good practice while society, decade by decade, moves on.

10–9 The problem was the persistence of many curators, and their advisers, in regarding preservation of the ward's estate as an overriding objective. The result was that the identified needs of many people

---

[27] Examples of resulting good practice, provided by the Accountant of Court, were with his permission quoted on pp.598–599 of *Mental Handicap and the Law*.

[28] In *B's Curator Bonis* (Sh. Ct), 1995 S.C.L.R. 671 special powers to agree to variation of a will were conferred, and in *D's Curator Bonis, Noter*, 1997 G.W.D. 13–538 and 1998 S.L.T. 2 powers to make gifts for Inheritance Tax planning purposes were conferred. See discussion of these cases in para.6–31 *supra*.

[29] *The Power to Act*, p.92.

[30] Addressed previously, and more fully, in *Mental Handicap and the Law*, pp.597–599.

with impairments of capacity were met inadequately, or only after much difficulty, or sometimes not at all. The inappropriateness of giving priority to preservation was emphasised by the example of estates consisting primarily of awards of compensation for costs and losses arising from permanent incapacity. Such awards are calculated on the basis that they will be used up during the period of loss or incapacity, not on the basis that income alone will provide adequate compensation, leaving the capital intact to be inherited by the beneficiaries in the ward's estate. To chart the route by which curatory practice navigated itself into this position, and much of it remained stranded there when the tide of human progress moved on, it is necessary to view the relevant history, firstly of judicial factors generally, and then of curatory in particular. Originally, judicial factors were appointed to preserve estates in an emergency, and in such cases "usual powers" were limited to those necessary to conserve the estate.[31] However, for each type of judicial factory the usual powers were those essential to carry out the purposes of the appointment, and use of judicial factory diversified to include situations where conservation was not the prime purpose, and even situations where the purpose was to distribute rather than to conserve the estate.[32] However, both in texts and in practice, over-emphasis of the aspect of preservation persisted, due to this historical background and to application to judicial factories generally of dicta appropriate to those where preservation was the principal purpose. A notable example of such dicta was the description of a factor as "a conservator merely" by Lord Justice-Clerk Inglis in *Neilson and others*.[33] Curatory was developed in the black-and-white era of "old law", described in para.3–1 above, when wards were labelled as "incapax" or "insane" and consigned to a category almost of non-persons, with no perceived needs other than costs of basic maintenance in an asylum. It was assumed that incapacity would be either total but temporary, in which case the ward would one day recover complete capacity, or total and permanent, in which case the only interests to consider were the interests of those who would inherit when the ward died. Such perceptions were consistent with an assumption that preservation, as a prime purpose, was in the ward's best interests. In society, such perceptions disappeared long ago and the reality is that there is often conflict between preservation and serving the ward's best interests. As the link between preservation and best interests dissolved, ancient cases and texts founded upon that link should have been seen as less and less relevant to modern society; but much curatory practice, blind or inert, remained ponderously beached where it had arrived long ago, leaving unresolved the incompatibility between the proposition that in such circumstances of conflict the ward's best interests should prevail, and assertions that the primary duty of a curator was to conserve the estate even when this might appear to be against the

---

[31] N.M.L. Walker, *Judicial Factors*, p.75.
[32] Such as a judicial factor to wind up a partnership (*Cooper & Sons' Judicial Factor*, 1931 S.L.T. 26) or administer a trust estate at point of distribution (*Wharrie's Judicial Factor*, 1916, 1 S.L.T. 345).
[33] (1865) 3 M. 559 at 560. See comment by Walker, *op.cit.*, p.76.

ward's best interests.[34] Even the concept of "best interests" is of limited relevance in adult incapacity law, and there are potential dangers if it is employed unthinkingly: see the comments on "best interests" in para.4–18 above and, in particular, the discussion in Chapter 15 below. In the context of the discussion in this paragraph, it was the view of this author[35] that the guiding principles should have been the duty of the curator to act in the best interests of the ward,[36] and the principle that the curator should act as the ward would have done if capable,[37] and that the potential conflict between those principles should have been resolved by addressing the question: "What would the ward, if not suffering from this particular impairment of capacity, consider to be in his or her best interests?" Those two principles of best interests and substituted judgement, the resolution of tension between them, and their relevance in the broader context of modern adult incapacity law, are further considered in Chapter 15.

The curatory régime

10–10   A curator required to be an individual.[38] An appointee under an intervention order must be one individual.[39] Guardians must be individuals or office holders,[40] joint and substitute appointments being competent.[41] Curators were required to find caution, a requirement continued for appointees with property or financial powers under intervention and guardianship orders, subject to a discretion to the sheriff to dispense with caution where the appointee satisfies the sheriff as to suitability but cannot find caution.[42] Curators were under the supervision of the Accountant of Court; under the Incapacity Act, the Accountant of Court became the Public Guardian and supervises appointees under intervention and guardianship orders with property and financial powers.[43] Curators were required to ingather the ward's estate, prepare an inventory, and lodge it with the Accountant of Court within six months of receipt by the Accountant of the bond of caution: a guardian with property and financial powers must lodge with the Public Guardian, within three months of registration of his appointment (or longer at the discretion of the Public Guardian), an inventory of the estate within the scope of the guardian's authority.[44] Curators' powers of investment were governed by the Trustee Investments Act 1961, and curators were subject to a régime of usual

---

[34] See *Stair Memorial Encyclopaedia*, Vol.24, para.247, where in relation to judicial factors generally those two principles are stated in the same paragraph, without comment upon the potential tension between them, though best interests is identified as the overriding principle.

[35] And of his senior author, G.R. Ashton, in *Mental Handicap and the Law*—see pp.6 and 598.

[36] *Encyclopaedia*, passage cited.

[37] See *Gordon's Curator Bonis* (1902) 4 F. 577 and comment thereon in Walker, *op.cit.*, p.110.

[38] *McFarlane v Donaldson* (1835) 13 S. 725; *Brogan, Petr*, 1986 S.L.T. 420.

[39] Incapacity Act, s.53(5)(b).

[40] ss.57(1) and 59.

[41] ss.62 and 63.

[42] ss.53(7) and 58(6).

[43] s.6(1) and (2).

[44] Sch.2, para.3.

powers, powers obtainable from the Accountant of Court, and special powers which might be conferred by the court, whereas the Incapacity Act replaces all of this with a new régime in which the "new law" concept of the individualised management plan is central.[45] Accounting requirements for financial guardians show the influence of curatory, but are much more flexible.[46] Recall and termination provisions under the Incapacity Act exhibit some parallels with curatory, but the time-limiting of appointments and the requirement to limit both powers conferred and their exercise to the minimum necessary, and to encourage use and development of skills, are all very necessary innovations. Discharge procedure under curatory was latterly simplified[47] with parallels under the Incapacity Act.[48] From 1880 both the Court of Session and the sheriff had curatory jurisdiction: the sheriff has sole jurisdiction to grant guardianship and intervention orders

Tutors-at-law

Tutors-at-law had fixed, plenary powers of personal guardianship **10–11** and fixed, plenary powers to manage property and finances. Penultimate in the ascending order of antiquity in which we here consider techniques current until they were superseded on April 1, 2002, tutors-at-law entered Scots law as part of the assimilation of principles from Roman law from about the fourteenth century onwards. The Curators Act 1585[49] confirmed the introduction, declaring that "the nearest agnates and kinsmen of natural fools, idiots and furious persons" should be appointed "to their tutory and curatory". From then until abolition on April 1, 2002, appointment was available only to the nearest male agnate[50] and a tutor-at-law, if appointed, superseded both tutors-dative[51] and a curator bonis.[52] Procedure could be initiated by any relative[53] and, until it was reformed in 1868, was by the process of cognition, described as "very absurd, very cumbrous, and very expensive",[54] requiring proof before a jury of the extreme conditions of furiosity or fatuity.[55] The Court of Session Act 1868, s.101 simplified the procedure[56] and widened the definition to cover a person "furious

---

[45] See paras 11–44 *et seq. infra*.

[46] See especially Sch.2, paras 4 and 5.

[47] Act of Sederunt (Rules of the Court of Session Amendment No. 8) (Discharge of Judicial Factors) 1991 and Act of Sederunt (Judicial Factors Rules) 1992.

[48] s.72.

[49] Referred to in older texts as the Act 1585 (c.18), and in the Record Edition of the Acts of the Parliament of Scotland as the Curators Act 1585 (c.25) (A.P.S. 111, 396, c.25), under which latter designation it was repealed by Sch.6 of the Incapacity Act.

[50] Except that a husband had prior claim to be appointed tutor-at-law to his wife, *Halliburton v Maxwell*, (1791) M. 16379.

[51] Stair's *Institutions* I, 6, 25.

[52] *Britton v Britton's Curator Bonis*, 1992 S.C.L.R. 947.

[53] *Bryce v Grahame* (1828) 6 S. 425; (1828) 3 W & S 323, which so defined, for this purpose, "any party having an interest".

[54] Fraser, *Parent and Child, and Guardian and Ward* (3rd ed.), p.654.

[55] According to Fraser *op.cit.* pp.659–660, in the case of *Lockhart* (there referred to by the reference SEP.REP.P236) "fatuous" referred to "a person without mind at all". Erskine (I, 7, 48) described fatuous persons as being "entirely deprived of the faculty of reason" and furious persons (in a passage which anticipates the modern distinction between a mental illness and any effect which it might have on capacity, described in paras 1–3 and 1–4 *supra*) as persons suffering from conditions which "obstruct the application of their reason to the ordinary purposes of life".

[56] See also Act of Sederunt, December 3, 1868.

or fatuous, or labouring under such unsoundness of mind as to render him incapable of managing his affairs". Doubt was created by the repeal of the 1868 Act by the Court of Session Act 1988 (on the assumption, apparently, that the 1868 Act was obsolete), resolved by the revival of tutor-at-law procedure, after a gap of over a century, in 1992.[57] By then tutors-at-law, although they were not judicial factors, had been brought under the same régime of supervision by the Accountant of Court as curators bonis and other judicial factors, by the Age of Legal Capacity (Scotland) Act 1991.[58]

10–12 That such an archetypally "old law" technique should be revived and used in the last decade of the twentieth century, as the best available measure for some—albeit few—adults with impaired capacity, emphasises how overdue was reform. Those few cases do however provide pointers for the new régime. They involved substantial estates, previously under curatory, belonging to relatively young adults whose significant abilities did not extend as far as assuming full management responsibility for their estates or full responsibility for deciding all personal matters, but who did have significant potential to benefit and develop under integration of personal guardianship and management powers in a responsible relative who was in a position to exercise those powers in the context of close day-to-day contact and general help and supervision.[59] What those appointments represented in practice was use of plenary "old law" powers in a carefully selective "new law" manner, and in accordance with the principles of good practice now embodied in s.1 of the Incapacity Act. Those principles now apply both when making the appointment and thereafter to discharge of their functions by appointees. Experience of the few modern tutors-at-law demonstrates that of the two, the conscientious application of the principles by appointees is ultimately the more important. Also, while the present author would not suggest (at least without further experience of the new régime) that there could be a presumption in favour of combining welfare and management powers, where both are needed, in a single appointment, the very limited modern experience of tutors-at-law exemplifies the benefits achieved when, and only when, such a combined appointment was in place. It also demonstrates the importance of the statutory criterion for appointment of accessibility of the appointee to the adult[60]: in some cases, to achieve the full potential of the appointment to benefit the adult, "accessibility" may mean residing with the adult or at least having virtually daily contact.

---

[57] *Britton v Britton's Curator Bonis*, *supra*. The last previous reported case was *Simpson v Simpson* (1891) 18 R. 1207.

[58] Sch.2. That such a reform of adult incapacity law should appear in the 1991 Act indicates that it may have been achieved inadvertently (particularly as the 1991 Act followed so soon after the 1988 Act), but nevertheless timeously.

[59] One of them, some years before her father was appointed her tutor-at-law, made the comment with which this author concluded *The Power to Act*: "I think it hurts inside you, not to be independent". About a decade after that appointment, the author was her visitor in her own independent home. After much thought and preparation for greater independence over several years, the house had recently been purchased, upgraded, and adapted to accommodate her physical disabilities. (Note added with the kind permission of her tutor, now guardian).

[60] Incapacity Act, s.59(4)(a).

Tutors-dative

Tutors-dative originally had plenary personal guardianship and management powers. Following revival in 1986, appointments took two forms. Firstly, most tutors-dative were appointed as personal guardians with limited powers shown in each individual case to be necessary, and for durations which generally did not exceed 10 years. Secondly, a smaller number were appointed for a single act of management, or to address a particular management matter over a relatively short period of time, for adults with no general or long-term management needs justifying appointment of a curator bonis. The first category were akin to welfare guardians under the Incapacity Act, and the second similar to appointees under intervention orders. Tutors-dative since 1986 were not appointed with plenary management powers: curators bonis, rather than tutors-dative, were held to be the appropriate appointment for that purpose.[61] The sovereign's jurisdiction to appoint tutors-dative was exercised by the Court of Exchequer from its establishment in 1708 until its abolition in 1856,[62] and thereafter by the Court of Session until further petitions for such appointment became incompetent on April 1, 2002. The convenience and lesser expense of the sheriff court was never available for appointment of tutors, which may have been a disadvantage for individual petitioners. Nevertheless, during the period of revival 1986–2002, which paved the way for the new régime, this area of law benefited from being developed with the coherence and authority which resulted from all petitions being heard by the Court of Session, rather than being scattered across Scotland's sheriffdoms. The *Morris* petition in 1986[63] was heard by the Inner House: all subsequent petitions were heard by Lords Ordinary in the Outer House, and this author is aware of no appeals.[64] Under the Incapacity Act the Court of Session has jurisdiction as described in para.5–22 above, including jurisdiction at first instance under the Specified Treatments Regulations, relevant to appointees under intervention and guardianship orders by virtue of s.64(2)(b).[65] Appeals under s.50 are also relevant to such appointees, and lie direct to the Court of Session.

10–13

Historical development

In earliest Scots law, the sovereign was guardian of adults with serious mental illness, and the feudal lord was guardian of those with serious learning disabilities. Later the sovereign became guardian of

10–14

---

[61] *Chapman Petitioners*, 1993 S.L.T. 955.

[62] See the Court of Exchequer (Scotland) Act 1856 (19 and 20 Vict. c.56), ss.1 and 2, see also the Court of Session (Scotland) Act 1857 (20 and 21 Vict. c.57).

[63] See para.10–18 *infra*.

[64] Doubts about the continued competence of procedure for appointment of tutors-dative were removed by the Inner House in *Law Hospital NHS Trust v Lord Advocate*, 1996 S.L.T. 848; 1996 S.C.L.R. 491 and 1996 S.C. 301. It was confirmed in that case that tutors-dative were appointed under the *parens patriae* jurisdiction—see para.14–25 *infra*. Rules of Court 14.2(i) and 14.7(3), added with effect from August 5, 1996, respectively confirmed that procedure should be by Outer House petition and provided that such petitions should not be intimated on the Walls of Court. Practice Note No.11 of 1994 had already required such petitions to be served on the Mental Welfare Commission. Lord Cullen reported in *Law Hospital* (S.L.T. at p.865, S.C.L.R. at p.516) that he had ascertained that there were 27 appointments of a tutor-dative during the three years 1993–1995.

[65] But see para.14–20 *infra*.

both categories. The sovereign delegated guardianship powers to tutors-dative,[66] a team of selected relatives who were both personal guardians and managers. The Parliament of Scotland attempted to abolish tutors-dative by the Curators Act 1585,[67] which sought to replace them, as guardians to adults with impaired capacity, by tutors-at-law, but failed. The Scottish Parliament repeated the attempt in 2001, and has certainly succeeded, because s.80 of the Incapacity Act is explicit and the Scottish Ministers brought it into force on April 1, 2002 (though of course existing appointments survive as guardianships by virtue of the transitional provisions). In relation to the long period from the first blow in 1585 to the coup de grâce in 2002, three questions remain relevant and point to characteristics and issues which are important to the new régime. Firstly, why did tutors-dative survive the attempt to replace them with tutors-at-law in 1585? Secondly, what was the effect upon them of the introduction of statutory guardianship in 1913? Thirdly, why, following the reform of statutory guardianship in 1984, did they celebrate the fourth centenary of their intended demise with a rejuvenated revival and period of inventive development which, far more than any other developments in our law, paved the way for the new régime of the Incapacity Act?

10–15 A recurring theme in adult guardianship law has been the question of the relative weight to be given to claims of kinship, on the one hand, and to assessment of suitability, on the other, when determining who should be personal guardian. Both in Roman law and originally in Scots law, kinship was given greater weight in relation to children, and suitability in relation to adults. Tutors-at-law were not only an introduction from Roman law, but an introduction from Roman child law.[68] Thus, the nearest male agnate was preferred as guardian to adults with incapacity, an appointment based on kinship, rather than the team of tutors-dative selected on the basis of suitability. This attempted reform was an early example of another recurring theme, the inappropriate infantilisation of adults with impaired capacity (with its counterpart in the form of equally inappropriate paternalism). Appointments of tutors-dative continued, notwithstanding the 1585 Act, for various reasons, including: that the nearest agnate was found to be unsuitable to act, or could not find caution, or declined to act, or considered himself unsuitable[69]; or as a temporary measure because of the time which it took to have a tutor-at-law appointed. After curators bonis became established as managers, if it was desired that a curatory should continue, the automatic termination of curatory by service of a tutor-at-law was avoided by appointing instead a tutor-dative with personal guardianship powers only.[70] The flexibility of tutors-dative, derived from their ancient origins as true guardians of adults with incapacity (as opposed to imports from child law), ensured their survival.

10–16 Statutory guardians entered Scots law in 1913, as described in para.10–2 above, as further imports from child law without reference to either form of adult tutory. The powers of statutory guardians were

---

[66] Originally termed "curators-dative". The shifts in terminology, and their significance, are followed in *The Power to Act*, Ch.4.
[67] See para.10–11 *supra*, and n.49 thereto.
[68] As the present author demonstrated in *The Power to Act*, Ch.4.
[69] *e.g. Graham* (1881) 8 R. 996.
[70] *Dick v Douglas*, 1924 S.C. 287; 1924 S.L.T. 578.

originally defined by reference to child law.[71] The pre-1913 law of personal guardianship of adults was not even recognised to the extent of clarifying which took precedence, until the Mental Health (Scotland) Act 1960 for the first time conferred powers on statutory guardians "to the exclusion of any other person".[72] Statutory guardians with the plenary powers which they held from 1913 to 1984 soon displaced tutors-dative as personal guardians (the last reported pre-1986 appointment apparently being in 1924[73]), and curators bonis appear already to have displaced tutors-dative as managers. However, just as tutors-dative had survived the introduction of tutors-at-law *inter alia* because of their greater flexibility as to whom might be appointed, they ultimately survived the introduction of statutory guardians because of their potential for flexibility as to powers granted, another advantage over the statutory imports from child law. This arose, however, by a curious route. The narrowing of the powers of statutory guardians, as described in para.10–3 above, was a clumsily ineffective response by Westminster to a dimly-perceived recognition that the fixed plenary personal powers which statutory guardians held until then often did not match needs. Instead of following the (by then) well-established international trend towards the flexibility of true personal guardianship, the 1983/1984 reforms took the "wrong turning" towards limited but still fixed powers.

Comparative influences

In contrast to legislators and officialdom, many families of people **10–17** with impaired capacity—and their voluntary organisations—were well aware of trends towards respecting and enhancing the rights, interests and quality of life of people with impaired capacity, and in moving from concepts of guardianship as "detention and restriction" to avoid supposed "injury to the community" or as interventionist "protection", towards guardianship as a right, as recognised by Article 5 of the UN Declaration, with which this chapter commences.[74] In 1969 a report by what is now Inclusion International had commented that: "... serious difficulty arises because the law usually represents incompetence in simple black and white terms, with the result that most guardianships of the person are looked on as plenary guardianships". It commented on the inadequate recognition in "most existing statutes pertaining to guardianship" of "the idea that the person himself can properly retain and exercise some personal and even property rights, selectively, according to his individual capacity". It urged that an adult should be permitted to act for himself in matters where he has competence, that "the limitations of legal capacity inherent in guardianship should not extend to these matters", and that an adult whose impairment of capacity is partial "should enjoy a

---

[71] See para.10–2 *supra*.
[72] Mental Health (Scotland) Act 1960, s.29(4).
[73] *Dick v Douglas, supra*.
[74] The full text of the Declaration is reproduced in SLC Discussion Paper, pp.4–5; *Mental Handicap and the Law*, p. xv, and *A New View*, Appendix 1 (p.183 of the English-language edition) where it is followed by the equivalent, and slightly longer, Declaration on General and Special Rights of the Mentally Retarded by the International League of Societies for Persons with Mental Handicap (now Inclusion International).

partial guardianship specifically adapted to his strengths and weaknesses".[75] Position papers issued by the American Association on Mental Deficiency in 1973–1975 included a valuable statement of general principles. These pointed to the restriction of personal liberty inherent in guardianship and stressed that every effort should be made to avoid the need for guardianship "through the use of social counselling services". A guardian should not be appointed unless the adult "is found to be significantly lacking the social competence necessary to make critical decisions respecting the conduct of his or her life", unless the appointment will be in the best interests of the adult ("and the community"), and unless required procedures have been followed. Adults should be permitted to participate in all decisions affecting them to the maximum extent of their capabilities. Those "who cannot assert their own rights should have individual guardians appointed, regardless of the setting in which they are living". The scope of each guardianship should be specified, "taking full cognisance of the social competencies and limitations of the individual", permitting the adult to act in all matters in which he has competence. "Particular care" should be taken to avoid treating adults under guardianship like children. Judgements as to competence should be based on careful evaluation by a multi-disciplinary team, and never on the judgement of a single professional.[76] A strong international consensus developed as to the guiding principles and principal characteristics for an appropriate "new law" régime of personal and financial guardianship for adults with impaired capacity. In 1976 such a "new law" form of guardianship appeared fully-fledged in the Dependent Adults Acts of Alberta.[77] The trend towards "new law" guardianship legislation accelerated during the 1980's. In 1985 the (English) Law Society's Group for the Welfare of People with a Mental Handicap produced a suggested modern guardianship code in the form of a draft Dependent Adults Act, never taken up by the legislature. Among reforming statutes in many jurisdictions, examples included New Zealand's Protection of Personal and Property Rights Act 1988[78] and Germany's Betreuungsgesetz of 1990. The main characteristics of these codes introduced at approximately the same time in these two countries were remarkably similar, notwithstanding that they appeared in countries on opposite sides of the world, from differing legal traditions (the common law and civilian traditions respectively) and apparently without significant reference to each other.[79]

Revival

10–18   For Scotland, the international trend outlined briefly in the preceding paragraph has significance in two important respects which are

---

[75] International League of Societies for Persons with Mental Handicap, *Report on Guardianship* (1969).
[76] *Guardianship for Mentally Retarded Persons, Position Papers of the American Association on Mental Deficiency*, approved by AAMD Council, 1973–1975. The principles are reproduced in full in *The Power to Act*, pp.33–34.
[77] Dependent Adults Acts, Chapter D–32. See also para.3–3 *supra*.
[78] Described in Ch.12 of *The Power to Act*.
[79] So far as the present author is aware. He described the similarities in *A New View*, para.4.2.

relevant here. Firstly, the guiding principles of "new law" guardianship and the examples (including those quoted) of their application in legislation were specifically drawn upon to shape the revival of tutors-dative in Scots law. Secondly, in combination with experience of that revival they largely shaped the new régime of guardianship and intervention orders, and remain essential to the full understanding and proper application of that régime. In the mid-1980's, two related events in Scotland were, so far as the present author is aware, unique.[80] As momentum gathered for progress from "old law" to "new law" provision, the 1983/1984 reforms to statutory guardianship—described in para.10–3 above—took Scotland in the opposite direction at the very time of growing demand here for a "new law" framework to respect the rights and meet the needs of adults with impaired capacity. The consequence was the second of those unique events, the achievement of a form of personal guardianship with significant "new law" characteristics not by legislation, but by the ability of Scots law—based fundamentally upon principles, rather than upon the precedents which exemplify them—to apply old principles in a manner consistent with modern needs and perceptions. In 1986 tutors-dative re-appeared in *Morris, Petitioner*,[81] in which both parents of a young adult with a learning disability were appointed his tutors-dative with specified powers only, which were shown to be necessary in his particular case, and for a period of five years only. In 1991 they initially sought re-appointment with one of their other children as substitute, though all three were in fact appointed joint tutors for a further 10 years.[82] In some early cases[83] appointments were made without limit of time, upon medical certification that no significant change in the capacity of the adult was foreseen such as to warrant limiting the duration of the appointment. However, in a 1991 petition seeking appointment for an unlimited duration, supported by medical certificates in such terms, Lord Penrose took the view that the court ought to be in a position to monitor the appointment, and limited the appointment to a period of 10 years.[84] This author is not aware of any appointment for longer than 10 years since 1992.[85] Under the Incapacity Act, appointment of guardians for an indefinite period is competent both upon initial appointment and upon renewal: there is however a presumption in favour of three years on initial appointment and five years upon renewal, appointments and renewals for any other period being competent on cause shown.[86] Sheriffs who take account of the approach of the Court of Session since 1991 in tutor-dative cases may require particularly good cause to be shown

---

[80] Except that the first applied also to England: see Mental Health Act 1983, s.8(1).
[81] 1986, unreported—see Ward, "Revival of Tutors-Dative", 1987 S.L.T. (News) 69.
[82] *Morris No.2* (1991), unreported: see Ward, "Tutors to Adults: Developments", 1992 S.L.T. (News) 325. The next renewal thereafter was granted initially on an interim basis, and then (*Morris No.3* (2002), unreported) for five years only, in common with many appointments and renewals in the months preceding implementation of Part 6 of the Incapacity Act, having regard to Sch.4, para.6(3) of the Act.
[83] Such as *Buchanan* (1989), unreported.
[84] *Emslie* (1991), unreported.
[85] The last appointment of unlimited duration of which the author is aware was *Millar* (April 16, 1992). Nevertheless, curators bonis continued to be appointed routinely without limit of time, regardless of developments in tutory practice.
[86] ss.58(4) and 60(4)(b).

Appointees

10–19 As to appointees, the Court of Session held true to the features of tutors-dative as true guardians to adults, established long before the tutor-at-law arrived as the first interloper from child law. In contrast to restriction of tutors-at-law and statutory guardians to single appointments, joint appointments of two or three tutors-dative predominated, a significant concern of many petitioners having been to provide for continuity in the event of absence, incapacity or death of one or more appointees. The court also made decisions on the basis of suitability rather than kinship, appointing one or more tutors not related to the adult where appropriate, and in one case appointing a non-relative in preference to a parent.[87] Quoting relationships (if any) to the adult, the range of appointments included both parents[88]; both parents and one sibling[89]; both parents and one grandparent[90]; a widowed parent and unrelated family friend[91]; sole surviving parent plus sibling plus family friend[92]; divorced parent and one sibling[93]; separated parent and sibling[94]; mother plus aunt plus sibling (where father worked abroad and both parents were petitioners)[95]; sister and her husband; three quite distant relatives who were testamentary trustees appointed by the adult's late mother[96]; and unrelated carers (a husband, wife and their daughter, with whom the unrelated adult resided on a long-term basis, appointed without opposition from any relatives).[97] Persons resident in England[98] and America[99] have been appointed. Appointments of a sole tutor-dative have been relatively rare, examples being mother[1] and unrelated curator bonis,[2] except where the appointment has been for a purpose for which an intervention order would now be appropriate (see para.10–35 below), where in each case known to this author a solicitor has been appointed sole tutor. In *Mrs X Petitioner, Mr and Mrs Y Petitioners*,[3] an unrelated carer petitioned for her own appointment as sole tutor to an adult with Angelman's Syndrome who had recently attained 16. The adult's mother and stepfather defended and cross-petitioned. The case turned not so much upon suitability to act as tutor *per se*, but on whether the adult's principal residence should remain with the carer,

---

[87] See *Mrs X, Petitioner, Mr and Mrs Y, Petitioners*, *infra*.
[88] *Morris, Petitioner* (1986), unreported.
[89] Perhaps the most common format, following *Morris No.2* (1991), unreported.
[90] *V and V, Petitioners* (1997), unreported.
[91] *Buchanan* (1989), unreported.
[92] *Alexander* (1992), unreported.
[93] *Millar* (1992), unreported.
[94] *V* (1995), unreported.
[95] *I and I, Petitioners* (1992), unreported.
[96] *S and others, Petitioners* (2000), unreported.
[97] *B and others, Petitioners* (2000), unreported.
[98] *I and I, Petitioners* (1992), unreported.
[99] *Alexander, supra*.
[1] *G, Petitioner* (1992), unreported; *L v L's curator ad litem*, 1997 S.L.T. 167.
[2] *Usher* (1989) unreported.
[3] (2001) unreported.

or should change to the home of her mother and stepfather. Lord Philip's approach was that he must decide the matter on the basis of the adult's welfare and best interests. He found it proved that there was between mother and adult a "level of intimate communication which is unique to them". On the other hand, the adult had resided with the carer and her family since the age of 6, and Lord Philip was of the view that the adult's best interests would be served "by achieving a situation in which [the adult's] home life remains as stable as possible while the changes which must inevitably occur in [the adult's] care are carefully considered and planned, and the necessary preparatory work done". He appointed the carer for a period of five years. On the relevance of "best interests" under the Incapacity Act, see para.4–18 above and Chapter 15, especially paras 15–26 and 15–27, below.

The Incapacity Act permits appointment of a single guardian, or of two or more persons as joint guardians, and joint guardians may share the same powers or have different powers,[4] but unless the joint guardians are all parents, siblings or children of the adult, the sheriff requires to be satisfied that it is in the circumstances appropriate to appoint as joint guardians persons not so related to the adult.[5] The diversity of appointments found to be appropriate as tutors-dative indicates that sheriffs may not infrequently be satisfied of the appropriateness of joint appointments of guardians beyond the particular relationships quoted. The Incapacity Act also provides for substitute guardians, without favouring particular relationships for this purpose.[6] As mentioned above,[7] the possibility of a substitute appointment as tutor-dative was raised in *Morris No.2* but not decided, the proposed substitute in that application being instead appointed joint tutor. Thereafter, so far as this author is aware, there were no further applications for a substitute appointment, joint appointments being favoured instead. Under the Incapacity Act, a shift is now likely from joint appointments towards substitute appointments. Interim appointments of tutors-dative were made,[8] and interim appointments of guardians are competent.[9] The Incapacity Act provisions regarding joint, substitute and interim appointments apply equally to welfare and financial guardians, and are discussed further in paras 11–6 *et seq.* below. **10–20**

Welfare powers

Experience of powers granted to tutors-dative in the period 1986–2002 is likely to be of assistance in considering and framing welfare powers to be sought in applications under the Incapacity Act. The Incapacity Act does not follow the pattern of legislation such as the Dependent Adults Acts of Alberta, mentioned in para.10–17 above, which lists powers from which the court may select those needed in **10–21**

---

[4] ss.58(5) and 62(1).
[5] s.62(2).
[6] s.63.
[7] para.10–18 *supra*.
[8] *e.g. Moir* (2000), unreported; *Morris No.3* (*supra*), where the interim appointment was made in 2001. In each of these examples, the interim appointment bridged the gap following expiry of a previous appointment.
[9] s.57(5). "Bridging" interim appointments are rendered unnecessary by s.60(1).

particular cases, though the court may also impose conditions or restrictions, and may "restrict, modify, change or add to" anything on the list. This "Alberta list" was drawn on for the original *Morris* petition in 1986, and to a greater or lesser extent in almost all appointments since.[10] Substantially the same powers appear in paras 2.1–2.5, 2.7 and 3.1 of the Schedule to the *Style* power of attorney in Appendix 5 to this book. Many tutors-dative have also been given powers similar to those in paras 2.6 and 2.9. The only power in the Alberta list not reflected in those *Style* powers is in the following terms: "The right to decide whether the dependent adult should (or should be permitted to) work and, if so, the nature or type of work, for whom he is to work and matters related thereto". In the phrase "should (or should be permitted to)" the brackets have been added by this author. The same phrase appears in a number of the Alberta powers: in some Scottish appointments of tutors-dative it has been amended to read "should (or should not)". The following is drawn from a typical interlocutor[11] which conferred powers based on all of the foregoing: *"The Lord Ordinary on the Motion of the Petitioners, and having resumed consideration of the Petition and Productions, no Answers having been lodged, appoints X, Y and Z to be joint tutors dative to A with the following powers (1) to decide where said A is to live, whether permanently or temporarily, (2) to decide with whom said A is to live and with whom she is to consort, (3) to decide whether said A should or should be permitted to engage in social activities and if so, the nature and extent thereof and related matters, (4) to decide whether the said A should or should be permitted to work and if so, the nature and type of work, for whom she is to work and matters related thereto, (5) to decide whether said A should or should be permitted to participate in any educational, vocational or other training and if so the nature and extent thereof and matters related thereto, (6) to decide whether the said A should or should be permitted to apply for any licence, permit, approval or any other consent or authorisation required by law, (7) to commence, compromise or settle any legal proceedings that do not relate to the estate of said A and to compromise or settle any proceedings taken against said A that do not relate to her estate, (8) to exercise all rights and powers competent to said A in relation to access to files, records and information, (9) to consent to any health care that is in the best interests of said A, (10) to open and read any mail or other communications addressed to or received by or on behalf of the said A, (11) to make normal day to day decisions on her behalf, including as to her diet and dress and (12) generally to provide support and guidance to said A and that for a period of ten years from this date hereof; reserves to any person claiming an interest the right to apply thereanent and decerns."*

10–22 Three specialities which arose in tutor-dative petitions as to powers conferred are worthy of note. Firstly, in *S and others, Petitioners*,[12] the application was initially opposed by the relevant local authority, and a curator ad litem was appointed and entered the process. Parties reached agreement that while the adult could make valid choices himself if appropriate alternatives were presented to him, he lacked full capacity to "set the agenda" of such choices. With the agreement

---

[10] The "Alberta list" is reproduced on p.38 of *The Power to Act*.
[11] Pronounced by Lord Abernethy on November 28, 1997.
[12] (2000) unreported.

of all parties, Lord Clarke conferred on the tutors powers *inter alia* in the following terms: *"insofar as it is reasonable and appropriate to do so, to represent the said B in the investigation, consideration and negotiation of the choices to be put to him for his own decision in relation to (a) whether he should or should not engage in social activities and, if so, the nature and extent thereof and related matters; (b) whether he should or should not work and, if so, the nature and type of work, for whom he is to work and matters related thereto; (c) whether he should or should not be part or participate in any educational, vocational or other training and, if so, the nature and extent thereof and matters related thereto"*. Lord Clarke commented that he believed it had been entirely the right approach to draft the petition powers to reflect the statutory framework of the Adults with Incapacity (Scotland) Act 2000. He also commented that it was apparent that a great deal of care had gone into the drafting of the powers to ensure that they reflected the particular needs and circumstances of B as an individual and did not go further than was necessary.[13]

Secondly, in the case of *V*,[14] the adult (C) was resident in a hospital. **10–23** There were concerns about the appropriateness of visits to C from D, a close relative, and about D taking C for outings. The petition was suggested by hospital authorities, brought by the relatives who were ultimately appointed, and opposed by D. The powers conferred by Lord MacLean included: *"the right to decide with whom the said C is to live and with whom she is to consort and how frequently subject to the Petitioners at all times acting in accordance with the advice of the Medical Consultant for the time being in charge of C's case"*.

Thirdly, in a number of cases powers were sought to consent to **10–24** surgical sterilisation of women with impaired capacity. In at least two early cases,[15] such powers were granted on the basis of substantial written medical evidence, but without appointment of a curator ad litem and without any hearing or discussion. In *L v L's curator ad litem*,[16] Lord MacLean appointed a curator ad litem, who opposed the proposed powers to consent to surgical sterilisation of the adult. Both Counsel were agreed that the correct test to be applied was whether the surgical sterilisation proposed was necessary and in the best interests of the adult.[17] Lord MacLean considered the decisive factor in the case to be not the need to avoid conception, but the need to avoid menstruation because of the adult's great difficulty in coming to terms with menstrual bleeding, due to her condition causing her to be very ritualistic in her behaviour and very fastidious. She would find

---

[13] In common with many appointments after the passing of the Incapacity Act, Lord Clarke's interlocutor also reflected the Act's general principles. It commenced: *"after satisfying themselves whenever exercising these powers that each such exercise will benefit said B, and that such benefit cannot reasonably be achieved without such exercise of these powers, after ascertaining that such exercise of these powers is the least restrictive option in relation to the freedom of said B, and after taking account of the present and past wishes and feelings of said B so far as they could be ascertained, and after taking account of the views of [the local authority] and any other primary carer of said B insofar as it is reasonable and practicable to do so; . . ."*
[14] *V* (1995) unreported.
[15] *D, Petr* (1991) unreported, *G, Petr* (1992) unreported.
[16] 1997 S.L.T. 167.
[17] They derived that test principally from passages in the speeches in *Re F (mental patient: sterilisation)* [1990] 2 A.C. 1; [1989] 2 W.L.R. 1025; [1989] 2 All E.R. 545, and *Re B (a minor) (wardship: sterilisation)* [1988] A.C. 199; [1987] 2 W.L.R. 1213; [1987] 2 All E.R. 206.

menstrual bleeding very distressing. Her mother "would never get her out of the bathroom if she bled". She would be likely to refuse to go to her training centre. Having been referred to an English Practice Note on the Official Solicitor's role in such cases, Lord MacLean commented: "In this jurisdiction I do not think that it is wise or beneficial to set down precise rules for particular situations, simply because these situations will vary so much according to their own facts. [The adult's] is a very unusual case. It is one in which, in my opinion, there is a continuing need for contraception and at the same time a need to prevent menstruation. I am clearly of the opinion, balancing all the considerations, including the desirability of avoiding a major invasive surgical procedure if it can be, that the only way of fulfilling these twin needs which are in [the adult's] best interests, is by means of the operation proposed by Doctor Lees, namely, sub-total or partial hysterectomy".[18] See para.10–13 above and Chapter 14 on the continuing role of the Court of Session in medical matters under the Incapacity Act.

Management powers

10–25   In a small number of cases following revival in 1986, tutors-dative were appointed for a single act of management, or to address a particular management matter over a relatively short period of time.[19] For both purposes an intervention order would now be appropriate. An example of the first was *Queen*,[20] where a tutor-dative was appointed for the sole purpose of executing a deed of family arrangement in respect of the estate of the adult's late mother. An example of the second was *W, Petr*,[21] where Mrs E's Will had made no provision in favour of her daughter Miss F, whose capacity was impaired. A tutor was appointed to Miss F with the following powers: *"(i) power and authority to negotiate with [Mrs E's trustees and the other persons with an interest in her estate] in respect of arrangements for a Trust to administer a sum equal to the legal rights of the said [Miss F] and the terms of documents to effect said purpose and (ii) to make further application to this Court for authority to execute such documents on behalf of [Miss F] and to discharge her legal rights in the estate of [Mrs E]"*. Upon subsequent presentation of a Note by the tutor, the tutor was authorised *"(i) to accept on behalf of [Miss F] the establishment of a Trust in terms of the draft Deed of Trust No 18/2 of process, appended hereto, and payment into that Trust of an amount equal to [Miss F's] legal rights entitlement in the estate of her mother [Mrs E], with interest thereon in lieu of her said legal rights entitlement; (ii) to do any further acts and execute any further documents on behalf of [Miss F] which may be reasonable and appropriate for the foregoing purposes"*. Following completion of those arrangements, the tutor was discharged. In both of the foregoing examples, the outcome was the establishment of a suitable trust to manage the fund in question. On

---

[18] Although Lord MacLean described this as a very unusual case, unbeknown to him a sheriff was at about the same time considering an application to authorise exercise of parental rights to consent to surgical sterilisation in very similar circumstances.

[19] In *Chapman, Petr*, 1993 S.L.T. 955 the court refused to confer general management powers on tutors-dative, holding that curatory remained the appropriate appointment for that purpose. See para.10–13 *supra*.

[20] (1992) unreported.

[21] (1997 and 1998), unreported.

such trusts see Chapter 13 and para.10–35 below, and on use of intervention orders to establish such trusts also see para.10–35 below. In neither case was the tutor required to receive or intromit with any funds, therefore neither caution nor supervision by the Accountant of Court was required.

CRITERIA, SCOPE AND COMMON PROVISIONS

10–26 The new régime outlined in para.10–1 above is comprehensive and integrated, therefore intervention and guardianship orders are best considered together as regards the criteria for granting each and their respective scopes, and as regards aspects to which the same or substantially similar provisions apply. These matters are addressed in the following paras 10–27 to 10–71, where "order" refers generically to any intervention or guardianship order unless the context clearly indicates otherwise. Remaining matters particular to intervention orders are considered in paras 10–72 to 10–78, and those particular to guardianship in Chapter 11.

Criteria

10–27 Intervention and guardianship orders may be granted by the sheriff. No order may be granted unless the granting of the order and the terms in which it is granted accord with the first four general principles.[22] Subject to compliance with those principles, an intervention order may be granted where the sheriff is satisfied that the adult is incapable of taking the action to which the application relates, or is incapable in relation to the decision about the adult's property, financial affairs or welfare to which the application relates.[23] Subject to compliance with those same principles, a guardianship order may be granted where the sheriff is satisfied as to the following matters. Firstly, the adult must be incapable in relation to decisions about his property, financial affairs or personal welfare, or incapable of acting to safeguard or promote his interests in such matters. Secondly, the adult must be likely to continue to be so incapable. Thirdly, guardianship is presumed to be the most restrictive of the options available under the Act,[24] and the sheriff must be satisfied that no other means provided by or under the Act would be sufficient to enable the adult's interests in his property, financial affairs or personal welfare to be safeguarded or promoted.[25]

Interpretation

10–28 "*Incapable*" for the above purposes has the meaning defined in s.1(6) and discussed in paras 4–23 to 4–28 above. In relation to an intervention order, the sheriff must be satisfied as to incapacity in relation to

---

[22] s.1(1)–(4): see paras 4–2 to 4–22 *supra*.
[23] s.53(1). Although s.53(5) implies that only orders under s.53(5)(b), and not those under s.53(5)(a), need relate to the adult's property, financial affairs or personal welfare, and although the punctuation of s.53(1) is ambiguous on the point, the long title of the Act limits its scope to provision for such matters and "connected purposes".
[24] See discussion of the second general principle, paras 4–12 to 4–15 *supra*.
[25] s.58(1).

the particular action or decision to which the application relates. In relation to a guardianship application, there must be incapacity in relation to some but not necessarily all matters within the first criterion for guardianship described above. In relation to the second of those criteria, *"likely to continue"* may in some cases raise questions of interpretation before the sheriff, or upon which medical certifiers may need guidance. It is suggested that the following guidelines could reasonably be applied to limit the area of doubt: (a) "likely" means simply on a balance of probabilities; (b) the word "continue" could, out of context, mean anything from a minimal continuation to a lifelong one, but the Parliament is unlikely to have intended either of those extremes; (c) "continue" refers to continuing incapacity in relation to some of the matters for which guardianship powers are sought, but not necessarily all of them[26]; (d) guardianship is precluded by s.1(2) where incapacity is likely only for so short a period that the adult would not benefit from it, and by ss.1(3) and 58(1)(c) where an intervention order or some other measure would suffice, but the whole purpose of the Act is to ensure that where an adult has needs within the scope of the Act's provisions, those needs will be appropriately met; and (e) where, having regard to (d), the adult has needs which can only be met by a guardianship order, "likely to continue" means for at least the duration of any order to be granted, bearing in mind that the norm (on first application) is three years but that there is no minimum duration.[27]

Scope

Orders

10–29 In this and the following sections, "relevant matters" means the adult's property, financial affairs or personal welfare. Intervention orders may take two forms. They may direct a specified action to be taken, or they may authorise an appointee to take specified action or make a specified decision in relation to relevant matters.[28] There appears to be no reason why both should not be combined in the same order, where appropriate. Section 64(1) states the powers which may be conferred on a guardian in five categories: (a) to deal with such particular matters as the order may specify in relation to relevant matters; (b) to deal with all aspects of the adult's personal welfare, or with such aspects as may be specified in the order; (c) to pursue or defend in the name of the adult an action of declarator of nullity of marriage, or of divorce or separation; (d) to manage the adult's whole property or financial affairs, or such parts as may be specified in the order; and (e) to authorise the adult to carry out such transactions or categories of transactions as the guardian may specify. Guardianship orders may, and frequently will, combine elements from two or more of the foregoing categories. The categories are referred to by the above lettering in the following paragraphs. In all applications, the sheriff may under s.3(2)(d) make such interim orders as appear to the sheriff

---

[26] s.1(5) envisages the development of new skills during the continuance of a guardianship order: see also ss.64(1)(e) and 67(1).
[27] s.58(4). See paras 11–22 and 11–33 *infra*.
[28] s.53(5). See comments in n.23 to para.10–27 *supra*.

to be appropriate.[29] In guardianship applications, the sheriff may under s.57(5) make an interim appointment as described in paras 11–19 to 11–21 below.

Combinations

More than one order may be granted or in force at the same time. There is no prohibition of such combinations. That they are permissible is implicit in ss.53(2) and 58(2), which require the sheriff, when considering any application for an order, to have regard to any order previously made in relation to the adult, and any orders varying any such previous order or ancillary to it. It is evidently intended that when granting a new order the sheriff should ensure that the whole scheme of provision remains appropriate, and that there will be no disco-ordination among orders simultaneously in force. It is to be anticipated that sheriffs will include powers under guardianship category (a), where appropriate, rather than simultaneously granting a guardianship order and an intervention order. The sheriff may grant an intervention order where guardianship has been sought[30] or is recalled.[31] **10–30**

Limitations

Section 64(2), applied to appointees under intervention orders by s.53(14), places restrictions upon appointees under both guardianship and intervention orders. They may not place the adult in a hospital for the treatment of mental disorder against the adult's will.[32] If the adult is a detained patient under MHSA 1984, they may not consent on the adult's behalf to any form of treatment to which Part X of that Act applies.[33] They may not consent on the adult's behalf to any medical treatment, or medical treatment of any class, specified in regulations under s.48(2).[34] By regulations the Scottish Ministers may define, and thus *inter alia* limit, the scope of the powers which may be conferred on a guardian as described in para.10–29 above, and define the conditions under which those powers may be exercised,[35] but the Scottish Ministers have indicated that they do not at present intend to make such regulations, and there is no equivalent power in relation to intervention orders. **10–31**

Summary

The range of orders and powers which may be granted, generally in ascending order of restrictiveness as defined in the second principle,[36] may be summarised as follows: **10–32**

(1) intervention order directing specified action (s.53(5)(a));

---

[29] See para.5–6 *supra*.
[30] s.58(3).
[31] s.71(4).
[32] s.64(2)(a).
[33] ss.64(2)(b) and 48(1).
[34] Per s.62(2)(b). Currently the Specified Treatments Regulations. See paras 14–48 *et seq. infra*.
[35] s.64(11).
[36] s.1(3), see paras 4–12 to 4–15 *supra*.

(2) intervention order nominating appointee to take specified action or make specified decision (s.53(5)(b));

(3) intervention order comprising both (1) and (2) (s.53(5));

(4) guardian with power to deal with specified particular matters (s.64(1)(a));

(5) guardian with power to
   — deal with specified aspects of personal welfare (s.64(1)(b)), or
   — pursue or defend action of nullity of marriage, divorce or separation (s.64(1)(c)), or
   — manage specified parts of property or financial affairs (s.64(1)(d));

(6) guardian with powers combining two or more elements from (4) and (5);

(7) guardian with power to
   — deal with all aspects of personal welfare (s.64(1)(b)), or
   — manage all property and financial affairs (s.64(1)(d));

(8) guardian with plenary management powers (category (7)) combined with limited personal powers from categories (4) and/or (5), or conversely (in theory, though less likely in practice) plenary personal powers combined with limited management powers;

(9) guardian with power to deal with all aspects of personal welfare and to manage all property and financial affairs (s.64(1)(b) and (d)).

Power under s.64(1)(c) in respect of nullity, divorce or separation proceedings may be combined with other guardianship powers, including powers under categories (7) and (9) above; and power under s.64(1)(e) to authorise the adult to transact may be conferred along with guardianship powers in any category, rendering the order to that extent less restrictive. Powers conferred on appointees under categories (2)–(6) above are limited powers. Powers in categories (7) and (9) above are plenary powers. Category (8) combines plenary management powers with limited personal powers (which could well become the most common form of combined powers) or vice versa. The combination of powers sought in Appendix 6, Style C, includes particular matters in category (4) without prejudice to the generality of plenary powers in category (7).

Uses and effect of intervention orders

10–33 An intervention order may direct any specified action to be taken.[37] It may authorise an appointee to take any specified action or make any specified decision in relevant matters, subject only to the limitations of s.64(2) described in para.10–31 above. Anything done under

---

[37] s.53(5)(a). See comment in n.23 to para.10–27 *supra*.

an intervention order has the same effect as if the adult had capacity to do it and did so.[38] There is no provision for the scope of intervention orders, or the conditions under which powers under them may be exercised, to be defined or limited by regulations, except only under s.48(2).[39] Taking the foregoing provisions together, the scope of intervention orders is potentially very wide. They are a new statutory creation, and are therefore circumscribed only by the statute which created them, and not by any previous law or by any law relating to other techniques or appointments. It would therefore appear that an intervention order may authorise anything, subject only to the following limitations. If it is the first type of order (directing the taking of a specified action), then it must be something which the adult could lawfully have done with unimpaired capacity; it must be possible to frame an order directing that it be done, without it being necessary to authorise someone to do it (which would put the order into the second category); and it should be something within the scope of the Act, having regard to the Act's long title and to the legislative competence of the Scottish Parliament. If it is the second type of order (authorising an appointee to take action or make a decision), then it must be something which the adult could lawfully have done with unimpaired capacity; it must relate to the adult's property, financial affairs or personal welfare; it must be possible to frame an order authorising someone to do it by taking specified action or making a specified decision; and it must not be prohibited by s.64(2) (see para.10–31 above). If it is either type of order, to grant it must accord with the general principles. Conversely, if the order is not excluded by any of the above criteria and it can be shown that to grant it would be in accordance with the general principles, then it should be granted, and not to do so would be a denial of justice.

It is expected that cases will arise to test the criteria suggested in the preceding paragraph, as regards both their validity and their limits. Indeed, where the granting of an intervention order would appear to accord with the general principles, advisers are likely to be under a professional duty to test those limits, if that should be necessary. One's approach to the new orders should not be limited by what could or could not be done under previous law for an adult with impaired capacity. The following hypothetical example will illustrate the point. Miss G is elderly, oldest of a large family, all of whom survive. She has only meagre savings but owns the family home and lives in it with one sister. Their siblings all left long ago to live independent lives, and have their own homes. Miss G consulted a solicitor for the first time in her life because of some pension and benefit problems. She confessed that she had never made a Will, and was dismayed to learn that on intestacy the house would not pass automatically to the sister who resided with her, as she had always assumed. She immediately instructed a Will leaving everything to the sister, whom failing to her other siblings. She was clearly fully capax at the time, and this was subsequently confirmed by her doctor. The Will was ready next day, but overnight she was taken suddenly and very seriously ill. She lost testamentary capacity and all means of communicating. She was expected neither to recover capacity nor to live very

10–34

---

[38] s.53(9).
[39] Referred to in s.64(2)(b). See paras 10–31 *supra* and 14–48 *et seq. infra*.

long. The solicitor immediately applied for an intervention order, and an interim order under s.3(2)(d), seeking authority to sign on Miss G's behalf the Will which had been prepared. In this hypothetical example, the criteria described in para.10–33 above were all met, and it was clearly in accordance with the general principles that the order be granted. The signing of the Will was an action relating to Miss G's property and financial affairs which she could and certainly would have taken if still capable. No provision of the Act would appear to prevent the granting of the order. The solicitor could well have been held in breach of duty to his client if he had not immediately sought the order.[40]

10–35 Intervention orders are appropriate in situations where management powers such as are described in paras 10–21 *et seq.* above were previously conferred on tutors-dative, and in situations where tutors-dative might previously have been authorised to deal with or decide specific welfare matters. They should be used in any situations where those concerned previously acted informally or relied on *negotiorum gestio*: adults with impaired capacity are entitled to the safeguards and protections of proper procedures when they have been created, rather than having powers imposed upon them *de facto*, which with reference to the second general principle will almost always be an option unacceptably restrictive of the adult's freedom.[41] Intervention orders can be used to enable less restrictive measures to be put in place, or to supplement other measures. Examples include: consolidating funds into a single account so that authority to intromit can thereafter be obtained and used[42]; dealing with a particular management matter outwith the statutory powers of managers of an establishment under Part 4[43]; allowing a medical team to deal with a non-medical welfare matter for a patient under authority to treat in terms of Part 5[44]; dealing with unforeseen matters not covered by the terms of a power of attorney or guardianship order; and in a similar situation of unforeseen circumstances, consenting to action by trustees or a variation of a trust. In relation to non-Act techniques generally, where procedure under s.3(3) is not available,[45] points of difficulty can be clarified and proposed action authorised by seeking an intervention order authorising the proposal on behalf of the adult: this could often be the simpler form of intervention order under s.53(5)(a). An intervention order may be appropriate to exercise rights or seek remedies

---

[40] A procedure to make a will on behalf of someone lacking testamentary capacity is available in England under the Mental Health Act 1983, s.96. The procedure is described, and examples of appropriate use of it given, in *Mental Handicap and the Law*, pp.573–576. The previous lack of any such procedure in Scotland was a serious deficiency, exacerbated by Scots law's adherence to fixed legal rights rather than judicial discretion. The matter was discussed in Part IV of the Scottish Law Commission's Consultative Memorandum No.70, *The Making and Revocation of Wills* (September 1986), but the hypothetical examples addressed there did not include elements such as those given in this paragraph (serious and unintended unfairness to one sibling if all were to inherit equally, and a clear testamentary intention frustrated by supervening incapacity) where the case for such a procedure, and the injustice created by its absence, would have been most clearly demonstrated.
[41] See paras 4–12 to 4–15 *supra*.
[42] See Ch.8.
[43] See Ch.9.
[44] See Ch.14.
[45] See para.5–14 above.

in a wide range of situations: for example, it has been suggested that an intervention order could be sought to remove an abuser where a vulnerable, incapable adult is the sole owner or tenant of his or her home and had previously permitted the abuser to live there.[46] An intervention order might be extensive in its scope, such as taking necessary personal welfare decisions and managing property and financial arrangements where loss of capacity is combined with a need to find a suitable residential placement, sell a house or give up a tenancy, dispose of contents, and re-arrange finances; yet where ongoing needs are not expected to justify continuing guardianship. For example, after completion of those matters funds might be consolidated into a single account and authority to intromit[47] might suffice for future management. Likewise, the order might authorise dealing with a legal rights claim or other rights in succession, and perhaps executing a deed of variation to establish a trust for ongoing management.[48] An intervention order would also be appropriate where incapacity is expected to be temporary, but something needs to be done or decided urgently and cannot be deferred pending recovery (where such deferment is possible, intervention would contravene the first and second general principles).

Intervention orders offer greater flexibility than guardianship as to **10–36** who may be appointed. The criteria for appointment as guardian are described in Chapter 11 (see in particular para.11–9). There are no equivalent criteria for appointment under an intervention order, where under s.53(5)(b) the sheriff simply has discretion to appoint (or not appoint) "the person nominated in the application", though the guardianship criteria may provide some assistance where suitability is an issue. On the other hand, s.53(5)(b) appears to be deliberately wider, using "person" where guardianship (except under Criminal Procedure (Scotland) Act 1995[49]) is limited to an "individual" or the chief social work officer of the local authority.[50]

Guardianship: uses and powers

The first and second general principles require guardianship to be **10–37** used only where no other measure less restrictive of the adult's freedom, whether within or outwith the scheme of the Act, would achieve the necessary benefit.[51] Section 58(1)(b) effectively places guardianship as the most restrictive of the Act's measures. This correctly cautious approach to the imposition of guardianship must however be balanced against the adult's entitlement to a guardian, where necessary, as formulated in the provision of the UN Declaration with which this chapter commences. The point made elsewhere in this book, including in discussion of the first and second principles in paras 4–9 and 4–12 above, bears repetition because it is important. It is a grave and unacceptable contravention of an adult's rights and

---

[46] Scottish Executive, *Consultation on Vulnerable Adults*, December 2001, para.41.
[47] See Ch.8.
[48] *cf.* cases where such powers were conferred on tutors-dative as described in para.10–25 *supra*.
[49] c.46. See paras 11–84 *et seq. infra*.
[50] s.59. See paras 11–3 to 11–5 *infra*.
[51] See paras 4–11 and 4–13 *supra*.

freedoms for powers which are truly guardianship powers to be imposed *de facto*, without due process[52] and the safeguards, protections and supervision which go with it, upon an adult unable to give valid consent to such imposition, regardless of whether the adult is compliant and regardless of who imposes such *de facto* control, whether family, carers, professionals, local authority or others.

10–38 The first four general principles[53] apply to whether a guardianship order is granted; if so, to which category or categories of s.64(1) powers (see paras 10–29 to 10–32 above) are applied; if a limited rather than a plenary category is selected, to precisely what powers are conferred; and to the extent of any power under category (e) to authorise transactions by the adult. Each of the powers conferred must be appropriate by reference to the general principles. Further comment is required on the s.64(1) categories.[54] Categories (c) and (e) are specialities. Categories (b) and (d) provide for plenary welfare guardianship and plenary management powers respectively, and also limited guardianship to deal with specified aspects of personal welfare and/or parts of property and financial affairs. Category (a) provides for limited guardianship to deal with particular matters. As to the difference between "aspects" and "parts", on the one hand, and "matters" on the other, it is suggested that "aspects" and "parts" are particular areas of responsibility and "matters" are specific issues, requiring action or decision, which may lie within one or more "aspects" or "parts". Thus, the various welfare powers quoted in paras 10–21 to 10–23 above as having been conferred on tutors-dative are all "aspects" within category (b), and particular items of property or areas of financial affairs would be "parts" within category (d). A "matter" would, for example, be dealing with the welfare aspects of a transition from one form of care and accommodation to another, or dealing with all the property and financial consequences of such a transition. Powers to deal with "matters" in category (a) will generally be combined with powers in categories (b) and/or (d), because if there were no other need for guardianship the "matter" would usually be dealt with by way of intervention order. Conversely, if there is need for ongoing guardianship, then the existence of category (a) indicates that it is to be preferred to a separate intervention order granted in parallel with the guardianship order. Some "matters" may be so substantial, complex or long-running as to justify guardianship in their own right.[55]

10–39 Issues may arise as to the scope of plenary guardianship: that is to say, as to what is encompassed within "all aspects of the personal welfare of the adult", or within unqualified powers to manage "the property or financial affairs of the adult". (In the latter phrase, there is a further question as to whether "or" should be read as "and", or whether two alternative plenary orders are envisaged in category (d): the second interpretation is literalistic but impracticable, and this discussion assumes that only one, comprehensive, form of plenary

---

[52] See ECHR Art.6 and para.1–47 *supra*.
[53] See paras 4–2 to 4–22 *supra*.
[54] Referred to by the lettering which appears in s.64(1) and is adopted in para.10–29 *supra*, as indicated in that paragraph.
[55] On the termination of an attorney's authority by a guardianship order with relevant powers, note that s.24(2) refers to "any matter" and "that matter".

management was intended in category (d)). It would appear that plenary welfare powers encompass everything in respect of which specific welfare powers could be granted, and that plenary management powers would encompass everything in respect of which specific property and/or financial powers could be granted, in both cases as referred to in the next paragraph. One can envisage difficulty, in relation to welfare powers, in justifying under the first and second principles[56] an order conferring unlimited powers which are not specified: the argument would be that if they can be shown to be justified, then they can be specified. Moreover, specification of the powers granted would remove uncertainty. While similar questions could arise in relation to plenary property and financial powers, there is the difference that those would in any event be limited by the extent of the adult's property and financial interests. Category (c) is referred to in para.10–43 below. Category (e) will always be a supplementary category: see the fifth principle[57] and ss.64(1)(e) and 67(1) and (5).

In some jurisdictions, statutes have provided lists of powers which **10–40** can be selected or adjusted for particular orders in individual cases. The Dependent Adults Acts of Alberta contain both the "Alberta list" of personal welfare powers referred to in para.10–17 above, and also a similar list of management powers.[58] New Zealand's Protection of Personal and Property Rights Act 1988,[59] in dealing with welfare guardianship, simply refers to "any aspect or aspects of personal care and welfare" without any list (though a lengthy list is offered of possible "personal orders", approximately akin to intervention orders), but on the other hand for "managers" (financial guardians) some fifty powers are listed in a Schedule. The Incapacity Act offers no lists, and regulations which might have done so[60] have not been made. For welfare powers, experience of tutors-dative as described in paras 10–21 to 10–24 above is likely to assist. The Part 6 Code offers both welfare and financial powers.[61] Statutory lists in other jurisdictions may assist, as may—with suitable adaptation—the styles of attorney's powers offered in Appendix 5 to this book.[62] No list can remove the necessity of carefully considering the adult's impairments of capacity, circumstances, needs and (for financial powers) assets and interests, and drafting powers which are precisely suited to that individual adult and which comply with the general principles.

Distinction between welfare and management powers

In all applications for intervention and guardianship orders, it is **10–41** essential to consider carefully whether the powers sought are welfare powers, or property and financial powers, or of both types. Many provisions of the Act differentiate between the two types, including as to application procedure and subsequent supervision. If an application

---

[56] See paras 4–6 to 4–15 *supra*.
[57] s.1(5): see para.4–22 *supra*.
[58] Reproduced in *The Power to Act*, pp.108–109.
[59] Described in *The Power to Act*, Ch. XII.
[60] Provided for in s.64(11).
[61] paras 3.57 and 3.53 respectively.
[62] *Style*, Schedule Parts 1, 2 and 3.

complies only with the formalities for property and financial powers, the sheriff will not be able to grant it if any of the powers sought are found to include welfare aspects. See paras 10–47 to 10–50 below.

Legal representative

10–42   A guardian has power to act as the adult's legal representative in relation to any matters within the scope of the powers conferred by the guardianship order, unless prohibited by an order of the sheriff, who can also order that conditions or restrictions be imposed. Failing such prohibition, conditions or restrictions, the power to act as legal representative is conferred automatically by virtue of the appointment, and does not require to be expressly included in it.[63] "Legal representative" is not defined for the purposes of the Act. Schedule 5 inserts references to "legal representative" in the Heritable Securities (Scotland) Act 1894 (c.44) by para.7 and in the Offices, Shops and Railway Premises Act 1963 (c.41) by para.9. There are many more insertions of express references to guardians. Legislation subsequent to the Incapacity Act may also be expected to refer to guardians where appropriate: for example, guardians are authorised by statute to attend private interviews (without compromising the status of the interview as private) between a person authorised by the Scottish Commission for the Regulation of Care and an adult in receipt of care, in pursuance of the Commission's powers of inspection under the Regulation of Care (Scotland) Act 2001.[64] It is clearly intended that "legal representative" should extend more widely than statutory references to the phrase. The Explanatory Notes to the Act include the example of instructing a solicitor on the adult's behalf.[65] The concept of "legal representative" is well developed in child law.[66] Great caution should be exercised in applying principles or precedents of child law to adults with incapacity, as they may often be inappropriate.[67] However, as demonstrated by Wilkinson and Norrie,[68] the concept of legal representation has its origins in tutory. Tutory in turn was in some of its origins a concept common both to children and to adults with incapacity,[69] therefore child law may (with appropriate caution) be a source of guidance in any difficulties in interpreting the scope of legal representation in relation to adults with incapacity.

Pursuit and defence of proceedings

10–43   This paragraph concerns not proceedings under the Act, where the provisions described in para.5–7 above apply, but the pursuit or defence of any other civil proceedings by or on behalf of the adult. Under the former law, where the adult had a curator bonis, the adult

---

[63] s.64(3).
[64] asp 8, s.25(6) and (7).
[65] Which may prompt review of para.5(a) of the Solicitors' Code of Conduct, which prescribes that solicitors must act (only) upon the "proper instructions" of the client or of another solicitor who acts for the client.
[66] See, for example, Children (Scotland) Act 1995 (c.36) and Age of Legal Capacity (Scotland) Act 1991 (c.50) as amended thereby.
[67] See, for example, paras 1–3, 10–15 and 10–16 *supra*.
[68] *Parent and Child* (2nd ed.), paras 15.28 *et seq*.
[69] See para.10–15 *supra*.

could not himself appear as pursuer or defender, and proceedings were brought by or against the curator bonis.[70] The same was understood to apply to proceedings within the powers of a tutor.[71] Proceedings in a matter within the scope of a guardian's powers will now be brought by or against the guardian. Under the former law, subject to the exception in para.10–44 below, if the adult had no curator bonis and no tutor with relevant powers but lacked sufficient capacity to sue or appear, then the adult could not competently do so,[72] and the court would either sist the action pending appointment of a curator bonis, or appoint a curator ad litem.[73] Curators ad litem are not abolished by the Incapacity Act, nor mentioned in it.[74] The options now, accordingly, would appear to be appointment of a guardian with relevant powers, the granting of an intervention order authorising an appointee to pursue or defend the action, or appointment of a curator ad litem. The existence of category (c) of guardian's powers appears to indicate that a guardianship order is now the preferred option in proceedings of divorce, separation and declaration of nullity of marriage.[75] It is suggested that guardianship should also be the preferred option where other guardianship powers are required or likely to be required, either during the proceedings or on a continuing basis thereafter. In other situations, it is suggested, an intervention order should normally be preferred over appointment of a curator ad litem. There are no procedural rules for the process of appointing curators ad litem, and sometimes in the past they have been appointed without a proof, though a proof on the issue is competent.[76] Having regard to ECHR Article 6 and the second general principle under the Incapacity Act, it would appear that the risks of contravention of the adult's rights and the restriction of the adult's freedom are likely to be less if the requirements of intervention order procedure are followed.[77]

The exception mentioned above is that proceedings within the scope of a management appointment other than as curator bonis or tutor have sometimes in practice been conducted in name of an adult with impaired capacity upon the instructions of the manager. For example, a social security appeal may be taken in name of the adult, upon the instructions of the DWP (formerly DSS) appointee.[78]

10–44

---

[70] *Anderson's Trs v Skinner* (1871) 8 S.L.R. 325; *Latta*, 1977 S.L.T. 127.

[71] See *Mental Handicap and the Law*, p.45.

[72] *Reid v Reid* (1839) 1 D. 400, followed in *McGaughey v Livingstone*, 1992 S.L.T. 386, though in the latter case Lord Coulsfield suggested (at p.387) that there "might be room for a different approach" where an incapax would otherwise suffer prejudice.

[73] *Moodie v Dempster*, 1931 S.C. 553.

[74] ss.3(4) and 5(1), on the appointment of safeguarders, are without prejudice to any existing powers to appoint a person to represent the interests of an adult.

[75] This does not sit easily with the mandatory requirements of Rule of the Court of Session 49.17 and Ordinary Cause Rule 33.16 to appoint a curator ad litem in an action of divorce or separation (rules made under Divorce (Scotland) Act 1976, s.11).

[76] *AB v CB*, 1937 S.C. 408. See also *Gibson v Gibson*, 1970 S.L.T. (N) 60.

[77] See also paras 12–26 and 12–35 *infra*.

[78] This occurred in *Moffat v Secretary of State for Social Services*, 1992 S.L.T. 393 in which an appellant with Down's Syndrome succeeded in an appeal to the Court of Session, after unsuccessful appeals to a Social Security Appeal Tribunal and a Social Security Commissioner. Strictly speaking, proceedings commenced in name of an incapax pursuer are normally incompetent.

Adult abroad

10–45 Where welfare powers are held by a guardian or by an appointee under an intervention order, those powers may be exercised in relation to the adult whether or not the adult is in Scotland at the time when they are exercised.[79]

Procedure

10–46 There is a unified procedure for applications for intervention and guardianship orders, and an intervention order may be granted where a guardianship order has been sought.[80] For convenience, in the remainder of this chapter "application" means either type of application; "order" means either type of order (as indicated in para.10–26); "nominee" means a person nominated in the application to be authorised under an intervention order or to be appointed guardian, as the case may be; "appointee" means the person so authorised or appointed; "welfare powers" means limited or plenary powers in relation to personal welfare, "management powers" means limited or plenary powers in relation to property and financial affairs, and "combined powers" means limited or plenary powers in respect of both welfare and management matters; "affairs or welfare" means property, financial affairs or personal welfare; and "Rules" means the Act of Sederunt (Summary Applications, Statutory Applications and Appeals etc. Rules) 1999 as amended by SSI 2001/142 and SSI 2002/146.[81] Described here are only the procedural provisions particular to applications for intervention and guardianship orders which apply in addition to the procedural and related matters described in paras 5–2 to 5–21, which should be read in conjunction with this section. Reference should be made to paras 4–2 to 4–22 on the general principles, and 4–23 to 4–29 on the definition of capacity. See also paras 10–72 to 10–78 below for further matters particular to intervention orders, and Chapter 11 for further matters particular to guardianship, including para.11–24 on renewal of guardianship. Styles of application are offered in Appendix 6.

Applicants, notice and nominees

10–47 Applications may be made by any person, including the adult, having an interest in the adult's affairs or welfare.[82] If the applicant claims an interest in the adult's personal welfare and is not the local authority, the applicant must give notice to the chief social work officer of intention to make the application.[83] The local authority must apply if it appears to the authority that the relevant criteria described in para.10–27 apply, no-one else has made or is likely to make an application, and an order is necessary for the protection of the adult's affairs or welfare.[84] It should be noted that although the role of the

---

[79] ss.53(14) and 67(3), applied to foreign guardians by s.67(7).
[80] ss.53(4) and 58(3).
[81] See para.5–5 *supra*.
[82] ss.53(1) and 57(1).
[83] s.57(4) (see also s.53(4)).
[84] ss.53(3) and 57(2). See s.60(2), described in para.11–24 *infra*, for the equivalent duty in relation to renewal of guardianship.

local authority under the Act in general terms relates to personal welfare matters (see paras 5–33 and 5–34), this duty also applies where management powers or combined powers appear to be needed. This is not however an innovation: local authorities had an equivalent duty to petition for appointment of a curator bonis under MHSA 1984, s.92(1).[85] Under all applications for guardianship where an individual is the nominee, the nominee must consent to such appointment[86] and must meet the criteria described in para.11–2 below, whereas the Act contains no such express requirements in relation to applications for intervention orders.[87] See paras 11–2 and 11–3 below for further requirements regarding nominees to be guardians.

Reports

Section 57(3), applied to applications for intervention orders by s.53(4) and for renewal of guardianship by s.60(3),[88] contains the principal provisions regarding reports. For all such applications, three reports require to be lodged in court with the application, all based on assessment of the adult within 30 days before lodging of the application, and each in the appropriate form prescribed by the Reports Regulations[89] and set out in the Schedules to those Regulations. Copies of all three reports must be served along with Form 20 (or Forms 20, 21 and 22).[90] Two of the reports must be medical reports, based on examination and assessment of the adult. Where the adult's incapacity results from mental disorder,[91] one of them must be from "a practitioner approved ... by a health board as having special experience in the diagnosis or treatment of mental disorder" under MHSA 1984, s.20(1)(b), here called "an approved psychiatrist". The prescribed form of medical report is in Reports Regulations, Schedule 1 (for both doctors and adaptable to all types of application). Information required includes the nature of the adult's mental disorder or inability to communicate, the findings of the examination and assessment, likely duration of incapacity, extent of communication with the adult and others mentioned in s.1(4), and a declaration of any relationship or pecuniary interest. The Act places no obligation on medical practitioners to produce such reports, or to do so within a particular time, but in case of difficulty it may be of assistance to refer to the practitioner's ethical duties and duty of care to the adult as patient, including any under the practitioner's terms of engagement,[92]

10–48

---

[85] Now repealed: Incapacity Act, Sch.6.
[86] s.59(1)(a)—see para.11–2 *infra*.
[87] See para.10–49 *infra*, n.4, regarding prescribed forms for the "third report".
[88] See para.11–24 *infra*.
[89] The Adults with Incapacity (Reports in Relation to Guardianships and Intervention Orders) (Scotland) Regulations 2002 (SSI 2002/96), made under s.57(3).
[90] Rule 3.16.4(6). This requirement also applies to applications for renewal of guardianship—Rule 3.16.8(4). On service generally, see para.5–5 *supra*.
[91] See para.4–24 *supra*.
[92] It appears that general practitioners have no such contractual obligation. Para.433 of the Financial Memorandum to the Bill stated: "Where a formal assessment is required for financial or guardianship reasons, or for obtaining a power of attorney, this would fall outwith the General Practitioner's contracted NHS duties. As a result it will not place a burden on the NHS. The cost of each assessment made will in general fall to the estate of the individual to be assessed. The exception will be assessments in connection with local authority applications for welfare guardianship, where the Bill provides that the local authority should meet the costs." Consultants' obligations will depend upon the terms of their contracts.

or to the sheriff's general powers under s.3.[93] The sheriff's powers under s.3 are likely also to be of assistance in resolving the "circular dilemma" sometimes encountered under former procedures, where there has been difficulty in obtaining reports to allow suspected incapacity to be addressed because doctors requested to examine the adult have doubted whether they have had the adult's competent consent, or other lawful authority, to carry out the examination. Of potential assistance would be one or more of the procedure to apply for directions under s.3(3),[94] the court's power to order assessment, interview and reports under s.3(2)(b), and the court's power to make interim orders under s.3(2)(d).[95] The requirement for two medical reports means that it will no longer be possible to proceed on the basis of one report from a medical practitioner and one report from a clinical psychologist (or clinical neuro-psychologist) as sometimes occurred under tutory procedure,[96] even when that would appear to be the best way of bringing relevant information before the court. However, the requirement under the Incapacity Act is a minimum, and it would be appropriate to submit additional reports where reasonably necessary to ensure that the court is adequately informed, whether the additional reports be from further medical practitioners with different areas of specialist expertise which are relevant, or from other relevant professions.[97] British Medical Association has suggested that it should be competent for certification under the Act to be provided by other practitioners such as appropriately trained specialist nurses and clinical psychologists.[98]

10–49 The third report is a report as to the general appropriateness of the order sought, based on an interview and assessment of the adult, and as to the suitability of the nominee.[99] Where welfare or combined powers are sought, this third report must be provided by the mental health officer[1] or (if the adult's affairs or welfare are in jeopardy only because of the adult's inability to communicate) the chief social work officer.[2] The reference to inability to communicate is likely to be interpreted as limited to such inability caused by physical disability (where the chief social work officer, upon receipt of intimation of the intention to apply, is able confidently to make that distinction), having regard to s.1(6) and the extent to which the scheme of the Act depends on the distinction there made between mental disorder and physical inability to communicate. Where only management powers are sought, anyone with sufficient knowledge to do so may provide the third report. There is a range of prescribed forms for these reports:

---

[93] See paras 5–6 and 5–14 *supra*.
[94] See para.5–14 *supra*.
[95] See para.5–6 *supra*.
[96] An example being *Britton v Britton's Curator Bonis*, 1992 S.C.L.R. 947.
[97] In *G, Petr*, referred to in para.10–24 *supra*, the petition was supported by four lengthy and detailed medical certificates, from the adult's general practitioner, a consultant psychiatrist, a consultant gynaecologist and a consultant clinical geneticist (and there was also a report from a school principal). Likewise in *D, Petr* (mentioned *ibid.*) there were four lengthy medical reports.
[98] See also para.14–43 *infra*.
[99] As with applications for authority to intromit, the same certifier must have knowledge of both the adult and the nominee: see discussion in para.8–7 *supra*.
[1] See para.5–37 *supra*.
[2] See para.5–35 *supra*.

for mental health officers, Reports Regulations, Schedule 2 for guardianship, Schedule 3 for renewal of guardianship, and Schedule 4 for an intervention order; for the chief social work officer, Schedules 5, 6 and 7 for those three purposes respectively; and for "a person with sufficient knowledge", Schedules 8, 9 and 10 respectively. All of these forms seek *inter alia* responses in some detail to the requirements of the first four general principles[3] and the criteria for appointment in s.59(3) and (4),[4] as well as seeking declarations of any relationship or pecuniary interest. The requirements of the forms should be considered before selecting "a person with sufficient knowledge", and explained when the selected person is first approached. To meet concerns about possible difficulties in progressing applications because of delays in obtaining reports, s.57(4) places a statutory duty on mental health officers and chief social work officers to produce their reports within 21 days of the date of notice under that section of intention to apply for an order.[5] Although the expertise and training of mental health officers and chief social work officers relate principally to personal welfare matters, their duty to report where combined powers are sought means that in those cases they are required to report on the "general appropriateness" of the management powers sought. It had been hoped that the Codes might have given guidance on this, but they do not. Likewise, the Codes do not give guidance on whether, and if so in what circumstances, it might be appropriate for "a person who has sufficient knowledge" providing the third report, in applications for management powers, to be the solicitor acting in the application, or a colleague in the same firm. There is nothing in the Act, regulations or guidance to prohibit this, and the general rule is that a solicitor acting in civil proceedings—even if personally conducting them in court—is not barred from giving evidence in those proceedings.[6] The absence of any prohibition may be inferred as deliberate from the fact that s.26(1)(c)(iii)(C) does explicitly prohibit a solicitor acting for anyone involved in relevant matters from countersigning an application for authority to intromit. Where the solicitor has been asked to investigate, consider and advise what course of action might be most appropriate, and the application accords with the advice thus given, there is unlikely to be any actual conflict of interest and the solicitor is likely already to have done what is required by s.57(3)(c). The solicitor would nevertheless be wise to obtain written authority from his client to act independently and with responsibility only to the court and to the adult's interests in relation to the report. Where the court is satisfied that the solicitor has so acted, that the report properly meets the Act's requirements, and that there are circumstances in which it is reasonable for the solicitor to provide the report, then it is tentatively suggested that the court should be willing to accept the report. Reasonable circumstances might be that the solicitor is the family's longstanding solicitor who

---

[3] s.1(2)–(4), see paras 4–2 *et seq. supra*.
[4] See para.11–2 *infra*. These criteria require to be addressed in the forms for intervention orders, although in terms of the Act they apply only to proposed guardians. For an intervention order under s.53(5)(a), where there is no appointee, these questions should be marked as inapplicable.
[5] See para.10–47 *supra*.
[6] *Campbell v Cochrane*, 1928 J.C. 25.

has known the adult for some time; or that to insist upon a report from someone else would have caused delay, difficulty or expense without in fact adding anything of value to the process. The public policy purposes of the Act included providing suitable protections but also removing unhelpful or unnecessarily expensive difficulties which might hinder or obstruct the route to appropriate solutions.

10–50   In summary,[7] the requirements for reports are as follows:

Welfare powers or combined powers sought, incapacity not caused solely by inability to communicate—

- two medical reports, at least one of them from an approved psychiatrist,

- report from mental health officer.

Management powers only sought, incapacity not caused solely by inability to communicate—

- two medical reports, at least one of them from an approved psychiatrist,

- report from person with sufficient knowledge.

Welfare powers or combined powers sought, incapacity caused solely by inability to communicate—

- two medical reports (neither need be by approved psychiatrist),

- report from chief social work officer.

Management powers only sought, incapacity caused solely by inability to communicate—

- two medical reports (neither need be by approved psychiatrist),

- report from person with sufficient knowledge.

The sheriff can order additional reports or information, further assessments or interviews, and make further enquiries.[8]

Other orders and measures

10–51   In considering an application, the sheriff must have regard to any intervention or guardianship order previously made in relation to the adult, and to any orders varying such previous order, or ancillary to

---

[7] This summary assumes that "incapacity ... by reason of mental disorder" in s.57(3)(a) and "jeopardy only because of inability of the adult to communicate" in s.57(3)(b) are mutually exclusive and that one or the other will apply to every application; but occasionally this might not be so, because these two criteria appear to differ through being carefully drawn to reflect the respective competencies of those who assess and certify (hence also, presumably, the absence of "because of physical disability" in s.57(3)(b)): see para.10–49.

[8] s.3(2). See para.5–6 *supra*.

it.[9] This applies whether or not the previous order is still in force. The sheriff thus requires to have regard both to the history of orders granted in respect of the adult, and also the present scheme of provision for the adult under such orders and what the scheme will be if the application is granted. There is no express obligation upon the sheriff to take account of any existing powers of attorney or other measures. However, guardianship orders expressly supersede powers of attorney insofar as they overlap,[10] and any intervention or guardianship order may affect or supersede any other measure in place. Accordingly, it would probably be difficult to demonstrate compliance with the general principles (particularly the first three) without having taken account of all measures, in addition to any intervention or guardianship orders, previously put in place. On the inter-relationship between such orders and other measures, and in particular the position where it is desired that an intervention order should supersede powers of an attorney, see para.10–70 below.

Caution

10–52 Where the sheriff makes any order relating to property or financial affairs, he must require the appointee to find caution, except where the appointee is unable to find caution but the sheriff is satisfied that the appointee is nevertheless suitable to be authorised (in the case of intervention orders) or appointed (in the case of guardianship).[11] The sheriff has discretion to require the appointee to find caution when making or varying any intervention order, not limited to orders concerning property or financial affairs.[12] The discretion to dispense with caution is particularly necessary in the context of concern about the continued availability of caution for lay appointees, or at all. The discretion relates only to the ability of the appointee to obtain caution, not the need for caution, so that it seems that the sheriff is obliged to order persons authorised under intervention orders to find caution (if able to do so) even where what is authorised in relation to property and financial affairs requires no intromissions, such as in the examples given in para.10–25 above where, under tutor-dative procedure, caution was not required. Perhaps, in some such cases, the sheriff might be persuaded that the appointee cannot obtain caution because it is not possible to demonstrate to any cautioner the nature of any financial risk in respect of which caution is sought, or any ascertainable quantification thereof. Unavailability of caution except at quite disproportionate cost might also be regarded as inability to obtain caution. As ever, in considering any such submissions the court should apply to the particular circumstances the Act's general principles, including the principle of benefit to the adult in s.1(2)—see para.4–2 above.

10–53 Where the sheriff requires caution to be found, Rule 3.16.10 applies. In the relevant interlocutor making or varying the appointment, the sheriff is required to specify the amount of caution and the period within which it is to be found. The sheriff can allow further time, on

---

[9] ss.53(2) and 58(2).
[10] s.24(2).
[11] ss.53(7) and 58(6).
[12] s.53(7).

application before expiry of the period originally allowed and upon cause shown. Caution must be lodged with the Public Guardian, who notifies the sheriff clerk. At any time while a requirement to find caution is in force, the sheriff may increase or decrease the amount, or require new caution to be found.

Registration with the Public Guardian

10–54 Forthwith upon the order being made, the sheriff clerk is required to send a copy of the interlocutor containing the order to the Public Guardian. The Public Guardian is required to enter prescribed particulars in the relevant register[13]; subject to s.11, to notify the adult; to notify the local authority; and except where incapacity arises solely from physical inability to communicate, to notify the Mental Welfare Commission.[14] In the case of guardianship, the Public Guardian is required to notify the adult "of the appointment of the guardian" and to notify the local authority and (where applicable) the Mental Welfare Commission "of the terms of the interlocutor".[15] The Act contains no equivalent specification of what is to be notified upon registration of an intervention order. Upon registration of a guardianship order, and when satisfied that the guardian has found caution if so required, the Public Guardian issues a certificate of appointment to the guardian.[16] There is no requirement to issue any equivalent certificate to a person authorised under an intervention order. There is no obvious reason for these discrepancies in relation to intervention orders. It is understood that the Public Guardian's systems are designed to operate on a consistent basis and that the Public Guardian gives similar notification in respect of intervention orders to that required for guardianship orders, and issues similar certificates. For the registration and notification provisions which apply upon appointment of an additional guardian and upon appointment of a substitute guardian subsequently to the original order, see paras 11–12 and 11–14 respectively below; and for registration and notification provisions upon grant or refusal of an application for renewal of guardianship, see para.11–24 below.

Heritable property and accommodation

Registration of orders relating to heritable property

10–55 Sections 56 and 61 make almost identical provision where intervention orders or guardianship orders, respectively, are made by the sheriff vesting in the appointee any right[17] to deal with, convey or manage any interest in heritable property which is recorded in the General Register of Sasines, registered in the Land Register of Scotland, or capable of being so recorded or registered.[18] The application and the order must specify each property affected by the order

---

[13] See s.6(2)(b)(iv) regarding guardianship orders and s.6(2)(b)(v) regarding intervention orders.
[14] ss.53(10) and 58(7).
[15] s.58(7)(c) and (d).
[16] s.58(7)(b).
[17] In the case of guardianship, "any right of the adult".
[18] ss.56(1) and 61(1).

"in such terms as enable it to be identified" in the relevant register,[19] for which purpose a proper conveyancing description will normally be appropriate. It is the duty of the appointee, after finding caution if so required, forthwith to apply to the Keeper of the Registers of Scotland for recording or registration in the relevant register of the interlocutor containing the order.[20] The application to the Keeper must contain the appointee's name and address; a statement that the appointee has powers relating to each property specified in the order; and a copy of the interlocutor.[21] Where the interlocutor is to be recorded in the Sasine register, the Keeper is required so to record it, to endorse the interlocutor to the effect that he has done so, and to send the endorsed interlocutor to the Public Guardian.[22] Where the interlocutor is to be registered in the Land Register, the Keeper is required to update the Title Sheet to show the interlocutor, and to send the updated Land Certificate or an Office Copy thereof to the Public Guardian.[23] The Public Guardian is required to enter prescribed particulars of the endorsed interlocutor, updated Land Certificate or updated Office Copy in the relevant register.[24] An initial order may confer powers in respect of property yet to be identified, for which no conveyancing description is thus yet available; or it may become appropriate for a guardian to acquire for the adult an interest in heritage at some time subsequent to the granting of plenary powers. In the case of intervention orders, this has been addressed in the manner followed in Style A of Appendix 6: an initial interim order, to be followed by a final order once the property has been identified and a conveyancing description can be provided. Other possibilities include an ancillary order under s.3(1) (see para.5–6 above) or, in the case of guardianship, an application under s.74 (see para.11–73 below) for a variation to the original order to include specific reference to the "new" property.

The Keeper of the Registers of Scotland has issued valuable guidance for conveyancers entitled *Guardianship and Intervention— Registration in the Land Register and Register of Sasines*, available *inter alia* on the Keeper's website www.ros.gov.uk. The following practice points are mentioned selectively, and are not a substitute for referring to the full guidance. The Keeper's policy is that orders are registrable only if they empower "dealings, conveyances or management activities . . . which alter the real or *quasi* real heritable rights of the adult". Examples are orders permitting the appointee to acquire or dispose of heritage; to grant, assign or renounce a long lease; to grant or vary a heritable security; to renounce or vary a proper liferent; to renounce, waive or vary a registered or recorded title condition; or to enter an agreement creating real or *quasi* real rights or conditions affecting heritage, such as an agreement under s.75 of the Town and Country Planning (Scotland) Act 1997 or a boundary agreement under s.19 of the Land Registration (Scotland) Act 1979. Orders are not registrable if (for example) they authorise dealings with tenancies not

---

[19] Rule 3.16.12 as regards the application and ss.56(2) and 61(2) as regards the order.
[20] ss.56(3) and 61(3).
[21] ss.56(4) and 61(4).
[22] ss.56(5) and (7) and 61(5) and (7).
[23] ss.56(6) and (7) and 61(6) and (7).
[24] Under s.6(2)(b)(iv) for guardianship orders and 6(2)(b)(v) for intervention orders.

capable of registration, or authorise matters of maintenance or insurance of heritage with no power to alter real rights or conditions. Where the order is in the form of a copy interlocutor rather than an extract decree, it must be certified a true copy by a solicitor, a clerk of court or a member of the Public Guardian's staff. Where orders are presented for Sasine recording, a warrant of registration should be added, Form CPB2 should be submitted (giving the appointee's name and address), a statement that the appointee has powers in relation to each property listed in the order[25] should be included in Form CPB2 or a covering letter, and a "miscellaneous event" recording fee should be paid. Requirements for Land Register registration are similar, subject to a requirement for Forms 2 and 4, submission of relevant Land and Charge Certificates, and (in the case of guardianship) evidence that caution has been found. The Keeper will normally require the order to be recorded or registered before or contemporaneously with any writ granted, or presented for recording or registration, on behalf of the adult by the appointee. Styles of dispositive and other clauses are offered in the guidance, as are checklists for recording and registration of deeds by the appointee or in favour of the adult. Note that question 12 on Form 1 and question 8(a) on Form 2 should be answered to the effect that the adult's capacity is impaired[26] and that the application is made, or the deed has been granted, by the appointee in terms of the order (both specified).

Amendment of registration (guardianship only)

10–57 Where an interlocutor containing a guardianship order relating to heritable property has been recorded or registered under s.61, s.78 requires the Public Guardian to apply to the Keeper for the recording or registration in the relevant register of the interlocutor or other document vouching various subsequent events. There is no equivalent provision in relation to intervention orders. The Public Guardian must so apply to the Keeper forthwith upon the Public Guardian having entered in his own register[27] the prescribed particulars of any of the following: an interlocutor under s.71 replacing or removing a guardian, recalling a guardianship order or otherwise terminating a guardianship[28]; recall by the Public Guardian himself under s.73 of a guardian's management powers[29]; variation by the sheriff under s.74 of the powers conferred by a guardianship order or any existing ancillary order[30]; or notification of resignation by a guardian to the Public Guardian under s.75.[31] The Public Guardian must also make such application to the Keeper forthwith upon the death of the adult (though there is no obligation on anyone to notify the Public Guardian of the death of the adult—see para.10–71 below).

---

[25] Per ss.56(4)(b) and 61(4)(b).
[26] The Keeper's guidance suggests "has restricted capacity".
[27] The register maintained under s.6(2)(b)(iv).
[28] See s.71(3)(a).
[29] See s.73(2)(a).
[30] See s.74(5)(a).
[31] See s.75(3)(a).

Protection of third parties

Sections 53(13) and 79 apply where a third party has acquired, in **10–58** good faith and for value, title to any interest in heritable property from, respectively, a person authorised under an intervention order or a guardian; and s.77(4) applies to such acquisition from either type of appointee. Under ss.53(13) and 79, such title is not challengeable on the ground only of any irregularity of procedure in making the order, or on the ground only that the appointee has acted outwith the scope of his authority.[32] Under s.77(4), such title is not challengeable on grounds only of the termination or ending of the appointee's authority. See also paras 10–68 and 10–69 below.

Accommodation

Section 53(6) applies where an intervention order directs the **10–59** "acquisition" of accommodation for the adult or the disposal of any accommodation used for the time being as a dwellinghouse by the adult. Schedule 2, para.6 applies to the "purchase" or disposal of such accommodation by a guardian. Under an intervention order the only requirement is for the consent of the Public Guardian "as respects the consideration", before the accommodation is acquired or disposed of, as the case may be.[33] The requirements and procedure under Schedule 2, para.6 relating to guardianship are described in paras 11–53 and 11–54 below: briefly, they require (firstly) the consent of the Public Guardian in principle to the purchase or disposal (with provision for intimation and dealing with objections), whereas in the case of an intervention order the transaction will have been authorised in principle by the order; and they require (secondly) the consent of the Public Guardian to "the purchase or selling price". As the Parliament has chosen to differentiate between "acquisition" and "consideration" under intervention orders, on the one hand, and "purchase" and "price" under guardianship, on the other, it would appear that the scope of the former is intended to be wider, covering tenancies and any other method of "acquisition". However, "disposal" in both sets of provisions, not limited to "sale" in the case of guardianship, indicates that the provisions of Schedule 2, para.6 should be followed for any disposal of accommodation, whether owned, rented, life-rented or otherwise held by the adult, and whether by sale, renunciation or any other method. "Accommodation used for the time being as a dwelling house, by the adult" in both s.53(6) and Schedule 2, para.6 is a relatively narrow definition which may nevertheless raise questions of interpretation on occasion. In a recent unreported case, it was held not to apply to the adult's one-half interest in her former home, where she had not resided and which she had not been able even to visit for some years. In difficult cases, consideration of the status of the adult's current accommodation may assist. A nursing or care home may be the adult's permanent and sole dwelling: a hospital, even during an extended stay, may not. It is of course within the sheriff's discretion to direct that acquisition or disposal of an interest in heritage be subject to the Public Guardian's approval as to consideration or other aspects, whether or not the definition applies, rendering

---

[32] Under an intervention order "the authority".
[33] s.53(6).

the distinction of little practical significance in such cases—see Style C in Appendix 6.

Duties, liabilities, supervision

10–60   Persons authorised under intervention orders are obliged to comply with the first four general principles, and guardians with all five (see paras 4–2 to 4–22 above). All appointees have the fiduciary duties and duty of care described in paras 4–31 et seq. above. They must not purport to act outwith the powers conferred on them by the sheriff or by the Act. They must repay, with interest at the rate applicable to sheriff court decrees, any funds of the adult used in breach of fiduciary duty, outwith their authority or power to intervene, or after receiving intimation of termination or suspension of such authority or power.[34] In the case of guardians, see also the provisions of s.69 and Schedule 2, paras 8(6) and (7).[35] All appointees are however exempted from liability for acts or omissions which are in breach of fiduciary duties or duties of care, if the act or omission is reasonable, in good faith and in accordance with the general principles.[36] An appointee with personal powers who ill-treats or wilfully neglects the adult is guilty of an offence and liable on summary conviction to imprisonment for a maximum of six months or a fine not exceeding the statutory maximum, or both; and upon conviction on indictment, to imprisonment for a maximum of two years or a fine, or both.[37] While the function of the Part 6 Code is to provide guidance as to the exercise of functions by appointees and related matters,[38] and while such guidance as to good practice is not binding, nevertheless a failure without good and proper reason to follow good practice as described in the Code could justify investigation or sanctions, including under the provisions described in paras 10–63 to 10–67 below and 11–68 to 11–73 below. Information and advice may be sought from the Public Guardian by appointees with management powers,[39] and from the Mental Welfare Commission[40] or local authority[41] by appointees with welfare powers.

Records

10–61   All appointees are required to keep records of the exercise of their powers.[42] The Part 6 Code gives guidance on the records to be kept in paras 2.86 et seq., 4.70 et seq. and 5.43 et seq.

Liability

10–62   Under s.67(4)[43] an appointee is personally liable under any transaction entered by him in two situations. Firstly, subject to the exception mentioned below he is so liable if he transacts without

---

[34] s.81.
[35] See paras 11–36 and 11–65 *infra*.
[36] s.82.
[37] s.83.
[38] s.13.
[39] s.6(2)(e).
[40] s.9(1)(g).
[41] s.10(1)(e).
[42] ss.54 and 65.
[43] Applied to appointees under intervention orders by s.53(14) and to foreign guardians by s.67(7).

disclosing that he is acting as such appointee. Secondly, he is so liable if the transaction falls outwith the scope of his authority. The exception relates to an appointee who enters a transaction without disclosing that he is acting in that capacity but who is not otherwise in breach of any requirement of the Act: in such a case, the appointee is still personally liable but is entitled to be reimbursed from the estate of the adult in respect of any loss suffered by him in consequence of a claim made upon him personally by virtue of s.67(4). Unless and until the adult's estate is able to reimburse him, he bears the liability personally.

The sheriff

In addition to the various functions and powers of the sheriff described in this and the next chapter, application may be made to the sheriff by an appointee, the adult or anyone else claiming an interest to give directions under s.3(3) to the appointee as to the exercise of the appointee's functions and the taking by the appointee of decisions or action in relation to the adult.[44] See para.5–15 on suggestions as to the principles which the Scottish courts might find it appropriate to apply in deciding when they should intervene by giving such directions to an appointee. The sheriff may also receive applications from the authorities mentioned in the next three paragraphs following investigation as there described.[45] **10–63**

The Public Guardian

In addition to his various specific functions described in this and the next chapter, the Public Guardian has a general function of supervising appointees with management powers[46]; and receiving and investigating complaints about such appointees.[47] Appointees, regardless of their powers, may be subject to investigation where the adult's property or financial affairs seem to the Public Guardian to be at risk.[48] See also paras 5–23 to 5–27 above. **10–64**

Mental Welfare Commission

In addition to particular functions mentioned elsewhere in this and the next chapter, Mental Welfare Commission has the following functions where an adult is subject to an intervention or guardianship order with welfare powers, except where incapacity is due only to physical inability to communicate. The Commission has the function of exercising protective functions in relation to the adult.[49] The visiting obligation of the Commission includes such adults.[50] The Commission **10–65**

---

[44] See para.5–14 *supra*.
[45] s.12(1).
[46] s.6(2), backed up, in the case of guardianship, with power to give orders or demands in relation to management powers with which the guardian must comply, s.64(7): see para.11–41 *infra*.
[47] s.6(2)(c).
[48] s.6(2)(d).
[49] s.9(1)(a)—note that this applies even where there is an intervention order with no appointee, under s.53(5)(a), if the order relates to personal welfare matters: but see para.5–32 *supra*.
[50] s.9(1)(b): but see para.5–32 *supra*.

can receive and investigate complaints about appointees with welfare powers if the local authority has failed to investigate or has not investigated to the Commission's satisfaction.[51] Appointees, regardless of their powers, may be subject to investigation where the adult's welfare seems to the Commission to be at risk.[52] See also paras 5–28 to 5–32.

Local authority

10–66   In addition to various functions described elsewhere in this and the next chapter, local authorities have a duty to supervise all guardians with welfare powers in the exercise of functions relating to the adult's personal welfare.[53] There is no equivalent general duty to supervise appointees under intervention orders with personal welfare functions, but such supervision may be ordered by the sheriff in particular cases: under s.3(2)(a) the sheriff may make any order subject to conditions, so that such supervision could be ordered either in the original intervention order or in any variation thereof under s.53(8), or possibly upon an application for directions under s.3(3).[54] The Adults with Incapacity (Supervision of Welfare Guardians etc. by Local Authorities) (Scotland) Regulations 2002 (SSI 2002/95)[55] apply both to welfare guardians and to appointees under intervention orders where supervision by the local authority has been ordered. Under regulation 2, the local authority must arrange for the adult and the guardian or the appointee under the intervention order to be visited on behalf of the local authority at specified times and intervals. Both the adult and the guardian or appointee may be visited at the same time where the local authority consider it appropriate. Under guardianship orders for one year or more, the adult must be visited from time to time, but in any case within three months of the granting of the order and at intervals not exceeding three months thereafter; and the guardian must be visited from time to time, but in any case at intervals not exceeding three months, except where the chief officer is guardian. Under guardianship orders for less than one year, both adult and guardian must be visited within 14 days either side of the mid-point of the period of appointment, and during the last 14 days of the appointment. Under an intervention order, the adult and the appointee must be visited as often as required by the sheriff; and if the sheriff has not specified the times or intervals for visits, at intervals not exceeding one month during the period for which local authority supervision has been ordered by the sheriff.[56] At consultation upon the Regulations, concerns were expressed that fixed requirements for visiting could disrupt reasonable activities by the adult, such as holidays, or could force local authorities to visit at a time when, in the local authority's reasonable judgement, it could for some reason be seriously inappropriate to do so. Regulation 2(5) permits the local

---

[51] s.9(1)(d).
[52] s.9(1)(e): but see para.5–32 *supra*.
[53] s.10(1)(a).
[54] See paras 5–14 and 5–15 *supra*.
[55] Made under s.10(3)(a) and (b)(i).
[56] The wording of reg.2(3) purports to cover supervision of the adult under an intervention order under s.53(5)(a) where there is no appointee, but that goes beyond the scope authorised by s.10(3)(b)(i).

authority some flexibility to visit the adult as close to the required time as the adult's circumstances will allow, where "the circumstances of an adult are such that it is not possible for a local authority to visit that adult within the time periods specified in this Regulation". Under regulation 3, guardians and appointees are required to provide to the local authority any reports or other information about the adult's personal welfare, or about the exercise by the guardian or appointee of powers and functions in relation to the adult's welfare, as the local authority may require to enable the local authority to carry out its supervisory functions.

Issues may arise as to the scope of "supervise" in terms of s.10(1)(a). Having regard to the terms of s.10(3) and the Regulations themselves, it would appear that supervisory powers are limited to visiting and receiving information as described in the preceding paragraph. The draft Bill annexed to the SLC Report contained, in clause 49(c), a requirement upon guardians to "comply with any order or demand made . . . by the local authority in relation to the personal welfare" of the adult. That provision was quite inappropriate, because guardians should not be the puppets of local authorities and on occasions may require, in the adult's best interests, to challenge local authorities. Accordingly, no equivalent provision was included in the Act, either as introduced or as enacted. This clearly contrasts with s.64(7), which retains a requirement upon financial guardians to comply with orders or demands made by the Public Guardian. On the other hand, an amendment at stage 2 to alter "supervise" to "monitor" was unsuccessful (though the official Explanatory Notes use "monitor"). Moreover, under s.73 the local authority may (subject to right of appeal to the sheriff) recall the welfare powers of a guardian if the criteria in s.73(3)(a) or (b) apply. Accordingly, it is probably reasonable to view the supervisory function under subs.(1)(a) as ensuring that guardians with welfare powers discharge their functions properly, but not inhibiting proper discharge of those functions even when that may entail conflict with the local authority. In any situation where there is a significant dispute between guardian and local authority as to whether the guardian is acting on the one hand inappropriately, or on the other hand properly but in a manner inconvenient to the local authority, it would probably be better for the matter to be referred to the Mental Welfare Commission under s.9(1), or to the sheriff for directions under s.3(3). The local authority has the function of receiving and investigating complaints about appointees with personal powers.[57] Appointees, regardless of their powers, may be subject to investigation where the adult's personal welfare seems to the local authority to be at risk.[58] See also paras 5–33 and 5–34. **10–67**

Protection of third parties

Third parties transacting in good faith and for value with an appointee purporting to act as such are afforded protection under s.53(11) in the case of intervention orders and s.67(6) in the case of guardianship, which are in substantially the same terms. Such transactions are not invalid on the ground only that (a) the appointee acted **10–68**

---

[57] s.10(1)(c).
[58] s.10(1)(d).

outwith the scope of his authority; or (b) the appointee failed to observe any requirement, whether substantive or procedural, imposed by or under the Act, or by the sheriff or by the Public Guardian; or (c) there was any irregularity, whether substantive or procedural, in the appointment of the appointee.

10–69 A third party in good faith is entitled to rely on the authority of an appointee with welfare and/or management powers, notwithstanding that such authority is terminated or has otherwise ended, if the third party is unaware of such termination or ending.[59] This would appear to cover *inter alia* expiry of a guardianship order, if the third party was aware of the order but unaware of its duration. See also para.10–58 on the protection of third parties in relation to heritable property, and para.11–10 where third parties deal with a joint guardian. See para.10–62 on appointees failing to disclose that they are acting as such, or acting outwith their authority.

Inter-relationship with other techniques

10–70 With some qualifications and one exception, the Act provides that powers granted under intervention or guardianship orders exclude and supersede other measures under the Act. Authority to intromit is excluded under s.34 where such powers already exist, and superseded under s.31(7) if they are granted. Management of residents' finances is disapplied under s.46. Authority to treat is disapplied under s.49, subject to the qualifications in that section, when the responsible medical practitioner[60] is aware of a pending application for relevant powers; and disapplied under s.50(2) where such powers are in force, unless the responsible medical practitioner is unaware of the appointment or it would be unreasonable or impracticable to obtain the appointee's consent.[61] The exception is in relation to powers of attorney. Under s.24(2), the authority of a continuing or welfare attorney in relation to any matter comes to an end on the appointment of a guardian with powers relating to that matter, but there is no equivalent provision in relation to intervention orders, therefore if it is desired to supersede an attorney's powers with an intervention order, simultaneous application to revoke the powers under s.20(2)(e)(i) would appear to be necessary. Where there is any possibility that it might in future be appropriate to allow an attorney's powers to revive, a guardianship order would be inappropriate (by reference *inter alia* to the first three general principles). In such a situation under an intervention order, no action would be necessary if the attorney were co-operative, and otherwise the sheriff could be asked to give appropriate directions to the attorney under s.3(3).[62] It appears that the principal enabling provisions of ss.53(5) and 64(1) and (3) mean that powers under an intervention or guardianship order, where they are competent and are conferred, will for the duration of the order supersede the same powers conferred under any non-Act measures.

---

[59] s.77(3).
[60] "The medical practitioner primarily responsible for the treatment of the adult"—see paras 14–2, 14–43 and 14–46 *infra*.
[61] See paras 14–46 and 14–54 to 14–57 *infra*, including as to procedures where there is disagreement between the responsible medical practitioner and the appointee, or with other persons having an interest.
[62] See para.5–14 *supra*.

Termination of authority (including death of adult)

10-71 An order ceases to have effect on the adult's death.[63] Where an appointee has management powers, the appointee is entitled to continue to act under those powers until he becomes aware of the adult's death or of any other event which has the effect of terminating his authority, if he acts in good faith.[64] The limitation of this provision to management powers appears to assume that an appointee with welfare powers would be immediately aware of the adult's death or other termination, though the provisions described in the next paragraph apply to both categories of powers. There is an apparent omission in the Act in that whereas s.22 obliges an attorney to notify the Public Guardian of the death of the grantor and obliges the attorney's personal representatives, if aware of the existence of the power of attorney, to notify the Public Guardian of the death of the attorney, there are no equivalent provisions in relation to the deaths of adults subject to intervention or guardianship orders or appointees under such orders, except for the obligation of a substitute guardian to notify the Public Guardian of the death (or incapacity) of the "original guardian".[65]

INTERVENTION ORDERS—FURTHER PROVISIONS

Interim orders

10-72 The sheriff's general powers under s.3 include power to make such interim order as appears to the sheriff to be appropriate.[66] While s.3 applies equally to guardianship applications, there are specific interim powers under guardianship procedure.[67]

Variation and recall

10-73 Under s.53(8) the sheriff may make an order varying the terms of an intervention order or recalling it, and may also recall or vary "any other order made for the purposes of the intervention order". The sheriff may make any such order on the application of the person authorised under the intervention order, or the adult, or any person claiming an interest in the adult's affairs or welfare.

Outlays

10-74 A person authorised under an intervention order may recover from the adult's estate the amount of such reasonable outlays as that appointee incurs in doing anything directed or authorised under the order.[68]

---

[63] s.77(1).
[64] s.77(2).
[65] s.63(8). See para.11–16 *infra*.
[66] s.3(2)(d)—see para.5–6 *supra*.
[67] See paras 11–19 to 11–21 *infra*.
[68] s.53(12).

Change of address

10–75 Once particulars of an intervention order have been registered with the Public Guardian,[69] the person authorised under the intervention order must notify the Public Guardian of any change in his or the adult's address. Surprisingly, there is no time limit for doing so, notwithstanding a seven-day time limit for guardians under their equivalent obligation.[70] Upon receiving notification, the Public Guardian enters prescribed particulars in the relevant register[71] and notifies the local authority and (except where incapacity results solely from physical inability to communicate) the Mental Welfare Commission.[72]

Appointee as "guardian"?

10–76 Issues may arise as to whether "guardian" in legislation prior to the Incapacity Act should now in some cases be interpreted as including an appointee under an intervention order with relevant powers. Possible candidates for such interpretation include the tax and other provisions referred to in para.11–60 below.

Intervention orders under criminal procedure

10–77 An intervention order may be made by the court under s.60B of the Criminal Procedure (Scotland) Act 1995.[73] This and other principally relevant sections of the 1995 Act are reproduced in Appendix 3. Under s.57(2)(c) of the 1995 Act, the court may make a guardianship order where the court acquits a person on the grounds of insanity at the time of alleged commission of the offence charged, or makes a finding at an examination of facts that the person did the act or made the omission constituting the offence and that there were no grounds for acquittal. Under s.58(1) and (1A) of that Act, where a person is convicted in the High Court or sheriff court of an offence which is punishable by the court with imprisonment or detention and which is not an offence for which the sentence is fixed by law, the court may make a hospital order or a guardianship order. Section 60B is in brief terms, and provides that "instead of making a hospital order . . . or a guardianship order" under the foregoing provisions, the court may make an intervention order as defined in s.53(1) of the Incapacity Act where the court considers that it would be appropriate to do so.[74] Under s.58A(1)(b) of the 1995 Act, the provisions of Parts 1, 5, 6 and 7 of the Incapacity Act apply to a person authorised under an intervention order under s.60B of the 1995 Act in the same way as they apply to a person authorised under an intervention order under s.53 of the Incapacity Act.

---

[69] See para.10–54 *supra*.
[70] Under s.64(4)—see para.11–27 *infra*.
[71] See s.6(2)(b)(v).
[72] s.55.
[73] c.46. Note that the relevant amendments to the 1995 Act contained in s.84 and in para.26(3) of Sch.5 to the Incapacity Act were in turn amended by para.23(5) and (7) of Sch.3 to ROCSA 2001. The further amendments included re-numbering of the relevant section from 60A to 60B, necessary because the Crime and Punishment (Scotland) Act 1997 (c.48), s.22 had already added a s.60A to the 1995 Act.
[74] The effect of s.58(1A)(b) of the 1995 Act is that the court must make an intervention order rather than a guardianship order if satisfied that the former will sufficiently safeguard or promote the person's welfare—see para.11–86 *infra*.

10-78 The guardianship provisions of the 1995 Act are described in paras 11–84 to 11–91 below. For guardianship, the procedural requirements of the 1995 Act substantially replicate those of the Incapacity Act. There is no equivalent replication of procedural requirements in relation to intervention orders. This points to an interpretation that "instead of making a hospital order . . . or a guardianship order" means that the sheriff may in his discretion make an intervention order only if the procedural requirements under the 1995 Act for a hospital or guardianship order have been followed.

CHAPTER 11

GUARDIANSHIP—FURTHER PROVISIONS

INTRODUCTION

This chapter should be read as a continuation, in relation to guardian- **11–1** ship only, of Chapter 10. In this chapter the chief social work officer of the local authority is for convenience referred to as "the chief officer". As in paras 10–46 *et seq.*, "welfare powers" means limited or plenary powers in relation to personal welfare, "management powers" means limited or plenary powers in relation to property and financial affairs, "combined powers" means limited or plenary powers in respect of both welfare and management matters, and "affairs or welfare" means property, financial affairs or personal welfare. A "welfare guardian" is a guardian with welfare powers only and a "financial guardian" is a guardian with management powers only. References to "the relevant register" mean the register established under s.6(2)(b)(iv), and references to "the Code" mean the Code of Practice for Persons authorised under Intervention Orders and Guardians.[1] The Rules referred to are (unless otherwise specified) those in the Act of Sederunt (Summary Applications, Statutory Applications and Appeals etc. Rules) 1999 as amended by SSI 2001/142 and SSI 2002/146.[2]

GUARDIANS

Individual as guardian

Except where the chief officer is appointed (see paras 11–3 *et seq.* **11–2** below), and except for appointments under Criminal Procedure (Scotland) Act 1995[3] under which the guardian is the local authority or a person approved by the local authority, only an individual can be guardian.[4] The individual may be any individual who has consented

---

[1] SE/2002/65, issued March 2002 pursuant to s.13(3). Elsewhere called "the Part 6 Code".

[2] See para.5–5 *supra*.

[3] (c.46), as amended by s.84 of and Sch.5, para.26 to the Incapacity Act (as further amended by the Regulation of Care (Scotland) Act 2001 (asp 8), Sch.3, para.23(7)). See paras 11–84 to 11–89 *infra*.

[4] s.59(1), which distinguishes between an "individual" (s.59(1)(a)) and the chief officer (s.59(1)(b)), so that the requirements of s.59(3) and (4) do not apply to the latter. That the Parliament intended these as alternatives, and the only alternatives, is confirmed by the terms of s.71(1)(a).

to be appointed and whom the sheriff considers to be suitable for appointment,[5] but the sheriff may not appoint an individual as guardian unless the sheriff is satisfied that the individual is aware of the adult's circumstances and condition, of the needs arising from the adult's circumstances and condition, and of the functions of a guardian.[6] Section 59(4) lists criteria to which the sheriff must have regard when determining suitability for appointment. The criteria are: (a) the accessibility of the individual to the adult and to the adult's primary carer; (b) the ability of the individual to carry out the functions of a guardian; (c) any likely conflict of interest between the adult and the individual; (d) any undue concentration of power which is likely to arise in the individual over the adult; (e) any adverse effects which the appointment of the individual would have on the interests of the adult; and (f) such other matters as appear to the sheriff to be appropriate. However, likely conflict of interest under criterion (c) and undue concentration of power under (d) are not to be regarded as applying to an individual only because the individual is a close relative of the adult, or resides with the adult.[7] Nominees may often be suitable, and in particular suitable by reference to criteria (a) and (b), precisely because *inter alia* they are closely related to the adult and/or reside with the adult, but in the exception "only" is nevertheless important, and close relationship or residing together could be relevant where there are other substantial reasons for considering that conflict of interest would be likely, or that there would be undue concentration of power. It is for the sheriff, in each case, to assess these criteria and the relative weight to be given to each, but it would be surprising if an individual were to be appointed if the sheriff formed a significantly negative view in relation to any of criteria (a), (b) or (e) or, subject to the disregard of "only" close relationship or living together, criteria (c) or (d). The provisions described in this paragraph all apply whether the nominee is to have welfare, management or combined powers. The remoteness and disengagement of some curators bonis was one of the serious deficiencies of curatory practice: nominees for financial guardianship, by contrast, must *inter alia* be demonstrably aware of the adult's circumstances, condition and needs, and their suitability must be assessed *inter alia* by reference to their accessibility to the adult. It is suggested that "accessibility" in criterion (a) means not merely proximity or theoretical availability, but a working relationship with appropriate levels of contact and communication.

Chief officer as guardian

11–3 The "chief social work officer of the local authority" ("chief officer") is not defined in the Incapacity Act, but may reasonably be presumed to be the person defined as such in Social Work (Scotland) Act 1968[8]: see para.5–35 above. For the purposes of the Act, the local authority is the council for the area in which the adult resides.[9] The chief officer

---

[5] s.59(1)(a).
[6] s.59(3).
[7] s.59(5).
[8] (c.49) s.3.
[9] s.87(1), under which the council is the council constituted under s.2 of the Local Government etc. (Scotland) Act 1994 (c.39).

may be appointed guardian only with personal powers, either upon an application for guardianship with personal powers only[10] or upon an application for appointment of joint guardians under which all management powers are conferred on one or more individuals.[11] Where the adult whose guardian is the chief officer moves to another local authority area, the chief officer of the new area becomes guardian under the procedure described in para.11–5 below, without further court order. For the purposes of investigative powers under s.10(1)(d) where the adult's welfare seems to be at risk, "local authority" is extended to include the authority for the area where the adult is present,[12] but there is no equivalent extension in relation to the Act's guardianship provisions. On the other hand, in an emergency an intervention order might be more appropriate, under which the appointee may be simply the "person nominated", without restriction.[13] The possibility of appointing the chief officer should be seen in the context of the local authority's duty under s.57(2) to apply for appointment when a guardian is needed and no-one else applies or is likely to,[14] and the provisions of s.68(3) that the appointment of the chief social work officer as guardian will not cost the adult anything.[15] These are "safety-net" provisions to ensure that the protection of welfare guardianship will be available without cost to those who need it. However the sheriff might require to consider competing applications, one proposing an individual as welfare guardian and the other proposing the chief officer. If the sheriff is satisfied that a welfare guardian is needed and that the individual meets the requirements of s.59(3), then assessment of the suitability of the individual in relation to the criteria in s.59(4) is likely to include comparative assessment of those criteria in relation to the alternative of the chief officer. If the adult is substantially dependent on local authority services, an individual who—considered alone—is suitable to be the guardian may frequently be more suitable than the chief social work officer as regards criteria (c) and (d) of s.59(4), and also criterion (b) (in that ability to carry out the function will reasonably include sufficient independence to represent the adult's interests effectively when dealing with authorities). Article V of the Declaration on General and Special Rights of the Mentally Retarded of Inclusion International, then named the International League of Societies for Persons with Mental Handicap (not incorporated into any international obligations, but persuasive) includes a provision that: "No person rendering direct services to the mentally retarded should also serve as his guardian".

Responsible officer

Where the chief officer is appointed welfare guardian, under s.64(9) **11–4** he must intimate the name of "the officer responsible at any time for carrying out the functions and duties of guardian". The intimation

---

[10] s.59(1)(b).
[11] s.59(2).
[12] s.10(2).
[13] s.53(5)(b)—see paras 10–47 and 10–49 *supra*.
[14] See para.10–47 *supra*.
[15] See para.11–34 *infra*.

must be given to the same persons to whom notification of the chief officer's appointment as guardian was given under s.58(7) (see para.10–54 above). Note that under s.64(10) the chief officer must not notify the adult if in the relevant proceedings the sheriff has directed that intimation or notification should not be given to the adult.[16] Intimation under s.64(9) must be given "not later than 7 working days after his appointment", but in view of the reference in that subsection to "the officer responsible at any time", it appears that "his appointment" may require to be construed as referring to the appointment of the responsible officer, rather than the appointment of the chief officer as guardian. However, even if that should be the correct interpretation, the importance attached to this matter in s.64 and in s.76[17] indicates that the Parliament envisaged that the adult and others should not be left longer than seven days in ignorance of the identity of the individual actually responsible for guardianship functions, and it would accordingly be inappropriate for the chief officer to delay appointing the responsible officer, or appointing a replacement when needed. A significant criticism of the previous law was that while even a curator bonis (the approximate equivalent of a guardian with property and financial powers) could only be an individual, and not an impersonal entity or even a partnership,[18] the local authority could be an MHSA guardian[19] and such impersonal appointments were actually made, and continued to be made. In relation to welfare powers even more than to property and financial powers, guardianship powers should only be exercised by an identified and known individual. Section 64(9) is designed to ensure this.[20]

Change of local authority area

11–5 Section 76 applies where the chief officer is guardian and the adult changes his place of habitual residence to another local authority area. Formerly, there was experience in practice of unsatisfactory discontinuity when an adult under MHSA guardianship made such a move. Under s.76, the chief officer for the original area must notify the chief officer of the local authority for the new area, termed the "receiving area". Upon receipt of such notification, the chief officer for the receiving area automatically becomes guardian. Within seven days of receipt of the notification, the chief officer for the receiving area must notify (a) the Public Guardian, (b) except where the adult is incapable only because of physical inability to communicate, the Mental Welfare Commission, and (c) the same persons to whom notification of the appointment as guardian of the original chief officer by the sheriff was given under s.58(7) (see para.10–54 above), subject to the exception under s.76(4) that the chief officer must not notify the adult if in the relevant proceedings the sheriff had directed that intimation or notification should not be given to the adult.[21] Subject to the same

---

[16] See also s.11 and paras 5–9 and 5–25 *supra*.
[17] See para.11–5 *infra*.
[18] *McFarlane v Donaldson* (1835) 13 S. 725; *Brogan, Petr*, 1986 S.L.T. 420.
[19] MHSA, s.37(2)(a).
[20] The subsection was strengthened at stage 3 to require notification within seven days of initial appointment, and any change, of the identity of the responsible officer.
[21] See also s.11 and paras 5–9 and 5–25 *supra*. These provisions mirror those of s.64(9) and (10), described in para.11–4 *supra*.

exception, the Public Guardian is also required to notify the adult, within seven days of receipt by the Public Guardian of the notification from the receiving authority. The Public Guardian is also required to enter prescribed particulars in the relevant register and to issue a certificate of appointment to the chief officer of the receiving authority as the new guardian.

Joint and concurrent guardians

Under s.58(5), two or more guardians may be appointed to act concurrently with different powers. Under s.62, two or more guardians may be appointed to act jointly, sharing the same powers. Section 58(5) is "without prejudice to the power under s.62(1) to appoint joint guardians", indicating that "joint" applies only to appointments under s.62, and not to appointments under s.58(5). The Act does not use the term "concurrent guardians", but it is adopted here to mark the distinction. There appears to be no reason why both possibilities should not be combined. Examples would be A and B appointed jointly as financial guardians and the chief officer appointed concurrently as welfare guardian; or A and B appointed jointly as welfare guardians and A also acting concurrently as sole financial guardian (an "overlapping appointment"). These provisions are in addition to the possibility of appointing a substitute guardian.[22] Under former law, a tutor-dative could be appointed with personal powers to act concurrently with a curator bonis, who of course had financial powers only.[23] Dual and triple joint appointments of tutors-dative with welfare powers were common, as described in paras 10–19 and 10–20 above, but (as suggested there) the availability of substitute appointments under the Incapacity Act may reduce the numbers appointed as joint guardians. In particular, appointments of two joint guardians with one substitute may largely replace triple appointments. Joint appointment of tutors-dative with management powers was competent under former law, though to the author's knowledge that did not occur in modern use. In practical terms, the availability of joint appointees as financial guardians is an innovation, not competent under curatory.[24]

11–6

Concurrent guardians

Section 58(5) is brief, and the Act contains no other explicit references to what are here termed concurrent appointments, except for the provisions of s.68 concerning allocation of costs under concurrent appointments where the chief officer is welfare guardian (see para.11–34 below). In particular, while s.62(7) provides for consultation among joint guardians, there is no equivalent provision in relation to concurrent appointments. However, it is difficult to conceive of a case where a sheriff would not consider it appropriate and necessary to make a direction under s.1(4)(c)(ii) that each concurrent guardian should act in consultation with the other.[25] An "overlapping

11–7

---

[22] s.63, see para.11–14 *infra*.
[23] As in *Dick v Douglas*, 1924 S.C. 287; 1924 S.L.T. 578.
[24] *McFarlane v Donaldson* (1835) 13 S. 725; *Brogan, Petr* 1986 S.L.T. 420.
[25] See para.4–20 *supra*.

appointment", as described in para.11–6 above, might sometimes be better. Under s.58(5) the concurrent guardians may be two or more individuals, or chief officer (as welfare guardian) plus one or more individuals. The allocation of powers need not be simply as between personal and management powers. Concurrent guardians could each have different personal powers allocated to them, or different management powers. This may well occur occasionally: some grantors of powers of attorney have found it appropriate to make such allocations. In general, concurrent appointments create concurrent but separate limited guardianships to each of which the relevant provisions of the Act's régime apply (including those regarding sole and joint guardians, as the case may be).

Joint guardians

11–8   Under s.62, joint guardians may be appointed in two ways. They may be appointed at the same time, or one may be appointed subsequently to the original appointment, as additional guardian. Both types of appointment may occur in relation to the same guardianship: for example, A and B may initially be appointed joint guardians, with C appointed later as additional joint guardian. Section 62(1) appears to make the following distinction. Under s.62(1)(a) "two or more individuals" may seek joint appointment, therefore it would not appear possible under that paragraph to appoint an individual as welfare guardian jointly with the chief officer. Under s.62(1)(b) additional appointment may be sought jointly with one or more "existing guardians", which would not appear to render incompetent an application by an individual for appointment as additional welfare guardian jointly with the chief officer as "existing guardian". Particular provisions for additional appointments are described in paras 11–11 and 11–12 below. Where the initial application seeks joint appointments under s.62(1)(a), the provisions of s.58 regarding disposal of the application[26] and of s.59 as to who may be appointed guardian[27] apply.[28] The provisions described in the next two paragraphs apply to all joint guardians, whether appointed initially or additionally.

Who may be appointed joint guardians

11–9   Section 62(2) provides that joint guardians shall not be appointed to an adult unless either (a) the individuals so appointed are parents, siblings or children of the adult, or (b) the sheriff is satisfied that, in the circumstances, it is appropriate to appoint as joint guardians individuals who are not related to the adult as mentioned in (a). The existence of (a) is peculiar. For sole appointments, which are more critical to the extent that all powers granted are concentrated in one individual, there is nothing in the Act to suggest that close relatives are to be preferred for appointment, and it would be naïve to assume that close relationship to the adult would by itself ensure harmonious discharge of joint responsibilities. It cannot be intended that the

---

[26] See paras 10–27 et seq. supra.
[27] See paras 11–2 and 11–3 supra.
[28] s.62(3).

sheriff should proceed under (a) without regard to the appropriateness in the circumstances of the joint appointments proposed, because he could hardly be satisfied under s.59 as to the appropriateness of each nominee without regard to the fact that a joint appointment is proposed. It is strange that where the adult is a widow with two children, they can be appointed under (a), whereas if her husband survives and they have one child, the husband and child would have to proceed under (b). As described in para.10–19 above, the majority of appointments of tutors-dative since revival in 1986 were joint appointments. Several individuals so appointed have been more distant relatives than specified in (a), or unrelated. Several strong appointments have comprised one close relative and one person, caring and concerned but with the greater objectivity of being more distantly related, or unrelated. The appointment of a couple, married to each other but unrelated to the adult for whom they care on a long-term basis, has also proved to be appropriate. It is suggested that s.62 does not create any presumption against joint appointees who are not relatives within (a), merely a requirement to satisfy the court as to appropriateness, and it is to be expected that in practice courts will frequently be so satisfied.

Actings, consultation, disagreement, third parties

Section 62(6) provides that, subject to the consultation provisions of **11–10** s.62(7), joint guardians may exercise their functions individually; and that each shall be liable for any loss or injury caused to the adult arising out of his own acts or omissions. Section 62(6) also imposes an obligation on each joint guardian to take reasonable steps to ensure that no other joint guardian breaches any duty of care or fiduciary duty owed to the adult: that obligation is created by providing that a joint guardian is liable for any loss or injury caused to the adult arising out of his failure to take such reasonable steps. Where more than one joint guardians incur liability under s.62(6), their liability is joint and several. Under s.62(7), a joint guardian is required to consult with the other joint guardian(s) before exercising any of his guardianship functions, unless (a) consultation would be impracticable in the circumstances, or (b) the joint guardians agree that consultation is not necessary. Under exception (b), it seems unlikely that joint guardians would simply agree that consultation is not necessary at all, and more likely that they would agree particular categories of matters in which consultation was unnecessary (or perhaps particular circumstances, though such circumstances would probably be covered by (a)). Joint guardians would be wise to record any such agreements.[29] Where joint guardians disagree as to the exercise of their functions, s.62(8) provides that either or both may apply for directions under s.3[30]: s.62(8) would seem to have been inserted as a signpost, because the wording of s.3(3) is sufficiently broad that the position would have been the same even without s.62(8).[31] A third party in good faith is

---

[29] As to the obligation to keep records, see s.65 and para.10–61 *supra*. *Cf.* the provisions of the *Style* Power of Attorney in Appendix 5 as to matters in which either joint attorney can act alone and matters where they must act together.

[30] See s.3(3) and para.5–14 *supra*.

[31] There seems no reason to doubt that joint attorneys could use s.3(3) similarly, in the absence of express provision equivalent to s.62(8). Concurrent guardians, or one or more of them, could likewise use s.3(3) in the event of disagreement.

entitled to rely on the authority to act of any one or more joint guardians.[32]

Additional guardian

11–11 As explained in para.11–8 above, joint guardians may be appointed when the guardianship order is first granted, or under s.62(1)(b) application may subsequently be made to the sheriff by an individual for his own appointment as an additional guardian jointly with one or more existing guardians. Such an application is an application for appointment of an additional guardian under an existing guardianship order, not an application for a new guardianship order, therefore the only provisions of other sections applied to such an application are those of s.59(3)–(5), as to the matters to which the sheriff should have regard in deciding whether the applicant is suitable for such appointment.[33] The relevant criteria are described in para.11–2 above. Section 59(1)(a), under which the nominee requires to be considered by the sheriff to be suitable and requires to have consented, is not applied to additional appointments. The requirement for suitability is clearly implied by the terms of s.62(4). Evidence of consent is not necessary because only the proposed appointee may apply under s.62(1)(b). See para.11–101 below on appointment of an additional guardian with a transitional guardian.

11–12 Where the sheriff appoints an additional guardian, the sheriff clerk is required to send a copy of the order to the Public Guardian. The Public Guardian is required to enter prescribed particulars in the relevant register. Upon registration, and when satisfied that the guardian has found caution if so required, the Public Guardian issues a certificate of appointment to the additional guardian and a new certificate of appointment "to the existing guardian". As s.62(1)(b) permits additional appointment "jointly with one or more existing guardians", it must be assumed that new certificates should be sent to each existing guardian where they are more than one. The intimation provisions are the same as for initial appointments and the Public Guardian is required, subject to s.11, to notify the adult; to notify the local authority; and except where incapacity arises solely from physical inability to communicate, to notify the Mental Welfare Commission.[34] For the equivalent registration and notification provisions upon original appointment, and comment on the Public Guardian's systems, see para.10–54 above.

Removal and resignation of joint guardian

11–13 Situations where a joint guardian is removed or resigns, the other joint guardian(s) being willing to continue, are provided for in s.71(1)(b)(i) (described in para.11–71 below) as regards removal, and s.75(1) and (2)(a)(i) (described in para.11–80 below) as regards resignation. See also paras 11–74 and 11–81 below on registration and intimation, and issue of a new certificate of appointment to the continuing guardian.

---

[32] s.62(9).
[33] s.62(4).
[34] s.62(5).

Substitute guardian

Section 63 provides for appointment of substitute guardians. For the purposes of that section, the guardian to whom the substitute is appointed is termed the "original guardian".[35] Application may be made to the sheriff to appoint a substitute guardian at the same time as the application for appointment of the original guardian, or at any time thereafter, and there is no distinction between substitutes appointed originally or subsequently. The substitute may be either an individual or the chief officer, but may be appointed only to an original guardian who is an individual. If the substitute is an individual, the substitute must satisfy the requirements of s.59 described in para.11–2 above.[36] The appointment of the substitute is for the same period as for the appointment of the original guardian,[37] which presumably means the remaining period of the original appointment where the substitute is appointed subsequently to the original appointment. Where the substitute is appointed at the same time as the original guardian, registration and notification is covered by the provisions described in para.10–54 above, under which there is no explicit requirement to notify the adult of the appointment of the substitute. Where the substitute is appointed subsequently, the sheriff clerk is required to send a copy of the interlocutor containing the substitute appointment to the Public Guardian. See para.11–101 below on appointment of a substitute to a transitional guardian. The Public Guardian is required to enter prescribed particulars in the relevant register; subject to s.11,[38] to notify the adult; to notify the local authority; and except where incapacity arises solely from physical inability to communicate, to notify the Mental Welfare Commission.[39]

11–14

Caution

As with original appointments, where the sheriff appoints a substitute with management powers, the sheriff must require the substitute to find caution, except where the appointee is unable to find caution but the sheriff is satisfied that the appointee is nevertheless suitable to be appointed.[40] It would appear that it is not necessary for the substitute to comply with this requirement unless and until the substitution is triggered, because the substitute requires to satisfy the Public Guardian that he has found caution before the Public Guardian registers the triggering of the substitution (see next paragraph), rather than prior to registering the appointment.[41] Where the sheriff did not dispense with caution in the original order, but caution cannot be obtained when the substitution is triggered, the sheriff could be asked to make an ancillary order under s.3(1) dispensing with caution, perhaps linked to a direction to the Public Guardian under s.3(3) confirming that the substitution should be registered notwithstanding that caution has not been found. It is doubtful whether the matter

11–15

---

[35] s.63(2) and (6).
[36] s.63(1), (4) and (6).
[37] s.63(3).
[38] See paras 5–9 and 5–25 *supra*.
[39] s.63(7).
[40] s.63(5).
[41] See ss.63(9)(b) and 63(7)(a) respectively.

could be addressed under the variation provisions of s.74 (see para.11–73 below) because those provisions relate to variation of the powers conferred. If however some variation, however minor, to the powers conferred were sought, then it appears that the sheriff would then have discretion to dispense with caution.[42]

Triggering the substitution

11–16 Section 63(1) refers to the substitution taking effect upon the original guardian "becoming unable to act", but the triggering provisions are more precise. Under s.63(8), substitution is triggered by the death or incapacity of the original guardian. As the definition of incapacity in s.1(6) is not disapplied, substitution will not be competent in the event of disabling physical incapacity. Substitution is triggered under s.71(1)(b)(ii) by the removal of the original guardian, and under s.75(1) and (2)(a)(ii) by the resignation of the original guardian. Under s.63(8) the substitute guardian is required to notify the Public Guardian without delay of the death or incapacity of the original guardian, and as to whether the substitute is prepared to act as guardian. If the original guardian has died, documentary evidence of death must be produced to the Public Guardian, but curiously there is no requirement to produce evidence of incapacity, though it would obviously be good practice to do so.[43] Under s.71(1), if the substitution is to be triggered the sheriff requires to be satisfied that the substitute is prepared to act, and upon the order under that section being made the sheriff clerk is required to send a copy of the interlocutor to the Public Guardian. Under s.75(1) and (2) the original guardian's resignation and evidence of the substitute's willingness to act are notified to the Public Guardian. Under ss.63, 71 and 75 registration and subsequent notification provisions are similar: the Public Guardian is required to enter prescribed particulars in the relevant register; subject to s.11,[44] to notify the adult; to notify the local authority; and except where incapacity arises solely from physical inability to communicate, to notify the Mental Welfare Commission. The substitute takes over with the same functions and powers as were exercised by the original guardian immediately before the substitution was triggered.[45]

Replacement guardian

11–17 The sheriff's powers under s.71 include power, upon application by the adult or anyone claiming a relevant interest, to replace a guardian by an individual meeting the criteria set out in s.59(3)–(5),[46] or by the chief officer. See para.11–70 below. Appointment of a replacement to a transitional guardian is referred to in para.11–101 below.

Transitional guardians

11–18 See paras 11–92 to 11–101 below for description of the transitional provisions under which pre-Act appointees become guardians, and of

---

[42] See s.74(2).
[43] The Part 6 Code is silent on this.
[44] See paras 5–9 and 5–25 *supra*.
[45] s.63(10).
[46] Described in para.11–2 *supra*.

the application of the Act to such guardians. The appointees referred to are curators bonis to adults, tutors-at-law, tutors-dative and MHSA guardians appointed before April 1, 2002 or under proceedings commenced before that date and determined after it, and also curators bonis appointed at any time to children whose appointment continues beyond the child's 16th birthday (who then become guardians under the Act).

Interim guardian

At any time before the disposal of an application for a guardianship **11–19** order, the sheriff may make an order appointing an interim guardian, on an application being made to the sheriff to do so.[47] The application may be made in the crave of the guardianship application or by subsequent motion.[48] The interim appointment lasts for a maximum of three months, and ceases to have effect earlier if recalled or if a guardian is duly appointed under s.58.[49] An interim guardian with management powers is required to report monthly to the Public Guardian as to the exercise of his powers, and an interim guardian with personal powers is required to report similarly to the local authority.[50]

The Act is not explicit as to whether, subject to the provisions **11–20** described in the preceding paragraph, an interim guardian is a guardian for the purposes of all relevant provisions of the Act, but it would appear appropriate to assume that this was the Parliament's intention.[51] On that basis, the criteria for appointment as a guardian described in para.11–2 above will apply. Also, it would appear that care should be taken to ensure that the sheriff is asked to confer upon the interim guardian such powers as will be required to address the matters necessitating the appointment, including any in terms of Schedule 2, para.1(4) (which limits the powers of a financial guardian prior to approval of the management plan unless the sheriff specifically confers wider powers—see para.11–45 below).

The availability of interim appointments may be valuable in urgent **11–21** situations, but "at any time before the disposal of the application" implies that the application requires first to have been competently initiated, so that the reports needed in terms of s.57(3)[52] would require to have been obtained, unless the sheriff were to be persuaded that his powers under s.3[53] enabled him to respond to an emergency before all the requirements of s.57(3) had been met. Having regard to the stipulation of s.58(1)(d) that a guardian should only be appointed

---

[47] s.57(5). This power is in addition to the sheriff's power under s.3(2)(d) to make such interim orders as appear to the sheriff to be appropriate: see paras 5–6 and 10–29 *supra*.
[48] Rule 3.16.11.
[49] s.57(6).
[50] s.64(8).
[51] The contrary argument would be that s.62(3), on joint guardians, specifically applies s.59 to them, whereas s.57(5) contains no such express reference in relation to interim guardians.
[52] See paras 10–48 to 10–50 *supra*.
[53] See para.5–6 *supra*.

if no other means under the Act would suffice, and also having regard to the second general principle,[54] it would appear that interim guardianship should not be sought where an interim order under s.3(2)(d) would suffice.[55] On the same basis, it could be argued that interim guardianship should not be sought where an intervention order would suffice, and indeed in some situations an intervention order might offer more flexibility than interim guardianship. Under s.3(2)(d) an interim order could be made in an application for an intervention order. Under s.58(3) an intervention order can be granted where guardianship has been sought, but this is achieved by empowering the sheriff to treat a guardianship application as an application for an intervention order, so that it might thereafter no longer be possible to seek a permanent guardianship order: it would accordingly appear to be better practice, if an intervention order is likely to be favoured by the sheriff to address immediate needs, to make an initial or concurrent application for an intervention order for that purpose. As to the sheriff's jurisdiction in emergencies, see Schedule 3, paras 1(1)(c), 2(1)(c) and (3), described in para.5–4 above.

DURATION AND RENEWAL

Duration of appointment

11–22 Upon granting a guardianship application, the sheriff is required to make a guardianship order appointing the nominee to be the adult's guardian "for a period of 3 years or such other period (including an indefinite period) as, on cause shown, he may determine".[56] Upon renewal (see para.11–24 below) the period is five years or such other period, including an indefinite period, as the sheriff on cause shown may determine.[57] It would appear that where management powers are conferred under variation procedure on a guardian hitherto having welfare powers only, or vice versa, the normal initial maximum for those new powers will be three years, because s.74(4) requires such variation to proceed as a fresh application under s.57. By inference from the wording of s.57(6), described in para.11–19 above, where there has been an initial interim appointment, the three years will run from the commencement of the full appointment.

11–23 Practice in relation to tutors-dative is described in para.10–18 above. Although a practice developed of appointing tutors-dative for a maximum of 10 years, it should be noted (firstly) that tutory lacked the supervisory and similar provisions of the Incapacity Act and (secondly) the Incapacity Act explicitly authorises appointment of indefinite duration. Situations in which the sheriff might be persuaded to grant an order of indefinite duration would include where the evidence demonstrates that the adult is elderly or has a terminal condition, and that the condition causing incapacity is irreversible. In such situations, even where life expectancy may be short, it may be

---

[54] s.1(3). See paras 4–12 et seq. supra.
[55] See paras 5–6 and 10–29 supra.
[56] s.58(4).
[57] s.60(4)(b).

inappropriate to risk putting all concerned to the trouble of a renewal application if the adult should survive longer than anticipated. On the other hand, and even in such a situation, if there are concerns about the appointment the sheriff may consider it safer to time-limit at least the initial appointment. On cause shown by any party appearing in the application, appointment (or renewal) could be for less than three years (or five years). In the case of a young adult with normal life expectancy and impairments of capacity expected to be lifelong, in considering duration of appointment and renewals it would be reasonable for the sheriff to have regard to the number of times it would be reasonable to require all concerned to go through renewal procedure. One could envisage cases where it might be appropriate to appoint initially for five years, with first renewal for 10 years, second renewal for 15 years, and an indefinite duration on third renewal. As described in the next paragraph, timeous lodging of a renewal application extends the duration of the current order until the renewal application has been determined.[58] The maximum duration for interim guardianship is three months.[59]

Renewal

Under s.60 the provisions for renewal of guardianship are the same **11–24** as for initial appointment, described in paras 10–46 *et seq.* above, subject to the provisions described in this paragraph. Application for renewal may be made at any time before expiry of the previous order. It would appear that if the application is late, then a fresh application rather than a renewal would be required. If the renewal application is made timeously the previous order remains in force until the renewal application has been determined, so that a "bridging" interim appointment is not necessary.[60] The renewal application may be made by the existing guardian[61] or by the local authority in accordance with its duty to apply for renewal if guardianship remains necessary but no renewal application has been made or is likely to be made.[62] Application is made by minute lodged in the original process.[63] Sections 57(3) and 58, described in paras 10–48 *et seq.* and 10–46 *et seq.* (also 10–28) respectively, apply to renewal applications with appropriate adaptation in terminology, the norm for duration being five years rather than three as described in the preceding paragraph.[64] Accordingly, the same requirements for reports apply as for initial appointment, and the same procedural provisions apply. Upon refusal, as well as on granting, of a renewal application the sheriff clerk is required forthwith to send a copy of the relevant interlocutor to the Public Guardian, who registers and notifies in the same manner as for appointment.[65]

---

[58] s.60(1) and (2).
[59] s.57(6). See para.11–19 *supra*.
[60] *cf.* the position under tutor-dative procedure as described in para.10–20.
[61] s.60(1).
[62] s.60(2).
[63] Rule 3.16.8(1). Ch.14 of the Ordinary Cause Rules applies to such minutes—Rule 3.16.8(1A). See para.5–5 *supra*.
[64] s.60(3) and (4).
[65] ss.58(7) and 60(4) and (5). See para.10–54 *supra*.

FUNCTIONS, ACTINGS AND DUTIES

11–25 The provisions and requirements described below apply to both welfare and financial guardianship in addition to those described in paras 10–42 and 10–60 to 10–67 above. Further provisions and requirements applicable to financial guardianship are described in paras 10–55 to 10–59 above and 11–39 to 11–67 below.

Delegation

11–26 A guardian may arrange for some or all of his functions to be exercised by one or more persons acting on his behalf, but the guardian may not surrender or transfer any part of his functions to anyone else.[66] This provision is helpful in relation to welfare powers, as well as management powers, and in a variety of situations, such as where the guardian is not the day-to-day carer, or where the adult goes for respite care or for a group holiday. The guardian may delegate the actual carrying out of functions, but not responsibility for them. The demarcation may not always be obvious. It may be unobjectionable for a guardian to delegate routine decisions about matters such as diet and dress, but there would be a question as to the extent of delegation competent to deal with an emergency. There could be a similar question as to the extent to which delegation of management of funds would be competent, though guardians are not trustees in terms of the Trusts (Scotland) Act 1921.[67] The Part 6 Code gives examples of delegation to carers (paying household bills, deciding when the adult needs services such as hairdressing or chiropody); recommends that every effort be made to inform the adult of the delegation; and stresses that the guardian remains responsible for ensuring that delegated functions are properly exercised.[68]

Change of address

11–27 Under s.64(4) the guardian must notify any change in his own address or in the adult's address to the Public Guardian, within seven days of the change occurring. If the guardian's address has changed, then subject to s.11[69] the Public Guardian is required to notify the adult of the change. Whether the change relates to the guardian or to the adult, the Public Guardian is required to notify the local authority; except where incapacity results from physical inability to communicate, to notify the Mental Welfare Commission; and to enter prescribed particulars in the relevant register. Where the adult has moved to another local authority area, the notice to the local authority under s.64(4) requires to be given to the local authority for the new area.[70] Where the chief officer is guardian and the adult moves to a different local authority area, s.76 (described in para.11–5 above) also applies. Section 64(4) refers to "address", s.76 to "place of habitual residence", and s.87(1) to "the area in which the adult resides", which could

---

[66] s.64(6).
[67] 11 and 12 Geo. 5 c.58.
[68] Part 6 Code, paras 4.75 and 5.21.
[69] See paras 5–9 and 5–25 *supra*.
[70] See definition of "local authority" in s.87(1).

occasionally raise questions as to whether there could be differences among address, residence and habitual residence.[71]

Effect of appointment; transactions of guardian and adult

Section 67 deals with the effects of a guardianship order in relation to four areas of decision-making or transactions: firstly, matters outwith the scope of the order; secondly, management matters within the scope of the appointment; thirdly, personal welfare matters within the scope of the appointment; and fourthly, matters within the scope of powers conferred on the guardian to authorise the adult to transact.[72] **11–28**

Matters outwith scope of the order

Outwith the scope of the guardianship order, the adult's capacity is unaffected by the order,[73] and thus the rebuttable presumption of capacity with which this book commenced continues to apply regardless of the existence of the order. **11–29**

Management within the scope of the order

Subject to the exception described in para.11–32 below, within the scope of the order the adult is deemed by s.67(1) to have no capacity "to enter into any transaction". Subject to the terms of the guardianship order, the certificate of authority issued to a financial guardian by the Public Guardian (a) authorises the guardian to take possession of, manage and deal with any moveable or immoveable estate (wherever situated) of the adult and (b) has the effect of requiring any payment due to the adult to be made to the guardian. Both (a) and (b) apply insofar as the estate, payment or matter falls within the scope of the guardian's authority.[74] **11–30**

Personal welfare matters within the scope of the order

Section 67(1) removes the adult's capacity "to enter any transaction" within the scope of the order, but declares that "nothing in this subsection shall be taken to affect the capacity of the adult in relation to any other matter". Accordingly, the rebuttable presumption of capacity is preserved not only outwith the scope of the order, as described in para.11–29 above, but also in relation to anything which is not a "transaction". While "transaction" is not defined for the purposes of the Act, few if any personal welfare decisions could be described as transactions. Accordingly, coupling the terms of s.67(1) with the general principles, including the obligation to encourage use and development of any capacity which an adult may have, welfare guardians and those dealing with them require to be particularly alert **11–31**

---

[71] *cf.* the provisions regarding jurisdiction, described in para.5–4 *supra*, under which the principal qualification is habitual residence, or presence in the sheriffdom in case of emergency.
[72] On s.67(3), see para.10–45 *supra*. On s.67(4), see para.10–62 *supra*. On s.67(6), see para.10–68 *supra*. On s.67(7), see paras 10–45 and 10–62 *supra*.
[73] s.67(1).
[74] s.67(2).

to the possibility of the adult being in fact capable of making a decision (or some parts of a composite decision) within the scope of the guardianship order. In matters other than entering "transactions", the order neither removes capacity nor creates any explicit presumption of incapacity. This may have significance *inter alia* in relation to the provisions of s.70 described in paras 11–37 and 11–38 below.

Matters within scope of power to authorise

11–32   Under s.64(1)(e) the guardianship order may empower the guardian to authorise the adult to carry out such transactions or categories of transactions as the guardian may specify. Under the fifth general principle, in terms of s.1(5),[75] a guardian is obliged to encourage the adult to exercise whatever skills the adult has concerning the adult's property, financial affairs or personal welfare, as the case may be, and to develop new such skills insofar as it is reasonable and practicable to do so. Section 67(1) excepts from the general rule described in para.11–30 above the situation where the adult has been authorised by the guardian under s.64(1)(e). Under s.67(5), where the adult transacts with a third party aware at the time of the transaction that authority has been granted under s.64(1)(e), the transaction "shall not be void only on the ground that the adult lacked capacity". Uniquely, in that situation there is an irrebuttable presumption of capacity, and consequently an onus upon guardians to exercise care when authorising transactions or categories of transactions where power to do so has been conferred under s.64(1)(e).

Reimbursement and remuneration of guardian

Individual as guardian

11–33   The provisions of s.68 on reimbursement and remuneration of guardians differentiate between guardians who are individuals and the chief officer as welfare guardian. This paragraph describes the provisions applicable to individuals as guardians (including concurrent and joint guardians, and presumably also interim guardians). See also paras 11–35 and 11–36. An individual who is guardian is entitled to be reimbursed from the adult's estate for any outlays reasonably incurred by the guardian in exercise of his guardianship functions, including payment for items and services other than those which the guardian is expected to provide as part of his functions.[76] As regards remuneration, there is a presumption against remuneration in relation to welfare powers and a presumption in favour of remuneration in relation to financial powers. A guardian may be remunerated from the adult's estate in respect of the exercise of welfare functions "only in a case where special cause is shown". A guardian may be remunerated from the adult's estate in respect of the exercise of management functions unless the sheriff directs otherwise in the guardianship order: in determining whether or not to make such a direction, the sheriff is required to take into account the value of the estate and the likely difficulty in managing it.[77] In considering such issues, the sheriff

---

[75] See para.4–22 *supra*.
[76] s.68(1) and (2)(a).
[77] s.68(4) and (5).

is likely to be guided *inter alia* by the first general principle[78]: where assets are small and remuneration likely to be disproportionately burdensome, the sheriff might not be satisfied that financial guardianship would benefit the adult unless the guardianship were unremunerated, but where difficulties require to be addressed it may be to the adult's benefit to expend a greater proportion of available funds either on recognising the time and effort required of a lay guardian or on employing a professional guardian.

Chief officer as guardian

The chief officer as guardian is also entitled to be reimbursed from **11-34** the adult's estate for any outlays reasonably incurred by the chief officer in exercise of his guardianship functions, but not for items or services unless they would not normally be provided free of charge by the local authority to a person who is in similar circumstances but does not have a guardian.[79] Remuneration is not payable to the local authority in respect of exercise of welfare functions by the chief officer as guardian.[80] Special provisions apply under s.68(3) to the costs of guardianship applications by the local authority (a) for appointment of the chief officer as welfare guardian or (b) for concurrent appointment of the chief officer as welfare guardian and one or more individuals as financial guardians. These provisions also apply to any subsequent application by the chief officer while acting as guardian. For (a), the local authority is required to meet the costs. For (b), the sheriff, in determining the application, apportions the costs as he thinks fit, and the local authority is entitled to recover from the adult's estate the proportion of costs relating to the financial appointment. At first sight, s.68(3)(b) might seem to apply to the whole costs, without apportionment, of an application for financial powers only, but s.68(3) cannot apply to such a situation, because it only applies where the local authority seeks appointment of the chief officer, and under s.59(1) and (2) the chief officer may only be appointed with welfare powers, therefore every case under s.68(3)(b) will require apportionment by the sheriff. Where the local authority petition for financial powers only, or nominates someone other than the chief officer as welfare guardian, the normal provisions regarding expenses described in paras 5–10 to 5–12 above apply.

Fixing amount, and payment

The Public Guardian fixes the amount of any remuneration **11-35** payable and outlays to be allowed under the provisions described in paras 11–33 and 11–34 above. The method of calculation currently adopted by the Public Guardian for both new and transitional appointments is described in Chapter 9 of *Guidance Notes for Curators Bonis*, published by the Public Guardian and referred to in para.11–96 below. Where "the guardian" is required to submit accounts, the Public Guardian fixes the sum payable when the accounts for the relevant period are audited. If "the guardian" is not required to

---

[78] s.1(2)—see paras 4–6 to 4–11 *supra*.
[79] s.68(1) and (2).
[80] s.68(4).

submit accounts, the Public Guardian fixes the sum payable upon application by the guardian. In fixing remuneration to be paid the Public Guardian is required to take account of the value of the estate.[81] Where there are concurrent guardians, only one of whom submits accounts, the other would require to apply to the Public Guardian. If it would be unreasonable to expect the guardian to wait for payment until the end of the relevant accounting period, the Public Guardian may allow payments to account to be made by way of remuneration during the accounting period.[82] Decisions by the Public Guardian in terms of the powers described in this paragraph may be appealed to the sheriff, whose decision is final.[83]

Forfeiture of remuneration

11–36 The sheriff may order forfeiture, in whole or in part, of any remuneration due to a guardian upon the application of any person claiming an interest. The sheriff may do so where the guardian is in breach of any duty of care, of fiduciary duty or of obligation imposed by the Act.[84]

Non-compliance with decisions of welfare guardian

11–37 Section 70 addresses the situation where any decision of a guardian with welfare powers, made within the scope of those powers, is not complied with by the adult or by any other person. The provisions of s.70 only apply if "the adult or other person might reasonably be expected to comply with the decision", a qualification inserted at stage 2 of the Bill's passage in response to expressions of concern by the Alliance and others that a guardian acting on behalf of an adult should not be empowered to make demands of third parties which the adult, if competent, would not be entitled to make, and that guardians should not in general terms be able to make unlimited demands. Without such qualification, the provisions of s.70 risked challenge that they breached ECHR. On the other hand there was consensus on the need to remedy the deficiency of provision to address non-compliance under MHSA 1984 guardianship, as described in para.10–3 above. Under s.70(1)(a), duplicated by s.70(2) as regards persons other than the adult,[85] the sheriff may make an order ordaining the adult or any other person named in the order to implement the decision of the guardian. Where the non-compliance relates to a decision as to place of residence of the adult by a guardian with power to decide the adult's place of residence, under s.70(1)(b) the sheriff may grant a warrant authorising a constable (i) to enter any premises where the adult is, or is reasonably supposed to be, and/or

---

[81] s.68(6).
[82] s.68(7).
[83] s.68(8).
[84] s.69. See also ss.81 and 82, described in para.10–60 *supra*, and Sch.2, paras 8(6) and (7), described in para.11–65 *infra*.
[85] In the Bill as introduced, subs.(1) dealt only with non-compliance by the adult, and subs.(2) only with non-compliance by others. At stage 2, subs.(1) was amended to refer also to "any other person". Assuming "any person other than the adult" in subs.(2) to be synonymous, subs.(2) would appear—as regards persons other than the adult—to add nothing to subs.(1).

(ii) to apprehend the adult and to remove him to such place as the guardian may direct. A constable executing a warrant under s.70(1)(b) may use such force as is reasonable in the circumstances and shall be accompanied by the guardian or such person as the guardian may authorise in writing. The granting and use of compulsive powers under this section should be seen as a last resort, and in relation to the adult must accord with the general principles in s.1. "Constable" is not defined in the Incapacity Act, but is defined in Social Work (Scotland) Act 1968[86] as "a constable of a police force within the meaning of the Police (Scotland) Act 1967".[87]

Procedure under section 70

11–38 An application under s.70 must be made in the form prescribed in the Adults with Incapacity (Non-Compliance with Decisions of Welfare Guardians) (Scotland) Regulations 2002.[88] Despite the serious nature of the order or warrant sought, the intimation provisions are more restricted than under most other provisions of the Act. The court is required to intimate the application only to the person (*i.e.* the adult or the other person) against whom the order or warrant is sought. In the case of the adult, intimation is subject to s.11(1).[89] The Act does not require intimation to the local authority or Mental Welfare Commission, or to the adult if the order is sought against someone other than the adult, but the general powers described in paras 5–6 and 5–7 apply to such an application, including the various discretionary powers of the sheriff under s.3(1) and (2) and the safeguarding provisions of s.3(4) and (5). Rule 3.16.13 applies to intimation of such applications. Intimation is in Form 20. Where the person to whom intimation requires to be given is within Scotland, intimation is by first class recorded delivery post or (where that is unsuccessful) by personal service. Where the person is furth of Scotland, Rule 2.12 applies. Under s.70(3),[90] the intimation of the application must advise the prescribed period of 21 days[91] within which the person receiving intimation may object to the granting of the application. The sheriff shall not grant the order or warrant without affording to any objector an opportunity of being heard. Having heard any such objections, the sheriff may grant the order, but in doing so the sheriff requires to comply with the first four general principles.[92]

MANAGEMENT BY FINANCIAL GUARDIANS

Introduction

11–39 Schedule 2[93] contains provisions regarding the management of the estate of an adult by a guardian with financial powers. Further such provisions are contained in Part 6, and there is no obvious reason why

---

[86] c.49, s.94(1).
[87] c.77.
[88] SSI 2002/98: see reg.2 and Sch.
[89] See para.5–9 *supra*.
[90] Unnecessarily duplicated by Rule 3.16.13(3).
[91] *ibid.* reg.3: the period of 21 days begins with the date of receipt of intimation.
[92] ss.1(1)–(4), 70(3) and (4). On the principles, see paras 4–2 *et seq. supra*.
[93] Introduced by s.64(12).

some of them are to be found there, rather than in Schedule 2. In this book, provisions common to guardianship and intervention orders have been described in Chapter 10, so that provisions regarding heritable property and accommodation appear in paras 10–55 to 10–59. Generally, the provisions described in this section apply to financial guardianship in addition to the provisions described in Chapter 10 and in the preceding and subsequent sections of this Chapter. As always, the general principles apply to those exercising functions under the Act in relation to management by financial guardians.[94]

11–40 The management régime for guardians with property and financial powers reflects the shift in emphasis, present throughout the Act, from fixed provision, applicable to all appointments, to an individualised package of provision.[95] Curators bonis operated within a generalised régime of usual powers, powers obtainable from the Accountant of Court and special powers obtainable from the court. Under the Act the emphasis has been shifted to the individual management plan. Investment provisions are less rigid than they were under curatory, and include a specific requirement that investments must be suitable for the adult's estate. The Public Guardian may adapt accounting requirements to particular cases. The management plan and investments must be kept under review. One of the purposes of these provisions, which are described in more detail below, is to ensure continuing compliance with the general principles and in particular that the assets of an individual adult are managed and applied in ways suitable to the circumstances and needs of that adult, both initially and as circumstances and needs change over time.

Public Guardian

11–41 The Public Guardian has the various specific functions described in the following paragraphs, as well as the general functions described in paras 5–23 to 5–27 and 10–64 above and the other functions, including registration and intimation functions, described elsewhere in Chapters 10 and 11. In addition, the Public Guardian has a general power under s.64(7) to make orders or demands in relation to the adult's financial affairs or property, with which a financial guardian must comply insofar as such compliance is within the scope of the guardian's authority. If the guardian fails to comply, the Public Guardian may apply to the sheriff, who may make an order to like effect. The sheriff's decision upon such an application is final. Procedure for applications to the sheriff is described in paras 5–5 *et seq.* above.

Inventory

11–42 Subject to the discretionary power of the Public Guardian described in the next paragraph, a financial guardian must submit to the Public Guardian for examination and approval a full inventory of the adult's estate insofar as within the scope of the guardian's authority. The guardian must submit the inventory as soon as possible, and in any

---

[94] See paras 4–2 *et seq. supra.*
[95] This is the shift from "old law" to "new law" provision, as those terms are described in paras 3–1 *et seq. supra.*

event within three months of the date of registration of the guardian's appointment[96] or within such other period as the Public Guardian may allow. The inventory must be accompanied by such supporting documents and additional information as the Public Guardian may require. The form of inventory is prescribed by the Public Guardian and is available from the Public Guardian's website and on disk.[97] If the guardian discovers any error in the inventory, or any omission from it, after the Public Guardian has approved the inventory, the error or omission must be intimated to the Public Guardian within six months of discovering it, or in the next accounts, whichever occurs sooner.[98]

Public Guardian's discretion

The Public Guardian may dispense with the need for the guardian to submit an inventory, or may require the guardian to take such other action as the Public Guardian thinks appropriate, in lieu of submitting an inventory.[99] **11–43**

Management plan

Unless the sheriff directs otherwise, a financial guardian must prepare a management plan for the management, investment and realisation of the adult's estate and for the application of the estate to the adult's needs, so far as the estate falls within the guardian's authority. The plan must take account of any directions given by the sheriff in the order appointing the guardian. The Public Guardian issues a style of management plan. The guardian is required to submit the plan in draft to the Public Guardian either along with the inventory, or within one month (or such longer period as the Public Guardian may allow) after submission of the inventory. The Public Guardian may approve the plan either as submitted in draft or with amendments. The guardian, in the exercise of his functions in relation to the adult, must take account of the plan as approved (with any amendments) by the Public Guardian,[1] and the guardian's powers are limited by the plan as described in para.11–49 below. **11–44**

Restrictions prior to approval of plan

The guardian's powers are limited until the management plan has been approved by the Public Guardian. The guardian has power only (a) to ingather and take control of the assets of the adult's estate so as to enable the guardian, when the management plan has been approved, to intromit with them, and (b) to make such payments as are necessary to provide for the adult's day-to-day needs. However, when appointing the guardian the sheriff may confer wider powers which may be exercised prior to approval of the management plan; and the Public Guardian may authorise the guardian to exercise any function within the scope of the guardian's authority (as conferred in **11–45**

---

[96] On registration of appointment, see para.10–54 *supra*.
[97] See para.5–27 *supra*.
[98] Sch.2, para.3(1)–(3).
[99] Sch.2, para.3(4).
[1] Sch.2, para.1(1)–(3).

the guardianship order) before the management plan is approved, if it would be unreasonable to delay the guardian exercising that function until the plan has been approved.[2]

Review and variation

11–46 The guardian is required to keep the management plan under review and to put forward to the Public Guardian proposals for variation of it whenever that appears to the guardian to be appropriate. The Public Guardian may at any time propose any variation to the management plan, and is required to review the plan whenever the guardian submits his accounts for audit. The Public Guardian must notify the guardian of any variation which the Public Guardian proposes to make to the management plan. The Public Guardian must not make any such variation without affording the guardian an opportunity to object. Having heard any objections raised by the guardian, the Public Guardian may make the variation with or without amendment.[3]

Directions from sheriff

11–47 Where the guardian disagrees with any decision made by the Public Guardian in relation to a management plan, the guardian may apply to the sheriff for a determination in relation to the matter. The sheriff's decision is final.[4]

General principles

11–48 While the provisions described in the preceding paras 11–44 to 11–47 might read as a dialogue between guardian and Public Guardian without formal notification to any other party, both guardian and Public Guardian must act in accordance with the general principles described in paras 4–2 *et seq.* above, as must the sheriff in giving directions and in making determinations.

Financial guardian's powers etc.

General

11–49 A financial guardian's powers are restricted as described in para.11–45 above until the management plan (if one is required) has been approved. This and the following paragraphs describe the position thereafter. A financial guardian is entitled to use the capital and income of the adult's estate for the purpose of purchasing assets, services or accommodation so as to enhance the adult's quality of life, subject to (a) such restrictions as may be imposed by the court, (b) the management plan, and (c) the provisions regarding acquisition or disposal of accommodation described in para.11–53 below.[5]

---

[2] Sch.2, para.1(4) and (5).
[3] Sch.2, para.1(6)–(9).
[4] Sch.2, para.2.
[5] s.64(5).

Money

The guardian is required to deposit all money received by him as **11–50** guardian in a bank or building society account in the name of the adult. The guardian must ensure that sums so deposited in excess of £500 (or such other sum as may be prescribed) shall earn interest.[6]

Investment

If the guardian proposes to retain any existing investment of the **11–51** adult, the guardian must first obtain and consider advice, given or subsequently confirmed in writing, from a person authorised to advise on investments[7] The adviser must not be guardian, an employer or employee of the guardian, or a business partner of the guardian. New investments may be made either in accordance with the management plan or with the Public Guardian's consent. The guardian must keep every investment under review, and in doing so must have regard to the following principles: (a) that the investment must be prudent, (b) that there must be a diversification of investments, and (c) that the investment must be suitable for the adult's estate. The Public Guardian may at any time direct the guardian to realise any investment. Such a direction may be appealed to the sheriff, whose decision is final.[8]

Carrying on of business

The guardian may carry on any business of the adult, subject to **11–52** any directions given by the Public Guardian. Any such direction may be appealed to the sheriff, whose decision is final.[9]

Purchase or disposal of accommodation

The guardian may not purchase accommodation for the adult, or **11–53** dispose of any accommodation used for the time being as a dwellinghouse by the adult, without the consent of the Public Guardian in principle and as to the purchase or selling price.[10] Guardians may choose to seek advice from the Public Guardian[11] before applying for each of these consents. The application for consent in principle should be made "in the prescribed form".[12] Upon receipt of the application, the Public Guardian intimates it (subject to s.11)[13] to the adult, to the adult's nearest relative and primary carer, and to any person whom the Public Guardian considers has an interest in the application. When intimating the application, the Public Guardian advises the prescribed period[14] within which they may object to the granting of the application. The Public Guardian is required to remit any objection to the

---

[6] Sch.2, para.4.
[7] For the purposes of the Financial Services and Markets Act 2000 (c.8) and any orders thereunder.
[8] Sch.2, para.5(1)–(4) and (6).
[9] Sch.2, para.5(5) and (6).
[10] Sch.2, para.6. See para.10–59 *supra* for comment on this provision, and paras 10–55 to 10–58 *supra* for provisions regarding heritable property.
[11] Under s.6(2)(e).
[12] The form and prescribed periods referred to in this paragraph are promulgated by the Public Guardian, not in regulations by the Scottish Ministers. See para.3–12 *supra*.
[13] See paras 5–9 and 5–25 *supra*.
[14] See n.12 above.

sheriff. If the sheriff upholds the objection, the Public Guardian is required to refuse the application, and if the sheriff dismisses the objection, the Public Guardian is required to grant the application. If the Public Guardian proposes to refuse the application otherwise than in consequence of a determination by the sheriff, the Public Guardian is required to intimate the proposed refusal to the applicant and to advise the applicant of the prescribed period[15] within which the applicant may object to the proposed refusal. If the applicant does object, the Public Guardian may not refuse the application without affording the applicant an opportunity to be heard. When the Public Guardian has heard any such objections, or where there are no objections from those to whom the application was intimated, the Public Guardian may grant the application. Alternatively, the Public Guardian may remit the application for determination by the sheriff. The Public Guardian may remit to the sheriff at his own instance, or at the instance of any person who objects to the granting or refusal of the application (but not where the refusal is consequent upon the upholding by the sheriff of an objection to the application). Also, the decision of the Public Guardian to grant or refuse the application may be appealed to the sheriff (except for a refusal which is consequent upon the upholding by the sheriff of an objection to the application). There are thus several possible routes to the sheriff: (a) mandatory referral of an objection to the application, (b) referral to the sheriff by the Public Guardian at his own instance or at the instance of a person who objects to grant or refusal, and (c) appeal to the sheriff against grant or refusal. Under all of these, the sheriff's decision is final.[16]

11–54 If consent in principle to the proposed purchase or disposal has been given, the guardian requires to make further application to the Public Guardian for consent to the purchase or selling price. The Public Guardian's decision on this is final.[17]

Gifts

11–55 Financial guardians may make gifts out of the adult's estate, but only if authorised to do so by the Public Guardian.[18] Making gifts, where it is reasonable to suppose that the adult would have done so if capable, is consistent with the interpretation of "benefit" in the first principle proposed in para.4–8 above, namely that "benefit" encompasses overcoming the limitations created by incapacity, so as to permit something which the adult could reasonably be expected to have chosen to do if capable, even though of a gratuitous or unselfish nature.

Procedure

11–56 The procedure for obtaining authorisation from the Public Guardian is set out in s.66. Such authorisation may be given generally, or in respect of a particular gift. Where an adult, while capable, established a pattern of making gifts to particular categories of people on

---

[15] See n.12 above.
[16] Sch.2, para.6(1)–(6) and (8).
[17] Sch.2, para.6(1)(b), (7) and (9).
[18] s.66(1).

particular occasions, and within a general level of expenditure, and where it would be reasonable to continue that practice having regard to the adult's assets, circumstances and needs, it would be appropriate to seek a general authority from the Public Guardian to continue that defined pattern.

Application for authority under s.66 requires to be made to the **11–57** Public Guardian in the prescribed form.[19] Subject to two exceptions, upon receipt of the application the Public Guardian is required to intimate it to the adult, to the adult's nearest relative and primary carer, and to any other person whom the Public Guardian considers has an interest in the application. When intimating the application, the Public Guardian is required to advise the prescribed period[20] within which objection may be made to the application. The first exception is that the Public Guardian may dispense with intimation where the Public Guardian is of the opinion that the value of the gift is such that intimation is not necessary. Normally, this would reasonably require consideration of the value of the gift in relation to the size of the estate and the extent to which it is required for the adult's own needs. The second exception is where intimation is not given to the adult under s.11.[21]

The Public Guardian must not grant the application without affording any objector an opportunity of being heard. Having heard any such objections, the Public Guardian may grant the application. Where the Public Guardian proposes to refuse the application, he is required to intimate that decision to the guardian and to advise the guardian of the prescribed period[22] within which the guardian may object to the proposed refusal. If the guardian objects, the Public Guardian may not refuse the application without affording the guardian an opportunity of being heard. **11–58**

The sheriff

The application may be remitted to the sheriff, and the decisions of **11–59** the Public Guardian may be appealed to the sheriff. The application may be remitted at the Public Guardian's own instance, or at the instance of the guardian or an objector. Decisions by the Public Guardian to grant the application, or refuse it, or to refuse to remit it to the sheriff, may be appealed to the sheriff. The sheriff's decisions on remits and appeals are final.

Powers and duties under other statutes etc.

References to guardians in pre-Act legislation are likely in general, **11–60** but perhaps not invariably, to be interpreted as applying to guardians under the Incapacity Act.[23] Thus guardians are responsible and

---

[19] Forms promulgated and issued by the Public Guardian: see paras 3–12 and 5–27 *supra*.

[20] No regulations have been made: the Public Guardian allows a period of 21 days. See para.3–12 *supra*.

[21] See paras 5–9 and 5–25 *supra*.

[22] No regulations have been made: the Public Guardian allows a period of 21 days. See para.3–12 *supra*.

[23] For possible extensions to include appointees under intervention orders, see para.10–76 *supra*. For an example in subsequent legislation, see para.10–42 *supra*.

assessable in respect of income tax matters,[24] and may claim reliefs.[25] See para.12–14 below on payment to guardians of damages paid in sheriff court actions. See also any references to guardians in regulations and provisions such as those referred to in para.12–17 below. The question arises whether references to curators bonis should now be construed as meaning financial guardians. That question arises, for example, in regulation 13 of the Individual Savings Account Regulations 1998,[26] which provides for applications by curators bonis and which, curiously, was inserted in those regulations after enactment of the Incapacity Act and indeed after the making of the Commencement No.1 Order which specified *inter alia* a commencement date for s.80 and Part 6.[27]

Accounting and auditing

11–61 The principal provisions regarding accounts and audit are contained in paras 7 and 8 of Schedule 2 to the Act. Subject to the Public Guardian's discretionary powers described below, a financial guardian is required to submit to the Public Guardian accounts in respect of each accounting period, within one month of the end of the accounting period. The first accounting period commences with the date of appointment of the guardian and ends on a date determined by the Public Guardian not later than 18 months after appointment. Subsequent accounting periods are each for one year, commencing on the first accounting date and subsequent anniversaries of it. The Public Guardian has discretion to allow longer than a month for submission of an account, and has a general power to give directions as to the frequency of accounting periods. More fundamentally, the Public Guardian may dispense with the need for submission of accounts by the guardian, and may require the guardian to do anything which the Public Guardian thinks appropriate in lieu of submitting accounts.

11–62 Accounts require to be in such form as is prescribed by the Public Guardian, who may prescribe forms for different cases or different descriptions of case.[28] With the accounts must be submitted such supporting documents as the Public Guardian may require. The Public Guardian may require the guardian to furnish the Public Guardian with such information in connection with the accounts as the Public Guardian may require.

Auditing

11–63 Except as regards the part of the account relating to any business (or interest in a business) forming part of the adult's estate, the accounts are audited by the Public Guardian or by an accountant appointed by the Public Guardian for the purpose, who is responsible to the Public

---

[24] Taxes Management Act 1970 (c.9), s.72. Note that this Act uses the antiquated and inappropriate definition of "incapacitated" described in n.6 to para.6–48 *supra*, which may not always coincide with the definition of "incapable" in the Incapacity Act (see paras 4–23 to 4–29 *supra*).
[25] *ibid.* s.42(6).
[26] SI 1998/1870.
[27] Reg.13 was inserted with effect from April 6, 2001 by the Individual Savings Account (Amendment) Regulations 2001 (SI 2001/908), reg.7(b).
[28] See paras 5–23 and 5–27 *supra* for the Public Guardian's address etc. and website.

Guardian. Where the adult's estate includes "a business or an interest in a business", the Public Guardian prescribes the person who shall audit the relevant part of the accounts, and prescribes the form of certificate by that person as to the accuracy of the relevant part of the accounts. The reference to "a business or an interest in a business" clearly includes a business of the adult which the Public Guardian has permitted the guardian to carry on.[29] It would appear that "an interest in a business" may go beyond a business of the adult carried on by the guardian, though the Act is silent on this point, and does not define the line between "an interest in a business" and an investment. One would anticipate that normally the Public Guardian's ruling would be accepted on such points, though an application to the sheriff for directions under s.3(3) would be competent.

Approval of accounts

11–64 Following audit of the accounts, two courses are open to the Public Guardian. The Public Guardian is required to approve the accounts and fix the remuneration due to the guardian, if the accounts appear to the Public Guardian to be a true and fair view of the guardian's management of the adult's estate; and the Public Guardian may so approve the accounts notwithstanding any minor inconsistencies or absence of full documentation in the accounts, if the Public Guardian is satisfied that the guardian acted reasonably and in good faith. If however it appears to the Public Guardian that the accounts are not a true and fair view of the guardian's management of the adult's estate, the Public Guardian is required to prepare a report. The report covers the extent to which the accounts do not represent such a true and fair view, and adjusts the accounts accordingly. The Public Guardian sends the report to the guardian, who may object to anything contained in the report within 28 days of it being sent to him. If the guardian does not object to the report, the accounts as adjusted by the Public Guardian are regarded as approved by the Public Guardian. If the guardian objects and the objection cannot be resolved between the guardian and the Public Guardian, the guardian may apply to the sheriff to determine the matter. The sheriff's decision is final.[30]

Deficiencies

11–65 In addition to the provisions of s.81 regarding liability to repay described in para.10–60 above, para.8(6) and (7) of Schedule 2 contains provisions regarding any deficiency revealed by the accounts as approved by the Public Guardian. Under para.8(6), the guardian is liable to make good the deficiency. Under para.8(7), the Public Guardian may require the guardian to pay interest to the adult's estate on the deficiency in respect of the period for which the deficiency appears to have existed. The rate of interest is the rate applicable to sheriff court decrees.[31] If the limitation of liability

---

[29] See para.11–52 *supra*.
[30] Sch.2, para.8(1)–(5).
[31] Currently 8 per cent under Act of Sederunt (Interest in Sheriff Court Decrees and Extracts) 1993 (SI 1993/769) (amending s.9 of the Sheriff Courts (Scotland) Extracts Act 1892 (55 & 56 Vict. c.17)).

Discharge

11–66 The Public Guardian may discharge a former financial guardian in respect of the former guardian's actings and intromissions with the adult's estate, in accordance with s.72. The Public Guardian may do so at any time after recall of the relevant order; or the resignation, removal or replacement of the guardian; or the death of the adult. Application may be made in the prescribed form[32] by the former guardian, or (where the former guardian has died) by the former guardian's representative. Upon receipt of the application, the Public Guardian intimates it (subject to s.11[33]) to the adult, if surviving; to the adult's nearest relative and primary carer; and to anyone else whom the Public Guardian considers has an interest. In each case the Public Guardian advises the prescribed period[34] within which they may object. The Public Guardian must not grant the application without affording any objector an opportunity of being heard. Having heard any objection, the Public Guardian may grant the application. Where the Public Guardian proposes to refuse the application, he is required to intimate the proposed refusal to the applicant and to advise the applicant of the prescribed period[35] within which the applicant may object. The Public Guardian may not refuse the application without affording the applicant an opportunity of being heard.[36]

The sheriff

11–67 The application may be remitted to the sheriff, and decisions of the Public Guardian may be appealed to the sheriff. The application may be remitted at the Public Guardian's own instance, or at the instance of the applicant or an objector. Decisions by the Public Guardian to grant the application, or refuse it, or to refuse to remit it to the sheriff, may be appealed to the sheriff. The sheriff's decisions on both remits and appeals are final.[37]

ALTERATIONS AND TERMINATION

11–68 This section describes provisions of the Incapacity Act dealing with replacement or removal of guardians, recall of guardianship orders and guardianship powers, variation of guardianship orders and resignation of a guardian. Except where otherwise indicated, these provisions apply to welfare, financial and combined guardianships. This section describes firstly the relevant powers of the sheriff; then the powers of the Public Guardian, Mental Welfare Commission and

---

[32] The form and prescribed periods referred to in this paragraph are promulgated by the Public Guardian, not in regulations by the Scottish Ministers. See paras 3–12 and 5–27 *supra*.

[33] See paras 5–9 and 5–25 *supra*.

[34] See n.32 above.

[35] See n.32 above.

[36] s.72(1)–(5).

[37] s.72(5) and (6).

local authority; and finally the provisions concerning resignation. Common themes are provisions to ensure that guardianship is not continued where it is no longer appropriate; conversely, that the adult is not left without a guardian where guardianship continues to be required; and that powers are adjusted where that is appropriate. All concerned in the application of these provisions are required to observe the first four general principles.[38]

The sheriff

The sheriff may under s.71 replace a guardian, remove a guardian **11–69** from office or recall the guardianship order or otherwise terminate a guardianship, and may under s.74 vary a guardianship order. The sheriff may exercise these powers upon application by the adult or by any other person claiming an interest in the adult's property, financial affairs or personal welfare.[39] Procedure under applications to the sheriff is described in paras 5–5 *et seq.* above.

Replacement

An application to replace a guardian requires to nominate the **11–70** proposed replacement guardian. As for original appointment, the nominee requires to be an individual or, as welfare guardian only, the chief officer, and the sheriff may replace the original guardian with the nominee if the sheriff is satisfied as to the matters set out in s.59(3)–(5) as described in para.11–2 above.[40] The application may be made by a guardian wishing to resign.[41] If the replacement guardian has financial powers, then similar provisions regarding caution to those described in paras 10–52 and 10–53 above apply.[42]

Removal

The sheriff may remove a guardian from office if the sheriff is **11–71** satisfied that there is a substitute guardian who is prepared to act or one or more joint guardians prepared to continue to act.[43] Where removal triggers substitution and the substitute has financial powers, similar provisions regarding caution to those described in paras 10–52 and 10–53 above apply.[44]

Recall

The sheriff may recall a guardianship order if satisfied that the **11–72** grounds for appointment of a guardian are no longer fulfilled, or that the interests of the adult in the adult's property, financial affairs or personal welfare can be satisfactorily safeguarded or promoted otherwise than by guardianship.[45] At the same time as recalling the guardianship order, the sheriff may make an intervention order.[46]

---

[38] See para.4–2 *et seq. supra.*
[39] ss.71(1) and 74(1). There are differences in the wording of those two subsections which do not appear to have any practical significance.
[40] s.71(1)(a).
[41] s.75(5). See para.11–80 *infra.*
[42] s.71(2).
[43] s.71(1)(b).
[44] s.71(2).
[45] s.71(1)(c).
[46] s.71(4).

Variation

11–73 The sheriff may vary the powers conferred by a guardianship order and may vary any existing ancillary order.[47] In considering the application to vary, the sheriff is required to have regard to any intervention or guardianship orders previously made and any previous variation orders, in each case whether still in force or not.[48] Where the proposed variation would confer welfare powers on a guardian previously holding management powers only, or vice versa, the procedure for a new guardianship order set forth in s.57 requires to be followed.[49] Where financial powers are varied, similar provisions regarding caution to those described in paras 10–52 and 10–53 above apply.[50]

Registration and intimation

11–74 Where the sheriff grants an application for replacement, removal, recall or variation, the sheriff clerk is required to send a copy of the relevant interlocutor to the Public Guardian. The Public Guardian enters prescribed particulars in the relevant register. After being satisfied that any requirements regarding caution have been met, the Public Guardian issues a certificate of appointment to a replacement or substitute guardian who takes over, or a new certificate of appointment where one or more joint guardians continue to act or a guardian's powers have been varied. Subject to s.11,[51] the Public Guardian is required to notify the adult. The Public Guardian is also required to notify the relevant local authority and (except where incapacity arises solely from physical inability to communicate) the Mental Welfare Commission.[52] Where the order relates to a guardianship order registered or recorded in the Land or Sasine Registers, the provisions of s.78 (described in para.10–57) apply.

Remits and appeals

11–75 The sheriff has the powers in relation to remits and appeals described in para.11–78 below.

The Public Guardian, Mental Welfare Commission and local authority

11–76 The Public Guardian may under s.73(1) recall a guardian's financial powers. The Mental Welfare Commission or relevant local authority may under s.73(3) recall a guardian's personal welfare powers, except that the local authority does not have this power where its own chief officer is guardian. In this and the following paras 11–77 and 11–78 the Public Guardian, Mental Welfare Commission or local authority, as the case may be, is referred to as "the relevant authority". The

---

[47] s.74(1).
[48] s.74(3).
[49] Per s.74(4). The procedure is described in paras 10–46 *et seq. supra*.
[50] s.74(2).
[51] See paras 5–9 and 5–25 *supra*.
[52] ss.71(3) and 74(5). Under the former (replacement, removal or recall), issue of certificates precedes notification, whereas under the latter (variation) notification precedes issue of the new certificate.

relevant authority may recall at its own instance, or on application by anyone (including the adult) claiming an interest in the adult's property and financial affairs, or the adult's personal welfare (as the case may be), if it appears to the relevant authority that the grounds for appointment of a guardian with management or welfare powers (as the case may be) are no longer fulfilled, or the interests of the adult in the adult's financial affairs or personal welfare (as the case may be) can be satisfactorily safeguarded or promoted otherwise than by guardianship.

Procedure

There are two different enabling provisions in the Act for procedural regulations, one for recall by the Public Guardian made under s.7(1)(c), and one for recall by the Mental Welfare Commission or local authority under s.73(10). No regulations have been made under s.7(1)(c). As is confirmed by the Part 6 Code,[53] the Office of the Public Guardian has prepared an application form and guidance notes for applications to the Public Guardian for recall of financial powers. In this paragraph "the Regulations" accordingly means the regulations under s.73(10)[54] which apply only to recall by the Mental Welfare Commission or the local authority. The Regulations contain forms for applications and intimations, and for recording decisions by the relevant authority. Under s.73(5), the relevant authority is required to intimate its intention to recall or (as the case may be) to intimate the application for recall to the adult, to the adult's nearest relative and primary carer, and to any other person whom the relevant authority considers to have an interest in the proposed recall. There is a discrepancy in the provisions regarding intimation to the adult in that in general the scheme of the Act provides for dispensation with intimation to (or service on) the adult where that would be likely to pose a serious risk to the adult's health,[55] but in the case of intimations under s.73 this applies only to the Public Guardian, under s.11(2), and not to the Mental Welfare Commission or local authority. Section 73(5) requires the intimation to advise the prescribed period for objecting, which under the Regulations is 21 days of receipt of the intimation.[56] The relevant authority must not recall the powers without affording any objector an opportunity of being heard, and having heard any objections may recall the guardian's powers. In the case of an application which the relevant authority proposes to refuse, the relevant authority must intimate that proposal to the applicant and to the adult, and advise the prescribed period for objecting, which under the Regulations is 21 days of receipt of the intimation.[57] The relevant authority must not refuse the application without affording the applicant or adult (if either objects) an opportunity of being heard.[58]

11–77

---

[53] para.6.33. See paras 3–12 and 5–27 *supra*.
[54] The Adults with Incapacity (Recall of Guardians' Powers) (Scotland) Regulations 2002 (SSI 2002/97).
[55] *e.g.* see ss.11, 37(8) and 64(10). For a similar omission in the Act, see s.23(1) and para.6–45 *supra*.
[56] The failure to prescribe a period in relation to recall by the Public Guardian could give rise to difficulty, but see para.3–12 *supra*.
[57] See preceding note.
[58] s.73(7).

The sheriff

11–78 A proposal to recall may be remitted to the sheriff, and decisions of the relevant authority may be appealed to the sheriff. The proposal to recall may be remitted by the relevant authority at its own instance or at the instance of an applicant or any objector. Decisions by the relevant authority to recall, or to remit or not to remit to the sheriff, may be appealed to the sheriff. The sheriff's decisions on both remits and appeals are final.[59]

Notification and intimation

11–79 Upon recall the following provisions apply. In the case of recall by the Mental Welfare Commission or local authority, each notifies the other and the Public Guardian. In all cases, the Public Guardian enters prescribed particulars[60] in the relevant register; subject to s.11[61] notifies the adult; and notifies the guardian. Where the Public Guardian has recalled, the Public Guardian also notifies the relevant local authority.[62] Where the recall relates to a guardianship order registered or recorded in the Land or Sasine Registers, the provisions of s.78 (described in para.10–57 above) apply.

Resignation

11–80 Section 75 permits a guardian to resign provided that either there is continuity of guardianship or a judicial determination that a guardian is no longer required. Accordingly, a guardian may resign if a joint or substitute guardian provides continuity, but otherwise requires to apply to the sheriff under s.71(1)(a) or (c) for his own removal and either replacement under s.71(1)(a) or a judicial determination that a guardian is no longer required under s.71(1)(c) as described in para.11–82 below.

11–81 A guardian who has a joint or substitute guardian may resign by giving notice in writing of his intention to do so to the Public Guardian and the local authority and (except where incapacity results solely from physical inability to communicate) to the Mental Welfare Commission. The resignation will not take effect unless "the remaining joint guardian is willing to continue to act" or the substitute guardian is willing to act. The relevant provisions do not refer explicitly to situations where there are more than one remaining joint guardians, but the requirements would presumably be satisfied in that situation if at least one joint guardian were willing to continue to act. The resignation takes effect upon receipt by the Public Guardian of both the guardian's notice of intention to resign and evidence that the joint guardian is willing to continue or the substitute is willing to take over. Upon the resignation taking effect, the Public Guardian is required to take the following steps. He enters prescribed particulars[63] in the relevant register. Where a substitute takes over, once any

---

[59] s.73(8) and (9).
[60] See para.3–12 *supra*.
[61] See paras 5–9 and 5–25 *supra*.
[62] s.73(2) and (4).
[63] See para.3–12 *supra*.

requirement for caution has been met the Public Guardian issues a certificate of appointment to the substitute.[64] Where a joint guardian continues to act, the Public Guardian issues a new certificate of appointment to the joint guardian. Finally, subject to s.11(2)[65] the Public Guardian notifies the adult. Where the resignation relates to a guardianship order registered or recorded in the Land or Sasine Registers, the provisions of s.78 (described in para.10–57 above) apply.

11–82 A guardian who has no joint guardian willing to continue to act or substitute willing to take over may not resign until a replacement has been appointed under the provisions of s.71 described in para.11–70 above.[66] Alternatively, the guardian wishing to resign in circumstances where guardianship is no longer required could apply for recall of the guardianship order under s.71(1)(c), described in para.11–71 above.

11–83 A substitute guardian whose appointment has not been triggered may resign by giving notice in writing to the Public Guardian and the local authority and (except where the adult's incapacity arises solely from physical inability to communicate) the Mental Welfare Commission. The resignation takes effect on the date of receipt of the notice by the Public Guardian. The Public Guardian notifies the existing guardian and (subject to s.11[67]) the adult, and enters prescribed particulars[68] in the relevant register.[69]

GUARDIANSHIP UNDER CRIMINAL PROCEDURE (SCOTLAND) ACT 1995

Circumstances in which order competent

11–84 The court may make a guardianship order under the Criminal Procedure (Scotland) Act 1995[70] in six situations: (a) under ss.57(1)(a) and 57(2)(c) of the 1995 Act, the court may make a guardianship order where the court acquits a person on the grounds of insanity at the time of alleged commission of the offence charged; (b) under ss.57(1)(b) and 57(2)(c) of the 1995 Act, the court may make a guardianship order where the court makes a finding at an examination of facts[71] that the person did the act or made the omission constituting the offence charged and that there were no grounds for acquittal; (c) under s.58, the court may make a guardianship order where a person is convicted in the High Court or sheriff court of an offence which is punishable by the court with imprisonment or detention and which is not an offence for which the punishment is fixed by law; (d) under s.58(2), the High Court may make a guardianship order where a case in category (c) has been remitted by the sheriff to the High Court for sentence; (e) under s.58(3), in the case of

---

[64] s.75(3)(b) refers to "a new certificate of appointment".
[65] See para.5–25 *supra*.
[66] s.75(5).
[67] See para.5–25 *supra*.
[68] See para.3–12 *supra*.
[69] s.75(4).
[70] "1995 Act", c.46, as amended by the Incapacity Act, which amendments were in turn amended by ROCSA. The principally relevant sections of the 1995 Act, as so amended, are reproduced in Appendix 3. On likely amendment by a new MHSA, see para.12–28 *infra*.
[71] Under ss.55 and 56.

a person charged summarily in the sheriff court with an offence punishable with imprisonment, the court may make a guardianship order without convicting him if satisfied that the person did the act or made the omission charged; and (f) under s.58(10), in the case of a person charged summarily before the District Court with an offence punishable with imprisonment, if it appears to that court that the person is suffering from mental disorder, that court must remit the person to the sheriff, who may make a guardianship order in the same manner as in category (c). Under all such guardianship orders, the court may place the person's personal welfare under the guardianship of a local authority or a person approved by a local authority, who in the case of (c) above only must be specified in the court order.[72] When making the order, the court may also appoint a joint guardian and/or a substitute guardian.[73]

11–85   A common régime set out in ss.58, 58A and 61 of the 1995 Act applies to guardianship orders made under all of the provisions quoted in the preceding paragraph. In the case of orders under s.57, the relevant provisions of s.58 are applied by s.57(4) and the relevant provisions of s.58A are applied by s.57(6). In the case of orders under s.58, s.58(11) provides that "Section 58A of this Act shall have effect as regards guardianship orders made under subsection (1) of this section", but the reference clearly should be to subs.(1A),[74] and the following description assumes that s.58(11) will be interpreted as referring to s.58(1A). Section 58A(1) provides that, subject to the provisions of s.58A, the provisions of Parts 1, 5, 6 and 7 of the Incapacity Act apply to guardians appointed under the 1995 Act as they apply to welfare guardians appointed under s.58 of the Incapacity Act; and they so apply whether the guardian under the 1995 Act was appointed before or after s.58A of the 1995 Act came into force on April 1, 2002.[75]

Criteria and procedure

11–86   The sheriff may make a guardianship order under the various provisions described in para.11–84 upon the evidence of two medical practitioners (here termed doctors), and the report of a mental health officer complying with the relevant requirements of s.57(3) of the Incapacity Act described in paras 10–48 and 10–49 above. The medical evidence must comply with the provisions of s.61 of the 1995 Act described in para.11–87 below. The court requires to be satisfied as to three matters: firstly, on the medical evidence that the person is incapable (as defined in the Incapacity Act) in relation to decisions about, or of acting to safeguard or promote his interests in, his personal welfare, and is likely to continue to be so incapable[76]; secondly, on the mental health officer's report giving his opinion as to the general appropriateness of the order sought, based on an interview and assessment of the person carried out not more than 30 days

---

[72] 1995 Act, ss.57(2)(c) and 58(1A).
[73] 1995 Act, s.58A(2)(b) and (c).
[74] s.58(1) covers hospital orders and s.58(1A) covers guardianship orders.
[75] Being the commencement date under the No.1 Commencement Order (SSI 2001/81 (C.2)) of s.84 of the Incapacity Act, which inserted s.58A into the 1995 Act.
[76] 1995 Act, s.58(1A)(a).

before the court makes the order, that guardianship is necessary in the interests of the person's personal welfare[77]; thirdly, that no other means provided by or under the 1995 Act[78] would be sufficient to enable "the offender's" personal welfare to be safeguarded or promoted[79]; fourthly, that any person nominated to be appointed guardian is suitable to be appointed as such[80]; fifthly, that the authority or person is willing to receive the person into guardianship[81]; and sixthly, that there is no other guardianship order under either the 1995 Act or the Incapacity Act in force relating to the person.[82]

Medical Reports

11–87 Section 61 of the 1995 Act contains requirements about the medical evidence for the purposes of the preceding sections, to which it refers. Paragraph 26(4) of Schedule 5 to the Incapacity Act sought to insert references to the new s.58(1A)(a). However, it erroneously purported to make such insertions in subss.(1), (2) and (3) of s.61, which would have been appropriate in relation to s.61 as originally enacted, but not to s.61 as amended by the Crime and Punishment Act 1997,[83] which *inter alia* introduced references to "the relevant provisions" and defined that term in a new subs.(6). The intention of para.26(4) of Schedule 5 to the Incapacity Act is clear. To give it meaning and to achieve its evident intent, it must be construed as inserting a reference to the new s.58(1A)(a) in s.61(6), the existence of which the Parliament clearly overlooked. The reproduction of s.61 in Appendix 3 proceeds on that basis. The requirements of s.61 in relation to making guardianship orders under s.58(1A) of the 1995 Act are accordingly as follows. One of the two doctors who give evidence must be an approved psychiatrist.[84] The evidence, whether written or oral, must include statements as to any relationship to "the accused" (here termed "the adult") or pecuniary interest in the "reception into guardianship".[85] A written report purporting to be signed by a doctor may be received in evidence without proof of the doctor's signature or qualifications, but the court or the adult may require the doctor to give oral evidence.[86] Where a written report is submitted, a copy must be given to the adult's counsel or solicitor; if the adult is unrepresented, the substance of the report must be disclosed to the adult; and the court must adjourn the case if it considers that more time is necessary,

---

[77] 1995 Act, s.58(6)(a).
[78] Which other means would include an intervention order under s.60B of the 1995 Act: see paras 10–77 and 10–78 *supra*.
[79] 1995 Act, s.58(1A)(b).
[80] 1995 Act, s.58(6)(b).
[81] 1995 Act, s.58(6)(c).
[82] 1995 Act, s.58(6)(d). This requirement appears to have the odd and unhelpful result that even though the sheriff were satisfied that guardianship is appropriate by reference to all of the other criteria, he would be prevented from making a guardianship order under the 1995 Act if the person already had a financial guardian.
[83] c.48, s.10, which came into force on January 1, 1998.
[84] *i.e.* approved for the purposes of s.20 of MHSA 1984—see para.14–2 *infra* (s.39 of MHSA 1984, referred to in s.61(1) of the 1995 Act, was repealed by the Incapacity Act, Sch.6). Per 1995 Act, s.61(1).
[85] 1995 Act, s.61(2).
[86] 1995 Act, ss.61(3) and 61(4)(c).

in the adult's interests, for consideration of the report.[87] Evidence to rebut the report may be called, for which purpose arrangements may be made for the adult to be examined by any doctor, and for such examination to be in private.[88]

The order

11–88 Section 58(7) of the 1995 Act provides that a guardianship order may only be made if the evidence of both doctors is in agreement that the person suffers from mental illness (including personality disorder) on the one hand or mental handicap on the other, or both, though it is acceptable for one certificate to state both but the other to state one only. The guardianship order must specify which alternative applies, or that both apply, as certified by both doctors. Section 58(7) is silent on incapacity resulting from physical inability to communicate. Section 58A(2) requires the court, in making the order, to have regard to any regulations under s.64(11) of the Incapacity Act.[89] The powers conferred must be welfare powers only and must be specified in the order.[90] Under s.58A(2)(d) and s.58A(3) of the 1995 Act the court has, in relation to guardianship orders under that Act, precisely the same discretionary powers as are conferred on the sheriff by s.3(1) and (2) of the Incapacity Act, as described in para.5–6 above. Sections 58A(4) and (5) of the 1995 Act contain similar provisions to those of the Incapacity Act ss.58(7) and (4) respectively regarding registration and duration, as described in paras 10–54 and 11–22 above.

Comment

11–89 The guardianship provisions of the 1995 Act remain in some respects unsatisfactory. They have not been fully updated to reflect the reforms in the Incapacity Act. Although the concept of impersonal guardianship by the local authority was rightly abolished under the Incapacity Act, it remains under the 1995 Act. As noted above, incapacity resulting solely from physical inability to communicate is overlooked. Inappropriate terminology includes "offender" in s.58(7), apparently in relation to people who have not been convicted as well as those convicted; and "he should be placed under guardianship" and "willing to receive that person into guardianship" in s.58(6), notwithstanding that (for example) the Incapacity Act amended s.57(2)(c) to refer to placing the person's personal welfare under guardianship, rather than "placing the person under . . . guardianship". The purely terminological anachronisms should prove harmless in practice provided that the general principles in s.1 of the Incapacity Act are duly adhered to.

---

[87] 1995 Act, s.61(4).
[88] 1995 Act, s.61(4) and (5).
[89] At time of writing the Scottish Ministers have not made such regulations, and it is understood that they do not at present intend to do so.
[90] 1995 Act, s.58A(2)(a).

Foreign Guardians

Directions

11-90 The power of the sheriff under s.3(3) to give directions[91] includes power to give directions to any person exercising functions conferred by the laws of any country of a like nature to functions conferred by the Incapacity Act.[92]

Other provisions

11-91 The provisions of the Incapacity Act described in this paragraph apply, in the same manner as they apply to a guardian under that Act, to "a guardian (however called) appointed under the law of any country to, or entitled under the law of any country to act for, an adult during his incapacity, if the guardianship is recognised by the law of Scotland".[93] The relevant provisions are: the right under the fourth principle to be consulted insofar as it is reasonable and practicable to do so[94]; the provisions regarding investigation of complaints by the Public Guardian,[95] Mental Welfare Commission[96] and local authority[97]; the provisions of Part 5 of the Act regarding medical treatment where there is a guardian[98] and authority for research[99]; the power of a welfare guardian to act whether or not the adult is in Scotland[1]; the provisions of s.67(4) regarding personal liability[2]; the provisions of s.70 regarding non-compliance with decisions of a welfare guardian[3]; the powers of the sheriff under s.71 to replace, remove or recall (but not the power to vary)[4]; the provisions of s.77 regarding the death of the adult and protection of third parties[5]; and the limitation of liability provisions of s.82.[6]

Transitional Provisions

Continuation of appointments

11-92 It has not been competent to appoint a curator bonis to an adult, or a tutor-dative or tutor at law, in proceedings begun after Part 6 of the Act was brought into force on April 1, 2002.[7] With effect on that date, the MHSA 1984 provisions regarding MHSA guardianship were

---

[91] See paras 5-14 and 5-15 *supra*.
[92] s.3(3)(b).
[93] See s.1(7) and the various other provisions specified in the following footnotes to this paragraph.
[94] s.1(4)(c)(i) applied by s.1(7). See para.4-20 *supra*.
[95] s.6(2)(c) applied by s.6(3)(a). See para.5-24 *supra*.
[96] s.9(1)(d) applied by s.9(3)(a). See para.5-30 *supra*.
[97] s.10(1)(c) applied by s.10(4)(a). See para.5-34 *supra*.
[98] s.50 applied by s.50(9)(a). See paras 14-54 *et seq. infra*.
[99] s.51 applied by s.51(8)(a). See para.14-69 *infra*.
[1] s.67(3) applied by s.67(7). See para.10-45 *supra*.
[2] Applied by s.67(7). See para.10-62 *supra*.
[3] Applied by s.70(6). See para.11-38 *supra*.
[4] Applied by s.71(5). See paras 11-70 to 11-72 *supra*.
[5] Applied by s.77(5). See paras 10-69 and 10-71 *supra*.
[6] Applied by s.82(2)(a). See para.10-60 *supra*.
[7] s.80 and Commencement Order No.1 (SSI 2001/81).

repealed.[8] All such appointees who were in office on that date became guardians under the Act on that date, subject to the provisions described in the following paragraphs. Proceedings for appointment of all such appointees commenced before that date were determined in accordance with the law as it stood immediately before that date, and appointees competently appointed after that date became, upon appointment, guardians under the Act subject to the provisions described below. As described in para.11–102, appointment of curators bonis to children remains competent, but on the child's 16th birthday (unless the appointment then terminates) such curators bonis also become guardians under the Act. Curators bonis who became (or become) guardians in any of these ways became (or become) plenary financial guardians; tutors-dative became guardians with the powers conferred by the court on them; tutors-at-law became plenary guardians with combined powers; and MHSA guardians became welfare guardians with the same powers as previously held, namely those set out in MHSA 1984, s.41(2) described in para.10–3 above, notwithstanding the repeal of that section.[9] All such guardians are referred to in this book as "transitional guardians".

Proceedings relating to previous appointments

11–93   As with proceedings for appointment, any proceedings relating to the functions of pre-Act appointees, which at April 1, 2002 had been commenced but not determined, were determined in accordance with the law immediately prior to that date. The appointees referred to are curators bonis, tutors and MHSA guardians.[10]

Application of the Act

11–94   The Act's provisions apply to transitional guardians subject only to the modifications set out in para.6 of Schedule 4 and described in this and the following paragraphs. None of the registration provisions of the Act apply to transitional guardians.[11] Paragraph 7 contained provisions applicable during phased implementation of the Act, some of which never came into force because the order of implementation rendered them unnecessary.

Guardians with management powers

11–95   Section 67(2), described in para.11–30 above, is modified to the effect that the court order making the appointment, rather than the certificate of appointment, authorises the transitional guardian to take possession of, manage and deal with the adult's estate and to require payment to the guardian of sums due to the adult.[12] The Public Guardian may determine that the provisions of Schedule 2, which are described in paras 11–39 to 11–59 above, shall apply to such cases and

---

[8] Sch.6, repealing MHSA 1984, ss.36–52.
[9] Sch.4, paras 1 and 2. As regards pending proceedings for appointment of a guardian under the Criminal Procedure (Scotland) Act 1995 (c.46), see s.58A(6) of that Act.
[10] Sch.4, para.3.
[11] para.6(8).
[12] para.6(2).

to such extent as he may decide, any such determination by the Public Guardian (or any decision not to make such a determination) being appealable to the sheriff, whose decision is final.[13] The circumstances in which the Public Guardian may make such a determination are not specified or limited. Unless and until the Public Guardian makes such a determination, Schedule 2 does not apply to a transitional financial guardianship. Note that the foregoing does not apply to the relevant provisions of Part 6 of the Act also described in paras 11–39 to 11–59, such as ss.64(7),[14] 64(5)[15] and 66,[16] 81 and 82,[17] and 72.[18] Those provisions do apply to transitional guardians.

Public Guardian's Guidance Notes

11–96 The Public Guardian has published *Guidance Notes for Curators Bonis*, issued to curators bonis becoming guardians under the Act's transitional provisions. This paragraph refers to a few particular points of interest. It does not summarise the whole guidance, which should be referred to by all such guardians and their advisers. Paragraphs 1.8 and 1.9 recommend re-assessment of capacity in appropriate cases, and possible replacement of guardianship with an alternative technique (limited guardianship, or a fresh appointment including power to authorise transactions under s.64(1)(e), are not mentioned, but might also be relevant). Paragraph 4.2 advises that although a curator who had already submitted a factorial inventory would not require to submit a management plan, a management plan would be required where the inventory was yet to be lodged. Section 6 advises that curators may either continue to use the previous style of account or the new schedule style of account developed by the Public Guardian; that only relevant bank statements, and no other vouchers or other productions, need be sent when the account is lodged; and that as from November 1, 2002 there should be lodged with the annual account a note giving details of the guardian's contact with the adult, the nearest relative and the primary carer during the accounting period. This last point is developed in section 8: para.8.2 advises that the Accountant of Court will expect full and comprehensive records to be kept, including minutes of the guardian's meetings with the adult and other interested parties. Section 9 on remuneration explains briefly the method of calculating remuneration for financial guardians appointed under the Act, and advises that as from November 1, 2002 transitional guardians might approach the Accountant of Court with a view to being remunerated in this new way, rather than in the same manner as previously. Paragraph 1.3 advises, without quoting authority, that curators (in context, evidently intended to include transitional guardians) "will still report to the Accountant of Court". As the Accountant of Court and the Public Guardian are the same person,[19] the significance of this would not appear to extend beyond relevant

---

[13] paras 6(6) and (7).
[14] See para.11–41 *supra*.
[15] See para.11–49 *supra*.
[16] See paras 11–55 *et seq. supra*.
[17] para.11–65 *supra*.
[18] paras 11–66 and 11–67 *supra*.
[19] s.6(1).

administrative arrangements, particularly as reference is made to the Accountant of Court's address in Edinburgh rather than the Public Guardian's address in Falkirk.

Former MHSA guardians

11–97 Under MHSA guardianship it was possible to appoint the local authority as guardian. Paragraph 6(5) includes the local authority as guardian, in the same manner as the chief officer as guardian, in the provisions regarding guardian's outlays in s.68(2) and costs in s.68(3), and provisions applicable where the adult moves from one local authority to another under s.76. These provisions are described in paras 11–34 and 11–5 respectively above. If a local authority had been appointed tutor-dative, the provisions described in this paragraph would have likewise applied. So far as the author is aware, no such appointment was made.[20]

Duration

11–98 The Act did not alter the duration of appointments under pre-Act law of curators bonis and tutors. Indefinite appointments, including (so far as is known) all appointments of curators bonis and tutors-at-law and a few appointments of tutors-dative, remain indefinite. Time-limited appointments, being most appointments of tutors-dative, retain their durations. Paragraph 6(3) of Schedule 4 however limits to a period of five years from April 1, 2002 the period within which renewal procedure under s.60 (described in para.11–24 above) may be followed. The only significance of para.6(3) is that where a time-limited appointment is due to expire after the five-year period and renewal proceedings are not commenced within the five-year period, then a fresh application rather than renewal procedure would be required. Most of the provisions for fresh applications apply to renewal procedure. Probably, the main advantage of renewal procedure is that once it has been commenced, the existing appointment continues until the renewal application has been determined.[21]

11–99 The effect of para.6(3) is curious, and perhaps not the intended effect. The official Explanatory Notes to the Act suggested that existing appointments of curators and tutors "will have to be re-considered by the court within 5 years". That appears to have been incorrect. The Bill as introduced provided (in para.6(4) of what was then Schedule 3) that existing appointments would continue for their duration, if the order creating them specified a duration, and otherwise indefinitely. That provision does not appear in the Act as enacted, but in the absence of any contrary provision its terms would still appear to represent the position under the Act. A further point is that para.6(3) as worded would appear to permit renewal procedure within five years of April 1, 2002 of a time-limited appointment which had already expired at some time after April 1, 2002. The Part 6 Code[22] recommends that: "Where the original appointment was not time

---

[20] Professor J. Thomson suggested that such appointment was competent in an article 1988 S.L.T. (News) 4.
[21] s.60(1).
[22] para.7.5.

limited, it is good practice to seek renewal of the powers within 5 years. At that point, all concerned, including the local authority, should consider whether a less intrusive measure than guardianship would be appropriate. If guardianship continues to be necessary, the sheriff will consider the precise powers to be conferred and the period for which the guardian is to be appointed, on the basis of an application for renewal of guardianship under s.60". This reads as a rather unconvincing attempt to justify the existence of para.6(3), because good practice requires review whenever there has been a significant change in needs or circumstances, the appropriate procedure for recall is that described in para.11–72 above, the appropriate procedure for variation is that described in para.11–73 above, and the first two general principles forbid procedures or other interventions which confer no benefit on the adult or are more than the minimum necessary intervention.

The position in relation to former MHSA guardians is clear. Powers continue in force for the duration under MHSA 1984 as if the Incapacity Act had not come into force, and renewal under s.60 is not competent.[23] If guardianship remains necessary, a fresh application is required. **11–100**

Replacement, additional and substitute guardians

It is competent to seek replacement under s.71(1)(a) of a transitional guardian,[24] to seek appointment under s.62(1)(b) of an additional guardian to act jointly with a transitional guardian,[25] or to seek appointment under s.63 of a substitute guardian to a transitional guardian.[26] It would appear that the provisions of the Act apply without modification to such replacement, additional or substitute guardians, because the modifications in para.6 of Schedule 4 apply only to "persons who have become guardians by virtue of [Schedule 4]".[27] Under all of the provisions referred to, the guardianship continues with a new, additional or substitute guardian, but para.6 appears to apply personally to the existing transitional guardian. Shortly after April 1, 2002 steps were initiated to have the mother of an adult appointed as additional guardian, jointly with the adult's father who had originally been appointed tutor-at-law, an appointment limited to the nearest male agnate.[28] **11–101**

Curators bonis to persons under 16

It remains competent to appoint a curator bonis to a person under 16.[29] Unless in terms of the appointment it ends on the ward's 16th birthday, the curator bonis then becomes a plenary financial guardian under the Act. This applies whether the original appointment was made before or after commencement of Part 6 on April 1, 2002.[30] The **11–102**

---

[23] Sch.3, para.6(4).
[24] See paras 11–17 and 11–70 *supra*.
[25] See paras 11–11 and 11–12 *supra*.
[26] See para.11–14 *supra*.
[27] Sch.4, para.6(1).
[28] See para.10–11 *supra*.
[29] s.80 rendered incompetent, after April 1, 2002, appointments "to a person who has attained the age of 16 years".
[30] Sch.4, para.1(2).

provisions of para.6 of Schedule 4, described in paras 11–94 and 11–95 above, apply to such guardians,[31] but in this context the references in s.88(1) to "existing powers" and in the heading to Schedule 4 to "existing curators" are misleading, because Schedule 4 (and the Act's provisions, except as modified by para.6) apply upon the ward attaining age 16 at any time on or after April 1, 2002 under appointments made, and powers conferred, before or after that date.

Comment

11–103 It is curious that appointments of curators bonis to persons under 16 should remain competent. There is no self-evident advantage in not having replaced all forms of curatory with the new form of guardianship, though provisions such as the general principles in s.1 would have required modification.[32] While the long title and scope of the Act restricts its provisions to persons aged 16 and over, the effect of the repeals in Schedule 6 of parts of the Judicial Factors Act 1849[33] appears to be to remove curators to both adults and children from relevant provisions, including the definition of judicial factors. Wilkinson and Norrie[34] recommend curatory for children where financial guardianship is likely to continue to be required into adulthood. They also point out that curatory, unlike appointment of a legal representative under the Children (Scotland) Act 1995,[35] is subject to the responsibilities of accounting and supervision contained in the Judicial Factors Act 1849—an advantage apparently now removed by the repeals in Schedule 6 to the Incapacity Act.

CHECKLIST

11–104 The following checklist is offered for guidance when an application for guardianship is contemplated. It is not complete, and should not be used in isolation from the remainder of this book, but may nevertheless be of assistance in ensuring that points of particular importance, best addressed before the application is lodged, are not overlooked.

- Is the person an adult (*i.e.* has attained the age of 16 years—s.1(6))?

- What guardianship or intervention orders have previously been granted, what variations or ancillary orders have there been, and which of them are still in force (s.58(2))?

- Are any other "interventions", under the Act or otherwise, in force; how will the application affect them (*e.g.* guardian

---

[31] Sch.4, para.6(1) applies to a "person who has become guardian by virtue of this Schedule".
[32] See, for example, the comments on "best interests" in para.4–18 *supra* and the passage from the SLC Report quoted in para.15–26 *infra*.
[33] 12 and 13 Vict. c.51.
[34] *Parent and Child* (2nd ed.), para.15.64.
[35] (c.36) s.11(2)(b).

superseding attorney under s.24(2)); and if they will continue, how will they inter-relate?

- Can guardianship be shown to be necessary (s.1(2))?

- Can guardianship be shown to be the least restrictive option (s.1(3))?

- Can the powers sought all be shown to be necessary and to represent the least restrictive option (ss.1(2) and 1(3))?

- Are the powers sought adequate to meet existing and reasonably foreseeable needs?

- In particular, are powers needed to access and/or divulge confidential information?

- If instructions have been given to seek management powers, are any welfare powers needed, and vice versa?

- Are the powers sought solely management powers, or solely welfare powers, or do they cover both categories?

- Does incapacity arise solely from physical inability to communicate (see s.57(3)(a) and (b))?

- Where the applicant claims an interest in the adult's personal welfare, has notice been given to the chief social work officer under s.57(4)?

- Having regard to powers sought and the cause of incapacity, have the appropriate reports been sought under s.57(3)?

- Have matters been planned and managed so that the application will be lodged in court within 30 days of the first examination or interview (s.57(3))?

- When received, do the reports comply with the forms in the regulations and do they confirm incapacity in terms of s.1(6) in relation to all of the powers sought?

- Have the present and past wishes and feelings of the adult been ascertained (s.1(4)(a))?

- Have the identities and views of the nearest relative and primary carer been ascertained (s.1(4)(b))?

- Should any other views be ascertained in terms of s.1(4)(c) and (d)?

- Can it be shown that the proposed guardian (or each proposed guardian) is suitable and has consented (s.59)?

- Should any interim order be sought under s.3(2)(d)?

- Should interim appointment be sought under s.57(5) and (6)?

- Should exercise of any other discretionary powers under s.3 be sought?

- Should a direction be sought that intimation should not be given to the adult (s.11(1)) and, if so, has appropriate medical certification been sought?

- Should the sheriff be asked to hold the hearing "in a hospital or other place" (Rule 3.16.3)?

- If financial or property powers are sought, is caution available, and—if not—should the sheriff be asked to dispense with caution (s.58(6))?

- Can sufficient information be provided to enable the level of caution to be fixed (Rule 3.16.10(1))?

- If property or financial powers are sought, should the sheriff be asked to dispense with a management plan (Schedule 2, para.1(1))?

- If any heritable property is to be covered by the order sought, has a proper conveyancing description been obtained for inclusion in the application (Rule 3.16.12)?

- Should the sheriff be asked to confer powers which may be exercised prior to approval of the management plan (Schedule 2, para.1(4))?

- Should the sheriff be asked to specify anyone whom the guardian should consult when exercising his functions (s.1(4)(c)(ii))?

- Should power be sought to enable the guardian to authorise transactions or categories of transactions by the adult (s.64(1)(e))?

- Should the appointment be for some period other than three years (in case of renewal, five years), and can cause be shown for this (ss.58(4) and 60(4)(b))?

- Which sheriff has jurisdiction (Schedule 3, para.2)?

- Does a court process require to be transferred from another sheriffdom (Rule 3.16.8(2) and (3))?

Chapter 12

OTHER RESPONSIVE MEASURES

Introduction

The range of anticipatory, responsive and third party measures in relation to both management and personal welfare was surveyed in para.3–9 above. They were allocated to categories of those abolished, created, amended or unaltered by the Incapacity Act. Those unaltered by the Act are nevertheless now substantially influenced by it, and the relevance of the Act to them is discussed in particular in Chapters 4 and 5. The investigatory and other provisions of the Act which may be exercised or invoked in relation to techniques and measures outwith the Act are summarised in para.5–41 above. **12–1**

Anticipatory measures outwith the Act were described in Chapter 7. The régime of responsive measures created by the Act is described in Chapters 8–11 inclusive, together with Chapter 14 which describes relevant law concerning medical treatment and research both within and outwith the Act. The remaining range of principal responsive measures is surveyed in this chapter, subject to three caveats. The first is that it would be almost impossible to identify every measure available in our law which could potentially, in one situation or another, be helpfully and properly employed in response to an adult's impairment of capacity. This chapter does not attempt to be comprehensive: instead, it seeks to identify and describe the measures most commonly used specifically in response to adult incapacity. The second caveat is that the statutory personal welfare measures described in paras 12–28 to 12–33 below proceed upon their own criteria, which are not explicitly criteria of incapacity, but are included here because some impairment of capacity is a frequent element in cases in which such measures are employed. Thirdly, there is obvious overlap between the categories of responsive and third party measures, recognised in the survey in para.3–9. The approach broadly adopted here is to classify as responsive those measures taken by a third party in relation to funds to which the adult is entitled as of right, and as third party measures those where the third party contributes funds by choice rather than by legal obligation. Even under that approach, some measures could fit equally well in either category. The allocation adopted between this and the next chapter is, in areas of overlap, based upon convenience.[1] **12–2**

---

[1] As explained at the end of para.3–9 *supra*, categorisations adopted in this book are not in all cases necessarily rigidly exclusive. For example, the author should not be understood as conclusively excluding the possible application of *negotiorum gestio* to a personal welfare matter or of the *parens patriae* jurisdiction to a management matter.

Good practice

12–3 In relation to decisions about the selection, operation, and continuation or discontinuation of the management measures described below, it is good practice for the adviser to apply the Act's general principles described in Chapter 5, and in doing so to have regard *inter alia* to the following:

- First to identify the circumstances and needs, and then to select the measure or combination of measures which will most accurately meet the identified need.

- To take account of possible use in combination of measures within and outwith the Act (such as an intervention order to permit transfer of funds into a trust).

- To ensure compatibility of proposed combinations of measures (for example, several measures—including DWP appointeeships—are not competent when there is a guardian whose authority is in force[2]).

- To ensure that the intervention proposed is the minimum necessary.

- To check carefully the powers which will become available under the proposed measure(s), and that they will be adequate for anticipated needs.

- To consider whether the formalities to be followed are proportional or disproportional, and whether they afford adequate protection in the particular circumstances of the case.

- To consider the adequacy of the protection offered by the régime of accountability and supervision (if any) for the proposed measure.

- To apply the third general principle.

- To apply the fourth general principle to the extent appropriate.

MANAGEMENT

Social security benefits

General

12–4 The provisions described below are contained in the Social Security (Claims and Payments) Regulations 1987, as amended, and are referred to by regulation number. "The Department" refers to the

---

[2] Such provisions should probably now be construed as referring to a guardian with relevant financial powers—see *e.g.* para.12–5 *infra*.

Department of Work and Pensions, formerly the Department of Social Security. Procedures to initiate these measures are relatively simple and informal. Once they are in place, they lack régimes of accountability and monitoring. Their scope is of course limited to receiving benefits (or part thereof). There are no proactive controls on how they are used by recipients.

Regulation 33

12–5 Where a person is incapable of acting in relation to social security matters, regulation 33 authorises the appointment of an appointee to apply for, receive and deal with benefits on that person's behalf. Appointment is not competent where the person's estate is being administered by a guardian acting or appointed in terms of law. It would appear that this must necessarily now be construed as referring to a guardian with relevant financial powers. There are no financial limits. The appointee must be aged over 18. Application is made by completing the appropriate form and submitting it to the local Benefits Agency, where staff are responsible for verifying the claimant's incapacity, usually by interview or medical certificate, and for ascertaining that the proposed appointee is suitable. The appointee may give one month's notice of termination to the Department. The Department may revoke the appointment at any time.

12–6 Promptly upon appointment, the appointee should check that all benefits to which the person may be entitled have been claimed. Otherwise, entitlement to backdating may be lost, because although mental incapacity is "good cause" for a late claim, once an appointee has been appointed it is for the appointee (rather than the incapacitated person) to show "good cause" for any delay.

12–7 On occasions, there are concerns that an adult appears to be trapped within the power of financial control exercised by the appointee. Such cases should be referred for investigation either by the Department or by the Public Guardian (under s.6(2)(d) of the Incapacity Act—see para.5–24 above). Another appointee, or other measures, may be appropriate. Conversely, difficulties have sometimes been encountered where it appears appropriate to end financial guardianship and for an appointee under regulation 33 to take over. Because an appointment cannot competently be made while guardianship is still in force, the Department require to see documentary confirmation of discharge or recall before formally making the appointment. It is therefore necessary to follow the appointment procedure up to, but not including, the actual appointment. The Department is then willing to provide written confirmation to the Public Guardian that the appointment will be made once the financial guardianship has been ended.

Regulation 34

12–8 Regulation 34 permits a benefit to be paid, wholly or in part, to another person acting for the claimant if that appears to be necessary to protect the interests of the claimant or dependants.

Regulation 34A

12–9 Regulation 34A permits payment of part of a person's benefit to a qualifying mortgage lender[3] to meet the person's liability to pay mortgage interest.

Regulation 35 (and Schedule 9)

12–10 Under regulation 35 of and Schedule 9 to the Regulations, costs of housing, accommodation, fuel and water may be deducted from benefits and paid direct.

Vaccine damage payments

12–11 If the requirements of the Vaccine Damage Payments Act 1979[4] are met, a single lump sum payment is made to those who become severely disabled as a result of a routine NHS vaccination against various specified diseases, or vaccination of the person's mother before birth, or infection from a vaccinated person. The amount of payment was formerly £30,000 and is currently £100,000: top up payments were made by the Vaccine Damage Payments Unit (of the Disability and Carer Benefits Directorate) to those who had previously received the lower amount. There are detailed rules regarding place and date of vaccination, and age. If the disabled person is unable to manage his own affairs, payment may be made to trustees appointed by the Department. Upon death, the payment falls into the estate of the disabled person. Commonly, the trustees appointed are the parents of the disabled person.

The deed of trust

12–12 The usual form of trust for the purpose is structured as a deed of trust between the Secretary of State and the trustees. The trustees are directed to hold the trust fund in trust for the disabled person until that person has attained the age of 18 years, and thereafter only as long as the disabled person is unable "by reason of any defect or illness of mind" to manage his own affairs. To determine this, it is declared to be sufficient for the trustees to act on a certificate purporting to be signed by a medical practitioner who has been in attendance on the beneficiary for at least one year. In addition to particular powers which are specified, the trustees have a general power under which they may "at their discretion, from time to time advance and pay to or apply for the behoof of the Beneficiary the whole or part of the income or capital of the Trust Fund for the proper maintenance, support, education, advancement in life, or otherwise for the benefit of the Beneficiary", and they have "the fullest powers of investment, realisation, appropriation, administration and management of the Trust Fund (as if they were absolute beneficial owners thereof)".

---

[3] As defined in the Social Security Administration Act 1992 (c.5), s.15A.
[4] c.17.

Damages payments in the sheriff court

Ordinary Cause Rules[5] 36.14–36.17 apply where a sum of money becomes payable to an adult who has attained the age of 18 and is "under legal disability", or becomes payable for the benefit of such an adult, under a decree for payment or of absolvitor or under an extrajudicial settlement, in a sheriff court action of damages. As is pointed out in MacPhail,[6] there is no provision for such persons aged 16 and 17: the provisions of OCR 36.14 and of the Children (Scotland) Act 1995, s.13, apply only up to age 16.[7] "Legal disability" is not defined, but would appear to encompass relevant incapacity. Rules 36.14–36.17 would benefit from updating with reference to the measures now available under the Incapacity Act.

12–13

Rule 36.14 requires the sheriff, in the circumstances described in para.12–13 above, to make such order regarding the payment and management of the sum in question for the benefit of the adult as the sheriff thinks fit. Under Rule 36.15 the sheriff may (a) appoint a judicial factor to apply, invest or otherwise deal with the money for the adult's benefit, (b) order that the money be paid to the Accountant of Court or to the adult's guardian, in either case as trustee, to apply, invest or otherwise deal with and administer the money under the sheriff's directions for the adult's benefit, (c) order the money to be paid to the sheriff clerk of the sheriff court district where the adult resides to be likewise managed, or (d) order the money to be paid directly to the adult. Power (a) may still be exercised to appoint a judicial factor other than a curator bonis—see para.12–25 below. The reference to guardians is now likely to be construed as referring to a guardian with financial powers under the Incapacity Act, but the requirement that the guardian administer "as trustee" rather than in accordance with the provisions of the Incapacity Act raises potential difficulties unlikely to be satisfactorily resolved except by amendment of these Rules. Fortunately, Rule 36.16 provides that where the sheriff has made an order under Rule 36.14, any person having an interest[8] may apply for an appointment or order under Rule 36.15, or for "any other order for the payment or management of the money". This provision would facilitate use of any appropriate techniques or appointments, including those under the Incapacity Act, and may well now prove to be the preferred option.

12–14

Damages payments: any competent court

Any competent court may, under Rule 36.17(2), request that the sheriff clerk accept custody of any sum in an action of damages, if the sum has been ordered to be paid to, applied, invested or otherwise dealt with by the sheriff clerk, for the benefit of a person "under legal disability".[9] Money received by the sheriff clerk in this way may

12–15

---

[5] Contained in first Schedule to Sheriff Courts (Scotland) Act 1907 (7 Edw. 7 c.51) as substituted for causes commenced from January 1, 1994 by SI 1993/1956 as amended, regarding rules referred to, by SI 1996/2167.

[6] MacPhail, *Sheriff Court Practice*, (Nicholson and Stewart, 2nd ed., 1998), Vol. I, para.21–37.

[7] Rule 36.17(2), described in para.12–15, might seem to offer a solution if construed out of context, but not in the context of the preceding Rules.

[8] See discussion in para.14–59.

[9] On interpretation of that phrase, see para.12–13 *supra*.

Criminal injuries compensation

12–16 There have been successive Criminal Injuries Compensation Schemes. The first was introduced in 1964, followed by successive amended Schemes in 1969, 1979 and 1990. The current Scheme is generally known as "the 1996 Scheme", and was introduced in terms of the Criminal Injuries Compensation Act 1995, under which administration passed from the former Criminal Injuries Compensation Board to the Criminal Injuries Compensation Authority.[10] Where the victim is an adult with impaired capacity, the arrangements for administration of the award depend upon which Scheme applied, which in turn depends upon the date of the incident or application. Broadly, the Criminal Injuries Compensation Board had, and the Criminal Injuries Compensation Authority now has, discretion to establish a trust or to make other arrangements. Under para.18 of the 1969 Scheme, which applied to injuries sustained up to September 30, 1979, the Board had "discretion to make special arrangements for the administration of any money awarded as compensation". The Board had discretion to pay the award to trustees or to make "special arrangements for its administration" under para.9 of the 1979 Scheme and para.9 of the 1990 Scheme, in similar terms and applicable where injuries were sustained on or after October 1, 1979 and application was made before April 1, 1996. Beneficiaries under any such trust were limited to the applicant and any spouse, widow, widower, relative claiming descent from the victim's grandparents, or dependant. The current 1996 Scheme, applicable to claims received on or after April 1, 1996, is less explicit. Paragraph 50 includes a provision that: "The claims officer may make such directions and arrangements, including the imposition of conditions, in connection with the acceptance, settlement, payment, repayment and/or administration of an award as he considers appropriate in all the circumstances". Paragraph 52 adds the option, by agreement between the Authority and the applicant or the applicant's representative, of using part or all of the award to purchase an annuity or annuities. Practice under para.50 appears largely to have followed previous practice. The establishment of a trust will often be the most appropriate arrangement where the applicant's capacity to manage the award is impaired, and may also be appropriate having regard to the potential impact of the award on entitlement to means-tested benefits.[11] It would be reasonable to expect the claims officer, and the Authority, to apply the general principles of the Incapacity Act as representing good practice when determining management arrangements for an adult with impaired capacity. If the claims officer, or the Authority, were to refuse to follow those principles to the disadvantage of the claimant, that (it is

---

[10] For a full account of the history of relevant Schemes, and of the subject, see Brown et al., *Claiming Criminal Injuries Compensation*, Legal Services Agency, 1997.

[11] See Brown et al. *op.cit.* paras 8.2–8.14.

submitted) would be *prima facie* cause to seek an intervention order containing an appropriate direction. This applies to any claimant who is an adult, that is to say 16 or over, notwithstanding that the 1996 Scheme contains special provisions in relation to applicants under 18 years of age, including the requirement under para.15(b) that the claims officer should only make an award where he is satisfied that it would be in the applicant's interest to do so, if the applicant is under 18 years of age when the application is determined.[12]

Miscellaneous statutory methods

Many statutes, and regulations made under statutes, provide for management of particular types of asset on behalf of a person whose management capacity is impaired. Typically, such provisions authorise the relevant fundholder to accept investments on behalf of the person whose capacity is impaired, and/or confer discretion on the fundholder to make payment to someone who is caring for the person, or to someone who will apply the payment for the person's benefit. This paragraph does not attempt to offer a comprehensive list. Common examples are these: (a) Savings Certificates Regulations 1991,[13] under regulation 9(4) of which the Director of Savings has discretion to make repayment to a recipient who has satisfied the Director that he will apply the payment for the maintenance, or otherwise for the benefit, of a "mentally disordered person"; (b) National Savings Bank Regulations 1972,[14] regulation 7(4) under which, where a depositor is a "mentally disordered person", the Director of Savings may pay sums to any person whom he may judge proper to receive them, if it is proved to his satisfaction that it is just and expedient to do so; (c) Premium Savings Bonds Regulations 1972,[15] under regulation 10(2) of which the Director of Savings may make payment to a person whom the Director is satisfied will apply it for the maintenance of the holder or otherwise for the holder's benefit, where the Director of Savings is satisfied as to "mental disorder" and as to the expediency of making the payment in such manner; (d) Industrial and Provident Societies Act 1965, s.26, under which, where a society's committee is satisfied that a member or claimant is "incapable through disorder or disability of mind of managing his own affairs" and there is no appointee with relevant powers, sums may be paid to any person judged proper to receive them if it is proved to the committee's satisfaction that it is just and expedient to do so; (e) Mental Health Act 1983 (c.20), s.142, which applies to Scotland, and which relates to any pay or pension from monies provided by Parliament or the Consolidated Fund or under the control or supervision of any government department; and (f) the Income Tax (Deposit-Takers) (Interest Payments) (Amendment) Regulations 1992[16] and Income Tax (Building Societies) (Dividends and

12-17

---

[12] It could reasonably be argued in relation to a Scottish applicant aged 16 or over, but under 18, that any reservations under para.15(b) regarding the applicant's capacity to safeguard his interests in relation to the award, and/or to manage it, cannot be related to his age, having regard to the Age of Legal Capacity (Scotland) Act 1991, and can only properly be considered in relation to the definition of incapacity in s.1(6) of the Incapacity Act.
[13] SI 1991/1031.
[14] SI 1972/764.
[15] SI 1972/65.
[16] Amending the principal regulations SI 1990/2232.

Interest) (Amendment) Regulations 1992,[17] under which a parent, guardian, spouse, son or daughter of a mentally incapacitated person may register on the person's behalf for interest to be paid without deduction of tax.

Negotiorum gestio

12–18   *Negotiorum gestio* is the principle under which someone, termed the gestor, spontaneously undertakes the management of a person's affairs without the person's knowledge, because the person either is absent or lacks capacity, in circumstances where it is a reasonable presumption that the person would have given authority if aware of the circumstances and able to do so.[18] In the case of incapacity, the principle applies both to single acts of management or short-term management, and also to long-term management. Reported cases contain examples of management for periods ranging from two years to over five years.[19] Acts by gestors in the years prior to the availability of intervention orders included acts now likely to be authorised by intervention orders, an example being a gestor who, with the consent of a landlord, executed a tenancy agreement expressly as gestor without incurring personal liability. Under former law the gestor was superseded by the appointment of a curator bonis[20] or tutor, and consequently would now probably be held to be superseded by appointment of a guardian with relevant powers. *Negotiorum gestio* may co-exist with other measures. While *negotiorum gestio* is not directly addressed in the Incapacity Act, it—like all other techniques— is subject to the investigatory and other provisions of the Act described in para.5–41 above, and the range of provision introduced by the Act has reduced the range of circumstances in which it would be reasonable to rely on *negotiorum gestio* and in which it would be reasonable to request third parties to transact with a gestor.

12–19   The gestor must show the same degree of care as a prudent person acting in relation to his own affairs, and provided that he does so he incurs no personal liability for any loss to the person's estate resulting from his actings.[21] The person's estate is liable for obligations and liabilities incurred by the gestor for the person's benefit. Third parties may seek payment from the person's funds, or the gestor may pay them and himself be reimbursed from the person's funds. The gestor may also be reimbursed for reasonable expenses, but is not entitled to remuneration.

12–20   The disadvantages of *negotiorum gestio* include the lack of any procedure to determine whether it is appropriate, the extent to which it is appropriate, and the suitability of the gestor; the lack of any controls or supervision to prevent detriment or misuse; and the lack of any evidence of authority—the gestor cannot insist that third parties recognise his authority or implement his instructions and directions.

---

[17] Amending the principal regulations SI 1990/2231.
[18] See Bell, *Principles*, para.540; also Scottish Law Commission Discussion Paper No.94, paras 4.21–4.23.
[19] *Maule v Graham*, 1757 Mor. 3529, *Fernie v Robertson* (1871) 9 M. 437, and *Dunbar v Wilson and Dunlop's Trs* (1887) 15 R. 210.
[20] *Dunbar v Wilson and Dunlop's Trs, supra.*
[21] *Smith's Reps v Earl of Winton*, 1714 Mor. 9275; *Bannatine's Trs v Cunningham* (1872) 10 M. 319; *Kolbin and Sons v The United Shipping Company Ltd*, 1931 S.C. (HL) 128.

Informal voluntary arrangements

12–21 Many transactions relating to adults with impaired capacity are conducted by agreement of those concerned without any identifiable legal basis. Prior to the Incapacity Act, such arrangements were often a practical response to the absence of suitable management techniques. However, such arrangements continue frequently to occur. Reasons include reluctance to use available techniques, a belief that they are unduly burdensome or restrictive in relation to the matters in question, or ignorance of them. Occasionally there may be less innocent motives.

12–22 Informal voluntary arrangements arise most often when a signature is required, for example to operate a bank or similar account, to grant a receipt or discharge for insurance proceeds or other sums, to claim a tax repayment, and so forth. It often happens in practice that a signature of some other person, or a signature or mark by the adult (notwithstanding lack of capacity), is accepted. Such arrangements depend upon the continuing co-operation of all concerned, and cannot be insisted upon. They may be combined with elements of *negotiorum gestio*.[22] They may operate satisfactorily for years, but remain precarious. For example, problems have arisen with operation of bank and building society accounts in this way upon appointment of a new manager.

Joint accounts

12–23 Accounts in joint names are discussed in paras 7–1 and 7–2 above, where they are categorised as an anticipatory technique, but in practice a joint account may be opened where one account holder has already lost incapacity. Section 32 of the Incapacity Act, described in paras 7–1 and 7–2 above, applies (reasonably and correctly) where an existing account holder "becomes incapable", but may in practice assist with management problems which formerly arose as described in those paragraphs in cases where the capacity of one account holder was already impaired when the account was opened. Potential problems remain in relation to the validity of the initial establishment of the account. On the death or incapacity of the other account holder, difficulties may arise as to future management. Typically, under such arrangements the funds are entirely the funds of the adult, but problems about entitlement may arise, including in relation to means-testing, income tax liability, or entitlement and inheritance tax liability on death of either party.

Bare trusts

12–24 A bare trust is established when title to a fund or asset is taken in name of someone "in trust for" a person with impaired capacity, with no document adequately setting out the terms and purposes of the trust. Common examples are where a relative or carer opens an account or takes an investment in this way. Problems may arise upon the death or incapacity of the trustee. There is also a risk that the fund may lie dormant, producing no significant benefit for the adult, then

---

[22] See preceding section.

become an embarrassment in its inter-relationship with the establishment of general arrangements for provision such as are described in Chapter 13.

Judicial factors

12–25 Only the appointment of curators and tutors to adults became incompetent from April 1, 2002 under s.80 of the Incapacity Act. Other forms of judicial factory remain competent. While there are, and have been, various specific types of judicial factors appointed for particular purposes, judicial factory is not limited to those specific types.[23] A judicial factor may be appointed whenever a collection of property, rights and obligations requires management or distribution by an independent factor supervised by the court.[24] A judicial factor may still be appointed to administer a particular fund or asset.[25] Given the comprehensive nature and purpose of the Incapacity Act and the flexibility of the new régime of guardianship and intervention orders, it seems unlikely that a court would be persuaded to appoint a judicial factor in relation to a fund or asset to which an adult with impaired capacity is solely entitled and where the only or principal reason for seeking intervention is the adult's incapacity. Judicial factory continues to be appropriate in many cases where the adult's incapacity is incidental to the need for a judicial factor, or where more persons than the adult have an interest in or claim against the fund or asset. While in many such cases a separate measure will be required in relation to management and safeguarding of the adult's interest, in some cases the judicial factory may adequately meet the adult's management needs. The judicial factory régime is not described in detail here. The main characteristics are those which applied to curatory, as outlined in para.10–10 above.

Curators ad litem

12–26 Curators ad litem remain competent, as described in para.10–43 above, but for the reasons given in that paragraph it is suggested that guardianship or an intervention order for the purpose of pursuing or defending proceedings should normally be preferred. To the extent that appointment of curators ad litem remains appropriate, they may act in litigation relating either to management or to personal welfare matters. MacPhail refers to such appointment being competent "in special circumstances and in actions affecting status".[26] The person other than the safeguarder appointed to convey the adult's views under s.3(5) of the Incapacity Act is described in the official guidance[27] as a curator ad litem.

---

[23] *Leslie's Judicial Factor*, 1925 S.C. 464 at 469.
[24] *Robertson v Robertson*, 2001 S.L.T. 797.
[25] See para.12–14 *supra* on appointment of a judicial factor to administer a damages payment.
[26] MacPhail, *Sheriff Court Practice* (Nicholson and Stewart, 2nd ed., 1998), Vol.I, para.4.07 citing *Moodie v Dempster*, 1931 S.C. 553 *per* Lord Sands at 555; *Drummond's Trustees v Peel's Trustees*, 1929 S.C. 484; and *Finlay v Finlay*, 1962 S.L.T. (Sh. Ct) 43.
[27] Explanatory Notes to the Act, para.26.

Parens patriae **jurisdiction**

On the *parens patriae* jurisdiction, see para.12–34 below. The jurisdiction would appear to remain relevant in relation to management matters, as well as personal welfare matters. 12–27

PERSONAL WELFARE

Introduction

Decision-making in relation to medical treatment and research is addressed in Chapter 14, where measures both within and outwith the Incapacity Act are considered. MHSA procedures are nevertheless outlined here, because they impose decisions about removal to and detention in hospital, as well as about treatment, and include a procedure for compulsory supervision in the community. Related measures under the Criminal Procedure (Scotland) Act 1995 ("the 1995 Act") are also outlined. Similarly, procedure under s.47 of the National Assistance Act 1948 ("the 1948 Act")[28] imposes a decision about removal to hospital and detention there, and is outlined here. Two general points require to be made about relevant procedures under these statutes. Firstly, the statutory criteria are not incapacity, but may encompass impaired capacity, so that these procedures can reasonably be included in a survey of measures which may be employed in response to impairment of capacity in relation to personal decision-making. Secondly, the relevant provisions of these statutes are subject to proposals for substantial reform in terms of the Mental Health (Scotland) Bill introduced in the Scottish Parliament on September 16, 2002. Reform of MHSA is referred to in para.3–31 above, and is expected to include reform of relevant 1995 Act provisions, and of s.47 of the 1948 Act in cases where vulnerability results from mental disorder. Scottish Executive have consulted with a view to reform of s.47 in cases where vulnerability arises otherwise than from mental disorder. Because of the likelihood of reform, existing law is outlined only briefly in the following paras 12–29 to 12–33, and criticisms of the existing law are not rehearsed, as they have been well explored in the reform process.[29] Any replacement provisions and procedures will also have a place in any consideration of measures responsive to impairment of capacity in relation to personal decision-making. 12–28

MHSA provisions

MHSA 1984 applies to people suffering, or appearing to suffer, from mental disorder, which is defined (as in the Incapacity Act) as meaning "mental illness (including personality disorder) or mental handicap however caused or manifested".[30] Additional criteria apply 12–29

---

[28] 11 and 12 Geo. 6 c.29, as amended by the National Assistance (Amendment) Act 1951.
[29] See reports and papers referred to in para.3–31 *supra*, and also Scottish Law Commission Report No.158 on *Vulnerable Adults*, 1997, and Scottish Executive Consultation Paper on *Vulnerable Adults*, published December 2001.
[30] MHSA 1984, s.1, as amended by the Mental Health (Public Safety and Appeals) (Scotland) Act 1999 (asp 1), s.3(1)(a). On anticipated change to the definition, see para.4–24 *supra*.

to particular procedures and provisions, but the starting-point is mental disorder (which may or may not result in some impairment of capacity) rather than incapacity caused by mental disorder.

12-30 The current MHSA provides for emergency detention for up to two hours by a nurse of a patient attempting to leave hospital[31]; emergency removal of a patient to hospital and detention there for up to 72 hours[32] or such emergency detention of a patient already in hospital as a voluntary patient[33]; short-term detention for up to 28 days,[34] extendable by three working days in the event of relapse late in the initial period[35] and by up to five working days if formal procedure has been initiated[36]; formal detention upon application to the sheriff for six months, renewable for six months and annually thereafter[37]; granting of leave of absence to a detained patient, which may in certain circumstances be revoked and the patient again detained[38]; and a community care order under which, in certain circumstances, the patient may be recalled to hospital for assessment for up to seven days and kept there for a further 21 days.[39]

12-31 MHSA 1984 also includes a right, exerciseable by a mental health officer[40] or medical commissioner of the Mental Welfare Commission, to demand admission to premises where a mentally disordered person is[41]; a procedure to confer powers of forcible entry upon a mental health officer or medical commissioner, with power to remove the mentally disordered person to a place of safety[42]; and a power exerciseable by the police to remove to a place of safety a mentally disordered person in need of care and control found in a public place.[43]

Criminal Procedure (Scotland) Act 1995

12-32 In addition to power to make guardianship orders as described in paras 11-84 *et seq.* above, under the Criminal Procedure (Scotland) Act 1995[44] the court has the following powers: (a) under s.52, the court may commit to hospital a person remanded or committed for trial who is charged with any offence and who appears to the court to be suffering from mental disorder, and to review such order if the circumstances subsequently change; (b) under s.53, the court may make an interim hospital order in respect of a mentally disordered offender where it may be appropriate for the offender to be detained

---

[31] MHSA 1984, s.25(2).
[32] *ibid.* s.24.
[33] *ibid.* s.25(1).
[34] *ibid.* s.26.
[35] *ibid.* s.26A, inserted by the Mental Health (Detention) (Scotland) Act 1991 (c.47), s.1.
[36] *ibid.* s.21(3B), inserted by the Mental Health (Detention) (Scotland) Act 1991 (c.47), s.2.
[37] *ibid.* ss.17-23 and 30.
[38] *ibid.* s.27.
[39] *ibid.* ss.35A-35K, inserted by the Mental Health (Patients in the Community) Act 1995, s.4.
[40] See para.5-37 *supra*.
[41] *ibid.* s.117(1).
[42] *ibid.* s.117(2).
[43] *ibid.* s.118.
[44] c.46, "the 1995 Act". See para.11-84 for a more detailed description of relevant provisions and Appendix 3 for selected sections of the 1995 Act.

in the State Hospital, which order may include a direction for the offender to be first conveyed to a place of safety pending admission to hospital; (c) under s.54, the court may make a temporary hospital order upon a finding of insanity in bar of trial, pending an examination of facts under ss.55 and 56, and to review such order upon change of circumstances; (d) under s.57(1)(a), upon acquittal on grounds of insanity at the time of alleged commission of the offence charged, and under s.57(1)(b) upon a finding at an examination of facts that the person did the act or made the omission constituting the offence charged and that there were no grounds for acquittal, the court may in terms of s.57(2) *inter alia* make an order with the same effect as a hospital order (see below), in addition to make an order with the same effect as a restriction order (see below), or to make a supervision and treatment order[45]; (e) under s.58, the court may make a hospital order upon conviction of an offence which is punishable with imprisonment or detention and which is not an offence for which the punishment is fixed by law, and may include in the order a direction for conveyance of the person to a place of safety pending admission to hospital; (f) under s.58(2), the High Court may make a hospital order (and direct conveyance to a place of safety) where a case in category (e) has been remitted by the sheriff to the High Court for sentence; (g) under s.58(3), in the case of a person charged summarily in the sheriff court with an offence punishable with imprisonment, the court may make a hospital order without convicting him if satisfied that the person did the act or made the omission charged; (h) under s.58(10), in the case of a person charged summarily before the district court with an offence punishable with imprisonment, if it appears to that court that the person is suffering from mental disorder, that court must remit the person to the sheriff, who may make a hospital order in the same manner as in category (e); (i) under s.59, the court may make a restriction order imposing special restrictions without limit of time where the court is satisfied that this is necessary for the protection of the public from serious harm; and (j) under s.59A, the court may give a hospital direction in addition to a sentence of imprisonment. See Part VI of the 1995 Act for further provisions in these matters. As indicated above, in terms of the Mental Health (Scotland) Bill introduced on September 16, 2002 substantial amendment to relevant provisions of the 1995 Act is proposed.

Removal under the National Assistance Act 1948

Procedure under s.47 of the 1948 Act (as amended) applies to **12–33** persons who are (a) suffering from grave chronic disease, or being aged, infirm or physically incapacitated, are living in insanitary conditions, and (b) are unable to devote proper care and attention to themselves, and are not receiving proper care and attention from anyone else. Application may be made to the sheriff by the local authority upon receipt of a certificate by a medical officer of health that, after thorough inquiry, he is satisfied that in the interests of the person concerned, or of preventing injury to the health of (or serious nuisance to) other people, it is necessary to remove the person from

---

[45] See Sch.4, para.1(1) to the 1995 Act.

the premises. The sheriff may authorise removal of the person to a hospital or other suitable premises for the purpose of securing necessary care and attention, and detention for up to three months, renewable for similar periods. Seven clear days' notice must be given, except under an emergency procedure.[46] The main components of a reformed scheme are likely to comprise a duty to investigate; powers to inspect, examine and assess; and power to remove the risk from the adult or, as a last resort, to remove the adult to a place of safety.[47]

Parens patriae **jurisdiction**

12–34 The *parens patriae* jurisdiction is an inherent jurisdiction of the Crown, exerciseable by the Court of Session, to do what is for the benefit of adults with impaired capacity.[48] The law is described in Chapter 14, paras 14–25 to 14–29 below, in the context of authorisation of withdrawal of life-preserving treatment. As mentioned in para.3–29 above, the Scottish Law Commission proposed that provisions regarding the withholding or withdrawal of life-supporting treatment should be included in the Incapacity Act, but such provisions were deliberately omitted from the Act. Development of the law in this respect therefore currently rests with *Law Hospital NHS Trust v Lord Advocate*,[49] which is described in Chapter 14. The range of provision introduced by the Incapacity Act, and in particular the wide potential scope of intervention orders, much reduces the likelihood of need arising to invoke the *parens patriae* jurisdiction, but it remains available if ever required as a jurisdiction of last resort, including in any circumstances as yet unforeseen where no other more appropriate remedy is available.

Curators ad litem

12–35 Paragraph 12–26 above, on curators ad litem in the context of management matters, applies equally to litigation concerning or including matters which would be classified as relating to personal welfare. See also para.10–43 above.

---

[46] Introduced by the National Assistance (Amendment) Act 1951.
[47] See for example Scottish Law Commission Report 158, *Vulnerable Adults*, 1997, para.2.8.
[48] See para.14–25 *infra*.
[49] 1996 S.L.T. 848, 1996 S.C.L.R. 491, 1996 S.C. 301.

Chapter 13

TRUSTS AND OTHER THIRD PARTY MEASURES

Introduction

The categorisations used in this book were set out in Chapter 3[1] and reviewed in the Introduction to Chapter 12 with particular reference to that chapter and this Chapter 13, where the broad approach was explained to the allocation adopted between measures classified as responsive and third party respectively. In relation to trusts, the difference is a matter of emphasis, and the allocation is one of convenience. Trusts established by a fundholder or other entity paying out sums to which an adult with impaired capacity is entitled are dealt with in Chapter 12, as are bare trusts. Formal trusts are considered in this chapter because in relation to incapacity they are more commonly created by persons seeking to make voluntary provision where the beneficiary or one of the intended beneficiaries (or sometimes more than one beneficiary) has impaired capacity; or where the possibility of future impairment of capacity is to be provided for. Such trusts may nevertheless contain elements here classed as responsive, such as where parents in establishing a trust have regard to entitlement to legal rights on each of their deaths; or where trustees are authorised to accept future contributions from any party, and such a future contribution could be a payment to which the beneficiary is entitled as of right.[2] At the end of this chapter, in paras 13–36 to 13–39, are described remaining techniques other than trusts which are or may be within the category described as third party measures. Although trusts and all those other third party measures lie outwith the scope of the Incapacity Act, the investigatory and other powers under that Act described in para.5–41 above may be invoked in relation to them.

13–1

Formal private trusts—general description

This work does not attempt a comprehensive treatment of trusts. It should be read in conjunction with works which do.[3] Likewise, it does not attempt a comprehensive general treatment of topics referred to as having particular relevance here, though it does consider aspects of

13–2

---

[1] paras 3–7 to 3–9.
[2] Conversely, a trust described in Ch.12 might permit the trustees subsequently to accept a voluntary contribution from another party. An example is the usual form of trust established initially to administer vaccine damage payments, described in para.12.12.
[3] Such as Wilson and Duncan, *Trusts, Trustees and Executors*, Scottish Universities Law Institute (2nd ed., 1995).

them which usually require to be taken into account by those considering the establishment of a trust as a third party measure in relation to incapacity, and considering what form the trust should take. First, the following introductory description of formal private trusts, provided without citation of authority, sets the scene for that consideration of those specific aspects, particularly for readers who are not lawyers.

13–3 Trusts are created in a great variety of circumstances and are used in many different ways. The following description is valid for the establishment of trusts for the purposes considered in this chapter. Note also that this description is valid for Scots law: the concept of the trust is well developed in Anglo-American legal systems, but less so elsewhere, and indeed still surprisingly little adopted or used in many Roman law based legal systems. In Europe, Scots law has been the pioneer among Roman law based systems in developing trusts into an advanced and much-used technique. Because of the particular advantages of trusts in relation to impaired capacity, there is growing interest in other European systems in the concept of the trust as it has been developed in Scotland. English and other Anglo-American concepts and precedents are not always relevant to Scots law. British tax law uses English terminology in relation to trusts: the Scots lawyer has to translate.

13–4 A formal trust is established when the creator of the trust (the truster) transfers and contributes funds or assets to one or more others (the trustees) to be held, administered and applied for the benefit of beneficiaries (or for the furtherance of a purpose) in accordance with such instructions and powers as are set out in the trust deed signed by the truster. There may be more than one truster, and lifetimes trusts as third party measures in relation to the incapacity of young adults are frequently created by both parents, but for simplicity this chapter generally refers to "the truster" in the singular. Essential to the concept of a trust is that a separate estate (or "patrimony") is created. The funds and assets within the trust are no longer the property of the truster. They are held and owned by the trustees, but as a separate estate or patrimony from the personal assets of the trustees, so that— for example—creditors of a trustee in his personal capacity cannot touch the trust assets. Conversely, a trustee's personal assets will only be liable to the trust if the trustee has acted wrongfully in relation to the trust, for example by contravening the terms of the trust deed or deriving some unauthorised personal profit from his position as trustee. The trust funds and assets retain the identity as the same separate estate or patrimony through changes in trustees and changes in those funds and assets, such as when they grow, diminish or are reinvested. While there can be linkage with the tax position of truster or beneficiaries, the trust estate usually bears taxes such as Income Tax and Capital Gains Tax in its own right, and some special tax provisions apply, or may apply, depending on the nature of the trust. Beneficiaries and potential beneficiaries have an interest in the trust, and a beneficiary's interest may become "vested" when the beneficiary becomes irrevocably entitled to an identifiable share or asset so that, for example, if the beneficiary dies before it is paid out, entitlement would pass to the beneficiary's successors. However, whether or not the beneficiary has a vested interest, ownership does not pass to the beneficiary (or the beneficiary's successors) until the funds or assets are actually transferred out of the trust, during the trust period or upon the trust ending.

The trust deed sets out the powers and duties of the trustees, and may contain a range of discretionary powers. There may be discretion not only as to how funds are invested and managed, but as to how, when and even to whom they are applied or paid out. The trustees are also subject to the applicable general law, but a characteristic of trust law in Scotland is the scope given to trusters to determine the terms and provisions of the trust, and the powers and duties of the trustees, with relatively few constraints of general law, though some such constraints are significant and are referred to below. The counterpart to the flexibility afforded to trusters is the relatively strict approach to the responsibilities of trustees. These include the fiduciary duties and duties of care described in paras 4–31 *et seq.* above. **13–5**

The truster can be a trustee (or can simply declare a trust so that he becomes sole trustee). He can retain right to change the trustees and appoint new trustees, or establish mechanisms by which that can be done. If all else fails and the trust finds itself with no trustees, it is described as having lapsed, but the court can be asked to appoint new trustees. A trustee, or the truster, may also be a beneficiary, though there may be disadvantages, particularly when the truster does not exclude himself from being a beneficiary. As already mentioned, two or more people may jointly be the trusters who create a trust. The trustees under one trust may have powers to create a second, new trust. Except for any linkages provided for in the relevant trust deeds, where there are several trusts the funds and assets of each represent a separate estate or patrimony, even though there may be shared trustees. **13–6**

The truster must have adequate capacity to establish the trust, but the trust is not adversely affected by the truster's subsequent incapacity, bankruptcy[4] or death (unless the trust deed specifies otherwise). Commencement of the trust may be deferred, for example until the truster's death. A trust which comes into force during the truster's lifetime is termed an *inter vivos* trust, and a trust which comes into force upon the truster's death is termed a *mortis causa* trust. Trustees should normally have attained the age of 18 when they commence to act.[5] Trustees can only act as such for so long as they have adequate capacity to do so. Entities such as companies or other bodies may act as trustees if authorised by their objects or equivalent. Impairment of capacity does not disqualify a beneficiary, but the trust deed may contain special provisions applicable in the event of a beneficiary having impairments of capacity. The potential advantages of trusts in relation to beneficiaries with impaired capacity include the following: **13–7**

- The initial trustees are chosen by the truster, who can create a team blending management skill with understanding of the beneficiary, of family and of other relevant circumstances.

---

[4] Unless the circumstances of the gift into the trust are such that it can be struck down.

[5] In terms of the Age of Legal Capacity (Scotland) Act 1991, a person who has attained 16 has capacity to act as a trustee, but there are significant potential difficulties if a person who has not attained 18 acts as a trustee. These are discussed by Wilson and Duncan *op.cit.* paras 18.06–18.11.

- The trustees manage funds and assets which the beneficiary may not have capacity to manage.

- The creation of the trust does not however affect the beneficiary's capacity in law.

- The creation of the trust does not affect the availability of other measures which might be beneficial to the beneficiary, but might obviate possible need for more restrictive measures.

- The trust can be structured so that trust funds are not vulnerable to means-testing in relation to benefits, accommodation or services provided to the beneficiary.[6]

- The truster can define the trustees' discretionary powers, and can give them wide-ranging powers which can be used proactively and inventively to the benefit of the beneficiary.

- Subject to the statutory provisions mentioned in para.13–17 below, the trustees can be authorised to accumulate funds in excess of those currently required for the benefit of the beneficiary.

- The trustees can be authorised to benefit other defined persons (commonly other members of the family) where (a) this is the best way of achieving benefit or ensuring support for the beneficiary with impaired capacity,[7] or (b) there are surplus funds above what the trustees judge will ever be required for the beneficiary with impaired capacity, or (c) circumstances arise in which it is appropriate to exercise discretionary powers in favour of another beneficiary.

- More broadly, the trust can be used as a more general vehicle for family provision, or to provide for two or more beneficiaries with impaired capacity or other special needs.[8]

- The trustees can be authorised, at their discretion, to benefit named or specified categories of charities.

- Particularly where it is anticipated that the trust may be of lengthy duration, the trustees can be given powers and discretions to adapt to significant changes in circumstances or in relevant legislation, including by renouncing powers or creating a new trust to better achieve the truster's original intention and purpose.

---

[6] See paras 13–31 to 13–35 *infra*.

[7] *e.g.* see para.13–35 *infra*.

[8] Examples in the author's experience have been a *mortis causa* trust providing *inter alia* both for an elderly parent (should she survive) and a young adult with mental health problems, and several *inter vivos* trusts where two sons or daughters both had impaired capacity resulting from genetic conditions.

- The trust may achieve tax advantages (though there may also be tax disadvantages).[9]

- The trustees can be authorised to accept future contributions into the trust, including from other parties (who may in turn, as well as benefiting the beneficiary with impaired capacity, achieve other advantages, including tax advantages).

- The trust deed can determine the application of trust funds upon the death of the beneficiary with impaired capacity, so that the beneficiary's lack of testamentary capacity will not be an issue.

All of the foregoing could be achieved by an *inter vivos* or *mortis causa* discretionary trust under which the trustees have discretion to apply income and/or capital to benefit a class of beneficiaries (typically the truster's descendants, and perhaps their spouses) with wide-ranging discretionary powers as to how such benefit may be achieved,[10] and with discretion also to benefit charities, either named charities or charities within a defined category. Variations on that pattern include limiting discretionary powers during the trust period to application of income only, not capital; limiting the range of beneficiaries and/or the circumstances in which they may be benefited; not including charities; and limiting the range of discretionary powers. For tax purposes, using the English terminology which is a feature of United Kingdom tax law, discretionary trusts are categorised as "non-interest in possession trusts", and are contrasted with trusts where the beneficiary has an absolute, non-discretionary, entitlement to trust income and/or the use of trust assets, that is to say a liferent, such liferent trusts being "interest in possession trusts" for tax purposes. Where there is only one beneficiary but the trustees have discretion whether, when and to what extent to make payments to or for the benefit of that beneficiary, that trust is still a non-interest in possession trust, but the statutory prohibition against accumulations (see para.13–17 below) may at some point have the effect of triggering an interest in possession. 13–8

Where a trust is identified as the appropriate vehicle for third party provision, the precise terms of the trust—within the broad range of possibilities described in the preceding paragraph—will be specific to each individual situation. Broadly, the principal factors influencing the type of trust adopted and its precise provisions will usually include the following: (a) the truster's overall circumstances and objectives, including family circumstances, assets and liabilities, any business interests, tax position and any tax-planning considerations, and so forth; (b) the capabilities and limitations of the adult with impaired capacity, his way of life and aspects of it which are important to his quality of life, the prognosis for his disabilities, anticipated future arrangements for his care and accommodation, the key elements of 13–9

---

[9] See paras 13–19 to 13–30 *infra*.
[10] Powers which frequently feature in such trusts include powers similar to several of those in Part 1 of the Schedule to the *Style* Power of Attorney in Appendix 5. For trust and related styles generally, see Appendices IIIA–V inclusive of Ashton and Ward, *Mental Handicap and the Law*.

financial provision which the truster would like to see continued for the beneficiary's lifetime,[11] and so on; and (c) the particular issues and constraints described in the following paras 13–11 to 13–35.

Delivery

13–10 For a trust to be effectively created, there must be delivery of the trust property to the trustees or something equivalent to delivery, normally intimation of the trust to the trustees, or where the truster is sole trustee, intimation to the beneficiaries.[12] If a truster puts property in the name of trustees but does not deliver the property or document of title to the trustees and does not intimate what he has done to the trustees or beneficiaries, no effectual trust is created.[13] The same applies if the truster simply puts funds in his own name "in trust for" another, without any delivery or intimation.[14] Best practice, it is suggested, in the case of an *inter vivos* trust is to have a written record, signed by the trustees, acknowledging intimation of the trust, accepting office as trustees, and acknowledging receipt in that capacity of the funds or assets comprising the initial trust fund. A problem remains where the truster(s) propose to be the only trustee(s). In such a case, the truster(s) require to do something which would be equivalent to delivery where a third party was trustee. "Intimation to the beneficiary of the execution of the deed or declaration of trust and of its terms, would clearly suffice for this purpose".[15] However, it is at best very doubtful whether it would be effective for this purpose to purport to intimate to a beneficiary lacking the capacity to understand the meaning and significance of such intimation. Safe practice is to have at least one trustee other than the truster(s), and to obtain written acknowledgement as recommended above, even if the additional trustee were to resign soon afterwards (if there should be some compelling reason for that).

Legal rights

13–11 It is necessary to consider the potential legal rights entitlements of the truster's spouse, and children or their issue, where they or any of them are among the beneficiaries, in particular where the capacity of one of them is impaired. Legal rights are common law rights of

---

[11] Often the truster will not have identified these as financial provision at all. The truster may take the beneficiary on holidays, paying both for the beneficiary and for companions; take the beneficiary for outings by car; fund hobbies, recreational activities and social activities; pay for special aids and equipment, or special adaptations to the house, or independent specialist assessment or provision; and so on.

[12] Most of the cases on this point are Inland Revenue cases: see *Inland Revenue v Wilson*, 1927 S.C. 733; 1928 S.C. (HL) 42; *Linton v Inland Revenue*, 1928 S.C. 209; *Allan's Trustees v Inland Revenue*, 1971 S.L.T. 62 (intimation to a beneficiary is equivalent to delivery); *Clark's Trustees v Inland Revenue*, 1972 S.L.T. 190 (intimation to an agent acting for the trustees may be sufficient); and *Kerr's Trustees v Inland Revenue*, 1974 S.L.T. 193 (decided in favour of Inland Revenue, contains useful review of position). See also *Gilpin v Martin* (1869) 7 M. 807; *Cameron's Trustees v Cameron*, 1907 S.C. 407; *Carmichael v Carmichael's Executrix*, 1920 S.C. (HL) 195; and the discussion of these and other cases in Wilson and Duncan *op.cit.* Ch.3.

[13] *Jarvie's Trustee v Jarvie's Trustees* (1887) 14 R. 411.

[14] *Graham's Trustees v Gillies*, 1956 S.C. 437 at 455 *per* Lord Sorn.

[15] *Clark Taylor & Co. Limited v Quality Site Development (Edinburgh) Limited*, 1981 S.C. 111 at 115 *per* Lord President Emslie.

ancient origin, but in present form were modified by the Succession (Scotland) Act 1964. They arise automatically on death, whether the deceased died testate or intestate, but a person with capacity to do so may discharge legal rights before death or renounce them upon death. If there is a Will, the relative may elect to accept the provisions of the Will or to claim legal rights, but cannot have both, unless the Will expressly says so. A relative with capacity to do so can—and should—be put to this election, but difficulties arise when a relative lacks the capacity to elect, or to discharge or renounce the legal rights claim. Legal rights may be claimed at any time within 20 years of date of death, with interest from that date until payment. If 20 years elapse, the right to claim will be irrevocably lost. For Inheritance Tax purposes, legal rights are presumed to have been claimed unless discharged or renounced within two years of death. This presumption sits uneasily with the general law. A person lacking capacity to elect may be presumed for Inheritance Tax purposes to have claimed legal rights, yet no such claim may in fact ever be made.

Calculation

Legal rights are exigible only from moveable estate. Where the deceased dies testate, legal rights are calculated as a proportion of the entire net moveable estate. Where the deceased dies intestate survived by his or her spouse, the prior rights of the surviving spouse are deducted first, and legal rights are calculated upon the remaining moveable estate. The proportions, whether of net moveable estate where there is a Will, or of net moveable estate after deduction of spouse's prior rights upon intestacy, are: (a) a surviving spouse's legal rights amount to one third when the deceased left children or other issue, and one half when there are no issue, and (b) the legal rights of children or other issue amount in total to one third when there is a surviving spouse, and one half when there is no surviving spouse. If a relative has discharged legal rights prior to death, that relative is left out of the computation as if he or she had predeceased. Accordingly, when a surviving spouse has discharged legal rights, the total fund for the children will be one half, not one third. The total legal rights fund for children is termed the legitim fund. It is divided into a number of equal shares, one share for each child who survives or has predeceased leaving issue who survive. This equal division is subject to collation. Children who have discharged legal rights prior to death, or predeceased without leaving issue who survive, are left out of the reckoning. Spouses of children have no claim on the legitim fund. The legitim fund is divided equally *per capita* at the level of the nearest surviving relatives. The principle of collation takes account of gifts from moveable estate made prior to death by the deceased to any child or issue of children. The amount or value of the gift, without interest, is added to the legitim fund, then deducted from the share of the recipient. Issue of children must collate advances to the person from whom they derive entitlement, as well as the amount of any advances to themselves. However, not all sums received from the deceased prior to death require to be collated. Maintenance payments do not, neither do loans (though they may require to be repaid). Marriage gifts and gifts of a capital nature do require to be collated.

13–12

The beneficiary with impaired capacity

13–13   In present context, the truster's concern is whether the scheme and purposes of the trust will be disrupted by a legal rights claim by or on behalf of the beneficiary with impaired capacity upon the truster's death. Such a claim could be pressed by a financial guardian with relevant powers, or an intervention order could be granted for the purpose. In the case of a *mortis causa* trust, there are two issues. The first is the question whether there should be an election to claim legal rights rather than accept the trust provisions. The second is the effect upon administration where no election is made.

13–14   On the first question, under former law a curator bonis could apply to the court for special powers to elect, and might ask the court to decide how the election should be made.[16] The court would only grant special powers to elect if it was necessary that a decision be made.[17] The executors might insist that the curator bonis elect, if necessary by seeking special powers to do so, if delay would be prejudicial to other beneficiaries. Such prejudice would arise if, for example, a decision was required to enable the estate to be distributed. The reluctance of the courts to authorise election unless necessary derived from the older view that the curator bonis should preserve the estate pending recovery or death of the ward.[18] Thus the decision would if possible be left for the ward to make upon recovery, or for the ward's executors to make upon the ward's death. The decision remained open even if the curator bonis in fact received payment in terms of the provisions of the Will, provided that the curator bonis did not formally elect. Under the Incapacity Act, the matter will now be governed by the general principles in that Act. If a parent has made testamentary provision less than legal rights entitlement for a son or daughter with impaired capacity, the court can be expected to authorise a guardian (or to grant authority in an intervention order) to elect to accept the testamentary provision if that can be shown to be appropriate having regard to the general principles. If the larger legal rights provision would be of no real benefit to the son or daughter, or would be absorbed in lost state or local authority funding, it would be reasonable to argue that under the general principles the more modest provisions of the Will should be accepted, thus preserving a scheme devised by the parent with due regard to the son or daughter's best interests and to the circumstances of the family as a whole. There appears to be no reported Scottish authority on this issue. Some assistance may be gained from English cases in relation to procedure under the Inheritance (Provision for Family and Dependants) Act 1975, under which (in contrast to the Scottish system of fixed legal rights) the courts have discretion to make provision for a relative from the deceased's estate. The general, though not consistent, trend of the English decisions has been not to order an award

---

[16] *Skinner's Curator Bonis* (1903) 5 F. 914; *Burns' Curator Bonis v Burns' Trustees*, 1961 S.L.T. 166.

[17] In *Mitchell*, 1939 S.L.T. 91 an application was refused on the grounds that there was no necessity to elect.

[18] See paras 10–8 and 10–9 *supra*, where it is suggested that this simplistic formulation never accurately expressed the law in this regard.

where the reality of the situation is that funds awarded would be absorbed in means-tested benefit lost and/or charges incurred.[19]

Where no election is made, there can be uncertainty for up to 20 years following death, during which the executors could be at risk of a legal rights claim by a guardian, under an intervention order, or by executors in the event of the beneficiary's death. Expressed in the commonly occurring context of parents whose children include a son or daughter with impaired capacity contemplating a *mortis causa* trust as part of their testamentary provision, techniques which may be adopted include the following (the son or daughter with impaired capacity, regardless of age, is referred to as the child):

- Leave in trust for the benefit of the child a fund defined as at least equal to the child's legal rights entitlement(s). If husband and wife leave their estates in the first instance outright to each other, then the trust fund established upon the death of the survivor would (under this option) at least equal legal rights in the first estate, interest thereon, and legal rights in the second.

- Ensure that the executors are the same persons as the residuary beneficiaries. They may then decide whether to set aside a contingency fund, or simply to bear in mind the contingency of a subsequent legal rights claim. Unless all the executors are also the beneficiaries from whom any legal rights claim would have to be retrieved, they would be likely to be advised to set aside a contingency fund, rather than risk having to pay out legal rights, with interest, from their personal funds, then attempt to reclaim from the beneficiaries. However, even then, one executor/beneficiary might have concerns about having to rely on rights of relief against others.

- Steps can be taken to minimise the legitim fund. During lifetime, moveable estate can be reduced, either by divesting or by converting to heritage. A direction to executors to sell heritage should be avoided, as should a discretion to sell if the purposes of the Will cannot be implemented without exercising the discretion. A married person may opt for intestacy, if the estate is such that children's entitlement would be less upon intestacy than their legal rights if there was a Will in favour of the spouse.

- Techniques have also been identified to minimise the child's share of the legitim fund, when there are other children. None of the other children should discharge legal rights

---

[19] *Re Collins (deceased)* [1990] 2 All E.R. 47. See also *Harrington v Gill* (1983) 4 F.L.R. 265, CA; *Re Watkins, Hayward v Chatterton* [1949] 1 All E.R. 695; and *Re E (deceased)* [1966] 2 All E.R. 44. On the test of whether the will made reasonable provision, see *Re Goodwin* [1968] 3 All E.R. 12 and *Millward v Shenton* [1972] 2 All E.R. 1025. For explanation and discussion of this topic in English law, as it relates to provision for persons with impaired capacity, see Ashton and Ward, *Mental Handicap and the Law*, pp.504–517. For discussion of the Scottish position in relation to legal rights, see *op.cit.* pp.517–526.

before death, and if there have been advances which should be collated, these should be recorded. Moreover, as collation only applies if more than one child claims legal rights, the Will should specifically permit the other children to claim legal rights without forfeiting any testamentary provisions in their favour.

- Maintenance payments and loans are not collatable, but it may be appropriate to treat maintenance and other payments during adulthood as loans repayable on demand, with a direction in the Will to the executors to demand repayment up to the amount of legal rights entitlement, and to waive any excess.

13–16   Where parents create an *inter vivos* discretionary trust of the kind described in para.13–8 above, they will commonly qualify the definition of "Beneficiaries" with a provision along the following lines: *"if at any time any legal rights entitlement of any person in the estate of either of us should be claimed by or on behalf of that person, such person shall thereupon cease to be one of the Beneficiaries hereunder"*.

Prohibition of accumulations

13–17   The maximum period during which trust income may be accumulated with capital is limited by statute[20] to one of the following alternatives: the life of the grantor; the period of 21 years from the grantor's death; the duration of the "minority" (for this purpose, still the period until age 21) or respective "minorities" of any person or persons who, under the deed creating the trust, would for the time being, if of full age, be entitled to the income directed to be accumulated; the period of 21 years from the date when the trust is made; or the duration of the "minority" or respective "minorities" of any person or persons living or *in utero* at the date when the trust is made. These limitations can become an issue where, under a discretionary trust, the principal intended beneficiary is a young adult whose needs are largely met by state provision, trust income is expected to exceed needs met from the trust for many years, but the trustees wish to ensure that adequate capital is available for possible changed circumstances decades ahead, perhaps as the beneficiary ages, or in the event of substantial shifts towards private resourcing of the provision of care. Provisions to address the risk of contravention of the statutory limitations might include powers to invest *inter alia* in capital bonds or other investments providing only capital appreciation rather than income.

13–18   Where the trustees are authorised to accept subsequent contributions to the trust, it may be helpful to provide that the trustees may (a) allocate to separate funds within the trust fund parts thereof received at different times and/or from different donors, and (b) accumulate with capital any income upon the trust fund or any separate fund comprised therein during the maximum period for which such

---

[20] Trusts (Scotland) Act 1961, s.5, as amended by the Law Reform (Miscellaneous Provisions) (Scotland) Act 1966, s.6.

accumulation is permitted by law in respect of the trust fund or the relevant separate fund comprised therein.

Taxation—general

The range of advantages listed in para.13–7 cannot be achieved **13–19** without some taxation disadvantages. Relevant tax aspects require to be considered in deciding whether to establish a trust and, if so, what form it should take; but where the advantages listed in para.13–7 are important, they may frequently outweigh consequential tax disadvantages. Means-testing aspects alone[21] may outweigh any taxation disadvantages. Depending upon circumstances and objectives, it may nevertheless be possible to avoid some taxation disadvantages or secure some taxation advantages. The following descriptions mention salient points but do not attempt to address in detail what are in several cases complex and technical provisions. In all cases, relevant statutes and regulations should be referred to and/or expert advice obtained.

Income tax

Liferent trust (interest in possession)

The trustees as recipients of the trust's income are liable to income **13–20** tax at basic rate on it.[22] In the case of dividend income, savings income and investment income received net of tax, the tax deducted at source satisfies the trustees' liability. They are required to pay tax at basic rate on income received gross. Personal allowances are not available to be deducted, but some expenses (though not the trust's own management expenses), reliefs and losses may be deducted. After the end of each tax year the trustees issue a Tax Deduction Certificate to the liferenter, who includes the income from the trust in his own Tax Return and may be able to reclaim tax, or alternatively if a higher rate payer may have to pay additional tax. Where liferented trust income is mandated direct to the liferenter, the liferenter is the recipient and the income forms part of the liferenter's income for tax purposes. In terms of the beneficiary's income tax position, the liferent trust is broadly neutral in its effect.

As with other tax matters, if one of the purposes of the trust is to **13–21** meet management needs, there may be an issue that the beneficiary lacks capacity to attend to his own tax affairs, including any repayment claims. Trustees under a trust established by a third party, particularly in the case of a discretionary trust, would not appear to fall within the provisions concerning the trustee "of an incapacitated person" or "of any incapacitated person having the direction, control or management of the property or concern of any such person" under ss.42(6) and 72, respectively, of Taxes Management Act 1970, authorising such a trustee to claim reliefs and rendering him assessable and

---

[21] See paras 13–31 to 13–35 *infra*.
[22] See Income and Corporation Taxes Act 1988, s.59 and Taxes Management Act 1970, ss.71–73.

chargeable.[23] Some *mortis causa* trusts attempt to address the need for a mechanism to deal with the beneficiary's own tax affairs, including repayment claims, with a provision along such lines as this example: *"The foregoing provisions in favour of said X are granted subject to the condition that he/she shall be deemed to have authorised the persons who may from time to time be my trustees (as a separate function from the performance of their duties as trustees) to perform the following functions for him/her and on his/her behalf, namely: (i) to claim, receive, hold and administer any repayment of tax deducted at source or by my said trustees in respect of income of or arising from this trust, and (ii) to administer on his/her behalf any income belonging to him/her in terms of the foregoing provisions and not expended by my trustees for his/her behoof".*

Discretionary trust (non-interest in possession)

13-22 Income received by accumulation trusts and discretionary trusts is subject to income tax at special rates. The principal relevant statutory provision is s.686 of Income and Corporation Taxes Act 1988. This tax régime was altered with effect from April 6, 1999 by Finance Act 1988, ss.24(4) and 55(3). A "rate applicable to trusts", currently 34 per cent, applies to all income except "Schedule F type income" (principally dividend income), to which a "special Schedule F trust rate", currently 25 per cent, applies. Expenses properly chargeable to income[24] can be set against tax at the special rates, but the income against which such relief is set remains subject to base rate, lower rate or ordinary Schedule F rate tax, as the case may be.[25] If income is retained in the trust, the tax paid is not reclaimable by the beneficiaries, and the relevant income is in future treated for tax purposes as capital. If the trustees use their discretion to pay income to a beneficiary, then (put simply) credit can be taken for all the tax paid at the rate applicable to trusts, but for income subject to the special Schedule F tax rate there is a 10 per cent notional non-repayable tax credit, which has the effect that the ultimate total tax burden, either in reduced payment to the beneficiary or further tax payable by the trustees, is increased. The comments in para.13–21 above may apply where a beneficiary with impaired capacity is entitled to reclaim tax.

Capital Gains Tax

13-23 A transfer of assets into a liferent trust (interest in possession trust) usually will not attract hold-over relief from Capital Gains Tax, but such relief is available for a transfer of assets into a discretionary trust (non-interest in possession trust).[26] If the truster is alive and the truster or the truster's spouse has an interest in the trust at any time during the relevant tax year, the trust's gains in that year are treated as accruing to the truster and taxed accordingly.[27] Otherwise, the

---

[23] These provisions do, it is suggested, apply to a trustee under a trust for administration (see para.7-3 *supra*) and trustees under trusts established as responsive measures in relation to funds or property to which the adult is entitled as of right, as described in Ch.12.

[24] *Carver v Duncan; Bosanquet v Allen*, HL 1985, [1985] A.C. 1082; 59 T.C. 125.

[25] For the order of set-off, see Income and Corporation Taxes Act 1988, s.689B.

[26] Taxation of Capital Gains Act 1992, ss.74 and 260.

[27] Taxation of Capital Gains Act 1992, ss.77–79.

trustees are liable for tax on the gains of the trust as a separate entity for tax purpose. Except as described in the next paragraph, the current exemption is half that for individuals, but if the same truster has created more than one trust the exemption is divided among them, subject to a minimum exemption for each trust of one-tenth of the current exemption for an individual.[28] The rate of tax on gains in excess of the exemption is the same "rate applicable to trusts" as is referred to in para.13–22 above, currently 34 per cent.[29]

The trust's annual exemption is doubled to the same as for individuals if the trust qualifies as a settlement for the disabled. A person qualifies as disabled if in receipt of Attendance Allowance, or the higher or middle rate of the care component of Disability Allowance, or is incapable of administering his property or managing his affairs by reason of the English definition of mental disorder in the Mental Health Act 1983. The trust qualifies if during all or part of a relevant tax year the terms of the trust secure that not less than one half of property which is applied is applied for the benefit of such a person, and either such a person is entitled to not less than half of the income arising from the property or none of the income is applied for the benefit of anyone else. Similar provisions as described in para.13–23 above apply where the truster has created more than one trust.[30] **13–24**

In the case of a *mortis causa* discretionary trust, it is generally unwise to transfer assets out of the trust to a beneficiary within three months of the truster's death, because within that period a charge to Capital Gains Tax will arise on any distribution of assets from the trust or acquisition of a right to income from the trust.[31] **13–25**

Inheritance Tax

If the truster transfers property into the trust subject to a reservation, that property is treated as part of the estate at his death for Inheritance Tax purposes (except that if it ceases earlier to be subject to a reservation, the truster is treated as then making a potentially exempt transfer of that property). A gift to a trust is treated as subject to a reservation *inter alia* if at any time it is not enjoyed by the trust to the entire exclusion, or virtually the entire exclusion, of the truster or any benefit to the truster by contract or otherwise. Trusters usually wish to ensure that their gift(s) into the trust will not be treated as subject to a reservation. If the trustees are authorised to accept contributions into the trust from others, it may be wise to allow the donor to decide: for example, a sibling of the beneficiary with impaired capacity may wish to make a gift into the trust of a particular item or for a particular purpose, but may be one of the class of discretionary beneficiaries and may not wish to be automatically disqualified as such. A declaration by the truster(s) in an *inter vivos* deed of trust could be in the following terms: "*This deed is irrevocable and none of the powers or discretions hereby or by law conferred upon the trustees shall at any time be exerciseable in any manner which might benefit us the grantors hereof or either of us and no part of the capital or income of* **13–26**

---

[28] Taxation of Capital Gains Act 1992, s.3, Sch.1, para.2.
[29] Taxation of Capital Gains Act 1992, ss.4 and 5.
[30] Taxation of Capital Gains Act 1992, s.3, Sch.1, para.1.
[31] *Frankland v Inland Revenue Commissioners*, 1996 S.T.C. 735.

the trust fund shall at any time be lent or paid to or applied for the benefit of us or either of us, declaring for the avoidance of doubt that the foregoing prohibition shall not apply to any person other than us or either of us who may hereafter have contributed any addition to the trust fund or to any spouse of such person unless such person should declare by irrevocable written intimation to the trustees that said prohibition (or such other prohibition as may be set forth in such intimation) shall apply to such person and/or any spouse of such person."

13–27 Inheritance Tax applies to transfer of property into a trust in the same way as it applies to gifts, subject to the following points. The gift is a potentially exempt transfer if made into (a) a liferent (interest in possession) trust or (b) a trust for a disabled person (as defined in para.13–24 above) which secures that not less than one half of the trust property which is applied during the disabled person's lifetime is applied for his benefit.[32] Except for (b) above, a gift into a discretionary (non-interest in possession) trust is a chargeable transfer, but the donor's nil-rate band and other exemptions and reliefs are available.

13–28 Under a liferent trust (an interest in possession trust) the liferenter is treated for Inheritance Tax purposes as beneficially entitled to the liferented capital, so that there is a charge to Inheritance Tax on the value of that capital when the liferent ends.[33]

13–29 Discretionary trusts (non-interest in possession trusts) which qualify as trusts for the disabled as described in para.13–24 above, where there is no liferent, are nevertheless treated for Inheritance Tax purposes as if the disabled person were liferenter, and the position described in para.13–28 above applies.[34]

13–30 Apart from trusts for the disabled as described in the preceding para.13–29, discretionary trusts (non-interest in possession trusts) are subject to a 10-yearly charge to Inheritance Tax. Put simplistically, the charge is at 30 per cent of the lifetime transfer rate (at current rates, a charge of 6 per cent) allowing for the truster's nil-rate band,[35] but taking account of related settlements (by the same truster commencing on the same day) and the value of chargeable transfers made by the truster in the seven years up to but not including the date when the trust commenced. Proportionate charges may arise on property transfers out of the trust: that is likely to happen if the size of the trust is such as to generate a 10-yearly charge, and if a proportionate charge occurs the property on which it has been made is included in the computation of the next 10-yearly charge.[36]

Means-testing

13–31 A third party contemplating making financial provision for a person with impaired capacity will frequently be concerned not to do so in such a way as might prejudice entitlement to means-tested benefits, and not to cause the beneficiary to incur means-tested charges for care costs or services.

---

[32] Inheritance Tax Act 1984, s.3A.
[33] Inheritance Tax Act 1984, ss.49(1), 51(1) and 52(1).
[34] Inheritance Tax Act 1984, s.89.
[35] But other exemptions and reliefs available in relation to the initial gift may not then be available.
[36] Inheritance Tax Act 1984, ss.58–69, 80–85.

The relevant means-tested benefits are income-related, the most **13–32** common being Income Support, Housing Benefit, Disabled Person's Tax Credit, Working Families Tax Credit, and income-based Job Seekers' Allowance. Means-tests for these follow a similar pattern, though there is some variation in the details. For all, income and capital are assessed, income above a given level disqualifies, capital above a given upper level disqualifies, and if capital is between that upper level and a given lower level a tariff income is assumed (currently £1 per week for each £250 or part of £250 of capital above the lower level) and added to actual income in calculating entitlement to the benefit.[37] Similar principles apply to the means assessment by the local authority in relation to costs of residential care.[38] Concerns in relation to such costs will in many cases have been reduced, but not necessarily eliminated, by the Community Care and Health (Scotland) Act 2002 (asp 5) and the introduction with effect from July 1, 2002 of non means-tested personal care payments for persons over 65, and nursing care payments.[39]

A common feature of all of these means-testing régimes is that **13–33** property is treated as notional capital, and added to the person's actual capital for purposes of the calculation, if the person has deprived himself of that capital in order to claim benefits, or to increase entitlement to benefits, or "for the purpose of decreasing the amount that he may be liable to pay for his accommodation".[40] There is however no reason, in law or ethically, why a third party making voluntary provision should not have regard to means-testing régimes and seek to avoid or minimise their impact; or, put another way, why the third party should not seek to ensure that his voluntary provision is available to achieve benefit for the intended beneficiary, rather than going indirectly or directly to the state or to local authorities as a consequence of means-testing.

If the third party makes an outright gift, the capital becomes the **13–34** donee's capital for all purposes. If the third party establishes a liferent trust, the income to which the liferenter is entitled is part of the liferenter's income for all purposes. Under a discretionary trust, where any payments of capital or income are at the trustees' discretion and the beneficiary has no right to demand them, only sums actually paid belong to the beneficiary, and only those sums are taken into account under current means-testing régimes.[41] Trusters may have concerns about possible future changes in assessment régimes, particularly if the beneficiary is a young person with impaired capacity who may

---

[37] Income Support (General) Regulations 1987 (SI 1987/1967) as multiply amended.
[38] National Assistance Act 1948, ss.22 and 26; National Assistance (Assessment of Resources) Regulations 1992 (SI 1992/2997); and Social Work (Scotland) Act 1968, s.87.
[39] Currently £145 per week and £65 per week respectively. Recipients of personal care payments cease to be eligible for the care component of disability living allowance. Eligibility for disability living allowance is unaffected by receipt of nursing care payments.
[40] Income Support (General) Regulations 1987, reg.51; National Assistance (Assessment of Resources) Regulations 1992, reg.25; see *Yule v South Lanarkshire Council (No.1)*, 1998 S.L.T. 490; 2000 S.L.T. 1249.
[41] Income Support (General) Regulations 1987, regs 40, 46 and 51(2)(a).

well live for very many decades.⁴² Possible future reforms over such a long timescale cannot be predicted, but features of past régimes can be noted. Under the former Supplementary Benefit régime, which preceded Income Support, discretionary trusts under which the claimant might benefit were assessed according to what were judged to be the real possibilities under the trust. In England, former guidance to local authorities in relation to assessment for residential care costs advised that when the resident had an interest in a discretionary trust the local authority should ascertain from the trust deed the extent of the trustees' discretion, and advised that it would be reasonable to treat the capital value of the trust fund as part of the resident's capital resources if there was discretion to release capital, or capital and interest, for the benefit of the resident.⁴³ It was considered helpful in relation to past means-testing régimes for there to be a range of potential beneficiaries of whom the person with impaired capacity was only one: for reasons already discussed, that might in any event be an appropriate arrangement, but a factor in adopting it might still be concern about possible future means-testing régimes. For similar reasons, discretion might be limited to application of income, and not application of capital.

13-35   Once a discretionary trust has been established, the trustees may require to have regard to the potential effect on means-testing of how they apply funds for the beneficiary's benefit. Regular payments may be classed as income, though under Income Support Regulations regular voluntary payments are ignored up to £20 per week⁴⁴ and also they may be ignored if not intended or used for certain categories of essential expenditure,⁴⁵ but there is a ceiling for aggregated disregards.⁴⁶ These provisions of the Income Support Regulations are substantially applied for residential care cost assessments.⁴⁷ Trustees may find it appropriate, for other reasons as well as these, to purchase items for the beneficiary's use in their own name, retaining ownership of the items and allowing the beneficiary to use them, rather than

---

⁴² Trusters may also have regard to the attempts by some local authorities to find new ways to extract payment of care costs from persons other than the adult. In *Robertson v Fife Council* (decision of the House of Lords, July 25, 2002, reported at 2002 S.L.T. 951, reversing decisions of the Lord Ordinary 2000 S.L.T. 1226 and of the Inner House on appeal 2001 S.L.T. 708) it had been necessary to restrain a local authority by interdict from refusing to provide care assessed as needed by an elderly lady with dementia no longer in fact able to pay for it, having previously gifted her house to her children. The local authority's tactics contravened government guidance (and the previous general understanding of the law) that "the provision of services, whether or not the local authority is under a statutory duty to make provision, should not be related to the ability of the user or their families to meet the costs. The assessment of financial means should, therefore, follow the assessment of need and decisions about service provision" (Social Work Services Group Circular SWSG 11/91, para.11). The matter nevertheless had to be taken to the House of Lords to prevent the local authority in question from depriving the lady of the services which she needed, or inappropriately coercing others into paying for them.

⁴³ *Residential Homes under Part III of the National Assistance Act: Charging and Assessment Procedures* issued by DHSS and Welsh Office (1978). This did not apply to Scotland, where there seemed to be no standard policy.

⁴⁴ Income Support (General) Regulations 1987, reg.38, Sch.9, para.15(4).

⁴⁵ *ibid.* Sch.9, para.15.

⁴⁶ *ibid.* Sch.9, para.36.

⁴⁷ National Assistance (Assessment of Resources) Regulations 1992, Sch.3, paras 10, 29 and 31.

gifting them outright. Sometimes it might be better to allow provision to be made by a relative who also happens to be within the class of discretionary beneficiaries, and who might on some other occasion happen to receive discretionary personal benefit from the trust.

Other third party measures

Nominations

The terms of employment or occupational pension arrangements of a third party contemplating making provision for a person with impaired capacity may include provision of death benefits or other entitlements. Typically, these will not form part of their estates, there may be enhanced entitlement when a dependent relative survives, and application of funds may be at the discretion of the pension fund trustees, with whom the employee can lodge a written nomination or request. It will usually be sensible for the third party to ensure that such arrangements are consistent with any overall scheme of provision made by the third party. Aspects of the foregoing discussion of trusts may be relevant, including the possibility of requesting or directing (as may be appropriate) that pension fund trustees make payment to an existing family discretionary trust. **13–36**

Gifts and bequests

Direct gifts or bequests to the person with impaired capacity may have the disadvantages identified previously in this chapter. Alternatively, the donor or testator may make a gift or bequest to some other person or persons (often siblings) in anticipation, and perhaps on the understanding, that they will in turn cater appropriately for the needs of the person with impaired capacity: all the risks and disadvantages of gifts discussed in para.2–20 above apply to such gifts and bequests. Also, if parents leave everything to other children with such intention, an issue will arise about the legal rights entitlement of the son or daughter with impaired capacity (see paras 13–11 to 13–16 above). **13–37**

Provisions for management of particular assets

Methods of management of particular types of asset are in this book categorised as responsive measures and covered in Chapter 12, although often they could reasonably be classed as third party measures. **13–38**

Informal voluntary arrangements and bare trusts

Informal voluntary arrangements and bare trusts are described and considered in Chapter 12.[48] Such techniques may be used as third party measures. They are vulnerable to the difficulties described in Chapter 12, and may also have undesired consequences in relation to the means-testing régimes described in paras 13–31 to 13–35 above. Typically, an adviser consulted about establishing a scheme of third party provision may discover that various such arrangements are **13–39**

---

[48] paras 12–21 to 12–24.

already in force. Sometimes, funds held in a bare trust can properly and appropriately be transferred into a formal *inter vivos* trust. Otherwise, it may be wise to use funds available under such informal arrangements first, until they have been exhausted or substantially exhausted, before drawing on the more appropriately structured formal provision.

CHAPTER 14

HEALTH-CARE DECISIONS AND MEDICAL RESEARCH

HEALTH-CARE DECISIONS

Introduction

"Health-care" is used here in the same broad way that "treatment" **14–1** was used by the Scottish Law Commission "to include surgery, prescribing and administering drugs, preliminary examinations, nursing care, physiotherapy, taking samples, psychological and psychiatric procedures, dental and optical treatment and also procedures to promote and safeguard health such as screening and preventative medicine".[1] That definition sets the overall scope of the main part of this chapter. For the purposes of the Incapacity Act, "medical treatment" has the statutory definition quoted in para.14–44 below, which is also in broad terms, but which may nevertheless give rise to issues requiring judicial determination of its precise scope, leaving "health-care" as a better term for a general description of the subject. Decisions about health-care are of course one category of personal welfare decisions, and it might reasonably be asked why they should warrant a separate chapter. One might point to many factors well-rehearsed in the public domain. Decisions about health-care are sometimes difficult and of critical importance. They can raise issues both of professional ethics for those providing or offering treatment, and of personal preferences, wishes and fears, and personal ethics, for the patient or those with a legitimate role in reaching decisions on behalf of the patient. Legislators face difficult issues about where to set the overall boundaries of what should be permissible and about how, within the full extent of those boundaries, to ensure:

— that patients with impaired capacity are not unfairly discriminated against by being denied, in consequence of their incapacities, the benefits of any medical intervention lawfully available to those who are capable (or by having treatment harmfully delayed);

— that non-discrimination is also achieved by ensuring that the processes of health-care decision-making respect and take account of present or past wishes and feelings of each patient, and of ethical viewpoints which may differ significantly one

---

[1] SLC *Report*, para.5.1.

from another, and which may be either the known ethical viewpoints of the individual, or those of the individual's family, cultural or religious background; and

— that the above are achieved within a régime which provides adequate checks and safeguards, avoids undue imbalances of powers, and provides for doubts and disagreements to be resolved by procedures which are trusted, respected and workable.[2]

During the passage of the Incapacity Act, the six sections comprising Part 5 required more parliamentary time and attracted more attention and comment than the whole of the rest of the Act, and were more significantly amended than other sections. Of the many sets of regulations made under the Act, only those under s.48(2) were opposed and amended.[3] However, of many potential reasons for allocating a separate chapter to the topic of health-care decisions, in a description of the law one is decisive. The practice of most professions is essentially lawful, subject to particular safeguards, controls and prohibitions. However, the intimately personal and physical nature of the practice of the health-care professions means that the acts essential to the actual delivery of much health-care would be assaults, in both civil and criminal law, unless they fall within one of the several categories in law which justify them. As to the criminal law of assault, the Scottish Law Commission in this context quoted Gordon: "There need not be substantial violence, and indeed an extremely trivial attack is sufficient. It is an assault to slap someone on the back, even perhaps to tap him on the shoulder, and to spit on someone is an assault in the eyes of the law."[4] The *Stair Memorial Encyclopaedia* states that: "Every medical treatment requires the consent of the patient to the touching which treatment entails: without such consent the patient may raise an action against the doctor for the assault entailed in non-consensual treatment".[5] However, while patient's consent is the most important category of authorisation where the patient is adult, competent, conscious and able to communicate, it is not the only category. The Scottish Law Commission put the position more accurately thus: "The invasion of a person's bodily integrity by treatment that he or she has not consented to (or that has not otherwise been authorised) amounts to a criminal offence and a civil wrong".[6] The categories of authorisation other than the patient's own

---

[2] Balanced consideration of such issues during the passage of the Incapacity Act was not helped by invective and misrepresentation from extremists outside the Parliament (and who had not engaged in the lengthy consultations of the preceding law reform process) who disregarded the distinction between the right to advocate one ethically based and sincerely held viewpoint, on the one hand, and seeking to impose that viewpoint by force of law to the exclusion of others, and to do so discriminatorily in relation to people with impaired capacity, on the other hand.

[3] See para.14–48 *infra*.

[4] Gordon, *Criminal Law* (2nd ed.) para.29–40, quoted in SLC Discussion Paper No.94, *Mentally Disabled Adults*, para.3.4

[5] *Stair Memorial Encyclopaedia*, Vol.14, para.1130, citing D.M. Walker, *The Law of Delict in Scotland* (2nd ed., 1981), p.493; J. Blackie in E Deutsch and H-L Schreiber (eds) *Medical responsibility in Western Europe* (1985), p.578.

[6] SLC Discussion Paper No.94, para.3.4, citing *S v S* [1970] 3 All E.R. 107 at 111, *per* Lord Reid; *W v Official Solicitor* [1972] A.C. 24 at 43 *per* Lord Reid.

consent are of particular significance in relation to adults who are not competent to give valid consent, or are unconscious, or are unable even with any possible assistance to communicate about the matter: that is to say, adults who are in terms of the Incapacity Act incapable[7] in relation to decisions about the particular health-care matter in question. The following sections of this chapter are structured by reference to those categories of justification which render health-care intervention lawful, but each category encompasses a process of health-care decision-making of which the authorisation of a proposed health-care intervention may be an outcome, and it is in each case the process of health-care decision-making as a whole which is here considered. There may be choices among alternative treatments; choices about when, where, how and by whom a treatment may be administered; decisions about whether a treatment should be refused, or should be discontinued; and so on. It nevertheless remains helpful to categorise methods of health-care decision-making by reference to the methods by which health-care intervention can be rendered lawful. In summary, the categories which existed immediately prior to the coming into force of the Incapacity Act, and which were expressly preserved by that Act (though subject to some modifications and clarifications),[8] are:

- The competent consent of the patient (in this chapter called *"patient's decision"*).

- Consent (*"appointee decision"*) on behalf of the patient by someone empowered to give it, being in relation to an adult a welfare attorney or tutor-dative with relevant powers, or a tutor-at-law (welfare attorneys became regulated by the Incapacity Act from April 2, 2001, and tutors became, and for new appointments were replaced by, welfare guardians from April 1, 2002, all prior to Part 5 of the Incapacity Act being brought into force on July 1, 2002). The fixed statutory powers of MHSA guardians included power to make certain health-care decisions, but not to consent to treatment: MHSA guardians also became, and for new appointments were replaced by, welfare guardians from April 1, 2002. Also included in this category are equivalent appointees under the laws of other countries, provided that the appointment is recognised by Scots law.

- Authorisation under the *parens patriae* jurisdiction.

- *Necessity*.

- Treatment for mental disorder in accordance with Part X of MHSA 1984 of a detained patient (*"Part X authority"*).

To these, the Incapacity Act added:

- Authorisation in terms of an *intervention order*.

---

[7] As defined in s.1(6): see paras 4–23 to 4–28 *supra*.
[8] s.47(2) and Parts 1, 2, 5 and 6 generally.

- Consent by an appointee under an intervention order empowering the appointee to give such consent (an addition to the existing category of *appointee decision*, "appointee" in this chapter—unless qualified—meaning a welfare attorney, welfare guardian or appointee under an intervention order, in each case with relevant powers).

- Authority under s.47(2) to safeguard or promote physical or mental health, upon certification by the medical practitioner primarily responsible for the medical treatment of the adult (in this chapter, such authority is called "*s.47(2) authority*" and such medical practitioner is called the "responsible doctor").

- Authority derived from s.48(3) in accordance with regulations made under s.48(2) (in this chapter called "*s.48(3) authority*", a category created by the interpretation of s.48(3) adopted in the Specified Treatments Regulations—see para.14–48 below).

- Authority under s.50(5) upon certification by a nominated medical practitioner following disagreement between the responsible doctor and an appointee with relevant powers (in this chapter called "*s.50(5) authority*").

- Judicial determination by the Court of Session under s.50(3) where a person having an interest challenges a decision agreed between the responsible doctor and an appointee, or under s.50(6) where the decision of a nominated medical practitioner as to s.50(5) authority is challenged; or judicial determination of an appeal against any other medical decision under Part 5 of the Incapacity Act by the sheriff (or on appeal by the Court of Session) under s.52 (all of the foregoing being here described as "*judicial determination*").

The Act, and regulations under it, set limitations on what may be authorised by appointees and under s.47(2) authority. It also adds to and clarifies the law on the inter-relationship between different methods of health-care decision-making. It addresses the relationship between appointee decisions and s.47(2) authority. It expressly preserves the principle of necessity in emergency situations where authority under the Act is otherwise disapplied.

Terminology

14–2   In this chapter "*health-care*" and "*treatment*" have the broad meaning described in para.14–1, "*medical treatment*" is used as defined in s.47(4) of the Incapacity Act,[9] "*practitioner*" means any professional health-care practitioner, and "*doctor*" means any medical practitioner. Particular categories of doctors are assigned roles by statute or regulation. As indicated above, the Incapacity Act refers to the medical practitioner primarily responsible for the medical treatment of the adult, in this chapter called "*the responsible doctor*". MHSA 1984,

---

[9] See para.14–44 *infra*.

s.20(1)(b) refers to "a practitioner approved . . . by a health board as having special experience in the diagnosis or treatment of mental disorder", in this chapter called an *"approved psychiatrist"*, who also has various roles under the Incapacity Act.[10] Section 50(9) of the Incapacity Act requires the Mental Welfare Commission to establish and maintain a list of doctors from whom to nominate doctors to give opinions under s.50(4),[11] here called a *"nominated practitioner"*. The Adults with Incapacity (Specified Medical Treatments) (Scotland) Regulations 2002[12] are here called the *"Specified Treatments Regulations"*, and they require the Mental Welfare Commission also to appoint doctors authorised to issue certificates in terms of regulation 4, here called an *"appointed practitioner"*. The appointed practitioner must not be the same person as the responsible doctor.[13] Regulation 6 refers to medical practitioners who have a qualification, or special experience, in child and adolescent psychiatry, who are here referred to as *"child and adolescent psychiatrists"*. On the roles of medical practitioners under the Incapacity Act, see also para.5–36 above. The summary in para.14–1 above explains the terms here adopted for the various categories of health-care decision-making, and also explains that *"appointee"*—unless qualified—here means a welfare attorney, welfare guardian or appointee under an intervention order, in each case with relevant powers. *"Patient"* refers to a patient who is an adult,[14] though some provisions apply only to persons who are 16 or 17 years of age.[15]

Patient's decision

The patient's decision may be overruled only by Part X treatment. **14–3** All other categories of health-care decision-making are excluded if the patient is competent to make a valid decision upon the matter in question, is conscious, and is able to communicate (by any means, and with any necessary assistance). The patient's right to make his own decision has been described as "a basic human right protected by the common law".[16] The effect of a patient's decision contained in an advance directive is discussed in Chapter 7, paras 7–5 to 7–12: broadly, an advance directive which is valid, still effective and applicable (as there discussed) will likewise exclude other categories of health-care decision-making, subject to a possible and as yet unresolved argument that it might be possible for s.47(2) authority to have effect notwithstanding the terms of an advance directive (see para.7–9 above and para.14–47 below). However, as pointed out in para.7–5 above, all patient's decisions have future effect. Unless explicitly time-limited, or unless the circumstances change materially, a valid health-care decision made by the patient today will hold good tomorrow,

---

[10] See para.5–36 *supra*.
[11] See paras 14–56 and 14–57 *infra*.
[12] SSI 2002/275, as amended by the Adults with Incapacity (Specified Medical Treatments) (Scotland) Amendment Regulations 2002 (SSI 2002/302), both of which came into force simultaneously with Part 5 of the Act on July 1, 2002.
[13] reg.4(2).
[14] *i.e.* over 16, as defined in the Incapacity Act, s.1(6).
[15] See reg.6 of the Specified Treatments Regulations.
[16] Lord Scarman in *Sidaway v Board of Governors of the Bethlem Royal Hospital* [1985] A.C. 871.

and will not cease to hold good only because of effluxion of time. An advance directive formalises and records the decision, but does not put it into a different legal category. Whatever the form which a patient's decision has taken, the issues—explored in more detail in para.7–5—are whether the decision was competently made, whether the factual situation which has arisen is within the scope of the decision, and whether the assumptions upon which the decision was based remain valid or have been falsified.[17] While advance directives are often self-proving documents and whilst health-care practitioners frequently, and sensibly, obtain written consent to invasive procedures, there is no requirement in law for a health-care decision to be in writing, and consent may be given verbally, or even impliedly by the patient allowing treatment to be administered.[18]

14–4 Where the patient has made a valid decision, practitioners acting in accordance with that decision are guilty neither of civil wrong nor criminal offence, whatever the outcome, provided that what they do is not something prohibited by law,[19] and provided that the treatment is performed by a recognised practitioner acting in accordance with accepted professional practice.[20] As to the converse, a practitioner is not obliged to give treatment requested by a competent patient but considered by the doctor to be clinically or ethically inappropriate,[21] but is obliged to abide by a competent refusal of treatment or request to discontinue treatment. The case of *Miss B*[22] in 2002 attracted much attention but in legal terms was unremarkable. It was held that Miss B, who had lain in hospital for a year with her survival dependent upon a ventilator, was entitled at a time of her choice to refuse consent to life-sustaining medical treatment, and that when she did so her ventilator should be switched off. The only real issue was whether she was competent to make that decision. Her counsel asserted that her doctors had "started from the position of looking at her decision and worked back from that to decide that she could not be competent". The court ruled that Miss B's decision was competent, and that by failing to implement her decision and keeping the ventilator switched on her doctors had committed an "unlawful trespass", for which damages of £100 were awarded. The position in Scotland was summarised by the Lord President in *Law Hospital* in the following terms: "Where the patient is of full age and capable of understanding and consenting to the procedures which on medical advice are for his or her benefit, or decides to refuse medical treatment, the right of self-determination provides the solution to all problems, at least so far as the court is concerned. It is not in doubt that a medical practitioner who acts or omits to act with the consent of his patient requires no sanction or other authority from the court. The patient's consent renders lawful that which would otherwise be unlawful. It is not for

---

[17] See the authorities referred to in para.7–5 *supra*.
[18] *Thomson v Devon* (1899) 15 Sh. Ct Rep 209.
[19] Such as administering drugs designed to kill a patient who no longer wishes to live, or carrying out an abortion contrary to the Abortion Act 1967.
[20] Gordon, *Criminal Law* (2nd ed.), para.29–40.
[21] See, for example, SLC Report, para.5.42.
[22] Decision of Dame Elizabeth Butler-Sloss, President of the Family Decision, March 22, 2002, reported in *The Times*, March 23, 2002 and now reported at [2002] 2 All E.R. 449.

the court to substitute its own views as to what may or may not be in the patient's best interests for the decision of the patient, if of full age and capacity".[23]

As with all other areas of decision-making, there is a rebuttable **14–5** presumption in favour of capacity,[24] and capacity to decide is specific to the particular matter. "People who are able to decide whether to undergo some minor surgical operation may not be able to decide about sterilisation, abortion or cosmetic surgery where many conflicting factors have to be considered. The ability to come to a decision on the treatment in question depends to some extent on the person's ability to comprehend, from information supplied by the doctor or others, the nature of the proposed treatment and its effects and risks. The patient does not need to have been given an exhaustive evaluation of the treatment. In particular, minimal risks need not be mentioned. What is required is that the patient is informed in broad terms of the nature of the proposed treatment".[25] MHSA 1984 recognises that detained patients may nevertheless have capacity to decide some health-care matters, and requires the detained patient's competent consent before specified treatments may be given.[26]

For health-care intervention to be justified on grounds of the **14–6** patient's consent, that consent must be adequately informed. Most of the relevant case law addresses issues of whether a doctor has adequately informed a competent patient about the risks of a particular treatment.[27] It is reasonable to suggest that such cases will provide assistance in determining issues of capacity to decide. If a competent patient requires a given amount of information about a proposed treatment for his consent to be valid so as to authorise it, then logic dictates that where capacity is in doubt the patient must not only receive but understand the required information, if his consent is to be valid and the treatment thus to be authorised.

A number of English cases consider the interface between patient's **14–7** decision and necessity in the form of the question: "Where doctors believe that treatment ought to be given, is the patient's refusal competent, in which case it must be respected, or is it incompetent, in which case the treatment may (though it may not) be justified on grounds of necessity?" In *St George's Healthcare National Health Service Trust v S; R v Collins, ex parte S*,[28] it was held that a woman may competently refuse a Caesarian section even though her own life and

---

[23] *Law Hospital NHS Trust v Lord Advocate*, 1996 S.L.T. 848 at 852; 1996 S.C.L.R. 491 at 495–6; 1996 S.C. 301.
[24] *Lindsay v Watson* (1843) 5 D. 1194. See also para.1–1 *supra*.
[25] SLC Report, para.5.2, citing *Chatterton v Gerson* [1981] Q.B. 432; referring also to *Sidaway v Governors of Bethlem Royal Hospital* [1985] A.C. 871 and *Moyes v Lothian Health Board*, 1990 S.L.T. 444.
[26] See MHSA 1984, ss.97(2) and 98(3). In *St George's Healthcare National Health Service Trust v S; R v Collins, ex parte S* [1998] 3 All E.R. 673, CA, it was confirmed that the English equivalent of Part X authority does not extend to health-care intervention unconnected with the patient's mental disorder, which may only be given with the patient's consent unless the patient does not have capacity to decide the matter.
[27] See *Sidaway* (above); *Moyes v Lothian Health Board*, 1990 S.L.T. 444, OH; *Cosgrove v Lothian Health Board*, 1990 G.W.D. 15–839, OH; *Goorkani v Tayside Health Board*, 1991 S.L.T. 94, OH; and *Cameron v Greater Glasgow Health Board*, 1993 G.W.D. 6–433, OH. The Stair Memorial Encyclopaedia (Vol.14, para.1130) refers to *Craig v Glasgow Victoria and Leverndale Hospitals Board of Management*, March 23, 1976 (unreported).
[28] Above. For an earlier, contrary decision see *re S* [1992] 4 All E.R. 671, CA.

that of the unborn child depend upon it. See that case for English guidelines to protect patients from invasive treatments against their wishes. In *Re MB*[29] the patient needed and desired a Caesarian section, but her fear of needles caused her to panic and refuse: the court held that her panic rendered her temporarily incompetent and that the Caesarian section could be authorised on grounds of necessity, a decision which might be seen as uncomfortably close to stretching too far the concepts of both incompetence and necessity, and to working backwards from the patient's decision in the manner criticised by *Miss B*'s counsel, as quoted in para.14–4 above.

14–8 The Incapacity Act definition of incapacity[30] is directly relevant in determining whether the patient is incapable of a health-care decision where the alternative is an appointee decision, an intervention order or s.47(2) authority, and in cases where s.50(5) authority or judicial determination under the Act may be invoked. While the Incapacity Act definition is not by statute the test where the alternative is necessity (or *parens patriae*, though in practice *parens patriae* is now only likely to be invoked where incapacity is beyond any doubt), nor the test where patient's consent is required for Part X authority, one cannot envisage any circumstances in which a court would consider it appropriate to come to a decision as to capacity differing from that which it would have reached if the Incapacity Act definition had mandatorily applied. If that view is correct, then it is appropriate for the court rigorously to apply the Incapacity Act criteria before concluding that a patient lacks capacity to make his or her own decision, whether or not the Incapacity Act criteria are mandatory in the proceedings in question. Indeed, it is important that courts and all others concerned in addressing questions of capacity should do so rigorously, in accordance with the Incapacity Act criteria, before depriving a patient on grounds of incapacity of the right to decide health-care matters for himself or herself; and it is important that courts and others be clearly seen to be doing so, given the criticisms and concerns (whether they be well or ill-founded) which have been frequently voiced and are, for example, implicit in the assertion by *Miss B*'s counsel quoted in para.14–4 above and in the concerns surrounding the decision in *Re MB* referred to in para.14–7 above.

14–9 A further point requires to be addressed where the Incapacity Act mandatorily applies. The requirements for s.47(2) authority are specific to the particular decision. Section 47(1) refers to the adult being "incapable in relation to a decision about the medical treatment in question". Likewise, an intervention order under s.53(5)(a), directing specified action to be taken without appointing an appointee, is specific to the particular matter and incapacity requires to be established in relation to the specific decision to be taken: s.53(1) refers to the adult being incapable in relation to "the decision", not "decisions". The provisions authorising welfare guardians and welfare attorneys to decide are not expressly specific to the particular decision in question. In the case of guardianship, the extent of incapacity is determined in the proceedings to grant the order, and powers are conferred accordingly, leaving the possibility that when a particular

---

[29] *Re MB* [1997] 8 Med. L.R. 217, CA.
[30] s.6(1), see paras 4–23 *et seq. supra*.

health-care matter subsequently arises, the adult may in fact have sufficient capacity to decide it, notwithstanding that it is within the scope of the authority conferred by the guardianship order. However, on the basis that a health-care decision is not a "transaction" (and this author is firmly of the view that it is not), the guardianship order neither removes the patient's capacity nor creates any explicit presumption of incapacity,[31] therefore the patient's decision remains competent and the Act's general principles would prohibit intervention in that particular matter.[32] In the case of a welfare attorney, the enabling provision of the Incapacity Act is expressed negatively: the welfare power is not exerciseable unless the grantor (in this context, the patient) "is incapable in relation to decisions about the matter to which the welfare power of attorney relates" or the welfare attorney reasonably believes this to be so.[33] The existence of the welfare power of attorney, and the fact that the welfare attorney has properly commenced to act under it, neither of themselves remove capacity nor create any presumption of incapacity in relation to particular matters, health-care or otherwise, subsequently arising, therefore the position is the same as suggested above in relation to guardians. Where there is an appointee with relevant powers under an intervention order in terms of s.53(5)(b), the position will usually be equally specific to that described above in relation to orders under s.53(5)(a), because the requirements of s.53(1) referred to apply to both types of order, but the possibility remains that by the time that a decision requires to be made (and, perhaps, when the nature of that decision has been clarified), the patient is in fact capable of it. In that situation, and indeed in such a situation under any category of authority within the provisions of the Act including s.47(2) authority, the patient's decision becomes the only competent authority, having regard to (a) the fact that, in contrast to "transactions" within the scope of a guardian's authority in terms of s.67(1), powers and authority under the Act in relation to welfare matters which are not transactions neither remove capacity nor explicitly create any presumption of incapacity, and (b) the first and second general principles, for reasons given in n.32 to this paragraph, prevent anyone acting under or in pursuance of the Act (appointees, practitioners or anyone else) from intervening to decide when the patient can in fact decide.

British Medical Association provides guidance to doctors on the assessment of capacity in relation to health-care decision-making in BMA's guidance on the Act.[34] BMA suggests that, in cases of doubt, a comprehensive psychological investigation may be needed, seeking to determine whether the adult: **14–10**

- is capable of making a choice;

---

[31] See para.11–31 *supra*, referring to s.67(1).
[32] See paras 4–2 *et seq. supra*. It is fundamental under the first and second principles that the patient's ability to decide means that no intervention is necessary and any intervention would be unnecessarily restrictive of the patient's freedom.
[33] s.16(5)(b)—see para.6–10 *supra*.
[34] *Medical treatment for adults with incapacity: Guidance on ethical and medico-legal issues in Scotland*, BMA, June 2002 (2nd ed., October 2002)—see s.4. See also BMA and Law Society (England and Wales), *Assessment of mental capacity: Guidance for doctors and lawyers*, 1995, the practical and medical content of which can be recommended notwithstanding that Scots law is not addressed in the legal sections.

- understands the nature of what is being asked;
- understands why a choice is needed:
- has memory abilities that allow the retention of information;
- is aware of any alternatives;
- has knowledge of the risks and benefits involved;
- is aware of the decision's personal relevance to him or herself;
- is aware of his or her right to refuse, as well as the consequences of refusal;
- is aware of how to refuse;
- is capable of communicating his or her choice;
- has ever expressed wishes relevant to the issue when greater capacity existed; and
- is expressing views consistent with previously preferred moral, cultural, family and experiential background.[35]

On assessment of capacity, see also paras 1–32 to 1–35 above.

Difficulty and debate

14–11 The line between competence and incapacity is of fundamental significance in relation to health-care matters, as it is in relation to all other decision-making. In law there is no middle area, only a clearcut divide. On either side of the line, the roles of deciding and advising are reversed. If the patient makes, or has made, a decision which is competent, lawful and applicable, then the patient's decision prevails and the input of doctors and others is advisory, subject only to the points made in para.14–4 above that patients can consent to and (except where Part X authority applies) refuse proposed treatment, and can insist that treatment which has commenced should cease, but cannot demand that a particular treatment be given. If however the patient lacks adequate capacity to decide the particular matter, incapacity being defined as in the Incapacity Act to include inability to communicate, then and (except as regards Part X authority) only then do other categories of decision-making apply, under all of which a decision will be made for the patient by someone else. Where the patient has wishes and feelings, present or past, then under the Incapacity Act they must be taken into account, but they are advisory, not decisive, and in the last resort—provided that they have been properly taken into account—a different decision may be made. However, although the law is precise as to the dividing line between

---

[35] *ibid.* p.3; based on the Part 5 Code, para.1.6, but helpfully broken down into more separate elements.

competence and incapacity, and its consequences, in many cases there can be considerable difficulties for clinicians and lawyers in placing a particular patient, in relation to a particular health-care decision, on one side of that line or the other. Taking the example of one particular condition, Dr Jim Dyer[36] wrote that: "The dividing line between consent and inability to consent, in the presence of severe depression, is thin and indistinct". In more general terms, the BMA guidance[37] points out that: "In cases where patients have borderline or fluctuating capacity, it can be difficult to assess whether the individual can make valid decisions on very serious issues". However difficult the task, it must be addressed rigorously and objectively. Many with experience of matters of adult incapacity will have noted situations where decisions about capacity, and sometimes mutually inconsistent decisions by the same practitioner or authority, appear to have been influenced by desired outcomes.[38] However honest, genuine and well motivated may be the belief in what would be an appropriate outcome and the desire to achieve it, and notwithstanding the potential relevance of these matters once a decision as to incapacity has been properly arrived at, such matters must be excluded from the determination of capacity, which must come first. Any decision on capacity which appears to be influenced by desired outcome is, to the extent so influenced, tainted and open to challenge. As is demonstrated by many of the cases cited in this chapter, and in relation to advance directives in Chapter 7,[39] patients competent to decide a particular matter are entitled to make decisions which may be contrary to professional advice, apparently perverse or even life-threatening; and the patient's decision, whatever it may be, determines the matter. In situations giving rise to concerns, difficulty or dispute, the Incapacity Act offers alternatives to litigation in the form of the investigatory and other powers and provisions which are applicable beyond the boundaries of the Act's own scheme of provision and are described in para.5–41 above.

Behind the issues identified in the preceding paragraph lurks the **14–12** debate about what should be the scope of patient autonomy. It is a debate which has been prominent in recent years, but which has not yet reached any clear and rationally consistent outcome. That debate needs to be carried forward. That is likely to occur both in the forthcoming reforms of mental health law and in other contexts. Aspects of the law on decision-making in this chapter may be

---

[36] Director and Medical Commissioner of the Mental Welfare Commission, article in the *Sunday Times* (Ecosse, p.2) on June 30, 2002.

[37] See n.34 to para.14–10 *supra*.

[38] Examples in the author's experience include a consultant who insisted that he could not discuss a patient except with the patient's consent, and after stating that he had obtained such consent proceeded to assert that the patient had no competence to make any health-care or other welfare decisions, nor to express any present wishes or feelings of sufficient relevance to be taken into account in relation to decisions requiring to be made; and a hospital authority which had without hesitation assumed authority to manage a patient's affairs under MHSA 1984, s.94 but refused to contemplate or address the possibility of impairment of the same patient's capacity to give competent and fully informed consent to major health-care and welfare decisions which happened to coincide in both time and nature with general management policies and decisions adopted by the authority.

[39] See in particular *Re C (Adult: Refusal of Treatment)* [1994] 1 W.L.R. 290.

influenced by the debate before even the most used copies of this book become shabby. Loudest in those debates hitherto have been those defending, rather than questioning, principles and ethical positions which have served well in the past, but the contemporary and future validity and relevance of which may depend upon careful re-examination in a changing world, not upon vociferous defence of them. The difficulty with resting satisfied once an entrenched position has been successfully defended is that consequences which may be undesirable, and undesired by those same defenders, are not addressed. Two examples current at time of writing will suffice to demonstrate this. The Specified Treatments Regulations as first laid included proposed controls on neurosurgery for mental disorder (NMD). The vociferous complaints of those opposed in principle to NMD resulted in it being dropped from the regulations, with the consequence that at that point NMD remained subject to no controls, rather than subject to the controls which had been proposed. That can hardly have been what the opponents intended. Moreover, as Dr Jim Dyer wrote[40]: "A patient who passes on one side of this line [between competence and incapacity] will get the treatment, but one who is more ill and therefore needs the treatment more will be denied it.... What [the opponents] are saying, to a patient with years of unremitting severe depression, who has been through at least a three-year treatment protocol of just about every known anti-depressant drug and other treatments, someone who may be at high risk of suicide, and is too ill to consider consent, is that they are to be prevented from having the one remaining treatment that might relieve their misery. I cannot see such a total ban as acceptable in a civilised society". The second example concerns patients with terminal conditions who do not fear death but do fear either the prolongation of life in a situation which they find unbearable, or the manner of dying in prospect if their terminal conditions are allowed to take their course (or both). The law, at least in England, at time of writing seems to be this. The case of *Miss B* in 2002, referred to in para.14–4 above, confirmed that a competent patient may insist upon the discontinuance of life-prolonging treatment, with the consequence that she will die. The case of *Pretty*, also in 2002,[41] upheld the right of patients to choose a time and way of dying if they can do so unaided, but for a patient such as Mrs Pretty who desires this but is unable to achieve it unaided, refused to declare that anyone else could with impunity give the help desired by the patient. It is doubtful whether even the most vehement defender of the principles applied in the latter decision would desire the potential consequences for a patient with an incurable and progressive disease, likely at some stage to result in the level of disability experienced by Mrs Pretty, and likely to be followed by a manner of dying which the patient fears more than death itself. The patient in such a situation who believes that he would in due course wish to be able to choose the manner and time of death now faces the prospect that his only option is to implement the preferred method of dying sooner than he would choose, while still physically able to do so unaided. He is denied the prospect of keeping his

---

[40] Dr Jim Dyer *ibid.*
[41] [2002] 1 A.C. 800; [2002] 1 All E.R. 1.

options open as his disease progresses further. Whatever one's personal values and beliefs in such matters, it cannot be right that a person in such a situation and with such views and feelings should be faced with the added, legally imposed, burden of deciding whether to end his life sooner than he would have chosen but for that legal constraint; and, if he does for that reason end his life because of future fears rather than present experience, that he should because of the current state of our law, rather than anything inherent in his condition, be denied a prolongation of life including the very real possibility that the latter stages might not be so unacceptable, or might not become unacceptable as soon, as he had expected. This book does not seek to advocate what the law should be in such matters. It does not suggest that well-established principles be set aside, but it does suggest that they must be fundamentally reviewed in a broader context. To the extent that they are retained following such review, their validity and authority will have been enhanced. Those seeking to engage meaningfully in such debate, rather than using it merely as an opportunity to proclaim entrenched positions, will require to distinguish among at least the following four elements. The first is the right, and the right of all, to hold and advocate ethical beliefs, to visualise various possible scenarios and to consider what parameters they would set for themselves, and might perhaps seek to urge upon others. The second is the pragmatic assessment of what might be appropriate and best for most people in most circumstances. The third is the question of the point at which ethical debate and scope for pragmatic decisions should both be closed off, and limitations set by law upon what should never be available even to one single citizen in any circumstances at all. The fourth is the question of what should never be available to any citizen with impaired capacity in any circumstances whatsoever, it being the view of this author—as asserted at the outset of this chapter—that there should in this respect be no discrimination on grounds of impairment of capacity, so that the answers to the third and fourth questions should be the same: but both questions require to be addressed. The challenge, to lawyers in particular, is not to take the easy option of prohibiting in all cases (or in all cases where capacity is impaired) something which could be used inappropriately or wrongfully in some circumstances, but instead—as has been done in the Incapacity Act in its broader application—to devise and introduce appropriate procedures, safeguards and controls, and to insist that best practice be followed in applying them.

Appointee decisions

As a category of health-care decision-making and a category of **14–13** authorisation for health-care intervention, appointee decisions were part of pre-Act law but aspects are now regulated by the Incapacity Act. Prior to implementation of Part 2 of the Act on April 2, 2001, welfare decisions (including health-care decisions) could competently be made by welfare attorneys.[42] As is described in Chapter 6, the granting and registration of welfare powers of attorney is now

---

[42] As is confirmed by the transitional provisions of Sch.4, para.4.

governed by Part 2 of the Act and, as described in para.14–17 below, the scope of what may be done and decided by a welfare attorney with powers in health-care matters is now limited by s.16(6) of the Act. Prior to implementation of Part 6 of the Act on April 1, 2002, powers to make health-care decisions were conferred by the courts upon most tutors-dative. Sometimes these included specific authority to consent to a particular medical intervention, and sometimes these were the only powers granted.[43] Powers to make health-care decisions were also included in the plenary welfare powers of tutors-at-law, and MHSA guardians had the fixed powers *inter alia* in relation to health-care matters (which did not include power to consent to treatment) described in para.10–3 above. On April 1, 2002 tutors-dative, tutors-at-law and MHSA guardians all became guardians in terms of the Incapacity Act, in each individual case with the same powers as were held immediately before that date.[44] From that date, powers to make health-care decisions may be conferred upon guardians and upon appointees under intervention orders, as described in para.14–15 below. The implementation of Part 5 of the Act on July 1, 2002 brought into force the provisions of s.49, which apply to medical treatment when an application is pending for a guardianship or intervention order with relevant powers (see para.14–46 below), and s.50, which confers certain rights of appeal on the responsible doctor and on persons having an interest who disagree with an appointee's decision in relation to proposed medical treatment (see paras 14–54 to 14–61 below). Appointee decisions may also be made by guardians, attorneys or their equivalents under the laws of other countries, provided that the appointment includes relevant powers and is recognised by Scots law: their status is expressly recognised for the purposes of the provisions of s.50.[45]

14–14 There is, or at least has been, a widespread practice among health-care providers of seeking a written form of "consent" to proposed health-care intervention from a relative, where an adult patient is for any reason unable to give written consent. It has never been the law that anyone has had any authority in law to make health-care decisions on behalf of an adult by reason of relationship. As the Scottish Law Commission put it in another context: "Medical practice does not make law".[46] Power to make health-care decisions, including power to consent to treatment, on behalf of an adult patient has only ever been conferred in Scots law by specific appointment by the patient or by the court. The categories of such appointees are limited to those described in para.14–2 above.[47]

Source of authority

14–15 For guardians appointed under the Incapacity Act, the source of their authority to make health-care decisions is s.64(1) of the Act, and is subject to the terms of the order appointing them and limitations in

---

[43] On powers conferred on tutors-dative see paras 10–21 to 10–24 *supra*.
[44] Sch.4, para.1.
[45] s.50(10).
[46] Consultative Memorandum No.65, *Legal Capacity and Responsibility of Minors and Pupils*, 1985, para.2.51.
[47] Throughout this book, "appointee" is used rather than "proxy", notwithstanding that the latter term has been adopted in codes of practice under the Incapacity Act.

terms of s.64(2).[48] Where the guardian has plenary welfare powers in terms of s.64(1)(b), then subject only to s.64(2) the guardian can make any welfare decisions—and thus any health-care decisions—which the adult, if competent, could have made for himself. Where the guardian's powers are limited to particular matters in terms of s.61(1)(a) or specified aspects of personal welfare in terms of s.64(1)(b), any powers to make health-care decisions are limited accordingly. For transitional guardians[49] the source of authority is the original appointment, limited from April 1, 2002 by s.64(2). Under an intervention order, the source of authority to exercise the powers specified in the order is s.53(5): the limitations in s.64(2) are applied by s.53(14). In the case of both pre-Act and post-Act welfare powers of attorney, the source of the attorney's authority is the power of attorney itself, the provisions of the Act being regulatory, though the competence of conferring and exercising powers to make health-care decisions is recognised by the terms of the statutory limitations in s.16(6), which specify steps which the welfare attorney may not take and treatments to which the attorney may not "consent on behalf of the grantor". The welfare attorney may make any other health-care decisions which the grantor, if competent, could have made for himself and may consent on behalf of the grantor to any other treatment; provided always that the decision or consent is within the scope of the powers conferred by the welfare power of attorney. The limitations under s.16(6) are the same as those under s.64(2), therefore both are treated together in paras 14–17 *et seq.* below.

Error in code of practice

The Part 5 Code of Practice,[50] at least in its first edition, contains a **14–16** potentially confusing error in para.2.25, the first sentence of which reads: "The Act requires that even where a proxy has been appointed, a certificate under s.47(1) should be completed". The Act contains no such provision. Certificates under s.47(1) are relevant only to s.47(2) authority. Section 47(2) authority is "without prejudice to any authority conferred by any other enactment or rule of law". In the case of guardianship and intervention orders, the only relevant medical certification is that provided for in s.57(3), and there is no requirement for further certification. Exercise of welfare powers conferred by a power of attorney is subject only to the limitations in ss.16(5)(b) and 16(6), which do not require any further certification for exercise of powers, subsequent to the certification at time of granting under s.16(3), and any requirement for further certification is a matter for the grantor.[51] The only explanation which has been tendered for the first sentence of para.2.25 of the Code[52] is the *non sequitur* that because s.50(2) disapplies s.47(2) *inter alia* where it would be reasonable and practicable for the responsible doctor to obtain an appointee's consent

---

[48] See para.14–17 *et seq. infra.*
[49] See para.11–18 *supra.*
[50] Code of Practice for Persons Authorised to Carry Out Medical Treatment or Research under Part 5 of the Act.
[51] See *e.g. Style* clause Four.
[52] Secretary's note incorporated in minute of meeting of National Implementation Steering Group held May 25, 2002.

but he has failed to do so, s.47(2) is somehow reapplied where appointee consent has been obtained. When competent appointee's consent is given, that consent is the authority for the treatment, and s.47(2) is unnecessary (and to invoke it would be an unnecessary intervention, prohibited under s.1(2)). The error appears only in the Part 5 Code of Practice and is not replicated in the relevant provisions of the Part 2 and Part 6 Codes.[53]

Sections 16(6) and 64(2) limitations

14–17 Sections 16(6) (which applies to appointees under welfare powers of attorney) and 64(2) (which applies to appointees under guardianship and intervention orders) are in similar terms to each other. All such appointees are prohibited from placing the patient for whom they act in a hospital for the treatment of mental disorder against his will and from consenting on behalf of the patient to any form of treatment mentioned in ss.48(1) or (2). "Against his will" has to be construed in the context that the issue will only arise where the patient is not capable of giving his own competent consent, and is therefore likely to be construed as referring to an expression of disagreement or resistance, howsoever communicated. In the case of non-verbal communication, this might necessitate evidence of how the patient is known to express disagreement or resistance. Conversely, an appointee acting properly and within his powers may place in hospital for such treatment a patient who gives no indication of disagreement or resistance.

14–18 Section 48(1), which applies also to s.47(2) authority, excludes any of the forms of treatment to which Part X of MHSA 1984 applies (see "Part X authority", paras 14–38 and 14–39 below). With reform of MHSA, reference to forms of treatment to which the procedures and provisions of the new MHSA apply is likely to be substituted.

14–19 Section 48(2), discussed in para.14–48 below, empowers Scottish Ministers to specify medical treatment, or a class or classes of medical treatment, to which s.47(2) authority shall not apply and to specify medical treatment, or a class or classes of medical treatment, to which s.47(2) authority does apply. Sections 16(6)(b) and 64(2) prohibit appointees from consenting to "any form of treatment mentioned in" s.48(2). Given the terms of s.48(2), this can only mean treatment specified in regulations under s.48(2) as treatments to which s.47(2) should not apply and treatments to which it does apply. The Specified Treatments Regulations have been made under s.48(2). The treatments specified in them are listed in Schedule 2 to the Regulations, so that subject to the issue discussed in the next paragraph, consent to those treatments is excluded from appointee authority. All of the specified treatments are treatments in respect of which s.47(2) authority is disapplied, and all of them may be authorised by s.48(3) authority, as described in paras 14–48 to 14–53 below. If it were ever desired to

---

[53] It is understood that both the Mental Welfare Commission and British Medical Association are also of the view that the first sentence of para.2.25 of the Part 5 Code is erroneous, and that both advise enquirers accordingly. BMA has amended accordingly its guidance, the first edition of which coincided with the Code: see *Medical treatment for adults with incapacity: Guidance on ethical and medico-legal issues in Scotland* (2nd ed., October 2002) (*cf.* 1st ed., June 2002).

remove a particular treatment from appointee decision-making and leave it within s.47(2) authority, that would be achieved by regulations specifying it as a treatment to which s.47(2) authority does apply.

The terms of the Specified Treatments Regulations give rise to an **14–20** issue as to whether they do indeed have the effect of removing consent to treatments specified in the Regulations from the powers which appointees would otherwise have been entitled to exercise in terms of their appointments. The Regulations appear to have been drafted with reference only to s.47(2) authority, either deliberately or inadvertently in terms which could be construed as excluding the cross-references in ss.16(6)(b) and 64(2)(b).[54] Regulation 2(1) limits the application of the Regulations to situations where the responsible doctor has granted a certificate in terms of s.47(1)[55] that the patient is incapable in relation to a decision about a treatment specified in Schedule 1 to the Regulations. As is explained in para.14–16 above, certification under s.47(1) is relevant only to s.47(2) authority, not to authority conferred by an appointee's consent. Moreover, regulation 2(2) not only provides that the medical treatments set out in Schedule 1 are specified for the purposes of s.48(2) of the Act, which would be sufficient without further elaboration if it was intended to specify them for the purposes of the cross-references in s.16(6) (as regards attorneys) and s.64(2) (as regards appointees under guardianship and intervention orders) as well as for the purposes of s.47(2) authority: Regulation 2(2) goes on to provide that they are so specified as treatments to which s.47(2) shall not apply, which by specifically and otherwise unnecessarily mentioning one of the three categories of authority to which such regulations would otherwise apply, could be construed as excluding the other two. Unless and until the Regulations are clarified by amendment or replaced, one is left with three possible interpretations: that they do not apply so as to limit appointee decisions at all; that they apply to limit appointee decisions only if the responsible doctor happens to have certified under s.47(1) in relation to the matter in question; or that they apply fully to appointee decisions (whether or not an irrelevant certificate under s.47(1) has been issued) as the scheme of the Incapacity Act clearly intended. In practice it would be prudent, and in the best interests of patients, to proceed in accordance with the last of these alternatives, unless and until a court should hold otherwise (or the poor drafting of

---

[54] As was explained in para.3–7 *supra*, the Act provides a coherent and integrated (but not comprehensive) code of provision. It has not helped the implementation of the Act that whereas the department at Scottish Executive primarily responsible was the Civil Law Division at the Justice Department, Part 5 was dealt with in isolation by the Public Health Division of the Health Department. There are indications that insufficient regard was paid by that department to the remainder of the Act, and the vital importance of considering each Part in the context of the remainder, or the equal importance of the wider context of incapacity law as a whole. That may well have contributed to the error in the Code of Practice discussed in para.14–16 *supra*. It is also possible that when the Specified Treatments Regulations were framed the cross-references in ss.16(6)(b) and 64(2)(b) were inadvertently overlooked. Certainly, the official Explanatory Notes appended to the draft Regulations and the accompanying Executive Note referred to the relevance of the Regulations to s.47(2) authority but made no mention of the cross-references in Parts 2 and 6 of the Act. The terms of both the Explanatory Note and the Executive Note are such that the cross-references would surely have been mentioned if they had not been overlooked.

[55] See para.14–43 *infra*.

Inter-relationship with other categories

14–21   For the reasons given in para.14–9 above, none of the appointees referred to in this section should make health-care decisions in respect of which the patient in fact has capacity (or has regained capacity); and even where the patient's relevant capacity remains impaired, any expression of disagreement or resistance would prevent the appointee from placing the patient in hospital for treatment of mental disorder.[56] On the effect of a competent and relevant advance directive, see paras 7–9 and 7–11 above. A decision under *parens patriae* jurisdiction would override an appointee decision, as would an intervention order under s.53(5)(a) of the Incapacity Act specifically directing particular action to be taken. Part X authority prevails to the exclusion of appointee decisions[57] and would override any inconsistent welfare decision already made by an appointee. Apart from the foregoing, it appears that an appointee's refusal of consent will prevail except where there is a mechanism which specifically overrides it: hence, for example, "notwithstanding the disagreement of [the appointee]" at the end of s.50(5), where a nominated practitioner has authorised treatment.

14–22   The principle of necessity would authorise treatment in emergency even though an appointee had relevant powers, whether or not the practitioner was aware of the appointment, but beyond that this author is unaware of authority on the relationship between the principle of necessity and appointee decision-making. On principle, one would argue that an appointee, within the powers conferred on him, stands in the same position as the adult by or to whom he is appointed, in matters of decision-making; that the appointee, where available to be consulted, should be consulted in the same manner as the patient (if competent, conscious and able to communicate) would have been consulted; and that the appointee's refusal would disapply the principle of necessity in the same way and to the same extent as would the patient's own competent refusal. Such issues are unlikely to be put to the test, as in situations other than emergency it would be better practice under the Incapacity Act to follow the Act's provisions and procedures. The Code of Practice recommends that it is "good practice to make use, so far as reasonable and practicable, of the procedures under Part 5 where this is without risk to the patient".[58] On the other hand, just as the Code of Practice explains that "It would be contrary to good practice to risk prejudice to a patient's health through any delay in providing necessary treatment, in order to give effect to the procedures under Part 5 of the Act", likewise it would be contrary to good practice to risk such prejudice trying to contact an appointee, or debating with an appointee, for longer than the circumstances permit.

14–23   The inter-relationship between appointee decision-making and s.47(2) authority, s.48(3) authority, s.50(5) authority and judicial determination under the Incapacity Act is discussed in the relevant sections

---

[56] ss.16(6)(a) and 64(2)(a)—see para.14–17 *supra*.
[57] s.48(1), as applied by ss.16(6), 53(14) and 64(2).
[58] Code of Practice, para.2.4, reproduced in Appendix 4 *infra*.

below. Note that *inter alia* appointee decisions are specifically preserved under s.47(9) of the Incapacity Act and regulation 5 of the Specified Treatments Regulations to authorise medical treatment to preserve life or prevent serious deterioration where any court proceedings have been commenced and not yet determined in relation to s.47(2) authority or s.47(3) authority (except that any relevant interdict which has been granted will prevail[59]). Also, *inter alia* a decision by a welfare attorney with relevant powers is specifically preserved by s.49(2) for the preservation of life or prevention of serious deterioration where application has been made to the sheriff, and not yet determined, for an intervention or guardianship order with relevant powers (again subject to any relevant interdict[60]).

General application of the Incapacity Act

All of the appointees referred to in this section are subject to the general provisions of the Act. All of them must accordingly comply with the general principles in relation to health-care matters within their powers, as in all other matters. They have the duties, and are subject to the supervision and controls, described in Chapters 6, 10 and 11, insofar as relevant to the particular category of appointment. They are in particular subject to s.3(3) directions.[61] Where they take decisions "for the purposes of" Part 5 of the Act as to the medical treatment of the adult, such decisions may be appealed under s.52 to the sheriff, and thence with leave of the sheriff to the Court of Session, by any person having an interest in the adult's personal welfare. Issues may arise as to whether a particular decision by an appointee about medical treatment was or was not "taken for the purposes of" Part 5. A person "having an interest" might for safety make application under both s.3(3) and s.52, whereas a person "claiming" but not "having" an interest does not have the option of s.52; which could in turn lead to arguments as to whether the Parliament intended that such a person, to whom the door to s.52 is closed, should be able to achieve the same purpose through the apparently open door to s.3(3). Section 14 could be available in some cases as providing a further alternative.

14–24

Parens patriae

The Court of Session confirmed in *Law Hospital NHS Trust v Lord Advocate*[62] that it remains competent to apply to the court to exercise the *parens patriae* jurisdiction, formerly termed the *pater patriae* jurisdiction. Both the Lord President in *Law Hospital*[63] and Lord Oliver of Aylmerton in *In Re B (a minor) (wardship: sterilisation)*[64] quoted with approval La Forest J in the Canadian case of *Mrs E v Eve*,[65] who said that the Crown has an inherent jurisdiction to do what is for the benefit of the incompetent and that its limits or scope have not, and

14–25

---

[59] s.47(10) and reg.5(3).
[60] s.49(3).
[61] See paras 5–14 and 5–15 *supra*.
[62] 1996 S.L.T. 848; 1996 S.C.L.R. 491; 1996 S.C. 301.
[63] 1996 S.L.T. 848 at 857–858; 1996 SCLR 491 at 504.
[64] [1988] 1 A.C. 199 at 211.
[65] (1986) 2 S.C.R. 388.

cannot, be defined. The Court of Session confirmed in *Law Hospital* that the jurisdiction of the court to appoint tutors-dative derived from the *parens patriae* jurisdiction,[66] and that within its broader, undefinable scope the *parens patriae* jurisdiction could also be invoked to seek authority to discontinue treatment for patients in a persistent vegetative state. Prior to the Incapacity Act, the *parens patriae* jurisdiction of the Court of Session was therefore analogous to the statutory jurisdiction of the sheriff under the Incapacity Act to grant direct authorisation under an intervention order or to appoint a guardian. Appointment of tutors-dative is no longer competent,[67] but otherwise the *parens patriae* jurisdiction would appear to remain in force, though apparently now parallel to the jurisdiction of the sheriff to grant intervention orders, so far as adults with impaired capacity are concerned. It is difficult to envisage matters which would lie beyond the reach of the statutory jurisdictions under the Incapacity Act and MHSA, but which would fall within the undefined scope of the *parens patriae* jurisdiction, but the development of human experience and human society can lead to unpredicted needs, and it is valuable that the *parens patriae* jurisdiction remains.

14–26 There appears to be no reason why applications might not now be made for an intervention order in the particular matter addressed in the *Law Hospital* case, namely a decision as to whether to discontinue treatment for a patient in a persistent vegetative state, or more generally as to whether any medical treatment should be withheld or withdrawn. The Scottish Law Commission's draft Bill[68] contained suggested provisions permitting medical practitioners to withhold or withdraw treatment (or authorise withholding or withdrawing) if satisfied that the treatment would not benefit the adult, even though that might result in the adult's death, subject to an obligation to consult in accordance with good medical practice, and subject to the right of anyone claiming an interest to apply to the Court of Session. No specific provisions on withholding or withdrawal of treatment were included in the Incapacity Act as introduced or enacted. This would appear to leave it open to those seeking a ruling in such matters either to apply for an intervention order or to invoke the *parens patriae* jurisdiction. Where the proposed withholding or withdrawal of treatment is likely to result in death, or to have other serious consequences, there are three potential reasons why an applicant might prefer the *parens patriae* jurisdiction. The first is that the *Law Hospital* decision was subsequent to the SLC Report, and it appears that the Scottish Executive, in deciding to exclude this topic from the Incapacity Act, did so on the basis that the courts should continue to develop the law in the light of the *Law Hospital* decision, with the implication that this would occur in the context of the *parens patriae* jurisdiction referred to in that decision. Secondly, the general scheme of the Act is to refer critical medical matters, such as appeals to court under s.50 or appeals from the sheriff under s.52, direct to the Court of Session. Thirdly, the Lord Advocate's decision not to prosecute in

---

[66] Lord President Hope, 1996 S.L.T. 848 at 856; 1996 S.C.L.R. 491 at 502, quoting *inter alia* Erskine I. 7. 8; Lord Clyde, 1996 S.L.T. 848 at 862–863; 1996 S.C.L.R. 491 at 511–512, quoting *inter alia* Bryce v Grahame (1828) 6 S. 425 at 433.
[67] Incapacity Act, s.80.
[68] Draft Bill annexed to SLC Report, clause 41.

terms of the policy statement referred to in para.14–28 below applies to actions "with the authority of the Court of Session". If application were nevertheless to be made for an intervention order in a matter of the type addressed in the *Law Hospital* case, one would expect the sheriff to have regard to the rulings of the Lord President in that case, to the extent relevant to intervention order procedure.

In *Law Hospital*, the Inner House authorised the Lord Ordinary to decide the matter by declarator, but directed that future such applications should be made under the *parens patriae* jurisdiction.[69] Pending promulgation of rules by Act of Sederunt,[70] the court set out a statement of practice[71] including *inter alia* that application should be by petition to the Outer House by the relevant health authority or NHS Trust or by any relative of the patient within the meaning of Schedule 1 to the Damages (Scotland) Act 1976; and that the petition should be served on such of the foregoing as are not petitioners, and upon the Lord Advocate. The petition should be supported by two medical certificates and should specify the proposed treatment or withdrawal of treatment. It should specify when persistent vegetative state was first diagnosed and for how long life-preserving treatment has been continued. Anticipating the requirements of the Incapacity Act, any known views of the patient should be narrated. Appointment of a curator ad litem should be sought. **14–27**

On April 11, 1996 the Lord Advocate issued a statement which is reproduced at the end of the reports of the decision of the Inner House.[72] The Lord Advocate intimated that he had decided that he would not authorise the prosecution of a qualified medical practitioner (or any person acting upon the instructions of such practitioner) who, acting in good faith and with the authority of the Court of Session, withdraws or otherwise causes to be discontinued life-sustaining treatment or other medical treatment from a patient in a persistent, or permanent, vegetative state, with the result that the patient dies. For the subsequent disposal of the *Law Hospital* case, see *Law Hospital NHS Trust v Lord Advocate (No.2)*[73] in which Lord Cameron of Lochbroom concluded: "In this case I am satisfied on the evidence and the facts which I have taken from it, that it is no longer possible to suggest that the continuance of the treatment which is presently being administered and has for some considerable time past been given to [J] to maintain her in her present condition, a condition in which she is permanently insensate, is of any benefit to her. That being so, there are no longer any best interests to be served by continuing such treatment". **14–28**

Although the *parens patriae* jurisdiction is described in this chapter, its undefined scope places it as the ultimate responsive measure of last resort, and it is thus referred to briefly in Chapter 12.[74] **14–29**

---

[69] 1996 S.L.T. 848 at 860; 1996 S.C.L.R. 491 at 507.
[70] Act of Sederunt (RCSA No.3) (Miscellaneous) 1996 (SI 1996/1756) with effect from August 5, 1996 added to the Rules of the Court of Session Rule 14.2 (i) that petitions for exercise of the *parens patriae* jurisdiction should be brought by way of Outer House petition and Rule 14.7(3) to the effect that such petitions should not be intimated on the Walls of Court.
[71] 1996 S.L.T. 848 at 860; 1996 S.C.L.R. 491 at 508.
[72] 1996 S.L.T. 848 at 867; 1996 S.C.L.R. 491 at 518.
[73] 1996 S.L.T. 869; 1996 S.C.L.R. 566.
[74] See paras 12–27 and 12–34 *supra*.

Necessity

14–30 There is no doubt about the proposition that in Scots law the principle of necessity authorises emergency treatment where the patient is temporarily unable to make a decision or give consent, and where that treatment cannot reasonably be delayed until the patient regains such capacity. It so applies where the patient is "unconscious, drunk or otherwise incapable of giving consent and is not known to have objected to receiving treatment".[75] If that can be called the "core extent" of the principle, it can reasonably be asserted that in the context of Scots law as it now stands with the relevant provisions of the Incapacity Act in force, necessity as a principle authorising treatment applies beyond the core extent, in relation to patients whose incapacity is not limited to temporary causes, in the following ways. Firstly, it would be fundamentally wrong in principle to discriminate among people with different causes of incapacity so as to deny essential treatment to some where it would be given to others, therefore within the other parameters of the "core extent" the principle of necessity authorises treatment regardless of the cause, nature or likely duration of incapacity. Secondly, the principle of necessity authorises treatment covered by the statement of good practice in para.2.4 of the Part 5 Code, the first sentence of which reads: "It would be contrary to good practice to risk prejudice to a patient's health through any delay in providing necessary treatment, in order to give effect to the procedures under Part 5 of the Act" (the entire paragraph is important, and is quoted in full with paras 2.5 and 2.6 in Appendix 4). Thirdly, the principle of necessity likewise authorises treatment (and it would likewise be contrary to good practice to delay) where there would be risk of prejudice to the patient's health if that treatment were to be delayed to ascertain whether there was an appointee with relevant powers, or to contact such appointee, or to discuss with and obtain a decision from such appointee.[76] Fourthly, the principle of necessity is included within the various references, in Part 5 of the Incapacity Act and in the Specified Treatments Regulations, to authorisation of treatment conferred "by any other enactment or rule of law" so that treatment is authorised on grounds of necessity in the circumstances addressed in ss.47(9), 49(2) and 50(7) and in regulation 5, all as described in para.14–35 below. Fifthly, however, in all cases the principle of necessity is subject to the patient's decision in that it is overridden by a competent refusal (including by advance directive) which remains in force and is applicable,[77] and is not available where there is a prospect of the patient regaining capacity and treatment can reasonably delayed until the patient does so. Treatment may not be given on grounds of necessity if forbidden by interdict.

14–31 There is doubt as to whether in Scots law the principle of necessity extends beyond the scope described in the preceding paragraph so as to authorise treatment where alternative authorisation could be

---

[75] See SLC Report, para.5.3, citing Hoggett, *Mental Health Law* (2nd ed.), p.202; Mason and McCall-Smith, *Law and Medical Ethics* (4th ed.) p.220; British Medical Association, *Medical Treatment and Incapable Adults: Interim Guidelines for the Medical Profession* (1990), p.2; NHS Scotland, *A Guide to Consent to Examination, Investigation, Treatment or Operation* (1992), para.16.1.

[76] See also para.14–22 *supra*.

[77] See para.14–3 *supra*.

sought without risk of prejudice to the patient's health through the delay necessary to obtain such alternative authorisation. Paragraph 2.4 of the Code, referred to above, advises that it "would ... be good practice to make use, so far as reasonable and practicable, of the procedures under Part 5 where this is without risk to the patient". Paragraph 2.6 concludes that: "It is recommended that the new authority be used in every case where it is reasonable and practicable to do so".[78] For the reasons given in the preceding paragraph and in para.14–33 below, it is also suggested that, both as a matter of good practice and as a matter of law, necessity neither should be relied on nor provides authority where it is reasonable and practicable, without risk to the patient, to ascertain whether there is an appointee with relevant powers, to contact such appointee, and to discuss with the appointee and seek consent. If such good practice is followed, the question would not in practice arise as to whether necessity extends to provide alternative authority where other methods of authority could be sought. That view of good practice may not be universally shared, or universally applied. The question is therefore addressed in the following paragraphs.

So far as this author is aware, there is no authority for the **14–32** proposition that the principle of necessity provides authority for treatment where some other authority could reasonably be invoked. In England, *Re F (mental patient: sterilisation)*[79] established a much broader scope for authority on grounds of necessity. In his leading judgement, Lord Brandon stated that: "A doctor can lawfully operate on, or give other treatment to, adult patients who are incapable, for one reason or another, of consenting to his doing so, provided that the operation or other treatment concerned is in the best interests of such patients. The operation or other treatment will be in their best interests if, but only if, it is carried out in order either to save their lives or to ensure improvement or prevent deterioration in their physical or mental health"; and he went on to equate "in the best interests of the patient" with "on ground of necessity".[80] In *Re F* the court authorised sterilisation of an adult woman with a learning disability whose reproductive organs were healthy. The decision drew criticism at the time,[81] but that is not the relevant point here. What is relevant is that English law then lacked, and at time of writing still lacks, any equivalent of appointee decision-making by a tutor-dative, tutor-at-law, welfare guardian or appointee under an intervention order; that it was (and is) apparently believed that appointment of a welfare attorney is not available in England; and that the *parens patriae* jurisdiction was abolished in England by the Mental Health Act 1959.[82]

---

[78] paras 2.4–2.6 of the Part 5 Code are reproduced in Appendix 4 *infra*.
[79] [1990] 2 A.C. 1; see also *In re B* (popularly known as "the Jeanette case") [1987] 2 All E.R. 206.
[80] *Re F* [1990] 2 A.C. 1 at 55.
[81] D. Carson, "Why the law lords said yes to sterilisation", Health Service Journal, June 8, 1989, pp.690–691; S.J. Gibson, "Sterilising the handicapped", *Independent*, May 31, 1989.
[82] On a point in which he was in a minority, in *Re F* Lord Griffiths was of the opinion that that case should in effect have created an English category of judicial authorisation, and that the particular operation authorised in that case (sterilisation of a mentally disabled woman with healthy reproductive organs) should have been declared unlawful unless the operation had been enquired into and sanctioned by the High Court.

Re F and other English decisions may not expressly enunciate any principle that authorisation on grounds of necessity is not available where some other authorisation could reasonably be sought, but at the very least they are consistent with such a principle. The existence of such a principle, and its application in *In re F*, is at least strongly implied by the comments of Lord Browne-Wilkinson in *Airedale NHS Trust v Bland*[83] that: "Faced with this lacuna in the law, this House in *In re F* developed and laid down a principle, based on concepts of necessity, under which a doctor can lawfully treat a patient who cannot consent to such treatment if it is in the best interests of the patient to receive such treatment". The significance of *In re F* in Scotland was addressed at the time by the present author in *The Power to Act* with the following conclusion:

> "Put simply, in England either a proposed operation is justified by the necessity principle, or it cannot be carried out. In Scotland, either it is justified by the necessity principle, or else the consent of a tutor-dative will be required, and then the operation may still be carried out. To avoid unacceptable consequences, English law needed a wider definition of necessity than is required in Scotland. It was right that, in the case of F, the House of Lords should seek to put in place in England a regime for treatment without consent which would not result in a mentally disabled patient failing, for want of consent, to receive treatment which was in the patient's 'best interests'.
> "Because of the difference between the Scottish and English positions, it is in my view unsafe to assume that the Scottish courts would adopt an equally broad definition of the area in which consent is not required. The Scottish courts may do so, but in my view it would be unwise to make that assumption unless and until a suitable case arises in Scotland, and is decided."[84]

14–33   The Incapacity Act has distanced the Scottish position much further from the English situation addressed by the court in *Re F*. At the time of *Re F*, tutors could only be appointed in the Court of Session. Not only may guardianship and intervention orders now be more conveniently sought in the sheriff court, but more importantly s.47(2) authority and the other authorisations under the Incapacity Act are available. Moreover, it is improbable that the Parliament intended to make provision for the controls authorised by s.48(2) and (3), and which have been implemented in the Specified Treatments Regulations, if those controls could be by-passed by invoking the principle of necessity, particularly where the operation actually considered in *Re F* now falls within Part 1 of Schedule 1 to the Specified Treatments Regulations and accordingly requires the approval of the Court of Session.[85] The issue could be described as being whether "necessity" means necessary only in medical terms, or also "legally necessary" in

---

[83] [1993] A.C. 789; [1993] 2 W.L.R. 316; [1993] 1 All E.R. 821; [1993] 1 F.L.R. 1026; [1993] 14 Med. LR 39.
[84] *The Power to Act*, pp.64–65.
[85] Thus adopting the minority view expressed by Lord Griffiths. On the Specified Treatments Regulations, see paras 14–48 *et seq. infra*.

the sense that it would not in the particular circumstances of the case be reasonable and practicable to seek authority by other means without the delay to do so risking prejudice to the patient's health. The undisputed "core extent" of the principle of necessity includes the element of "legal necessity" in relation to patient's decision: if the patient can be consulted, or if delaying until the patient can be consulted would not risk prejudice to health, then the principle of necessity does not apply. There does not appear to be any logical reason why "legal necessity" should be required in relation to the patient's own decision-making but not in relation to specific powers conferred by the patient or by the court upon an appointee to make the same decision for the patient, or in relation to other methods of authorisation now created—with appropriate procedures and controls—by the Parliament. It is the view of this author that necessity is the safety net available when, but only when, no other source of lawful authority is reasonably available, but that whether alternative authority is reasonably available should be construed in this way: where an emergency demands that the practitioner act immediately, the principle of necessity always applies unless the practitioner already knows that the intervention which he proposes to make is forbidden by interdict or the competent and applicable decision of the patient; that as urgency decreases the boundary will be set reasonably having regard to the circumstances presenting to the practitioner, and his knowledge, at the time; and that in cases of doubt the boundary should always be set so as not to create risk that a practitioner acting competently and in accordance with good practice as recommended in the Part 5 Code might prejudice his patient's health by hesitating or delaying. While it would be unrealistic to expect practitioners to carry the whole Part 5 Code in their heads, it seems highly advisable that all practitioners should be aware of the advice in paras 2.4–2.6 inclusive of the Code. Those paragraphs are reproduced in Appendix 4. Put another way, it will at times be reasonable to allow some leeway between the requirements of good practice and the point at which a practitioner should be held to have acted unlawfully, enough to avoid creating the risk of prejudice to patients which the principle of necessity exists to prevent, but not too much.

Application of the Incapacity Act

14-34 Section 47(2) authority is without prejudice to authorisation of treatment on grounds of necessity.[86]

14-35 There are four situations in which the Incapacity Act and the Specified Treatments Regulations specifically permit medical treatment on grounds of necessity to preserve the patient's life or prevent serious deterioration in the patient's medical condition. In each case, the Act (and the Regulations) refer to treatment "authorised by any other enactment or rule of law". That phrase includes the principle of necessity, but does not extend it, so that a competent and applicable refusal by the patient (including by advance directive) remains effective. Also, in each of the four cases, treatment may not be given where prohibited by an interdict which has been granted and

---

[86] s.47(2).

continues to have effect.[87] The first of the four situations, under s.47(9), is where any question about the authority of anyone to provide medical treatment under s.47(2) is subject to proceedings in any court and has not been determined (though proceedings under regulations made under s.48[88] are excluded from the provisions of s.47(9), and are covered instead by regulation 5). The second situation, under s.49(2), is where the responsible doctor is aware that an application has been made to the sheriff, and not yet determined, for an intervention or guardianship order with powers in relation to any medical treatment which would be subject to s.47(2) authority. The third situation, under s.50(7), applies to medical treatment authorised by s.47(2) authority where an appeal under s.50(3) or an application under s.50(6) (described in paras 14–60 and 14–61 below) has been made to the Court of Session. In each of the first three situations, treatment is prohibited unless authorised by "any other enactment or rule of law" as described in this paragraph. The fourth situation, under regulation 5 of the Specified Treatments Regulations, applies to the treatments listed in Schedule 1 to the Regulations. Regulation 5(1) declares the Regulations to be without prejudice to authorisation on other grounds in emergency to preserve life or prevent serious deterioration, and regulation 5(2)—described in para.14–53 below—requires notification within seven days to the Mental Welfare Commission.

14–36 The investigatory and other powers and provisions of the Incapacity Act which apply beyond the boundaries of the Act's own scheme of provision, and which are described in para.5–41 above, may be invoked in relation to issues concerning or arising from the application of the principle of necessity. Note also that where the principle of necessity applies by virtue of the provisions described in the preceding paragraph, it would appear that compliance with the s.1 principles is mandatory on the basis that treatment in such circumstances is an intervention "under or in pursuance of" the Incapacity Act.[89] Otherwise, the s.1 principles represent good practice but are not mandatory where treatment is contemplated or given on grounds of necessity.

14–37 MHSA 1984, s.102 explicitly preserves the principle of necessity in emergencies in relation to treatments otherwise subject to the controls of ss.97 or 98, as described in para.14–39 below.

Part X authority

14–38 As in Chapter 12,[90] because of anticipated reform of the current MHSA referred to in para.3–31 above, existing law under Part X of MHSA 1984 is outlined only briefly in the next paragraph. Under existing law, Part X authority prevails over all other categories of health-care decision-making, including (with only the limited exceptions mentioned in the next paragraph) the patient's own competent decision. On the basis of the draft Bill published by Scottish Executive on June 27, 2002, a pattern broadly similar to the existing provision is

---

[87] ss.47(10), 49(3) and 50(8), and reg.5(3).
[88] Currently, the Specified Treatments Regulations.
[89] s.1(1).
[90] See para.12–28 *supra*.

likely to be adopted, but in restructured form with additional elements and safeguards. It is likely still to be the case that, with the exception of specified treatments to which special provisions will apply, medical treatment for mental disorder may be given to detained patients (other than those detained under emergency powers and power to remove to a place of safety) notwithstanding that the patient does not consent or is incapable of consenting. Of the specified treatments subject to special provisions, it is likely that some will require the consent of the patient if capable, or require that the patient be unlikely to resist the treatment if incapable, whereas others may be imposed upon a patient who resists or does not consent. There are likely to be special provisions for emergencies. It is likely to continue to be the case that there will be a category of authorisation of treatment under mental health legislation which will prevail over all other categories of health-care decision-making, including (subject to some exceptions) the patient's own competent decision. The gravity of any decision to impose treatment upon a competent, non-consenting patient has been emphasised in *R. v Feggetter Ex p. Wooder*,[91] where it was held that, having regard to ECHR, reasons should be given for any such decision. Written reasons are likely to be required under the new MHSA.

The current MHSA 1984 provides that, except for specified treatments to which special provisions apply, patients detained under the Act, subject to exceptions in s.96(1), may under s.103 be given medical treatment without consent for the mental disorders from which they are suffering. This authorises treatment of a patient not capable of consenting and compulsory treatment of a competent patient who refuses consent. There are two categories of specified treatments to which special provisions apply. Under s.97, treatment specified in that section or in regulations made under it may only be given if both the patient is competent to consent and is certified as having done so, and also a medical practitioner appointed for the purpose by the Mental Welfare Commission has certified that the treatment should be given. Under s.98, treatment specified in that section or in regulations made under it may only be given if either the patient is competent to consent and is certified as having done so or alternatively a medical practitioner appointed for the purpose by the Mental Welfare Commission has certified that the treatment should be given. Section 102 disapplies ss.97 and 98 in relation to various categories of emergency defined in that section, subject to a requirement for the responsible medical officer to notify Mental Welfare Commission within seven days. **14–39**

Intervention order

An intervention order made under s.53(5)(a) of the Incapacity Act may "direct the taking of any action specified in the order". The matter could be a health-care matter. On intervention orders under s.53(5)(a), and intervention orders generally, see Chapter 10. (Health-care decisions by an appointee under the other type of intervention **14–40**

---

[91] Court of Appeal April 25, 2002, briefly reported 2002 Scolag Journal p.130; see also *R. v Responsible Medical Officer Broadmoor Hospital Ex p. Wilkinson* [2002] 1 W.L.R. 419.

order, made in terms of s.53(5)(b) where an appointee is appointed, fall within the category of appointee decisions discussed in paras 14–13 to 14–24 above.) On the relationship between s.53(5)(a) intervention orders and the *parens patriae* jurisdiction, see para.14–26 above.

Section 47(2) authority

14–41   Section 47(2) is an addition to the range of ways in which medical treatment may be authorised, and does not detract from any of the other categories of authority.[92] It is conferred by a single medical certificate as described in para.14–43 below, and is subject to the limitations described in paras 14–45 to 14–47. Within those limitations, and except in cases of emergency or urgency where any delay in proceeding under the doctrine of necessity would risk causing prejudice to the patient,[93] s.47(2) authority is likely to be the preferred method of obtaining authorisation for (and thus rendering lawful) proposed medical treatment of patients who are incapable, within the broad definition in s.1(6) of the Incapacity Act,[94] in relation to a decision about that treatment. Section 47(2) authority is particularly valuable in removing worries and doubts which previously existed about giving treatment in situations not falling clearly within the principle of necessity. It is suggested in para.14–33 above that necessity applies where delays to follow s.47 procedure (or obtain an appointee's consent) would risk prejudice to the patient. The Code of Practice sensibly recommends a similar approach to the point at which s.47 procedure should be followed.[95]

General application of Incapacity Act

14–42   The Act's general principles[96] apply to s.47 procedure and s.47(2) authority, as they apply to all interventions under the Act. In particular, the general principles apply to the decision and procedure to invoke s.47(2) authority, and to any interventions contemplated or effected once s.47(2) authority is in place. As described in Chapter 4, "intervention" encompasses decisions to refrain from acting as well as decisions to act, and "benefit" encompasses overcoming the limitations created by incapacity, so as to permit something which the patient could reasonably be expected to have chosen to do (or not to do) if capable. As regards the requirement to adopt the option least restrictive of the patient's freedoms, s.58(1)(b) places guardianship as the most restrictive option under the Act, so that guardianship should not be sought where the patient's welfare would be adequately safeguarded or promoted by obtaining s.47(2) authority. There is no equivalent declaration in relation to intervention orders: it is possible to envisage health-care decisions of such difficulty and importance that, where there would be no prejudice in taking the time required to obtain an intervention order, the greater safeguards of intervention order procedure would be less restrictive of the patient's freedom

---

[92] See the "Without prejudice . . ." proviso to s.47(2).
[93] See para.14–33 *supra*.
[94] See paras 4–23 *et seq. supra*.
[95] Code of Practice, paras 2.4–2.6, which are reproduced in Appendix 4 *infra*.
[96] s.1(1)–(5)—see paras 4–2 *et seq. supra*.

than s.47(2) procedure. An alternative would be to put s.47(2) authority in place, then seek directions under s.3(3).[97] Other general provisions of the Act meriting mention here are the procedure to appeal against decisions about incapacity under s.14[98]; the investigatory powers of the Mental Welfare Commission under s.9(1)(e) and the local authority under s.10(1)(d), with related provisions in s.12; and the offence of ill-treatment and wilful neglect under s.83 (which would apply *inter alia* to anyone exercising powers conferred by s.47 where failure to provide care or treatment amounted to wilful neglect). Any decision taken for the purposes of s.47 procedure may be appealed under s.52: see para.14–62 below.

Procedure and duration

Section 47(2) authority applies where the responsible doctor is of **14–43** the opinion that the patient is incapable in relation to a decision about the medical treatment for which he is responsible, and issues a certificate in the prescribed form.[99] Guidance on good practice in following the procedure is given in the Part 5 Code. The certificate must specify the duration of the authority conferred by it, being the period which the responsible doctor considers appropriate to the condition or circumstances of the patient subject to a maximum of one year from the date of the examination on which the certificate is based.[1] If during the duration of the authority the responsible doctor considers that the patient's condition or circumstances have changed, he may revoke the certificate, and he may also issue a new certificate, for such period as he considers appropriate to the new condition or circumstances, up to a maximum of one year from revocation of the old certificate.[2] There are no limitations in the Act upon issuing successive certificates, whether similar or different. British Medical Association has suggested that it is inappropriate that certification may be by any doctor, irrespective of experience and training, but not by other practitioners such as appropriately trained specialist nurses and clinical psychologists. The Association has also suggested that in some cases the one year maximum is too short, quoting the examples of severe learning disability or established and severe dementia, where recovery is impossible. The Association has requested review of these aspects of the Act's provisions.

Scope of authority

Subject to the exclusions described in paras 14–45 to 14–47 below, **14–44** for the duration of the period covered by the certificate medical treatment within the scope of the certificate[3] is authorised as follows. Firstly, the responsible doctor may do what is reasonable in the

---

[97] See para.5–14 *supra*.
[98] See para.5–18 *supra*.
[99] s.47(1) and (5). The prescribed form of certificate is set out in the Adults with Incapacity (Medical Treatment Certificates) (Scotland) Regulations 2002 (SSI 2002/208) (see Appendix 2).
[1] s.47(5).
[2] s.47(6).
[3] s.47(2) refers to "the medical treatment" (not "medical treatment"), referring to "the medical treatment in question" in s.47(1).

circumstances, in relation to that medical treatment, to safeguard or promote the physical or mental health of the adult.[4] Secondly, medical treatment may be carried out by any other person who is authorised by the responsible doctor and who is acting either on his behalf under his instructions, or with his approval or agreement.[5] This covers those directly responsible to the responsible doctor, colleagues who are not, and persons who are not health-care professionals such as family or carers. "Medical treatment", throughout Part 5 of the Act, is defined as including "any procedure or treatment designed to safeguard or promote physical or mental health".[6]

Exclusions

14–45 Excluded from s.47(2) authority is: (a) the use of force or detention, unless it is immediately necessary and only for so long as is necessary in the circumstances, (b) action which would be inconsistent with any decision by a competent court, and (c) placing an adult in a hospital for the treatment of mental disorder against his will.[7] Any use of force or detention under the exception to (a) must be strictly in accordance with s.1 principles, including the requirement that it must in all respects be limited to the minimum necessary restriction of the adult's freedom. In (c), it is suggested that "against his will" refers to any expression of disagreement or resistance, howsoever communicated (see para.14–17 above on the same phrase in ss.16(6) and 64(2)). Section 47(9) excludes s.47(2) authority where any question as to the authority of any person to provide medical treatment under s.47(2) is the subject of court proceedings which have not been determined. See paras 14–23 and 14–35 above on the extent to which, respectively, authorisation by appointees and the principle of necessity are explicitly preserved in such circumstances, in the absence of an interdict forbidding the treatment in question. Also excluded from s.47(2) authority is giving any treatment to which Part X of MHSA 1984 applies (see para.14–38 above).[8] Section 47(8) provides that s.47(2) authority does not authorise medical treatment "prescribed in regulations made under s.48". That could be inconsistent with the provision of s.48(2) that such regulations may *inter alia* make provision about treatment to which s.47(2) authority "does apply", but that difficulty remains hypothetical as the current Specified Treatments Regulations specify only treatments to which s.47(2) authority does not apply.[9] However, none of those treatments are prohibited altogether: the Regulations contain procedures under which all of them may be authorised, putting them all into the separate category of authorisation here termed "s.48(3) authority", described in paras 14–48 *et seq.* below.

14–46 Sections 49 and 50 define the relationship between s.47(2) authority and appointee decision-making, and in course of doing so further limit the scope of s.47(2) authority. Section 49 disapplies s.47(2)

---

[4] s.47(2).
[5] s.47(2) and (3).
[6] s.47(4).
[7] s.47(7).
[8] s.48(1).
[9] reg.2(2).

authority where, to the knowledge of the responsible doctor, an application for an intervention or guardianship order with relevant powers has been made to the sheriff and has not been determined. See paras 14–23 and 14–35 above on the extent to which, respectively, decision-making by a welfare attorney and the principle of necessity are expressly preserved in such circumstances. Section 50(1) and (2) disapplies s.47(2) authority where all of the following three conditions apply: (a) an appointee[10] has relevant powers, (b) the responsible doctor is aware of the relevant appointment or authorisation, and (c) it would be reasonable and practicable for the responsible doctor to obtain the appointee's consent to the proposed medical treatment but the responsible doctor has failed to do so. Put conversely, where an appointee has relevant powers, s.47(2) authority will nevertheless be available if either under (b) the responsible doctor is unaware of the appointment (or unaware that the appointee has relevant powers) or under (c) it would not be reasonable and practicable for the responsible doctor to obtain the appointee's consent. With reference to (b), with one exception the Act places no obligation on the responsible doctor to go out of his way to ascertain whether there is a relevant appointment, so that in practical terms the onus is upon the appointee to notify the appointment and terms thereof, in such manner and to such extent as may be appropriate. The exception is that the responsible doctor's unqualified obligation under the third principle[11] to ascertain and take account of the patient's past and present wishes and feelings would appear to place an obligation on the responsible doctor *inter alia* to ascertain whether the patient had granted a welfare power of attorney conferring relevant powers. With reference to (c), it is to be anticipated that "obtain" is likely to be interpreted as broadly synonymous with "seek", except that in a situation of urgency it might be reasonable and practicable to obtain consent where the appointee is willing and able to give it immediately, but not where (without refusing) the appointee is unwilling to commit to a decision without more explanation or discussion than the urgency of the situation permits. See paras 14–54 *et seq.* below where the responsible doctor and the appointee are in disagreement, or where they agree but a person having an interest challenges their agreed decision.

The Act is not explicit as to the relationship between s.47(2) **14–47** authority and advance directives. Legislative provision on advance directives was proposed by the Scottish Law Commission, and was included in the draft Bill annexed to the SLC Report, but on the basis explained in para.7–5 above was excluded from the Incapacity Act. The excision has left some uncertainties, of which this is one. It is suggested in para.7–9 above that it would be reasonable to argue that a valid and applicable advance directive would prevail over s.47(2) authority. On the one hand, in the absence of clarification to the contrary, practitioners would be unwise to do under s.47(2) authority something forbidden by an advance directive. On the other hand, patients seeking to ensure the effectiveness of an advance directive might wish to link it to a power of attorney as suggested in para.7–9

---

[10] Under a welfare power of attorney, intervention order or guardianship order, or (s.50(10)) the equivalent of a guardian or attorney under the law of any other country.
[11] s.1(4)(a).

above. More important in practice is that patients discuss matters with medical advisers before framing advance directives, and that they and any relevant appointees should thereafter ensure that practitioners are aware of the advance directive and the patient's reasons for the content, including relevant wishes and feelings. Treatment not desired by the patient is most effectively blocked by an interdict,[12] which might be sought following upon the granting of an advance directive by the patient or by an appointee with relevant powers.

Section 48(3) authority

14–48   Section 48(2) and (3) empowers the Scottish Ministers by regulations to do three things. Firstly, it empowers them to specify medical treatment, or classes of medical treatment, to which s.47(2) authority shall not apply. Secondly, they may specify medical treatment, or classes of medical treatment, to which s.47(2) authority does apply. Thirdly, s.48(3) provides that regulations under s.48(2) may provide for the circumstances in which the treatment, or class or classes of treatment, may be carried out. Section 48(3) as drafted has two possible interpretations. The first is that it provides an alternative mechanism for authorising treatments to which s.47(2) authority, in terms of the regulations, does not apply (thus creating the separate category of authorisation here termed "s.48(3) authorisation"). The second is that particular requirements could be applied to treatments specified as treatments to which s.47(2) authority does apply. It would seem theoretically possible to adopt both interpretations, applying the first to one list of treatments and the second to another list, though it is doubtful whether such complexity would serve any useful purpose. In practice, the first method has been adopted by the Adults with Incapacity (Specified Medical Treatments) (Scotland) Regulations 2002[13] as amended by the Adults with Incapacity (Specified Medical Treatments) (Scotland) Amendment Regulations 2002,[14] here termed the Specified Treatments Regulations. On the applicability of s.48(3) authority, and the Specified Treatments Regulations, to appointee decision-making see paras 14–19 and 14–20 above. It would be possible for regulations under s.48(3) to remove specified treatments from s.47(2) authority without making alternative provision, or to remove specified treatments from appointee decision-making and to confirm the applicability to them of s.47(2) authority without further qualifications, but neither of these options has been adopted or proposed. The Specified Treatments Regulations create two sets of requirements, one for approval by the Court of Session and the other for a certificate from a practitioner appointed by the Mental Welfare Commission, referred to in this chapter as an "appointed practitioner" (see para.14–2 above, which also explains other terminology adopted in this chapter, including in particular references to "the responsible doctor" and to "child and adolescent psychiatrists"). Except with the competent consent of the patient, or under Part X authority where applicable, or in emergency as described in para.14–53 below, the medical treatments listed in Schedule 1 to the Specified Treatments

---

[12] ss.47(10), also 49(3) and 50(8), and reg.5(3) of the Specified Treatments Regulations.
[13] SSI 2002/275.
[14] SSI 2002/302.

Regulations may be carried out in relation to an adult only in accordance with the relevant provisions of the Regulations, and only where they are designed to safeguard or promote the adult's physical or mental health.[15] The general principles of the Incapacity Act must be observed in seeking, granting and implementing s.48(3) authority.

Treatments requiring application to the Court of Session

Regulation 3 requires the authority of the Court of Session to carry out the treatments specified in Part 1 of Schedule 1 to the Regulations. Even with such authority, those treatments are prohibited if the patient resists.[16] Application to the court may be made by the responsible doctor. The court requires to be satisfied that the patient is an adult who is incapable in relation to a decision about the proposed treatment, that the treatment will safeguard or promote the adult's physical or mental health, and that the adult does not oppose the treatment. It is suggested that reference to resistance or opposition by the patient will be construed as any expression of disagreement or resistance, however communicated, having regard in the case of non-verbal communication to any relevant evidence of how the patient is known to express disagreement or resistance.[17] Issues of interpretation might arise where the adult is expected to exhibit some degree of resistance or opposition to something peripheral to, but necessary for the purposes of, the specified medical treatment. It would be sensible to disclose such concerns in the application, or to make further application for directions.[18] It would appear that use of the present tense in "does not oppose" would not exclude opposition expressed in the past but continuing to apply in terms of an advance directive which is valid and applicable.[19] If the patient is a 16 or 17-year old and the proposed specified treatment is a treatment for mental disorder, then the responsible doctor either must be a child and adolescent psychiatrist, or must have sought and obtained a written opinion from a child and adolescent psychiatrist that the treatment is reasonably required to safeguard or promote that young adult's mental health.[20] In considering the application, the court must afford to any person having an interest in the adult's personal welfare an opportunity to make representations in respect of the application.[21] Any certificates or opinions given in accordance with the Regulations may subsist for a maximum of one year, and the responsible doctor must send copies of

14–49

---

[15] reg.2(3).
[16] reg.3(1)(b).
[17] *cf.* discussion of "against his will" in paras 14–17 and 14–45 *supra*. See Scottish Parliament Subordinate Legislation Committee Official Report, Meeting No.22, 2002 (June 25, 2002) for suggestions that "opposition" would probably be expressed by the adult either verbally or in an advance directive, and that "resist" refers to physical resistance: both of which seem unduly narrow in the context of adults who may have physical or communication difficulties.
[18] While applications to the sheriff under s.3(3) would appear to be technically competent, it would be helpful for authorisations granted by the Court of Session to be in terms expressly permitting subsequent application by the responsible doctor or anyone having an interest.
[19] See Scottish Parliament Subordinate Legislation Committee Official Report, Meeting No.22, 2002 (above).
[20] reg.6(1).
[21] reg.3(2).

14-50 Two treatments are specified in Part 1 of Schedule 1 to the Regulations: sterilisation where there is no serious malfunction or disease of the reproductive organs; and surgical implantation of hormones for the purpose of reducing sex drive.[23] Such sterilisation was addressed by the Court of Session in *L v L's curator ad litem*[24] and in the English cases of *Re F* and *In re B*.[25] During the passage of the *Betreuungsgesetz*, the German legislature gave full and anxious consideration as to whether such sterilisation should be prohibited, or permitted subject to controls, and concluded that it was better that it should be permitted but regulated by careful controls. The Scottish Law Commission translated and summarised the resulting preconditions as follows: (a) the sterilisation must not be opposed by the patient, (b) the patient must be permanently incapable of consenting (*i.e.* not likely to recover relevant capacity), (c) there must be a definite risk of pregnancy without a sterilisation, (d) a pregnancy must lead to a serious risk to the patient's physical or mental health which could not be averted in another way, and (e) a pregnancy must not be reasonably preventable by other means such as contraception or restrictions on sexual activity.[26] It should be noted that any medical treatment likely to result in sterilisation which does not fall within Part 1 of the Schedule to the Specified Treatments Regulations nevertheless falls within Part 2, and that any drug treatment to reduce sex drive other than by surgical implantation also falls within Part 2 (see para.14–52 below).

Treatment requiring a certificate from an appointed practitioner

14-51 Under regulation 4, treatments specified in Part 2 of Schedule 1 to the Regulations require a certificate from an approved practitioner in the form set out in Schedule 2 to the Regulations that the patient is incapable in relation to a decision about the treatment in question and that the treatment should be carried out, having regard to the likelihood of its safeguarding or promoting the patient's physical or mental health. The appointed practitioner must not be the same person as the responsible doctor. Where the patient is aged 16 or 17, and the proposed treatment is a treatment for mental disorder, the appointed practitioner must be a child and adolescent psychiatrist and the responsible doctor either must also be a child and adolescent psychiatrist, or must have sought and obtained a written opinion from a child and adolescent psychiatrist that the treatment is reasonably required to safeguard or promote the patient's mental health.[27] Every certificate and opinion given in accordance with the Regulations may subsist for a maximum of one year, and the responsible doctor must

---

[22] reg.7.
[23] Neurosurgery for mental disorder was removed by the amending Regulations SSI 2002/302, thus removing this controversial treatment from all special controls, though with the intention that the matter be addressed in the forthcoming new MHSA.
[24] 1997 S.L.T. 167: see para.10–24 *supra*.
[25] [1990] 2 A.C. 1 and [1987] 2 All E.R. 206 respectively: see para.14–32 *supra*.
[26] SLC Discussion Paper para.3.33, referring to BGB s.1905, inserted by Betreuungsgesetz 1990.
[27] reg.6.

send copies of each to the Mental Welfare Commission within seven days of its date.[28] Regulation 4 contains no provisions equivalent to those of regulation 3 prohibiting the treatment where the patient opposes or resists. The surprising implication is that although those concerned are obliged to adhere to the general principles in s.1 of the Incapacity Act, they may nevertheless impose treatment authorised by regulation 4 under s.48(3) authority in the face of opposition or resistance from the adult, notwithstanding that the adult is not subject to MHSA Part X and its protections and notwithstanding that the Parliament has strictly limited the use of force or detention in relation to s.47(2) authority in terms of s.47(7)(a).

Four treatments are specified in Part 2 of Schedule 1 to the Regulations: drug treatment for the purpose of reducing sex drive, other than surgical implantation of hormones (which is included in Part 1—see para.14–50 above); electro-convulsive therapy for mental disorder; abortion (to which the requirements and provisions of the Abortion Act 1967 also apply in full); and any medical treatment which is considered likely by the responsible doctor to lead to sterilisation as an unavoidable result (as opposed to sterilisation of the kind included in Part 1—see para.14–50 above). **14–52**

Emergencies

Regulation 5 permits any of the treatments specified in the Regulations to be given to preserve the patient's life or prevent serious deterioration in the patient's medical condition, if authorised under "any other enactment or rule of law". This would include authorisation under the principle of necessity.[29] However, the treatment may not be given if prohibited by an interdict which has been granted and continues to have effect.[30] See also para.14–30 above, including as regards the effect of an advance directive. Where such emergency treatment has been given, the responsible doctor must within seven days notify the Mental Welfare Commission in writing (which may be in electronic form) of the patient's name and address, the nature of the treatment, the place where it took place and the reasons for giving it.[31] **14–53**

Section 50(5) authority

Section 50(5) authority may be conferred by a certificate by a nominated practitioner following disagreement between the responsible doctor and an appointee with relevant powers. The terms "nominated practitioner", "responsible doctor" and "appointee" are used as described in para.14–2 above. References to an appointee include a guardian, attorney or equivalent with relevant powers under the law of any country, provided (in the case of a guardian or equivalent) that the guardianship is recognised by Scots law.[32] **14–54**

---

[28] reg.7.
[29] See para.14–35 *supra*: authorisation by an appointee is disapplied by the references in ss.16(6) and 64(2) to treatments "mentioned in" s.48(2) (meaning treatments specified in the Specified Treatments Regulations).
[30] reg.5(3).
[31] reg.5(2).
[32] s.50(10).

14-55 The relationship between appointees and medical practitioners regarding medical decisions, and the resolution of disagreements between them, attracted lively debate throughout the law reform process and the ensuing parliamentary proceedings. In these matters the Incapacity Act as enacted differs radically from the Bill as introduced, which in turn differed substantially from the draft Bill annexed to the SLC Report. The SLC draft Bill proposed that the medical practitioner, upon obtaining a second opinion, could override the appointee. The SLC proposal "evolved from discussion with representatives of some of the Royal Colleges in Scotland" (para.5.38), without any of the wider consultation which had characterised the SLC's work generally, and ran into wide-ranging and strong opposition on the grounds that doctors should not be able to override either an attorney expressly empowered by the patient to decide such matters, or a guardian or appointee under an intervention order expressly empowered by the court to do so, at least without the involvement of the court. It was also asserted that people likely to be appointed attorneys and guardians are more likely to know well the patient and the patient's medical history, and many examples were given of imposition by consultants, without discussion, of treatments already known to have failed or to have had undesirable consequences. Accordingly, the Act as introduced equated refusal by the appointee with refusal by the patient, subject to application to the Court of Session by the doctor. This prompted fears that inappropriate refusals by appointees might go unchallenged, to the detriment of the patient, because doctors lacked the will or resources to apply to the Court of Session. Suggestions that the Executive might revert substantially to the SLC proposal appeared to suit no-one. The Alliance adhered to the original objection to the SLC proposal, but also took the view that if appointees were to be overruled by anyone other than a court, that should only be done by someone who was—and was clearly seen to be—competent, independent and independently appointed, and there should be right of further recourse to the courts. Another element which emerged was the need to allow input from other parties with a clear interest, such as close relatives other than the appointee. The final form of s.50 was adopted by amendment at stage 3, and sought reasonably to accommodate all of these concerns. On recourse to the courts, including by a person having an interest, see paras 14–58 *et seq.* below.

14-56 Where there is an appointee with relevant powers and the other requirements of s.50(2), as described in para.14–46 above, are met, s.47(2) authority is disapplied. If an appointee with relevant powers consents, that consent provides authority for the proposed treatment.[33] Section 50(4) addresses the situation where there is a disagreement between the responsible doctor and the appointee. Because a doctor cannot be forced by an appointee (or a competent patient) to administer treatment which the doctor considers to be clinically or ethically inappropriate,[34] and because no form of authorisation to treat is an instruction to treat, a disagreement subject to s.50(4) will normally arise where the responsible doctor believes that the treatment should be given but the appointee refuses consent. However it

---

[33] On the limitations upon appointee decisions, see paras 14–17 *et seq. supra.*
[34] See para.14–4 *supra.*

is not impossible to envisage converse situations, such as where there are alternatives, the doctor accepts that one of the alternatives should be applied and that doing nothing is not an option, but the doctor disagrees with the appointee's choice. In such a situation, it would be appropriate to refer all of the options to the nominated practitioner.

14–57 Section 50(4) requires the responsible doctor to request the Mental Welfare Commission to nominate a practitioner from the list maintained under s.50(9)[35] to give an opinion as to the medical treatment proposed. It is not open to the appointee or anyone else to make such request. On the other hand, the responsible doctor may not leave a disagreement unresolved: if there is unresolved disagreement between responsible doctor and appointee about the patient's medical treatment, the responsible doctor "shall request" the appointment of a nominated practitioner. The nominated practitioner is required to have regard to all the circumstances and to consult the appointee. The appointee may nominate a person whom the nominated practitioner should consult if it is reasonable and practicable to do so. The Part 5 Code suggests that such consultee could be the patient's general practitioner, a consultant in a relevant speciality, a relative or carer, an independent advocate or someone else who knows the patient well.[36] The nominated practitioner must also comply with the general principles in s.1 of the Act. If the nominated practitioner then certifies that in his opinion the proposed medical treatment should be given, that certificate permits the treatment to be given by the responsible doctor or by any other person authorised by the responsible doctor, notwithstanding the appointee's disagreement.[37] However, the nominated practitioner may not authorise treatment prohibited by an interdict which has been granted and continues to have effect,[38] and on the same basis as indicated in para.14–47 above it is suggested that a valid and applicable refusal by the patient, including a refusal by way of advance directive, would continue to prohibit the treatment. Regarding appeal to the Court of Session against the decision of the nominated practitioner, see the next section.

Judicial determination

14–58 Part 5 of the Incapacity Act contains three provisions specific to that Part for appeal to the courts. They are described in the following paras 14–60 to 14–62. They are in addition to other provisions for appeal and application to the courts, contained elsewhere in the Act, which may nevertheless be applicable and appropriate in relation *inter alia* to health-care matters. These include the procedures under s.3(3) to seek directions[39] and under s.14 to appeal against a decision as to incapacity,[40] and the various powers of the court in relation to appointees under Parts 2 and 6.[41] Except under Part 5, the court of first instance is the sheriff court, and where appeal is competent it lies

---

[35] See para.14–2 *supra*.
[36] Part 5 Code, para.3.6.
[37] s.50(5).
[38] s.50(8).
[39] See para.5–14 *supra*.
[40] See para.5–18 *supra*.
[41] See Chapters 6, 10 and 11.

to the sheriff principal, and thence with leave of the sheriff principal to the Court of Session. Under Part 5, however, including under the Specified Treatments Regulations as described in paras 14–48 *et seq.* above, jurisdiction lies exclusively with the Court of Session except under s.52, where appeal lies to the sheriff and thence, with leave of the sheriff, direct to the Court of Session.

Persons having an interest

14–59 Another speciality of the provisions described in the next three paragraphs is that whereas elsewhere under the Act rights of application and appeal are generally available to anyone "claiming" an interest in the affairs or welfare of the adult, the provisions described below refer to a person "having" an interest in the adult's personal welfare. Likewise, the right to make representations to the Court of Session in relation to treatments listed in Part 1 of Schedule 1 to the Specified Treatments Regulations is limited to persons "having" an interest in the adult's personal welfare.[42] Outwith Part 5 of the Act, a person "having" an interest may under s.37(7)(a) cause review of a certificate authorising management of a resident's affairs under Part 4, if it appears to such person that there has been a material change.[43] While "person having an interest" is clearly intended to exclude those merely claiming an interest, the term is defined neither in the Act nor in the Specified Treatments Regulations, indicating that the Parliament preferred to leave precise definition of the term in particular circumstances to the Court of Session. In one old case "any party having an interest" was held to mean any relative,[44] but the Part 5 Code suggests that "any person having an interest in the personal welfare of the adult" in s.50 refers to persons "close to an adult", and might be "a close relation of the adult, or a person who has lived with, or cared for or about them, over a significant period".[45] It would be difficult in modern society to justify including or excluding people only because they are or are not relatives, and one would expect the court to have regard to the terms of the Part 5 Code, but to concentrate upon the circumstances of the individual case. The Code assumes that an appointee with relevant powers has an interest, which would appear to be correct, and would appear to be the basis on which s.50(6), described below, does not specifically mention such appointees—who in the circumstances addressed in s.50(6) would surely be specified if separate mention was necessary in order to include them. One would not expect any disagreement with the assertion in the Code that: "The term does not extend to those whose interest is that of an onlooker, such as interested pressure-groups, uninvolved neighbours, or those seeking to achieve objectives which are of wider import than the welfare of the particular adult".[46] Section 87(1) defines "person claiming an interest" as including the local authority, Mental Welfare Commission and personal guardian: the absence of any similar provision in relation to "person having an

---

[42] See para.14–49 *supra.*
[43] See para.9–19 *supra.*
[44] *Bryce v Grahame* (1828) 6 S. 425, relating to cognition—see para.10–11 *supra.*
[45] Part 5 Code, para.3.2.
[46] *ibid.*

interest" might be founded upon as excluding them from that category. Where someone held not to have an interest claims to be able to present evidence or argument relevant to the specific matter before the court, then although the wide-ranging powers under s.3 apply only to sheriff court proceedings, the provisions of s.5 regarding the appointment of a safeguarder (and of another person to convey the adult's views) apply to all proceedings before the Court of Session under the Incapacity Act, and thus to proceedings under ss.50 and 52, and under the Specified Treatments Regulations made under the Act: the safeguarder would be in a position to ascertain and bring before the court any evidence or argument clearly relevant to the matter in question.

Section 50(3)

Where the responsible doctor has consulted an appointee[47] with relevant powers about proposed medical treatment and there is no dispute between them, any person having an interest in the personal welfare of the patient may appeal "the decision" reached between them to the Court of Session. As s.47(2) authority is disapplied in the circumstances addressed by s.50(3), "the decision" referred to would appear to be the decision of the appointee to consent on behalf of the patient to the proposed treatment agreed between the responsible doctor and the appointee.

14–60

Section 50(6)

A decision by a nominated practitioner under the procedure described in para.14–57 above, following disagreement between the responsible doctor and an appointee with relevant powers, either that proposed medical treatment should be given or that it should not be given, may be appealed to the Court of Session by the responsible doctor or any person having an interest in the personal welfare of the patient. As indicated in para.14–59 above, "person having an interest" is clearly intended to include the appointee, in the absence of separate mention of the appointee.

14–61

Section 52

Section 52 provides a general right of appeal against any decision as to medical treatment of an adult taken for the purposes of Part 5 of the Act, except for a decision "by a medical practitioner" under s.50. The exception means that s.52 does not provide an alternative to the routes of appeal set out in s.50 except for an appeal under s.50(3) against an appointee's decision to consent to proposed treatment. Appellants under s.50(3) might feel it more appropriate and safer to go to the Court of Session under that section, as the legislature probably intended, rather than in the first instance to the sheriff under s.52. Appeals under s.52 may be brought by any person having an interest.[48] Appeal lies in the first instance to the sheriff and then, with leave of the sheriff, direct to the Court of Session. Where there is

14–62

---

[47] Including a foreign appointee, under s.50(10) described in para.14–54 *supra*.
[48] See para.14–59 *supra*.

dispute about a decision as to the patient's incapacity, then as mentioned in para.14–58 above the alternative of an appeal under s.14 remains available to any person claiming an interest. It remains to be seen how a sheriff would view an appeal by a person claiming but not having an interest, if it appeared that the appeal was brought under s.14 only because the Parliament had closed the door to s.52 to such a person. It is vitally important that a person who has capacity to make his own decision, albeit with difficulty or requiring assistance in communication, should never be subjected to any responsive measures predicated upon impairment of relevant capacity. Accordingly, it would seem reasonable to argue that the sheriff should never refuse to entertain an apparently serious assertion that a decision as to incapacity was wrong, notwithstanding that the decision was relevant to a matter under Part 5: under s.14 there is still a route to the Court of Session, albeit via the sheriff principal. It would be less easy to justify an application to the sheriff to give directions under s.3(3) if used as an alternative to an appeal under s.52, and if made by someone excluded from appealing under the latter section.[49]

AUTHORITY FOR RESEARCH

14–63 The Scottish Law Commission commented in its Report that: "There is virtually no authority in Scotland as to the legality of research on people incapable of consenting to their participation", and proposed that: "There should be legislative authority and regulation of research on mentally incapable people in place of the present legal near-vacuum".[50] Section 51 contains provisions about the carrying out of surgical, medical, nursing, dental or psychological research upon an adult who is incapable in relation to a decision about participation in the research. Section 51 stipulates (though without specifying sanctions[51]) that such research shall not be carried out upon such an adult unless (a) research of a similar nature cannot be carried out on an adult who is capable in relation to a decision about participation in the research,[52] (b) the purpose of the research is to obtain knowledge either of the causes, diagnosis, treatment or care of the adult's incapacity or of the effect of any treatment or care given during incapacity which relates to that incapacity,[53] and (c) the following six conditions are met.[54]

14–64 The first condition is stated as alternatives[55]: either the research is likely to produce real and direct benefit to the adult, or alternatively the research is not likely to produce real and direct benefit to the adult but will contribute, through significant improvement in the scientific understanding of the adult's incapacity, to the attainment of real and direct benefit to the adult or to other persons having the same incapacity. All of the remaining requirements apply under either

---

[49] See also para.14–24 *supra*.
[50] SLC Report, para.5.65.
[51] See para.14–71 *infra*.
[52] s.51(1)(a).
[53] ss.51(1)(b) and 51(2)(a).
[54] ss.51(1)(b) and 51(2)(b). The conditions are set out in ss.51(3) and (4).
[55] ss.51(3)(a) and 51(4).

alternative. Examples given in the course of discussion of the second alternative included research into Alzheimer's Disease which can only be carried out upon people in an advanced state of the disease, and likely to benefit people in an early stage or not yet suffering from the disease; and research which can only be carried out upon people following serious head injuries, likely to benefit others as to precautions or best initial treatment.

The second condition is that the adult does not indicate unwillingness to participate in the research. "Indicate unwillingness" should, it is suggested, be construed similarly to, but perhaps even more widely than, the references to "against his will" discussed in paras 14–17 and 14–45 above. See also the references to objection and resistance in the Specified Treatments Regulations discussed in para.14–49 above. **14–65**

The third condition is that the research has been approved by the Ethics Committee, constituted by the Adults with Incapacity (Ethics Committee) (Scotland) Regulations 2002.[56] In terms of regulation 6, before approving any research the Committee must take into account: (a) the objectives, design, methodology, statistical considerations and organisation of the research; (b) the relevance of the research and the study design; (c) the justification of predictable risks and inconveniences weighed against the anticipated benefits for the research participants and future participants; (d) the suitability of the lead researcher; (e) the adequacy of the written information to be given and the procedure for obtaining consent; and (f) the arrangements for the recruitment of research participants. The Committee may attach such conditions as it thinks fit to any approval which it grants.[57] **14–66**

The fourth condition is that the research entails no foreseeable risk, or only a minimal foreseeable risk, to the adult. The latter element is potentially ambiguous, encompassing either an extremely low risk of something nevertheless of significant severity if it were to occur, or no risk of anything other than something of minimal disadvantage to the adult—though it would seem that the risk must be of something more than minimal discomfort, as that is covered by the fifth condition. The only guidance given in the Part 5 Code is that this and the fifth condition "should be seen in the context of the adult's standard treatment, if that is appropriate".[58] On risk, see also element (c) in para.14–66 above. **14–67**

The fifth condition is that the research imposes no discomfort, or only minimal discomfort, on the adult: see the reference to the Part 5 Code in the preceding paragraph. **14–68**

The sixth requirement, under s.51(2)(f), is that if there is an appointee with relevant powers under a welfare power of attorney or guardianship order (or foreign equivalent of either[59]) or an intervention order, then the appointee shall have consented to the adult's participation in the research; or that if there is no such appointee, then **14–69**

---

[56] SSI 2002/190, made in terms of ss.51(6) and (7) of the Act. The Regulations make provision for the membership, required qualifications for some members, length of service, appointment of chair and vice-chair, payment of expenses and various procedural matters, including provisions permitting the Committee to determine the form of application and to consider applications in such manner as it thinks fit.
[57] s.51(5).
[58] Part 5 Code, para.4.3(d).
[59] s.51(8).

the adult's nearest relative[60] shall have consented. This requirement has caused concern that it creates significant difficulties for research in acute care settings, linked to concern about the similar requirement in European Union Directive 2001/20/EC.[61] The Act is an enabling provision which does not create difficulties which did not exist before: the question is whether it goes far enough in providing a procedure to overcome them. The Act is helpful in clarifying who may provide the required consent, compared with the situation under the Directive in countries lacking such provision, but is perceived as unhelpful in relation to emergency treatment when the appointee or nearest relative is not immediately available to consent. "It is unethical to create a Europe behind walls, which leaves others to solve research problems and then makes use of their work".[62] Some assistance in addressing these concerns may be provided by considering the linked questions of what is research, and what is wrongful.

What is research?

14–70 Section 51 applies to research, not to treatment. The Scottish Law Commission accepted that: "The distinction between medical research and medical practice is not an easy one to make".[63] It suggested that the distinguishing feature is the intent of the doctor, and adopted the following analysis by the Royal College of Physicians of London: "The distinction derives from the intent. In medical practice the sole intention is to benefit the individual patient consulting the clinician, not to gain knowledge of general benefit, though such knowledge may incidentally emerge from the clinical experience gained. In medical research the primary intention is to advance knowledge so that patients in general may benefit; the individual patient may or may not benefit directly".[64] However, the Commission then pointed out that this definition includes observational research, and stated that observational research "raises issues of confidentiality and privacy and therefore requires approval by a local research ethics committee, but because no consent is required from the patients concerned there are no special issues arising in connection with incapable patients. We are therefore content to leave the regulation of such research to the existing regime and exclude it from the ambit of this report".[65] It seems reasonable to interpret "research" in s.51 on the basis that the Parliament used the term in the same sense as Scottish Law Commission to mean research which is not treatment and which would

---

[60] See paras 5–38 and 5–39 *supra*.
[61] Directive of the European Parliament and of the Council of April 4, 2001 on the approximation of laws, regulations and administrative provisions of the member states relating to the implementation of good clinical practice in the conduct of clinical trials on medicinal products for human use, Art.5. On the Directive, see Singer and Mullner, *Implications of the EU Directive on Clinical Trials for Emergency Medicine*, British Medical Journal 2002; 324: 1169–1170 (May 18, 2002). On applicability of those concerns to the provisions of the Incapacity Act, see Warlow, Teasdale and Cobbe, *Evaluation of Treatments is Threatened by EC Directive*, British Medical Journal 2002; 325: 222 (July 27, 2002).
[62] Singer and Mullner *op.cit*.
[63] SLC Report, para.5.63.
[64] *Guidelines on the Practice of Ethics Committees in Medical Research Involving Human Subjects* (2nd ed., 1990), para.3.1.
[65] SLC Report, para.5.64.

require consent if carried out in relation to a capable patient. This takes us to the second question.

What is wrongful?

As pointed out in para.14–63 above, s.51 specifies no sanctions. The effect of s.51(1), accordingly, is that a researcher is not protected from any criminal or civil consequences which his actions might have, in the absence of s.51 and of compliance with its requirements. Any research in an acute situation is likely to be carried out in conjunction with emergency treatment authorised under the principle of necessity (if an appointee with relevant powers is unavailable to consent, there being no difficulty under s.51(2)(f) where such appointee is available). Treatment, it is suggested, has the broad definition quoted in the first sentence of this chapter. Anything which is treatment and which is justified under the principle of necessity is not wrongful for the purposes of s.51, even though a contribution to research may be gained from data properly obtained for the purposes of the treatment, including assessment of its effectiveness, or data obtained not as part of the treatment but by non-invasive observation. If in a particular type of situation doctors do not know which of two alternative possible treatments might be the better, allocate the two treatments randomly to their patients, and assess the outcome on the basis of analysis of proper follow-up examination and/or non-invasive observation, then (it is suggested) the question is not whether the outcome contributed to research, but whether the treatment of one or other set of patients was wrongful. It will not (it is suggested) be wrongful unless it fails the tests in Scots law as to what is covered by the principle of necessity and is not wrongful. For it to be wrongful, it would require *inter alia* to be shown that the course adopted "is one which no professional man of ordinary skill would have taken if he had been acting with ordinary care".[66] Such issues, it is suggested, must be determined in the context described by Lord Cameron: "The practice of medicine is not an exact science and methods of practice and treatment vary with the movement of professional opinion and the expansion of the horizon of scientific knowledge".[67] **14–71**

These considerations may not eliminate the concerns expressed about s.51(2)(f), but may help to limit them. Moreover, researchers are in all respects better placed in law following the Incapacity Act than before it. The Act provides a procedure to authorise research where it was not previously authorised by any identifiable principle of law, and has not rendered unlawful any research which previously has been lawfully authorised. Any remaining area of difficulty is one which has always existed: if it has now been thrown into sharper focus, that is only because it is all that remains of a much wider area where lawful authority for research was previously lacking. **14–72**

---

[66] *Hunter v Hanley*, 1955 S.C. 200 at 206.
[67] *Morrisons Associated Companies Limited v James Rome & Sons Limited*, 1964 S.C. 160; 1964 S.L.T. 249 at 255.

Chapter 15

CONSTRUCTING DECISIONS

In the practical application of adult incapacity law there is always a **15–1** continuum from the general to the particular. Definitions and general principles take us from starting-points of whether capacity is impaired and whether to intervene at all, through selection of particular techniques and (where they offer flexibility) selection of the form which they should take, to their application in practice. However, the principles and rules and procedures and technicalities are all preliminaries to engagement with the vital human task of making specific decisions or groups of decisions. They are essential preliminaries, but only acquire meaning when carried through to practical application. Likewise, no-one professionally or otherwise involved in these matters can properly stop short at the boundary of those preliminaries and fail to engage in the human reality of specific decisions and their consequences.

No text can foresee all the circumstances and dimensions of even **15–2** one specific decision yet to be made. It can however suggest a methodology which attempts to synthesise essential concepts and principles of good practice (including those now embodied in the Incapacity Act) that can take us from before any decision that there is a relevant impairment of capacity through to making or confirming specific choices and decisions.

Choices and decisions may be made or contributed to, in each case, **15–3** by one or more of a court, an appointee, anyone with any specific role in any procedure, people acting in official and professional capacities, relatives and carers, and others; and always, at least in some degree, by the adult. Principal elements in the synthesis are the concepts and definitions of capacity and incapacity; the concept of intervention; the concept and principles of benefit, of minimum necessary intervention and least restrictive alternative, of communication, and of the adult's wishes and feelings; and the relevance of the views of family, carers and others. Central to the synthesis are the principles of autonomy, empowerment, non-discrimination and respect for the essential human rights of every individual, and particularly the adult by or for whom a decision is to be made.

Every adult has the right, circumscribed only by limitations expres- **15–4** sly set by the law, to make whatever choices and decisions he or she wishes. Incapacity may impair the exercise of that right, but does not detract from the right itself. The purpose of incapacity law and its procedures, techniques, roles and appointments is to endeavour to make good that impairment so far as possible; never simply to take that right from the adult and pass it to another. That distinction must always be observed to the maximum possible extent. In some cases where the distinction is a narrow one, it remains critical.

15–5 One must always start with basic questions. Can the adult make and communicate a valid choice or decision in the particular matter? If so, that choice or decision applies. If not, what is the reason? Ability to communicate may be impaired; other elements of capacity may each in some degree be limited; or they may be distorted so seriously by mental illness as to raise questions as to whether apparent choices and decisions are nullified by those distortions. All of these are value judgements. They are value judgements by someone other than the adult. To question the apparent choices and decisions of an adult is an intervention, which must be justified. The presumption of capacity, with which this book commenced, must be actively supported, encouraged and facilitated before the possibility of rebutting it is seriously contemplated. If the principal difficulty is one of communication only, the matter is relatively clearcut. Whatever assistance is required, by any party to the communication in question, should be provided. But even here the matter is only relatively clearcut, not always absolutely clearcut. Some forms of serious communication difficulty require interpretative elements based on past knowledge of the adult, or upon skilled professional judgement, or a combination of both, to an extent that involves a degree of intervention, so that aspects of the following discussion become relevant.

15–6 "Intervention", in this context, means any involvement of any third party anywhere from the initial stages of questioning and assessing the adult's capacity through to making specific choices and decisions. The principles of no intervention except for benefit, and of minimum necessary intervention, are of fundamental importance, but it is necessary to pick out some of the individual strands which combine to form those principles.

15–7 The methodology proposed below applies only in situations where appropriate professional evidence has confirmed that there is some impairment of capacity. In approaching specific choices and decisions, it is still necessary to commence with an assessment of the extent to which the adult may nevertheless be able competently to decide the particular matter, or decide elements of it. Judgements about such particular matters can usefully be seen as including a comparison between what the adult communicates, when best assisted to do so, with a construct of what that same adult, with unimpaired capacity, could and would communicate. However, the methodology applies principally to the process of arriving at particular choices and decisions which the adult cannot competently make in their entirety. Such specific choices and decisions are, as stressed above, never merely someone else's, but still the adult's "own" choices and decisions which are at least to some extent constructed for the adult by the intervention of others.

15–8 Clearly, the adult's own input should be maximised. We have two constructs: the shadow construct against which the adult's input may be evaluated, and the actual construct in the form of the choice or decision made. Put another way, the first guides us in identifying elements of the choice or decision which will be supplied by the intervention of others rather than by the adult, and the second guides us in deciding those elements and constructing the final choice or decision. The first helps shape the second, and similar principles apply to both. The following suggested methodology is generalised, and is likely to require intelligent adaptation in some particular circumstances.

The possible elements of the construct can be stated hierarchically **15–9** as follows:

(1) The adult's present competent decision.

(2) The adult's past competent decision.

(3) The adult's decisive present choice.

(4) The adult's significant present choice.

(5) The adult's present wishes and feelings.

(6) The adult's past wishes and feelings.

(7) Information about the adult from, and the views of, the persons closest to the adult.

(8) Input of others with significant personal or professional knowledge of the adult, or specific appointments or roles in relation to the adult.

(9) The shared views and ethos of the adult's family.

(10) The shared views and ethos of any other grouping with which the adult is immediately and substantially associated.

(11) The shared views and ethos of any religious, ethnic or other group of which the adult, or the adult's family, is a member.

(12) The norms of the society of which the adult is a member.

In general terms, an element higher in the list will prevail over an **15–10** element lower; and at each step down the hierarchy, lower elements will only impinge upon a higher one if and to the extent that they strongly and persuasively indicate that it would be appropriate for them to do so. However the steps are not equal. For example, there are qualitative differences between competent decisions, past and present, and the other elements. There are also qualitative differences between elements (1)–(6), which all relate to the adult's own input, and the subsequent elements which do not. On the other hand, in some circumstances and for some purposes consecutive elements represent points along a continuum, rather than separately definable steps.

Taking firstly the difference between elements (1) and (2) and the **15–11** others, we can set aside situations where the adult can competently decide a particular matter, or all the components of a composite decision. That is the end of the matter: the adult decides. We can also set aside situations where the adult has made a competent decision in the past which remains valid and applicable and is not overruled by a competent subsequent or present decision. The past decision stands. The effects of supervening incapacity were briefly referred to in para.1–23 above. The circumstances in which a decision to appoint and empower an attorney survives incapacity are described in Chapter 6. The circumstances in which an advance directive or other specific anticipatory measure allows decisions to remain effective after loss of capacity are described in Chapter 7. It would seem reasonable to apply to past decisions generally the tests described in para.7–5 above in relation to advance directives: in general, a past decision decides the present matter if it was competently made, it has not been revoked, it addresses the factual situation which has arisen, and the assumptions on which it was based have not been falsified.

15–12 The list in para.15–9 comes into play when a matter is not decided in its entirety by a present or past competent decision. It will be helpful at this point to refer back to the general list of factors likely to be necessary for a competent decision suggested in para.1–30 above. Referring to the elements in that list by their lettering, in relation to a particular matter an adult may be capable of all necessary elements except (d) and (g). Presented with an appropriate list of options about the matter in question, the adult can make a competent choice, but the adult cannot set the agenda, add relevant options to it, or (if appropriate) decline to take any of the choices. Such a situation was addressed in *S and Others, Petitioners*[1] described in para.10–22 above, and in the terms of the powers conferred, as quoted in that paragraph. In such a situation, the elements requiring to be constructed for the adult are the elements of what alternatives to present, and whether and when to present them, for the adult then to make the adult's own competent choice.

15–13 In the situation described in the preceding paragraph, the separation between aspects decided by the adult and aspects where a decision has to be constructed for the adult are clearcut, and in *S and Others, Petitioners* that separation was formalised in the terms of an interlocutor. Other situations can be less clearcut. Most decisions, or decision-making processes, comprise several components, and an adult may be able to decide a few elements only. It may be possible to regard some of those as representing competent decisions, which stand, and around which remaining aspects require to be constructed for the adult. If however the components "decided" by the adult are interdependent with others which the adult cannot competently decide, then inability to understand that interdependence will probably be inconsistent with treating any of the adult's input as being competent decisions. We may instead be looking at wishes and feelings, which may nevertheless be clearly and strongly held, and persuasive.

15–14 This is a situation where we may be looking at a continuum rather than separate steps. In practical terms there may be no significant difference between a competent decision by the adult as to one dominant element in a process of composite decision-making, and a decisive choice which might not fit into any theoretical model of competent decision-making, but which may nevertheless be decisive to the extent that other related decisions require to be arranged around it. While analyses of the processes of competent decision-making, such as that offered in para.1–30 above, can be helpful in addressing the validity of particular decisions, the most important decisions of all may not be susceptible to such analysis. Made by people whose competence and capacity is not in doubt, those most

---

[1] (2000), unreported.

important decisions are often made instinctively. Such an instinctive decision becomes the "given", around which other decisions are made, logically and systematically, as best as circumstances permit. Instinctive elements are frequently decisive in decisions about the most important personal relationships in one's life, about the general nature of a preferred career, the preferred type of home environment and living arrangements, the general nature of preferred hobbies and leisure activities, and so forth. When such an instinctive decision is made, it is likely to be irrelevant to analyse the "decision-making process" by which it has been reached, and may well be impossible to do so. It is probably better to describe it as a choice, rather than as the outcome of a decision-making process which can be analysed; and because decision-making processes which are capable of analysis are irrelevant, the person's capacity in relation to such processes is also irrelevant. The continuum runs from such instinctive decisions, or choices, which are decisive and are a "given", around which other related decisions will be arranged (whether those decisions be competently made by the adult or constructed for the adult), through various degrees of persuasiveness to the level at which those instinctive choices should reasonably be treated, in the terminology of the Incapacity Act, as wishes and feelings of which account should be taken.

However, at one end of the continuum there are some situations in **15–15** which a choice by an adult will be decisive even though the adult has severe impairments of capacity. Such a choice will be decisive if a similar choice, by a competent adult, would have equally decisive status. To proceed otherwise would be to discriminate against, and indeed to de-personalise, the adult with impairments of capacity, however severe. Respect for such instinctive and entirely individual expressions of one particular person's personality is one of the fundamental elements of non-discrimination. Such choices are no less valid because they are communicated with difficulty and understood only by someone who knows the adult well, or who has advanced skills in understanding non-verbal communication or otherwise establishing communication. If these are the only ways in which a severely disabled adult can have some control over his own life, then it will be a grave and cruel injustice not to facilitate the communication of such decisive choices, and to respect them.

Along the continuum from choices which are decisive (and thus **15–16** equivalent in their effect to competent decisions) through choices which are significant to wishes and feelings, the weight given to the choice—or to the wishes and feelings—should be the same when constructing a decision for an adult with impaired capacity as it would be given to the same "level" of choice, or of wishes and feelings, by a competent person making his own decision. In other words, when constructing a decision for an adult unable to make the full decision competently for himself, within the construct the weight given to a particular "level" of choice, or of wishes and feelings, should be the same regardless of the degree of impairment of capacity. The degree of incapacity defines the extent to which other elements may require to be supplied other than by the direct contribution of the adult; not the weight to be given to those elements which the adult can supply. That weight should be determined both by objective assessment of the importance of the element in question and also by reference to the relative importance actually attached to it by the adult, whether the adult has full competence or impaired capacity.

15–17 This is a suitable point at which to consider the potential tension between past decisions, choices and wishes and feelings, on the one hand, and present ones, on the other. Usually present views will override past views. As was observed in para.4–17, an adult's choices and views when directly experiencing the realities of a situation may differ from distantly theoretical views expressed in the past about such a situation without direct personal experience of it. Moreover, the illness or injury causing the impairment of capacity may itself have altered the adult's personality and changed the adult's views. As is suggested in para.4–17, the present adult should not be treated as unequivocally "owned" by the past adult.

15–18 Conversely, however, there are situations such as that described in para.7–3 above, where an adult has a fluctuating illness and a tendency to make decisions and choices when unwell which are regretted when well. In these cases, the adult goes through phases when capacity and judgement are impaired. The adult lacks insight during those phases, but between them well understands what was happening. In the context of imposition of compulsory measures under mental health law, the Millan Committee considered and contrasted concepts of lack of capacity, lack of insight and impaired judgement, favouring the last-mentioned as a criterion for imposition of compulsory measures.[2] The distinctions are less relevant in incapacity law: in terms of the Incapacity Act, impairment of judgement may be a factor rendering an adult "incapable of . . . making decisions".[3] The vociferous assertion during a phase of illness may be neither a competent decision nor a decisive choice. It seems reasonable to make a distinction between the rational decision or decisive choice of a permanently altered personality, albeit combined with significant impairment of capacity, on the one hand, with temporary distortions of the adult's known views during phases of impaired judgement, on the other: but of course not every situation will fall neatly into one category or the other. Use of the "shadow construct" referred to in para.15–8 may assist, particularly in conjunction with professional assessment, but it can be difficult to avoid subjectivity.

15–19 The remainder of this discussion moves down the list in para.15–9 beyond items (1)–(3), that is to say away from cases where a decision or a component of a decision is clearly settled by the adult. Three examples may help to conclude consideration of elements (1)–(3) and set the scene for the following discussion. Firstly, one could take the simple hypothetical example of an adult whose physical disabilities and condition require that a special chair be acquired. The adult can non-verbally communicate feelings of comfort when seated in a suitably adapted and adjusted special chair, but beyond that her impairments of capacity do not permit her to participate meaningfully in the process of assessing needs, considering the alternatives offered by different manufacturers, considering cost-effectiveness, and so on. She can however make one contribution to the decision-making process. She is consistently adamant that she wants to have a green

---

[2] Millan Report, Ch.5, paras 25–45.
[3] Incapacity Act, s.1(6)(b).

chair. If the preferred model of chair, as assessed by others, is available in green, then that is either a competent decision, or at least a decisive choice, by the adult. Having regard to the s.1 principles and definitions of the Incapacity Act, it would be quite wrongful for anyone exercising functions under the Act to buy her a chair of the preferred model, but coloured red. She can competently choose her preferred colour of chair. She may have difficulty in communicating her choice, but must be assisted to do so, both in the context of the definition of capacity and in the context of the third general principle. To impose someone else's choice of colour, whether unthinkingly or arrogantly, would contravene the first principle: it would not benefit the adult. In terms of the second principle, the intervention of choosing a chair for the adult will not be the least restrictive intervention if it extends to an aspect of the decision which the adult can decide for herself. However, the position under this first example is different if (for example) the second best choice of chair, on all other grounds, is available in green but the best is not, or if a green chair of the preferred design will not be available for some time and either the adult's condition is deteriorating or her expected lifespan is limited. Those scenarios would be complicated further if the adult strongly preferred green, but was less averse to blue than to any other colour, and the preferred choice of chair (on all other grounds) was readily available in blue. As soon as we move into those areas, we have a situation of persuasive choice rather than decisive choice, or of strongly held wishes and feelings which must be taken into account but may not be decisive. The second and third examples take elements which one would normally regard as more fundamentally important than the choice of colour in the first example. The second would be a very strongly held desire by the adult to return to her own home, which was a dominant factor in the case described in para.5–2 above.[4] The third would be exemplified by the finding in one of the cases described in para.10–19 above[5] that there was between a young adult and one of the competing candidates to be her tutor (her mother) a "level of intimate communication which is unique to them". In both cases the capacity of each adult was without doubt in general terms very substantially impaired. However, setting those cases themselves to one side and considering simply the factors of an adult's overwhelming desire to return to her own home or strong attachment to one person above all others to a degree of unique intimacy, then there will be cases where either factor will be found to be a decisive choice, provided that its fulfilment is possible of achievement, so that the decisive choice becomes a "given" and a range of other decisions, largely made by others, will require to be constructed around it. Alternatively, depending upon the facts and circumstances of each case, that choice—like the simplistic choice of green for the chair—may move down the continuum from decisive choice to persuasive choice, or to wishes and feelings which must be ascertained and taken into account, but which may not necessarily decide the matter.

As one moves further along that continuum, the general principles **15–20** of the Incapacity Act apply fully in relation to all decisions or elements of decisions not settled at levels (1), (2) or (3). The principles apply

---

[4] *Millborrow, Applicant(for appointment of guardian to D)*, unreported, 2000.
[5] *Mrs X petitioner, Mr and Mrs Y petitioners*, unreported, 2001.

mandatorily to matters and procedures within the scope of the Incapacity Act's provisions, and—outwith that scope—as good practice, with the potential sanction of invocation of the Act's provisions if failure to follow good practice disadvantages the adult. Accordingly, as soon as a proposed choice or decision is not entirely or principally that of the adult, that proposed intervention—and each option under consideration, where there are several—must be something which will benefit the adult, and without which that benefit cannot reasonably be achieved, in accordance with the first principle.[6] The selected option must be the choice, among those which are consistent with the purpose of the intervention, which in accordance with the second principle is least restrictive of the adult's freedom. It is suggested that the methodology proposed in this chapter will contribute towards meeting that requirement, by ensuring that as far as possible the suggested choice accords with the adult's wishes and all that is known and can be ascertained about the adult: though the second principle of course goes beyond that aspect and must be fully and demonstrably complied with in its own terms.[7] The process of selecting from the options and constructing a decision must also comply with the third and fourth principles,[8] and where applicable the fifth principle[9]: it is suggested that compliance with these necessitates an approach such as the methodology proposed here.

15–21 When decisions and choices are not settled at levels (1), (2) or (3), the full range of elements (4)–(12) comes into play. If all identifiable elements should point in the same general direction, it should be possible to construct a decision accordingly with confidence that it is appropriate. One will probably be able to do likewise if the preponderance of elements, particularly those higher in the list, all point in the same direction. It would be absurd to attempt to create a mathematical model based upon the list. It may nevertheless be helpful in general terms to run through the list, locate the level of any discordant elements, and in general terms give them weight according to their level in the hierarchy. One seeks to ascertain a general direction, if not a precise answer, by assessing relevant elements at each level, giving progressively less weight to those lower down.

15–22 At levels (7) and (8), and sometimes at (9) and (10), it is helpful to recognise the different types of contribution, each valid, which the same person might be able to make. People in these categories may be able to help ascertain and understand the adult's present choices, wishes and feelings; to contribute information about the adult's past wishes and feelings; to express opinions of their own which may contribute; and to explain the potential impact of different choices on themselves and on their own relationship with the adult (and thus upon the family and social support systems which are usually so important to vulnerable and disabled people). These can all be matters which should reasonably be taken into account in constructing a decision. It can be helpful to reassure people that each of these categories of contribution can be relevant and valuable, but to ask

---

[6] See paras 4–6 to 4–11 *supra*.
[7] As to which see paras 4–12 to 4–15 *supra*.
[8] See paras 4–16 to 4–21 *supra*.
[9] See para.4–22 *supra*.

them to make clear the distinctions, so that (for example) they do not blur the difference between identifying the adult's views and expressing their own.

15–23 In contemplating situations where decisions require largely or wholly to be constructed for the adult, it is often helpful to make the distinction between identifying and evaluating options, on the one hand, and making a choice from those options, on the other. In the first task, the role of those with professional and specialist expertise will often be important. Doctors may identify medical options and provide an evaluation of them. Social workers and housing professionals may identify available options for housing and care, and provide an evaluation of them. The process of constructing a decision for the adult commences when the options have been identified and an evaluation of them has been provided. In this author's experience, the process of constructing a decision for an adult with impaired capacity can often be made easier and more effective by asking simple questions. What, realistically, are the options? What are the main characteristics, advantages and disadvantages of each? What, in the particular circumstances of the adult, is the best way of going about making a choice from the options and constructing a decision for the adult on the basis of that information?

15–24 It is rarely appropriate to adopt an unnecessarily adversarial approach to constructing decisions for an adult with impaired capacity. Experience shows that such an approach is likely to be inefficient and ineffective: it may cause participants to adopt and defend entrenched positions rather than proceeding with the open-mindedness and receptiveness which are generally essential, and it may damage relationships which are important to the adult. It can be particularly inappropriate for anyone in a role such as that of safeguarder or perhaps (if for some reason one is appointed) curator ad litem, to adopt a stance which no-one who knows the adult can recognise as representing the real person whom the adult is, playing the role of contradictor for the sake of doing so, and abdicating from the much more relevant and meaningful (though often difficult) task of drawing together the many threads which may lead through to an appropriate constructed decision for the particular person for whom that decision requires to be constructed. Where a decision is being constructed in a court setting, doing justice to the adult is likely to require a proactive and well-informed judicial role: hence, in part, the favoured option of "designated sheriffs" described in para.5–21 above.

15–25 The principle of the preceding paragraph also applies as one moves down the list in para.15–9. Some aspects of element (8) are in this respect "external": for example, professional input may contribute objective assessment rather than contributing towards the picture of the real person whom the adult is. However, a stance which is unrecognisable to people who know the adult as representing the real person whom the adult is, becomes even more inappropriate if it also conflicts with elements (7) and (9), and—albeit with gradually reducing force—as one moves down to elements (10) and then (11). Elements (7) and (9), then (10), then (11), become more important where the adult's disabilities are significant and long-term, weakening the extent to which a picture of the "real person" can be gained directly from the adult, in the context of issues and decisions beyond the adult's ability to understand or decide. Provided that there is nothing conflicting with what can nevertheless be gained directly from the adult, it will generally be appropriate to rely heavily on levels (7) and (9), and upon (8) so far as contributing close personal knowledge, in forming a picture of the ethos and standards against which decisions should be made; and quite inappropriate to allow the intrusion of an ethos, standards and viewpoints which are discordant with the background and way of life of the adult and those close to the adult. Similar considerations apply, provided in each case that there is no significant conflict at higher levels, as one moves down to levels (10), (11) and even (12). It is necessary also to have regard to the potential consequences, where there is choice, of selecting an option discordant with the shared views and ethos of family and others at levels (9), (10) and (11). Where family and other groups are close to and supportive of the adult, the adult's life and wellbeing are likely to be closely intertwined with them, and the family and social support systems which they provide to the adult are likely to be important to the adult. As mentioned above, such systems are usually particularly important to vulnerable and disabled people. Where the adult, if capable, would be unlikely to risk unnecessarily causing upset or conflict within those support systems, it will generally be quite inappropriate—and contrary to the first and second general principles of the Incapacity Act—for anyone playing any particular role in a decision-making process to risk causing disruption in such ways. Only in exceptional circumstances, and for very good reason, would it ever be appropriate to risk any ongoing damage to long-term family and social support systems, particularly if that is likely to be caused by someone playing a particular role for a limited duration, leaving others to suffer and cope with the longer-term consequences. Where level (8) pulls in a different direction from a consensus at levels (7) and (9) which is not discordant with the adult's own input, that consensus view should generally be favoured, provided that it is feasible when viewed with reasonable objectivity, and is consistent with the Act's general principles. The most difficult cases generally arise where there is conflict at levels (7), (8) and (9), and in particular where at levels (7) and (9) there are two camps pulling in opposite directions, each with a reasonably justifiable viewpoint. The judge or other arbiter must in such situations still focus upon the individual whom the adult is and proceed carefully by way of the general principles, in which task use of the whole of the construct based on the hierarchy in para.15–9 above, and described in this chapter as a whole, may still assist.

15–26 In a court setting, as in any other, the Act's general principles are mandatory in proceedings under the Act, and represent good practice in any other proceedings concerning an adult with impairment of capacity. The general principles must be complied with by the sheriff. They must be complied with in selecting a person to play, in the task of constructing decisions for the adult, particular roles such as those of safeguarder and person to convey the adult's views, and they must be complied with by any such appointees. If, despite the availability of a safeguarder, appointment of a curator ad litem is in contemplation, the decision—and any appointment—must comply with the general principles, and be demonstrably conducive to assisting the court in complying with them. The choice of persons appointed to any such roles should have regard to their ability to ensure compliance with the general principles, and to participate—proactively and rigorously, but without causing inappropriate or harmful disruption—in the process of constructing decisions for the adult by methods such as that proposed in this chapter.

So far, this discussion has not employed the term "best interests". As was pointed out in Chapter 4, that term does not appear in the Incapacity Act. In the past, those who enjoy adversarial debate have joined the camps advocating "best interests" or "substituted judgement" approaches to making decisions for people with impaired capacity. "Substituted judgement", in this context, means ascertaining and applying the choice or decision which, it is believed, the adult would have arrived at if able to make and communicate a choice or decision in the matter in question.[10] The English Law Commission set out the alternatives of best interests and substituted judgement in its preliminary consultation paper *Mentally Incapacitated Adults and Decision-making: An Overview*[11] and returned to the topic in its subsequent consultation paper *Mentally Incapacitated Adults and Decision-making: A New Jurisdiction*,[12] in which the English Commission wrote (para.2.14): " . . . the best interests test is often presented in opposition to the substituted judgement test. The latter was preferred by many of our respondents, though it was conceded that it was hard to apply to persons who had never been able to form judgements of their own. We doubt that the two tests need be mutually exclusive, and favour a compromise whereby a best interests test is modified by a requirement that the substitute decision-maker first goes through an exercise in substituted judgement". The Scottish Law Commission favoured an approach based upon the principles now embodied in the Incapacity Act, rather than upon a concept of best interests. They wrote[13]: "Our general principles do not rely on the concept of best interests of the incapable adult . . . We consider that 'best interests' by itself is too vague and would require to be supplemented by further factors which have to be taken into account. We also consider that 'best interests' does not give due weight to the views of the adult, particularly to wishes and feelings which he or she had expressed while capable of doing so. The concept of best interests was developed in the context of child law where a child's level of understanding may not be high and will usually have been lower in the past. Incapable adults such as those who are mentally ill, head-injured, or suffering from dementia at the time when a decision has to be made in connection with them, will have possessed full mental powers before their present incapacity. We think it is wrong to equate such adults with children, and for that reason would avoid extending child law concepts to them. Accordingly, the general principles we set out below are framed without

15–27

---

[10] This was the test adopted by Lord Nimmo Smith in the passage quoted in para.6–31 *supra* from his judgement in *D's Curator Bonis*, Noter, 1997 G.W.D. 13–538 and 1998 S.L.T. 2; though he also extended this to consideration in addition of what a reasonable and prudent person, aware of the circumstances and professionally advised, might decide. For an example of application of a "best interests" test, see the decision of Lord Phillip in *Mrs X petitioner, Mr and Mrs Y petitioners*, unreported, 2001 described in para.10–19 *supra*. Both cases predated implementation of relevant provisions of the Incapacity Act.

[11] (1991) Consultation Paper No.119.

[12] (1993) Consultation Paper No.128. See also the discussion of these alternatives in para.10–9 *supra*.

[13] SLC Report, para.2.50.

express reference to best interests." The general principles referred to are those now set forth in the Incapacity Act. The approach of the Scottish Law Commission is to be preferred both on its merits and because Scots law in this regard now implements the Commission's recommendations. The approach favoured by the English Commission is nevertheless helpful to the extent of identifying a "best interests" approach as a last resort. Even at that level, however, it is necessary to look more closely at what is meant by a "best interests" approach. It is an inherently subjective and paternalistic approach. Except where the choice of decision is beyond doubt, it entails a choice by someone other than the adult. If that choice is in any way reflective of the personal views and background of whoever makes it, it is to that extent flawed; but even if the person making the choice is rigorously objective, that choice will inevitably be a reflection of level (12) of the list in para.15–9. In other words, it will be a contribution from the lowest level of the list, and should be accorded no higher status than that. If inconsistent even with level (11), or with the preponderant view to be derived from higher levels, then usually it should not prevail. It is worthy of repetition that the requirement of modern Scots law is that any judge, safeguarder, curator ad litem (if for some clear, good and justified reason one should ever be appointed), or appointee, or any other authority or person exercising functions under the Incapacity Act, should proceed in all respects in accordance with the general principles of the Incapacity Act, and not by simply interjecting their personal views as to the adult's "best interests".

15–28 In the discussion in para.10–9 above of approaches to former curatory practice, "best interests" was contrasted with "preservation". Apart from that curious relic from times and perceptions long past, within recent decades the focus was on the alternatives of "best interest" and "substitute judgement", generally resolved by the early 1990's in formulations such as that quoted in para.10–9, or—more authoritatively—that of the English Law Commission quoted above. On occasions, Scottish courts nevertheless continued to apply, in adult incapacity cases, a best interests test. They appear to have done so without consideration or debate as to whether it was the appropriate test, what it meant, or by what methodology "best interests" should be determined. It is doubtful whether any cases which in fact applied a "best interests" test in such an uncritical way could be regarded as precedents that it was ever the proper approach, rather than as evidence only that it was the approach in fact adopted. Beyond doubt, in this century—with the Incapacity Act in force—a simplistic "best interests" formulation is not the appropriate approach in the law of Scotland to making choices or decisions for adults whose impairments of capacity disable them from doing so for themselves. The standing of "best interests" is that accorded by the Scottish Law Commission in the passage quoted above, and the correct approach in Scots law is that proposed by the Commission and adopted in the Incapacity Act, namely an approach which requires the application of the general principles set out in s.1 of the Incapacity Act. It is also necessary to comply with other relevant principles of law such as respect for the adult's human rights, and avoidance of discrimination. This chapter has sought to suggest a methodology for constructing decisions which accords with those requirements. Reference to the Act's general principles, and to the principles of respect for human rights and non-discrimination, should be the constant theme, as well as forming an appropriate conclusion, in an account of the modern Scots law of adult incapacity.

APPENDIX 1

ADULTS WITH INCAPACITY (SCOTLAND) ACT 2000

(2000 asp 4)

ARRANGEMENT OF SECTIONS

PART 1

GENERAL

General

Section
1. General principles and fundamental definitions

Judicial proceedings

2. Applications and other proceedings and appeals
3. Powers of sheriff
4. Power of Court of Session or sheriff with regard to nearest relative
5. Safeguarding of interests in Court of Session appeals or proceedings

The Public Guardian

6. The Public Guardian and his functions
7. The Public Guardian: further provision

Expenses in court proceedings

8. Expenses in court proceedings

The Mental Welfare Commission

9. Functions of the Mental Welfare Commission

Local authorities

10. Functions of local authorities

Intimation

11. Intimation not required in certain circumstances

Investigations

12. Investigations

Codes of practice

13. Codes of practice

Appeal against decision as to incapacity

14. Appeal against decision as to incapacity

PART 2

CONTINUING POWERS OF ATTORNEY AND WELFARE POWERS OF ATTORNEY

15. Creation of continuing power of attorney
16. Creation and exercise of welfare power of attorney
17. Attorney not obliged to act in certain circumstances
18. Power of attorney not granted in accordance with this Act
19. Registration of continuing or welfare power of attorney
20. Powers of sheriff
21. Records: attorneys
22. Notification to Public Guardian
23. Resignation of continuing or welfare attorney
24. Termination of continuing or welfare power of attorney

PART 3

ACCOUNTS AND FUNDS

25. Authority to intromit with funds
26. Application for authority to intromit
27. Notification of change of address
28. Purposes of intromissions with funds
29. Withdrawal and use of funds
30. Records and inquiries
31. Duration and termination of registration
32. Joint accounts
33. Transfer of funds
34. Disapplication of Part 3

PART 4

MANAGEMENT OF RESIDENTS' FINANCES

35. Application of Part 4
36. Registration for purposes of managing residents' finances
37. Residents whose affairs may be managed
38. Financial procedures and controls in registered establishments
39. Matters which may be managed
40. Supervisory bodies
41. Duties and functions of managers of authorised establishment
42. Authorisation of named manager to withdraw from resident's account
43. Statement of resident's affairs
44. Resident ceasing to be resident of authorised establishment
45. Appeal, revocation etc.
46. Disapplication of Part 4

PART 5

MEDICAL TREATMENT AND RESEARCH

47. Authority of persons responsible for medical treatment
48. Exceptions to authority to treat
49. Medical treatment where there is an application for intervention or guardianship order
50. Medical treatment where guardian etc. has been appointed
51. Authority for research
52. Appeal against decision as to medical treatment

Part 6

Intervention Orders and Guardianship Orders

Intervention orders

53. Intervention orders
54. Records: intervention orders
55. Notification of change of address
56. Registration of intervention order relating to heritable property

Guardianship orders

57. Application for guardianship order
58. Disposal of application
59. Who may be appointed as guardian
60. Renewal of guardianship order by sheriff
61. Registration of guardianship order relating to heritable property

Joint and substitute guardians

62. Joint guardians
63. Substitute guardian

Functions etc. of guardian

64. Functions and duties of guardian
65. Records: guardians
66. Gifts
67. Effect of appointment and transactions of guardian
68. Reimbursement and remuneration of guardian
69. Forfeiture of guardian's remuneration
70. Non-compliance with decisions of guardian with welfare powers

Termination and variation of guardianship and replacement, removal or resignation of guardian

71. Replacement or removal of guardian or recall of guardianship by sheriff
72. Discharge of guardian with financial powers
73. Recall of powers of guardian
74. Variation of guardianship order
75. Resignation of guardian
76. Change of habitual residence

Termination of authority to intervene and guardianship on death of adult

77. Termination of authority to intervene and guardianship on death of adult
78. Amendment of registration under section 61 on events affecting guardianship or death of adult
79. Protection of third parties: guardianship

Part 7

Miscellaneous

80. Future appointment of curator bonis etc. incompetent
81. Repayment of funds
82. Limitation of liability
83. Offence of ill-treatment and wilful neglect
84. Application to guardians appointed under Criminal Procedure (Scotland) Act 1995
85. Jurisdiction and private international law
86. Regulations
87. Interpretation
88. Continuation of existing powers, minor and consequential amendments and repeals
89. Citation and commencement

Schedule 1 Managers of an establishment
Schedule 2 Management of estate of adult
Schedule 3 Jurisdiction and private international law
Schedule 4 Continuation of existing curators, tutors, guardians and attorneys under this Act
Schedule 5 Minor and consequential amendments
Schedule 6 Repeals

An Act of the Scottish Parliament to make provision as to the property, financial affairs and personal welfare of adults who are incapable by reason of mental disorder or inability to communicate; and for connected purposes.

PART 1

GENERAL

General

General principles and fundamental definitions

A1–01 1.—(1) The principles set out in subsections (2) to (4) shall be given effect to in relation to any intervention in the affairs of an adult under or in pursuance of this Act, including any order made in or for the purpose of any proceedings under this Act for or in connection with an adult.

(2) There shall be no intervention in the affairs of an adult unless the person responsible for authorising or effecting the intervention is satisfied that the intervention will benefit the adult and that such benefit cannot reasonably be achieved without the intervention.

(3) Where it is determined that an intervention as mentioned in subsection (1) is to be made, such intervention shall be the least restrictive option in relation to the freedom of the adult, consistent with the purpose of the intervention.

(4) In determining if an intervention is to be made and, if so, what intervention is to be made, account shall be taken of—
  (a) the present and past wishes and feelings of the adult so far as they can be ascertained by any means of communication, whether human or by mechanical aid (whether of an interpretative nature or otherwise) appropriate to the adult;
  (b) the views of the nearest relative and the primary carer of the adult, in so far as it is reasonable and practicable to do so;
  (c) the views of—
    (i) any guardian, continuing attorney or welfare attorney of the adult who has powers relating to the proposed intervention; and
    (ii) any person whom the sheriff has directed to be consulted,
  in so far as it is reasonable and practicable to do so; and
  (d) the views of any other person appearing to the person responsible for authorising or effecting the intervention to have an interest in the welfare of the adult or in the proposed intervention, where these views have been made known to the person responsible, in so far as it is reasonable and practicable to do so.

(5) Any guardian, continuing attorney, welfare attorney or manager of an establishment exercising functions under this Act or under any order of the sheriff in relation to an adult shall, in so far as it is reasonable and practicable to do so, encourage the adult to exercise whatever skills he has concerning his property, financial affairs or personal welfare, as the case may be, and to develop new such skills.

(6) For the purposes of this Act, and unless the context otherwise requires—
"adult" means a person who has attained the age of 16 years;

"incapable" means incapable of—
 (a) acting; or
 (b) making decisions; or
 (c) communicating decisions; or
 (d) understanding decisions; or
 (e) retaining the memory of decisions,
as mentioned in any provision of this Act, by reason of mental disorder or of inability to communicate because of physical disability; but a person shall not fall within this definition by reason only of a lack or deficiency in a faculty of communication if that lack or deficiency can be made good by human or mechanical aid (whether of an interpretative nature or otherwise); and
"incapacity" shall be construed accordingly.
 (7) In subsection (4)(c)(i) any reference to—
 (a) a guardian shall include a reference to a guardian (however called) appointed under the law of any country to, or entitled under the law of any country to act for, an adult during his incapacity, if the guardianship is recognised by the law of Scotland;
 (b) a continuing attorney shall include a reference to a person granted, under a contract, grant or appointment governed by the law of any country, powers (however expressed), relating to the granter's property or financial affairs and having continuing effect notwithstanding the granter's incapacity;
 (c) a welfare attorney shall include a reference to a person granted, under a contract, grant or appointment governed by the law of any country, powers (however expressed) relating to the granter's personal welfare and having effect during the granter's incapacity.

Judicial proceedings

Applications and other proceedings and appeals

2.—(1) This section shall apply for the purposes of any application which may be made to and any other proceedings before the sheriff under this Act.

(2) An application to the sheriff under this Act shall be made by summary application.

(3) Unless otherwise expressly provided for, any decision of the sheriff at first instance in any application to, or in any other proceedings before, him under this Act may be appealed to the sheriff principal, and the decision upon such appeal of the sheriff principal may be appealed, with the leave of the sheriff principal, to the Court of Session.

(4) Rules made under section 32 of the Sheriff Courts (Scotland) Act 1971 (c.58) may make provision as to the evidence which the sheriff shall take into account when deciding whether to give a direction under section 11(1).

Powers of sheriff

3.—(1) In an application or any other proceedings under this Act, the sheriff may make such consequential or ancillary order, provision or direction as he considers appropriate.

(2) Without prejudice to the generality of subsection (1) or to any other powers conferred by this Act, the sheriff may—
 (a) make any order granted by him subject to such conditions and restrictions as appear to him to be appropriate;
 (b) order that any reports relating to the person who is the subject of the application or proceedings be lodged with the court or that the person be assessed or interviewed and that a report of such assessment or interview be lodged;
 (c) make such further inquiry or call for such further information as appears to him to be appropriate;

A1–02

A1–03

(d) make such interim order as appears to him to be appropriate pending the disposal of the application or proceedings.

(3) On an application by any person (including the adult himself) claiming an interest in the property, financial affairs or personal welfare of an adult, the sheriff may give such directions to any person exercising—
   (a) functions conferred by this Act; or
   (b) functions of a like nature conferred by the law of any country,
as to the exercise of those functions and the taking of decisions or action in relation to the adult as appear to him to be appropriate.

(4) In an application or any other proceedings under this Act, the sheriff—
   (a) shall consider whether it is necessary to appoint a person for the purpose of safeguarding the interests of the person who is the subject of the application or proceedings; and
   (b) without prejudice to any existing power to appoint a person to represent the interests of the person who is the subject of the application or proceedings may, if he thinks fit, appoint a person to act for the purpose specified in paragraph (a).

(5) Safeguarding the interests of a person shall, for the purposes of subsection (4), include conveying his views so far as they are ascertainable to the sheriff; but if the sheriff considers that it is inappropriate that a person appointed to safeguard the interests of another under this section should also convey that other's views to the sheriff, the sheriff may appoint another person for that latter purpose only.

(6) The sheriff may, on an application by—
   (a) the person authorised under the order;
   (b) the adult; or
   (c) any person entitled to apply for the order,
make an order varying the terms of an order granted under subsection (2)(a).

Power of Court of Session or sheriff with regard to nearest relative

4.—(1) On an application by an adult, the court may, having regard to section 1 and being satisfied that to do so will benefit the adult, make an order that—
   (a) certain information shall not be disclosed, or intimation of certain applications shall not be given, to the nearest relative of the adult;
   (b) the functions of the nearest relative of the adult shall, during the continuance in force of the order, be exercised by a person, specified in the application, who is not the nearest relative of the adult but who—
      (i) is a person who would otherwise be entitled to be the nearest relative in terms of this Act;
      (ii) in the opinion of the court is a proper person to act as the nearest relative; and
      (iii) is willing to so act; or
   (c) no person shall, during the continuance in force of the order, exercise the functions of the nearest relative.

(2) An order made under subsection (1) shall apply only to the exercise of the functions under this Act of the nearest relative.

(3) The court may, on an application by an adult, make an order varying the terms of an order granted under subsection (1).

(4) No application shall be made under this section by an adult who is not incapable within the meaning of this Act at the time of making the application.

Safeguarding of interests in Court of Session appeals or proceedings

5.—(1) In determining any appeal or in any other proceedings under this Act the Court of Session—
   (a) shall consider whether it is necessary to appoint a person for the purpose of safeguarding the interests of the person who is the subject of the appeal or other proceedings; and

(b) without prejudice to any existing power to appoint a person to represent the interests of the second mentioned person, may if it thinks fit appoint a person to act for the purpose specified in paragraph (a).

(2) Safeguarding the interests of a person shall, for the purposes of subsection (1), include conveying his views so far as they are ascertainable to the court; but if the court considers that it is inappropriate that a person appointed to safeguard the interests of another under this section should also convey that other's views to the court, the court may appoint another person for that latter purpose only.

The Public Guardian

The Public Guardian and his functions

6.—(1) The Accountant of Court shall be the Public Guardian.

(2) The Public Guardian shall have the following general functions under this Act—
  (a) to supervise any guardian or any person who is authorised under an intervention order in the exercise of his functions relating to the property or financial affairs of the adult;
  (b) to establish, maintain and make available during normal office hours for inspection by members of the public on payment of the prescribed fee, separate registers of—
    (i) all documents relating to continuing powers of attorney governed by the law of Scotland;
    (ii) all documents relating to welfare powers of attorney governed by the law of Scotland;
    (iii) all authorisations to intromit with funds under Part 3;
    (iv) all documents relating to guardianship orders under Part 6;
    (v) all documents relating to intervention orders under Part 6,
    in which he shall enter any matter which he is required to enter under this Act and any other matter of which he becomes aware relating to the existence or scope of the power, authorisation or order as the case may be;
  (c) to receive and investigate any complaints regarding the exercise of functions relating to the property or financial affairs of an adult made—
    (i) in relation to continuing attorneys;
    (ii) concerning intromissions with funds under Part 3;
    (iii) in relation to guardians or persons authorised under intervention orders;
  (d) to investigate any circumstances made known to him in which the property or financial affairs of an adult seem to him to be at risk;
  (e) to provide, when requested to do so, a guardian, a continuing attorney, a withdrawer or a person authorised under an intervention order with information and advice about the performance of functions relating to property or financial affairs under this Act;
  (f) to consult the Mental Welfare Commission and any local authority on cases or matters relating to the exercise of functions under this Act in which there is, or appears to be, a common interest.

(3) In subsection (2)(c) any reference to—
(a) a guardian shall include a reference to a guardian (however called) appointed under the law of any country to, or entitled under the law of any country to act for, an adult during his incapacity, if the guardianship is recognised by the law of Scotland;
(b) a continuing attorney shall include a reference to a person granted, under a contract, grant or appointment governed by the law of any country, powers (however expressed), relating to the granter's property or financial affairs and having continuing effect notwithstanding the granter's incapacity.

The Public Guardian: further provision

A1-07 7.—(1) The Scottish Ministers may prescribe—
(a) the form and content of the registers to be established and maintained under section 6(2)(b) and the manner and medium in which they are to be established and maintained;
(b) the form and content of any certificate which the Public Guardian is empowered to issue under this Act;
(c) the forms and procedure for the purposes of any application required or permitted to be made under this Act to the Public Guardian in relation to any matter;
(d) the evidence which the Public Guardian shall take into account when deciding under section 11(2) whether to dispense with intimation or notification to the adult.

(2) The Public Guardian may charge the prescribed fee for anything done by him in connection with any of his functions under this Act and he shall not be obliged to act until such fee is paid.

(3) Any certificate which the Public Guardian issues under this Act shall, for the purposes of any proceedings, be conclusive evidence of the matters contained in it.

Expenses in court proceedings

Expenses in court proceedings

A1-08 8.—(1) Where in any court proceedings (other than, in the case of a local authority, an application under section 68(3)) the Public Guardian, Mental Welfare Commission or local authority is a party for the purpose of protecting the interests of an adult, the court may make an award of expenses against the adult or against any person whose actings have resulted in the proceedings.

(2) Where in any court proceedings (other than, in the case of a local authority, an application under section 68(3)) the Public Guardian, Mental Welfare Commission or local authority is a party for the purpose of representing the public interest, the court may make an award of expenses against any person whose actings have resulted in the proceedings or on whose part there has been unreasonable conduct in relation to the proceedings.

The Mental Welfare Commission

Functions of the Mental Welfare Commission

A1-09 9.—(1) Without prejudice to their functions under the 1984 Act, the Mental Welfare Commission shall have the following general functions under this Act in relation to any adult to whom this Act applies by reason of, or by reasons which include, mental disorder—
(a) to exercise protective functions in respect of the adult if the adult is the subject of an intervention or guardianship order, in so far as the order relates to the personal welfare of the adult;
(b) to visit the adult as often as they think appropriate and bring to the attention of the Health Board for the area in which the adult resides, or the local authority, or any other body any matter relating to the personal welfare of the adult which they consider ought to be brought to their attention;
(c) to consult the Public Guardian and any local authority on cases or matters relating to the exercise of functions under this Act in which there is, or appears to be, a common interest;
(d) where they are not satisfied with any investigation made by a local authority into a complaint made under section 10(1)(c), or where the local authority have failed to investigate the complaint, to receive and

investigate any complaints relating to the exercise of functions relating to the personal welfare of the adult made—
  (i) in relation to welfare attorneys;
  (ii) in relation to guardians or persons authorised under intervention orders;
(e) to investigate any circumstances made known to them in which the personal welfare of the adult seems to them to be at risk;
(f) to investigate any circumstances made known to them in which the property of the adult may, by reason of the mental disorder of the adult, be exposed to a risk of loss or damage;
(g) to provide a guardian, welfare attorney or person authorised under an intervention order, when requested to do so, with information and advice in connection with the performance of his functions in relation to personal welfare under this Act.
(2) A guardian or welfare attorney of such an adult or a person authorised under an intervention order in relation to such an adult or the local authority shall afford the Mental Welfare Commission all facilities necessary to enable them to carry out their functions in respect of the adult.
(3) In subsection (1)(d) any reference to—
(a) a guardian shall include a reference to a guardian (however called) appointed under the law of any country to, or entitled under the law of any country to act for, an adult during his incapacity, if the guardianship is recognised by the law of Scotland;
(b) a welfare attorney shall include a reference to a person granted, under a contract, grant or appointment governed by the law of any country, powers (however expressed) relating to the granter's personal welfare and having effect during the granter's incapacity.

Local authorities

Functions of local authorities

10.—(1) A local authority shall have the following general functions under this Act—
  (a) to supervise a guardian appointed with functions relating to the personal welfare of an adult in the exercise of those functions;
  (b) to consult the Public Guardian and the Mental Welfare Commission on cases or matters relating to the exercise of functions under this Act in which there is, or appears to be, a common interest;
  (c) to receive and investigate any complaints relating to the exercise of functions relating to the personal welfare of an adult made—
    (i) in relation to welfare attorneys;
    (ii) in relation to guardians or persons authorised under intervention orders;
  (d) to investigate any circumstances made known to them in which the personal welfare of an adult seems to them to be at risk;
  (e) to provide a guardian, welfare attorney or person authorised under an intervention order, when requested to do so, with information and advice in connection with the performance of his functions in relation to personal welfare under this Act.
(2) For the purposes of subsection (1)(d),"local authority" includes a local authority for an area in which the adult is present.
(3) The Scottish Ministers may make provision by regulations as regards the supervision by local authorities of the performance of their functions—
  (a) by guardians, in relation to the personal welfare of adults under this Act;
  (b) where the supervision has been ordered by the sheriff—
    (i) by persons authorised under intervention orders;
    (ii) by welfare attorneys.

(4) In subsection (1)(c) any reference to—
(a) a guardian shall include a reference to a guardian (however called) appointed under the law of any country to, or entitled under the law of any country to act for, an adult during his incapacity, if the guardianship is recognised by the law of Scotland;
(b) a welfare attorney shall include a reference to a person granted, under a contract, grant or appointment governed by the law of any country, powers (however expressed) relating to the granter's personal welfare and having effect during the granter's incapacity.

Intimation

Intimation not required in certain circumstances

A1–11 11.—(1) Where, apart from this subsection, intimation of any application or other proceedings under this Act, or notification of any interlocutor relating to such application or other proceedings, would be given to an adult and the court considers that the intimation or notification would be likely to pose a serious risk to the health of the adult the court may direct that such intimation or notification shall not be given.

(2) Where, apart from this subsection and subsection (1), any intimation or notification to him under this Act would be given by the Public Guardian to an adult and the Public Guardian considers that the intimation or notification would be likely to pose a serious risk to the health of the adult the Public Guardian shall not give the intimation or notification.

Investigations

Investigations

A1–12 12.—(1) In consequence of any investigation carried out under—
(a) section 6(2)(c) or (d) by the Public Guardian;
(b) section 9(1)(d) or (e) by the Mental Welfare Commission; or
(c) section 10(1)(c) or (d) by a local authority,
the Public Guardian, Mental Welfare Commission or local authority, as the case may be, may take such steps, including the making of an application to the sheriff, as seem to him or them to be necessary to safeguard the property, financial affairs or personal welfare, as the case may be, of the adult.

(2) For the purposes of any investigation mentioned in subsection (1), the Public Guardian, Mental Welfare Commission and local authority shall provide each other with such information and assistance as may be necessary to facilitate the investigation.

Codes of practice

Codes of practice

A1–13 13.—(1) The Scottish Ministers shall prepare, or cause to be prepared for their approval, and from time to time revise, or cause to be revised for their approval, codes of practice containing guidance as to the exercise by—
(a) local authorities and their chief social work officers and mental health officers;
(b) continuing and welfare attorneys;
(c) persons authorised under intervention orders;
(d) guardians;
(e) withdrawers;
(f) managers of authorised establishments;
(g) supervisory bodies;
(h) persons authorised to carry out medical treatment or research under Part 5,

of their functions under this Act and as to such other matters arising out of or connected with this Act as the Scottish Ministers consider appropriate.

(2) Before preparing or approving any code of practice under this Act or making or approving any alteration in it the Scottish Ministers shall consult such bodies as appear to them to be concerned.

(3) The Scottish Ministers shall lay copies of any such code and of any alteration in it before the Parliament.

(4) The Scottish Ministers shall publish every code of practice made under this Act as for the time being in force.

Appeal against decision as to incapacity

Appeal against decision as to incapacity

14. A decision taken for the purposes of this Act, other than by the sheriff, as to the incapacity of an adult may be appealed by— **A1–14**
 (a) the adult; or
 (b) any person claiming an interest in the adult's property, financial affairs or personal welfare relating to the purpose for which the decision was taken,
to the sheriff or, where the decision was taken by the sheriff, to the sheriff principal and thence, with the leave of the sheriff principal, to the Court of Session.

PART 2

CONTINUING POWERS OF ATTORNEY AND WELFARE POWERS OF ATTORNEY

Creation of continuing power of attorney

15.—(1) Where an individual grants a power of attorney relating to his property or financial affairs in accordance with the following provisions of this section that power of attorney shall, notwithstanding any rule of law, continue to have effect in the event of the granter's becoming incapable in relation to decisions about the matter to which the power of attorney relates. **A1–15**

(2) In this Act a power of attorney granted under subsection (1) is referred to as a "continuing power of attorney" and a person on whom such power is conferred is referred to as a "continuing attorney".

(3) A continuing power of attorney shall be valid only if it is expressed in a written document which—
 (a) is subscribed by the granter;
 (b) incorporates a statement which clearly expresses the granter's intention that the power be a continuing power;
 (c) incorporates a certificate in the prescribed form by a solicitor or by a member of another prescribed class that—
  (i) he has interviewed the granter immediately before the granter subscribed the document;
  (ii) he is satisfied, either because of his own knowledge of the granter or because he has consulted other persons (whom he names in the certificate) who have knowledge of the granter, that at the time the continuing power of attorney is granted the granter understands its nature and extent;
  (iii) he has no reason to believe that the granter is acting under undue influence or that any other factor vitiates the granting of the power.

(4) A solicitor or member of another prescribed class may not grant a certificate under subsection (3)(c) if he is the person to whom the power of attorney has been granted.

Creation and exercise of welfare power of attorney

16.—(1) An individual may grant a power of attorney relating to his personal welfare in accordance with the following provisions of this section. **A1–16**

(2) In this Act a power of attorney granted under this section is referred to as a "welfare power of attorney" and an individual on whom such power is conferred is referred to as a "welfare attorney".

(3) A welfare power of attorney shall be valid only if it is expressed in a written document which—
  (a) is subscribed by the granter;
  (b) incorporates a statement which clearly expresses the granter's intention that the power be a welfare power to which this section applies;
  (c) incorporates a certificate in the prescribed form by a solicitor or by a member of another prescribed class that—
    (i) he has interviewed the granter immediately before the granter subscribed the document;
    (ii) he is satisfied, either because of his own knowledge of the granter or because he has consulted other persons (whom he names in the certificate) who have knowledge of the granter, that at the time the welfare power of attorney is granted the granter understands its nature and extent;
    (iii) he has no reason to believe that the granter is acting under undue influence or that any other factor vitiates the granting of the power.

(4) A solicitor or member of another prescribed class may not grant a certificate under subsection (3)(c) if he is the person to whom the power of attorney has been granted.

(5) A welfare power of attorney—
  (a) may be granted only to an individual (which does not include a person acting in his capacity as an officer of a local authority or other body established by or under an enactment); and
  (b) shall not be exercisable unless—
    (i) the granter is incapable in relation to decisions about the matter to which the welfare power of attorney relates; or
    (ii) the welfare attorney reasonably believes that sub-paragraph (i) applies.

(6) A welfare attorney may not—
  (a) place the granter in a hospital for the treatment of mental disorder against his will; or
  (b) consent on behalf of the granter to any form of treatment mentioned in section 48(1) or (2).

(7) A welfare power of attorney shall not come to an end in the event of the bankruptcy of the granter or the welfare attorney.

(8) Any reference to a welfare attorney—
  (a) in relation to subsection (5)(b) in a case where the granter is habitually resident in Scotland; and
  (b) in subsection (6),
shall include a reference to a person granted, under a contract, grant or appointment governed by the law of any country, powers (however expressed) relating to the granter's personal welfare and having effect during the granter's incapacity.

Attorney not obliged to act in certain circumstances

A1–17   17. A continuing or welfare attorney shall not be obliged to do anything which would otherwise be within the powers of the attorney if doing it would, in relation to its value or utility, be unduly burdensome or expensive.

Power of attorney not granted in accordance with this Act

A1–18   18. A power of attorney granted after the commencement of this Act which is not granted in accordance with section 15 or 16 shall have no effect during any period when the granter is incapable in relation to decisions about the matter to which the power of attorney relates.

Registration of continuing or welfare power of attorney

19.—(1) A continuing or welfare attorney shall have no authority to act until **A1–19** the document conferring the power of attorney has been registered under this section.

(2) For the purposes of registration, the document conferring the power of attorney shall be sent to the Public Guardian who, if he is satisfied that a person appointed to act is prepared to act, shall—
   (a) enter prescribed particulars of it in the register maintained by him under section 6(2)(b)(i) or (ii) as the case may be;
   (b) send a copy of it with a certificate of registration to the sender;
   (c) if it confers a welfare power of attorney, send a copy of it to the Mental Welfare Commission.

(3) The document conferring a continuing or welfare power of attorney may contain a condition that the Public Guardian shall not register it under this section until the occurrence of a specified event and in that case the Public Guardian shall not register it until he is satisfied that the specified event has occurred.

(4) A copy of a document conferring a continuing or welfare power of attorney authenticated by the Public Guardian shall be accepted for all purposes as sufficient evidence of the contents of the original and of any matter relating thereto appearing in the copy.

(5) The Public Guardian shall—
   (a) on the registration of a document conferring a continuing or welfare power of attorney, send a copy of it to the granter; and
   (b) where the document conferring the continuing or welfare power of attorney so requires, send a copy of it to not more than two specified individuals or holders of specified offices or positions.

(6) A decision of the Public Guardian under subsection (2) as to whether or not a person is prepared to act or under subsection (3) as to whether or not the specified event has occurred may be appealed to the sheriff, whose decision shall be final.

Powers of sheriff

20.—(1) An application for an order under subsection (2) may be made to the **A1–20** sheriff by any person claiming an interest in the property, financial affairs or personal welfare of the granter of a continuing or welfare power of attorney.

(2) Where, on an application being made under subsection (1), the sheriff is satisfied that the granter is incapable in relation to decisions about, or of acting to safeguard or promote his interests in, his property, financial affairs or personal welfare insofar as the power of attorney relates to them, and that it is necessary to safeguard or promote these interests, he may make an order—
   (a) ordaining that the continuing attorney shall be subject to the supervision of the Public Guardian to such extent as may be specified in the order;
   (b) ordaining the continuing attorney to submit accounts in respect of any period specified in the order for audit to the Public Guardian;
   (c) ordaining that the welfare attorney shall be subject to the supervision of the local authority to such extent as may be specified in the order;
   (d) ordaining the welfare attorney to give a report to him as to the manner in which the welfare attorney has exercised his powers during any period specified in the order;
   (e) revoking—
      (i) any of the powers granted by the continuing or welfare power of attorney; or
      (ii) the appointment of an attorney.

(3) Where the sheriff makes an order under this section the sheriff clerk shall send a copy of the interlocutor containing the order to the Public Guardian who shall—
   (a) enter prescribed particulars in the register maintained by him under section 6(2)(b)(i) or (ii) as the case may be;

(b) notify—
    (i) the granter;
    (ii) the continuing or welfare attorney;
    (iii) where it is the welfare attorney who is notified, the local authority and (in a case where the incapacity of the granter is by reason of, or reasons which include, mental disorder) the Mental Welfare Commission;
    (iv) where the sheriff makes an order under subsection (2)(c), the local authority.

(4) A decision of the sheriff under subsection (2)(a) to (d) shall be final.

(5) In this section any reference to—
(a) a continuing power of attorney shall include a reference to a power (however expressed) under a contract, grant or appointment governed by the law of any country, relating to the granter's property or financial affairs and having continuing effect notwithstanding the granter's incapacity;
(b) a welfare power of attorney shall include a reference to a power (however expressed) under a contract, grant or appointment governed by the law of any country, relating to the granter's personal welfare and having effect during the granter's incapacity,

and "continuing attorney" and "welfare attorney" shall be construed accordingly.

Records: attorneys

21. A continuing or welfare attorney shall keep records of the exercise of his powers.

Notification to Public Guardian

22.—(1) After a document conferring a continuing or welfare power of attorney has been registered under section 19, the attorney shall notify the Public Guardian—
(a) of any change in his address;
(b) of any change in the address of the granter of the power of attorney;
(c) of the death of the granter of the power of attorney; or
(d) of any other event which results in the termination of the power of attorney,

and the Public Guardian shall enter prescribed particulars in the register maintained by him under section 6(2)(b)(i) or (ii) as the case may be and shall notify the granter (in the case of an event mentioned in paragraph (a) or (d)) and, where the power of attorney relates to the personal welfare of the adult, both the local authority and (in a case where the incapacity of the granter is by reason of, or reasons which include, mental disorder) the Mental Welfare Commission.

(2) If, after a document conferring a continuing or welfare power of attorney has been registered under section 19, the attorney dies, his personal representatives shall, if aware of the existence of the power of attorney, notify the Public Guardian who shall enter prescribed particulars in the register maintained by him under section 6(2)(b)(i) or (ii) as the case may be, and shall notify the granter and, where the power of attorney relates to the personal welfare of the adult, both the local authority and (in a case where the incapacity of the granter is by reason of, or reasons which include, mental disorder) the Mental Welfare Commission.

Resignation of continuing or welfare attorney

23.—(1) A continuing or welfare attorney who wishes to resign after the document conferring the power of attorney has been registered under section 19 shall give notice in writing of his intention to do so to—

(a) the granter of the power of attorney;
(b) the Public Guardian;
(c) any guardian or, where there is no guardian, the granter's primary carer;
(d) the local authority, where they are supervising the welfare attorney.

(2) Subject to subsection (4), the resignation shall not have effect until the expiry of a period of 28 days commencing with the date of receipt by the Public Guardian of the notice given under subsection (1); and on its becoming effective the Public Guardian shall enter prescribed particulars in the register maintained by him under section 6(2)(b)(i) or (ii) as the case may be.

(3) Where the resignation is of a welfare attorney, the Public Guardian shall notify the local authority and (in a case where the incapacity of the adult is by reason of, or reasons which include, mental disorder) the Mental Welfare Commission.

(4) The resignation of a joint attorney, or an attorney in respect of whom the granter has appointed a substitute attorney, shall take effect on the receipt by the Public Guardian of notice under subsection (1)(b) if evidence that—
(a) the remaining joint attorney is willing to continue to act; or
(b) the substitute attorney is willing to act,
accompanies the notice.

Termination of continuing or welfare power of attorney

24.—(1) If the granter and the continuing or welfare attorney are married to each other the power of attorney shall, unless the document conferring it provides otherwise, come to an end upon the granting of—
(a) a decree of separation to either party;
(b) a decree of divorce to either party;
(c) declarator of nullity of the marriage.

(2) The authority of a continuing or welfare attorney in relation to any matter shall come to an end on the appointment of a guardian with powers relating to that matter.

(3) In subsection (2) any reference to—
(a) a continuing attorney shall include a reference to a person granted, under a contract, grant or appointment governed by the law of any country, powers (however expressed), relating to the granter's property or financial affairs and having continuing effect notwithstanding the granter's incapacity;
(b) a welfare attorney shall include a reference to a person granted, under a contract, grant or appointment governed by the law of any country, powers (however expressed) relating to the granter's personal welfare and having effect during the granter's incapacity.

(4) No liability shall be incurred by any person who acts in good faith in ignorance of—
(a) the coming to an end of a power of attorney under subsection (1); or
(b) the appointment of a guardian as mentioned in subsection (2),
nor shall any title to heritable property acquired by such a person be challengeable on those grounds alone.

PART 3

ACCOUNTS AND FUNDS

Authority to intromit with funds

25.—(1) Subject to section 34, an individual (which does not include a person acting in his capacity as an officer of a local authority or other body established by or under an enactment) may apply to the Public Guardian for authority under this Part to intromit with funds held by a person or organisation (the "fundholder") on behalf of an adult who is incapable in relation to decisions about the funds or of safeguarding his interests in the funds, and is the sole holder of an account in his name.

(2) An application for authority under this section shall be made in respect of a specified account with the fundholder and shall not be made if there is an existing authority to intromit under this Part.

Application for authority to intromit

26.—(1) An application form for authority to intromit with funds shall—
(a) state the purposes of the proposed intromission, setting out the specific sums relating to each purpose;
(b) be signed by the applicant;
(c) be countersigned by a member of such class of persons as is prescribed, who shall declare in the form that—
   (i) he knows the applicant and has known him for at least 2 years prior to the date of the application;
   (ii) he knows the adult;
   (iii) he is not—
      (A) a relative of or person residing with the applicant or the adult; or
      (B) a director or employee of the fundholder; or
      (C) a solicitor acting on behalf of the adult or any other person mentioned in this sub-paragraph in relation to any matter under this Act; or
      (D) the medical practitioner who has issued the certificate under sub-paragraph (f);
   (iv) he believes the information contained in the document to be true; and
   (v) he believes the applicant to be a fit and proper person to intromit with the funds;
(d) contain the names and addresses of the nearest relative and primary carer of the adult, if known;
(e) identify the account with the fundholder in relation to which the authority is sought;
(f) be accompanied by a certificate in prescribed form from a medical practitioner that the adult is—
   (i) incapable in relation to decisions about; or
   (ii) incapable of acting to safeguard or promote his interests in,
the funds;
(g) contain an undertaking that he will open an account (the "designated account") solely for the purposes of—
   (i) receiving funds transferred under section 29(1); and
   (ii) intromitting with those funds.

(2) The applicant shall, not later than 14 days after the form has been countersigned as mentioned in subsection (1)(c), send the completed form to the Public Guardian.

(3) On receipt of a properly completed form sent timeously to him under subsection (2), the Public Guardian shall intimate the application to the adult, his nearest relative, his primary carer and any person who the Public Guardian considers has an interest in the application and advise them of the prescribed period within which they may object to the granting of the application; and he shall not grant the application without affording to any objector an opportunity of being heard.

(4) Having heard any objections as mentioned in subsection (3), the Public Guardian may grant the application and where he does so he shall—
(a) enter prescribed particulars in the register maintained by him under section 6(2)(b)(iii); and
(b) issue a certificate of authority to the withdrawer.

(5) A certificate of authority issued under subsection (4) shall instruct—
(a) the fundholder that the account held in the name of the adult; and
(b) the withdrawer that the designated account,
must not be overdrawn; and if either account is overdrawn, the fundholder of that account shall have a right of relief against the withdrawer.

(6) A certificate of authority issued under subsection (4) shall instruct the fundholder of the account held in the name of the adult that no operations shall be carried out on the account other than those carried out in accordance with the certificate by the person authorised under this section.

(7) Where the Public Guardian proposes to refuse the application he shall intimate his decision to the applicant and advise him of the prescribed period within which he may object to the refusal; and he shall not refuse the application without affording to the applicant, if he objects, an opportunity of being heard.

(8) The Public Guardian may at his own instance or at the instance of the applicant or of any person who objects to the granting of the application remit the application for determination by the sheriff, whose decision shall be final.

(9) A decision of the Public Guardian—
- (a) to grant an application under subsection (4) or to refuse an application; or
- (b) to refuse to remit an application to the sheriff under subsection (8) above,

may be appealed to the sheriff, whose decision shall be final.

(10) In this Act an individual in respect of whom a form is registered under subsection (4) is referred to as a "withdrawer".

Notification of change of address

27. After the name of a withdrawer has been registered under section 26 the withdrawer shall notify the Public Guardian—
- (a) of any change in his address; and
- (b) of any change in the address of the adult,

and the Public Guardian shall enter prescribed particulars in the register maintained by him under section 6(2)(b)(iii).

Purposes of intromissions with funds

28.—(1) The purposes of intromissions with funds may include any or all of the following—
- (a) the payment of central and local government taxes for which the adult is responsible;
- (b) the provisions of sustenance, accommodation, fuel, clothing and related goods and services for the adult;
- (c) the provision of other services provided for the purposes of looking after or caring for the adult;
- (d) the settlement of debts owed by or incurred in respect of the adult, including any prescribed fees charged by the Public Guardian in connection with the application to intromit.

(2) The Public Guardian may, in any case, authorise payment for the provision of items other than those mentioned in subsection (1).

(3) Subject to subsection (4), any funds used by the withdrawer shall be applied only for the benefit of the adult.

(4) Where the withdrawer lives with the adult, he may, to the extent authorised by the certificate, apply any funds withdrawn towards household expenses.

Withdrawal and use of funds

29.—(1) On presentation to it of the certificate issued under section 26(4)(b), the fundholder of the account held in the name of the adult specified in the form may make arrangements to transfer to the designated account such sums as the Public Guardian shall authorise.

(2) The fundholder of an account held by an adult shall be liable to the adult for any funds removed from the account under this section at any time when it was aware that the withdrawer's authority had been terminated or

suspended by the Public Guardian under section 31(3), but, on meeting such liability, the fundholder of the account shall have a right of relief against the withdrawer.

(3) The Public Guardian may authorise a method of payment other than a method mentioned in subsection (1).

(4) A decision of the Public Guardian not to authorise—
(a) a method of payment other than a method mentioned in subsection (1); or
(b) a payment under subsection (3),

may be appealed to the sheriff, whose decision shall be final.

Records and inquiries

30.—(1) The Scottish Ministers may by regulations provide that a withdrawer shall keep a record of his intromissions with the funds and that the Public Guardian may at any time require a withdrawer to produce such record for the Public Guardian's inspection.

(2) The Public Guardian may—
(a) make inquiries from time to time as to the manner in which a withdrawer has exercised his functions under this Part; and
(b) ask the withdrawer to produce any records which he has relating to his intromissions.

(3) The Public Guardian may require a fundholder of an account in the name of an adult or of a designated account to make its records of the account available for inspection by the Public Guardian.

(4) A fundholder complying with a requirement under subsection (3) may charge a reasonable fee for doing so and may recover that fee from the account concerned.

Duration and termination of registration

31.—(1) Subject to the following provisions of this section, the authority of a withdrawer to intromit with funds under section 26 shall be valid for a period of 3 years commencing with the date of issue of the certificate by the Public Guardian under subsection (4)(b) of that section.

(2) The Public Guardian may reduce or extend the period of validity mentioned in subsection (1); and an extension may be without limit of time.

(3) The Public Guardian may suspend or terminate the authority of a withdrawer and shall forthwith intimate such suspension or termination to—
(a) the withdrawer;
(b) the fundholder of the designated account,

and such suspension or termination shall have the effect of suspending or, as the case may be, terminating all operations on that account.

(4) The Public Guardian may on terminating the authority of the withdrawer grant the withdrawer interim authority to continue to intromit with the funds of the adult for a period not exceeding 4 weeks from the date of the termination; and paragraphs (a) and (b) of section 26(4) shall apply in the case of a grant of interim authority under this subsection as they apply to the grant of an application under that section.

(5) Subsections (1) and (2) are without prejudice to the right of the withdrawer to make subsequent applications under the said section 26 after the end of a valid period of authority to withdraw or, as the case may be, a suspension or termination of the authority.

(6) A decision of the Public Guardian to reduce or extend a period of validity mentioned in subsection (1) or to suspend or terminate the authority of a withdrawer under subsection (3) may be appealed to the sheriff, whose decision shall be final; and the suspension or termination shall remain in force until the appeal is determined.

(7) The authority of a withdrawer to withdraw funds under section 26 shall come to an end—

(a) on the appointment of a guardian with powers relating to the funds or account in question;
(b) on the granting of an intervention order relating to the funds or account in question; or
(c) on a continuing attorney's acquiring authority to act in relation to the funds or account in question,

but no liability shall be incurred by any person who acts in good faith under this Part in ignorance of the coming to an end of a withdrawer's authority under this subsection.

(8) In subsection (7) any reference to—
(a) a guardian shall include a reference to a guardian (however called) appointed under the law of any country to, or entitled under the law of any country to act for, an adult during his incapacity, if the guardianship is recognised by the law of Scotland;
(b) a continuing attorney shall include a reference to a person granted, under a contract, grant or appointment governed by the law of any country, powers (however expressed), relating to the granter's property or financial affairs and having continuing effect notwithstanding the granter's incapacity.

Joint accounts

32. Where an individual who along with one or more others is the holder of a joint account with a fundholder becomes incapable in relation to decisions about, or of safeguarding his interests in, the funds in the account, any other joint account holder may continue to operate the account unless— **A1–32**
   (a) the terms of the account provide otherwise; or
   (b) he is barred by an order of any court from so doing.

Transfer of funds

33.—(1) The Public Guardian may, on an application made at the same time as, or at any time after, an application for authority to intromit with funds held in a specified account by a fundholder, authorise the transfer of funds from that account to another specified account. **A1–33**

(2) In subsection (1),"specified" means specified in the application to transfer funds and in the authorisation of that transfer; and the account to which funds are transferred may be specified as to kind of account.

(3) A decision of the Public Guardian under subsection (1) may be appealed to the sheriff, whose decision shall be final.

Disapplication of Part 3

34.—(1) This Part shall not apply in the case of an adult in relation to whom— **A1–34**
   (a) there is a guardian or continuing attorney with powers relating to the funds or account in question; or
   (b) an intervention order has been granted relating to the funds or account in question,

but no liability shall be incurred by any person who acts in good faith under this Part in ignorance of any such appointment or grant.

(2) In this section any reference to—
(a) a guardian shall include a reference to a guardian (however called) appointed under the law of any country to, or entitled under the law of any country to act for, an adult during his incapacity, if the guardianship is recognised by the law of Scotland;
(b) a continuing attorney shall include a reference to a person granted, under a contract, grant or appointment governed by the law of any country, powers (however expressed), relating to the granter's property or financial affairs and having continuing effect notwithstanding the granter's incapacity.

Part 4

Management of Residents' Finances

Application of Part 4

A1–35 **35.**—(1) Subject to subsection (3), this Part applies to the management of the matters set out in section 39 relating to any resident of any of the following establishments—
   (a) a health service hospital;
   (b) an independent hospital or private psychiatric hospital;
   (c) a State hospital;
   (d) a care home service; and
   (e) a limited registration service.

(2) In this Part establishments mentioned in paragraph (b), (d) or (e) of subsection (1) are referred to as "registered establishments", all other establishments mentioned in subsection (1) are referred to as "unregistered establishments", and registered and unregistered establishments together are referred to as "authorised establishments".

(3) This Part shall not apply to a registered establishment where notice in writing is given to the supervisory body by—
   (a) the managers of the registered establishment; or
   (b) an applicant, under section 7(1) of the Regulation of Care (Scotland) Act 2001 (asp 8), for registration of the service which comprises that establishment,
that it shall not apply.

(4) The Scottish Ministers may by regulations amend the list of authorised establishments set out in subsection (1).

(5) In this Part, "the managers" has the meaning set out in schedule 1; and "resident" in relation to an authorised establishment means an adult whose main residence for the time being is the authorised establishment or who is liable to be detained there under the 1984 Act.

(6) Expressions used in subsection (1) and in the Regulation of Care (Scotland) Act 2001 have the same meanings in that subsection as in that Act.

NOTE
This section was amended by the Regulation of Care (Scotland) Act 2001 (asp 8), s.79 and Sch.3, para.23(2).

Registration for purposes of managing residents' finances

A1–36 **36.** [. . .]

NOTE
This section was repealed by the Regulation of Care (Scotland) Act 2001 (asp 8), s.80 and Sch.4.

Residents whose affairs may be managed

A1–37 **37.**—(1) The managers of an authorised establishment shall be entitled to manage on behalf of any resident in the establishment in relation to whom a certificate has been issued under subsection (2) any of the matters set out in section 39.

(2) Where the managers of an authorised establishment, having considered all other appropriate courses of action, have decided that management on behalf of the resident of the matters set out in section 39 by them is the most appropriate course of action, they shall cause to be examined by a medical practitioner any resident in the establishment who they believe may be incapable in relation to decisions as to, or of safeguarding his interest in, any of the resident's affairs referred to in section 39; and if the medical practitioner finds that the resident is so incapable he shall issue a certificate in prescribed form to that effect.

(3) Subject to subsection (8), the managers of the authorised establishment shall intimate their intention of requiring an examination under subsection (2) to the resident and to the resident's nearest relative.

(4) Subject to subsection (8), the managers of the authorised establishment shall—
  (a) send a copy of the certificate to the resident and to the supervisory body, who shall notify the resident's nearest relative;
  (b) notify the resident and the supervisory body that they intend to manage the resident's affairs.

(5) Notification under subsection (4)(b) shall include a statement as to what other courses of action had been considered and why they were not considered appropriate.

(6) The medical practitioner who certifies under this section shall not—
  (a) be related to the resident or to any of the managers of the authorised establishment;
  (b) have any direct or indirect financial interest in the authorised establishment.

(7) A certificate—
  (a) shall be reviewed where it appears to the managers of the authorised establishment, the medical practitioner who certifies under this section or any person having an interest in any of the resident's affairs mentioned in section 39 that there has been any change in the condition or circumstances of the resident bearing on the resident's incapacity; and
  (b) shall expire 3 years after it was issued.

(8) If the managers of the authorised establishment consider that intimation to the resident under subsection (3) or any action under subsection (4) would be likely to pose a serious risk to the health of the resident they may apply to the supervisory body for a direction that they need not make the intimation or take the action.

(9) The Scottish Ministers may prescribe the evidence which the supervisory body shall take into account in reaching a decision under subsection (8).

Financial procedures and controls in registered establishments

38. [. . .]

NOTE
This section was repealed by the Regulation of Care (Scotland) Act 2001 (asp 8), s.80 and Sch.4.

Matters which may be managed

39.—(1) The matters which may be managed under this Part by the managers of an authorised establishment are—
  (a) claiming, receiving, holding and spending any pension, benefit, allowance or other payment other than under the Social Security Contributions and Benefits Act 1992 (c.4);
  (b) claiming, receiving, holding and spending any money to which a resident is entitled;
  (c) holding any other moveable property to which the resident is entitled;
  (d) disposing of such moveable property,
and in this Part these matters, or any of them, are referred to as residents' affairs; and cognate expressions shall be construed accordingly.

(2) In managing these matters, the managers of an authorised establishment shall—
  (a) act only for the benefit of the resident; and
  (b) have regard to the sentimental value that any item might have for the resident, or would have but for the resident's incapacity.

(3) The managers of an authorised establishment shall not, without the consent of the supervisory body, manage any matter if that matter has a value greater than that which is prescribed for the purposes of this subsection.

(4) The supervisory body may in relation to an individual resident permit the managers of the authorised establishment to manage any matter which has a value greater than that which is prescribed in relation to it under subsection (3).

(5) For the purpose of this section, "manage" denotes no greater responsibility than complying with the duties set out in this section.

Supervisory bodies

A1–40 40.—(1) The supervisory body for the purposes of this Part is, in relation to—
  (a) a registered establishment, the Scottish Commission for the Regulation of Care; and
  (b) an unregistered establishment, the Health Board for the area in which the establishment is situated;
and any reference in this Part to an authorised establishment in relation to a supervisory body is a reference to an authorised establishment for which the supervisory body is responsible.

(2) The supervisory body shall from time to time make inquiry as to the manner in which the managers of an authorised establishment are carrying out the management of residents' affairs and in particular the manner in which they are carrying out their functions under section 41.

(3) The supervisory body shall investigate any complaint received as to the manner in which the managers of an authorised establishment are managing residents' affairs.

(4) The Scottish Ministers may, as respects any authorised establishment, amend subsection (1) by substituting for the supervisory body allotted to that establishment a different supervisory body.

NOTE
This section was amended by the Regulation of Care (Scotland) Act 2001 (asp 8), s.79 and Sch.3, para.23(3).

Duties and functions of managers of authorised establishment

A1–41 41. The managers of an authorised establishment shall, in relation to residents whose affairs they are managing under section 39—
  (a) claim, receive and hold any pension, benefit, allowance or other payment to which the resident is entitled other than under the Social Security Contributions and Benefits Act 1992 (c.4);
  (b) keep the funds of residents separate from the funds of the establishment;
  (c) comply with any requirements of the supervisory body as respects keeping the funds of residents separate or distinguishable from each other;
  (d) ensure that where, at any time, the total amount of funds held on behalf of any resident exceeds such sum as may from time to time be prescribed they shall be placed so as to earn interest;
  (e) keep records of all transactions made in relation to the funds held by them in respect of each resident for whose benefit the funds are held and managed and, in particular, ensure that details of the balance and any interest due to each resident can be ascertained at any time;
  (f) produce such records when requested to do so by the resident, his nearest relative or the supervisory body;
  (g) spend money only on items or services which are of benefit to the resident on whose behalf the funds are held;
  (h) not spend money on items or services which are provided by the establishment to or for such resident as part of its normal service;
  (i) make proper provision for indemnifying residents against any loss attributable to—
    (i) any act or omission on the part of the managers of the establishment in exercising the powers conferred by this Part or of others for whom

the managers are responsible or attributable to any expenditure in breach of paragraph (g);
(ii) any breach of duty, misuse of funds or failure to act reasonably and in good faith on the part of the managers.

Authorisation of named manager to withdraw from resident's account

42.—(1) On an application in writing by the managers of an authorised establishment the supervisory body may issue a certificate of authority under this section in relation to any resident named in the application.

(2) An application under subsection (1) shall specify one or more persons (being managers, officers or members of staff of the establishment) who shall exercise the authority conferred by this section.

(3) A certificate of authority shall be signed by the officer of the supervisory body authorised by the body to do so and shall—
(a) specify accounts or other funds of the resident;
(b) name the persons specified in the application (the "authorised persons");
(c) specify the period of validity of the certificate of authority, being a period not exceeding the period of validity of the certificate issued under section 37(2).

(4) The authorised persons may make withdrawals from such account or source of funds of the named resident as is specified in the certificate of authority and the fundholder may make payments accordingly.

(5) The supervisory body may at any time after it has issued a certificate of authority, revoke it and if it does so it shall notify the fundholder of the revocation.

Statement of resident's affairs

43.—(1) In this section, "resident" means a resident of an authorised establishment whose affairs are being managed in accordance with the provisions of this Part and "statement" means a statement of the affairs of the resident.

(2) Where a resident ceases to be incapable of managing his affairs, the managers of the establishment shall prepare a statement as at the date on which he ceases to be incapable and shall give a copy to him.

(3) Where a resident moves from an authorised establishment to another authorised establishment, the managers of the establishment from which he moves shall, except where he has ceased to be incapable, prepare a statement as at the date on which he moves and shall send a copy of the statement to the managers of the other establishment.

(4) Where a resident leaves an authorised establishment, other than to move to another authorised establishment and except where he has ceased to be incapable, the managers of the establishment shall prepare a statement as at the date on which he leaves and shall give a copy of the statement to any person who appears to them to be the person who will manage his affairs.

Resident ceasing to be resident of authorised establishment

44.—(1) Where a resident ceases to be a resident of an authorised establishment, or ceases to be incapable, the managers of the establishment shall continue, for a period not exceeding 3 months from the date on which he ceases to be a resident or, as the case may be, to be incapable, to manage his affairs while such other arrangements as are necessary for managing his affairs are being made.

(2) At the end of the period referred to in subsection (1) during which the managers of the establishment have continued to manage the resident's affairs, they shall prepare a statement and shall give a copy of it to—
(a) the resident, if he has ceased to be incapable; or
(b) any person who appears to them to be the person who will manage his affairs.

(3) Where a resident ceases to be a resident of an authorised establishment and his affairs are to be managed by another establishment, authority or person (including himself) the managers of the establishment shall take such steps as are necessary to transfer his affairs to that establishment, authority or person, as the case may be.

(4) Where a resident ceases to be a resident of an authorised establishment the managers of the establishment shall within 14 days of that event inform—
 (a) the supervisory body; and
 (b) where the resident has not ceased to be incapable and has moved neither—
  (i) to another authorised establishment; nor
  (ii) into the care of a local authority,
the local authority of the area in which they expect him to reside.

Appeal, revocation etc.

45.—(1) Where it appears to the supervisory body that the managers of an authorised establishment are no longer operating as such or have failed to comply with any requirement of this Part or that, for any other reason, it is no longer appropriate that they should continue to manage residents' affairs it may revoke that power to manage.

(2) [. . .]

(3) Where [. . .] a power to manage has been revoked under this section, the supervisory body shall within a period of 14 days from such revocation take over management of the residents' affairs and, where they do so, comply with the requirements imposed by and under this Part upon the managers of an authorised establishment.

(4) The supervisory body shall, within the period of 3 months after taking over management of residents' affairs under subsection (3), cause that management to be transferred to such other establishment, authority or person (who may be the resident) as they consider appropriate.

(5) Where the supervisory body is satisfied that the circumstances mentioned in subsection (1) no longer apply in relation to an establishment whose power to manage it has revoked, it may annul the revocation of the power and, where necessary, of the registration.

(6) Any decision of the supervisory body may be appealed to the sheriff, whose decision shall be final.

NOTE
This section was amended and repealed in part by the Regulation of Care (Scotland) Act 2001 (asp 8), s.79 and Sch.3, para.23(4).

Disapplication of Part 4

46.—(1) This Part shall not apply to any of the matters which may be managed under section 39 if—
 (a) there is a guardian, continuing attorney, or other person with powers relating to that matter; or
 (b) an intervention order has been granted relating to that matter,
but no liability shall be incurred by any person who acts in good faith under this Part in ignorance of any guardian, continuing attorney, other person or intervention order.

(2) In this section any reference to—
 (a) a guardian shall include a reference to a guardian (however called) appointed under the law of any country to, or entitled under the law of any country to act for, an adult during his incapacity, if the guardianship is recognised by the law of Scotland;
 (b) a continuing attorney shall include a reference to a person granted, under a contract, grant or appointment governed by the law of any country, powers (however expressed), relating to the granter's property

or financial affairs and having continuing effect notwithstanding the granter's incapacity.

PART 5

MEDICAL TREATMENT AND RESEARCH

Authority of persons responsible for medical treatment

47.—(1) This section applies where the medical practitioner primarily responsible for the medical treatment of an adult—
 (a) is of the opinion that the adult is incapable in relation to a decision about the medical treatment in question; and
 (b) has certified in accordance with subsection (5) that he is of this opinion.

(2) Without prejudice to any authority conferred by any other enactment or rule of law, and subject to sections 49 and 50 and to the following provisions of this section, the medical practitioner primarily responsible for the medical treatment of the adult shall have, during the period specified in the certificate, authority to do what is reasonable in the circumstances, in relation to the medical treatment, to safeguard or promote the physical or mental health of the adult.

(3) The authority conferred by subsection (2) shall be exercisable also by any other person who is authorised by the medical practitioner primarily responsible for the medical treatment of the adult to carry out medical treatment and who is acting—
 (a) on his behalf under his instructions; or
 (b) with his approval or agreement.

(4) In this Part "medical treatment" includes any procedure or treatment designed to safeguard or promote physical or mental health.

(5) A certificate for the purposes of subsection (1) shall be in the prescribed form and shall specify the period during which the authority conferred by subsection (2) shall subsist, being a period which—
 (a) the medical practitioner primarily responsible for the medical treatment of the adult considers appropriate to the condition or circumstances of the adult; but
 (b) does not exceed one year from the date of the examination on which the certificate is based.

(6) If after issuing a certificate, the medical practitioner primarily responsible for the medical treatment of the adult is of the opinion that the condition or circumstances of the adult have changed he may—
 (a) revoke the certificate;
 (b) issue a new certificate specifying such period not exceeding one year from the date of revocation of the old certificate as he considers appropriate to the new condition or circumstances of the adult.

(7) The authority conferred by subsection (2) shall not authorise—
 (a) the use of force or detention, unless it is immediately necessary and only for so long as is necessary in the circumstances;
 (b) action which would be inconsistent with any decision by a competent court;
 (c) placing an adult in a hospital for the treatment of mental disorder against his will.

(8) The authority conferred by subsection (2) shall not authorise medical treatment prescribed in regulations made under section 48.

(9) Subject to subsection (10), where any question as to the authority of any person to provide medical treatment in pursuance of subsection (2)—
 (a) is the subject of proceedings in any court (other than for the purposes of any application to the court made under regulations made under section 48); and
 (b) has not been determined,
medical treatment authorised by subsection (2) shall not be given unless it is authorised by any other enactment or rule of law for the preservation of the

life of the adult or the prevention of serious deterioration in his medical condition.

(10) Nothing in subsection (9) shall authorise the provision of any medical treatment where an interdict has been granted and continues to have effect prohibiting the provision of such medical treatment.

Exceptions to authority to treat

A1–48   48.—(1) The authority conferred by section 47(2) does not extend to the giving of any of the forms of treatment to which Part X of the 1984 Act applies to a patient to whom that Part applies (which Part authorises certain treatments for mental disorder for certain patients detained under that Act).

(2) The Scottish Ministers may by regulations specify medical treatment, or a class or classes of medical treatment, in relation to which the authority conferred by section 47(2) shall not apply and make provision about the medical treatment, or a class or classes of medical treatment, in relation to which that authority does apply.

(3) Regulations made under subsection (2) may provide for the circumstances in which the specified medical treatment or specified class or classes of medical treatment may be carried out.

Medical treatment where there is an application for intervention or guardianship order

A1–49   49.—(1) Section 47(2) shall not apply if, to the knowledge of the medical practitioner primarily responsible for the medical treatment of the adult, an application for an intervention order or a guardianship order with power in relation to any medical treatment referred to in that subsection has been made to the sheriff and has not been determined.

(2) Until the application has been finally determined, medical treatment authorised by section 47(2) shall not be given unless it is authorised by any other enactment or rule of law for the preservation of the life of the adult or the prevention of serious deterioration in his medical condition.

(3) Nothing in subsection (2) shall authorise the provision of any medical treatment where an interdict has been granted and continues to have effect prohibiting the provision of such medical treatment.

Medical treatment where guardian etc. has been appointed

A1–50   50.—(1) This section applies where a guardian or a welfare attorney has been appointed or a person has been authorised under an intervention order with power in relation to any medical treatment referred to in section 47.

(2) The authority conferred by section 47(2) shall not apply where—
(a) subsection (1) applies;
(b) the medical practitioner primarily responsible for the medical treatment of the adult is aware of the appointment or, as the case may be, authorisation; and
(c) it would be reasonable and practicable for that medical practitioner to obtain the consent of the guardian, welfare attorney or person authorised under the intervention order, as the case may be, to any proposed medical treatment but he has failed to do so.

(3) Where the medical practitioner primarily responsible for the medical treatment of the adult has consulted the guardian, welfare attorney or person authorised under the intervention order and there is no disagreement as to the medical treatment of the adult, any person having an interest in the personal welfare of the adult may appeal the decision as to the medical treatment to the Court of Session.

(4) Where the medical practitioner primarily responsible for the medical treatment of the adult has consulted the guardian, welfare attorney or person authorised under the intervention order and there is a disagreement as to the

medical treatment of the adult, the medical practitioner shall request the Mental Welfare Commission to nominate a medical practitioner (the "nominated medical practitioner") from the list established and maintained by them under subsection (9) to give an opinion as to the medical treatment proposed.

(5) Where the nominated medical practitioner certifies that, in his opinion, having regard to all the circumstances and having consulted the guardian, welfare attorney or person authorised under the intervention order as the case may be and, if it is reasonable and practicable to do so, a person nominated by such guardian, welfare attorney or person authorised under the intervention order as the case may be, the proposed medical treatment should be given, the medical practitioner primarily responsible for the medical treatment of the adult may give the treatment or may authorise any other person to give the treatment notwithstanding the disagreement with the guardian, welfare attorney, or person authorised under the intervention order, as the case may be.

(6) Where the nominated medical practitioner certifies that, in his opinion, having regard to all the circumstances and having consulted the guardian, welfare attorney or person authorised under the intervention order as the case may be and, if it is reasonable and practicable to do so, a person nominated by such guardian, welfare attorney or person authorised under the intervention order as the case may be, the proposed medical treatment should or, as the case may be, should not be given, the medical practitioner primarily responsible for the medical treatment of the adult, or any person having an interest in the personal welfare of the adult, may apply to the Court of Session for a determination as to whether the proposed treatment should be given or not.

(7) Subject to subsection (8), where an appeal has been made to the Court of Session under subsection (3) or an application has been made under subsection (6), and has not been determined, medical treatment authorised by section 47(2) shall not be given unless it is authorised by any other enactment or rule of law for the preservation of the life of the adult or the prevention of serious deterioration in his medical condition.

(8) Nothing in subsection (7) shall authorise the provision of any medical treatment where an interdict has been granted and continues to have effect prohibiting the giving of such medical treatment.

(9) The Mental Welfare Commission shall establish and maintain a list of medical practitioners from whom they shall nominate the medical practitioner who is to give the opinion under subsection (4).

(10) In this section any reference to—
(a) a guardian shall include a reference to a guardian (however called) appointed under the law of any country to, or entitled under the law of any country to act for, an adult during his incapacity, if the guardianship is recognised by the law of Scotland;
(b) a welfare attorney shall include a reference to a person granted, under a contract, grant or appointment governed by the law of any country, powers (however expressed) relating to the granter's personal welfare and having effect during the granter's incapacity.

Authority for research

51.—(1) No surgical, medical, nursing, dental or psychological research shall be carried out on any adult who is incapable in relation to a decision about participation in the research unless—
 (a) research of a similar nature cannot be carried out on an adult who is capable in relation to such a decision; and
 (b) the circumstances mentioned in subsection (2) are satisfied.
(2) The circumstances referred to in subsection (1) are that—
 (a) the purpose of the research is to obtain knowledge of—
  (i) the causes, diagnosis, treatment or care of the adult's incapacity; or
  (ii) the effect of any treatment or care given during his incapacity to the adult which relates to that incapacity; and

(b) the conditions mentioned in subsection (3) are fulfilled.
(3) The conditions are—
(a) the research is likely to produce real and direct benefit to the adult;
(b) the adult does not indicate unwillingness to participate in the research;
(c) the research has been approved by the Ethics Committee;
(d) the research entails no foreseeable risk, or only a minimal foreseeable risk, to the adult;
(e) the research imposes no discomfort, or only minimal discomfort, on the adult; and
(f) consent has been obtained from any guardian or welfare attorney who has power to consent to the adult's participation in research or, where there is no such guardian or welfare attorney, from the adult's nearest relative.

(4) Where the research is not likely to produce real and direct benefit to the adult, it may nevertheless be carried out if it will contribute through significant improvement in the scientific understanding of the adult's incapacity to the attainment of real and direct benefit to the adult or to other persons having the same incapacity, provided the other circumstances or conditions mentioned in subsections (1) to (3) are fulfilled.

(5) In granting approval under subsection (3)(c), the Ethics Committee may impose such conditions as it sees fit.

(6) The Ethics Committee shall be constituted by regulations made by the Scottish Ministers and such regulations may make provision as to the composition of, appointments to and procedures of the Ethics Committee and may make such provision for the payment of such remuneration, expenses and superannuation as the Scottish Ministers may determine.

(7) Regulations made by the Scottish Ministers under subsection (6) may prescribe particular matters which the Ethics Committee shall take into account when deciding whether to approve any research under this Part.

(8) In this section any reference to—
(a) a guardian shall include a reference to a guardian (however called) appointed under the law of any country to, or entitled under the law of any country to act for, an adult during his incapacity, if the guardianship is recognised by the law of Scotland;
(b) a welfare attorney shall include a reference to a person granted, under a contract, grant or appointment governed by the law of any country, powers (however expressed) relating to the granter's personal welfare and having effect during the granter's incapacity.

Appeal against decision as to medical treatment

52.—Any decision taken for the purposes of this Part, other than a decision by a medical practitioner under section 50, as to the medical treatment of the adult may be appealed by any person having an interest in the personal welfare of the adult to the sheriff and thence, with the leave of the sheriff, to the Court of Session.

PART 6

INTERVENTION ORDERS AND GUARDIANSHIP ORDERS

Intervention orders

Intervention orders

53.—(1) The sheriff may, on an application by any person (including the adult himself) claiming an interest in the property, financial affairs or personal welfare of an adult, if he is satisfied that the adult is incapable of taking the action, or is incapable in relation to the decision about his property, financial affairs or personal welfare to which the application relates, make an order (in this Act referred to as an "intervention order").

(2) In considering an application under subsection (1), the sheriff shall have regard to any intervention order or guardianship order which may have been previously made in relation to the adult, and to any order varying, or ancillary to, such an order.

(3) Where it appears to the local authority that—
(a) the adult is incapable as mentioned in subsection (1); and
(b) no application has been made or is likely to be made for an order under this section in relation to the decision to which the application under this subsection relates; and
(c) an intervention order is necessary for the protection of the property, financial affairs or personal welfare of the adult,
they shall apply under this section for an order.

(4) Section 57(3) and (4) shall apply to an application under this section and, for this purpose, for the reference to the individual or office holder nominated for appointment as guardian there shall be substituted a reference to a person nominated in such application.

(5) An intervention order may—
(a) direct the taking of any action specified in the order;
(b) authorise the person nominated in the application to take such action or make such decision in relation to the property, financial affairs or personal welfare of the adult as is specified in the order;

(6) Where an intervention order directs the acquisition of accommodation for, or the disposal of any accommodation used for the time being as a dwelling house by, the adult, the consent of the Public Guardian as respects the consideration shall be required before the accommodation is acquired or, as the case may be, disposed of.

(7) In making or varying an intervention order the sheriff may, and in the case of an intervention order relating to property or financial affairs shall, except where—
(a) the person authorised under the intervention order is unable to find caution; but
(b) the sheriff is satisfied that nevertheless he is suitable to be authorised under the order,
require the person authorised under the order to find caution.

(8) The sheriff may, on an application by—
(a) the person authorised under the intervention order; or
(b) the adult; or
(c) any person claiming an interest in the property, financial affairs or personal welfare of the adult,
make an order varying the terms of, or recalling, the intervention order or any other order made for the purposes of the intervention order.

(9) Anything done under an intervention order shall have the same effect as if done by the adult if he had the capacity to do so.

(10) Where an intervention order is made, the sheriff clerk shall forthwith send a copy of the interlocutor containing the order to the Public Guardian who shall—
(a) enter in the register maintained by him under section 6(2)(b)(v) such particulars of the order as may be prescribed; and
(b) notify the adult, the local authority and (in a case where the adult's incapacity is by reason of, or reasons which include, mental disorder and the intervention order relates to the adult's personal welfare or factors which include it) the Mental Welfare Commission.

(11) A transaction for value between a person authorised under an intervention order, purporting to act as such, and a third party acting in good faith shall not be invalid on the ground only that—
(a) the person acted outwith the scope of his authority;
(b) the person failed to observe any requirement, whether substantive or procedural, imposed by or under this Act or by the sheriff or by the Public Guardian; or

(c) there was any irregularity whether substantive or procedural in the authorisation of the person.

(12) A person authorised under an intervention order may recover from the estate of the adult the amount of such reasonable outlays as he incurs in doing anything directed or authorised under the order.

(13) Where a third party has acquired, in good faith and for value, title to any interest in heritable property from a person authorised under an intervention order that title shall not be challengeable on the ground only—
- (a) of any irregularity of procedure in the making of the intervention order; or
- (b) that the person authorised under the intervention order has acted outwith the scope of the authority.

(14) Sections 64(2) and 67(3) and (4) shall apply to an intervention order as they apply to a guardianship order and, for this purpose, for any reference to a guardian there shall be substituted a reference to the person authorised under the order.

Records: intervention orders

54. A person authorised under an intervention order shall keep records of the exercise of his powers.

Notification of change of address

55. After particulars relating to an intervention order are entered in the register under section 53 the person authorised under the intervention order shall notify the Public Guardian—
- (a) of any change in his address; and
- (b) of any change in the address of the adult,

and the Public Guardian shall enter prescribed particulars in the register maintained by him under section 6(2)(b)(v) and notify the local authority and (in a case where the adult's incapacity is by reason of, or reasons which include, mental disorder and the intervention order relates to the adult's personal welfare or factors which include it) the Mental Welfare Commission.

Registration of intervention order relating to heritable property

56.—(1) This section applies where the sheriff makes an intervention order which vests in the person authorised under the order any right to deal with, convey or manage any interest in heritable property which is recorded or is capable of being recorded in the General Register of Sasines or is registered or is capable of being registered in the Land Register of Scotland.

(2) In making such an order the sheriff shall specify each property affected by the order, in such terms as enable it to be identified in the Register of Sasines or, as the case may be, the Land Register of Scotland.

(3) The person authorised under the order shall forthwith apply to the Keeper of the Registers of Scotland for recording of the interlocutor containing the order in the General Register of Sasines or, as the case may be, for registering of it in the Land Register of Scotland.

(4) An application under subsection (3) shall contain—
- (a) the name and address of the person authorised under the order;
- (b) a statement that the person authorised under the order has powers relating to each property specified in the order;
- (c) a copy of the interlocutor.

(5) Where the interlocutor is to be recorded in the General Register of Sasines, the Keeper shall—
- (a) record the interlocutor in the Register; and
- (b) endorse the interlocutor to the effect that it has been so recorded.

(6) Where the interlocutor is to be registered in the Land Register of Scotland, the Keeper shall update the title sheet of the property to show it.

(7) The person authorised under the order shall send the endorsed interlocutor or, as the case may be, the updated Land Certificate or an office copy thereof to the Public Guardian who shall enter prescribed particulars of it in the register maintained by him under section 6(2)(b)(v).

Guardianship orders

Application for guardianship order

57.—(1) An application may be made under this section by any person (including the adult himself) claiming an interest in the property, financial affairs or personal welfare of an adult to the sheriff for an order appointing an individual or office holder as guardian in relation to the adult's property, financial affairs or personal welfare.

(2) Where it appears to the local authority that—
  (a) the conditions mentioned in section 58(1)(a) and (b) apply to the adult; and
  (b) no application has been made or is likely to be made for an order under this section; and
  (c) a guardianship order is necessary for the protection of the property, financial affairs or personal welfare of the adult,
they shall apply under this section for an order.

(3) There shall be lodged in court along with an application under this section—
  (a) reports, in prescribed form, of an examination and assessment of the adult carried out not more than 30 days before the lodging of the application by at least two medical practitioners one of whom, in a case where the incapacity is by reason of mental disorder, must be a medical practitioner approved for the purposes of section 20 of the 1984 Act as having special experience in the diagnosis or treatment of mental disorder;
  (b) where the application relates to the personal welfare of the adult, a report, in prescribed form, from the mental health officer, (but where it is in jeopardy only because of the inability of the adult to communicate, from the chief social work officer), containing his opinion as to—
    (i) the general appropriateness of the order sought, based on an interview and assessment of the adult carried out not more than 30 days before the lodging of the application; and
    (ii) the suitability of the individual nominated in the application to be appointed guardian; and
  (c) where the application relates only to the property or financial affairs of the adult, a report, in prescribed form, based on an interview and assessment of the adult carried out not more than 30 days before the lodging of the application, by a person who has sufficient knowledge to make such a report as to the matters referred to in paragraph (b)(i) and (ii).

(4) Where an applicant claims an interest in the personal welfare of the adult and is not the local authority, he shall give notice to the chief social work officer of his intention to make an application under this section and the report referred to in subsection (3)(b) shall be prepared by the chief social work officer or, as the case may be, the mental health officer, within 21 days of the date of the notice.

(5) The sheriff may, on an application being made to him, at any time before the disposal of the application made under this section, make an order for the appointment of an interim guardian.

(6) The appointment of an interim guardian in pursuance of this section shall, unless recalled earlier, cease to have effect—
  (a) on the appointment of a guardian under section 58; or
  (b) at the end of the period of 3 months from the date of appointment,
whichever is the earlier.

Disposal of application

A1-58 **58.**—(1) Where the sheriff is satisfied in considering an application under section 57 that—
  (a) the adult is incapable in relation to decisions about, or of acting to safeguard or promote his interests in, his property, financial affairs or personal welfare, and is likely to continue to be so incapable; and
  (b) no other means provided by or under this Act would be sufficient to enable the adult's interests in his property, financial affairs or personal welfare to be safeguarded or promoted,
he may grant the application.

(2) In considering an application under section 57, the sheriff shall have regard to any intervention order or guardianship order which may have been previously made in relation to the adult, and to any order varying, or ancillary to, such an order.

(3) Where the sheriff is satisfied that an intervention order would be sufficient as mentioned in subsection (1), he may treat the application under this section as an application for an intervention order under section 53 and may make such order as appears to him to be appropriate.

(4) Where the sheriff grants the application under section 57 he shall make an order (in this Act referred to as a "guardianship order") appointing the individual or office holder nominated in the application to be the guardian of the adult for a period of 3 years or such other period (including an indefinite period) as, on cause shown, he may determine.

(5) Where more than one individual or office holder is nominated in the application, a guardianship order may, without prejudice to the power under section 62(1) to appoint joint guardians, appoint two or more guardians to exercise different powers in relation to the adult.

(6) In making a guardianship order relating to the property or financial affairs of the adult the sheriff shall, except where—
  (a) the individual is unable to find caution; but
  (b) the sheriff is satisfied that nevertheless he is suitable to be appointed guardian,
require an individual appointed as guardian to find caution.

(7) Where the sheriff makes a guardianship order the sheriff clerk shall forthwith send a copy of the interlocutor containing the order to the Public Guardian who shall—
  (a) enter prescribed particulars of the appointment in the register maintained by him under section 6(2)(b)(iv);
  (b) when satisfied that the guardian has found caution if so required, issue a certificate of appointment to the guardian;
  (c) notify the adult of the appointment of the guardian; and
  (d) notify the local authority and (in a case where the incapacity of the adult is by reason of, or reasons which include, mental disorder and the guardianship order relates to the adult's personal welfare or factors which include it) the Mental Welfare Commission of the terms of the interlocutor.

Who may be appointed as guardian

A1-59 **59.**—(1) The sheriff may appoint as guardian—
  (a) any individual whom he considers to be suitable for appointment and who has consented to being appointed;
  (b) where the guardianship order is to relate only to the personal welfare of the adult, the chief social work officer of the local authority.

(2) Where the guardianship order is to relate to the property and financial affairs and to the personal welfare of the adult and joint guardians are to be appointed, the chief social work officer of the local authority may be appointed guardian in relation only to the personal welfare of the adult.

(3) The sheriff shall not appoint an individual as guardian to an adult unless he is satisfied that the individual is aware of—
(a) the adult's circumstances and condition and of the needs arising from such circumstances and condition; and
(b) the functions of a guardian.
(4) In determining if an individual is suitable for appointment as guardian, the sheriff shall have regard to—
(a) the accessibility of the individual to the adult and to his primary carer;
(b) the ability of the individual to carry out the functions of guardian;
(c) any likely conflict of interest between the adult and the individual;
(d) any undue concentration of power which is likely to arise in the individual over the adult;
(e) any adverse effects which the appointment of the individual would have on the interests of the adult;
(f) such other matters as appear to him to be appropriate.
(5) Paragraphs (c) and (d) of subsection (4) shall not be regarded as applying to an individual by reason only of his being a close relative of, or person residing with, the adult.

Renewal of guardianship order by sheriff

60.—(1) At any time before the end of a period in respect of which a guardianship order has been made or renewed, an application may be made to the sheriff under this section by the guardian for the renewal of such order, and where such an application is so made, the order shall continue to have effect until the application is determined.

(2) Where it appears to the local authority that an application for renewal of a guardianship order under subsection (1) is necessary but that no such application has been made or is likely to be made, they shall apply under subsection (1) for the renewal of such an order and, where such an application is so made, the order shall continue to have effect until the application is determined.

(3) Section 57(3) shall apply for the purposes of an application made under this section as it applies for the purposes of an application made under that section; and for the purposes of so applying that subsection references to the appointment of a guardian (however expressed) shall be construed as references to the continuation of appointment.

(4) Section 58 shall apply to an application under this section as it applies to an application under section 57; and for the purposes of so applying that section—
(a) references to the making of a guardianship order and the appointment of a guardian (however expressed) shall be construed as references to, respectively, the renewal of the order and the continuation of appointment;
(b) for subsection (4) there shall be substituted—
"(4) Where the sheriff grants an application under section 60, he may continue the guardianship order for a period of 5 years or for such other period (including an indefinite period) as, on cause shown, he may determine.".

(5) Where the sheriff refuses an application under this section, the sheriff clerk shall forthwith send a copy of the interlocutor containing the refusal to the Public Guardian who shall—
(a) enter prescribed particulars in the register maintained by him under section 6(2)(b)(iv); and
(b) notify the adult and the local authority and (in a case where the adult's incapacity is by reason of, or reasons which include, mental disorder and the guardianship order relates to the adult's personal welfare or factors which include it) the Mental Welfare Commission.

Registration of guardianship order relating to heritable property

A1–61 **61.**—(1) This section applies where the sheriff makes a guardianship order which vests in the guardian any right of the adult to deal with, convey or manage any interest in heritable property which is recorded or is capable of being recorded in the General Register of Sasines or is registered or is capable of being registered in the Land Register of Scotland.

(2) In making such an order the sheriff shall specify each property affected by the order, in such terms as enable it to be identified in the Register of Sasines or, as the case may be, the Land Register of Scotland.

(3) The guardian shall, after finding caution if so required, forthwith apply to the Keeper of the Registers of Scotland for recording of the interlocutor containing the order in the General Register of Sasines or, as the case may be, registering of it in the Land Register of Scotland.

(4) An application under subsection (3) shall contain—
(a) the name and address of the guardian;
(b) a statement that the guardian has powers relating to each property specified in the order;
(c) a copy of the interlocutor.

(5) Where the interlocutor is to be recorded in the General Register of Sasines, the Keeper shall—
(a) record the interlocutor in the Register; and
(b) endorse the interlocutor to the effect that it has been so recorded.

(6) Where the interlocutor is to be registered in the Land Register of Scotland, the Keeper shall update the title sheet of the property to show the interlocutor.

(7) The guardian shall send the endorsed interlocutor or, as the case may be, the updated Land Certificate or an office copy thereof to the Public Guardian who shall enter prescribed particulars of it in the register maintained by him under section 6(2)(b)(iv).

Joint and substitute guardians

Joint guardians

A1–62 **62.**—(1) An application may be made to the sheriff—
(a) by two or more individuals seeking appointment, for their appointment as joint guardians to an adult; or
(b) by an individual seeking appointment, for his appointment as an additional guardian to an adult jointly with one or more existing guardians.

(2) Joint guardians shall not be appointed to an adult unless—
(a) the individuals so appointed are parents, siblings or children of the adult; or
(b) the sheriff is satisfied that, in the circumstances, it is appropriate to appoint as joint guardians individuals who are not related to the adult as mentioned in paragraph (a).

(3) Where an application is made under subsection (1)(a), sections 58 and 59 shall apply for the purposes of the disposal of that application as they apply for the disposal of an application under section 57.

(4) In deciding if an individual is suitable for appointment as additional guardian under subsection (1)(b), the sheriff shall have regard to the matters set out in section 59(3) to (5).

(5) Where the sheriff appoints an additional guardian under this section, the sheriff clerk shall send a copy of the order appointing him to the Public Guardian who shall—
(a) enter prescribed particulars in the register maintained by him under section 6(2) (b)(iv) of this Act;

(b) when satisfied that the additional guardian has found caution if so required, issue a certificate of appointment to the additional guardian and a new certificate of appointment to the existing guardian;
(c) notify the adult and the local authority and (in a case where the adult's incapacity is by reason of, or reasons which include, mental disorder and the guardianship order relates to the adult's personal welfare or factors which include it) the Mental Welfare Commission.

(6) Joint guardians may, subject to subsection (7), exercise their functions individually, and each guardian shall be liable for any loss or injury caused to the adult arising out of—
(a) his own acts or omissions; or
(b) his failure to take reasonable steps to ensure that a joint guardian does not breach any duty of care or fiduciary duty owed to the adult,
and where more than one such guardian is so liable they shall be liable jointly and severally.

(7) A joint guardian shall, before exercising any functions conferred on him, consult the other joint guardians, unless—
(a) consultation would be impracticable in the circumstances; or
(b) the joint guardians agree that consultation is not necessary.

(8) Where joint guardians disagree as to the exercise of their functions, either or both of them may apply to the sheriff for directions under section 3.

(9) Where there are joint guardians, a third party in good faith is entitled to rely on the authority to act of any one or more of them.

Substitute guardian

63.—(1) In any case where an individual is appointed as guardian under **A1–63** section 58 the sheriff may, on an application, appoint to act as guardian in the event of the guardian so appointed becoming unable to act any individual or office holder who could competently be appointed by virtue of section 59.

(2) In this Act an individual appointed under section 58 and an individual or office holder appointed under this section are referred to respectively as an "original guardian" and a "substitute guardian".

(3) The appointment of a substitute guardian shall be for the same period as the appointment of the original guardian under section 58(4).

(4) An application for appointment as a substitute guardian may be made at the time of the application for the appointment of the original guardian or at any time thereafter.

(5) In making an order appointing an individual as substitute guardian with powers relating to the property or financial affairs of the adult the sheriff shall, except where—
(a) the individual is unable to find caution; but
(b) the sheriff is satisfied that nevertheless he is suitable to be appointed substitute guardian,
require an individual appointed as substitute guardian to find caution.

(6) Subsection (1) shall apply to an individual who, having been appointed as a substitute guardian subsequently, by virtue of this section, becomes the guardian as it applies to an individual appointed under section 58 and, for this purpose, any reference in this section to the "original guardian" shall be construed accordingly.

(7) Where the sheriff appoints a substitute guardian (other than a substitute guardian appointed in the same order as an original guardian) under subsection (1), the sheriff clerk shall send a copy of the interlocutor containing the order appointing the substitute guardian to the Public Guardian who shall—
(a) enter prescribed particulars in the register maintained by him under section 6(2)(b)(iv); and
(b) notify the adult, the original guardian and the local authority and (in a case where the adult's incapacity is by reason of, or by reasons which include, mental disorder and the guardianship order relates to the

adult's personal welfare or factors which include it) the Mental Welfare Commission.

(8) On the death or incapacity of the original guardian, the substitute guardian shall, without undue delay, notify the Public Guardian—
   (a) of the death or incapacity (and where the original guardian has died, provide the Public Guardian with documentary evidence of the death); and
   (b) whether or not he is prepared to act as guardian.

(9) The Public Guardian on being notified under subsection (8) shall, if the substitute guardian is prepared to act—
   (a) enter prescribed particulars in the register maintained by him under section 6(2)(b)(iv);
   (b) when satisfied that the substitute guardian has found caution if so required, issue the substitute guardian with a certificate of appointment;
   (c) notify the adult, the original guardian, the local authority and (in a case where the adult's incapacity is by reason of, or by reasons which include, mental disorder and the guardianship order relates to the adult's personal welfare or factors which include it) the Mental Welfare Commission that the substitute guardian is acting.

(10) Unless otherwise specified in the order appointing him, the substitute guardian shall have the same functions and powers as those exercisable by the original guardian immediately before the event mentioned in subsection (1).

Functions etc. of guardian

Functions and duties of guardian

A1–64 64.—(1) Subject to the provisions of this section, an order appointing a guardian may confer on him—
   (a) power to deal with such particular matters in relation to the property, financial affairs or personal welfare of the adult as may be specified in the order;
   (b) power to deal with all aspects of the personal welfare of the adult, or with such aspects as may be specified in the order;
   (c) power to pursue or defend an action of declarator of nullity of marriage, or of divorce or separation in the name of the adult;
   (d) power to manage the property or financial affairs of the adult, or such parts of them as may be specified in the order;
   (e) power to authorise the adult to carry out such transactions or categories of transactions as the guardian may specify.

(2) A guardian may not—
   (a) place the adult in a hospital for the treatment of mental disorder against his will; or
   (b) consent on behalf of the adult to any form of treatment mentioned in section 48(1) or (2).

(3) A guardian shall (unless prohibited by an order of the sheriff and subject to any conditions or restrictions specified in such an order) have power by virtue of his appointment to act as the adult's legal representative in relation to any matter within the scope of the power conferred by the guardianship order.

(4) The guardian shall not later than 7 days after any change of his own or the adult's address notify the Public Guardian who shall—
   (a) notify the adult (in a case where it is the guardian's address which has changed), the local authority and (in a case where the adult's incapacity is by reason of, or reasons which include, mental disorder and the guardianship order relates to the adult's personal welfare or factors which include it) the Mental Welfare Commission of the change; and
   (b) enter prescribed particulars in the register maintained by him under section 6(2)(b)(iv).

(5) A guardian having powers relating to the property or financial affairs of the adult shall, subject to—
   (a) such restrictions as may be imposed by the court;
   (b) any management plan prepared under paragraph 1 of schedule 2; or
   (c) paragraph 6 of that schedule,
be entitled to use the capital and income of the adult's estate for the purpose of purchasing assets, services or accommodation so as to enhance the adult's quality of life.

(6) The guardian may arrange for some or all of his functions to be exercised by one or more persons acting on his behalf but shall not be entitled to surrender or transfer any part of them to another person.

(7) The guardian shall comply with any order or demand made by the Public Guardian in relation to the property or financial affairs of the adult in so far as so complying would be within the scope of his authority; and where the guardian fails to do so the sheriff may, on the application of the Public Guardian, make an order to the like effect as the order or demand made by the Public Guardian, and the sheriff's decision shall be final.

(8) An interim guardian appointed under section 57(5) having powers relating to—
   (a) the property or financial affairs of an adult shall report to the Public Guardian;
   (b) the personal welfare of an adult shall report to the chief social work officer of the local authority,
every month as to his exercise of those powers.

(9) Where the chief social work officer of the local authority has been appointed guardian he shall, not later than 7 working days after his appointment, notify any person who received notification under section 58(7) of the appointment of the name of the officer responsible at any time for carrying out the functions and duties of guardian.

(10) If, in relation to the appointment of the chief social work officer as guardian, the sheriff has directed that that intimation or notification of any application or other proceedings should not be given to the adult, the chief social work officer shall not notify the adult under subsection (9).

(11) The Scottish Ministers may by regulations define the scope of the powers which may be conferred on a guardian under subsection (1) and the conditions under which they shall be exercised.

(12) Schedule 2 (which makes provision as to the guardian's management of the estate of an adult) has effect.

Records: guardians

65. A guardian shall keep records of the exercise of his powers.   **A1–65**

Gifts

66.—(1) A guardian having powers relating to the property or financial affairs **A1–66** of an adult may make a gift out of the adult's estate only if authorised to do so by the Public Guardian.

(2) Authorisation by the Public Guardian under subsection (1) may be given generally, or in respect of a particular gift.

(3) On receipt of an application in the prescribed form for an authorisation to make a gift, the Public Guardian shall, subject to subsection (4), intimate the application to the adult, his nearest relative, his primary carer and any other person who the Public Guardian considers has an interest in the application and advise them of the prescribed period within which they may object to the granting of the application; and he shall not grant the application without affording to any objector an opportunity of being heard.

(4) Where the Public Guardian is of the opinion that the value of the gift is such that intimation is not necessary, he may dispense with intimation.

(5) Having heard any objections as mentioned in subsection (3), the Public Guardian may grant the application.

(6) Where the Public Guardian proposes to refuse the application he shall intimate his decision to the guardian and advise him of the prescribed period within which he may object to the refusal; and he shall not refuse the application without affording to the guardian, if he objects, an opportunity of being heard.

(7) The Public Guardian may at his own instance or at the instance of the guardian or of any person who objects to the granting of the application remit the application for determination by the sheriff, whose decision shall be final.

(8) A decision of the Public Guardian—
   (a) to grant an application under subsection (5) or to refuse an application; or
   (b) to refuse to remit an application to the sheriff under subsection (7),
may be appealed to the sheriff, whose decision shall be final.

Effect of appointment and transactions of guardian

67.—(1) The adult shall have no capacity to enter into any transaction in relation to any matter which is within the scope of the authority conferred on the guardian except in a case where he has been authorised by the guardian under section 64(1)(e); but nothing in this subsection shall be taken to affect the capacity of the adult in relation to any other matter.

(2) Where the guardian has powers relating to the property or financial affairs of the adult, the certificate of appointment issued to him by the Public Guardian shall, subject to the terms of the order appointing him, have the effect of—
   (a) authorising the guardian to take possession of, manage and deal with any moveable or immoveable estate (wherever situated) of the adult;
   (b) requiring any payment due to the adult to be made to the guardian,
in so far as the estate, payment or matter falls within the scope of the guardian's authority.

(3) A guardian having powers relating to the personal welfare of an adult may exercise these powers in relation to the adult whether or not the adult is in Scotland at the time of the exercise of the powers.

(4) The guardian shall be personally liable under any transaction entered into by him—
   (a) without disclosing that he is acting as guardian of the adult; or
   (b) which falls outwith the scope of his authority,
but where a guardian has acted as mentioned in paragraph (a) and is not otherwise in breach of any requirement of this Act relating to such guardians, he shall be entitled to be reimbursed from the estate of the adult in respect of any loss suffered by him in consequence of a claim made upon him personally by virtue of this subsection.

(5) Where a third party with whom the adult entered into a transaction was aware at the date of entering into the transaction that authority had been granted by the guardian under section 64(1)(e), the transaction shall not be void only on the ground that the adult lacked capacity.

(6) A transaction for value between the guardian purporting to act as such and a third party acting in good faith shall not be invalid on the ground only that—
   (a) the guardian acted outwith the scope of his authority; or
   (b) the guardian failed to observe any requirement, whether substantive or procedural, imposed by or under this Act, or by the sheriff or by the Public Guardian; or
   (c) there was any irregularity whether substantive or procedural in the appointment of the guardian.

(7) In subsections (3) and (4) any reference to a guardian shall include a reference to a guardian (however called) appointed under the law of any country to, or entitled under the law of any country to act for, an adult during his incapacity, if the guardianship is recognised by the law of Scotland.

Reimbursement and remuneration of guardian

68.—(1) A guardian shall be entitled to be reimbursed out of the estate of the adult for any outlays reasonably incurred by him in the exercise of his functions.

(2) In subsection (1),"outlays", in relation to a guardian—
(a) who is someone other than the chief social work officer of a local authority, includes payment for items and services other than those items and services which the guardian is expected to provide as part of his functions;
(b) who is the chief social work officer of a local authority, includes payment for items and services only if they would not normally be provided free of charge by the local authority to a person who is in similar circumstances but who does not have a guardian.

(3) The local authority shall, in relation to the cost of any application by them for appointment of their chief social work officer as guardian or of any subsequent application by that officer while acting as guardian—
(a) where the application relates to the personal welfare of the adult, meet such cost;
(b) where the application relates to the property or financial affairs of the adult, be entitled to recover such cost from the estate of the adult,
and where the application relates to the personal welfare and to the property or financial affairs of the adult the sheriff shall, in determining the application, apportion the cost as he thinks fit.

(4) Remuneration shall be payable out of the adult's estate—
(a) in respect of the exercise of functions relating to the personal welfare of the adult, only in a case where special cause is shown;
(b) in respect of the exercise of functions relating to the property or financial affairs of the adult, unless the sheriff directs otherwise in the order appointing the guardian,
but shall not be payable to a local authority in respect of the exercise by their chief social work officer of functions relating to the personal welfare of the adult.

(5) In determining whether or not to make a direction under subsection (4)(b), the sheriff shall take into account the value of the estate and the likely difficulty of managing it.

(6) Any remuneration payable to the guardian and the amount of outlays to be allowed under subsection (1) shall be fixed by the Public Guardian—
(a) in a case where the guardian is required to submit accounts, when the guardian's accounts for that period are audited;
(b) in any other case, on an application by the guardian,
and in fixing the remuneration to be paid to the guardian the Public Guardian shall take into account the value of the estate.

(7) The Public Guardian may allow payments to account to be made by way of remuneration during the accounting period if it would be unreasonable to expect the guardian to wait for payment until the end of an accounting period.

(8) A decision by the Public Guardian—
(a) under subsection (6) as to the remuneration payable and the outlays allowable to the guardian;
(b) under subsection (7) as to payments to account to the guardian
may be appealed to the sheriff, whose decision shall be final.

Forfeiture of guardian's remuneration

69. Where a guardian is in breach of any duty of care, fiduciary duty or obligation imposed by this Act the sheriff may, on an application being made to him by any person claiming an interest in the property, financial affairs or personal welfare of the adult, order the forfeiture (in whole or in part) of any remuneration due to the guardian.

Non-compliance with decisions of guardian with welfare powers

A1–70 **70.**—(1) Where any decision of a guardian with powers relating to the personal welfare of the adult is not complied with by the adult or by any other person, and the adult or other person might reasonably be expected to comply with the decision, the sheriff may, on an application by the guardian—
   (a) make an order ordaining the adult or any person named in the order to implement the decision of the guardian;
   (b) where the non-compliance relates to a decision of the guardian as to the place of residence of the adult, grant a warrant authorising a constable—
      (i) to enter any premises where the adult is, or is reasonably supposed to be;
      (ii) to apprehend the adult and to remove him to such place as the guardian may direct.

(2) Where any decision of a guardian with powers relating to the personal welfare of the adult is not complied with by any person other than the adult, and that person might reasonably be expected to comply with the decision, the sheriff may, on an application by the guardian make an order ordaining the person named in the order to implement the decision of the guardian.

(3) On receipt of an application in the prescribed form for an order or warrant under subsection (1) or for an order under subsection (2), the court shall intimate the application to the adult or, as the case may be, to the person named in the application as a person against whom the order or warrant is sought and shall advise them of the prescribed period within which they may object to the granting of the application; and the sheriff shall not grant the order or warrant without affording to any objector an opportunity of being heard.

(4) Having heard any objections as mentioned in subsection (3), the sheriff may grant the application.

(5) A constable executing a warrant under subsection (1)(b) may use such force as is reasonable in the circumstances and shall be accompanied by the guardian or such person as the guardian may authorise in writing.

(6) In this section any reference to a guardian shall include a reference to a guardian (however called) appointed under the law of any country to, or entitled under the law of any country to act for, an adult during his incapacity, if the guardianship is recognised by the law of Scotland.

Termination and variation of guardianship and replacement, removal or resignation of guardian

Replacement or removal of guardian or recall of guardianship by sheriff

A1–71 **71.**—(1) The sheriff, on an application made to him by an adult subject to guardianship or by any other person claiming an interest in the adult's property, financial affairs or personal welfare, may—
   (a) replace a guardian by an individual or office holder nominated in the application if he is satisfied, in relation to an individual, that he is suitable for appointment having regard to the matters set out in section 59(3) to (5);
   (b) remove a guardian from office if he is satisfied—
      (i) that there is a substitute guardian who is prepared to act as guardian; or
      (ii) in a case where there are joint guardians, that the remaining guardian is or remaining guardians are prepared to continue to act; or
   (c) recall a guardianship order or otherwise terminate a guardianship if he is satisfied—
      (i) that the grounds for appointment of a guardian are no longer fulfilled; or
      (ii) that the interests of the adult in his property, financial affairs or personal welfare can be satisfactorily safeguarded or promoted otherwise than by guardianship,

and where an application under this subsection is granted, the sheriff clerk shall send a copy of the interlocutor to the Public Guardian.

(2) In making an order replacing a guardian by an individual with powers relating to the property or financial affairs of the adult or removing a guardian from office where there is a substitute guardian with such powers prepared to act as guardian, the sheriff shall, except where—
   (a) the individual or substitute guardian is unable to find caution; but
   (b) the sheriff is satisfied that nevertheless he is suitable to be appointed guardian or substitute guardian, as the case may be,
require an individual appointed as guardian or the substitute guardian to find caution.

(3) The Public Guardian on receiving a copy of the interlocutor under subsection (1) shall—
   (a) enter prescribed particulars in the register maintained by him under section 6(2)(b)(iv);
   (b) where the sheriff—
      (i) replaces the guardian by the individual or office holder nominated in the application, when satisfied that, in the case of an individual, the individual has found caution if so required, issue him with a certificate of appointment;
      (ii) removes a guardian from office and a substitute guardian is prepared to act, when satisfied that the substitute guardian has found caution if so required, issue the substitute guardian with a certificate of appointment;
      (iii) removes a joint guardian from office and there is a joint guardian who is prepared to continue to act, issue a remaining joint guardian with a new certificate of appointment;
   (c) notify the adult and the local authority and (in a case where the incapacity of the adult is by reason of, or reasons which include, mental disorder and the guardianship order relates to the adult's personal welfare or factors including it) the Mental Welfare Commission.

(4) Where the sheriff recalls the guardianship order he may at the same time make an intervention order.

(5) In this section any reference to a guardian shall include a reference to a guardian (however called) appointed under the law of any country to, or entitled under the law of any country to act for, an adult during his incapacity, if the guardianship is recognised by the law of Scotland; and "guardianship order" shall be construed accordingly.

Discharge of guardian with financial powers

72.—(1) At any time after—　　　　　　　　　　　　　　　　　　　　　　　　A1–72
   (a) the recall of a guardianship order appointing a guardian with powers relating to the property or financial affairs of an adult;
   (b) the resignation, removal or replacement of such a guardian; or
   (c) the death of the adult,
the Public Guardian may, on an application by the former guardian or, if the former guardian has died, his representative, grant a discharge in respect of the former guardian's actings and intromissions with the estate of the adult.

(2) On receipt of an application in the prescribed form, the Public Guardian shall intimate the application to the adult, his nearest relative, his primary carer and any other person who the Public Guardian considers has an interest in the application and advise them of the prescribed period within which they may object to the granting of the application; and he shall not grant the application without affording to any objector an opportunity of being heard.

(3) Having heard any objections as mentioned in subsection (2) the Public Guardian may grant the application.

(4) Where the Public Guardian proposes to refuse the application he shall intimate his decision to the applicant and advise him of the prescribed period within which he may object to the refusal; and he shall not refuse the

application without affording to the applicant, if he objects, an opportunity of being heard.

(5) The Public Guardian may at his own instance or at the instance of the applicant or of any person who objects to the granting of the application remit the application for determination by the sheriff, whose decision shall be final.

(6) A decision of the Public Guardian—
  (a) to grant a discharge under subsection (1) or to refuse a discharge;
  (b) to grant an application under subsection (3) or to refuse an application;
  (c) to refuse to remit an application to the sheriff under subsection (5)
may be appealed to the sheriff, whose decision shall be final.

Recall of powers of guardian

A1–73 73.—(1) The Public Guardian, at his own instance or on an application by any person (including the adult himself) claiming an interest in the property and financial affairs of an adult in respect of whom a guardian has been appointed, may recall the powers of a guardian relating to the property or financial affairs of the adult if it appears to him that—
  (a) the grounds for appointment of a guardian with such powers are no longer fulfilled; or
  (b) the interests of the adult in his property and financial affairs can be satisfactorily safeguarded or promoted otherwise than by guardianship.

(2) Where the Public Guardian recalls the powers of a guardian under subsection (1) he shall—
  (a) enter prescribed particulars in the register maintained by him under section 6(2)(b)(iv);
  (b) notify the adult, the guardian and the local authority.

(3) The Mental Welfare Commission or the local authority in whose area an adult in respect of whom a guardian has been appointed habitually resides (other than a local authority whose chief social work officer has been appointed guardian), at their own instance or on an application by any person (including the adult himself) claiming an interest in the personal welfare of the adult, may recall the powers of a guardian relating to the personal welfare of the adult if it appears to them that—
  (a) the grounds for appointment of a guardian with such powers are no longer fulfilled; or
  (b) the interests of the adult in his personal welfare can be satisfactorily safeguarded or promoted otherwise than by guardianship.

(4) Where the Mental Welfare Commission or the local authority recall the powers of a guardian under subsection (3) they shall notify the other and the Public Guardian who shall—
  (a) enter prescribed particulars in the register maintained by him under section 6(2)(b)(iv);
  (b) notify the adult and the guardian.

(5) The Public Guardian, Mental Welfare Commission or local authority, as the case may be, shall—
  (a) where acting on an application, on receipt of the application in the prescribed form intimate it;
  (b) where acting at his or their own instance, intimate the intention to recall the powers of a guardian,
to the adult, his nearest relative, his primary carer and any person who he or they consider has an interest in the recall of the powers and advise them of the prescribed period within which they may object to such recall; and he or they shall not recall the powers without affording to any objector an opportunity of being heard.

(6) Having heard any objections as mentioned in subsection (5) the Public Guardian, Mental Welfare Commission or local authority may recall the powers of a guardian.

(7) Where the Public Guardian, Mental Welfare Commission or local authority proposes or propose to refuse the application he or they shall

intimate the decision to the applicant and the adult and advise them of the prescribed period within which they may object to the refusal; and he or they shall not refuse the application without affording to the applicant or the adult, if he objects, an opportunity of being heard.

(8) The Public Guardian, Mental Welfare Commission or local authority may at his or their own instance or at the instance of an applicant or of any person who objects to the recall of the powers of the guardian remit the matter for determination by the sheriff whose decision shall be final.

(9) A decision of—
(a) the Public Guardian, Mental Welfare Commission or local authority to recall the powers of a guardian under subsection (6);
(b) the Public Guardian, Mental Welfare Commission or local authority to remit or not to remit the matter to the sheriff under subsection (8),

may be appealed to the sheriff, whose decision shall be final, and the decision of the Public Guardian, Mental Welfare Commission or local authority as to the recall of the powers of a guardian shall remain in force pending the final determination of the appeal.

(10) The Scottish Ministers may prescribe the forms and procedure for the purposes of any recall of guardianship powers by the Mental Welfare Commission or the local authority.

Variation of guardianship order

74.—(1) The sheriff, on an application by any person (including the adult himself) claiming an interest in the property, financial affairs or personal welfare of the adult, may vary the powers conferred by the guardianship order and may vary any existing ancillary order. **A1–74**

(2) In varying powers relating to the property or financial affairs of the adult conferred by the guardianship order or in varying any ancillary order in relation to such powers the sheriff shall, except where—
(a) the guardian is unable to find caution; but
(b) the sheriff is satisfied that nevertheless it is appropriate to vary the powers conferred by the guardianship order or to vary the ancillary order,

require the guardian to find caution.

(3) In considering an application under subsection (1), the sheriff shall have regard to any intervention order or guardianship order which may have been previously made in relation to the adult or any other order varying such an order, and to any order ancillary to such an order.

(4) Notwithstanding subsection (1), an application which seeks to vary the powers conferred by a guardianship order or to vary an ancillary order so that—
(a) a guardian, appointed only in relation to the personal welfare of an adult, shall be appointed also or instead in relation to the property or financial affairs of the adult; or
(b) a guardian, appointed only in relation to the property or financial affairs of an adult, shall be appointed also or instead in relation to the personal welfare of the adult;

shall be made under section 57.

(5) Where the sheriff varies the powers conferred by a guardianship order or varies an ancillary order under this section, the sheriff clerk shall send a copy of the interlocutor containing the order to the Public Guardian who shall—
(a) enter prescribed particulars in the register maintained by him under section 6(2)(b)(iv);
(b) notify the adult and the local authority and (in a case where the incapacity of the adult is by reason of, or reasons which include, mental disorder and the guardianship order relates to the adult's personal welfare or factors including it) the Mental Welfare Commission; and
(c) if he is satisfied that the guardian has caution, if so required, which covers the varied order, issue a new certificate of appointment where necessary.

Resignation of guardian

A1-75 **75.**—(1) A joint guardian, or a guardian in respect of whom a substitute guardian has been appointed, may resign by giving notice in writing of his intention to do so to the Public Guardian and the local authority and (in a case where the incapacity of the adult is by reason of, or reasons which include, mental disorder and the guardianship order relates to the adult's personal welfare or factors including it) the Mental Welfare Commission.

(2) The resignation of a guardian as mentioned in subsection (1)—
 (a) shall not take effect unless—
  (i) the remaining joint guardian is willing to continue to act; or
  (ii) the substitute guardian is willing to act;
 (b) shall take effect on the receipt by the Public Guardian of notice in writing under subsection (1) together with evidence as to the matters contained in paragraph (a)(i) or (ii).

(3) On receiving notice in writing and evidence as mentioned in subsection (2)(b), the Public Guardian shall—
 (a) enter prescribed particulars in the register maintained by him under section 6(2)(b)(iv);
 (b) if satisfied that the substitute guardian has found caution if so required, issue him with a new certificate of appointment;
 (c) issue a remaining joint guardian with a new certificate of appointment;
 (d) notify the adult.

(4) A substitute guardian who has not subsequently become guardian by virtue of section 63 may resign by giving notice in writing to the Public Guardian and the local authority and (in the case mentioned in subsection (1)) the Mental Welfare Commission and the resignation shall take effect on the date of receipt of the notice by the Public Guardian; and on its becoming effective, the Public Guardian shall—
 (a) notify the guardian and the adult; and
 (b) enter prescribed particulars in the register maintained by him under section 6(2)(b)(iv).

(5) A guardian—
 (a) who has no joint guardian; or
 (b) in respect of whom no substitute guardian has been appointed; or
 (c) being a joint guardian or guardian in respect of whom a substitute has been appointed who cannot effectively resign by reason of subsection (2)(a)(i) or (ii),
shall not resign until a replacement guardian has been appointed under section 71.

Change of habitual residence

A1-76 **76.**—(1) Where the guardian is the chief social work officer of the local authority and the adult changes his place of habitual residence to the area of another local authority, the chief social work officer of the first mentioned local authority shall notify the chief social work officer of the second mentioned local authority (the "receiving authority") who shall become guardian on receipt of the notification and shall within 7 days of that receipt notify the Public Guardian and (in a case where the incapacity of the adult is by reason of, or reasons which include, mental disorder and the guardianship order relates to the adult's personal welfare or factors which include it) the Mental Welfare Commission.

(2) The Public Guardian shall—
 (a) enter prescribed particulars in the register maintained by him under section 6(2)(b)(iv) and issue a certificate of appointment to the new guardian; and
 (b) subject to subsection (4), notify the adult within 7 days of receipt of the notification from the receiving authority.

(3) Subject to subsection (4), the chief social work officer of the receiving authority shall, within 7 working days of receipt of the notification, notify any

person who received notification under section 58(7) of the appointment of the name of the officer responsible at any time for carrying out the functions and duties of guardian.

(4) If, in relation to the original application for a guardianship order, the sheriff has directed that intimation or notification of any application or other proceedings should not be given to the adult, the Public Guardian and the chief social work officer shall not notify the adult under subsection (2)(b) or (3) as the case may be.

Termination of authority to intervene and guardianship on death of adult

Termination of authority to intervene and guardianship on death of adult

77.—(1) An intervention order or a guardianship order in respect of an adult under this Part shall cease to have effect on his death.

(2) A person authorised under an intervention order or a guardian having powers relating to the property or financial affairs of the adult shall, until he becomes aware of the death of the adult or of any other event which has the effect of terminating his authority, be entitled to act under those powers if he acts in good faith.

(3) Where the authority of a person authorised under an intervention order or of a guardian (including a joint guardian) is terminated or otherwise comes to an end, a third party in good faith is entitled to rely on the authority of the person or guardian if he is unaware of the termination or ending of that authority.

(4) No title to any interest in heritable property acquired by a third party in good faith and for value from a person authorised under an intervention order or from a guardian having powers relating to the property or financial affairs of the adult shall be challengeable on the grounds only of the termination or coming to an end of the authority of the person or of the guardian.

(5) In this section any reference to a guardian shall include a reference to a guardian (however called) appointed under the law of any country to, or entitled under the law of any country to act for, an adult during his incapacity, if the guardianship is recognised by the law of Scotland.

Amendment of registration under section 61 on events affecting guardianship or death of adult

78.—(1) The Public Guardian shall—
    (a) where under section 71(3)(a), 73(2)(a), 74(5)(a) or 75(3)(a) he enters in the register maintained by him under section 6(2)(b)(iv) prescribed particulars relating to a guardianship order in respect of which the appointment of the guardian was recorded or registered under section 61; or
    (b) where an adult in respect of whom there was such a guardianship order has died,
apply forthwith to the Keeper of the Registers of Scotland for the recording of the interlocutor or other document vouching the event giving rise to the entry or, as the case may be, the certificate of the death or, as the case may be, the registering of the event or the death in the Land Register of Scotland.

(2) On an application under subsection (1), the Keeper shall, as appropriate—
    (a) record the interlocutor or other document or certificate in the Register of Sasines and endorse it that it has been so recorded;
    (b) update the title sheet of the heritable property accordingly.

Protection of third parties: guardianship

79. Where a third party has acquired, in good faith and for value, title to any interest in heritable property from a guardian that title shall not be challengeable on the ground only—

(a) of any irregularity of procedure in making the guardianship order; or
(b) that the guardian has acted outwith the scope of his authority.

PART 7

MISCELLANEOUS

Future appointment of curator bonis etc. incompetent

A1–80 80. In any proceedings begun after the commencement of this Act it shall not be competent to appoint a curator bonis, tutor-dative or tutor-at-law to a person who has attained the age of 16 years.

Repayment of funds

A1–81 81.—(1) Where—
(a) a continuing attorney;
(b) a welfare attorney;
(c) a withdrawer;
(d) a guardian;
(e) a person authorised under an intervention order; or
(f) the managers of an authorised establishment within the meaning of Part 4,

uses or use any funds of an adult in breach of their fiduciary duty or outwith their authority or power to intervene in the affairs of the adult or after having received intimation of the termination or suspension of their authority or power to intervene, they shall be liable to repay the funds so used, with interest thereon at the rate fixed by Act of Sederunt as applicable to a decree of the sheriff, to the account of the adult.

(2) Subsection (1) shall be without prejudice to sections 69 and 82.

Limitation of liability

A1–82 82.—(1) No liability shall be incurred by a guardian, a continuing attorney, a welfare attorney, a person authorised under an intervention order, a withdrawer or the managers of an establishment for any breach of any duty of care or fiduciary duty owed to the adult if he has or they have—
(a) acted reasonably and in good faith and in accordance with the general principles set out in section 1; or
(b) failed to act and the failure was reasonable and in good faith and in accordance with the said general principles.
(2) In this section any reference to—
(a) a guardian shall include a reference to a guardian (however called) appointed under the law of any country to, or entitled under the law of any country to act for, an adult during his incapacity, if the guardianship is recognised by the law of Scotland;
(b) a continuing attorney shall include a reference to a person granted, under a contract, grant or appointment governed by the law of any country, powers (however expressed), relating to the granter's property or financial affairs and having continuing effect notwithstanding the granter's incapacity; and
(c) a welfare attorney shall include a reference to a person granted, under a contract, grant or appointment governed by the law of any country, powers (however expressed) relating to the granter's personal welfare and having effect during the granter's incapacity.

Offence of ill-treatment and wilful neglect

A1–83 83.—(1) It shall be an offence for any person exercising powers under this Act relating to the personal welfare of an adult to ill-treat or wilfully neglect that adult.

(2) A person guilty of an offence under subsection (1) shall be liable—
(a) on summary conviction, to imprisonment for a term not exceeding 6 months or to a fine not exceeding the statutory maximum or both;
(b) on conviction on indictment, to imprisonment for a term not exceeding 2 years or to a fine, or both.

Application to guardians appointed under Criminal Procedure (Scotland) Act 1995

84.—(1) Parts 1, 5, 6 and 7 shall apply to a guardian appointed under section 57(2)(c) or section 58(1) of the Criminal Procedure (Scotland) Act 1995 (c.46) ("the 1995 Act") as they apply to a guardian with powers relating to the personal welfare of an adult appointed under Part 6; and accordingly the 1995 Act shall be amended as follows.
(2) After section 58 there shall be inserted—
"58A. **Application of Adults with Incapacity (Scotland) Act 2000**
(1) Subject to the provisions of this section, the provisions of Parts 1, 5, 6 and 7 of the Adults with Incapacity (Scotland) Act 2000 (asp 4) ("the 2000 Act") apply—
(a) to a guardian appointed by an order of the court under section 57(2)(c), 58(1) or 58(1A) of this Act (in this section referred to as a "guardianship order") whether appointed before or after the coming into force of these provisions, as they apply to a guardian with powers relating to the personal welfare of an adult appointed under section 58 of that Act;
(b) to a person authorised under an intervention order under section 60B of this Act as they apply to a person so authorised under section 53 of that Act.
(2) In making a guardianship order the court shall have regard to any regulations made by the Scottish Ministers under section 64(11) of the 2000 Act and—
(a) shall confer powers, which it shall specify in the order, relating only to the personal welfare of the person;
(b) may appoint a joint guardian;
(c) may appoint a substitute guardian;
(d) may make such consequential or ancillary order, provision or direction as it considers appropriate.
(3) Without prejudice to the generality of subsection (2), or to any other powers conferred by this Act, the court may—
(a) make any order granted by it subject to such conditions and restrictions as appear to it to be appropriate;
(b) order that any reports relating to the person who will be the subject of the order be lodged with the court or that the person be assessed or interviewed and that a report of such assessment or interview be lodged;
(c) make such further inquiry or call for such further information as appears to it to be appropriate;
(d) make such interim order as appears to it to be appropriate pending the disposal of the proceedings.
(4) Where the court makes a guardianship order it shall forthwith send a copy of the interlocutor containing the order to the Public Guardian who shall—
(a) enter prescribed particulars of the appointment in the register maintained by him under section 6(2)(b)(iv) of the 2000 Act;
(b) unless he considers that the notification would be likely to pose a serious risk to the person's health notify the person of the appointment of the guardian; and
(c) notify the local authority and the Mental Welfare Commission of the terms of the interlocutor.
(5) A guardianship order shall continue in force for a period of 3 years or such other period (including an indefinite period) as, on cause shown, the court may determine.

(6) Where any proceedings for the appointment of a guardian under section 57(2)(c) or 58(1) of this Act have been commenced and not determined before the date of coming into force of section 84 of, and paragraph 26 of schedule 5 to, the Adults with Incapacity (Scotland) Act 2000 (asp 4) they shall be determined in accordance with this Act as it was immediately in force before that date.".

NOTE
This section was amended by the Regulation of Care (Scotland) Act 2001 (asp 8), s.79 and Sch.3, para.23(5).

Jurisdiction and private international law

A1–85 85. Schedule 3 shall have effect for the purposes of defining the jurisdiction, in respect of adults who are incapable within the meaning of this Act, of the Scottish judicial and administrative authorities and for making provision as to the private international law of Scotland in that respect.

Regulations

A1–86 86.—(1) Any power of the Scottish Ministers to make regulations under this Act shall be exercisable by statutory instrument subject to annulment in pursuance of a resolution of the Scottish Parliament.

(2) Any such power may be exercised to make different provision for different cases or classes of case and includes power to make such incidental, supplemental, consequential or transitional provision or savings as appear to the Scottish Ministers to be appropriate.

Interpretation

A1–87 87.—(1) In this Act, unless the context otherwise requires—
"adult" shall be construed in accordance with section 1;
"continuing attorney" shall be construed in accordance with section 15;
"guardianship order" shall be construed in accordance with section 58;
"incapable" and "incapacity" shall be construed in accordance with section 1;
"intervention order" shall be construed in accordance with section 53;
"local authority" means a council constituted under section 2 of the Local Government etc. (Scotland) Act 1994 (c.39), and references to a local authority shall be construed as references to the local authority for the area in which the adult resides;
"managers of an establishment" shall be construed in accordance with schedule 1;
"mental disorder" means mental illness (including personality disorder) or mental handicap however caused or manifested; but an adult shall not be treated as suffering from mental disorder by reason only of promiscuity or other immoral conduct, sexual deviancy, dependence on alcohol or drugs, or acting as no prudent person would act;
"Mental Welfare Commission" means the Mental Welfare Commission for Scotland continued in being by section 2 of the 1984 Act;
"nearest relative" means, subject to subsection (2), the person who would be, or would be exercising the functions of, the adult's nearest relative under sections 53 to 57 of the 1984 Act if the adult were a patient within the meaning of that Act and notwithstanding that the person neither is nor was caring for the adult for the purposes of section 53(3) of that Act;
"office holder", in relation to a guardian, means the chief social work officer of the local authority;
"person claiming an interest" includes the local authority, the Mental Welfare Commission and the Public Guardian;
"power of attorney" includes a factory and commission;

"prescribe", except for the purposes of anything which may be or is to be prescribed by the Public Guardian, means prescribe by regulations; and "prescribed" shall be construed accordingly;

"primary carer" in relation to an adult, means the person or organisation primarily engaged in caring for him;

"Public Guardian" shall be construed in accordance with section 6;

"State hospital" shall be construed in accordance with section 102 of the National Health Service (Scotland) Act 1978 (c.29);

"substitute guardian" shall be construed in accordance with section 63;

"welfare attorney" shall be construed in accordance with section 16;

"withdrawer" shall be construed in accordance with section 26;

"the 1984 Act" means the Mental Health (Scotland) Act 1984 (c.36).

(2) Where—

(a) an adult has no spouse or has a spouse but subsection (3) applies; and

(b) a person of the same sex as the adult—

(i) is and has been, for a period of not less than 6 months, living with the adult in a relationship which has the characteristics, other than that the persons are of the opposite sex, of the relationship between husband and wife; or

(ii) if the adult is for the time being an in-patient in a hospital, had so lived with the adult until the adult was admitted;

then that person shall be treated as the nearest relative.

(3) This subsection applies where the adult's spouse is permanently separated from the adult, either by agreement or under an order of a court, or has deserted, or been deserted by, the adult for a period and the desertion persists.

(4) For the purposes of this Act, a person is bankrupt if his estate has been sequestrated for insolvency or he has granted a trust deed which has become a protected trust deed under Schedule 5 to the Bankruptcy (Scotland) Act 1985 (c.66), or he has been adjudged bankrupt in England and Wales, or he has become bankrupt (however expressed) under the law of any other country.

Continuation of existing powers, minor and consequential amendments and repeals

88.—(1) Schedule 4, which contains provisions relating to the continuation of existing powers, shall have effect.

(2) Schedule 5, which contains minor amendments and amendments consequential on the provisions of this Act, shall have effect.

(3) The enactments mentioned in schedule 6 are hereby repealed to the extent specified in the second column of that schedule.

NOTE
Section 88(3) as amended by correction slip

Citation and commencement

89.—(1) This Act may be cited as the Adults with Incapacity (Scotland) Act 2000.

(2) This Act shall come into force on such day as the Scottish Ministers may by order made by statutory instrument appoint and different days may be appointed for different purposes.

(3) Without prejudice to the provisions of schedule 4, an order under subsection (2) may make such transitional provisions and savings as appear to the Scottish Ministers necessary or expedient in connection with any provision brought into force by the order; and where it does so, the statutory instrument under which it is made shall be subject to annulment in pursuance of a resolution of the Scottish Parliament.

SCHEDULE 1

MANAGERS OF AN ESTABLISHMENT

1. For the purposes of Part 4"the managers" of an establishment means—
   (a) in relation to a hospital vested in the Scottish Ministers under the National Health Service (Scotland) Act 1978 (c.29), the Health Board responsible for the administration of that hospital;
   (b) in relation to a hospital managed by a National Health Service trust established under section 12A of the said Act of 1978, the directors of the trust;
   (c) in relation to a State hospital—
      (i) the Scottish Ministers; or
      (ii) if a State Hospital Management Committee has been appointed to manage that hospital, that Committee; or
      (iii) if the management of that hospital has been delegated to a Health Board, to a Special Health Board, to a National Health Service trust or to the Common Services Agency for the Scottish Health Service, that Board, trust or Agency, as the case may be, or any person appointed by the Board, trust or agency, as the case may be, to manage the hospital;
   (d) in relation to a care service or limited registration service—
      (i) the person identified under section 7(2)(b) of the Regulation of Care (Scotland) Act 2001 (asp 8) in the application for registration of the service;
      (ii) if the application is made under section 33(1) of that Act, the local authority or any person appointed by the local authority to manage the service; or
      (iii) if another person has been identified in pursuance of regulations under section 29(7)(j) of that Act, the other person so identified,
   and in paragraph (d) above "care service" and "limited registration service" have the same meanings as in the Regulation of Care (Scotland) Act 2001.
   (e) [. . .]
   (f) [. . .]
   (g) [. . .]

2. The Scottish Ministers may by regulations amend the list of managers in paragraph 1.

NOTE
This Schedule was amended by the Regulation of Care (Scotland) Act 2001 (asp 8), s.79 and Sch.3, para.23(6).

SCHEDULE 2

MANAGEMENT OF ESTATE OF ADULT

Management plan

1.—(1) A guardian with powers relating to the property and financial affairs of the adult shall, unless the sheriff otherwise directs, prepare a plan (a "management plan"), taking account of any directions given by the sheriff in the order appointing him, for the management, investment and realisation of the adult's estate and for the application of the estate to the adult's needs, so far as the estate falls within the guardian's authority.

(2) The management plan shall be submitted in draft by the guardian to the Public Guardian for his approval, along with the inventory of the adult's estate prepared under paragraph 3, not more than one month, or such other period as the Public Guardian may allow, after the submission of the inventory.

(3) The Public Guardian may approve the management plan submitted to him under sub-paragraph (2) or he may approve it with amendments and the plan as so approved or as so amended shall be taken account of by the guardian in the exercise of his functions in relation to the adult.

(4) Before the management plan is approved, the guardian shall, unless the sheriff on appointing him has conferred wider powers, have power only to—
   (a) ingather and take control of the assets of the adult's estate so as to enable him, when the management plan has been approved, to intromit with them;
   (b) make such payments as are necessary to provide for the adult's day to day needs.

(5) The Public Guardian may authorise the guardian to exercise any function within the scope of his authority before the management plan is approved, if it would be unreasonable to delay him exercising that function until the plan had been approved.

(6) The guardian shall keep the management plan under review and shall put forward to the Public Guardian proposals for variation of it whenever it appears to him to be appropriate.

(7) The Public Guardian—
(a) may at any time propose any variation to the management plan; and
(b) shall review the plan whenever the guardian submits his accounts for audit.

(8) The Public Guardian shall notify the guardian of any variation which he proposes to make to the management plan and shall not make any such variation without affording the guardian an opportunity to object.

(9) Having heard any objections by the guardian as mentioned in sub-paragraph (8) the Public Guardian may make the variation with or without amendment.

Directions from sheriff

2. Where the guardian disagrees with any decision made by the Public Guardian in relation to a management plan prepared under paragraph 1, he may apply to the sheriff for a determination in relation to the matter and the sheriff's decision shall be final.

Inventory of estate

3.—(1) A guardian with powers relating to the property or financial affairs of the adult shall, as soon after his appointment as possible and in any event within 3 months of the date of registration of his appointment or such other period as the Public Guardian may allow, submit to the Public Guardian for examination and approval a full inventory of the adult's estate in so far as it falls within the scope of the guardian's authority, along with such supporting documents and additional information as the Public Guardian may require.

(2) The inventory shall be in a form, and contain information, prescribed by the Public Guardian.

(3) Errors in and omissions from the inventory which are discovered by the guardian after the inventory has been approved by the Public Guardian shall be notified by him to the Public Guardian within 6 months of the date of discovery or when submitting his next accounts to the Public Guardian, whichever occurs sooner.

(4) The Public Guardian may dispense with the need for the guardian to submit an inventory under sub-paragraph (1) or may require the guardian to take such other action as he thinks appropriate in lieu of submitting an inventory.

Money

4. The guardian shall deposit all money received by him as guardian in a bank or a building society in an account in the name of the adult and shall ensure that all sums in excess of £500 (or such other sum as may be prescribed) so deposited shall earn interest.

Powers relating to investment and carrying on of business by guardian

5.—(1) Subject to the following provisions of this paragraph, a guardian with powers relating to the property or financial affairs of the adult shall be entitled—
  (a) after obtaining and considering proper advice, to retain any existing investment of the adult;
  (b) to use the adult's estate to make new investments in accordance with the management plan prepared under paragraph 1 or with the consent of the Public Guardian.

(2) For the purpose of sub-paragraph (1)—
  (a) proper advice is the advice of a person who has permission for the purposes of the Financial Services and Markets Act 2000 to advise on investments who is not the guardian or any person who is an employer, employee or business partner of the guardian; and
  (b) the advice must be given or subsequently confirmed in writing.

(2A) Sub-paragraph (2) must be read with—
  (a) section 22 of the Financial Services and Markets Act 2000;
  (b) any relevant order under that section; and
  (c) Schedule 2 to that Act.

(3) The guardian shall keep every investment under review and in doing so shall have regard to the following principles—
  (a) that the investment must be prudent;

(b) that there must be diversification of investments; and
(c) that the investment must be suitable for the adult's estate.
(4) The Public Guardian may at any time direct the guardian to realise any investment.
(5) The guardian may, subject to any direction given by the Public Guardian, carry on any business of the adult.
(6) Any decision by the Public Guardian—
 (a) under sub-paragraph (4) as to directing the guardian to realise investments;
 (b) under sub-paragraph (5) as to giving directions to the guardian in carrying on the business of the adult,
may be appealed to the sheriff, whose decision shall be final.

NOTE
Para.5(2) was amended and para.5(2A) added by the Financial Services and Markets Act 2000 (Consequential Amendments and Repeals) Order 2001 (SI 2001/3649), art.235.

Purchase or disposal of accommodation

6.—(1) The guardian shall not, without the consent of the Public Guardian—
 (a) in principle; and
 (b) to the purchase or selling price,
purchase accommodation for, or dispose of any accommodation used for the time being as a dwelling house by, the adult.
(2) On receipt of an application for consent in principle under sub-paragraph (1)(a) in the prescribed form, the Public Guardian shall intimate the application to the adult, his nearest relative, his primary carer and any person who the Public Guardian considers has an interest in the application and advise them of the prescribed period within which they may object to the granting of the application.
(3) The Public Guardian shall remit any objection under sub-paragraph (2) for determination by the sheriff (whose decision shall be final) and—
 (a) if the sheriff upholds the objection, shall refuse the application;
 (b) if the sheriff dismisses the objection, shall grant the application.
(4) Where the Public Guardian proposes to refuse the application other than under sub-paragraph (3)(a) he shall intimate his decision to the applicant and advise him of the prescribed period within which he may object to the refusal; and he shall not refuse the application without affording the applicant, if he objects, an opportunity of being heard.
(5) Having heard any objections as mentioned in sub-paragraph (4) or where there is no objection as mentioned in sub-paragraph (2), the Public Guardian may grant the application.
(6) The Public Guardian may at his own instance or at the instance of any person who objects to the granting or refusal (other than a refusal under sub-paragraph (3)(a)) of the application remit the application to the sheriff for determination by the sheriff, whose decision shall be final.
(7) If consent in principle to the purchase or disposal of the accommodation is given, the guardian shall apply to the Public Guardian for consent under sub-paragraph (1)(b) to the purchase or selling price.
(8) A decision of the Public Guardian—
 (a) to grant or to refuse (other than under sub-paragraph (3)(a)) an application; or
 (b) to refuse to remit an application to the sheriff under sub-paragraph (6),
may be appealed to the sheriff, whose decision shall be final.
(9) A decision of the Public Guardian to give or to refuse consent under sub-paragraph (1)(b) shall be final.

Accounting and auditing

7.—(1) A guardian with powers relating to the property or financial affairs of the adult shall submit accounts in respect of each accounting period to the Public Guardian within one month from the end of the accounting period or such longer period as the Public Guardian may allow.
(2) There shall be submitted with the accounts under sub-paragraph (1) such supporting documents as the Public Guardian may require, and the Public Guardian may require the guardian to furnish him with such information in connection with the accounts as the Public Guardian may determine.
(3) For the purposes of this paragraph, the first accounting period shall commence with the date of appointment of the guardian and end at such date not later than 18

months after the date of registration of the guardian's appointment as the Public Guardian may determine; and thereafter each accounting period shall be a year commencing with the date on which the immediately previous accounting period ended.

(4) Notwithstanding the foregoing provisions of this paragraph, the Public Guardian may at any time—
   (a) give directions as to the frequency of accounting periods;
   (b) dispense with the need for the submission of accounts by the guardian; or
   (c) require the guardian to do anything which the Public Guardian thinks appropriate in lieu of submitting accounts.

(5) The accounts shall be in such form as is prescribed by the Public Guardian and different forms may be prescribed for different cases or descriptions of case.

(6) Where the estate of the adult includes a business or an interest in a business that part of the accounts which relates to the business or to the interest in the business shall be accompanied by a certificate from such person and in such form as may be prescribed by the Public Guardian, certifying the accuracy of that part of the accounts.

(7) The accounts submitted to the Public Guardian under sub-paragraph (1) (other than any part to which a certificate as mentioned in sub-paragraph (6) relates) shall be audited by the Public Guardian or by an accountant appointed by, and responsible to, the Public Guardian for that purpose.

Approval of accounts

8.—(1) After the accounts of the guardian have been audited, the Public Guardian shall, if the accounts appear to him—
   (a) to be a true and fair view of the guardian's management of the adult's estate, approve them and fix the remuneration (if any) due to the guardian;
   (b) not to be a true and fair view of the guardian's management of the adult's estate, prepare a report as to the extent to which they do not represent such a true and fair view and adjusting the accounts accordingly.

(2) The Public Guardian may approve the accounts, notwithstanding any minor inconsistencies or absence of full documentation in the accounts, if he is satisfied that the guardian acted reasonably and in good faith.

(3) The Public Guardian shall send any report prepared by him under sub-paragraph (1)(b) to the guardian, who may object to anything contained in the report within 28 days of it being sent to him.

(4) If no objection is taken to the report, the accounts as adjusted by the Public Guardian shall be regarded as approved by him.

(5) Where any objection taken to the report cannot be resolved between the guardian and the Public Guardian, the matter may be determined by the sheriff on an application by the guardian, and the sheriff's decision shall be final.

(6) Without prejudice to sub-paragraph (7), the guardian shall be liable to make good any deficiency revealed by the accounts as approved by the Public Guardian under sub-paragraph (1)(a).

(7) Where a deficiency is revealed as mentioned in sub-paragraph (6), the Public Guardian may require the guardian to pay interest to the adult's estate on the amount of the deficiency at the rate fixed by Act of Sederunt as applicable to a decree of the sheriff in respect of the period for which it appears that the deficiency has existed.

SCHEDULE 3

JURISDICTION AND PRIVATE INTERNATIONAL LAW

General

1.—(1) The Scottish judicial and administrative authorities shall have jurisdiction to dispose of an application or other proceedings and otherwise carry out functions under this Act in relation to an adult if—
   (a) the adult is habitually resident in Scotland; or
   (b) property which is the subject of the application or proceedings or in respect of which functions are carried out under this Act is in Scotland; or
   (c) the adult, although not habitually resident in Scotland is there or property belonging to the adult is there and, in either case, it is a matter of urgency that the application is or the proceedings are dealt with; or

A1–92

(d) the adult is present in Scotland and the intervention sought in the application or proceedings is of a temporary nature and its effect limited to Scotland.

(2) As from the ratification date, the Scottish judicial and administrative authorities shall, in addition to the jurisdiction mentioned in sub-paragraph (1) in the circumstances set out therein, have the jurisdiction mentioned in that sub-paragraph in the following circumstances—
(a) the adult—
  (i) is a British citizen; and
  (ii) has a closer connection with Scotland than with any other part of the United Kingdom; and
(b) Article 7 of the Convention has been complied with,

or if the Scottish Central Authority, having received a request under Article 8 of the Convention from an authority of the State in which the adult is habitually resident and consulted such authorities in Scotland as would, under this Act, have functions in relation to the adult, have agreed to the request.

(3) As from the ratification date, the provisions of the Convention shall apply to the exercise of jurisdiction under this schedule where the adult—
(a) is habitually resident in a Contracting State other than the United Kingdom; or
(b) not being habitually resident in Scotland, is or has been the subject of protective proceedings in such a Contracting State.

(4) As from the ratification date, any application made to a Scottish judicial or administrative authority under this Act which—
(a) relates to an adult who is not habitually resident in Scotland; and
(b) does not require to be determined as a matter of urgency,

shall be accompanied by information as to which State the adult habitually resides in and as to any other application relating to the adult which has been dealt with or is being made, or proceedings so relating which have been or are being brought, in any Contracting State other than the United Kingdom.

(5) For the purposes of this paragraph, an adult—
(a) whose habitual residence cannot be ascertained; or
(b) who is a refugee or has been internationally displaced by disturbance in the country of his habitual residence,

shall be taken to be habitually resident in the State which he is in.

Appropriate sheriff

2.—(1) The sheriff having jurisdiction under this schedule to take measures is the sheriff in whose sheriffdom—
(a) in relation to a case falling within paragraph 1(1)(a), the adult is habitually resident;
(b) in relation to a case falling within paragraph 1(1)(b), the property is located;
(c) in relation to a case falling within paragraph 1(1)(c), the adult or property belonging to the adult is present;
(d) in relation to a case falling within paragraph 1(1)(d), the adult is present.

(2) The sheriff shall also have jurisdiction to vary or recall any intervention order or guardianship order made by him under this Act if no Contracting State other than the United Kingdom has, by way of its judicial or administrative authorities, jurisdiction; and—
(a) no other court or authority has jurisdiction; or
(b) another court or authority has jurisdiction but—
  (i) it would be unreasonable to expect an applicant to invoke it; or
  (ii) that court or authority has declined to exercise it.

(3) Notwithstanding that any other judicial or administrative authority has jurisdiction under sub-paragraph (1)(a) to take measures, a sheriff shall have jurisdiction to take measures if—
(a) the adult is present in the sheriffdom; and
(b) the sheriff considers that it is necessary, in the interests of the adult, to take the measures immediately.

(4) Where, by operation of paragraph 1, jurisdiction falls to be exercised by a sheriff but the case is one appearing to fall outside sub-paragraphs (1) and (2), the sheriff having jurisdiction is the Sheriff of the Lothians and Borders at Edinburgh.

Applicable law

3.—(1) The law applicable to anything done under this Act by a Scottish judicial or administrative authority in relation to an adult is the law of Scotland.

(2) Sub-paragraph (1) does not prevent a Scottish judicial or administrative authority from applying the law of a country other than Scotland if, in circumstances which demonstrate a substantial connection with that other country and having regard to the interests of the adult, it appears appropriate to do so.

(3) Such an authority shall, however, in the exercise of the powers conferred by section 18 of this Act, take into consideration to the extent possible the law which, as provided in paragraph 4, governs the power of attorney.

(4) Where a measure for the protection of an adult has been taken in one State and is implemented in another, the conditions of its implementation are governed by the law of that other State.

(5) Any question whether a person has authority by virtue of any enactment or rule of law to represent an adult shall be governed—
- (a) where such representation is for the purposes of the immediate personal welfare of the adult and the adult is in Scotland, by the law of Scotland; and
- (b) in any other case, by the law of the country in which the adult is habitually resident.

4.—(1) The law governing the existence, extent, modification and extinction of continuing or welfare powers of attorney (including like powers, however described) shall be that of the State in which the granter habitually resided at the time of the grant of these powers.

(2) Where, however, the granter of such a power of attorney so provides in writing, the law so applicable shall instead be the law of a State—
- (a) of which the granter is a national;
- (b) in which the granter was habitually resident before the grant; or
- (c) in which the property of the granter is located.

(3) The manner of exercise of such a power shall be governed by the law of the State in which its exercise takes place.

(4) The law of a State may be applied under sub-paragraph (2)(c) above only in respect of the property referred to in that provision.

(5) Nothing in sub-paragraphs (1) and (2) prevents the sheriff from exercising powers under section 20 of this Act if a power of attorney is not being exercised so as to safeguard the welfare or property of the granter.

(6) It is not an objection to the validity of any contract or other transaction between a person acting or purporting to act as the representative of an adult and any other person that the person so acting or purporting to act was not entitled so to act under the law of a country other than the country where the contract or other transaction was concluded.

(7) Sub-paragraph (6) does not, however, apply where the other person knew or ought to have known that the entitlement so to act of the person acting or purporting to act as representative was governed by the law of that other country.

(8) Sub-paragraph (6) applies only if the persons entering into the contract or other transaction were, when they did so, both (or all) in the same country.

5. Nothing in this schedule displaces any enactment or rule of law which has mandatory effect for the protection of an adult with incapacity in Scotland whatever law would otherwise be applicable.

6. Nothing in this schedule requires or enables the application in Scotland of any provision of the law of a country other than Scotland so as to produce a result which would be manifestly contrary to public policy.

Recognition and enforcement

7.—(1) Any measure taken under the law of a country other than Scotland for the personal welfare or the protection of property of an adult with incapacity shall, if one of the conditions specified in sub-paragraph (2) is met, be recognised by the law of Scotland.

(2) These conditions are—
- (a) that the jurisdiction of the authority of the other country was based on the adult's habitual residence there;
- (b) that the United Kingdom and the other country were, when the measure was taken, parties to the Convention and the jurisdiction of the authority of the other country was based on a ground of jurisdiction provided for in the Convention.

(3) Recognition of a measure may, however, be refused—
- (a) if, except in a case of urgency—
  - (i) the authority which took it did so without the adult to whom it related being given an opportunity to be heard; and
  - (ii) these circumstances constituted a breach of natural justice;

(b) if it would be manifestly contrary to public policy to recognise the measure;
(c) if the measure conflicts with any enactment or rule of law of Scotland which is mandatory whatever law would otherwise be applicable;
(d) if the measure is incompatible with a later measure taken in Scotland or recognised by the law of Scotland;
(e) if the measure would have the effect of placing the adult in an establishment in Scotland and—
   (i) the Scottish Central Authority has not previously been provided with a report on the adult and a statement of the reasons for the proposed placement and has not been consulted on the proposed placement; or
   (ii) where the Authority has been provided with such a report and statement and so consulted, it has, within a reasonable time thereafter, declared that it disapproves of the proposed placement.

8.—(1) A measure which is enforceable in the country of origin and which is recognised under paragraph 7 by the law of Scotland may, in accordance with rules of court, be registered.

(2) A measure so registered shall be as enforceable as a measure having the like effect granted by a court in Scotland.

9.—(1) For the purposes of recognition or enforcement of a measure taken outside Scotland in relation to an adult, findings of fact going to jurisdiction made by the authority taking the measure are conclusive of the facts found.

(2) The validity or merits of a measure falling to be recognised by the law of Scotland by virtue of this schedule shall not be questioned in any proceedings except for the purposes of ascertaining its compliance with any provision of this schedule.

10.—(1) The Scottish Ministers may, by order, provide for the recognition and enforcement of orders made and other measures taken by authorities in any part of the United Kingdom other than Scotland.

(2) The provision so made shall accord no less recognition and secure that these orders and measures are no less enforceable than if they were measures which are recognised by the law of Scotland under paragraph 7.

Co-operation, avoidance of conflict of jurisdiction and compliance with the Convention

11.—(1) Her Majesty may by Order in Council confer on the Scottish Central Authority, and the Scottish judicial and administrative authorities such powers, and impose on them such duties additional, in each case, to those which they have under this Act, as are necessary or expedient to enable them to give effect in Scotland to the Convention on and after the ratification date.

(2) An Order in Council under sub-paragraph (1) shall be subject to annulment in pursuance of a resolution of the Scottish Parliament.

(3) A certificate delivered in pursuance of Article 38 of the Convention by a designated authority of a Contracting State other than Scotland shall be proof of the matters stated in it unless the contrary is proved.

General

12. No provision of this schedule deriving from or giving effect to the Convention extends to any matter to which the Convention, by Article 4 thereof, does not apply.

13. Orders or regulations under this schedule shall be made by statutory instrument subject to annulment in pursuance of a resolution of the Scottish Parliament.

14. In this schedule—

"the Convention" means the Hague Convention of 13 January 2000 on the International Protection of Adults;

a "measure for the personal welfare or protection of the property" of an adult with incapacity includes any order, direction or decision effecting or relating to—
   (a) the determination of the incapacity and the institution of appropriate measures of protection;
   (b) the placing of the adult under the protection of a judicial or administrative authority;
   (c) guardianship, curatorship or analogous institutions;
   (d) the appointment and functions of any person or body having charge of the adult's person or property or otherwise representing the adult;
   (e) the placement of the adult in an establishment or other place where the personal welfare of the adult is safeguarded;
   (f) the administration, conservation or disposal of the adult's property; or
   (g) the authorisation of a specific intervention for the personal welfare or protection of the property of the adult;

the "ratification date" means the date when the Convention is ratified as respects Scotland;
the "Scottish Central Authority" means—
(a) an authority designated under Article 28 of the Convention for the purposes of acting as such; or
(b) if no authority has been so designated any authority appointed by the Scottish Ministers for the purposes of carrying out the functions to be carried out under this schedule by the Scottish Central Authority;
the "Scottish judicial and administrative authorities" means the courts having functions under this Act and the Public Guardian, the Mental Welfare Commission, local authorities and supervisory bodies.

SCHEDULE 4

CONTINUATION OF EXISTING CURATORS, TUTORS, GUARDIANS AND ATTORNEYS UNDER THIS ACT

Curators and tutors

1.—(1) On the relevant date, any person holding office as curator bonis to an adult shall become guardian of that adult with power to manage the property or financial affairs of the adult.   **A1–93**
(2) Where a person—
(a) before the relevant date, holds office as curator bonis to a person who has not attained the age of 16 years and does not hold such office for the sole reason that the person has not attained the age of 16 years; or
(b) after the relevant date, is appointed as curator bonis to such a person,
he shall become guardian of that person when that person attains the age of 16 years, with power to manage his property or financial affairs.
(3) Where any proceedings for the appointment of a curator bonis to an adult have been commenced and not determined before the relevant date, they shall be determined in accordance with the law as it was immediately before that date; and any person appointed curator bonis shall become guardian of that adult with power to manage the property or financial affairs of the adult.
(4) On the relevant date, any person holding office as tutor-dative to an adult shall become guardian of that adult and shall continue to have the powers conferred by the court on his appointment as tutor-dative.
(5) Where any proceedings for the appointment of a tutor-dative to an adult have been commenced and not determined before the relevant date, they shall be determined in accordance with the law as it was immediately before that date; and any person appointed tutor-dative shall become guardian of that adult with such power to manage the property, financial affairs or personal welfare of the adult as the court may determine.
(6) On the relevant date, any person holding office as tutor-at-law to an adult shall become guardian of that adult with power to manage the property, financial affairs or personal welfare of the adult.
(7) Where any proceedings for the appointment of a tutor-at-law to an adult have been commenced and not determined before the relevant date, they shall be determined in accordance with the law as it was immediately before that date; and any person appointed tutor-at-law shall become guardian of that adult with power to manage the property, financial affairs or personal welfare of the adult.

Guardians

2.—(1) On the relevant date, any person holding office as guardian of an adult under the 1984 Act shall become guardian of that adult under this Act and shall continue to have the powers set out in paragraphs (a) to (c) of section 41(2) of that Act notwithstanding the repeal of that section by this Act.
(2) Where any proceedings for the appointment of such a guardian of an adult have been commenced and not determined before the relevant date, they shall be determined in accordance with the 1984 Act as it was in force immediately before that date; and any person appointed guardian shall become guardian of that adult under this Act with the powers set out in the said paragraphs (a) to (c) of section 41(2) of the 1984 Act.

Proceedings relating to existing appointments

3. Where any proceedings in relation to the functions of an existing curator bonis, tutor-dative, tutor-at-law or guardian have been commenced and not determined before the relevant date, they shall be determined in accordance with the law as it was immediately before that date.

Attorneys

4.—(1) On the relevant date, any person holding office as—
  (a) an attorney under a contract of mandate or agency with powers relating solely to the property or financial affairs of an adult shall become a continuing attorney under this Act;
  (b) an attorney under a contract of mandate or agency with powers relating solely to the personal welfare of an adult shall become a welfare attorney under this Act;
  (c) an attorney under a contract of mandate or agency with powers relating both to the property and financial affairs and to the personal welfare of an adult shall become a continuing attorney and a welfare attorney under this Act.
  (2) Where, under the provisions of a contract of mandate or agency executed before the relevant date, a person is appointed as an attorney after that date he shall be a continuing attorney, a welfare attorney or a continuing and welfare attorney, as provided for in sub-paragraph (1), under this Act.
  (3) For the purposes of their application to persons who have become continuing attorneys by virtue of sub-paragraph (1)(a) or (c), the following provisions shall have effect as modified or disapplied by sub-paragraph (3).
  (4) Sections 6(2)(c)(i), 15, 19, 20(3)(a), 21, 22 and 23 shall not apply.
  (5) For the purposes of their application to persons who have become welfare attorneys by virtue of sub-paragraph (1)(b) or (c) the following provisions shall have effect as modified or disapplied by sub-paragraph (5).
  (6) Sections 16(1) to (4) and (7), 19, 20(3)(a), 21, 22 and 23 shall not apply.

NOTE
Sch.4, para.4 as amended by correction slip

Managers

5.—(1) Any managers of a hospital who have received and hold money and valuables on behalf of any person under section 94 of the 1984 Act may continue to do so under this Act for a period not exceeding 3 years from the relevant date.
  (2) This Act applies to managers as mentioned in sub-paragraph (1) notwithstanding that no certificate has been issued under section 37 in respect of the owner of the money or valuables.
  (3) Sections 35 and 38 shall not apply in the case of managers who continue to hold money by virtue of sub-paragraph (1).
  (4) Where the managers have authority from the Mental Welfare Commission to hold and manage money and other property in excess of the aggregate value mentioned in section 39 they may do so in relation to the money and valuables of any person which they continue to hold under sub-paragraph (1).

NOTE
Sch.4, para.5(4) as amended by correction slip.

Application of Act to persons who become guardians by virtue of this schedule

6.—(1) For the purposes of their application to persons who have become guardians by virtue of this schedule, the following provisions shall have effect as modified or disapplied by this paragraph.
  (2) In section 67(2) the reference to the certificate of appointment issued under section 58 shall be construed as a reference to the order of the court appointing the person as curator bonis, tutor-dative, tutor-at-law or guardian under the 1984 Act, as the case may be.
  (3) Section 60 shall apply to a person who has become a guardian to an adult by virtue of this schedule and who was a curator bonis, tutor dative or tutor-at-law to that adult; and, for the purpose of that application, for the reference in section 60(1) to a period in respect of which a guardianship order has been made or renewed there shall be substituted a reference to the period of 5 years from the relevant date or (in the case

of a curator bonis who has under paragraph 1(2), became guardian to a person on his attaining the age of 16 years) from the date on which the person attained the age of 16 years.

(4) Section 60 shall not apply to a person who has become a guardian to an adult by virtue of this schedule and who was a guardian of that adult under the 1984 Act, in which case the powers shall continue until such time as they would have continued had he not become a guardian by virtue of this schedule to this Act.

(5) In sections 68(2) and (3) and 76 the references to the chief social work officer of the local authority shall be construed as including references to the local authority.

(6) Schedule 2 shall apply only—
(a) in a case where; and
(b) to the extent that,
the Public Guardian has determined that it should apply.

(7) Any determination by the Public Guardian under sub-paragraph (6), or a decision by him not to make such a determination, may be appealed to the sheriff, whose decision shall be final.

(8) No reference in this Act to registration shall have effect in relation to any person who becomes a guardian by virtue of this schedule.

Transitional Provisions

7. Until Part 6 comes into force—
   (a) the references in section 23(1)(c) to a guardian shall be omitted;
   (b) in section 31(7), the reference in paragraph (a) to the appointment of a guardian shall be construed as a reference to the appointment of a curator bonis or tutor-dative or tutor-at-law with powers relating to the funds or accounts in question and paragraph (b) shall be omitted;
   (c) in section 34(1), the reference in paragraph (a) to a guardian shall be construed as a reference to a curator bonis or tutor-dative or tutor-at-law with powers relating to the funds or account in question and paragraph (b) shall be omitted;
   (d) in section 46(1), the reference in paragraph (a) to a guardian shall be construed as a reference to a curator bonis or tutor-dative or tutor-at-law with powers relating to the matter and paragraph (b) shall be omitted.

Interpretation

8. In this schedule the "relevant date" in relation to any paragraph in which it appears means the date of coming into force of that paragraph.

SCHEDULE 5

MINOR AND CONSEQUENTIAL AMENDMENTS

General

1. With effect from the commencement of this paragraph any reference in any enactment or document to a curator bonis or a tutor or curator of a person of or over the age of 16 years shall be construed as a reference to a guardian with similar powers appointed to that person under this Act.

A1–94

Defence Act 1842 (c.94)

2.—(1) In section 15 of the Defence Act 1842—
   (a) after "nonage" in both places there shall be inserted "or mental incapacity";
   (b) "or not of whole mind" shall be repealed;
   (c) for "out of prison, within this land, or of whole mind" there shall be substituted "within this land".
(2) In section 27 of that Act for "lunacy" there shall be substituted "mental incapacity".

Judicial Factors Act 1849 (c.51)

3. In section 34A of the Judicial Factors Act 1849 for "recovery, death or coming of age of the ward" there shall be substituted "coming to an end of the situation giving rise to it".

Improvement of Land Act 1864 (c.114)

4.—(1) In section 24 of the Improvement of Land Act 1864—
   (a) "tutors,", "curators," "tutor," and "curator," shall be repealed;
   (b) for "persons suffering from mental disorder within the meaning of the Mental Health (Scotland) Act, 1960" there shall be substituted "adults who are incapable within the meaning of the Adults with Incapacity (Scotland) Act 2000 (asp 4)".
   (2) In section 68 of that Act for "Mental Health (Scotland) Act 1984" there shall be substituted "Adults with Incapacity (Scotland) Act 2000 (asp 4)".

Titles to Land (Consolidation) (Scotland) Act 1868 (c.101)

5.—(1) In section 24 of the Titles to Land (Consolidation) (Scotland) Act 1868 for "mental disorder within the meaning of the Mental Health (Scotland) Act 1960" there shall be substituted "mental or other incapacity".
   (2) In section 62 of that Act for "of insane mind" there shall be substituted "mental or other incapacity".

Judicial Factors (Scotland) Act 1889 (c.39)

6.—(1) In section 2 of the Judicial Factors (Scotland) Act 1889 at the beginning there shall be inserted "Without prejudice to section 6(1) of the Adults with Incapacity (Scotland) Act 2000 (asp 4) (Accountant of Court to be Public Guardian)".
   (2) In section 6 of that Act, in the proviso, after "apply to" there shall be inserted "guardians appointed under the Adults with Incapacity (Scotland) Act 2000 (asp 4), to".

Heritable Securities (Scotland) Act 1894 (c.44)

7. In section 13 of the Heritable Securities (Scotland) Act 1894—
   (a) after "(b) trustees" there shall be inserted—
      "(c) the person entitled to act as the legal representative of any such person";
   (b) "tutors, curators," shall be repealed.

National Assistance Act 1948 (c.29)

8. In section 49 of the National Assistance Act 1948 as it applies to Scotland—
   (a) immediately before "the council" where last occurring there shall be inserted "or applies for an intervention order or for appointment as a guardian under the Adults with Incapacity (Scotland) Act 2000 (asp 4)";
   (b) immediately before "in so far as" there shall be inserted "or his functions under the intervention order or as guardian".

Offices, Shops and Railway Premises Act 1963 (c.41)

9. In section 90(1) of the Offices, Shops and Railway Premises Act 1963 in the definition of "owner" for ", tutor or curator" there shall be substituted "or person entitled to act as legal representative of a person under disability by reason of nonage or mental or other incapacity".

Social Work (Scotland) Act 1968 (c.49)

10. [. . .]
11. [. . .]

NOTE
Paras 10 and 11 were repealed by the Regulation of Care (Scotland) Act 2001 (asp 8), s.80 and Sch.4.

Medicines Act 1968 (c.67)

12. In section 72 of the Medicines Act 1968—
   (a) in subsection (1) for "curator bonis" there shall be substituted "guardian";
   (b) in subsections (3)(d) and (4)(c) "curator bonis," shall be repealed.

Sheriff Courts (Scotland) Act 1971 (c.58)

13. In section 32(1) of the Sheriff Courts (Scotland) Act 1971 after paragraph (j) there shall be inserted—

Appendix 1

"(k) prescribing the procedure to be followed in appointing a person under section 3(4) of the Adults with Incapacity (Scotland) Act 2000 (asp 4) and the functions of such a person.".

Land Registration (Scotland) Act 1979 (c.33)

14. In section 12(3) of the Land Registration (Scotland) Act 1979 after paragraph (k) there shall be inserted—
"(kk) the loss is suffered by an adult within the meaning of the Adults with Incapacity (Scotland) Act 2000 (asp 4) because of the operation of sections 24, 53, 67, 77 or 79 of that Act, or by any person who acquires any right, title or interest from that adult;".

NOTE
Sch.5, para.14 as amended by correction slip.

Solicitors (Scotland) Act 1980 (c.46)

15. In section 18(1) of the Solicitors (Scotland) Act 1980—
(a) in paragraph (a) "or becomes subject to guardianship" shall be repealed;
(b) for paragraph (b) there shall be substituted—
"(b) a guardian is appointed to a solicitor under the Adults with Incapacity (Scotland) Act 2000 (asp 4);".

Law Reform (Miscellaneous Provisions) (Scotland) Act 1980 (c.55)

16. In group C of Part I of Schedule 1 to the Law Reform (Miscellaneous Provisions) (Scotland) Act 1980 for paragraphs (b) and (c) there shall be substituted—
"(b) persons for the time being subject to guardianship under the Adults with Incapacity (Scotland) Act 2000 (asp 4).".

Mental Health (Scotland) Act 1984 (c.36)

17.—(1) In section 3 of the Mental Health (Scotland) Act 1984—
(a) in subsection (1) "guardianship or" shall be repealed;
(b) in subsection (2) in paragraph (b) "or who are subject to guardianship" shall be repealed.
(2) In section 5(2) of that Act "and the guardian of any person subject to guardianship under this Act" shall be repealed.
(3) In section 19 of that Act—
(a) in subsection (1) for "either by the nearest relative of the patient or by a mental health officer" there shall be substituted "by the nearest relative of the patient, by a mental health officer, or by a guardian or welfare attorney of the patient who has powers to do so";
(b) in subsection (2) after "relative" there shall be inserted ", guardian or welfare attorney, as the case may be,";
(c) in subsection (3) after "relative" in both places there shall be inserted ", guardian or welfare attorney, as the case may be";
(d) in subsection (4) after "patient" where second occurring there shall be inserted "or by a guardian or welfare attorney of the patient";
(e) in subsection (5)(b) after "relative" there shall be inserted "and any guardian or welfare attorney".
(4) In section 20(1)(a) of that Act for "or his nearest relative" there shall be substituted ", his nearest relative, guardian or welfare attorney, as the case may be".
(5) In section 21(2)(b) of that Act—
(a) after "relative" where first occuring there shall be inserted ", guardian or welfare attorney, as the case may be";
(b) after "relative" where second and third occurring there shall be inserted "guardian or welfare attorney".
(6) In section 22(4)(c) of that Act after "relative" there shall be inserted "and any guardian or welfare attorney".
(7) In section 24 of that Act—
(a) in subsection (2) after "relative" there shall be inserted ", of any guardian or welfare attorney who has powers to do so,";
(b) in subsection (5) after "relative" there shall be inserted "and any guardian or welfare attorney".

(8) In section 26 of that Act—
(a) in subsection (1)(b) after "patient" there shall be inserted ", by any guardian or welfare attorney of the patient who has power so to consent,";
(b) in subsection (4)(b) after "relative" where first occurring there shall be inserted "and any guardian or welfare attorney" and after "relative" where second occurring there shall be inserted ", guardian or welfare attorney, as the case may be".
(9) In section 26A of that Act—
(a) in subsection (4) after "relative" there shall be inserted "or any guardian or welfare attorney who has powers to do so";
(b) in subsection (6)(b) after "relative" where first occurring there shall be inserted "and any guardian or welfare attorney" and after "relative" where second occurring there shall be inserted ", guardian or welfare attorney, as the case may be".
(10) In section 29 of that Act—
(a) in subsection (2) after "relative" there shall be inserted ", to any guardian or welfare attorney";
(b) in subsection (4) after "relative" there shall be inserted ", guardian or welfare attorney".
(11) In section 30(5) of that Act after "relative" there shall be inserted "and any guardian or welfare attorney of his".
(12) In section 31B(3) of that Act after "relative" there shall be inserted ", and any welfare attorney,".
(13) In section 33(5) of that Act for "or by the nearest relative" there shall be substituted ", by the nearest relative or by any guardian or welfare attorney who has powers to do so".
(14) In section 34 of that Act—
(a) in subsection (1) after "relative" wherever occurring there shall be inserted ", or guardian or welfare attorney with powers to do so";
(b) in subsection (2) after "relative" where first occurring there shall be inserted ", guardian or welfare attorney, as the case may be" and after "relative" where second occurring there shall be inserted ", guardian or welfare attorney";
(c) in subsection (3) after "relative" there shall be inserted "or by any guardian or welfare attorney".
(15) In section 35 of that Act—
(a) in subsection (1) for "or his nearest relative or both" there shall be substituted ", his nearest relative, his guardian or his welfare attorney or all of them";
(b) in subsection (3) after "relative" there shall be inserted "or any guardian or welfare attorney".
(16) In section 35B of that Act—
(a) in subsection (3)(a) after "patient" where first occurring there shall be inserted "or any guardian of the patient" and after "relative" there shall be inserted "and any welfare attorney of the patient";
(b) in subsection (4) after "relative" there shall be inserted "and any welfare attorney of the patient,".
(17) In section 35C of that Act—
(a) in subsection (3)(b)(i) after "patient" where first occurring there shall be inserted "or any guardian of the patient" and after "relative" there shall be inserted "and any welfare attorney of the patient";
(b) in subsection (4) after "relative" there shall be inserted "and any welfare attorney of the patient,".
(18) In section 35D of that Act—
(a) in subsection (1)(a) after "patient" where first occurring there shall be inserted "or any guardian of the patient" and after "relative" there shall be inserted "and any welfare attorney of the patient";
(b) in subsection (2) after "relative" there shall be inserted "and any welfare attorney of the patient,".
(19) In section 35E of that Act—
(a) in subsection (3)(a) after "patient" where first occurring there shall be inserted "or any guardian of the patient" and after "relative" there shall be inserted "and any welfare attorney of the patient";
(b) in subsection (4)(a) after "patient" where first occurring there shall be inserted "or any guardian of the patient" and after "relative" there shall be inserted "and any welfare attorney of the patient";
(c) in subsection (5) after "relative" there shall be inserted "and any welfare attorney of the patient,".

(20) In section 35G of that Act—
(a) in subsection (2)(a) at the beginning there shall be inserted "any guardian of the patient, and" and after "relative" there shall be inserted "and any welfare attorney of the patient";
(b) in subsection (3) after "relative" there shall be inserted "and any welfare attorney of the patient,".
(21) In section 35I of that Act—
(a) in subsection (2)(a) after "patient" where first occurring there shall be inserted "or any guardian of the patient" and after "relative" there shall be inserted "and any welfare attorney of the patient";
(b) in subsection (3) after "relative" there shall be inserted "and any welfare attorney of the patient,";
(c) in subsection (5)(a) at the beginning there shall be inserted "any guardian of the patient, and" and after "relative" there shall be inserted "and any welfare attorney of the patient".
(22) In section 55(3) of that Act for "apart from section 41(2) of this Act" there shall be substituted "but for the appointment of a guardian under the Adults with Incapacity (Scotland) Act 2000 (asp 4)".
(23) In section 95 of that Act—
(a) in subsection (1) after "tutor" there shall be inserted ", guardian";
(b) in subsection (2) after "tutor" there shall be inserted ", guardian".
(24) In section 125(1) of that Act—
(a) for the definition of "application for admission" and "guardianship application" there shall be substituted—
" 'application for admission' has the meaning assigned to it by section 18 of this Act";
(b) in the appropriate place, there shall be inserted—
" 'guardian' includes a guardian (however called) appointed under the law of any country to, or entitled under the law of any country to act for an adult during his incapacity, if the guardianship is recognised by the law of Scotland;";
" 'welfare attorney' includes a person granted, under a contract, grant or appointment governed by the law of any country, powers (however expressed) relating to the granter's personal welfare and having effect during the granter's incapacity;".

Insolvency Act 1986 (c.45)

18. In section 390(4)(c) of the Insolvency Act 1986 at the end there shall be added "or has had a guardian appointed to him under the Adults with Incapacity (Scotland) Act 2000 (asp 4).".

Legal Aid (Scotland) Act 1986 (c.47)

19. In section 36(3) of the Legal Aid (Scotland) Act 1986, after paragraph (b) there shall be inserted—
"(bb) is concerned as claiming or having an interest in the property, financial affairs or personal welfare of an adult under the Adults with Incapacity (Scotland) Act 2000 (asp 4);".

Financial Services Act 1986 (c.60)

20. In section 45(1)(d) of the Financial Services Act 1986 at the end there shall be added "or when acting in the exercise of his functions as Public Guardian under the Adults with Incapacity (Scotland) Act 2000 (asp 4);".

Access to Health Records Act 1990 (c.23)

21. In section 3 of the Access to Health Records Act 1990, in subsection (3) after paragraph (e) there shall be inserted—
"(ee) where the record is held in Scotland and the patient is incapable, within the meaning of the Adults with Incapacity (Scotland) Act 2000 (asp 4) in relation to making or authorising the application, any person entitled to act on behalf of the patient under that Act.".

Child Support Act 1991 (c.48)

22. In section 50 of the Child Support Act 1991 in subsection (8)(c) for paragraphs (i) and (ii) there shall be substituted "a guardian or other person entitled to act on behalf of the person under the Adults with Incapacity (Scotland) Act 2000 (asp 4).".

Social Security Administration Act 1992 (c.5)

23. In section 123 of the Social Security Administration Act 1992 in subsection (10)(c) for paragraphs (i) and (ii) there shall be substituted "a guardian or other person entitled to act on behalf of the person under the Adults with Incapacity (Scotland) Act 2000 (asp 4).".

Health Service Commissioners Act 1993 (c.46)

24. In section 7A of the Health Service Commissioners Act 1993 after "patients)" there shall be inserted "or", "or 50 (orders discharging patients from guardianship)" shall be repealed, and at the end there shall be inserted "or section 73 of the Adults with Incapacity (Scotland) Act 2000 (asp 4)".

Clean Air Act 1993 (c.11)

25. In section 64 of the Clean Air Act 1993 in subsection (1) in the definition of "owner" for "tutor or curator" there shall be substituted "or person entitled to act as the legal representative of a person under disability by reason of nonage or mental or other incapacity".

Criminal Procedure (Scotland) Act 1995 (c.46)

26.—(1) In section 57 of the Criminal Procedure (Scotland) Act 1995—
 (a) in subsection (2)(c) for first "person" there shall be substituted "person's personal welfare";
 (b) in subsection (4) after "58(1)," there shall be inserted "58(1A),";
 (c) at the end there shall be added—
  "(6) Section 58A of this Act shall have effect as regards guardianship orders made under subsection (2)(c) of this section.".
(2) In section 58 of that Act—
(a) for subsection (1) there shall be substituted—
 "(1) Where a person is convicted in the High Court or the sheriff court of an offence, other than an offence the sentence for which is fixed by law, punishable by that court with imprisonment, and the court—
 (a) is satisfied on the written or oral evidence of two medical practitioners (complying with section 61 of this Act) that the grounds set out in section 17(1) of the Mental Health (Scotland) Act 1984 apply in relation to the offender;
 (b) is of the opinion, having regard to all the circumstances including the nature of the offence and the character and antecedents of the offender and to the other available methods of dealing with him, that the most suitable method of disposing of the case is by means of an order under this subsection,
the court may, subject to subsection (2) below, by order authorise his admission to and detention in such hospital as may be specified in the order.
(1A) Where a person is convicted as mentioned in subsection (1) above and the court is satisfied—
 (a) on the evidence of two medical practitioners (complying with section 61 of this Act and with any requirements imposed under section 57(3) of the Adults with Incapacity (Scotland) Act 2000 (asp 4)) that the grounds set out in section 58(1)(a) of that Act apply in relation to the offender;
 (b) that no other means provided by or under this Act would be sufficient to enable the offender's interests in his personal welfare to be safeguarded or promoted,
the court may, subject to subsection (2) below, by order place the offender's personal welfare under the guardianship of such local authority or of such other person approved by a local authority as may be specified in the order.";
(b) in subsections (2), (3) and (10) for "subsection (1)" there shall be substituted "subsection (1) or (1A)";
(c) in subsections (5) and (7) after "subsection (1)" there shall be inserted "or paragraph (a) of subsection (1A),";
(d) for subsection (6) there shall be substituted—
 "(6) An order placing a person under the guardianship of a local authority or of any other person (in this Act referred to as "a guardianship order") shall not be made under this section unless the court is satisfied—
 (a) on the report of a mental health officer (complying with any requirements imposed by section 57(3) of the Adults with Incapacity (Scotland) Act 2000 (asp

4)) giving his opinion as to the general appropriateness of the order sought, based on an interview and assessment of the person carried out not more than 30 days before it makes the order, that it is necessary in the interests of the personal welfare of the person that he should be placed under guardianship;
(b) that any person nominated to be appointed a guardian is suitable to be so appointed;
(c) that the authority or person is willing to receive that person into guardianship; and
(d) that there is no other guardianship order, under this Act or the Adults with Incapacity (Scotland) Act 2000 (asp 4), in force relating to the person.";
(e) at the end there shall be added—
"(11) Section 58A of this Act shall have effect as regards guardianship orders made under subsection (1) of this section.".
(3) After section 60A of that Act there shall be inserted—
"**Intervention orders**
60B. The court may instead of making a hospital order under section 58(1) of this Act or a guardianship order under section 57(2)(c) or 58(1A) of this Act, make an intervention order (as defined in section 53(1) of the Adults with Incapacity (Scotland) Act 2000 (asp 4)) where it considers that it would be appropriate to do so.".
(4) In section 61 of that Act—
(a) in subsection (1), for "and 58(1)(a)" there shall be substituted ", 58(1)(a) and 58(1A)(a)";
(b) in subsection (2), after "section 58(1)(a)" there shall be inserted "or 58(1A)(a)"; and
(c) in subsection (3) for "and 58(1)(a)" there shall be substituted ", 58(1)(a) and 58(1A)(a)".

NOTE
Para.26(3) was amended by the Regulation of Care (Scotland) Act 2001 (asp 8), s.79 and Sch.3, para.23(7).

SCHEDULE 6

REPEALS

Enactment	Extent of Repeal
Curators Act 1585 (c.25(S))	The whole Act.
Judicial Factors Act 1849 (12 & 13 Vict. c.51)	In section 1, "and curator bonis" and the words from "the word "tutor"" to "Act 1960" where second occurring. In section 7, the words from "and if any factor" to "not subject to appeal". In section 10, "tutors and curators". Section 25(1). Section 26. In section 27, "or Court of Exchequer, as the case may be," and "tutors and curators". Section 28. In section 31, "tutor or curator" and "or curator bonis". In section 32, "tutor or curator". In section 33, "tutor or curator". In section 34, "tutor, or curator". In section 34A, "tutors and curators" and "tutory or curatory". In section 36, "tutories, and curatories". In section 37, "tutor, or curator". In section 40, the words from "and the manner of applying" to "curators" where first occurring and "tutors, and curators,".
Improvement of Land Act 1864 (27 & 28 Vict. c.114)	In section 24, "tutors,", "curators,", "tutor," and "curator,".
Titles to Land (Consolidation) (Scotland) Act 1868 (31 & 32 Vict. c.101)	In section 3 in the definition of "judicial factor", "or curators bonis".
Judicial Factors (Scotland) Act 1880 (43 & 44 Vict. c.4)	In section 3, "a curator bonis".
Judicial Factors (Scotland) Act 1889 (52 & 53 Vict. c.39)	In section 13, "tutor, curator" in both places.
Heritable Securities (Scotland) Act 1894 (57 & 58 Vict. c.44)	In section 13, "tutors, curators".
Trusts (Scotland) Act 1921 (11 & 12 Geo.5 c.58)	In section 2 in each of the definitions of "trust" and "trust deed" the words "tutor, curator, guardian or" and in the definition of "trustee" the words "tutor, curator, guardian"; in the definition of "judicial factor" the words "or curator"; the definitions of "curator", "tutor" and "guardian".
U.S.A. Veterans' Pensions Act 1949 (12 & 13 Geo.6 c.45)	In section 1(4), "tutor, factor loco tutoris," and "curator bonis or".
Medicines Act 1968 (c.67)	In section 72(3)(d) and (4)(c), "curator bonis,".
Solicitors (Scotland) Act 1980 (c.46)	In section 18(1)(a), "or becomes subject to guardianship".
Mental Health Act 1983 (c.20)	In section 110, in subsection (1) "curator bonis, tutor or"; in subsection (2) "curator bonis, tutor, or".
Mental Health (Scotland) Act 1984 (c.36)	In section 3 in subsection (1) "guardianship or"; in subsection (2)(b), "or who are subject to guardianship". In section 5(2) "or subject to guardianship under the following provisions of this Act". In section 7(1)(b), "under the following provisions of this Act". In section 10(1)(b) "the following provisions of this Act or under".

Mental Health (Scotland) Act 1984 (c.36)—cont.	In section 29 in subsection (1), paragraphs (b) and (c) and "or" which precedes them; in subsection (2), "or, as the case may be, by the local authority concerned"; in subsection (3), paragraph (b). Sections 36 to 52. In section 53(3), "or his reception into guardianship". Section 55(3). In section 57(4), "or subject to guardianship" and "or so subject" wherever occurring. In section 59, subsections (1)(b) and (2) and in subsection (3), "or 44". Section 61. In section 76(1) paragraph (b) and ", a guardianship order". In section 77, in subsection (1) "or subject to guardianship" and "or, as the case may be, for receiving him into guardianship"; subsection (3). In section 78, in subsection (1), "or reception into guardianship"; in subsection (2), "or his reception into guardianship". In section 80(1), "or subject to guardianship" and "or, as the case may be, for receiving him into guardianship". Section 84(4). In section 87(1), "or subject to guardianship" and "or placed under guardianship." In section 92, subsection (1) and in subsection (2)(a), "or subject to guardianship thereunder". Sections 93 and 94. In section 105(2), "subject to his guardianship under this Act or otherwise". In section 107(1)(b), "subject to his guardianship under this Act or is otherwise". In section 108(1)(a), "or being subject to guardianship". In section 110 in subsection (1), ", or in the case of a patient subject to guardianship, the local authority concerned", "or subject to guardianship", "or guardianship" in both places, "or his reception into guardianship"; in subsection (4), "or, as the case may be, the local authority concerned in relation to a patient subject to guardianship as aforesaid". In section 112, "or his reception into guardianship". In section 113(1), "or for reception into guardianship". In section 119, "guardianship under this Act". In section 121 in subsection (1)(b), "or subject to guardianship", "or 44"; in subsection (2), "or subject to guardianship", "or 44", "and subsection (2) of the said section 44"; in subsection (6), the words from "(in the case of" where first occurring to "guardianship)", "or section 44", "respectively", "or the said section 44 (as the case may be)". In section 125 in subsection (4), "or subject to guardianship"; in subsection (5), "or received, or liable to be received, into guardianship", "(other than under Part V thereof)", "or received or liable to be received into guardianship".
Law Reform (Miscellaneous Provisions) (Scotland) Act 1990 (c.40)	Section 71.
Criminal Procedure (Scotland) Act 1995 (c.46)	In section 59(2), "or section 39". In section 61(1), "or section 39". In section 230(1), "or 39". In schedule 4, in paragraph 2(1)(b), "or 39".

APPENDIX 2

STATUTORY INSTRUMENTS

ADULTS WITH INCAPACITY (PUBLIC GUARDIAN'S FEES) (SCOTLAND) REGULATIONS 2001

(SSI 2001/75)

Made	7th March 2001	**A2–01**
Laid before the Scottish Parliament	8th March 2001	
Coming into force	2nd April 2001	

The Scottish Ministers, in exercise of the powers conferred by section 7(2) of the Adults with Incapacity (Scotland) Act 2000 and of all other powers enabling them in that behalf, hereby make the following Regulations:

Citation, commencement and interpretation

1.—(1) These Regulations may be cited as the Adults with Incapacity (Public Guardian's Fees) (Scotland) Regulations 2001 and shall come into force on 2nd April 2001.

(2) In these Regulations, "the Act" means the Adults with Incapacity (Scotland) Act 2000 and references to sections are references to sections in that Act.

Fees payable to Public Guardian

2. The fees payable to the Public Guardian in respect of the matters specified in column 1 of the Schedule shall be the fees specified in relation to those matters in column 2 of that Schedule.

SCHEDULE

Regulation 2

TABLE OF FEES PAYABLE TO PUBLIC GUARDIAN

Column 1	Column 2
1. Search of registers under section 6(2)(b) of the Act (per half hour or any part thereof)	£5.00
2. Registration of a document conferring a continuing or welfare power of attorney under section 19 of the Act	£35.00
3. Provision of a duplicate or replacement of a certificate issued under the Act	£10.00
4. Audit of accounts submitted by a continuing attorney under section 20(2)(b) of the Act	£75.00

Column 1—cont.	Column 2—cont.
5. Processing of an application for authorisation to intromit with funds under section 26 of the Act, and where such an application is granted, the issue of a certificate of authority to the withdrawer	£35.00
6. Provision of a duplicate or replacement of a certificate of authority issued under section 26(4) of the Act	£10.00
7. Provision of first copy— (a) each of first 10 pages (b) each page after first 10	£1.00 £0.30
8. Subsequent copies: each page	£0.30
9. Registration under section 6(2) of the Act of— (a) guardianship order; (b) an intervention order; (c) a variation of a guardianship order; (d) a variation of an intervention order; or (e) a renewal of a guardianship order, made under Part 6 of the Act (including, where appropriate, checking caution and issuing certificates)	£35
10. Authorisation of a gift out of the adult's estate under section 66(1) of the Act, where the gift has a value in excess of £2,500	£35
11. Grant of discharge of a guardian under section 72(1) of the Act— (a) for an estate with no heritable property (b) for an estate with heritable property	£35 £75
12. Recall of the powers of a guardian under section 73 of the Act— (a) for an estate with no heritable property (b) for an estate with heritable property	£35 £75
13. Approval of guardian's management plan and inventory, in accordance with paragraphs 1 and 3 of schedule 2 to the Act— Estate value (excluding heritable property) £0 to £30,000 £30,001 to £50,000 £50,001 to £100,000 £100,001 to £500,000 £500,001 and over	£35 £150 £300 £500 £750
14. Granting an application for consent made in accordance with paragraph 6 of schedule 2 to the Act	£100
15. Audit of accounts submitted in accordance with paragraph 7 of schedule 2 to the Act— Estate value (excluding heritable property) £0 to £30,000 £30,001 to £50,000 £50,001 to £100,000 £100,001 to £250,000 £250,001 to £750,000 £750,001 to £2,000,000 £2,000,001 and over	£50 £125 £350 £450 £600 £1,200 £1,750

NOTE
This Schedule was amended by the Adults with Incapacity (Public Guardian's Fees) (Scotland) Amendment Regulations 2002 (SSI 2002/131)

Appendix 2

ADULTS WITH INCAPACITY (CERTIFICATES FROM MEDICAL PRACTITIONERS) (ACCOUNTS AND FUNDS) (SCOTLAND) REGULATIONS 2001

(SSI 2001/76)

Made	7th March 2001
Laid before the Scottish Parliament	8th March 2001
Coming into force	2nd April 2001

The Scottish Ministers, in exercise of the powers conferred by sections 26(1)(f) and 86(2) of the Adults with Incapacity (Scotland) Act 2000 and of all other powers enabling them in that behalf, hereby make the following Regulations:

Citation and commencement

1. These Regulations may be cited as the Adults with Incapacity (Certificates from Medical Practitioners) (Accounts and Funds) (Scotland) Regulations 2001 and shall come into force on 2nd April 2001.

Certificate from a medical practitioner

2. The certificate from a medical practitioner for the purposes of section 26(1)(f) of the Adults with Incapacity (Scotland) Act 2000 shall be in the form set out in the Schedule.

SCHEDULE

Regulation 2

ADULTS WITH INCAPACITY (SCOTLAND) ACT 2000 ("THE ACT")

Certificate of incapacity to accompany an application to the Public Guardian under section 26 of the Act for authority to intromit with funds

I _____
(full name)

of _____
(professional address)

have examined the following patient on _____
(date), in my capacity as

* _____

_____
(patient's name)

of _____
(address)

/ _____

/ _____

_____

(date of birth)

I am of the opinion that he/she is incapable in relation to decisions about, or incapable of acting to safeguard or promote his/her interests in, the funds specified in the accompanying application for authority to intromit with funds under section 26 of the Act.

I am of the opinion that the patient named above is incapable in terms of section 26(1)(f) of the Act because of:
 mental disorder**
 inability to communicate because of physical disability**

Brief description of mental disorder/inability to communicate
_____

_____
(signed)

_____
(date)

* the person signing the certificate must be a medical practitioner; insert as appropriate, e.g. GP, specialist in mental disorder

** one of these **must** be deleted unless both apply

ADULTS WITH INCAPACITY (SUPERVISION OF WELFARE ATTORNEYS BY LOCAL AUTHORITIES) (SCOTLAND) REGULATIONS 2001

(SSI 2001/77)

Made	7th March 2001
Laid before the Scottish Parliament	8th March 2001
Coming into force	2nd April 2001

The Scottish Ministers, in exercise of the powers conferred by sections 10(3)(b)(ii) and 86(2) of the Adults with Incapacity (Scotland) Act 2000 and of all other powers enabling them in that behalf, hereby make the following Regulations:

Citation and commencement

1. These Regulations may be cited as the Adults with Incapacity (Supervision of Welfare Attorneys by Local Authorities) (Scotland) Regulations 2001 and shall come into force on 2nd April 2001.

Duties of local authority

2.—(1) Where the local authority is supervising a welfare attorney by virtue of an order made by the sheriff under section 20(2)(c) of the Adults with Incapacity (Scotland) Act 2000, that local authority shall arrange for the adult who is subject to the welfare power of attorney and the welfare attorney to be visited on behalf of the local authority as often as required by the sheriff and, where no such requirement has been specified, at intervals of not more than one calendar month for the period of time fixed by the sheriff for supervision by the local authority.

(2) Where the local authority considers it appropriate, any visit to the adult in accordance with this regulation may take place at the same time as the visit to the welfare attorney.

Information to be provided

3. For the purpose of enabling a local authority to carry out its supervisory function, a welfare attorney shall from time to time provide the local authority with any reports or other information about the personal welfare of the adult or the exercise by that attorney of that attorney's functions as the local authority may reasonably require.

ADULTS WITH INCAPACITY (COUNTERSIGNATORIES OF APPLICATIONS FOR AUTHORITY TO INTROMIT) (SCOTLAND) REGULATIONS 2001

(SSI 2001/78)

Made	7th March 2001
Laid before the Scottish Parliament	8th March 2001
Coming into force	2nd April 2001

The Scottish Ministers, in exercise of the powers conferred by section 26(1)(c) of the Adults with Incapacity (Scotland) Act 2000 and of all other powers enabling them in that behalf, hereby make the following Regulations:

Citation and commencement

1. These Regulations may be cited as the Adults with Incapacity (Countersignatories of Applications for Authority to Intromit) (Scotland) Regulations 2001 and shall come into force on 2nd April 2001.

Interpretation

2. In these Regulations—
"the Act" means the Adults with Incapacity (Scotland) Act 2000;
"advocate" means a practising member of the Faculty of Advocates;
"councillor" means a member of a council constituted by section 2 of the Local Government etc. (Scotland) Act 1994;
"executry practitioner" has the same meaning as in section 23 of the Law Reform Miscellaneous Provisions (Scotland) Act 1990;
"mental health officer" has the same meaning as in section 125 of the Mental Health (Scotland) Act 1984;
"qualified conveyancer" has the same meaning as in section 23 of the Law Reform (Miscellaneous Provisions) (Scotland) Act 1990;
"registered European lawyer" has the same meaning as in regulation 2 of the European Communities (Lawyer's Practice) (Scotland) Regulations 2000;
"solicitor" has the same meaning as in section 65(1) of the Solicitors (Scotland) Act 1980;
"registered teacher" has the same meaning as in section 135 of the Education (Scotland) Act 1980.

Classes of persons who may countersign an application under section 26 of the Act

3. An application made under section 26 of the Act shall be countersigned by a person who is a member of a class of persons referred to in the Schedule to these Regulations.

SCHEDULE

Regulation 3

CLASSES OF PERSONS WHO MAY COUNTERSIGN AN APPLICATION UNDER SECTION 26 OF THE ACT

Advocates
Constables of a police force
Established civil servants
Executry practitioners
Justices of the peace
Councillors
Members of Parliament
Members of the European Parliament
Members of the Scottish Parliament
Mental health officers
Ministers of religion
Qualified conveyancers
Registered European lawyers
Registered medical practitioners
Registered nurses
Solicitors
Registered Teachers

ADULTS WITH INCAPACITY (EVIDENCE IN RELATION TO DISPENSING WITH INTIMATION OR NOTIFICATION) (SCOTLAND) REGULATIONS 2001

(SSI 2001/79)

Made 7th March 2001
Laid before the Scottish Parliament 8th March 2001
Coming into force 2nd April 2001

The Scottish Ministers, in exercise of the powers conferred by sections 7(1)(d) and 86(2) of the Adults with Incapacity (Scotland) Act 2000 and of all other powers enabling them in that behalf, hereby make the following Regulations:

Citation and commencement

1. These Regulations may be cited as the Adults with Incapacity (Evidence in Relation to Dispensing with Intimation or Notification) (Scotland) Regulations 2001 and shall come into force on 2nd April 2001.

Evidence to be taken into account

2.—(1) For the purposes of section 11(2) of the Adults with Incapacity (Scotland) Act 2000, the evidence which the Public Guardian shall take into account when deciding whether to dispense with intimation or notification to the adult shall be two medical certificates stating that intimation or notification could be likely to pose a serious risk to the health of the adult.

(2) Those medical certificates shall be prepared by medical practitioners independent of each other.

(3) In any case where the incapacity of the adult is by reason of mental disorder, one of the two medical practitioners must be a medical practitioner approved for the purposes of section 20 of the Mental Health (Scotland) Act

1984 as having special experience in the diagnosis or treatment of mental disorder.

ADULTS WITH INCAPACITY (CERTIFICATES IN RELATION TO POWERS OF ATTORNEY) (SCOTLAND) REGULATIONS 2001

(SSI 2001/80)

Made   7th March 2001
Laid before the Scottish Parliament   8th March 2001
Coming into force   2nd April 2001

The Scottish Ministers, in exercise of the powers conferred by sections 15(3)(c) and 16(3)(c) of the Adults with Incapacity (Scotland) Act 2000 and of all other powers enabling them in that behalf, hereby make the following Regulations:

Citation, commencement and interpretation

1.—(1) These Regulations may be cited as the Adults with Incapacity (Certificates in Relation to Powers of Attorney) (Scotland) Regulations 2001 and shall come into force on 2nd April 2001.

(2) In these Regulations, "the Act" means the Adults with Incapacity (Scotland) Act 2000.

Certificates for use in connection with continuing and welfare powers of attorney

2. For the purposes of section 15(3)(c) of the Act, the certificate to be incorporated in a written document granting a continuing power of attorney shall be in the form set out in Schedule 1.

3. For the purposes of section 16(3)(c) of the Act, the certificate to be incorporated in a document granting a welfare power of attorney shall be in the form set out in Schedule 2.

Classes of persons for the purposes of sections 15(3)(c) or 16(3)(c) of the Act

4. For the purposes of sections 15(3)(c) and 16(3)(c) of the Act, the following classes are hereby prescribed—
(a) practising members of the Faculty of Advocates; and
(b) registered medical practitioners.

SCHEDULE 1

Regulation 2

CERTIFICATE UNDER SECTION 15(3)(C) OF THE ADULTS WITH INCAPACITY (SCOTLAND) ACT 2000 TO BE INCORPORATED IN A DOCUMENT GRANTING A CONTINUING POWER OF ATTORNEY

Insert names and date	This certificate is incorporated in the document subscribed by _____ ("the granter") on _____ that confers a continuing power of attorney on _____
Insert date	I certify that: A. I interviewed the granter on_____ immediately before he/she subscribed this continuing power of attorney AND B. I am satisfied that, at the time this continuing power of attorney was granted, the granter understood its nature and extent I have satisfied myself of this:
Delete either (a) or (b) if not applicable. Both may apply but one must apply	(a) because of my own knowledge of the granter; (b) because I have consulted the following persons, who have knowledge of the granter on the matter:
Insert names, designations, addresses and relationship with granter, if any	AND C. I have no reason to believe that the granter was acting under undue influence or that any other factor vitiates the granting of this continuing power of attorney
Include full name, and state whether address given is business or personal	Signed: Date: Print name: Profession: Address: Note: any person signing this certificate should not be the person to whom this continuing power of attorney has been granted.

Appendix 2

SCHEDULE 2

Regulation 3

CERTIFICATE UNDER SECTION 16(3)(C) OF THE ADULTS WITH INCAPACITY (SCOTLAND) ACT TO BE INCORPORATED IN A DOCUMENT GRANTING A WELFARE POWER OF ATTORNEY

Insert names and date	This certificate is incorporated in the document subscribed by ("the granter") on that confers a welfare power of attorney on
Insert date	I certify that: **A.** I interviewed the granter on_____ immediately before he/she subscribed this welfare power of attorney AND **B.** I am satisfied that, at the time this welfare power of attorney was granted, the granter understood its nature and extent I have satisfied myself of this:
Delete either (a) or (b) if not applicable. Both may apply but one must apply	(a) because of my own knowledge of the granter; (b) because I have consulted the following persons, who have knowledge of the granter on the matter:
Insert names, designations, addresses and relationship with granter, if any	AND **C.** I have no reason to believe that the granter was acting under undue influence or that any other factor vitiates the granting of this welfare power of attorney
Include full name, and state whether address given is business or personal	Signed: Date: Print name: Profession: Address: Note: any person signing this certificate should not be the person to whom this welfare power of attorney has been granted.

ADULTS WITH INCAPACITY (SCOTLAND) ACT 2000 (COMMENCEMENT NO. 1) ORDER 2001

(SSI 2001/81 (C. 2))

Made   7th March 2001

The Scottish Ministers, in exercise of the powers conferred by section 89(2) of the Adults with Incapacity (Scotland) Act 2000, and all other powers enabling them in that behalf, hereby make the following Order:

Citation and interpretation

1.—(1) This Order may be cited as the Adults with Incapacity (Scotland) Act 2000 (Commencement No. 1) Order 2001.

(2) In this Order, "the Act" means the Adults with Incapacity (Scotland) Act 2000.

Commencement

2. The provisions of the Act which are specified in column 1 of Schedule 1 to this Order and the subject matter of which is described in column 2 of that Schedule shall come into force on 2nd April 2001, and where a particular purpose is specified in relation to any provision in Column 3 of that Schedule, that provision shall come into force on that day for that purpose only.

3. The provisions of the Act which are specified in column 1 of Schedule 2 to this Order and the subject matter of which is described in column 2 of that Schedule shall so far as not then in force come into force on 1st April 2002, and where a particular purpose is specified in relation to any provision in Column 3 of that Schedule, that provision shall come into force on that day for that purpose only.

SCHEDULE 1

Article 2

PROVISIONS OF THE ACT BROUGHT INTO FORCE BY ARTICLE 2 OF THIS ORDER ON 2ND APRIL 2001

Column 1	Column 2	Column 3
Provision of the Act	*Subject matter*	*Purposes*
Section 1	General principles and fundamental definitions	
Section 2	Applications and other proceedings and appeals	
Section 3	Powers of sheriff	
Section 4	Power of Court of Session or sheriff with regard to nearest relative	
Section 5	Safeguarding of interests in Court of Session appeals or proceedings	

Column 1	Column 2	Column 3
Provision of the Act–cont.	*Subject matter*–cont.	*Purposes*—cont.
Section 6(1), (2)(b)(i)to (iii), (2)(c)(i) and (ii), (2)(d)	The Public Guardian and his functions	
Section 6(2)(e)	" "	Only for the purpose of bringing into force this provision insofar as it relates to continuing attorneys or withdrawers
Section 6(2)(f), (3)(b)	" "	
Section 7	The Public Guardian: further provision	
Section 8	Expenses in court proceedings	
Section 9(1)(a) to (c), (d)(i), (e), (f)	Functions of the Mental Welfare Commission	
Section 9(1)(g)	" "	Only for the purpose of bringing into force this provision insofar as it relates to welfare attorneys
Section 9(2)	" "	Only for the purpose of bringing into force this provision insofar as it relates to welfare attorneys
Section 9(3)(b)	" "	
Sections 10(1)(b), (1)(c)(i), (1)(d)	Functions of local authorities	
Section 10(1)(e)	" "	Only for the purpose of bringing into force this provision insofar as it relates to welfare attorneys
Section 10(2), (3)(b)(ii), (4)(b)	Functions of local authorities	
Section 11	Intimation not required in certain circumstances	
Section 12	Investigations	Only for the purpose of bringing into force this provision insofar as it relates to investigations in relation to continuing attorneys, welfare attorneys and intromission with funds under Part 3 of the Act
Section 13	Codes of practice	
Section 14	Appeal against decision as to incapacity	
Section 15	Creation of continuing power of attorney	
Section 16	Creation and exercise of welfare power of attorney	
Section 17	Attorney not obliged to act in certain circumstances	

Column 1	Column 2	Column 3
Provision of the Act–cont.	Subject matter–cont.	Purposes—cont.
Section 18	Power of attorney not granted in accordance with this Act	
Section 19	Registration of continuing or welfare power of attorney	
Section 20	Powers of sheriff	
Section 21	Records: attorneys	
Section 22	Notification to Public Guardian	
Section 23	Resignation of continuing or welfare attorney	
Section 24(1) and (4)	Termination of continuing or welfare power of attorney	
Section 25	Authority to intromit with funds	
Section 26	Application for authority to intromit	
Section 27	Notification of change of address	
Section 28	Purposes of intromission with funds	
Section 29	Withdrawal and use of funds	
Section 30	Records and inquiries	
Section 31	Duration and termination of registration	
Section 32	Joint accounts	
Section 33	Transfer of funds	
Section 34	Disapplication of Part 3 of the Act	
Section 81(1)(a) to (c)	Repayment of funds	
Section 81(2)	" "	Only for the purpose of bringing into force this provision insofar as it relates to section 82 of the Act
Section 82(1)	Limitation of liability	Only for the purpose of bringing into force this provision insofar as it relates to continuing attorneys, welfare attorneys and withdrawers
Section 82(2)(b) and (c)	" "	
Section 83	Offence of ill treatment and wilful neglect.	

Appendix 2

Column 1	Column 2	Column 3
*Provision of the Act–*cont.	*Subject matter–*cont.	*Purposes–*cont.
Section 85	Jurisdiction and private international law	Only for the purpose of bringing into force the provisions of Schedule 3 to the Act specified below
Section 86	Regulations	
Section 87	Interpretation	
Section 88	Continuation of existing powers, minor and consequential amendments and repeals	Only for the purpose of bringing into force the provisions of Schedules 4, 5 and 6 to the Act specified below
Schedule 3, paragraphs 1(1) and (5), 2(1), (3) and (4), 3, 4, 5, 6, 7(1), (2)(a), (3)(a) to (d), 8, 9, 10, 13 and 14	Jurisdiction and private international law	
Schedule 4, paragraphs 4, 7(a) to (c), and 8	Continuation of existing curators, tutors, guardians and attorneys under this Act	
Schedule 5:	Minor and Consequential Amendments—	
Paragraph 2	Defence Act 1842 (c.94)	
Paragraph 3	Judicial Factors Act 1849 (c.51)	
Paragraph 5	Titles to Land (Consolidation) (Scotland) Act 1868 (c.101)	
Paragraph 6	Judicial Factors (Scotland) Act 1889 (c.39)	
Paragraph 7	Heritable Securities (Scotland) Act 1894 (c.44)	Only for the purpose of bringing into force this provision insofar as it relates to continuing and welfare attorneys and withdrawers
Paragraph 9	Offices Shops and Railway Premises Act 1963 (c.41)	Only for the purpose of bringing into force this provision insofar as it relates to continuing and welfare attorneys and withdrawers
Paragraph 13	Sheriff Courts (Scotland) Act 1971 (c.58)	
Paragraph 14	Land Registration (Scotland) Act 1979 (c.33)	
Paragraph 17(3) to (21), (24)(b)	Mental Health (Scotland) Act 1984 (c.36)	Only for the purpose of bringing into force these provisions insofar as they relate to welfare attorneys
Paragraph 19	Legal Aid (Scotland) Act 1986 (c.47)	
Paragraph 22	Child Support Act 1991 (c.48)	Only for the purpose of bringing into force this provision insofar as it relates to welfare attorneys

Column 1	Column 2	Column 3
Provision of the Act—cont.	Subject matter—cont.	Purposes—cont.
Paragraph 23	Social Security Administration Act 1992 (c.5)	Only for the purpose of bringing into force this provision insofar as it relates to welfare attorneys
Paragraph 25	Clean Air Act 1993 (c.11)	
Schedule 6	Repeals	Only for the purpose of bringing into force the repeal of section 71 of the Law Reform (Miscellaneous Provisions) (Scotland) Act 1990 (c.40)

SCHEDULE 2

Article 3

Provisions of the Act Brought into Force by Article 3 of this Order on 1st April 2002

Column 1	Column 2	Column 3
Provision of the Act	Subject matter	Purposes
Section 6	The Public Guardian and his functions	
Section 9	Functions of the Mental Welfare Commission	
Section 10	Functions of local authorities	
Section 12	Investigations	
Section 24	Termination of continuing or welfare power of attorney	
Section 53	Intervention orders	
Section 54	Records: intervention orders	
Section 55	Notification of change of address	
Section 56	Registration of intervention order relating to heritable property	
Section 57	Application for guardianship order	
Section 58	Disposal of application	
Section 59	Who may be appointed as guardian	
Section 60	Renewal of guardianship order by sheriff	
Section 61	Registration of guardianship order relating to heritable property	

Column 1	Column 2	Column 3
Provision of the Act—cont.	Subject matter—cont.	Purposes—cont.
Section 62	Joint guardians	
Section 63	Substitute guardian	
Section 64	Functions and duties of guardian	
Section 65	Records: guardians	
Section 66	Gifts	
Section 67	Effect of appointment and transactions of guardian	
Section 68	Reimbursement and remuneration of guardian	
Section 69	Forfeiture of guardian's remuneration	
Section 70	Non-compliance with decisions of guardian with welfare powers	
Section 71	Replacement or removal of guardian or recall of guardianship by sheriff	
Section 72	Discharge of guardian with financial powers	
Section 73	Recall of powers of guardian	
Section 74	Variation of guardianship order	
Section 75	Resignation of guardian	
Section 76	Change of habitual residence	
Section 77	Termination of authority to intervene and guardianship on death of adult	
Section 78	Amendment of registration under section 61 on events affecting guardianship or death of an adult	
Section 79	Protection of third parties: guardianship	
Section 80	Future appointment of curator bonis etc. incompetent	
Section 81	Repayment of funds	For all purposes other than bringing into force this provision insofar as it relates to the managers of an authorised establishment.
Section 82	Limitation of liability	For all purposes other than bringing into force this provision insofar as it relates to the managers of an authorised establishment.
Section 84	Application to guardians appointed under Criminal Procedure (Scotland) Act 1995	

Column 1	Column 2	Column 3
Provision of the Act—cont.	Subject matter—cont.	Purposes—cont.
Section 88	Continuation of existing powers, minor and consequential amendments and repeals	Only for the purpose of bringing into force the provisions of Schedules 4, 5 and 6 to the Act specified below
Schedule 2	Management of estate of adult	
Schedule 4, paragraphs 1, 2, 3 and 6	Continuation of existing curators, tutors, guardians and attorneys under this Act	
Schedule 5:	Minor and Consequential Amendments—	
Paragraph 1	General	
Paragraph 7	Heritable Securities (Scotland) Act 1894 (c.44)	
Paragraph 8	National Assistance Act 1984 (c.29)	
Paragraph 9	Offices, Shops and Railway Premises Act 1963 (c.41)	
Paragraph 12	Medicines Act 1968 (c.67)	
Paragraph 15	Solicitors (Scotland) Act 1980 (c.46)	
Paragraph 16	Law Reform (Miscellaneous Provisions) (Scotland) Act 1980 (c.55)	
Paragraph 17(1), (2), (3) to (21) and (24)	Mental Health (Scotland) Act 1984 (c.36)	
Paragraph 18	Insolvency Act 1986 (c.45)	
Paragraph 20	Financial Services Act 1986 (c.60)	
Paragraph 21	Access to Health Records Act 1990 (c.23)	
Paragraph 22	Child Support Act 1991 (c.48)	
Paragraph 23	Social Security Administration Act 1992 (c.5)	
Paragraph 24	Health Service Commissioners Act 1993 (c.46)	
Paragraph 26	Criminal Procedure (Scotland) Act 1995 (c.46)	
Schedule 6	Repeals	For all purposes, other than bringing into force the repeal of provisions in the Improvement of Land Act 1864 (27&28 Vict. c.114) and in sections 5(2) and 94 of the Mental Health (Scotland) Act 1984 (c.36)

NOTE
Schedule 2 was amended by the Adults with Incapacity (Scotland) Act 2000 (Commencement No.1) (Amendment) Order 2002 (SSI 2002/172).

Appendix 2 429

CIVIL LEGAL AID (SCOTLAND) AMENDMENT REGULATIONS 2001

(SSI 2001/82)

Made	7th March 2001	A2–08
Laid before the Scottish Parliament	8th March 2001	
Coming into force	2nd April 2001	

The Scottish Ministers, in exercise of the powers conferred by section 36(1), (2)(h) and (3)(bb) of the Legal Aid (Scotland) Act 1986 and of all other powers enabling them in that behalf, hereby make the following Regulations:

Citation and commencement

1. These Regulations may be cited as the Civil Legal Aid (Scotland) Amendment Regulations 2001 and shall come into force on 2nd April 2001.

Amendment of the Civil Legal Aid (Scotland) Regulations 1996

2. After regulation 14 of the Civil Legal Aid (Scotland) Regulations 1996 there shall be inserted—

"**14A.**—(1) Where the applicant is a person concerned in any of the proceedings set out in paragraph (2) below only as claiming or having an interest in the property, financial affairs or personal welfare of an incapable adult under the Adults with Incapacity (Scotland) Act 2000 (in this regulation referred to as "the 2000 Act") then for the purpose of determining his disposable income and disposable capital, and the amount of any contribution required under section 17 of the Act, the personal resources of the applicant shall be disregarded, but regard shall be had to the personal resources of the incapable adult.

(2) The proceedings referred to in paragraph (1) above are proceedings where—
  (a) an application is made to the sheriff under section 3(3) of the 2000 Act;
  (b) a decision as to the incapacity of an adult is appealed under section 14(b) of the 2000 Act;
  (c) an application is made to the sheriff for an order under section 20(2) of the 2000 Act;
  (d) an application is made to the sheriff under section 3(6) of the 2000 Act to vary the terms of an order made under section 20(2) of that Act;
  (e) an application under section 26(1) of the 2000 Act for authority to intromit with funds is remitted for determination by the sheriff under section 26(8) of that Act;
  (f) the decision of the Public Guardian to grant or refuse an application under section 26(1) of the 2000 Act for authority to intromit with funds is appealed under section 26(9)(a) of the 2000 Act;
  (g) the decision of the Public Guardian to refuse to remit an application to the sheriff under section 26(8) is appealed under section 26(9)(b) of the 2000 Act;
  (h) an application is made to the sheriff under section 53(1) of the 2000 Act for an intervention order;
  (i) an application is made to the sheriff under section 57(1) of the 2000 Act for a guardianship order;
  (j) an application is made to the sheriff under section 71(1) of the 2000 Act for the replacement or removal of a guardian, or the recall or other termination of a guardianship order; and
  (k) an application is made to the sheriff under section 74(1) of the 2000 Act for variation of a guardianship order;
  (l) a decision as to the medical treatment of an adult is appealed to the Court of Session under section 50(3) of the 2000 Act;

430   Adult Incapacity

(m) an application for a determination is made to the Court of Session under section 50(6) of the 2000 Act; and
(n) any decision as to the medical treatment of an adult is appealed to the sheriff or to the Court of Session under section 52 of the 2000 Act.".

NOTE
This section was amended by the Civil Legal Aid (Scotland) Amendment Regulations 2002 (SSI 2002/88) and the Civil Legal Aid (Scotland) Amendment (No.2) Regulations 2002 (SSI 2002/254).

ACT OF SEDERUNT (SUMMARY APPLICATIONS, STATUTORY APPLICATIONS AND APPEALS ETC. RULES) AMENDMENT (ADULTS WITH INCAPACITY) 2001

(SSI 2001/142)

A2–09   Made   30th March 2001
         Coming into force   2nd April 2001

The Lords of Council and Session, under and by virtue of the powers conferred by section 32 of the Sheriff Courts (Scotland) Act 1971 and section 2(4) of the Adults with Incapacity (Scotland) Act 2000 and of all other powers enabling them in that behalf, having approved draft rules submitted to them by the Sheriff Court Rules Council in accordance with section 34 of the Sheriff Courts (Scotland) Act 1971, do hereby enact and declare:

Citation and commencement

1.—(1) This Act of Sederunt may be cited as the Act of Sederunt (Summary Applications, Statutory Applications and Appeals etc. Rules) Amendment (Adults with Incapacity) 2001 and shall come into force on 2nd April 2001.
(2) This Act of Sederunt shall be inserted in the Books of Sederunt.

Interpretation

2. In this Act of Sederunt—
"the principal Rules" means the Act of Sederunt (Summary Applications, Statutory Applications and Appeals etc. Rules) 1999.

Amendment of the principal Rules

3.—(1) The principal Rules shall be amended in accordance with the following paragraphs.
(2) In Chapter 3 (rules on applications under specific statutes), after Part XV (Race Relations Act 1976), insert—

"PART XVI

ADULTS WITH INCAPACITY (SCOTLAND) ACT 2000

Interpretation

3.16.1 In this Part—
"the 1984 Act" means the Mental Health (Scotland) Act 1984;
"the 2000 Act" means the Adults with Incapacity (Scotland) Act 2000;

"adult" means a person who has attained the age of 16 years and who is the subject of an application under the 2000 Act;

"authorised establishment" has the meaning ascribed to it in section 35(2) of the 2000 Act;

"continuing attorney" means a person on whom there has been conferred a power of attorney granted under section 15(1) of the 2000 Act;

"guardianship order" means an order made under section 58(4) of the 2000 Act;

"incapable" has the meaning ascribed to it at section 1(6) of the 2000 Act, and "incapacity" shall be construed accordingly;

"intervention order" means an order made under section 53(1) of the 2000 Act;

"local authority" has the meaning ascribed to it by section 87(1) of the 2000 Act;

"managers" has the meaning ascribed to it in paragraph 1 of Schedule 1 to the 2000 Act;

"Mental Welfare Commission" has the meaning ascribed to it by section 87(1) of the 2000 Act;

"nearest relative" means, subject to section 87(2) of the 2000 Act, the person who would be, or would be exercising the functions of, the adult's nearest relative under sections 53 to 57 of the 1984 Act if the adult were a patient within the meaning of that Act and notwithstanding that the person neither is or was caring for the adult for the purposes of section 53(3) of that Act;

"power of attorney" includes a factory and commission;

"primary carer" means the person or organisation primarily engaged in caring for an adult;

"Public Guardian" shall be construed in accordance with section 6 of the 2000 Act; and

"welfare attorney" means a person on whom there has been conferred a power of attorney granted under section 16(1) of the 2000 Act.

NOTE
This rule was amended by the Act of Sederunt (Summary Applications, Statutory Applications and Appeals etc. Rules) Amendment (No.3) (Adults with Incapacity) 2002 (SSI 2002/146).

Appointment of hearing

3.16.2 On an application or other proceedings being submitted under or in pursuance of the 2000 Act the sheriff shall—
   (a) fix a hearing;
   (b) order answers to be lodged (where he considers it appropriate to do so) within a period that he shall specify; and
   (c) appoint service and intimation of the application or other proceedings.

Place of any hearing

3.16.3 The sheriff may, where he considers it appropriate in all the circumstances, appoint that the hearing of an application or other proceedings shall take place in a hospital or other place.

Service of application

3.16.4—(1) Service of the application or other proceedings shall be made in Form 20 on—
   (a) the adult;
   (b) the nearest relative of the adult;
   (c) the primary carer of the adult (if any);
   (d) any guardian, continuing attorney or welfare attorney of the adult who has any power relating to the application or proceedings;

(e) the Public Guardian;
(ea) where appropriate, the Mental Welfare Commission;
(eb) where appropriate, the local authority; and
(f) any other person directed by the sheriff.

(2) Where the applicant is an individual person without legal representation service shall be effected by the sheriff clerk.

(3) Where the adult is in an authorised establishment the person effecting service shall not serve Form 20 on the adult under paragraph (1)(a) but shall instead serve Forms 20 and 21, together with Form 22, on the managers of that authorised establishment by—
(a) first class recorded delivery post; or
(b) personal service by a sheriff officer.

(4) On receipt of Forms 20 and 21 in terms of paragraph (3) the managers of the authorised establishment shall, subject to rule 3.16.5—
(a) deliver the notice in Form 20 to the adult; and
(b) as soon as practicable thereafter complete and return to the sheriff clerk a certificate of such delivery in Form 22.

(5) Where the application or other proceeding follows on a remit under rule 3.16.9 the order for service of the application shall include an order for service on the Public Guardian or other party concerned.

(6) Where the application is for an intervention order or a guardianship order, copies of the reports lodged in accordance with section 57(3) of the 2000 Act (reports to be lodged in court along with application) shall be served along with Form 20, or Forms 20, 21 and 22 as the case may be.

NOTE
This rule was amended by the Act of Sederunt (Summary Applications, Statutory Applications and Appeals etc. Rules) Amendment (No.3) (Adults with Incapacity) 2002 (SSI 2002/146).

Dispensing with service on adult

3.16.5—(1) Where, in relation to any application or proceeding under or in pursuance of the 2000 Act, two medical certificates are produced stating that intimation of the application or other proceeding, or notification of any interlocutor relating to such application or other proceeding, would be likely to pose a serious risk to the health of the adult the sheriff may dispense with such intimation or notification.

(2) Any medical certificates produced under paragraph (1) shall be prepared by medical practitioners independent of each other.

(3) In any case where the incapacity of the adult is by reason of mental disorder, one of the two medical practitioners must be a medical practitioner approved for the purposes of section 20 of the 1984 Act as having special experience in the diagnosis or treatment of mental disorder.

Hearing

3.16.6—(1) A hearing to determine any application or other proceeding shall take place within 28 days of the interlocutor fixing the hearing under rule 3.16.2 unless any person upon whom the application is to be served is outside Europe.

(2) At the hearing referred to in paragraph (1) the sheriff may determine the application or other proceeding or may order such further procedure as he thinks fit.

NOTE
This rule was amended by the Act of Sederunt (Summary Applications, Statutory Applications and Appeals etc. Rules) Amendment (No.3) (Adults with Incapacity) 2002 (SSI 2002/146).

Prescribed forms of application

3.16.7—(1) An application submitted to the sheriff under or in pursuance of the 2000 Act, other than an appeal or remitted matter, shall be in Form 23.

(2) An appeal to the sheriff under or in pursuance of the 2000 Act shall be in Form 24.

Subsequent applications

3.16.8—(1) Unless otherwise prescribed in this Part or under the 2000 Act, any application or proceedings subsequent to an initial application or proceeding considered by the sheriff, including an application to renew an existing order, shall take the form of a minute lodged in the process.

(1A) Except where the sheriff otherwise directs, any such minute shall be lodged in accordance with, and regulated by, Chapter 14 of the Ordinary Cause Rules.

(2) Where any subsequent application or proceedings under paragraph (1) above are made to a court in another sheriffdom the sheriff clerk shall transmit the court process to the court dealing with the current application or proceeding.

(3) Transmission of the process in terms of paragraph (2) shall be made within 4 days of it being requested by the sheriff clerk of the court in which the current application or proceedings have been raised.

(4) Where the application is for renewal of a guardianship order, copies of the reports lodged in accordance with section 57(3) shall be served along with the minute.

NOTE
This rule was amended by the Act of Sederunt (Summary Applications, Statutory Applications and Appeals etc. Rules) Amendment (No.3) (Adults with Incapacity) 2002 (SSI 2002/146).

Remit of applications by the Public Guardian etc.

3.16.9 Where an application is remitted to the sheriff by the Public Guardian or by any other party authorised to do so under the 2000 Act the party remitting the application shall, within 4 days of the decision to remit, transmit the papers relating to the application to the sheriff clerk of the court where the application is to be considered."

Caution

3.16.10—(1) Where the sheriff requires a person authorised under an intervention order or any variation of an intervention order, or appointed as a guardian, to find caution he shall specify the amount and period within which caution is to be found in the interlocutor authorising or appointing the person or varying the order (as the case may be).

(2) The sheriff may, on application made by motion before the expiry of the period for finding caution and on cause shown, allow further time for finding caution in accordance with paragraph (1).

(3) Caution shall be lodged with the Public Guardian.

(4) Where caution has been lodged to the satisfaction of the Public Guardian he shall notify the sheriff clerk.

(5) The sheriff may at any time while a requirement to find caution is in force—

(a) increase the amount of, or require the person to find new, caution; or

(b) authorise the amount of caution to be decreased.

Appointment of interim guardian

3.16.11 An application under section 57(5) of the 2000 Act (appointment of interim guardian) may be made in the crave of the application for a guardianship order to which it relates or, if made after the submission of the application for a guardianship order, by motion in the process of that application.

Registration of intervention order or guardianship order relating to heritable property

3.16.12 Where an application for an intervention order or a guardianship order seeks to vest in the person authorised under the order, or the guardian, as the case may be, any right to deal with, convey or manage any interest in heritable property which is recorded or capable of being recorded in the General Register of Sasines or is registered or capable of being registered in the Land Register of Scotland, the applicant must specify the necessary details of the property in the application to enable it to be identified in the Register of Sasines or the Land Register of Scotland, as the case may be.

Non-compliance with decisions of guardians with welfare powers

3.16.13—(1) Where the court is required under section 70(3) of the 2000 Act to intimate an application for an order or warrant in relation to non-compliance with the decision of a guardian with welfare powers, the sheriff clerk shall effect intimation in Form 20 in accordance with paragraphs (2) and (3).

(2) Intimation shall be effected—
(a) where the person is within Scotland, by first class recorded delivery post, or, in the event that intimation by first class recorded delivery post is unsuccessful, by personal service by a sheriff officer; or
(b) where the person is furth of Scotland, in accordance with rule 2.12 (service on persons furth of Scotland).

(3) Such intimation shall include notice of the period within which any objection to the application shall be lodged."

(3) In Schedule 1 to the principal Rules, after Form 19, insert the forms as set out in the Schedule to this Act of Sederunt.

NOTE
Rules 3.16.10—3.16.13 were inserted by the Act of Sederunt (Summary Applications, Statutory Applications and Appeals etc. Rules) Amendment (No.3) (Adults with Incapacity) 2002 (SSI 2002/146).

SCHEDULE

Rule 3(3)

FORM 20

Rule 3.16.4(1)

FORM OF NOTICE OF AN APPLICATION UNDER THE ADULTS WITH INCAPACITY (SCOTLAND) ACT 2000

To *(insert name and address)*

Attached to this notice is a copy of an application for (insert type of application) under the Adults with Incapacity (Scotland) Act 2000.

The hearing will be held at (insert place) on (insert date) at (insert time)
You may appear personally at the hearing of this application.

In any event, if you are unable or do not wish to appear personally you may appoint a legal representative to appear on your behalf.

If you are uncertain as to what action to take you should consult a solicitor. You may be eligible for legal aid, and you can obtain information about legal aid from any solicitor. You may also obtain information from any Citizens Advice Bureau or other advice agency.

If you do not appear personally or by legal representative, the sheriff may consider the application in the absence of you or your legal representative.

(insert place and date)

(signed)

Sheriff Clerk

or

[P.Q.] Sheriff Officer

or

[X.Y.], Solicitor

FORM 21

Rule 3.16.4(3)

FORM OF NOTICE TO MANAGERS

To *(insert name and address of manager)*

A copy of an application made under the Adults with Incapacity (Scotland) Act 2000 and notice of hearing is sent with this notice.

1. You are requested to deliver it personally to (name of adult) and to explain the contents of it to him or her.

2. You are further requested to complete and return to the sheriff clerk in the enclosed envelope the certificate (Form 22) appended hereto before the date of the hearing.

(insert place and date) (signed)

Sheriff Clerk

or

[P.Q.], Sheriff Officer

or

[X.Y.], Solicitor

FORM 22

Rule 3.16.4(4)

FORM OF CERTIFICATE OF DELIVERY BY MANAGER

I, *(insert name and designation)*, certify that—

I have on *(insert date)* personally delivered to (name of adult) a copy of the application and the intimation of the hearing and have explained the contents to him/her.

Date *(insert date) (signed)*

Manager

(add designation and address)

FORM 23

Rule 3.16.7(1)

SUMMARY APPLICATION UNDER THE ADULTS WITH INCAPACITY (SCOTLAND) ACT 2000

SHERIFFDOM OF *(insert name of sheriffdom)*
AT *(insert place of Sheriff Court)*
[A.B.] *(design and state capacity in which the application is made)*, Pursuer

The applicant craves the court *(state here the specific order(s) sought by reference to the provisions in the Adults with Incapacity (Scotland) Act 2000.)*

STATEMENTS OF FACT
(State in numbered paragraphs the facts on which the application is made, including:

1. The designation of the adult concerned *(if other than the applicant).*

(a) *the adult's nearest relative;*

(b) *the adult's primary carer;*

(c) *any guardian, continuing attorney or welfare attorney of the adult; and*

(d) *any other person who may have an interest in the application.*

3. *The adult's place of habitual residence and/or the location of the property which is the subject of the application.)*

(insert place and date) (signed)

[A.B.], Pursuer or

[X.Y.], *(state designation and business address)*

Solicitor for the Pursuer

Note. This Form should not be used for appeals to the Sheriff. Appeals should be made in Form 24.

FORM 24

Rule 3.16.7(2)

APPEAL TO THE SHERIFF UNDER THE ADULTS WITH INCAPACITY (SCOTLAND) ACT 2000

SHERIFFDOM OF *(insert name of sheriffdom)*
AT *(insert place of Sheriff Court)*
[A.B.] *(design and state capacity in which the appeal is being made)*, Pursuer

This appeal is made in respect of *(state here the decision concerned, the date on which it was intimated to the pursuer, and refer to the relevant provisions in the Adults with Incapacity (Scotland) Act 2000).*

(State here, in numbered paragraphs:

1. *The designation of the adult concerned (if other than the applicant).*

2. *The designation of:*

(a) *the adult's nearest relative;*

(b) *the adult's primary carer;*

(c) *any guardian, continuing attorney or welfare attorney of the adult; and*

(d) *any other person who may have an interest in the application.*

3. *The adult's place of habitual residence and/or the location of the property which is the subject of the application.)*

The pursuer appeals against the decision on the following grounds *(state here in separate paragraphs the grounds on which the appeal is made).*

The pursuer craves the court *(state here orders sought in respect of appeal).*

(insert place and date) (signed)

[A.B.], Pursuer

or

[X.Y.], *(state designation and business address)*

Solicitor for the Pursuer

ADULTS WITH INCAPACITY (SUPERVISION OF WELFARE GUARDIANS ETC. BY LOCAL AUTHORITIES) (SCOTLAND) REGULATIONS 2002

(SSI 2002/95)

Made	5th March 2002
Laid before the Scottish Parliament	7th March 2002
Coming into force	1st April 2002

The Scottish Ministers, in exercise of the powers conferred by sections 10(3)(a) and (b)(i) and 86(2) of the Adults with Incapacity (Scotland) Act 2000 and of all other powers enabling them in that behalf, hereby make the following Regulations:

Citation and commencement

1. These Regulations may be cited as the Adults with Incapacity (Supervision of Welfare Guardians etc. by Local Authorities) (Scotland) Regulations 2002 and shall come into force on 1st April 2002.

Duties of local authority

2.—(1) Where a guardian with functions in relation to the personal welfare of an adult has been appointed for a period of one year or more the local authority shall arrange for—
  (a) that adult to be visited on behalf of the local authority from time to time but in any case within three months of the guardianship order being granted and thereafter at intervals of not more than three months; and
  (b) that guardian (except where the guardian is the chief social work officer) to be visited on behalf of the local authority from time to time but in any case at intervals of not more than three months.

(2) Where that guardian has been appointed for a period of less than one year the local authority shall arrange for the adult and guardian to be visited on behalf of the local authority—
  (a) within fourteen days before or after the midpoint of that period of appointment; and
  (b) within fourteen days before the end of that period of appointment.

(3) Where the local authority is supervising a person authorised under an intervention order, it shall arrange for the adult who is the subject of the intervention order, and where appropriate the person authorised under the intervention order, to be visited on behalf of the local authority as often as required by the sheriff and, where no such requirement has been specified, at intervals of not more than one month for the period of time fixed by the sheriff for supervision by the local authority.

(4) Where the local authority considers it appropriate, any visit to the adult in accordance with this regulation may take place at the same time as a visit to the guardian or person authorised under an intervention order as the case may be.

(5) Where the circumstances of an adult are such that it is not possible for a local authority to visit that adult within the time periods specified in this regulation, that local authority shall visit the adult at a time as close to the time when the visit should have taken place, as the adult's circumstances will allow.

Information to be provided

3. For the purpose of enabling the local authority to carry out its supervisory functions—
  (a) a guardian shall from time to time provide the local authority with any reports or other information about the personal welfare of the adult, or the exercise by that guardian of that guardian's powers in relation to the personal welfare of the adult, as the local authority may reasonably require; and
  (b) a person authorised under an intervention order shall from time to time provide the local authority with any reports or other information about the personal welfare of the adult, or the exercise by that person of that person's functions, as the local authority may reasonably require.

Revocation

4. Regulations 4, 5, 6 and 7 of the Mental Health (Specified Treatments, Guardianship Duties etc.) (Scotland) Regulations 1984 are hereby revoked.

Appendix 2

ADULTS WITH INCAPACITY (REPORTS IN RELATION TO GUARDIANSHIP AND INTERVENTION ORDERS) (SCOTLAND) REGULATIONS 2002

(SSI 2002/96)

Made	5th March 2002	**A2–11**
Laid before the Scottish Parliament	7th March 2002	
Coming into force	1st April 2002	

The Scottish Ministers, in exercise of the powers conferred by sections 57(3) and 86(2) of the Adults with Incapacity (Scotland) Act 2000 and of all other powers enabling them in that behalf,
hereby make the following Regulations:

Citation and commencement

1. These Regulations may be cited as the Adults with Incapacity (Reports in Relation to Guardianship and Intervention Orders) (Scotland) Regulations 2002 and shall come into force on 1st April 2002.

Interpretation

2. Any reference in these Regulations—
   (a) to a numbered section is a reference to the section bearing that number in the Adults with Incapacity (Scotland) Act 2000; and
   (b) to a numbered Schedule is a reference to the Schedule bearing that number in these Regulations.

Report from medical practitioner

3. The reports by medical practitioners under section 57(3)(a) in relation to an application for—
   (a) a guardianship order;
   (b) renewal of a guardianship order; or
   (c) an intervention order,
shall be in the form set out in Schedule 1.

Report from mental health officer

4. A report by the mental health officer under section 57(3)(b) in relation to an application for—
   (a) a guardianship order shall be in the form set out in Schedule 2;
   (b) renewal of a guardianship order shall be in the form set out in Schedule 3; and
   (c) an intervention order shall be in the form set out in Schedule 4.

Report from chief social work officer

5. A report by the chief social work officer under section 57(3)(b) in relation to an application for—
   (a) a guardianship order shall be in the form set out in Schedule 5;
   (b) renewal of a guardianship order shall be in the form set out in Schedule 6; and
   (c) an intervention order shall be in the form set out in Schedule 7.

Report from person with sufficient knowledge

6. A report, by a person with sufficient knowledge as to the matters referred to in section 57(3)(b)(i) and (ii), under section 57(3)(c) in relation to an application for—
   (a) a guardianship order shall be in the form set out in Schedule 8;
   (b) renewal of a guardianship order shall be in the form set out in Schedule 9; and
   (c) an intervention order shall be in the form set out in Schedule 10.

SCHEDULE 1

Regulation 3

Report of incapacity to accompany
application for guardianship*
application for renewal of guardianship*
application for intervention order*

AWI[1]
ADULTS WITH INCAPACITY
(SCOTLAND) ACT 2000
Section 57(3)(a)

PART A   **DETAILS OF REPORT WRITER AND ADULT**

I [_____] (name)

being a medical practitioner with the following professional address:

[_____] (state full postal address for contact)

Telephone [_____]   E-mail [_____]

[complete the following box if applicable[1]; otherwise, delete]

and being approved by the [_____] Health Board for the purposes of section 20 of the Mental Health (Scotland) Act 1984 as having special experience in the diagnosis or treatment of mental disorder,

hereby confirm that I examined and assessed the following adult ("the adult")

Name [_____]

Residing at [_____] (state full postal address)

Date of birth [_____]

On [_____] (give date of examination and assessment)

---

* delete the two which do not apply

[1] Where the incapacity is by reason of mental disorder, one of the medical practitioners must be approved for the purposes of section 20 of the 1984 Act as having special experience in the diagnosis or treatment of mental disorder (section 57 (3)(a) of the Act)

Appendix 2

SCHEDULE 1

Regulation 3

PART B   **PURPOSE OF EXAMINATION AND ASSESSMENT**

The examination and assessment was in connection with a proposed application for (tick whichever applies)

A guardianship order*/renewal of guardianship order*/an intervention order

a)   with power over personal welfare

b)   with power over property and/or financial affairs

c)   with power over personal welfare, property and/or financial affairs.

Name of applicant or person requesting report

Name(s) of person or persons nominated in application (if known)

PART C   **FINDINGS OF EXAMINATION AND ASSESSMENT**

On the basis of my examination and assessment I am of the opinion that the adult named in Part A has

(tick box for whichever of the following applies and add comments on nature

a)   Mental disorder[2]

Nature

And /or

b)   Inability to communicate because of physical disability

Nature

---

* delete the two which do not apply

[1] mental disorder means mental illness (including personality disorder) or mental handicap however caused or manifested; but an adult shall not be treated as suffering from mental disorder by reason only of promiscuity or other immoral conduct, sexual deviancy, dependence on alcohol or drugs, or acting as no prudent person would act.

SCHEDULE 1

Regulation 3

I am of the opinion that the condition mentioned in Part C has impaired the capacity of the adult named in Part A to make decisions about or to act to safeguard or promote his/her interests in his/her property, financial affairs or personal welfare in relation to the matters covered in the proposed application. The reason for my opinion is given below.

Please indicate the findings of your examination and assessment, so far as they relate to the adult's capacity in relation to the matters which are the subject of the application.

Please indicate the likely duration of the incapacity

Please indicate the extent to which you have been able to communicate with the adult.

Please indicate the extent to which you have been able to consult the nearest relative, primary carer, and anyone else having an interest in, or knowledge of, the adult.

Appendix 2

SCHEDULE 1

Regulation 3

PART D   **DECLARATION OF INTEREST**

Delete (a) or (b)   (a) I am not related to the adult

(b) I am related to the adult being his/her *(state relationship)*

AND

Delete (c) or (d)   (c) I have no pecuniary interest
in the appointment of a guardian or guardians*
in the renewal of guardianship*
in the intervention order sought*

(d) I have a pecuniary interest
in the appointment of a guardian or guardians*
in the renewal of guardianship*
in the intervention order sought*
The nature and extent of that interest is

Signed[3]

Date

---

* delete the two which do not apply.
[3] Please note that the application and accompanying reports will be served on interested parties.

Note: Schedules 2–7 have not been reproduced here.

Regulation 6(a)

SCHEDULE 8

Report to accompany application for guardianship relating to property and financial affairs

AWI[8]

ADULTS WITH INCAPACITY (SCOTLAND) ACT 2000

Section 57(3)(c)

PART A — AUTHOR OF THE REPORT

I [_____]

am a person with sufficient knowledge to make this report, because of my position as:

[_____]

(Give contact address) Address [_____]

Tel No [_____] E-mail [_____]

PART B — THE ADULT

On [_____] (Give date of interview and assessment of the adult)

I interviewed and assessed the adult who is the subject of this application

[_____] (name)

(Give full name, address and date of birth of the adult, as on the application) of

[_____] (address)

[_____] (DOB)

PART C — THE APPLICANT

This report is written in relation to the application by

(Name of applicant) [_____]

Appendix 2

SCHEDULE 8

Regulation 6(a)

PART D

Please state your opinion in terms of the general principles as set out in section (1) of the Act where possible.

APPROPRIATENESS OF THE ORDER APPLIED FOR

I have read the application, have taken note of the powers sought and the period of guardianship being applied for. My opinion as to the appropriateness of the order sought is as follows:-

1. Will the proposed order (a) benefit the adult and (b) will the benefit be unable to be reasonably achieved without the order?

(a) Describe how the proposed order will benefit the adult.

(b) Describe how the benefit will be unable to be reasonably achieved without the order.

2. Whether the proposed order is the least restrictive option in relation to the freedom of the adult, consistent with the purpose of the order.

(Describe any alternatives considered. These may include a measure outwith the 2000 Act, a different measure under the 2000 Act or an order containing less restrictive powers. State whether you support the terms of the order sought or support it subject to amendment.)

SCHEDULE 8

Regulation 6(a)

| 3 | What are the past and present wishes and feelings of the adult? |

State
(a) the past and present wishes and feelings of the adult about the order sought and the powers requested, so far as you have been able to ascertain them.

(b) If you have not been able to ascertain the adult's wishes and feelings, please explain the barriers to this.

(c) Describe the efforts you made to overcome these barriers.

Appendix 2

Regulation 6(a)

SCHEDULE 8

| 4 | What are the views of the nearest relative of the adult? |

Name:

Relationship:

State
(a) the views of the nearest relative about the order sought if you have obtained these. Note this section relates to the relative's own views. Information which the relative wishes to provide about the adult's wishes and feelings should be included (and attributed) in section 3(a).

(b) Do you agree with these views?

(c) If you have not obtained these views, why was it not reasonable or practicable to do so?
Note: the nearest relative should not be consulted where an order to that effect has been made under section 4 of the Act.

Regulation 6(a)

SCHEDULE 8

5 | What are the views of the primary carer of the adult?

Name:

Relationship:

State
(a) the views of the primary carer about the order sought if you have obtained these.

(b) Do you agree with these views?

(c) If you have not obtained these views, why was it not reasonable or practicable to do so?

Appendix 2

Regulation 6(a)

SCHEDULE 8

Complete if applicable

| 6 | What are the views of any guardian, continuing attorney or welfare attorney? |

Name:

Appointment (e.g. financial guardian:)

State
(a) the views of such a person about the order sought if you have obtained these.

(b) Do you agree with these views?

(c) If you have not obtained these views, why was it not reasonable or practicable to do so? (Continue on a separate sheet if there is more than one such person).

SCHEDULE 8

Regulation 6(a)

Complete if applicable

| 7 | What are the views of any other relevant person which have been made known to you? |

Name:

Connection to adult:

State
(a) the views of any other relevant person which have been made known to you and which are relevant to the order sought.

(b) Do you agree with these views? (Continue on a separate sheet if there is more than one such person.)

| 8 | Are there any other matters which seem to you to be relevant? |

Appendix 2 451

Regulation 6(a)

SCHEDULE 8

PART E   **PROPOSED GUARDIAN'S SUITABILITY**

(If there is more than one proposed guardian with powers over property and/or financial affairs please duplicate Part E and complete for each proposed guardian.)

Name of proposed guardian:

Relationship to adult:

Sections 59(3) & (4) of the Act require the sheriff to consider certain factors before appointing an individual as a guardian; comment on the suitability of the person nominated under the headings in Part E where possible. Refer as appropriate to discussion with him or her.

My opinion as to the suitability of the person nominated is as follows:-

1. Awareness of the adult's circumstances and conditions and of the needs arising from such circumstances and conditions.

2. Awareness of the functions of a guardian.

Regulation 6(a)

SCHEDULE 8

| 3 | Accessibility to adult and primary carer. |

| 4 | Ability to carry out the functions of a guardian with personal welfare powers. |

| 5 | Any likely conflict of interest between the guardian and the adult. (NB: Being a close relative or living in the same household as the adult does *not* on its own count as conflict of interest.) |

| 6 | Any undue concentration of power which is likely to arise in the proposed guardian over the adult. (NB: Being a close relative or living in the same household as the adult does *not* on its own count as undue concentration of power.) |

Appendix 2 Regulation 6(a)

SCHEDULE 8

7 | Any adverse effects which the appointment of the proposed guardian would have on the interests of the adult.

8 | Any other matters which seem to you to be relevant.

SCHEDULE 8

Regulation 6(a)

PART F: **CONCLUSION**

My general conclusion on the appropriateness of the order sought and the suitability of the proposed guardian(s) are as follows:

[   ]

PART G: **DECLARATION OF INTEREST**

Delete (a) or (b)   (a) I am not related to the adult

(b) I am related to the adult being his/her

(state relationship)

[   ]

AND

Delete (c) or (d)   (c) I have no pecuniary interest in the appointment of a guardian or guardians

(d) I have a pecuniary interest in the appointment of a guardian or guardians

The nature and extent of that interest is

[   ]

Signed[1]   [   ]

Dated   [   ]

---

[1] Please note that the application and accompanying reports will be served on interested parties.

Appendix 2

SCHEDULE 9

Regulation 6(b)

Report to accompany application for renewal of guardianship relating to property and financial affairs

AWI[9]
ADULTS WITH INCAPACITY (SCOTLAND) ACT 2000
Section 57(3)(c)

PART A — AUTHOR OF THE REPORT

I [_____]

am a person with sufficient knowledge to make this report, because of my position as:

[_____]

(Give contact address)   Address [_____]

Tel No [_____]   E-mail [_____]

PART B — THE ADULT

On [_____] (Give date of interview and assessment of the adult)

I interviewed and assessed the adult who is the subject of this application

[_____] (name)

(Give full name, address and date of birth of the adult, as on the application) of

[_____] (address)

[_____] (DOB)

PART C — THE APPLICANT

This report is written in relation to the application by

(Name of applicant) [_____]

SCHEDULE 9

Regulation 6(b)

PART D
Please state your opinion in terms of the general principles as set out in section (1) of the Act where possible.

APPROPRIATENESS OF THE ORDER APPLIED FOR
I have read the application, have taken note of the powers sought and the renewal of guardianship being applied for. My opinion as to the appropriateness of the order sought is as follows:-

1. Will the proposed order (a) benefit the adult and (b) will the benefit be unable to be reasonably achieved without the order?

(a) Describe how the proposed order will benefit the adult.

(b) Describe how the benefit will be unable to be reasonably achieved without the order.

2. Whether the proposed order is the least restrictive option in relation to the freedom of the adult, consistent with the purpose of the order.

(Describe any alternatives considered. These may include a measure outwith the 2000 Act, a different measure under the 2000 Act or an order containing less restrictive powers. State whether you support the terms of the order sought or support it subject to amendment.)

Regulation 6(b)

SCHEDULE 9

3 | What are the past and present wishes and feelings of the adult?

State
(a) the past and present wishes and feelings of the adult about the order sought and the powers requested, so far as you have been able to ascertain them.

(b) If you have not been able to ascertain the adult's wishes and feelings, please explain the barriers to this.

(c) describe the efforts you made to overcome these barriers.

Regulation 6(b)

SCHEDULE 9

| 4 | What are the views of the nearest relative of the adult? |

Name:

Relationship:

State
(a) the views of the nearest relative about the order sought if you have obtained these. Note this section relates to the relative's own views. Information which the relative wishes to provide about the adult's wishes and feelings should be included (and attributed) in section 3(a).

(b) Do you agree with these views?

(c) If you have not obtained these views, why was it not reasonable or practicable to do so?
Note: the nearest relative should not be consulted where an order to that effect has been made under section 4 of the Act.

Appendix 2

Regulation 6(b)

SCHEDULE 9

| 5 | What are the views of the primary carer of the adult? |

Name:

Relationship:

State
(a) the views of the primary carer about the order sought if you have obtained these.

(b) Do you agree with these views?

(c) If you have not obtained these views, why was it not reasonable or practicable to do so?

Adult Incapacity

Regulation 6(b)

SCHEDULE 9

Complete if applicable

| 6 | What are the views of any guardian, continuing attorney or welfare attorney? |

Name:

Appointment (e.g. financial guardian:)

State
(a) the views of such a person about the order sought if you have obtained these.

(b) Do you agree with these views?

(c) If you have not obtained these views, why was it not reasonable or practicable to do so? (Continue on a separate sheet if there is more than one such person).

Appendix 2

Regulation 6(b)

SCHEDULE 9

Complete if applicable

| 7 | What are the views of any other relevant person which have been made known to you? |

Name:

Connection to adult:

State
(a) the views of any other relevant person which have been made known to you and which are relevant to the order sought.

(b) Do you agree with these views? (Continue on a separate sheet if there is more than one such person.)

| 8 | Are there any other matters which seem to you to be relevant? |

Regulation 6(b)

SCHEDULE 9

PART E **PROPOSED GUARDIAN'S SUITABILITY**

(If there is more than one proposed guardian with powers over property and/or financial affairs please duplicate Part E and complete for each proposed guardian.)

Name of proposed guardian: [ ]

Relationship to adult: [ ]

Sections 59(3) & (4) of the Act require the sheriff to consider certain factors before appointing an individual as a guardian; comment on the suitability of the person nominated under the headings in Part E where possible. Refer as appropriate to discussion with him or her.

My opinion as to the suitability of the person nominated is as follows:-

1. Awareness of the adult's circumstances and conditions and of the needs arising from such circumstances and conditions.

[ ]

2. Awareness of the functions of a guardian.

[ ]

Appendix 2

SCHEDULE 9

Regulation 6(b)

| 3 | Accessibility to adult and primary carer. |

| 4 | Ability to carry out the functions of a guardian with personal welfare powers |

| 5 | Any likely conflict of interest between the guardian and the adult. (NB: Being a close relative or living in the same household as the adult does *not* on its own count as conflict of interest.) |

| 6 | Any undue concentration of power which is likely to arise in the proposed guardian over the adult. (NB: Being a close relative or living in the same household as the adult does *not* on its own count as undue concentration of power.) |

Regulation 6(b)

SCHEDULE 9

| 7 | Any adverse effects which the appointment of the proposed guardian would have on the interests of the adult. |

| 8 | Any other matters which seem to you to be relevant. |

Appendix 2

SCHEDULE 9

Regulation 6(b)

PART F: **CONCLUSION**

My general conclusions on the appropriateness of the order sought and the suitability of the proposed guardian(s) are as follows:

[   ]

PART G: **DECLARATION OF INTEREST**

Delete (a) or (b)   (a) I am not related to the adult

                       (b) I am related to the adult being his/her

                       (state relationship)

[   ]

AND

Delete (c) or (d)   (c) I have no pecuniary interest in the appointment of a guardian or guardians

                       (d) I have a pecuniary interest in the appointment of a guardian or guardians

                       The nature and extent of that interest is

[   ]

Signed[1]   [   ]

Dated   [   ]

---

[1] Please note that the application and accompanying reports will be served on interested parties.

Adult Incapacity

SCHEDULE 10

Regulation 6(c)

Report to accompany application for intervention order relating to property and financial affairs

AWI[10]

ADULTS WITH INCAPACITY (SCOTLAND) ACT 2000

Section 57(3)(c)

PART A   **AUTHOR OF THE REPORT**

I _____

am a person with sufficient knowledge to make this report, because of my position as:

_____

(Give contact address)   Address _____

Tel No _____   E-mail _____

PART B   **THE ADULT**

On _____   (Give date of interview and assessment of the adult)

I interviewed and assessed the adult who is the subject of this application

_____ (name)

(Give full name, address and date of birth of the adult, as on the application) of

_____ (address)

_____ (DOB)

PART C   **THE APPLICANT**

This report is written in relation to the application by _____

(Name of applicant)

Appendix 2

SCHEDULE 10

Regulation 6(c)

PART D

Please state your opinion in terms of the general principles as set out in section (1) of the Act where possible.

APPROPRIATENESS OF THE ORDER APPLIED FOR

I have read the application, have taken note of the powers sought and the period being applied for (if applicable). My opinion as to the appropriateness of the order sought is as follows:-

1. Will the proposed order (a) benefit the adult and (b) will the benefit be unable to be reasonably achieved without the order?

(a) Describe how the proposed order will benefit the adult.

(b) Describe how the benefit will be unable to be reasonably achieved without the order.

2. Whether the proposed order is the least restrictive option in relation to the freedom of the adult, consistent with the purpose of the order.

(Describe any alternatives considered. These may include a measure outwith the 2000 Act, a different measure under the 2000 Act or an order containing less restrictive powers. State whether you support the terms of the order sought or support it subject to amendment.)

Regulation 6(c)

SCHEDULE 10

| 3 | What are the past and present wishes and feelings of the adult? |

State
(a) the past and present wishes and feelings of the adult about the order sought and the powers requested, so far as you have been able to ascertain them.

(b) If you have not been able to ascertain the adult's wishes and feelings, please explain the barriers to this.

(c) describe the efforts you made to overcome these barriers.

Appendix 2 469

Regulation 6(c)

SCHEDULE 10

| 4 | What are the views of the nearest relative of the adult? |

Name:

Relationship:

State
(a) the views of the nearest relative about the order sought if you have obtained these. Note this section relates to the relative's own views. Information which the relative wishes to provide about the adult's wishes and feelings should be included (and attributed) in section 3(a).

(b) Do you agree with these views?

(c) If you have not obtained these views, why was it not reasonable or practicable to do so?
Note: the nearest relative should not be consulted where an order to that effect has been made under section 4 of the Act.

SCHEDULE 10

Regulation 6(c)

| 5 | What are the views of the primary carer of the adult? |

Name:

Relationship:

State
(a) the views of the primary carer about the order sought if you have obtained these.

(b) Do you agree with these views?

(c) If you have not obtained these views, why was it not reasonable or practicable to do so?

Appendix 2

Regulation 6(c)

SCHEDULE 10

Complete if applicable

| 6 | What are the views of any guardian, continuing attorney or welfare attorney? |

Name:

Appointment (e.g. financial guardian:)

State
(a) the views of such a person about the order sought if you have obtained these.

(b) Do you agree with these views?

(c) If you have not obtained these views, why was it not reasonable or practicable to do so? (Continue on a separate sheet if there is more than one such person).

Adult Incapacity

Regulation 6(c)

SCHEDULE 10

Complete if applicable

| 7 | What are the views of any other relevant person which have been made known to you? |

Name:

Connection to adult:

State
(a) the views of any other relevant person which have been made known to you and which are relevant to the order sought.

(b) Do you agree with these views? (Continue on a separate sheet if there is more than one such person.)

| 8 | Are there any other matters which seem to you to be relevant? |

Appendix 2

Regulation 6(c)

SCHEDULE 10

PART E   **SUITABILITY OF PERSON NOMINATED TO BE AUTHORISED UNDER IN INTERVENTION ORDER**

(Complete in all cases where under section 53(5)(b) a person is nominated in the application to take action or make a decision, including those where the person nominated is an officer of the local authority.)

Name of nominee:

Relationship to adult:

Sections 59(3) & (4) of the Act require the sheriff to consider certain factors before appointing an individual as a guardian; These provide useful guidance as to what information should be contained in the report on the suitability of a person named in an application for an intervention order. Please therefore comment on the suitability of the person nominated under the headings in Part E where possible. Refer as appropriate to discussion with him or her.

My opinion as to the suitability of the person nominated is as follows:-

| 1 | Awareness of the adult's circumstances and conditions and of the needs arising from such circumstances and conditions. |

| 2 | Awareness of the functions of a person authorised under an intervention order. |

SCHEDULE 10 **Regulation 6(c)**

3 | Accessibility to adult and primary carer.

4 | Ability to carry out the functions of a person authorised under an intervention order with power over property and/or financial powers.

5 | Any likely conflict of interest between the person nominated and the adult. (NB: Being a close relative or living in the same household as the adult does *not* on its own count as conflict of interest.)

6 | Any undue concentration of power which is likely to arise in the person nominated over the adult. (NB: Being a close relative or living in the same household as the adult does *not* on its own count as undue concentration of power.)

Appendix 2

Regulation 6(c)

SCHEDULE 10

7 | Any adverse effects which the appointment of the person nominated would have on the interests of the adult.

8 | Any other matters which seem to you to be relevant.

SCHEDULE 10

Regulation 6(c)

PART F: **CONCLUSION**

My general conclusions on the appropriateness of the order sought and the suitability of the person nominated (if any) are as follows:

PART G: **DECLARATION OF INTEREST**

Delete (a) or (b)   (a) I am not related to the adult

    (b) I am related to the adult being his/her

    (state relationship)

AND

Delete (c) or (d)   (c) I have no pecuniary interest in the order sought

    (d) I have a pecuniary interest in the order sought

    The nature and extent of that interest is

Signed[1]

Dated

---

[1] Please note that the application and accompanying reports will be served on interested parties.

Appendix 2

ADULTS WITH INCAPACITY (RECALL OF GUARDIANS' POWERS) (SCOTLAND) REGULATIONS 2002

(SSI 2002/97)

Made 5th March 2002
Laid before the Scottish Parliament 7th March 2002
Coming into force 1st April 2002

The Scottish Ministers, in exercise of the powers conferred by sections 73(5), (7) and (10) and 86(2) of the Adults with Incapacity (Scotland) Act 2000 and of all other powers enabling them in that behalf, hereby make the following Regulations:

Citation and commencement

1. These Regulations may be cited as the Adults with Incapacity (Recall of Guardians' Powers) (Scotland) Regulations 2002 and shall come into force on 1st April 2002.

Interpretation

2. Any reference in these Regulations—
  (a) to a numbered section is a reference to the section bearing that number in the Adults with Incapacity (Scotland) Act 2000; and
  (b) to a numbered Schedule is a reference to the Schedule bearing that number in these Regulations.

Applications for recall

3. An application under section 73(3) for recall of a guardian's powers—
  (a) by the Mental Welfare Commission shall be in the form set out in Schedule 1; or
  (b) by the local authority shall be in the form set out in Schedule 2,
and, where the person making the application considers that the adult is no longer incapable, shall be accompanied by a medical report in the form set out in Schedule 3.

Intimation of application to recall or intention to recall by the Mental Welfare Commission

4. An intimation by the Mental Welfare Commission under section 73(5) of—
  (a) an application for recall of a guardian's powers; or
  (b) their intention at their own instance to recall the powers of a guardian,
shall be in the form set out in Schedule 4.

Intimation of application to recall or intention to recall by the local authority

5. An intimation by the local authority under section 73(5) of—
  (a) an application for recall of a guardian's powers; or
  (b) its intention at its own instance to recall the powers of a guardian,
shall be in the form set out in Schedule 5.

Period for objection to recall

6. A person may object under section 73(5) to the recall of a guardian's powers within 21 days of receipt of intimation of the application for recall, or intention to recall, by the Mental Welfare Commission or local authority, as the case may be.

Intimation of a decision by the Mental Welfare Commission to refuse recall

7. Where the Mental Welfare Commission proposes to refuse an application for recall under section 73(7), the intimation of that decision shall be in the form set out in Schedule 6.

Intimation of a decision by the local authority to refuse recall

8. Where the local authority proposes to refuse an application for recall under section 73(7), the intimation of that decision shall be in the form set out in Schedule 7.

Period for objection to decision as to recall

9. A person may object under section 73(7) to the decision by the Mental Welfare Commission or local authority, as the case may be, to refuse an application for recall of a guardian's powers within 21 days of receipt of intimation of that decision.

Form for recording decision by the Mental Welfare Commission

10. A decision by the Mental Welfare Commission to—
    (a) recall the powers of a guardian under section 73(6);
    (b) refuse an application to recall such powers; or
    (c) remit, or not remit, the decision on recall to the sheriff under section 73(8),
shall be in the form set out in Schedule 8.

Form for recording decision by the local authority

11. A decision by the local authority to—
    (a) recall the powers of a guardian under section 73(6);
    (b) refuse an application to recall such powers; or
    (c) remit, or not remit, the decision on recall to the sheriff under section 73(8),
shall be in the form set out in Schedule 9.

Notification of decisions

12.—(1) Where the Mental Welfare Commission decides to recall the powers of a guardian they shall send a copy of the form provided for at regulation 10 above to the applicant, the local authority and the Public Guardian.

(2) Where the local authority decides to recall the powers of a guardian it shall send a copy of the form provided for at regulation 11 above to the applicant, the Mental Welfare Commission and the Public Guardian.

Appendix 2

SCHEDULE 1

Regulation 3(a)

Application to Mental Welfare Commission for recall of powers of a guardian relating to personal welfare

AWI[11]
ADULTS WITH INCAPACITY (SCOTLAND) ACT 2000

Section 73(3)

PART A PERSON MAKING THE APPLICATION

(Give your full name and name of local authority for whom you are acting in this case if applicable or provide details of your interest in the personal welfare of the adult.)

Name

Local authority/ statement of interest

Address

Post Code

Tel No

E-mail

PART B THE ADULT

This application is for recall of the powers of a guardian/guardians relating to the personal welfare of:

(name)

of

(Give full name, address and date of birth of the adult or insert "as above" if adult is person making the application)

(address including postcode)

(DOB)

SCHEDULE 1   Regulation

PART C   DETAILS OF GUARDIANSHIP

(Insert date, court and court case number if known)

> The guardianship order currently in force to which this application relates was made on:
> Court :
> Court case number:

(Insert name and address)

> The guardianship order appointed the following person(s) as guardian(s) with powers relating to personal welfare:
>
> Name:
> Address:
>
> Post Code:
> Tel no:
> Fax No:
> e-mail address:
>
> **Note: If available please provide a copy of the guardianship order**

Where the chief social work officer was appointed guardian, the officer responsible under section 64(9) of the Act to carry out the functions and duties of guardian is:

(Insert name and contact details or delete as applicable)

> Name:
> Address:
>
> Post Code:
> Tel no:
> Fax No:
> e-mail address:

The guardianship order also appointed the following person(s) as guardian(s) with powers relating to property or financial affairs:

(Insert details or delete as applicable)

> Name(s):
> Address(es):
>
> Post Code
> Tel no:
> Fax No:
> e-mail address:

Regulation 3(a)

SCHEDULE 1

PART D GROUNDS ON WHICH RECALL IS SOUGHT

(Delete (a) or (b), unless both apply.)	I apply for the powers relating to personal welfare in the order described in Part C above to be recalled because:
	(a) the grounds for appointment of a guardian with such powers are no longer fulfilled (this could relate to either the adult's capacity or the adult's needs).
NB: the applicant must ensure that the doctor providing such a report is informed of the powers in the order.	(Explain why this is the case and, if applicable, attach a report by a medical practitioner stating that the adult is no longer incapable in relation to decisions about, or of acting to safeguard or promote his interests in his/her personal welfare, in relation to the matters covered in the guardianship order.)
(Describe alternatives proposed)	(b) the interests of the adult in his/her personal welfare can be satisfactorily safeguarded or promoted otherwise than by guardianship. (Describe the alternative means by which the adult's interests are to be safeguarded or promoted.)

SCHEDULE 1

Regulation 3(a)

PART E   CONSULTATION

In making the application, I have consulted the following persons:

1. the adult

(State the past and present wishes and feelings of the adult about the proposed recall of guardianship, so far as you have been able to ascertain them. If you have not been able to ascertain the adult's wishes and feelings, please explain the barriers to this and explain the efforts you made to help the adult overcome these barriers.)

2. The nearest relative of the adult

Name:

Address

Relationship to adult:

(State the views of the nearest relative on the proposed recall if you have obtained these. Do you agree with these views? If you have not obtained these views, why was it not reasonable or practicable to do so?) Note: the nearest relative of the adult should not be consulted where an order to that effect has been made under section 4 of the Act.

Regulation 3(a)

SCHEDULE 1

3. | The views of the primary carer of the adult |

Name:
Address

Relationship to adult:

(State the views of the primary carer on the proposed recall if you have obtained these. Do you agree with these views? If you have not obtained these views, why was it not reasonable or practicable to do so?)

4. | The views of the guardian(s) at Part C |

Name(s):

Appointment e.g. financial guardian

(State the views of any guardian named at Part (C) on the proposed recall if you have obtained these. Do you agree with these views? If you have not obtained these views, why was it not reasonable or practicable to do so?).

Regulation 3(a)

SCHEDULE 1

5. The views of any other relevant person including any other guardian, continuing or welfare attorney which have been made known to you and any person whom the sheriff has directed to be consulted

Name:
Address:

Connection to adult

(State the views of any other relevant person which have been made known to you and which are relevant to the proposed recall. Do you agree with these views?) (Continue on a separate sheet if there is more than one such person.)

PART F CONCLUSION

List any other matters which seem to you to be relevant.

Sign and date the form

Signed:

Date:

Application to local authority for recall of powers of a guardian relating to personal welfare

SCHEDULE 2

Regulation 3(b)

AWI[12]
ADULTS WITH INCAPACITY (SCOTLAND) ACT 2000

Section 73(3)

PART A PERSON MAKING THE APPLICATION

(Give your full name and the name of the local authority for whom you are acting in this case if applicable or provide details of your interest in the personal welfare of the adult.[1])

Name

Local authority/ statement of interest

Address

Post Code

Tel No

E-mail

PART B THE ADULT

This application is for recall of the powers of a guardian/guardians relating to the personal welfare of:

(name)

of

(address including postcode)

(Give full name, address and date of birth of the adult or insert "as above" if adult is person making application)

(DOB)

---

[1] Note that a local authority may not be asked to recall welfare powers conferred on its own chief social work officer. In such a case an application for recall should be made to the sheriff or to the Mental Welfare Commission.

Regulation 3(b)

SCHEDULE 2

PART C DETAILS OF GUARDIANSHIP

(Insert date, court and court case number if known)	The guardianship order currently in force to which this application relates was made on: Court: Court case number:
(Insert name and address)	The guardianship order appointed the following person(s) as guardian(s) with powers relating to personal welfare: Name: Address: Post Code: Tel no: Fax No: e-mail address: **Note: If available please provide a copy of the guardianship order**

The guardianship order also appointed the following person(s) as guardian(s) with powers relating to property or financial affairs:

(Insert details or delete as applicable)	Name(s): Address(es): Post Code: Tel no: Fax No: e-mail address:

Regulation 3(b)

SCHEDULE 2

PART D GROUNDS ON WHICH RECALL IS SOUGHT

(Delete (a) or (b), unless both apply.)	I apply for the powers relating to personal welfare in the order described in Part C above to be recalled because: (a) the grounds for appointment of a guardian with such powers are no longer fulfilled(this could relate to either the adult's capacity or the adult's needs).
NB: the applicant must ensure that the doctor providing such a report is informed of the powers in the order.	(Explain why this is the case and, if applicable, attach a report by a medical practitioner stating that the adult is no longer incapable in relation to decisions about, or of acting to safeguard or promote his interests in his/her personal welfare, in relation to the matters covered in the guardianship order.)
(Describe alternatives proposed)	(b) the interests of the adult in his/her personal welfare can be satisfactorily safeguarded or promoted otherwise than by guardianship. (Describe the alternative means by which the adult's interests are to be safeguarded or promoted).

SCHEDULE 2 Regulation 3(b)

PART E CONSULTATION

In making the application, I have consulted as follows:

1. the adult

(State the past and present wishes and feelings of the adult about the proposed recall of guardianship, so far as you have been able to ascertain them. If you have not been able to ascertain the adult's wishes and feelings, please explain the barriers to this and explain the efforts you made to help the adult overcome these barriers.)

2. The nearest relative of the adult

Name:
Address:

Relationship to adult:

(State the views of the nearest relative on the proposed recall if you have obtained these. Do you agree with these views? If you have not obtained these views, why was it not reasonable or practicable to do so?) Note : the nearest relative of the adult should not be consulted where an order to that effect has been made under section 4 of the Act.

SCHEDULE 2

Regulation 3(b)

3. | The views of the primary carer of the adult

Name:
Address:

Relationship to adult:

(State the views of the primary carer on the proposed recall if you have obtained these. Do you agree with these views? If you have not obtained these views, why was it not reasonable or practicable to do so?)

4. | The views of the guardian(s) at Part C

Name(s):

Appointment e.g. financial guardian

(Only complete if applicable.)

(State the views of any guardian(s) named at Part (C) on the proposed recall if you have obtained these. Do you agree with these views? If you have not obtained these views, why was it not reasonable or practicable to do so?)

SCHEDULE 2 Regulation 3(b)

5. The views of any other relevant person, including any other guardian, continuing attorney or welfare attorney which have been made known to you and any person whom the sheriff has directed to be consulted

Name:
Address:

Connection to adult:

(State the views of any other relevant person which have been made known to you and which are relevant to the proposed recall. Do you agree with these views?) (Continue on a separate sheet if there is more than one such person.)

PART F CONCLUSION

List any other matters which seem to you to be relevant.

Sign and date the form

Signed:

Date:

Appendix 2 491

SCHEDULE 3 Regulation 3

Report of capacity to accompany applications to the Mental Welfare Commission or local authority under section 73(3) of the Act for recall of powers of a guardian relating to personal welfare

AWI[13]
Adults with Incapacity (Scotland) Act 2000
Section 73(3)

PART A   DETAILS OF REPORT WRITER AND ADULT

I [_____] (name)

being a medical practitioner with the following professional address:

[_____] (state full postal address for contact)

Telephone [_____]   E-mail [_____]

hereby confirm that I examined and assessed the following adult ("the adult")

Name   [_____]

Residing at   [_____] (state full postal address)

Date of birth [_____]

On   [_____] (give date of examination and assessment)

SCHEDULE 3   Regulation 3

PART B   DETAILS OF APPLICATION

Name of applicant or person requesting report

Date of application (if known)

PART C   FINDINGS OF EXAMINATION AND ASSESSMENT

On the basis of my examination and assessment I am of the opinion that the adult named in Part A is no longer incapable in relation to decisions about, or of acting to safeguard or promote his/her interests in his/her personal welfare in relation to the matters covered in the guardianship order. The reason for my opinion is given below.

Please indicate the findings of your examination and assessment, so far as they relate to the adult's capacity in relation to the matters which are the subject of the guardianship order.

Please indicate the extent to which you have been able to communicate with the adult,

Please indicate the extent to which you have been able to consult the nearest relative, primary carer, and anyone else having an interest in, or knowledge of, the adult.

Signed

Date

Appendix 2 493

SCHEDULE 4   Regulation 4

Intimation by Mental Welfare Commission of   **AWI[14]**
(i) application or
(ii) intention to recall powers of a guardian
relating to personal welfare

ADULTS WITH INCAPACITY
(SCOTLAND) ACT 2000

Section 73(5)

PART A   PERSONS TO WHOM THIS INTIMATION IS ADDRESSED

(Insert details of those listed in section 73(5) of the Act – see notes on Part A, at end of form.)

Name	
Status under section 73(5)	
Address	
Name	
Status under section 73(5)	
Address	
Name	
Status under section 73(5)	
Address	

SCHEDULE 4 Regulation 4

PART B PERSON WHO IS THE SUBJECT OF THE APPLICATION OR INTENTION TO RECALL ("THE ADULT")

This intimation is in respect of the powers relating to personal welfare conferred on the guardian(s) of:

[   ] (name)

(Give full name, address and date of birth of the adult, as on the application)

[   ] (address)

[   ] DOB

PART C DETAILS OF GUARDIANSHIP

The guardian(s) with powers relating to the personal welfare of the adult is/are:

Name(s):

Address(es):

Note: If available please provide a copy of the guardianship order

Appendix 2 495

SCHEDULE 4   Regulation 4

PART D   APPLICATION RECEIVED OR INTENTION TO RECALL

(Delete (a) or (b))

(a)   The Mental Welfare Commission has received an application for recall of the powers relating to personal welfare conferred on the guardian(s) of the adult named in Part B. The application was made by:

(Insert details of applicant)

Name:

Address:

The application was made on:

Date:

The reason(s) why the application was made is (are):

OR

(b)   The Mental Welfare Commission, acting at its own instance intends to recall the powers relating to personal welfare conferred on the guardian(s) of the adult named in Part B.

The reason(s) why it is intended to recall the powers are:

Regulation 4

SCHEDULE 4

PART E   **OBJECTIONS TO RECALL**

> You may object to recall of the powers relating to personal welfare conferred on the guardian(s) of the adult named in Part B.
>
> Objections must be made within 21 days of the date of receipt of this form. Objections must be made in writing, and should be sent to:
>
> Name:
>
> Address:
>
>
> Tel No:
>
> e-mail address:
>
> Fax:

NOTES ON PART A

Under section 73(5) of the Adults with Incapacity (Scotland) Act 2000, the following should receive intimation of applications for recall or the intention of the Mental Welfare Commission to recall the powers of a guardian relating to personal welfare:

(a)   the adult, unless the sheriff has determined under section 11(1) of the Act that he/she should not be so notified;

(b)   the adult's nearest relative as defined in the Act. The nearest relative should not receive intimation of this form, however, where a court has made an order to that effect under section 4 of the Act;

(c)   the adult's primary carer;

(d)   any guardian(s) with powers relating to personal welfare (unless an application for recall has been received from that person);

(e)   any person who the Mental Welfare Commission considers has an interest in the recall of the powers.

Appendix 2 497

SCHEDULE 5

Regulation 5

Intimation by local authority of
(i) application or
(ii) intention to recall powers of a guardian
relating to personal welfare

AWI[15]
ADULTS WITH INCAPACITY (SCOTLAND) ACT 2000

Section 73(5)

PART A PERSONS TO WHOM THIS INTIMATION IS ADDRESSED

(Insert details of those listed in section 73(5) of the Act – see notes on Part A, at end of form.)

Name

Status under section 73(5)

Address

Name

Status under section 73(5)

Address

Name

Status under section 73(5)

Address

SCHEDULE 5

Regulation 5

PART B PERSON WHO IS THE SUBJECT OF THE APPLICATION OR INTENTION TO RECALL ("THE ADULT")

This intimation is in respect of the powers relating to personal welfare conferred on the guardian(s) of:

[   ] (name)

(Give full name, address and date of birth of the adult, as on the application)

[   ] (address)

[   ] DOB

PART C DETAILS OF GUARDIANSHIP

The guardian(s) with powers relating to the personal welfare of the adult is/are:

Name(s):

Address(es):

Note: If available please provide a copy of the guardianship order

Appendix 2

SCHEDULE 5   Regulation 5

PART D   APPLICATION RECEIVED OR INTENTION TO RECALL

(Delete (a) or (b))
(Insert name of local authority)

(a) _____ has received an application for recall of the powers relating to personal welfare conferred on the guardian(s) of the adult named in Part B. The application was made by:

(Insert details of applicant)

Name:

Address:

The application was made on:

Date:

The reasons why the application was made is (are):

OR

(Insert name of local authority)

(b) _____ acting at its own instance intends to recall the powers relating to personal welfare conferred on the guardian(s) of the adult named in Part B.

The reason(s) why it is intended to recall the powers is (are):

SCHEDULE 5

Regulation 5

PART E OBJECTIONS TO RECALL

> You may object to recall of the powers relating to personal welfare conferred on the guardian(s) of the adult named in Part B.
>
> Objections must be made within 21 days of the date of receipt of this form. Objections must be made in writing, and should be sent to:
>
> Name:
>
> Address:
>
> Tel No:
>
> e-mail address:
>
> Fax:

NOTES ON PART A

Under section 73(5) of the Adults with Incapacity (Scotland) Act 2000, the following should receive intimation of applications for recall or the intention of the Mental Welfare Commission to recall the powers of a guardian relating to personal welfare:

(a) the adult, unless the sheriff has determined under section 11(1) of the Act that he/she should not be so notified;

(b) the adult's nearest relative as defined in the Act. The nearest relative should not receive intimation of this form, however, where a court has made an order to that effect under section 4 of the Act;

(c) the adult's primary carer;

(d) any guardian(s) with powers relating to personal welfare (unless an application for recall has been received from that person);

(e) any person who the Mental Welfare Commission considers has an interest in the recall of the powers.

Appendix 2

SCHEDULE 6

Regulation 7

Intimation by Mental Welfare Commission of proposal to refuse application for recall of powers of a guardian relating to personal welfare

AWI[16]

ADULTS WITH INCAPACITY (SCOTLAND) ACT 2000

Section 73(7)

PART A PERSON WHO IS THE SUBJECT OF THE APPLICATION TO RECALL ("THE ADULT")

This intimation is in respect of the powers relating to personal welfare conferred on the guardian(s) of:

(Give full name, address and date of birth of the adult, as on the application)

(name)

(address)

(DOB)

PART B PERSONS TO WHOM THIS INTIMATION IS ADDRESSED

(a) Adult (see details above) unless the sheriff has determined under section 11(1) of the Act that he/she should not be so notified;

(b) the person who submitted the application for recall.

Name :
Address:

PART C DETAILS OF GUARDIANSHIP

The guardian(s) with powers relating to the personal welfare of the adult is/are:

Name(s):

Address(es):

SCHEDULE 6

Regulation 7

PART D REASONS FOR PROPOSAL TO REFUSE APPLICATION FOR RECALL

(Insert details of applicant)

The Mental Welfare Commission has received an application for recall of the powers relating to personal welfare conferred on the guardian(s) of the adult named in Part B. The application was made by:

Name:

Address:

The application was made on:

Date:

The reason(s) why it is proposed to refuse the application for recall is (are):

PART E OBJECTIONS TO REFUSAL TO RECALL

You may object to the proposed refusal to recall the powers relating to personal welfare conferred on the guardian(s) of the adult named in Part B.

Objections must be made within 21 days of the date of receipt of this form. Objections must be made in writing, and should be sent to:

Name:

Address:

Tel No:
e-mail address:
Fax:

Appendix 2

SCHEDULE 7

Regulation 8

Intimation by local authority of proposal to refuse application for recall of powers of a guardian relating to personal welfare

ADULTS WITH INCAPACITY (SCOTLAND) ACT 2000

AWI[17]

Section 73(7)

PART A   PERSON WHO IS THE SUBJECT OF THE APPLICATION TO RECALL ("THE ADULT")

(Give full name, address and date of birth of the adult, as on the application)

This intimation is in respect of the powers relating to personal welfare conferred on the guardian(s) of:

_____ (name)

_____ (address)

_____ (DOB)

PART B   PERSONS TO WHOM THIS INTIMATION IS ADDRESSED

(a) Adult (see details above) unless the sheriff has determined under section 11(1) of the Act that he/she should not be so notified;

(b) the person who submitted the application for recall.

Name :
Address:

PART C   DETAILS OF GUARDIANSHIP

The guardian(s) with powers relating to the personal welfare of the adult is/are:

Name(s):

Address(es):

SCHEDULE 7

Regulation 8

PART D   REASONS FOR PROPOSAL TO REFUSE APPLICATION FOR RECALL

(Insert name of local authority)

_____ has received an application for recall of the powers relating to personal welfare conferred on the guardian(s) of the adult named in Part B. The application was made by:

(Insert details of applicant)

Name:

Address:

The application was made on:

Date:

The reason(s) why it is proposed to refuse the application for recall is (are):

PART E   OBJECTIONS TO REFUSAL TO RECALL

You may object to the proposed refusal to recall the powers relating to personal welfare conferred on the guardian(s) of the adult named in Part B.

Objections must be made within 21 days of the date of receipt of this form. Objections must be made in writing, and should be sent to:

Name:

Address:

Tel No:
e-mail address:
Fax:

Appendix 2 505

SCHEDULE 8   Regulation 10

Decision by Mental Welfare Commission on recall of powers of a guardian relating to personal welfare

AWI[18]
ADULTS WITH INCAPACITY (SCOTLAND) ACT 2000

Section 73(6)

PART A   ADULT UNDER GUARDIANSHIP

This decision concerns the powers of a guardian/guardians relating to the personal welfare of:

[_____] (name)

(Give full name, address and date of birth of the adult under guardianship)

of

[_____] (address)

[_____] (DOB)

PART B   DETAILS OF GUARDIANSHIP

(Insert date, court and court case number if known)

The guardianship order currently in force to which this application relates was made on:
Court:
Court case number:

(Insert name and address)

The guardianship order appointed the following person(s) as guardian(s) with powers relating to personal welfare:

Name:
Address:

SCHEDULE 8

Regulation 10

PART C APPLICATION FOR RECALL

Delete part C if not applicable

(Insert details of applicant)

The Mental Welfare Commission has received an application for recall of the powers relating to personal welfare conferred on the guardian(s) named in Part B.

The application was made by:

Name

Address:

(Insert details from application)

The capacity in which the applicant claimed an interest in the adult's personal welfare was:

The application was made on: (date)

PART D CONFIRMATION OF INTIMATIONS TO POTENTIAL OBJECTORS

I confirm that the application OR the Mental Welfare Commission's intention to recall the personal welfare powers at Part B was intimated to:

(Insert names and details of those who received intimations under sections 73(5) and (7) of the Act)

SCHEDULE 8 Regulation 10

PART E **OBJECTIONS RECEIVED**

(Insert details of objections including name of objector(s) and capacity in which he/she/they objected)

The following objections to recall were received:

Regulation 10

SCHEDULE 8

PART F   DECISION

Please delete those sections (a) – (d) which are not applicable.

The decision of the Mental Welfare Commission is as follows:-

(a) to recall the personal welfare powers of the guardian(s) named at Part B in relation to the adult named at Part A.

> The decision was made because either (i) or (ii) or both are applicable (delete as necessary)
>
> (i) the grounds for appointment of the guardian with personal welfare powers named at Part B are no longer fulfilled
>
> (ii) the interests of the adult named at Part A in his/her personal welfare can be satisfactorily safeguarded or promoted otherwise than by guardianship

(b) to refuse to recall the personal welfare powers at Part B of the guardian(s) of the adult at Part A.

> The decision was made because either (i) or (ii) or both are applicable (delete as necessary)
>
> (i) the grounds for appointment of a guardian with the personal welfare powers at Part B are still fulfilled
>
> (ii) the interests of the adult at Part A in his/her personal welfare cannot be satisfactorily safeguarded or promoted otherwise than by guardianship

(c) to remit to the sheriff the decision on recall of the personal welfare powers of the guardian(s) named at Part B in relation to the adult named at Part A

> Insert the reasons why the decision at (c) was made

(d) not to remit to the sheriff the decision on recall of the personal welfare powers of the guardian(s) named at Part B in relation to the adult named at Part A where the issue of remit has been considered.

> Insert the reasons why the decision at (d) was made

Local Authority and Public Guardian hereby notified in terms of section 73(4) of the Act.

Signed   Date

On behalf of the Mental Welfare Commission.

SCHEDULE 9

Regulation 11

Decision by local authority on recall of powers of a guardian relating to personal welfare

AWI[19]
ADULTS WITH INCAPACITY (SCOTLAND) ACT 2000
Section 73(6)

PART A ADULT UNDER GUARDIANSHIP

This decision concerns the powers of a guardian/guardians relating to the personal welfare of:

(Give full name, address and date of birth of the adult under guardianship)

☐ (name)
of
☐ (address)
☐ (DOB)

PART B DETAILS OF GUARDIANSHIP

(Insert date, court and court case number if known)

The guardianship order currently in force to which this application relates was made on:
Court:
Court case number:

(Insert name and address)

The guardianship order appointed the following person(s) as guardian(s) with powers relating to personal welfare:

Name:
Address:

SCHEDULE 9   Regulation 11

PART C   APPLICATION FOR RECALL

Delete part C if not applicable

(Insert name of local authority)

_____ has received an application for recall of the powers relating to personal welfare conferred on the guardian(s) named in Part B.

(Insert details of applicant)

The application was made by:

Name

Address:

(Insert details from application)

The capacity in which the applicant claimed an interest in the adult's personal welfare was:

The application was made on: (date)

PART D   CONFIRMATION OF INTIMATIONS TO POTENTIAL OBJECTORS

I confirm that the application OR the authority's intention to recall the personal welfare powers at Part B was intimated to:

(Insert names and details of those who received intimations under sections 73(5) and (7) of the Act)

Appendix 2

SCHEDULE 9

Regulation 11

PART E OBJECTIONS RECEIVED

(Insert details of objections including name of objector(s) and capacity in which he/she/they objected)

The following objections to recall were received:

Regulation 11

SCHEDULE 9

PART F   DECISION

Please delete those sections (a) – (d) which are not applicable.

The decision of the local authority is as follows:-

(a) to recall the personal welfare powers of the guardian(s) named at Part B in relation to the adult named at Part A.

> The decision was made because either (i) or (ii) or both are applicable (delete as necessary)
>
> (i) the grounds for appointment of the guardian with personal welfare powers named at Part B are no longer fulfilled
>
> (ii) the interests of the adult named at Part A in his/her personal welfare can be satisfactorily safeguarded or promoted otherwise than by guardianship

(b) to refuse to recall the personal welfare powers at Part B of the guardian(s) of the adult at Part A.

> The decision was made because either (i) or (ii) or both are applicable (delete as necessary)
>
> (i) the grounds for appointment of a guardian with the personal welfare powers at Part B are still fulfilled
>
> (ii) the interests of the adult at Part A in his/her personal welfare cannot be satisfactorily safeguarded or promoted otherwise than by guardianship

(c) to remit to the sheriff the decision on recall of the personal welfare powers of the guardian(s) named at Part B in relation to the adult named at Part A

> Insert the reasons why the decision at (c) was made

(d) not to remit to the sheriff the decision on recall of the personal welfare powers of the guardian(s) named at Part B in relation to the adult named at Part A where the issue of remit has been considered.

> Insert the reasons why the decision at (d) was made

Mental Welfare Commission and Public Guardian hereby notified in terms of section 73(4) of the Act.

Signed   Date

On behalf of the local authority.

Appendix 2

ADULTS WITH INCAPACITY (NON-COMPLIANCE WITH DECISIONS OF WELFARE GUARDIANS) (SCOTLAND) REGULATIONS 2002

(SSI 2002/98)

Made   5th March 2002
Laid before the Scottish Parliament   7th March 2002
Coming into force   1st April 2002

The Scottish Ministers, in exercise of the powers conferred by section 70(3) of the Adults with Incapacity (Scotland) Act 2000 and of all other powers enabling them in that behalf, hereby make the following Regulations:

Citation and commencement

1. These Regulations may be cited as the Adults with Incapacity (Non-compliance with Decisions of Welfare Guardians) (Scotland) Regulations 2002 and shall come into force on 1st April 2002.

Form of application

2. An application for an order or warrant under section 70(1), or an order under section 70(2), of the Adults with Incapacity (Scotland) Act 2000 shall be in the form set out in the Schedule to these Regulations.

Period for objection

3. The period for the purposes of section 70(3) of the Adults with Incapacity (Scotland) Act 2000 shall be 21 days beginning with the date of receipt of intimation under that subsection.

SCHEDULE

Regulation 2

COURT REF NO:

APPLICATION UNDER SECTION 70 OF THE ADULTS WITH INCAPACITY (SCOTLAND) ACT 2000

SHERIFF OF *(insert name of sheriffdom)*
AT *(insert place of Sheriff Court)*

Name and address of applicant (who must be the guardian of the adult):

Name and address of adults:

If applicable, name and address of any person other than the adult who is failing to comply with the guardian's decision

ORDER OR WARRANT SOUGHT

(State here the order or warrant that you seek from the sheriff — delete as appropriate)

- an order under section 70(1)(a) — requiring the adult to comply with a decision of the guardian
- an order under section 70(2) — requiring a person other than the adult to comply with a decision of the guardian
- a warrant under section 70(1)(b) — authorising a constable:
  (i) to enter any premises where the adult is, or is reasonably supposed to be;
  (ii) to apprehend the adult and to remove him/her to such place as the guardian may direct

REASON FOR APPLICATION

Explain why you are seeking this order or warrant. Include here: details of the decisions by the guardian which is not being complied with; a statement as to who is not complying (i.e. the adult or another person named above); details of action already taken to try to effect compliance. If the decision relates to the place of residence of the adult, the adult's current whereabouts must be stated, if different from the address given above.

(insert place and date)   (signed)
                                          .... (applicant)
                                       or
                                          .... (solicitor for applicant)

ADULTS WITH INCAPACITY (SCOTLAND) ACT 2000 (COMMENCEMENT NO. 2) ORDER 2002

(SSI 2002/189 (C. 14))

A2–14   Made   15th April 2002

The Scottish Ministers, in exercise of the powers conferred by section 89(2) of the Adults with Incapacity (Scotland) Act 2000 and all other powers enabling them in that behalf, hereby make the following Order:

Citation

1. This Order may be cited as the Adults with Incapacity (Scotland) Act 2000 (Commencement No. 2) Order 2002.

Commencement

2. Sections 47 (authority of persons responsible for medical treatment), 48 (exceptions to authority to treat), 49 (medical treatment where there is an application for intervention or guardianship order), 50 (medical treatment where guardian etc. has been appointed), 51 (authority for research) and 52 (appeal against decision as to medical treatment) of the Adults with Incapacity (Scotland) Act 2000 shall come into force on 1st July 2002.

Appendix 2

ADULTS WITH INCAPACITY (ETHICS COMMITTEE) (SCOTLAND) REGULATIONS 2002

(SSI 2002/190)

Made	*15th April 2002*	
Laid before the Scottish Parliament	*17th April 2002*	
Coming into force	*1st July 2002*	

The Scottish Ministers, in exercise of the powers conferred by sections 51(6) and (7) and 86(2) of the Adults with Incapacity (Scotland) Act 2000 and of all other powers enabling them in that behalf, hereby make the following Regulations:

Citation and commencement

1. These Regulations may be cited as the Adults with Incapacity (Ethics Committee) (Scotland) Regulations 2002 and come into force on 1st July 2002.

Ethics Committee

2. There is hereby constituted an Ethics Committee ("the Committee") for the purposes specified in section 51 of the Adults with Incapacity (Scotland) Act 2000.

Membership of the Committee

3.—(1) The members of the Committee may be appointed by the Scottish Ministers on such terms and conditions as the Scottish Ministers consider appropriate.
 (2) No more than 18 members shall be appointed to the Committee at any time.
 (3) The membership of the Committee shall, so far as practical, include at least—
  (a) one person who has experience in relation to the treatment of adults who are incapable;
  (b) one medical practitioner who provides personal, or general, medical services under sections 17C or 19 of the National Health Service (Scotland) Act 1978;
  (c) one registered nurse or registered midwife;
  (d) one registered medical practitioner having experience in clinical pharmacology;
  (e) one registered pharmaceutical chemist as defined by section 24(1) of the Pharmacy Act 1954 or a registered person as defined by Article 2(2) of the Pharmacy (Northern Ireland) Order 1976;
  (f) one registered medical practitioner who holds the position of hospital consultant;
  (g) one registered medical practitioner having experience in the field of public health medicine;
  (h) one member who is registered as a member of a profession to which the Professions Supplementary to Medicine Act 1960 applies; and
  (i) three lay members.
 (4) Each member may be appointed for a period not exceeding 5 years but no member may be appointed for consecutive periods exceeding 10 years.

(5) Where a person has been appointed as a member for a total of 10 years consecutively that person may only be appointed again as a member under paragraph (4) above after the expiration of a period of 2 years from the end of the person's previous membership.

Chair and Vice-Chair

4. Subject to regulation 3(4) and (5) above, the Scottish Ministers may appoint, from among the members of the Committee, a Chair and a Vice-Chair of the Committee for such period or periods as the Scottish Ministers consider appropriate.

Remuneration

5. The Scottish Ministers may pay, to members of the Committee, such expenses related to their membership of the Committee as the Scottish Ministers consider appropriate.

Approval of Research

6. Before approving any research under section 51 of the Adults with Incapacity (Scotland) Act 2000 the Committee must take into account—
  (a) the objectives, design, methodology, statistical considerations and organisation of the research;
  (b) the relevance of the research and the study design;
  (c) the justification of predictable risks and inconveniences weighed against the anticipated benefits for the research participants and future participants;
  (d) the suitability of the lead researcher;
  (e) the adequacy of the written information to be given and the procedure for obtaining consent; and
  (f) the arrangements for the recruitment of research participants.

Procedures

7.—(1) Subject to the provision of this regulation, the Committee shall consider applications in such manner as it considers appropriate in the circumstances.
  (2) No approval of research shall be granted by the Committee unless at least one half of its membership is present and those members include—
  (a) the Chair, or in the Chair's absence, the Vice-Chair;
  (b) two members from among those appointed under sub-paragraphs (a) to (h) of regulation 3(3) above; and
  (c) two members from among those appointed under sub-paragraph (i) of regulation 3(3) above.
  (3) The proceedings of the Committee shall not be invalidated by death or other vacancy in its membership.
  (4) Application to the Committee for approval of research shall be in such form as the Committee may determine.
  (5) The Committee may call for such information from an applicant as it may reasonably require in order to determine the application and may seek such assistance from other persons as it considers necessary for that determination.
  (6) The Committee may refer to one or more of its members for report or recommendation on such matters as it considers appropriate in relation to its consideration of an application.

Appendix 2

ADULTS WITH INCAPACITY (MEDICAL TREATMENT CERTIFICATES) (SCOTLAND) REGULATIONS 2002

(SSI 2002/208)

Made	*30th April 2002*
Laid before the Scottish Parliament	*3rd May 2002*
Coming into force	*1st July 2002*

The Scottish Ministers, in exercise of the powers conferred by section 47(5) of the Adults with Incapacity (Scotland) Act 2000 and of all other powers enabling them in that behalf, hereby make the following Regulations:

Citation and commencement

1. These Regulations may be cited as the Adults with Incapacity (Medical Treatment Certificates) (Scotland) Regulations 2002 and come into force on 1st July 2002.

Medical treatment certificates

2. The certificate of a medical practitioner primarily responsible for the medical treatment of an adult for the purposes of section 47 of the Adults with Incapacity (Scotland) Act 2000 (authority of persons responsible for medical treatment) shall be in the form set out in the Schedule to these Regulations.

SCHEDULE

Regulation 2

CERTIFICATE OF INCAPACITY UNDER SECTION 47 OF THE ADULTS WITH INCAPACITY (SCOTLAND) ACT 2000

I _____

(name)

of

_____

(address)

being the medical practitioner primarily responsible for the medical treatment of

_____

(name)

of

_____

(address)

/ _____

/ _____

_____

(date of birth)

for whom the guardian/welfare attorney/person appointed by intervention order/nearest relative/carer is

_____

have today examined the patient named above. I am of the opinion that he/she is incapable in terms of the Adults with Incapacity (Scotland) Act 2000 ("the Act") because of

_____

(nature of incapacity)

in relation to a decision about the following medical treatment

_____

_____

This incapacity is likely to continue for

_____

months. I therefore consider it appropriate for medical treatment to be authorised by this certificate until

/_____

/_____

(a date not more than one year later than the date of the examination on which this certificate is based) or until such earlier date as this certificate is revoked.

In assessing the capacity of the patient I have observed the principles set out in section 1 of the Act.

Signed _____

Date

/_____

/_____

_____

ADULTS WITH INCAPACITY (SPECIFIED MEDICAL TREATMENTS) (SCOTLAND) REGULATIONS 2002

(SSI 2002/275)

Made	6th June 2002	A2–17
Laid before the Scottish Parliament	7th June 2002	
Coming into force	1st July 2002	

The Scottish Ministers, in exercise of the powers conferred by section 48(2) and (3) of the Adults with Incapacity (Scotland) Act 2000 and of all other powers enabling them in that behalf, hereby make the following Regulations:

Citation, commencement and interpretation

1.—(1) These Regulations may be cited as the Adults with Incapacity (Specified Medical Treatments) (Scotland) Regulations 2002 and come into force on 1st July 2002.

(2) In these Regulations "the Act" means the Adults with Incapacity (Scotland) Act 2000.

Specified Medical Treatments

2.—(1) These Regulations apply where the medical practitioner primarily responsible for the medical treatment of an adult has certified, in accordance with section 47(1) (authority of persons responsible for medical treatment) of the Act, that he is of the opinion that the adult is incapable in relation to a decision about a treatment specified in Schedule 1 to these Regulations.

(2) The medical treatments set out in Schedule 1 to these Regulations are specified, for the purposes of section 48(2) of the Act, as treatments to which section 47(2) of the Act (authority of persons responsible for medical treatment) shall not apply.

(3) The medical treatments so specified may be carried out only in accordance with the following provisions of these Regulations and where they are designed to safeguard or promote the physical or mental health of the adult.

Treatments requiring application to the court

3.—(1) Subject to regulations 5 and 6 below, a treatment of a kind set out in Part 1 of Schedule 1 to these Regulations may be carried out in relation to an adult who is incapable in relation to a decision about that treatment if—
 (a) the Court of Session is satisfied, on application to it by the medical practitioner primarily responsible for the medical treatment, that the treatment will safeguard or promote the physical or mental health of the adult and that the adult does not oppose the treatment; and
 (b) the adult does not resist the carrying out of the treatment.

(2) The Court of Session shall, in considering such an application, afford an opportunity to any person having an interest in the personal welfare of the adult to make representations in respect of it.

Treatments requiring a certificate from a practitioner appointed by the Mental Welfare Commission

4.—(1) Subject to regulations 5 and 6 below, a treatment of a kind set out in Part 2 of Schedule 1 to these Regulations may be carried out in relation to an adult who is incapable in relation to a decision about that treatment where a medical practitioner appointed by the Mental Welfare Commission certifies, in the form set out in Schedule 2 to these Regulations, that—
 (a) the adult is incapable in relation to such a decision, and

(b) having regard to the likelihood of its safeguarding or promoting the adult's physical or mental health, the treatment should be carried out.

(2) The medical practitioner referred to in paragraph (1) above shall not be the medical practitioner primarily responsible for any medical treatment of the adult.

Treatment in emergencies

5.—(1) Subject to paragraph (3) below, these Regulations are without prejudice to any authority conferred by any other enactment or rule of law for the preservation of the life of the adult or the prevention of serious deterioration in the adult's medical condition, which may apply to any of the medical treatments set out in Schedule 1 to these Regulations.

(2) Where treatment of a kind set out in Schedule 1 to these Regulations, is carried out under such an authority, the medical practitioner primarily responsible for the treatment shall within 7 days after the treatment has taken place notify the Mental Welfare Commission in writing (including in electronic form) of—
(a) the name and address of the adult;
(b) the nature of the treatment;
(c) the place at which it took place; and
(d) the reasons for its having been given.

(3) Nothing in this regulation shall authorise the carrying out of any medical treatment where an interdict has been granted and continues to have effect prohibiting the provision of such medical treatment.

Young persons

6.—(1) No treatment for mental disorder set out in Schedule 1 to these Regulations may be carried out in relation to an adult who is 16 or 17 years of age and is incapable in relation to a decision about that treatment unless either—
(a) the medical practitioner primarily responsible for that treatment has a qualification, or special experience, in child and adolescent psychiatry; or
(b) that practitioner has sought and obtained an opinion in writing from a practitioner having such a qualification or special experience that the treatment is reasonably required to safeguard or promote the mental health of the adult.

(2) No treatment for mental disorder set out in Part 2 of Schedule 1 to these Regulations may be carried out in relation to an adult who is 16 or 17 years of age and is incapable in relation to a decision about that treatment unless the medical practitioner appointed by the Mental Welfare Commission who certifies that the treatment should be carried out has a qualification, or special experience, in child and adolescent psychiatry or in another specialism appropriate to the treatment of the adult.

Certificates by medical practitioners

7.—(1) The medical practitioner primarily responsible for the medical treatment of the adult shall send a copy of any certificate or opinion given in accordance with these Regulations to the Mental Welfare Commission within 7 days of the date of that certificate or opinion.

(2) A certificate or opinion given in accordance with these Regulations may subsist for a period not exceeding one year.

Appendix 2

SCHEDULE 1

Regulation 2(1) and (2)

MEDICAL TREATMENTS SPECIFIED FOR THE PURPOSES OF SECTION 48(2) OF THE ACT

PART 1

TREATMENTS SUBJECT TO APPROVAL BY THE COURT OF SESSION

1. [. . .]

2. Sterilisation where there is no serious malfunction or disease of the reproductive organs.

3. Surgical implantation of hormones for the purpose of reducing sex drive.

NOTE
Para. 1 was deleted by the Adults with Incapacity (Specified Medical Treatments) (Scotland) Amendment Regulations 2002 (SSI 2002/302).

PART 2

TREATMENTS APPROVED BY A PRACTITIONER APPOINTED BY MENTAL WELFARE COMMISSION

1. Drug treatment for the purpose of reducing sex drive, other than surgical implantation of hormones.

2. Electro-convulsive therapy (ECT) for mental disorder.

3. Abortion.

4. Any medical treatment which is considered likely by the medical practitioner primarily responsible for that treatment to lead to sterilisation as an unavoidable result.

SCHEDULE 2

Regulation 4(1)

CERTIFICATE OF MEDICAL PRACTITIONER APPOINTED BY MENTAL WELFARE COMMISSION

I, (name and professional address)

_____

_____

_____

am a medical practitioner appointed by the Mental Welfare Commission for the purposes of the Adults with Incapacity (Specified Medical Treatments) (Scotland) Regulations 2002 ("the Regulations")

(and, in a case to which regulation 6 of the Regulations (adults aged 16 or 17) applies, have a qualification, or special experience, in child and adolescent psychiatry or in another specialism appropriate to the treatment of the adult) and have today examined

_____
(name of adult)

_____
(adult's address)

_____

_____
(adult's date of birth)

_____
("the adult")

I certify that the adult is incapable in relation to a decision about the treatment proposed which is a treatment to which the Regulations apply namely—

(describe treatment)

_____

_____

and that having regard to the likelihood of that treatment safeguarding or promoting the adult's physical or mental health, the treatment should be carried out. In coming to this decision I have observed the principles set out in section 1 to the Adults with Incapacity (Scotland) Act 2000.

This certificate shall subsist until

_____
(a date not exceeding 1 year from the date of certificate).

_____
(signed)

_____
(date)

APPENDIX 3

CRIMINAL PROCEDURE (SCOTLAND) ACT 1995, ss.57, 58, 58A, 60B and 61

Disposal in case of insanity

Disposal of case where accused found to be insane

57.—(1)This section applies where—
 (a) a person is, by virtue of section 54(6) or 55(3) of this Act, acquitted on the ground of his insanity at the time of the act or omission; or
 (b) following an examination of facts under section 55, a court makes a finding under subsection (2) of that section.
 (2) Subject to subsection (3) below, where this section applies the court may, as it thinks fit—
 (a) make an order (which shall have the same effect as a hospital order) that the person be detained in such hospital as the court may specify;
 (b) in addition to making an order under paragraph (a) above, make an order (which shall have the same effect as a restriction order) that the person shall, without limit of time, be subject to the special restrictions set out in section 62(1) of the Mental Health (Scotland) Act 1984;
 (c) make an order (which shall have the same effect as a guardianship order) placing the person's personal welfare under the guardianship of a local authority or of a person approved by a local authority;
 (d) make a supervision and treatment order (within the meaning paragraph 1(1) of Schedule 4 to this Act); or
 (e) make no order.
 (3) Where the offence with which the person was charged is murder, the court shall make orders under both paragraphs (a) and (b) of subsection (2) above in respect of that person.
 (4) Sections 58(1), 58(1A), (2) and (4) to (7) and 59 and 61 of this Act shall have effect in relation to the making, terms and effect of an order under paragraph (a), (b) or (c) of subsection (2) above as those provisions have effect in relation to the making, terms and effect of, respectively, a hospital order, a restriction order and a guardianship order as respects a person convicted of an offence, other than an offence the sentence for which is fixed by law, punishable by imprisonment.
 (5) Schedule 4 to this Act shall have effect as regards supervision and treatment orders.
 (6) Section 58A of this Act shall have effect as regards guardianship orders made under subsection (2)(c) of this section

NOTE
Section 57 as amended by the Adults with Incapacity (Scotland) Act (asp 4), s.88 and Sch.5, para.26.

Hospital orders and guardianship

Order for hospital admission or guardianship

A3–02 58.—(1) Where a person is convicted in the High Court or the sheriff court of an offence, other than an offence the sentence for which is fixed by law, punishable by that court with imprisonment, and the court—
  (a) is satisfied on the written or oral evidence of two medical practitioners (complying with section 61 of this Act) that the grounds set out in section 17(1) of the Mental Health (Scotland) Act 1984 apply in relation to the offender;
  (b) is of the opinion, having regard to all the circumstances including the nature of the offence and the character and antecedents of the offender and to the other available methods of dealing with him, that the most suitable method of disposing of the case is by means of an order under this subsection,
the court may, subject to subsection (2) below, by order authorise his admission to and detention in such hospital as may be specified in the order.

(1A) Where a person is convicted as mentioned in subsection (1) above and the court is satisfied—
  (a) on the evidence of two medical practitioners (complying with section 61 of this Act and with any requirements imposed under section 57(3) of the Adults with Incapacity (Scotland) Act 2000 (asp 4)) that the grounds set out in section 58(1)(a) of that Act apply in relation to the offender;
  (b) that no other means provided by or under this Act would be sufficient to enable the offender's interests in his personal welfare to be safeguarded or promoted,
the court may, subject to subsection (2) below, by order place the offender's personal welfare under the guardianship of such local authority or of such other person approved by a local authority as may be specified in the order

(2) Where the case is remitted by the sheriff to the High Court for sentence under any enactment, the power to make an order under subsection (1) or (1A) above shall be exercisable by that court.

(3) Where in the case of a person charged summarily in the sheriff court with an act or omission constituting an offence the court would have power, on convicting him, to make an order under subsection (1) or (1A) above, then, if it is satisfied that the person did the act or made the omission charged, the court may, if it thinks fit, make such an order without convicting him.

(4) An order for the admission of a person to a hospital (in this Act, referred to as "a hospital order") shall not be made under this section in respect of an offender or of a person to whom subsection (3) above applies unless the court is satisfied that that hospital, in the event of such an order being made by the court, is available for his admission thereto within 7 days of the making of such an order.

(5) A State hospital shall not be specified in a hospital order in respect of the detention of a person unless the court is satisfied, on the evidence of the medical practitioners which is taken into account under paragraph (a) of subsection (1) or paragraph (a) of subsection (1A) above, that the offender, on account of his dangerous, violent or criminal propensities, requires treatment under conditions of special security, and cannot suitably be cared for in a hospital other than a State hospital.

(6) An order placing a person under the guardianship of a local authority or of any other person (in this Act referred to as "a guardianship order") shall not be made under this section unless the court is satisfied—
  (a) on the report of a mental health officer (complying with any requirements imposed by section 57(3) of the Adults with Incapacity (Scotland) Act 2000 (asp 4)) giving his opinion as to the general appropriateness of the order sought, based on an interview and assessment of the person carried out not more than 30 days before it makes the order, that it is necessary in the interests of the personal welfare of the person that he should be placed under guardianship;

(b) that any person nominated to be appointed a guardian is suitable to be so appointed;
(c) that the authority or person is willing to receive that person into guardianship; and
(d) that there is no other guardianship order, under this Act or the Adults with Incapacity (Scotland) Act 2000 (asp 4), in force relating to the person.

(7) A hospital order or guardianship order shall specify the form of mental disorder, being mental illness (including personality disorder) or mental handicap or both, from which, upon the evidence taken into account under paragraph (a) of subsection (1) or paragraph (a) of subsection (1A) above, the offender is found by the court to be suffering; and no such order shall be made unless the offender is described by each of the practitioners, whose evidence is taken into account as aforesaid, as suffering from the same form of mental disorder, whether or not he is also described by either of them as suffering from the other form.

(8) Where an order is made under this section, the court shall not pass sentence of imprisonment or impose a fine or make a probation order or a community service order in respect of the offence, but may make any other order which the court has power to make apart from this section; and for the purposes of this subsection "sentence of imprisonment" includes any sentence or order for detention.

(9) The court by which a hospital order is made may give such directions as it thinks fit for the conveyance of the patient to a place of safety and his detention therein pending his admission to the hospital within the period of 7 days referred to in subsection (4) above; but a direction for the conveyance of a patient to a residential establishment shall not be given unless the court is satisfied that the authority is willing to receive the patient therein.

(10) Where a person is charged before the district court with an act or omission constituting an offence punishable with imprisonment, the district court, if it appears to it that that person may be suffering from mental disorder, shall remit him to the sheriff court in the manner provided by section 7(9) and (10) of this Act, and the sheriff court shall, on any such remit being made, have the like power to make an order under subsection (1) or (1A) above in respect of him as if he had been charged before that court with the said act or omission as an offence, or in dealing with him may exercise the like powers as the district court.

(11) Section 58A of this Act shall have effect as regards guardianship orders made under subsection (1) of this section.

NOTES
Subss.(4) and (9) amended by the Crime and Punishment (Scotland) Act 1997 (c.48), s.62(1) and Sch.1, para.21(6), with effect from January 1, 1998 in terms of the Crime and Punishment (Scotland) Act 1997 (Commencement No. 2 and Transitional and Consequential Provisions) Order 1997 (SI 1997/2323) art. 4, Sch.2.)
Subs.(7) as amended by the Mental Health (Public Safety and Appeals) (Scotland) Act 1999 (asp 1), s.3(b) (effective September 13, 1999).
Section 58 as amended by the Adults with Incapacity (Scotland) Act 2000 (asp 4), s.88 and Sch.5, para.26.
Subs.(11) inserted by the Adults with Incapacity (Scotland) Act 2000 (asp 4), s.88 and Sch.5, para.26 and should refer to subs.(1A)—see para.11-85 *supra*.

Application of Adults with Incapacity (Scotland) Act 2000

58A.—(1) Subject to the provisions of this section, the provisions of Parts 1, 5, 6 and 7 of the Adults with Incapacity (Scotland) Act 2000 (asp 4) ("the 2000 Act") apply—
(a) to a guardian appointed by an order of the court under section 57(2)(c), 58(1) or 58(1A) of this Act (in this section referred to as a "guardianship order") whether appointed before or after the coming into force of these provisions, as they apply to a guardian with powers relating to the personal welfare of an adult appointed under section 58 of that Act;

A3–03

(b) to a person authorised under an intervention order under section 60A of this Act as they apply to a person so authorised under section 53 of that Act.

(2) In making a guardianship order the court shall have regard to any regulations made by the Scottish Ministers under section 64(11) of the 2000 Act and—

(a) shall confer powers, which it shall specify in the order, relating only to the personal welfare of the person;
(b) may appoint a joint guardian;
(c) may appoint a substitute guardian;
(d) may make such consequential or ancillary order, provision or direction as it considers appropriate.

(3) Without prejudice to the generality of subsection (2), or to any other powers conferred by this Act, the court may—

(a) make any order granted by it subject to such conditions and restrictions as appear to it to be appropriate;
(b) order that any reports relating to the person who will be the subject of the order be lodged with the court or that the person be assessed or interviewed and that a report of such assessment or interview be lodged;
(c) make such further inquiry or call for such further information as appears to it to be appropriate;
(d) make such interim order as appears to it to be appropriate pending the disposal of the proceedings.

(4) Where the court makes a guardianship order it shall forthwith send a copy of the interlocutor containing the order to the Public Guardian who shall—

(a) enter prescribed particulars of the appointment in the register maintained by him under section 6(2)(b)(iv) of the 2000 Act;
(b) unless he considers that the notification would be likely to pose a serious risk to the person's health notify the person of the appointment of the guardian; and
(c) notify the local authority and the Mental Welfare Commission of the terms of the interlocutor.

(5) A guardianship order shall continue in force for a period of 3 years or such other period (including an indefinite period) as, on cause shown, the court may determine.

(6) Where any proceedings for the appointment of a guardian under section 57(2)(c) or 58(1) of this Act have been commenced and not determined before the date of coming into force of section 84 of, and paragraph 26 of schedule 5 to, the Adults with Incapacity (Scotland) Act 2000 (asp 4) they shall be determined in accordance with this Act as it was immediately in force before that date.

NOTE
Section 58A inserted by the Adults with Incapacity (Scotland) Act 2000 (asp 4), s.84.

Intervention orders

A3–04 **60B.** The court may instead of making a hospital order under section 58(1) of this Act or a guardianship order under section 57(2)(c) or 58(1A) of this Act, make an intervention order where it considers that it would be appropriate to do so.

NOTE
Section 60B inserted by the Adults with Incapacity (Scotland) Act 2000 (asp 4), s.88 and Sch.5, para.26.

Medical evidence

Requirements as to medical evidence

61.—(1) Of the medical practitioners whose evidence is taken into account in making a finding under section 54(1)(a) of this Act or under any of the relevant provisions, at least one shall be a practitioner approved for the purposes of section 20 or section 39 of the Mental Health (Scotland) Act 1984 by a Health Board as having special experience in the diagnosis or treatment of mental disorder.

A3–05

(1A) Of the medical practitioners whose evidence is taken into account under section 53(1), 54(1)(c), 58(1)(a)(i) or 59A(3)(a) and (b) of this Act, at least one shall be employed at the hospital which is to be specified in the order or, as the case may be, direction.

(2) Written or oral evidence given for the purposes of any of the relevant provisions shall include a statement as to whether the person giving the evidence is related to the accused and of any pecuniary interest which that person may have in the admission of the accused to hospital or his reception into guardianship.

(3) For the purposes of making a finding under section 54(1)(a) of this Act or of any of the relevant provisions a report in writing purporting to be signed by a medical practitioner may, subject to the provisions of this section, be received in evidence without proof of the signature or qualifications of the practitioner; but the court may, in any case, require that the practitioner by whom such a report was signed be called to give oral evidence.

(4) Where any such report as aforesaid is tendered in evidence, otherwise than by or on behalf of the accused, then—
  (a) if the accused is represented by counsel or solicitor, a copy of the report shall be given to his counsel or solicitor;
  (b) if the accused is not so represented, the substance of the report shall be disclosed to the accused or, where he is a child under 16 years of age, to his parent or guardian if present in court;
  (c) in any case, the accused may require that the practitioner by whom the report was signed be called to give oral evidence, and evidence to rebut the evidence contained in the report may be called by or on behalf of the accused,
and where the court is of the opinion that further time is necessary in the interests of the accused for consideration of that report, or the substance of any such report, it shall adjourn the case.

(5) For the purpose of calling evidence to rebut the evidence contained in any such report as aforesaid, arrangements may be made by or on behalf of an accused person detained in a hospital or, as respects a report for the purposes of the said section 54(1), remanded in custody for his examination by any medical practitioner, and any such examination may he made in private.

(6) In this section the "relevant provisions" means sections 53(1), 54(1)(c), 58(1)(a), 58(1A)(a) and 59A(3)(a) and (b) of this Act.

NOTES
Subss. (1), (2) and (3) as amended by the Crime and Punishment (Scotland) Act 1997 (c. 48) s.10(2) with effect from January 1, 1998 by the Crime and Punishment (Scotland) Act 1997 (Commencement No. 2 and Transitional and Consequential Provisions) Order 1997 (SI 1997/2323), art.4, Sch.2.
Subss. (1A) and (6) as inserted by the above Act.
Section 61 as amended by Adults with Incapacity (Scotland) Act 2000 (asp 4) s.88 and Sch.5, para.26, but see para.11–87 *supra*.

APPENDIX 4

PART 5 CODE OF PRACTICE

EXTRACT FROM PART 2, MEDICAL TREATMENT UNDER PART 5

Emergencies

2.4 It would be contrary to good practice to risk prejudice to a patient's health through any delay in providing necessary treatment, in order to give effect to the procedures under Part 5 of the Act. The Act specifically preserves existing grounds on which treatment may be given without consent. In such circumstances the provisions of the Act are an addition to, rather than a substitute for normal procedures. This is particularly so in the case of emergencies. However, the provisions of the Act were introduced with a view to avoiding the uncertainties which existed under the law as to the precise circumstances in which treatment could be given. It could therefore offer added confidence to the practitioner and would also be good practice to make use, so far as reasonable and practicable, of the procedures under Part 5 where this is without risk to the patient.

2.5 The division between cases where treatment is necessary for the preservation of life or to prevent serious deterioration, urgent cases, a necessity to treat and routine matters is not always as clear-cut. What underlies the concepts of emergency and necessity is the issue of immediacy. The definition of emergency will vary slightly from speciality to speciality. There will of course be clinical situations where urgent treatment is required to save life—for example in labour wards or Accident & Emergency Departments, or when the patient is found unconscious through illness or injury. In such circumstances a decision must be taken and acted upon within seconds or minutes, if a fatality or severe damage is to be avoided. In other specialities, however, situations can take much longer to develop. An adult could require lifesaving surgery but there may be a period while they are being rehydrated and given antibiotics before they have an anaesthetic and operation. In this time, the medical practitioner responsible should have time to consult and complete the form. What is possible in the way of consultation will vary according to time of day—the opportunities are likely to be fewer at night or during weekends.

2.6 In all normal circumstances, the procedures set out in Part 5 of the Act should be followed. The basic judgement as to whether or not there is time to complete the appropriate form and undertake the processes associated with its completion is essentially a medical judgement in the first instance. Ultimately, however it will be for the courts to decide whether a practitioner has acted improperly in failing to secure the authority provided by a certificate under section 47 of the Act. It will obviously be good practice and potentially a legal necessity to use the new authority in any situation where there is room for doubt. It is recommended that the new authority be used in every case where it is reasonable and practicable to do so.

Appendix 5

STYLE OF POWER OF ATTORNEY

Note: *This style should be read in conjunction with Chapter 6, and in particular paras* **A5–01**
6–28 to 6–30. It is not offered as a recommended style, but rather as one combining a range of elements and possibilities, including the more complex of possible options, which a competent draftsman, proceeding in accordance with an individual client's instructions, might find it helpful to draw upon selectively, simplify, or alter or adapt as required. Examples of further clauses for particular purposes are offered in paras 6–21, 6–29 and 7–9. By way of contrast, an example of a simpler style is offered in para.6–19. Some of the provisions in the following style follow, or are adapted from, those drafted by the late Professor Halliday and appearing in "Conveyancing Law and Practice", 2nd ed., Chapter 13: the author gratefully acknowledges the permission of the publishers of that work to draw upon that material.

I, A, residing at [–], whereas I consider it appropriate to grant this continuing and welfare Power of Attorney, HEREBY PROVIDE as follows:

One I hereby nominate and appoint B, residing at [–] (hereinafter called **"my First Attorney"**) to be my true and lawful attorney with the powers aftermentioned.

Two I hereby nominate and appoint as my substitute attorneys and attorney to act as my attorneys and attorney in the event of the said B for any reason not taking up office as my attorney or at any time and for any reason ceasing to act as my attorney, C, residing at [–] and D, residing at [–] (hereinafter called **"my Substitute Attorneys"**) with the powers aftermentioned, declaring (a) that my Substitute Attorneys shall act in consultation with each other but either may act alone if and to the extent that the other has so agreed, except that they may only competently act jointly in entering any contract or executing any document relating to heritable property, in any acts or decisions concerning any gift, renunciation, lending or borrowing, in commencing and/or pursuing any judicial or other proceedings and in making any appointment and/or authorising any remuneration or reimbursement in terms of the powers set forth in paragraphs 3.2 and 3.4 of the Schedule hereto, **(b)** that if one of my Substitute Attorneys shall for any reason not take up office as attorney or at any time and for any reason cease to act as attorney, my other Substitute Attorney may act alone in all matters and the foregoing provision (a) shall not apply, and **(c)** references hereinafter and in said Schedule to "Attorneys" mean my First Attorney for so long as my First Attorney shall act, my Substitute Attorneys for so long as they shall act, and any remaining Substitute Attorney for so long as that Substitute Attorney shall act, and references in said Schedule hereto to "Attorney" shall mean the attorney then acting and (notwithstanding the use of that term in the singular) shall mean both of my Substitute Attorneys where they both act.

Three Subject to provision Five below, I confer upon my Attorneys the whole powers in relation to my affairs, including my property and financial affairs, which can competently be granted upon a continuing attorney without limitation, including without prejudice to that generality the powers set forth in Parts 1 and 3 of said Schedule, and that with effect from the earlier of **(a)** issue by me of a written request (or, if in the circumstances it is not reasonably feasible for me to make a written request, a verbal request) to any of my Attorneys that my Attorneys should commence to act as my continuing attorney or continuing attorneys, or **(b)** issue of a certificate by a medical practitioner or clinical psychologist (or, in case of emergency, verbal or other confirmation to my Attorney) that I am incapable (as defined in section 1(6) of the Adults with Incapacity (Scotland) Act 2000) in relation to some or all of my property and financial affairs. Following such request, certification or confirmation, my Attorneys may act in all of the matters in respect of which powers are conferred in terms of this provision Three and may continue to do so notwithstanding that I may have subsequently regained capacity in relation to any of them. I expressly declare that it is my intention that the powers conferred in terms of this provision Three be continuing powers in terms of section 15 of said Act.

Four Subject to provision Five below, I confer upon my Attorneys the whole powers of personal decision-making, including the whole powers in relation to my personal welfare, which can competently be granted upon a welfare attorney without limitation, including without prejudice to that generality the powers set forth in Parts 2 and 3 of said Schedule, and that with effect from issue of a certificate (or, in case of urgency, verbal or other confirmation to any of my Attorneys) by a medical practitioner or clinical psychologist that I am incapable (as defined in section 1(6) of the Adults with Incapacity (Scotland) Act 2000) in relation to the matters in respect of which powers are conferred in terms of this provision Four. If such certification or confirmation is to the effect that I am incapable as aforesaid in relation to some but not all of said matters, my Attorneys may exercise powers only in relation to matters of which I am incapable as aforesaid, but it shall be competent for my Attorneys to act upon subsequent such certification or confirmation of my incapacity in relation to further matters or all other relevant matters. My Attorneys may only continue to exercise powers in terms of this provision Four for so long as I remain incapable (or my Attorneys reasonably believe that I remain incapable) of the matters in respect of which they are exercised, but if my Attorneys subsequently reasonably believe that I have again lost capacity in respect of any matter or matters of which I have previously been so certified or confirmed as incapable, my Attorneys may resume acting whether or not they have received fresh such certification or confirmation. I expressly declare that it is my intention that the powers conferred in terms of this provision Four be welfare powers in terms of section 16 of said Act.

Five Notwithstanding the terms of the foregoing provisions Three and Four:
  (a) My Attorneys shall not have the powers set forth in Part 4 of said Schedule.
  (b) Exercise of the powers specifically set forth in Parts 1, 2 and 3 of said Schedule shall be subject to such qualifications, declarations, provisos and others (insofar as they apply to each of said powers) as are set forth in said Parts of said Schedule.
  (c) The fact that I have specifically conferred any power in terms of said Parts 1, 2 and 3 of said Schedule does not for that reason alone imply any wish that such power be exercised.

Six I provide and declare: **(a)** that all acts and deeds done or granted by my Attorneys and all decisions made by them in virtue of the powers hereby conferred shall be as valid and binding as if done, granted or made by myself; **(b)** that as evidence of my Attorneys' entitlement to act, third parties may rely without further enquiry **(i)** upon any letter bearing to be a written request by me in terms of provision Three above commence to act, or **(ii)** upon a statement by any of my Attorneys that in terms of provision Three above my

Attorneys or any of them have received a verbal request from me that my Attorneys should commence acting, or **(iii)** upon production of any certificate or certificates issued in terms of provisions Three and/or Four above, or **(iv)** upon a statement by any of my Attorneys that in terms of provisions Three and/or Four above any of my Attorneys have received verbal or other confirmation of my incapacity from a medical practitioner or clinical psychologist named by that Attorney; **(c)** that as evidence of the entitlement of my Substitute Attorneys or either of them to act, third parties may rely without further enquiry upon evidence that the Public Guardian has been notified that my First Attorney has ceased to act or ceased to be available to act and that both or either of my Substitute Attorneys have provided to the Public Guardian evidence of willingness to act; **(d)** that in matters where my Attorneys are required to consult with each other the acts, deeds and decisions of each shall be valid and binding in questions with third parties whether or not they have so consulted, and third parties shall not require to enquire as to whether they have so consulted; **(e)** that except where in terms hereof anything requires to be done, executed or decided by more than one of my Attorneys, third parties may accept without further enquiry a statement by one of my Attorneys that that Attorney is at the time my sole Attorney or that that Attorney has been authorised by any other Attorney to act alone in the matter in question; and **(f)** that persons paying money or transferring property to my Attorney or Attorneys shall not be concerned with or be bound to see to the application thereof; and I bind myself to ratify, approve of and confirm all that my Attorneys shall do or cause to be done in virtue of the powers herein contained.

Seven I further provide and declare that this Power of Attorney shall remain in force until recalled by me in writing or terminated by my death, and that all of the powers conferred hereunder shall remain exerciseable unless and until revoked by me or by a competent court; but until my Attorney or Attorneys shall have received notice of such recall or of other termination hereof, or of revocation of any appointment or powers hereunder, my Attorney or Attorneys shall be entitled to continue to act hereunder; and (subject to provision Six hereof) all powers herein conferred shall be operative and may be acted and relied upon by third parties upon production of a copy hereof certified as required by the Powers of Attorney Act 1971 or an extract hereof from the Books of Council and Session or a copy hereof authenticated by the Public Guardian in accordance with section 19(4) of the Adults with Incapacity (Scotland) Act 2000 until they shall have had notice of such recall or other termination however occasioned or of revocation of one or more of the appointments hereunder or powers hereby conferred.

Eight My Attorneys shall each be bound as by their respective acceptances hereof they bind themselves to account to me or to my executors for their respective intromissions in virtue hereof and to make payment to me or to my executors of whatever balance may be due to me after deduction of all outlays and expenses upon being relieved of all obligations and liabilities undertaken or incurred on my behalf; but declaring that none of my Attorneys shall incur any responsibility whatever in respect of the actings, intromissions or management of any bankers, brokers or other agents employed by that Attorney.

Nine I direct that my Attorneys shall comply inter alia with the provisions of section 1 of the Adults with Incapacity (Scotland) Act 2000 and in particular that **(a)** they should take account of the wishes and feelings recorded in Part 5 of said Schedule except to the extent that I may subsequently indicate by any means of communication (verbal or non-verbal) that any of such wishes and feelings have altered and **(b)** they should take account of the views of the persons named in part 6 of said Schedule insofar as it is reasonable and practicable to do so.

Ten I declare that certificates to be annexed hereto in terms of ss.15(3)(c) and 16(3)(c) of the Adults with Incapacity (Scotland) Act 2000 shall be deemed to be incorporated herein in terms of those sections; and I consent to registration hereof and of any letter issued in terms of provision Three above and any certificate or certificates issued in terms of provisions Three and/or Four above for preservation, but exercise by my Attorneys of the powers hereby conferred shall not be conditional upon such registration; And I confirm that these presents may be registered with the Public Guardian at any time after execution hereof, and in terms of section 19(5)(b) of said Act I require that copies hereof be sent by the Public Guardian to E, residing at [–] and to F, residing at [–]: **IN WITNESS WHEREOF**

SCHEDULE
referred to in the foregoing Power of Attorney
by
A
in favour of
B as First Attorney and C and D as Substitute Attorneys

Part 1

Continuing Powers

Without prejudice to the generality of provision Three of the foregoing Power of Attorney, I confer upon my Attorney the following powers, all to be exercised or not and, if exercised, then at such time or times and in such manner and generally on such terms and conditions all as my Attorney may in my Attorney's sole discretion think fit, namely:

1.1 To demand, sue for and recover all debts, claims and sums of money due or that may become due to me or exigible by me on any account or in any way, to give time for payment of any debt or claim and to grant receipts or discharges therefor.

1.2 To open accounts with any banker or banking company or any building society or any other fundholder in the United Kingdom in my name or in my Attorney's name as my Attorney and to operate thereon, or to operate on any such account wherever located already opened in my name or to which I am a party, and for that purpose to lodge or deposit monies and to draw, sign, endorse or negotiate all cheques, coupons, bills of exchange, promissory notes, deposit receipts, interest or dividend warrants, money orders or postal orders and generally all cash and other documents of whatever description which may require to be signed or endorsed by me.

1.3 To meet my general household and living expenses.

1.4 To apply all or any part of my capital or income towards any scheme or plan which in my Attorney's opinion may provide a sufficient degree of security, protection and care for me during the whole or some part of my life.

1.5 To alter or adapt any residential accommodation in the ownership of any person or body for my more convenient occupation thereof as a home.

1.6 To purchase domestic appliances or procure domestic assistance for me or the person or persons with whom I from time to time reside.

1.7 To purchase, hire or otherwise acquire equipment, appliances, aids or the like for my use or benefit.

1.8 To purchase caravans or motor cars appropriate to my needs and/or those of the person or persons with whom I from time to time reside.

1.9 To purchase or otherwise secure the provision of facilities or services of any kind for my support, care, occupation, training, recreation, enjoyment or otherwise for my benefit, or for the support or assistance of my carers.

1.10 To provide holidays for me or to meet the expenses incurred by any person or persons to enable them to accompany me on holiday or to provide holidays unaccompanied by me for any person who bears the daily burden of caring for me.

1.11 To exercise powers for my benefit notwithstanding that any other person may also benefit from such exercise.

1.12 To sell or concur with others in selling by public auction or by private sale any property, heritable or moveable, real or personal, of any kind or description and wherever situated which may belong to me or in which I may be or become interested and whether the title thereto may be in my name or in the names of myself and others or in the name of any person as nominee or trustee for me, and that at such prices and upon such terms as my Attorney may think proper.

1.13 To purchase or concur with others in purchasing heritable property or real estate in any part of the United Kingdom or to invest in the purchase of government stocks or funds of the United Kingdom, any country of the British Commonwealth or any foreign country or in stocks, securities or funds of any municipal corporation or public trust in the United Kingdom, or in the stocks, shares, debentures or other securities of public or private companies registered in the United Kingdom or elsewhere or in shares, bonds or other securities of unit or other trusts, provided that the certificates for such investments are registered and not to bearer and that the liability incurred is limited to the amount invested, and generally to act in relation to any such purchases or investments made in virtue of the powers hereby conferred upon my Attorney.

1.14 To accept on my behalf any stocks, shares or securities allotted or provisionally allotted to me, to undertake liability for and make any payments that may be due in respect thereof and to procure the registration thereof in my name or in my Attorney's name as my Attorney, or to renounce or sell any rights to such stocks, shares or securities; and to attend, act and vote for me at all meetings of and with regard to all matters affecting any company, corporation, trust or other undertaking in which I may be or become interested as a holder of stocks, shares, debentures or other securities or as a creditor or otherwise, or at any class meeting of such holders or creditors, and to grant proxies for others to act on my behalf at any of such meetings, and generally to act for me in the premises as fully and freely as I could have done myself, including without prejudice to the foregoing generality power to agree to liquidation, amalgamation, reconstruction or transfer of any such company, corporation, trust or undertaking.

1.15 To grant or accept feus or leases, to excamb land, to consolidate interests of superiority and property, to improve or reconstruct or concur with others in improving or reconstructing heritable or real property, to accept renunciations of leases, input and output tenants, pay and receive rents, feuduties, ground annuals and ground rents, to redeem or accept redemption of feuduties or ground annuals, to alter or vary rents, and all on such terms and conditions as my Attorney may think proper, and generally to do all acts or things which my Attorney may consider necessary or desirable in relation to the management of heritable or real property in which I may be interested.

1.16 To lend money upon the security of any moveable or personal property or upon the security of any heritable property or real estate in the United Kingdom, on such terms and conditions as my Attorney shall think proper, and to rearrange or vary all loans or securities, whether made by myself or by my Attorney on my behalf, from time to time or to require repayment thereof or enforce the security therefor and generally to do all such acts or things in relation thereto as my Attorney may deem fit.

1.17 To borrow money on my behalf binding me and my executors and representatives jointly and severally for repayment thereof and that on such terms and conditions as my Attorney may think fit, and to grant security therefor over any part of my property, heritable or moveable, real or personal, and to rearrange or vary the terms of any borrowings whether made by myself or by my Attorney on my behalf, or the securities therefor, including without prejudice to that generality to make repayment thereof or arrange for loans or advances in substitution therefor and generally to do all such acts or things in relation thereto as my Attorney may deem fit.

1.18 To grant, execute and deliver or to accept any deeds or documents necessary or appropriate to the exercise of any of the powers hereby conferred upon my Attorney, including without prejudice to that generality feu grants, dispositions, deeds of conditions relating to land or buildings, deeds of excambion, leases, standard securities, mortgages, assignations, variations, discharges, deeds of restriction or disburdenment, transfers of stocks, shares or other securities, renunciations, acceptances, applications for registration and receipts.

1.19 To make on my behalf all returns required for government or local taxation or rating, to adjust valuations and assessments, to claim all repayments, rebates or allowances to which I may be entitled and to make any relevant appeals, and that as regards all periods past, current or future.

1.20 To claim and receive on my behalf all pensions, benefits, allowances, insurance and other entitlements and proceeds, services, financial contributions, repayments, rebates and the like to which I may at any time be entitled or for which I may at any time be entitled to apply, to complete and submit all forms, give any necessary undertakings, make any relevant appeals, and generally do anything else necessary or appropriate in connection therewith, and that as regards all periods past, current or future.

1.21 To appear and claim for me in the bankruptcy or liquidation of any person or company indebted to me and to concur in any arrangement in connection therewith.

1.22 To examine, prepare and adjust all accounts between me and any other person or persons and to claim or pay any sums which my Attorney may be satisfied are payable to or by me, and to compound, compromise, submit to arbitration and settle claims of any kind due to or payable by me.

1.23 To make any arrangements which my Attorney considers appropriate for the suitable management of my estate, including without prejudice to that generality (a) making arrangements of any kind which will subsist after termination for any reason of this Power of Attorney, and (b) placing any or all of my assets or estate in a trust for administration created by my Attorney on my behalf, under which my Attorney may appoint such trustee or trustees (including or not including himself) as my Attorney may consider appropriate, which trustees may be empowered to assume additional trustees, and otherwise upon such terms as my Attorney may consider appropriate.

1.24 To claim or renounce testamentary or other entitlements (including without prejudice to that generality to claim, discharge or renounce any entitlement to legal rights), execute Deeds of Arrangement in any terms, consent to any variation of any trust in which I have any interest (including any prospective or contingent interest), enter any other arrangements, make gifts, grant deeds of covenant, or make other provision from my estate (including without prejudice to that generality, to create any form of trust, discretionary or non-discretionary, charitable or non-charitable) of any kind and in favour of any beneficiary or beneficiaries if in the judgement of my Attorney, acting reasonably, I myself would have done so if consulted or able to be consulted; declaring that (a) in the case of a trust, the beneficiaries may include myself, but that (b) my Attorney may not exercise any powers in terms of this paragraph so as to benefit himself or herself except in accordance with advice in writing from an appropriate professional instructed to advise with professional responsibility to me alone.

1.25 In accordance with such professional advice as my Attorney may consider it appropriate to seek, to implement such tax-planning or similar arrangements as my Attorney may deem suitable, including without prejudice to that generality to do for such purposes anything authorised in terms of the preceding paragraph 1.24 hereof.

1.26 To grant (or refuse to grant) any consent or renunciation in terms of the Matrimonial Homes (Family Protection) (Scotland) Act 1981.

1.27 To make any alimentary payments to my spouse and/or children and/or other dependants for which I may be liable and to continue any such payments customarily made by me without legal liability to do so.

1.28 To conduct, dispose of or otherwise deal with, or to wind up, any business or interest in a business belonging to me.

1.29 To meet the costs of private medical, nursing or other care.

1.30 To agree any common repairs or improvement scheme in relation to any property interest of mine and to meet the expenses thereof.

1.31 To acquire, whether by purchase, lease or otherwise, for my residential use whether alone or jointly with any other person or persons any accommodation without being required to insist upon the payment by any other person, whether or not a joint occupier thereof, of any consideration, but my Attorney shall have a complete discretion as to the terms on which my Attorney permits such residential accommodation to be occupied and the arrangements established to facilitate such occupation (which arrangements may, without prejudice to that generality, include entering leasing or other arrangements with a suitable provider of care or housing).

1.32 To pay the premiums on any policies of assurance belonging to me and to effect any such policies on any lives in which I have an insurable interest.

1.33 To insure any of my property for such amount and against such risks as my Attorney thinks fit.

Part 2

Welfare Powers

Without prejudice to the generality of provision Four of the foregoing Power of Attorney, I confer upon my Attorney the powers set out below, all to be exercised or not and, if exercised, then at such time or times and in such manner and generally on such terms and conditions all as my Attorney may in my Attorney's sole discretion think fit, but subject to the declarations that **(a)** notwithstanding issue of a certificate in terms of provision Four of the foregoing Power of Attorney, my Attorney shall not make any decisions which at the time when it is appropriate or necessary that the decision be made I am capable of making and communicating myself, and **(b)** my Attorney shall not make any decision which does not accord with my known and clearly expressed (by any means of communication, verbal or non-verbal) wishes and feelings present or (if not superseded by subsequent or present wishes and feelings) past. The powers conferred as aforesaid are powers:

2.1 To make decisions generally about my accommodation and care including about where I should live, whether permanently or temporarily, with whom I should live and consort, and what services I should receive.

2.2 To make decisions about my social and cultural activities, including the nature and extent thereof and matters related thereto.

2.3 To make decisions regarding my healthcare, to consent to any healthcare that is in my best interests, to refuse consent to any proposed healthcare that is not in my best interests or does not accord with my known wishes and feelings, to arrange for me to attend for any healthcare (including investigation, assessment and the like) and to arrange access to me for the purpose of any healthcare (including investigation, assessment and the like).

2.4 To decide whether I should (or should be permitted to) take or participate in any educational, vocational or other training and, if so, the nature and extent thereof and matters related thereto.

2.5 To decide whether I should (or should be permitted to) apply for any licence, permit, approval or other consent or authorisation required by law.

2.6 To open, read, attend to and as appropriate reply to any mail or other communications addressed to or received by me or on my behalf, or to make arrangements for such mail to be dealt with.

2.7 To make normal day-to-day decisions on my behalf including as to my diet, dress and personal appearance and to do whatever is necessary to preserve my personal dignity so far as it is reasonable and practicable to do so (regardless of any degree of impairment of my ability still to appreciate such matters).

2.8 To take me on holidays, excursions or the like or authorise someone else to do so.

2.9 To exercise all rights and powers competent to me and/or to an attorney of mine under statute, and in particular under the Data Protection Act 1998, Access to Personal Files Act 1987, Access to Medical Reports Act 1988, Environment and Safety Information Act 1988 and Access to Health Records Act 1990, and any statutes amending, re-enacting or replacing any of them.

2.10 **[On possible linkage to an advance directive, see Chapter 7, para.7–9]**

Part 3

Continuing and Welfare Powers

Without prejudice to the generality of provisions Three and Four of the foregoing Power of Attorney, I confer upon my Attorney the following powers, all to be exercised or not and, if exercised, then at such time or times and in such manner and generally on such terms and conditions all as my Attorney may in my Attorney's sole discretion think fit, namely:

3.1 To raise or defend all actions or judicial or other proceedings in which I am or may be interested so far as my Attorney may consider necessary or expedient and to refer to arbitration any questions or disputes in which I am or may become involved, to appeal against, enforce or implement any judgement, order or award and to appear or instruct appearance on my behalf before any tribunal, commission or other official inquiry.

3.2 To employ bankers, brokers, solicitors, counsel, accountants, managers, factors or agents of any kind for the management of any of my affairs and to pay them appropriate remuneration for their services.

3.3 To require disclosure to my Attorney of any document or information, however confidential, which I could require or (if competent to do so) could have required to be disclosed to me, including without prejudice to that generality (a) my Will, any Codicils thereto and any other documents or writings of a testamentary effect and (b) any medical or other healthcare information **[on possible inclusion of advance directive, see Chapter 7, para.7–9]**; to make decisions regarding disclosure or release of any document or information (whether confidential or not); and to attach conditions to such disclosure or release, or to stipulate or require that any documents or information pertaining to me or my affairs be kept confidential.

3.4 To reimburse to my Attorney any out-of-pocket costs reasonably and necessarily incurred in consequence of acting as my Attorney.

3.5 To act as my legal representative in relation to any and all matters within the scope of the powers conferred by this Power of Attorney.

Part 4

Powers Specifically Excluded

Notwithstanding anything contained in the foregoing Power of Attorney or in any other Part or Parts of this Schedule thereto, and in addition to any limitations by law upon the powers which can competently be conferred on and exercised by continuing and welfare attorneys, I specifically provide that my Attorney shall have no power to do any of the following:

Excluded Power (a): To [–]

Excluded Power (b): To [–]

Part 5

Wishes and Feelings

I record the wish that if at any time two medical practitioners are of the opinion, independently from each other, that:
   (a) I have become unable to participate effectively in decisions about my medical care, and
   (b) I am unlikely to regain the ability to participate effectively in decisions about my medical care, and
   (c) there is no reasonable prospect of my recovery from severe physical illness, or from impairment expected to cause me severe distress or render me incapable of rational existence,
then and in those circumstances my wishes are: **(Firstly)** that I be allowed to die and not be kept alive by artificial means such as life support systems, tube feeding, antibiotics, resuscitation or blood transfusions; **(Secondly)** that any treatment which has no benefit other than a mere prolongation of my existence should be withheld or withdrawn, even if it means that my life is shortened; and **(Thirdly)** that I should however be given basic care and aggressive palliative care, drugs or any other measures to keep me free of pain or distress, even if they shorten my life.

2 I record that I accept the risk that I may not be able to change my mind in the future when I am no longer able to speak for myself, and I accept the risk that improving medical technology may offer increased hope, but I record that I personally consider the risk of unwanted treatment to be a greater risk. I record that I fear degradation and indignity far more than death.

3 I record the following wishes about specific treatments or investigation:
. . .

4 I record the wish that my Attorney, medical practitioners responsible for my treatment and for decisions about my treatment, and any other person making or participating in decisions about treatment which I should or should not receive, or any intervention which should or should not be made, should have regard to the terms of this Part 5 of this Schedule and any written statement by me amending it or adding to it, both in making and participating in any decisions and also in considering, in any uncertain situation, what my wishes or intentions would be or what would constitute benefit to me.

5 I understand and accept that decisions made in accordance with my wishes may have the consequence that my life is or may be shortened. I confirm that it is within the authority of my Attorney to make such decisions notwithstanding that in consequence thereof my life is or may be shortened.

Part 6

Persons to be Consulted

E, residing at [–]

F, residing at [–]

G, residing at [–]

This is the Schedule referred to in the foregoing Power of Attorney

APPENDIX 6

STYLES: INTERVENTION ORDER AND GUARDIANSHIP

These styles are offered as examples for guidance, each addressing a particular hypothetical situation. They should be drawn on selectively, and read in conjunction with all relevant parts of this book, particularly paras 4–2 to 4–30, paras 5–2 to 5–21, and Chapters 10, 11 and 15. The approach is similar to that of Appendix 5: see the note at the beginning of that Appendix. Pleas-in-law are not required, though some practitioners include them.

STYLE A — APPLICATION FOR INTERVENTION ORDER   A6–01

SUMMARY APPLICATION

under

THE ADULTS WITH INCAPACITY (SCOTLAND) ACT 2000

by

A [design]

Pursuer

The Pursuer craves the court:

(FIRST): To grant an intervention order under section 53 of the Adults with Incapacity (Scotland) Act 2000 authorising the Pursuer to take the following action and to make the following decisions in relation to the property and financial affairs of the Pursuer's wife, B, residing sometime at [–] and now at [–], namely:

1. To sell at such price on such other terms as may be approved by the Public Guardian B's one-half *pro indiviso* share in and to **ALL and WHOLE** [conveyancing description] (the whole of said subjects of which said B is proprietrix of a one-half *pro indiviso* share being hereinafter called "**the existing house**").

2. In the event that the existing house is sold as aforesaid, to purchase a one-half *pro indiviso* share in and to such residential property (hereinafter called "**the new house**") at such price and on such other terms as the Public Guardian may approve, title to the new house to be taken in name of the Pursuer and said B equally between them and to their respective disponees and executors.

3 To do everything reasonably required for the purposes of marketing the existing house, and negotiating, concluding and implementing a sale of the existing house and the purchase of the new house, including:
   (a) To employ, instruct and appropriately remunerate estate agents, solicitors, surveyors and any tradesmen, specialists or experts whom surveyors might recommend be instructed.
   (b) To employ, instruct and appropriately remunerate removal contractors.
   (c) To arrange for termination of responsibility for services to the existing house and to arrange for provision of services to the new house.
   (d) To execute on behalf of said B, *quoad* her interest in the existing house, a Disposition in favour of the purchaser(s) of the existing house.
   (e) To execute on behalf of said B any other deeds or documents which solicitors employed as aforesaid might advise should properly be so executed.

4 To pay and apply said B's one-half share of the price received for the existing house as follows:
   (a) In meeting the expenses of this Application.
   (b) In meeting a one-half share of the price of the new house.
   (c) In meeting a one-half share of the whole costs of purchase, sale and removal, including all costs properly incurred in consequence of exercise of the powers conferred on the Pursuer.
   (d) In investing any remainder thereof for the benefit of said B in such manner and on such terms as the Public Guardian may approve.

5 To do anything ancillary to or consequential upon the powers above specified which may reasonably be necessary or appropriate for the full and proper exercise thereof.

(SECOND): To grant an interim intervention order under sections 3(2)(d) and 53 of said Act in the terms (FIRST) herein craved and thereafter, upon submission of a description of "the new house" (as hereinbefore defined), to grant a final intervention order incorporating such description and authorising the Pursuer on behalf of said B to acquire a one-half *pro indiviso* share in and to said new house and to register her interest therein in the Land Register of Scotland.

STATEMENTS OF FACT

1 This Application is made under section 53(1) of said Act. The Pursuer claims an interest in the property and financial affairs of his wife the said B. The Pursuer seeks an intervention order in terms of said Act in respect of the said B. B was born on [–]. She is an adult. She is habitually resident at C Nursing Home, [address], which is within the territory of this court. This court accordingly has jurisdiction in terms of paragraphs 1 and 2 of Schedule 3 to said Act. To the Pursuer's knowledge, no proceedings are pending before any other court involving the present cause of action and to which the Pursuer is a party or which relate to B. To the Pursuer's knowledge, no agreement exists prorogating jurisdiction over the whole or any part of the subject-matter of this Application to another court.

2 No guardianship or intervention orders in terms of said Act and no appointments which have become guardianship appointments in accordance with the transitional provisions of said Act are in force or have ever been granted in respect of B. B has no continuing attorney or welfare attorney.

3   The Pursuer is B's nearest relative. B's primary carers are said C Nursing Home. The Pursuer and B have [–] children, all of whom have an interest in this Application, namely: [specify]. B has, and has had, no other children. No other persons have an interest in this Application.

4   As verified by the medical reports submitted with this Application, [narrate impairments]. In consequence of said impairments, B is incapable, as defined in section 1(6) of said Act, of taking any of the action or making any of the decisions for which authority is sought in this Application.

5   Title to the existing house is held in joint names of the Pursuer and B in terms of a Disposition [specify]. They took entry to the existing house in terms of said Disposition on [–]. The Pursuer has resided there since then. B resided there until [–], but since then has been continuously in hospital or nursing home care. She will require such care for the remainder of her life and will not for the remainder of her life be able to resume living in a domestic residential setting. The Pursuer has been advised by Messrs [–] that the existing house would be likely to achieve a price of £[–] on the open market. Reference is made to report and valuation by said Messrs [–] dated [–], which is produced herewith. The value of said B's one-half share may accordingly be reasonably estimated at £[–]

6   The Pursuer now resides alone in the existing house. He is elderly. His physical mobility is restricted. He no longer feels able to drive. The existing house is too large for his needs and inconvenient for his use. It is situated an inconvenient distance from shops and other facilities, from public transport and from C Nursing Home. The Pursuer desires that the existing house be sold and the proceeds applied in whole or in part to acquire a new house of more convenient size, layout and location. It would be of benefit to B that the Pursuer should be housed more appropriately, and in a location from which he can more conveniently continue to visit her. The Pursuer seeks the intervention order craved so that he may *quoad* the interests of himself and B sell the existing house, purchase a new house, and do everything necessary to conclude and implement the sale and purchase transactions, the removal, and other matters ancillary thereto. The household contents which would be removed comprise items belonging to the Pursuer, items belonging to B and items the joint property of both of them.

7   It is appropriate in the circumstances that B's one-half share of the price received for the existing house be applied in meeting the expenses of this Application, in meeting a one-half share of the price of the new house, and in meeting a one-half share of the whole costs of purchase, sale and removal, including all costs properly incurred in consequence of exercise of the powers sought in this Application, insofar as conferred on the Pursuer. The Pursuer intends that the price for the new house should be such, and matters on behalf of B should be so managed, that her one-half share of the price received for the existing house will be sufficient to meet all of the foregoing. If however there should be a shortfall, the Pursuer intends to meet that shortfall. If there should be a surplus, it is appropriate that such surplus be invested for the benefit of B in such manner and on such terms as the Public Guardian may approve.

8   B is unable to comprehend what is proposed and unable to express any wishes or feelings in the matter. To the best of the Pursuer's knowledge, information and belief, B has not at any time in the past contemplated or expressed views about circumstances, such as those which have now arisen, as described in Statement 6 above. Prior to B's impairment of capacity, she and the Pursuer managed their affairs jointly, in full

communication with each other, for their joint benefit as a married couple. The Pursuer, from his knowledge of B, believes that if it were possible to consult her about the present proposal, she would agree with it. From all of his knowledge about her, he has no reason to believe that she would disagree. He has discussed this proposal with their children the said [–]. Each of them has confirmed that they believe that if B could be consulted, she would agree. Each of them has confirmed that, from their whole knowledge of her, they have no reason to believe that she would in any way disagree. Each of them has confirmed in writing that he or she agrees that the intervention order now sought is appropriate and that there should be conferred upon the Pursuer the powers and interim powers sought herein. Each has confirmed that he or she does not intend to oppose this Application or to enter the process. Letters from each of them to the foregoing effect are produced herewith. The Pursuer has discussed this proposal with said primary carers, who consider that they would be unaffected by it and have offered no views upon it, beyond general comments that it seems sensible and that they would encourage anything which would be conducive to maintaining regular contact between the Pursuer and both B and themselves.

9 As the purpose of the intervention proposed in terms of this Application includes *inter alia* the sale of heritable property vested in B and the purchase of heritable property in her name, an intervention order in the terms sought represents an intervention which will benefit B, which will confer a benefit which cannot reasonably be achieved without such intervention, and which is the intervention least restrictive in relation to the freedom of B, consistent with the purpose thereof.

10 B has no other property or financial affairs requiring formal intervention in terms of said Act. Her state benefits are received and dealt with by [–] as appointee in terms of regulation 33 of the Social Security (Claims and Payments) Regulations 1987. Her occupational pension from the [–] Pension Scheme is paid to the Pursuer to hold and administer on her behalf in accordance with discretionary powers held and so exercised by the Trustees of said Scheme. She has no other income. Apart from her interest in said house, she has no funds or capital except for accumulated state benefits and pension received and held as aforesaid, which do not at any one time exceed £[–] in total. She does not have, nor is it anticipated that she will have, any needs for welfare intervention which cannot be properly and satisfactorily addressed in terms of section 47 of said Act.

11 This Application is supported by the accompanying reports, as required by section 57(3) of said Act: [specify]

IN RESPECT WHEREOF

STYLE B — APPLICATION TO REPLACE GUARDIAN

This style may be adapted for appointment of an additional guardian under s.62(1)(b) or a subsequent substitute guardian under s.63.

SUMMARY APPLICATION

under

THE ADULTS WITH INCAPACITY (SCOTLAND) ACT 2000

by

D [design]

Pursuer

The Pursuer craves the court:

To grant an order under section 71(1)(a) of the Adults with Incapacity (Scotland) Act 2000 replacing E [design] with the Pursuer as guardian to F [design]; And finding any party opposing this Application liable in the expenses thereof; And otherwise authorising the expenses of this Application to be charged against the estate of the said F.

STATEMENTS OF FACT

1 The Pursuer seeks an order in terms of section 71(1)(a) of the Adults with Incapacity (Scotland) Act 2000 replacing the Pursuer's mother E with the Pursuer as guardian to the Pursuer's brother F. The Pursuer claims an interest in F's property and financial affairs. F was born on [-]. He is an adult. He is habitually resident at G [-], which is within the territory of this court. This court accordingly has jurisdiction in terms of paragraphs 1 and 2 of Schedule 3 to said Act. To the Pursuer's knowledge, no proceedings are pending before any other court involving the present cause of action and to which the Pursuer is a party or which relate to F. To the Pursuer's knowledge, no agreement exists prorogating jurisdiction over the whole or any part of the subject-matter of this Application to another court.

2 By interlocutor dated [-], a copy of which is produced herewith, the Sheriff of [-] appointed E to be curator bonis to F. E duly found caution and thereafter acted as curator bonis aforesaid. On April 1, 2002 E became guardian to F with power to manage his property and financial affairs, in accordance with section 88(1) of said Act and paragraph 1(1) of Schedule 4 to said Act. She continues to act as such guardian.

3 E now considers that in view of her advancing years it is appropriate that she be replaced as F's guardian by a suitable person who is younger and fitter. She has confidence in the Pursuer's care and concern for F, and in the Pursuer's suitability to take over the role of F's guardian. She has requested the Pursuer to proceed accordingly. Reference is made to letter dated [-] from E to the Pursuer, which is produced herewith.

4 F has severe disabilities. He requires 24-hour care. He has no capacity to make decisions about or to manage his property or financial affairs. He has been resident at G for many years. It is likely that for the rest of his life he will continue to require accommodation there, or similar accommodation,

and to require considerable care and support services. His estate amounts to approximately £[–]. Management needs include need to ensure that said estate is properly and appropriately invested, to meet his regular accommodation, care and other costs, and from time to time to make decisions about and pay for the acquisition of clothing and other requisites for him, and facilities and services for him.

5   The Pursuer maintains close contact with F. She normally visits him every week. For about the last two years she has attended care review meetings about him in place of E. She maintains contact with relevant staff at G, including by telephone when there are health or other concerns regarding F. She [specify any qualifications, experience or other factors demonstrating suitability]. She is suitable for appointment as guardian to F. In particular, she is aware of the circumstances and condition of F and of the needs arising from such circumstances and condition, and she is aware of the functions of a guardian; she is and will continue to make herself accessible to F and to his primary carer; she is able to carry out the functions of guardian; she is a close relative of F, but in terms of said Act there is no likely conflict of interest between F and her, and her appointment would give rise to no undue concentration of power in the Pursuer over the adult; and the appointment of the Pursuer as guardian would have no adverse effect on the interests of F.

6   In the circumstances hereinbefore averred, the replacement of E with the Pursuer as guardian to F represents an intervention which will benefit F, which will confer a benefit which cannot reasonably be achieved without such intervention, and which is the intervention least restrictive in relation to the freedom of F consistent with the purpose thereof.

7   Except for said appointment of E as guardian, no guardianship or intervention orders in terms of said Act, and no appointments which have become guardianship appointments in accordance with the transitional provisions of said Act, are in force or have ever been granted in respect of F. F has no continuing attorney or welfare attorney.

8   F does not have, nor is it anticipated that he will have, any needs for welfare intervention which cannot be properly and satisfactorily addressed in terms of section 47 of said Act.

9   The Pursuer was born on [–]. She is the younger of the two siblings of F. His older sibling is his brother H, who was born on [–] and who resides at [–]. Said H is F's nearest relative. F's primary carers are said G [address]. His mother is said E. She has an interest in this Application. F's father [–] died on [–]. F has never been married and has never had any children. He has never had any siblings other than the Pursuer and said H. The cautioners to E as guardian foresaid are [–], who have an interest in this Application. No other persons have an interest in this Application.

10 F cannot meaningfully be consulted, or express views, about this Application, but has a good relationship with the Pursuer and enjoys her visits. Said E proposed this Application. Said H and said G have both been consulted about this Application, and both have indicated that they support it.

11 A copy of E's last accounts as guardian foresaid, being accounts for the year to [–], as approved by the Accountant of Court, are produced herewith. The current level of caution as fixed by the Accountant of Court and in place is £[–]. It remains an appropriate level of caution.

IN RESPECT WHEREOF

Appendix 6

STYLE C — APPLICATION FOR GUARDIANSHIP ORDER   A6–03

This style combines a range of proposed provisions and powers. Many applications are simpler. Applications for financial guardianship often seek only power to manage specified parts of the adult's property and financial affairs, in terms of s.64(1)(d) of the Act. Statement 3 is only required if the applicant claims an interest in the adult's personal welfare, which the applicant should only do if welfare powers are sought.

A style of application is offered on the Public Guardian's website: for comment, see editor's note to "Guardianship and Intervention Orders under the Adults with Incapacity (Scotland) Act 2000" by Donald N. Gordon (Scottish Law Gazette, Vol.70, No.3 (June 2002) p.62, at p.67).

SUMMARY APPLICATION

under

THE ADULTS WITH INCAPACITY
(SCOTLAND) ACT 2000

by

J [design]
K [design]
L [design]

Pursuers

The Pursuers crave the court:

To grant a guardianship order under Part 6 of the Adults with Incapacity (Scotland) Act 2000 appointing the Pursuers J & K joint guardians and the Pursuer L substitute guardian to M [design] with the following powers:

1. Power in terms of section 64(1)(d) of said Act to manage the property and financial affairs of said M, subject to power 2 below.

2. Power in terms of section 64(1)(e) of said Act to authorise said M to carry out such transactions or categories of transactions as the guardians or guardian acting for the time being may specify.

3. Without prejudice to the generality of power 1 above, power in terms of section 64(1)(a) of said Act to deal with the following particular matters on behalf of said M:

    3.1 To sell ALL and WHOLE [conveyancing description] (hereinafter called "M's dwellinghouse"), including but not limited to power to [see Style A, Crave (FIRST) 3].

    3.2 As regards each item of corporeal moveable property belonging to said M, in the discretion of the guardians or guardian then acting: (a) to sell same to the purchaser(s) of said dwellinghouse, (b) to sell same to any other party, (c) to retain same in accordance with such arrangements as such guardians or guardian may determine, or (d) to seek authority under section 66 of said Act to make a gift thereof.

    3.3 To do everything reasonable and necessary to seek and obtain reparation for loss, injury and damage sustained by said M in, or in consequence of, a road traffic incident on or about [date] in which he sustained injury, including but not limited to power to instruct investigations and reports; to negotiate and agree terms of settlement;

if advised that said M qualifies or is likely to qualify for Legal Aid, to apply for Legal Aid on his behalf; and to pursue an action or actions of reparation in such court or courts as may be appropriate.

3.4 To claim, negotiate and accept such payments as M may be entitled to receive in terms of (a) any policy or policies of insurance, (b) his contract of employment, or (c) any arrangements established or entered by his employers.

4 Power in terms of section 64(1)(b) of said Act to deal with the following aspects of said M's personal welfare [or with specified personal welfare matters under section 64(1)(a), as the case may be], namely:

4.1 Etc. [See examples of welfare powers conferred on tutors-dative quoted in paragraphs 10–21 to 10–23 above; the styles of attorneys' powers in Appendix 5; and styles in paragraph 3.57 of the Part 6 Code]

and that for the period of five years from date of appointment, or for such other period as the sheriff may consider appropriate; and finding any party opposing this Application liable in the expenses thereof; and otherwise authorising the expenses of this Application to be charged against the estate of said M.

STATEMENTS OF FACT

1 This Application is made under Part 6 of said Act. The Pursuers J, K and L are respectively father, mother and sister of said M. They each claim an interest in the property, financial affairs and personal welfare of said M.

2 The Pursuers seek a guardianship order in terms of said Act in respect of said M. M was born on [continue as in Style A, Statement 1].

3 The local authority for the area in which said M resides is N Council. The Pursuers gave notice to said N Council in terms of section 57(4) of said Act on [date].

4 [Particulars of any previous orders—see style A, Statement 2]

5 [Specify nearest relative, primary carers and other persons having an interest—see Style A, Statement 3 and Style B, Statement 9]

6 On [date] said M was involved in a road traffic incident as more particularly described in Statement 9 below, in which he sustained injuries, including serious head injuries as described in the medical reports submitted with this Application. As verified by said medical reports [narrate impairments]. In consequence of said impairments, he is incapable, as defined in section 1(6) of said Act, of managing his property and financial affairs but may, with encouragement, support and guidance, develop some skills to carry out some transactions or categories of transactions. He is incapable, as so defined, of acting and making decisions about the sale of M's dwellinghouse, about the retention or disposal of his corporeal moveable assets, the pursuit of a claim to reparation, or the claiming of any sums which may be due to him under policies of assurance, his terms of employment or arrangements established or entered by his employers. As verified by said medical reports, he is incapable (as so defined) of acting and making decisions in relation to the matters specified in Crave 4 of this Application. All of said matters are matters in respect of which action or decisions are required or are likely to be required during the forthcoming five years. It will be of benefit to M, and will represent the minimum restriction of his freedom, that such action be taken and decisions made by

suitable persons lawfully empowered to do so and subject to the supervisory and other provisions of said Act.

7 [M purchased M's dwellinghouse in [month and year]; description of type and accommodation; price paid, loan, present valuation; M only occupant at time of his accident, house now unoccupied; house unlikely ever to be suitable for M's accommodation needs; to his benefit to sell it]

8 [Summary of M's corporeal moveable belongings; total estimated value thereof; explanation why each of the alternatives in Crave 3.2 likely to be appropriate for some items; to M's benefit to provide for or dispose of all such items]

9 [Description of accident and its consequences, of further investigations proposed, and of potential grounds for pursuing reparation; to M's benefit that any reparation to which he is entitled should be obtained]

10 [Particulars, so far as available, of relevant insurances, and possibility of benefit from employers or arrangements made by employers; to M's benefit to claim, negotiate and accept payments]

11 [Particulars, with values or estimated values, of all other assets so far as known; concluding with total estimated value of whole estate]

12 It will be of benefit to M that management of his property and finances and decisions about his personal welfare should be continuously co-ordinated and taken by persons in regular or continuous contact with him, who are able to respond promptly and appropriately to his circumstances and needs as they change and develop, and who are able to use their powers on a continuing basis to encourage and support such recovery of effective capacity and development of skills and independence as he may be able to achieve. The Pursuers J and K are able to perform those functions in that manner. They undertake to do so. They are willing to accommodate M in their own home if at any time it should become appropriate that he be so accommodated. They have been married to each other for [–] years. They are accustomed to making joint decisions and managing affairs jointly, and have always done so effectively and without unresolved disagreement. They are related to said M as specified in section 62(1)(a) of said Act. [Further averments of suitability—see Style B, Statement 5]

13 The Pursuer J is aged [–] and the Pursuer K is aged [–]. It will be of benefit to M that he should have a substitute guardian able and suitable to commence acting promptly should either J or K die or resign or otherwise cease to act. L is the sister of M. She is related to said M as specified in section 62(1)(a) of said Act. [Averments of suitability—see Style B, Statement 5]

14 Prior to his accident, M usually discussed matters of importance in his own life with his parents J and K. From time to time, he sought and valued their opinions in such matters. He discussed his choice of career, and subsequent career decisions, with them in this way. He discussed with them the acquisition of his own house, and aspects of that transaction. He and his sister L from time to time discussed personal aspects of their lives with each other. They valued each other's views and trusted each other's confidentiality. So far as is known to the Pursuers, M never expressed views about the arrangements which should apply in circumstances such as have now arisen. It is however evident that his past wishes and feelings were that J, K and L should generally be informed of matters of importance in his life, and that they should generally be the persons who should provide such assistance as he might require in making decisions about such matters.

15 In consequence of his impairments, M now has only very limited ability to formulate and express relevant wishes and feelings. His speech is severely impaired, though it is anticipated that it may gradually improve. He responds to simple statements and questions by gestures. He still knows and recognises J, K and L. He reacts with greater pleasure and warmth to visits from them and from his best personal friends, than he does to visits from others. He has responded consistently on a number of occasions to simple questions about the arrangements proposed in terms of this Application, though the extent of his understanding of them is doubtful. He consistently responds affirmatively to questions as to whether J, K and L should help in managing matters and making decisions for him. He consistently responds positively to questions about whether he wishes to return "home" if possible, but appears to relate these to the parental home of J and K, and his responses do not indicate a memory of his own home ("M's dwellinghouse"). It has not proved possible, by any means of communication, to ascertain from M any wishes or feelings about other aspects of this Application. The Pursuers, from their knowledge of M, believe that if it were possible to consult him fully about the arrangements proposed in this Application he would agree with them, and that he would not in any respect disagree with them.

16 M has a wide circle of friends. X, Y and Z are all particularly close and long-standing friends. They are significantly closer to M than his other friends. They all continue to visit M regularly. They all have an interest in his welfare. The Pursuers have shown to each of them a draft of this Application and have discussed with each of them the proposals embodied in this Application. Each of them supports this Application. Letters from each to that effect are produced herewith and referred to for their terms. [Narrate also any other views which are relevant in terms of section 1(4)]

17 The powers sought in this Application can only be conferred and exercised in the integrated manner described in Statement 12 hereof if a guardianship order is granted. A guardianship order in the terms sought represents an intervention which will benefit M, which will confer a benefit which cannot reasonably be achieved without such intervention, and which is the intervention least restrictive in relation to the freedom of M, consistent with the purpose thereof.

18 M is likely for the remainder of his life to require guardians with powers in relation to his property, financial affairs and personal welfare. Any recovery of capacity is likely to be slow and of limited extent. The Pursuers, if appointed guardians, undertake to act in accordance with the general principles in section 1 of said Act and in particular not to intervene in any matter in which M may develop capacity to act for himself. They undertake to encourage the development and exercise by him of such capacity. It would not be of benefit to M that applications for renewal of guardianship should be required with undue frequency during his lifetime. The pursuit of reparation may well take more than three years until concluded. In the foregoing circumstances it is appropriate that a guardianship order should be granted initially for a period of five years.

19 This Application is supported by the accompanying reports, as required by section 57(3) of said Act: [specify]

IN RESPECT WHEREOF

INDEX

Accounts
  financial guardianship, and
    approval, 11–64
    audit, 11–63
    deficiencies, 11–65
    generally, 11–61—11–62
Accumulations
  trusts, and, 13–17—13–18
Actings
  attorneys, and, 6–33—6–36
  guardians, and
    change of address, 11–27
    delegation, 11–26
    duty of care, 10–60
    fiduciary duty, 10–60
    heritable property, 10–55—10–59
    introduction, 11–25
    legal representation, 10–42
    liability, 10–62
    non-compliance with welfare
      guardian's decisions,
      11–37—11–38
    records, 10–61
    remuneration, 11–33—11–36
    transactions, 11–28—11–32
  joint guardians, and, 11–10
  withdrawers, and, 8–12—8–13
Acute conditions
  intellectual impairments, and, 1–13
Additional guardians
  joint guardians, and, 11–11—11–12
  transitional provisions, 11–101
Adolescent practitioner
  meaning, 14–2
Adult
  affairs and welfare, *see* Financial
    Guardianship, Personal welfare
  disagreement or resistance, 6–23
  treatment, 14–17—14–20
    and see Health-care decisions
  identification of client, and, 2–12—2–13
  impairment of capacity, *see* Capacity,
    Incapacity
  meaning, 1–2
  personal decision-making, *see*
    Health-care decisions, Personal
    welfare
  transactions, 4–22, 11–28—11–32
  wishes and feelings
    constructing decisions, 15–1—15–28
    statement of, 3–9, 7–13
    taking into account, 4–16—4–19
Adults with Incapacity (Scotland) Act
  2000
  accounts and funds, A1–25—A1–34
  authority for medical treatment, A1–51
  authority to treat, A1–47—A1–52
  citation, A1–89
  commencement
    generally, A1–89
    Order No.1, A2–07
    Order No.2, A2–14

Adults with Incapacity (Scotland) Act
  2000—*cont.*
  consequential amendments, A1–88
  general provisions
    appeals, A1–14
    Codes of Practice, A1–13
    court expenses, A1–08
    definitions, A1–01
    general principles, A1–01
    intimation, A1–11
    investigations, A1–12
    judicial proceedings, A1–02—A1–05
    local authorities, A1–10
    Mental Welfare Commission, A1–09
    Public Guardian, A1–06—A1–07
  guardianship
    function and duties of guardians,
      A1–64—A1–70
    generally, A1–57—A1–62
    joint guardians, A1–62
    substitute guardians, A1–63
    termination, A1–71—A1–79
  health-care decisions, A1–47—A1–52
  interpretation, A1–87
  intervention orders, A1–53—A1–56
  introduction
    applicable law, 3–22—3–25
    Codes of Practice, 3–14—3–18
    commencement, 3–19
    criminal offences, 3–27
    English law, 3–32
    excluded matters, 3–28—3–29
    generally, 3–1—3–2
    historical background, 3–3—3–6
    jurisdiction, 3–20—3–21
    layout, 3–10—3–11
    legal aid, 3–30
    overview, 3–7—3–9
    recognition and enforcement, 3–26
    reform of mental health law, 3–31
    regulations, 3–12—3–13
  jurisdiction, A1–85
  management of residents' finances,
    A1–35—A1–46
  medical treatment, A1–47—A1–52
  minor amendments, A1–88
  miscellaneous, A1–80—A1–84
  powers of attorney, A1–15—A1–24
  private international law, A1–85
  regulations, A1–86
  repeals, A1–88
  schedules
    consequential amendments, A1–94
    continuation of existing
      officeholders, A1–93
    jurisdiction, A1–92
    managers of establishment, A1–90
    management of estate of adult,
      A1–91
    minor amendments, A1–94
    private international law, A1–92
    repeals, A1–95

Advance directives
  BMA policy, 7–6
  excluded matters, and, 3–29
  generally, 3–29, 7–5, 14–3, 14–47
  guardianship, 7–12
  intervention orders, 7–12
  links to power of attorney, 7–9
  mental health legislation, 7–11
  Styles, 7–8
  taking instructions, 7–7
  use of interdict, 7–10
Age-related conditions
  intellectual impairments, and,
    1–11—1–12
Agency
  powers of attorney, and
    generally, 6–47
    income tax, 6–48
Agency and mandate
  and see Powers of attorney
  generally, 6–1
Alcohol abuse
  intellectual impairments, and, 1–13
Alliance for the Promotion of the
  Incapable Adults Bill, 3–4, 3–5, 3–32,
    11–37, 14–55
Angelman's Syndrome
  tutors-dative, and, 10–19
Anticipatory measures
  advance directives
    BMA policy, 7–6
    generally, 7–5
    guardianship, 7–12
    intervention orders, 7–12
    links to power of attorney, 7–9
    mental health legislation, 7–11
    Styles, 7–8
    taking instructions, 7–7
    use of interdict, 7–10
  gifts
    generally, 7–4
    introduction, 2–20
  introduction, 1–25
  joint bank accounts, 7–1—7–2
  powers of attorney
    and see Powers of attorney
    agency, 6–47—6–48
    attorneys, 6–20—6–22, 6–33—6–37
    creation and registration, 6–9—6–18
    good practice, 6–32
    grantor, 6–19
    introduction, 6–1—6–5
    nature, 6–6—6–8
    non-Scottish powers, 6–49—6–53
    other authorities, 6–41
    powers, 6–23—6–31
    sheriff, 6–38—6–40
    termination, 6–43—6–46
    transitional provisions, 6–54—6–58
  professional issues, and
    gifts, 2–20
    taking instructions, 2–19
  statement of wishes and feelings, 7–13
  summary, 3–9
  taking instructions, 2–19
  trusts for administration, 7–3
Anti-social personality disorder
  intellectual impairments, and, 1–8

Anxiety states
  intellectual impairments, and, 1–8
Appeals
  incapacity, and, 4–29
  regulatory amendments, A2–09
  sheriffs, and
    generally, 5–13
    incapacity decisions, 5–18
    medical treatment decisions, 5–19
    miscellaneous, 5–20
Applicable law
  generally, 3–22—3–25
  powers of attorney, and, 6–53
Applications
  guardianship, and, 10–47
  intervention orders, and, 10–47
  sheriffs, and, 5–21
Appointed practitioner
  meaning, 14–2
Appointee
  meaning, 14–2
Appointee decisions
  'appointee', 14–2
  Code of Practice, 14–16
  general principles, and, 14–24
  generally, 14–13—14–14
  inter-relationships, 14–21—14–23
  limitations, 14–17—14–20
  source of authority, 14–15
Approved psychiatrists
  meaning, 14–2
  role and function, 5–36
Assault
  health-care decisions, and, 14–1
Attorney, powers of
  agency, and
    generally, 6–47
    income tax, 6–48
  applicable law, and, 6–53
  attorneys
    actings and duties, 6–33—6–36
    agents, as, 6–47
    duty of care, 6–5
    fiduciary duty, 6–5
    generally, 6–20—6–22
    indemnification, 6–37
    general principles, and, 6–5
    remuneration, 6–37
  authority to intromit, and, 6–42
  authority to treat, and, 6–42
  Books of Council, and, 6–18
  categories, 6–4
  certifiers, 6–12—6–14
  Code of Practice, 6–4
  contract, and, 6–7
  copies, 6–17
  creation
    certificates, 6–12—6–15
    certifiers, 6–12—6–14
    introduction, 6–11
  duty of care, 6–5
  enduring, 6–49—6–50
  English law, and, 6–49—6–50
  express powers, 6–25—6–126

Attorney, powers of—*cont.*
  fiduciary duty, 6–5
  foreign law, and, 6–51—6–52
  general principles, and, 6–5
  gifts, and, 6–31
  good practice, 6–32
  grantor, 6–19
  income tax, and, 6–48
  interpretation
    contract model, 6–7
    grant model, 6–8
    introduction, 6–6
  introduction, 6–1—6–5
  investigation of complaints, 6–41
  joint bank accounts, and, 6–42
  management of resident's finances, and, 6–42
  Mental Welfare Commission
    investigation of complaints, 6–41
  professional issues, and, 6–28—6–30
  Public Guardian
    general principles, and, 6–5
    investigation of complaints, 6–41
    registration, 6–16
  registration
    Books of Council, in, 6–18
    certificate, 6–17
    continuing attorney, 6–9
    generally, 6–16
    Public Guardian, with, 6–16
    welfare attorney, 6–10
  restrictions, 6–23—6–24
  sheriff, and
    general principles, and, 6–5
    powers, 6–38—6–40
  solicitor attorneys, and, 6–35
  Style, and
    form, A5–01
    generally, 6–28—6–30
  tax powers, 6–27
  termination
    effect, 6–46
    generally, 6–43—6–45
    transitional provisions, 6–54—6–58
Audit
  financial guardianship, and, 11–63
Authorisation of health-care
  introduction, 14–1
  necessity
    application of Act, 14–34—14–37
    appointee decision, and, 14–22
    generally, 14–30—14–33
  parens patriae
    appointee decision, and, 14–21
    generally, 14–25—14–29
    intervention order, and, 14–21
    patient's decision, and, 14–8
  Part X MHSA 1984, under
    appointee decision, and, 14–21
    generally, 14–38—14–39
    necessity, and, 14–37
    patient's decision, and, 14–3
  s.47(2), under
    application of Act, 14–42
    appointee decision, and, 14–23
    duration, 14–43

Authorisation of health-care—*cont.*
  s.47(2), under—*cont.*
    exclusions, 14–45—14–47
    general principles, and, 14–42
    generally, 14–41
    necessity, and, 14–34—14–35
    patient's decision, and, 14–3
    procedure, 14–43
    scope, 14–44
  s.48(3), under
    appointee decision, and, 14–23
    emergencies, 14–53
    generally, 14–48
    treatments requiring certificate, 14–51—14–52
    treatments requiring court application, 14–49—14–50
  s.50(5), under
    appointee decision, and, 14–23
    generally, 14–54—14–58
    patient's decision, and, 14–8
Authority for medical research
  Ethics Committee, A2–15
  generally, 14–63—14–69
  'research', 14–70
  summary of measures, and, 3–9
  wrongful research, 14–71—14–72
Authority to intromit
  applications
    countersignature, 8–6—8–7
    introduction, 8–4
    medical certificate, 8–8
    Part A, 8–5
    Part B, 8–6—8–7
    post-receipt procedure, 8–9
  certificate of authority, 8–10
  duration, 8–15
  guardianship, and, 10–70
  intervention orders, and, 10–70
  introduction, 8–1
  limitations, 8–3
  powers of attorney, and, 6–42
  Public Guardian, and
    duration, 8–15
    intimation to adult, 8–9
    introduction, 8–1
    supervision, 8–14
    termination, 8–16
  purposes, 8–11
  related provisions
    joint accounts, 8–18
    managers of establishments, 8–19
    summary of measures, and, 3–9
  supervision, 8–14
  suspension, 8–16
  termination, 8–16
  terminology, 8–2
  withdrawers
    actings and duties, 8–12—8–13
    generally, 8–1
Authority to transfer
  generally, 8–17
  introduction, 8–1
  limitations, 8–3
  terminology, 8–2
Authority to treat
  and see Health-care decisions

Authority to treat—*cont.*
  guardianship, and, 10–70
  intervention orders, and, 10–70
  powers of attorney, and, 6–42
  summary of measures, and, 3–9

Bare trusts
  responsive measures, and
    generally, 12–24
    good practice, 12–3
  third party measures, and, 13–39
Bequests
  and see Gifts
  third party measures, and, 13–37
Best interests
  construction of decisions, and,
    15–27—15–28
Bi-polar disorder
  intellectual impairments, and, 1–8
BMA policy
  advance directives, and, 7–6
Books of Council
  powers of attorney, and, 6–18
Borderline personality disorder
  intellectual impairments, and, 1–9
Brain injuries
  intellectual impairments, and, 1–7

Capacity
  and see Incapacity
  assessment, 1–32—1–35
  communication difficulties, and, 1–14
  health-care decisions, and, 14–5—14–10
  intellectual impairments and
    disabilities, and
    acute conditions, 1–13
    age-related conditions, 1–11—1–12
    brain injuries, 1–7
    distortions, 1–19
    effect, 1–15
    induced conditions, 1–13
    introduction, 1–5
    learning disabilities, 1–6
    legal significance, 1–20—1–27
    mental illness, 1–8
    personality disorder, 1–9—1–10
    temporary conditions, 1–13
  introduction, 1–1—1–4
  minimising impairment, 1–16—1–18
  tests, 1–28—1–31
Capital gains tax
  trusts, and, 13–23—13–25
Carrying on business
  financial guardianship, and, 11–52
Caution
  guardianship, and, 10–52—10–53
  intervention orders, and, 10–52—10–53
  substitute guardian, and, 11–15
Certificates
  authority to intromit, and
    generally, 8–10
    medical practitioners, A2–02
  powers of attorney, and
    generally, 6–12—6–14
    regulation, A2–06

Change of address
  guardians, and, 11–27
  intervention order, and, 10–75
Changes in capacity
  management of resident's affairs, and
    resident leaves without regaining
      capacity, 9–21
    resident regains capacity, 9–20
    review of certificate, 9–19
Chief social work officers
  guardian, as
    change of local authority area by
      adult, 11–5
    generally, 11–3
    remuneration of guardian, 11–34
    responsible officer, 11–4
  role and function, 5–35
Child practitioner
  meaning, 14–2
Children
  capacity, and, 1–2
Client, identification of
  adult, 2–12—2–13
  hybrid situations, 2–15—2–18
  interested person, 2–14
  introduction, 2–11
  relative, 2–14
Clinical psychologists
  role and function, 5–36
Codes of Practice
  fiduciary duty, and
    confidentiality, 4–38
    conflicts of interest, 4–37
  generally, 3–14—3–18
  health-care decisions, A4–01
  management of resident's affairs, and,
    9–1
  powers of attorney, and, 6–4
Combination orders
  guardianship, and, 10–30
  intervention orders, and, 10–30
Combined powers
  meaning, 10–46
Commencement of the Act
  generally, 3–19
Communication difficulties
  sensory impairment, 1–13
Concurrent guardians
  generally, 11–7
  introduction, 11–6
Confidentiality
  fiduciary duty, and, 4–38
Conflicts of interest
  fiduciary duty, and, 4–37
Consent to health-care
  appointee decision
    'appointee', 14–2
    Code of Practice, 14–16
    general principles, and, 14–24
    generally, 14–13—14–14
    inter-relationships, 14–21—14–23
    limitations, 14–17—14–20
    source of authority, 14–15
  introduction, 14–1

Consent to health-care—*cont.*
  patient's decision
    advance directives, and, 7–5—7–12
    generally, 14–3—14–10
    problem areas, 14–11—14–12
Construction of decisions
  generally, 15–1—15–28
Consultation
  concurrent guardians, and, 11–7
  joint guardians, and, 11–10
Continuing powers of attorney
  and see Powers of attorney
  agency, 6–47—6–48
  attorneys, 6–20—6–22, 6–33—6–37
  Code of Practice, 3–15
  creation and registration, 6–9—6–18
  good practice, 6–32
  grantor, 6–19
  introduction, 6–1—6–5
  nature, 6–6—6–8
  non-Scottish powers, 6–49—6–53
  other authorities, 6–41
  powers, 6–23—6–31
  sheriff, 6–38—6–40
  summary of measures, and, 3–9
  termination, 6–43—6–46
  transitional provisions, 6–54—6–58
Contract
  powers of attorney, and, 6–7
Correspondence, respect for
  human rights, and, 1–48
Council of Europe recommendations
  principles of legal protection, 3–6
Countersignature
  authority to intromit, and, 8–6—8–7
  regulation, A2–04
Court of Session
  role and function, 5–22
Criminal injuries compensation
  generally, 12–16
  good practice, 12–3
  summary of measures, and, 3–9
Criminal offence
  generally, 3–27
Criminal procedure
  guardianship, and
    comment, 11–89
    criteria, 11–86
    generally, 11–84—11–85
    medical reports, 11–87
    order, 11–88
    statutory provision, A3–02—A3–03
  intervention order, and
    generally, 10–77—10–78
    statutory provision, A3–04
  responsive measures, and, 12–32
Criminal Procedure (Scotland) Act 1995
  disposal in case of insanity, A3–01
  guardianship, A3–02—A3–03
  hospital orders, A3–02—A3–03
  intervention orders, A3–04
  medical evidence, A3–05
Curators *ad litem*
  good practice, 12–3
  management, 12–26
  personal welfare, 12–35

Curators *ad litem—cont.*
  safeguarders, and, 5–7
  summary of measures, and, 3–9
Curators bonis
  abolition of measures, and, 3–9
  curatory regime, 10–10
  generally, 10–5—10–6
  historical development, 10–7
  'preservation' issue, 10–8—10–9
  transitional provisions, 11–102—11–103

Damages payments
  good practice, 12–3
  other courts, in, 12–13
  sheriff court, in, 12–13—12–14
Death of adult
  guardianship, and, 10–71
  intervention orders, and, 10–71
Decision-making process
  generally, 15–1—15–28
Deed of trust
  vaccine damage payments, and, 12–12
Defence of proceedings
  guardianship and intervention orders, and, 10–43
Degenerative brain disorders
  intellectual impairments, and, 1–8
Delegation
  guardians, and, 11–26
Delivery
  trusts, and, 13–10
Dementia
  intellectual impairments, and
    age-related conditions, 1–11
    mental disorders, 1–8
Detention of persons of unsound mind
  human rights, and, 1–48
Directions
  sheriffs, and, 5–14—5–15
Disability
  meaning, 1–3
Disability discrimination
  disabled person, 1–42
  introduction, 1–41
  less favourable treatment, 1–44
  other provisions, 1–46
  provision of goods, facilities and services, 1–43
  reasonable adjustments, 1–45
  solicitor's services, and, 2–6
Disagreements
  joint guardians, and, 11–10
Discharge of financial guardian
  generally, 11–66
  sheriff's role, 11–67
Discretionary trust
  income tax, and, 13–22
Dispensation with intimation
  evidence, A2–05
Disposal of accommodation
  guardianship, and, 11–53—11–54
  intervention order, and, 10–59
Doctors
  certificates, A2–02
  meaning, 14–2

Doctors—*cont.*
  role and function, 5–36
Down's syndrome
  intellectual impairments, and, 1–6
Duty of care
  generally, 4–35
  guardianship, and, 10–60
  intervention orders, and, 10–60
  introduction, 4–31—4–34
  powers of attorney, and, 6–5

Enduring powers of attorney, 6–49—6–50
Enforcement of foreign measures
  generally, 3–26
English law
  enduring powers of attorney,
    6–49—6–50
  generally, 3–32
Ethics Committee
  regulation, A2–15
European Convention on Human Rights
  generally, 1–47—1–48
  inspection of registers, and, 5–23
Expenses
  intervention order, and, 10–74
  sheriffs, and, 5–10—5–12

Facility and circumvention
  elements, 1–37
  generally, 1–36
  introduction, 1–21
  personal welfare, 1–40
Factory and commission
  and see Powers of attorney
  generally, 6–1
Fair hearing, right to
  human rights, and, 1–47
Family life, respect for
  generally, 1–48
  inspection of registers, and, 5–23
Fees
  Public Guardian, A2–01
Fiduciary duty
  confidentiality, 4–38
  conflicts of interest, 4–37
  generally, 4–36
  guardianship, and, 10–60
  intervention orders, and, 10–60
  introduction, 4–31—4–34
  powers of attorney, and, 6–5
Financial guardianship
  accounts
    approval, 11–64
    audit, 11–63
    deficiencies, 11–65
    generally, 11–61—11–62
  audit, 11–63
  carrying on business, 11–52
  discharge of guardian
    generally, 11–66
    sheriff's role, 11–67
  disposal of accommodation
    generally, 11–53—11–54
    introduction, 10–59

Financial guardianship—*cont.*
  general principles, and
    generally, 11–39
    management plan, 11–48
  gifts
    generally, 11–55
    procedure, 11–56—11–58
    sheriff's role, 11–59
  guardian's powers
    carrying on business, 11–52
    disposal of accommodation,
      11–53—11–54
    general, 11–49
    investment, 11–51
    money, 11–50
    purchase of accommodation,
      11–53—11–54
  heritable property, and
    accommodation, 10–59
    amendment of registration, 10–57
    registration of orders, 10–55—10–56
    third party protection, 10–58
  income tax, 11–60
  introduction, 11–39—11–40
  inventory, 11–42—11–43
  investment, 11–51
  management plan
    directions, 11–47
    general principles, 11–48
    introduction, 11–44
    pre-approval restrictions, 11–45
    review, 11–46
    variation, 11–46
  money, 11–50
  Public Guardian, and
    generally, 11–41
    inventory, 11–43
    management plan, 11–44
  purchase of accommodation
    generally, 11–53—11–54
    introduction, 10–59
  tax powers, 11–60
Foreign guardians
  directions, 11–90
  other provisions, 11–91
Forfeiture
  remuneration of guardians, and, 11–36

'Gateway' definition
  generally, 3–10
General principles
  application
    consequences of non-compliance,
      4–4—4–5
    intervention, 4–3
    introduction, 4–2
  consequences of non-compliance,
    4–4—4–5
  fifth principle, 4–22
  financial guardianship, and
    generally, 11–39
    management plan, 11–48
  first principle
    'benefit', 4–8
    introduction, 4–6

General principles—*cont.*
  first principle—*cont.*
    'person responsible for authorising intervention', 4–7
    'such benefit not reasonably be achieved with intervention', 4–9
    wider application, 4–10—4–11
  fourth principle, 4–20—4–21
  guardianship, and
    duties, 10–60
    generally, 10–27
  health-care decisions, and necessity, 14–34—14–37
  s.47(2) authority, 14–42
  intervention, and, 4–3
  intervention orders, and
    duties, 10–60
    generally, 10–27
  introduction, 4–1
  powers of attorney, and, 6–5
  second principle
    choice of powers, 4–14
    choice of procedure, 4–13
    exercise of powers, 4–15
    introduction, 4–12
  sheriffs, and, 5–8
  third principle, 4–16—4–19
Gifts
  anticipatory measures, and
    generally, 7–4
    introduction, 2–20
  financial guardianship, and
    generally, 11–55
    procedure, 11–56—11–58
    sheriff's role, 11–59
  powers of attorney, and, 6–31
  summary of measures, and, 3–9
  third party measures, and, 13–37
Good practice
  incapacity, and, 4–30
  powers of attorney, and, 6–32
Goods, facilities and services, provision of
  disability discrimination, and, 1–43
Grantor
  powers of attorney, and, 6–19
Guardians
  and see Guardianship
  change of address, 11–27
  chief social work officer
    change of local authority area by adult, 11–5
    generally, 11–3
    remuneration, 11–34
    responsible officer, 11–4
  Code of Practice, and, 3–15
  concurrent
    generally, 11–7
    introduction, 11–6
  delegation, 11–26
  duration of appointment
    generally, 11–22—11–2
    transitional provisions, 11–98—11–100
  duty of care, 10–60

Guardians—*cont.*
  fiduciary duty, 10–60
  financial management
    and see Financial guardianship
    accounting, 11–61—11–65
    audit, 11–63
    discharge of guardian, 11–66—11–67
    gifts, 11–55—11–60
    guardian's powers, 11–49—11–54
    introduction, 11–39—11–40
    inventory, 11–42—11–43
    management plan, 11–44—11–48
    Public Guardian's role, 11–41
  functions, actings and duties
    change of address, 11–27
    delegation, 11–26
    duty of care, 10–60
    fiduciary duty, 10–60
    heritable property, 10–55—10–59
    introduction, 11–25
    legal representation, 10–42
    liability, 10–62
    local authority, of, 10–66—10–67
    Mental Welfare Commission, of, 10–65
    non-compliance with welfare guardian's decisions, 11–37—11–38
    Public Guardian, of, 10–64
    records, 10–61
    remuneration, 11–33—11–36
    sheriff, of, 10–63
    transactions, 11–28—11–32
  heritable property
    accommodation, 10–59
    amendment of registration, 10–57
    registration of orders, 10–55—10–56
    third party protection, 10–58
  individuals
    generally, 11–2
    remuneration, 11–33
  interim, 11–19—11–21
  joint
    actings, 11–10
    additional appointment, 11–11—11–12
    appointees, 11–9
    consultation, 11–10
    disagreements, 11–10
    generally, 11–8
    introduction, 11–6
    liability, 11–10
    removal, 11–13
    resignation, 11–13
    third party protection, 11–10
  legal representation, 10–42
  limitations, 10–31
  limited powers, 10–38
  liability, 10–62
  non-compliance with welfare guardian's decisions
    generally, 11–37—11–38
    regulation, A2–13
  plenary powers, 10–38, 10–39
  records, 10–61

Guardians—*cont.*
  removal
    generally, 11–68
    introduction, 11–17
    joint guardians, 11–13
    sheriff's powers, 11–71
  remuneration
    calculation, 11–35
    chief social work officer, 11–34
    forfeiture, 11–36
    individual, 11–33
    payment, 11–35
  renewal of appointment, 11–22
  replacement
    generally, 11–68
    introduction, 11–17
    joint guardians, 11–13
    sheriff's powers, 11–69—11–70
    transitional provisions, 11–101
  resignation
    generally, 11–80—11–83
    joint guardians, 11–13
  substitute
    caution, and, 11–15
    generally, 11–14
    transitional provisions, 11–101
  transactions
    introduction, 11–28
    matters outwith scope of order, 11–29
    matters within scope of order, 11–30
    matters within scope of power to authorise, 11–32
    personal welfare matters within scope of order, 11–31
  transitional, 11–18
  transitional provisions
    additional guardians, 11–101
    application of, 11–94
    continuation of pre-Act appointments, 11–92
    curators bonis, 11–102—11–103
    duration, 11–98—11–100
    former MHSA guardians, 11–97
    guardians with management powers, 11–95
    Guidance Notes, 11–96
    proceedings relating to pre-Act appointments, 11–93
    replacement guardians, 11–101
    substitute guardians, 11–101
Guardianship
  adult abroad, 10–45
  advance directives, and, 7–12
  application, 10–47
  authority to intromit, and, 10–70
  authority to treat, and, 10–70
  caution, 10–52—10–53
  change of address, 11–27
  combination orders, 10–30
  criminal procedure, and
    comment, 11–89
    criteria, 11–86
    generally, 11–84—11–85
    medical reports, 11–87
    order, 11–88

Guardianship—*cont.*
  criminal procedure, and—*cont.*
    statutory provision, A3–02—A3–03
  criteria
    generally, 10–27
    'incapable', 10–28
    'likely to continue', 10–28
  death of adult, and, 10–71
  delegation, 11–26
  duration, 11–22—11–23
  duty of care, and, 10–60
  effects
    introduction, 11–28
    matters outwith scope of order, 11–29
    matters within scope of order, 11–30
    matters within scope of power to authorise, 11–32
    personal welfare matters within scope of order, 11–31
  fiduciary duty, and, 10–60
  financial management
  and see Financial guardianship
    accounting, 11–61—11–65
    audit, 11–63
    discharge of guardian, 11–66—11–67
    gifts, 11–55—11–60
    guardian's powers, 11–49—11–54
    introduction, 11–39—11–40
    inventory, 11–42—11–43
    management plan, 11–44—11–48
    Public Guardian's role, 11–41
  foreign guardians
    directions, 11–90
    other provisions, 11–91
  further provisions
    alterations and termination, 11–68—11–83
    checklist, 11–104
    criminal procedure, 11–84—11–89
    duration, 11–22—11–23
    financial management, 11–39—11–67
    foreign guardians, 11–90—11–91
    functions, actings and duties, 11–25—11–38
    guardians, 11–2—11–21
    introduction, 11–1
    renewal, 11–24
    transitional provisions, 11–92—11–103
  generally, 10–26
  general principles, and
    duties, 10–60
    generally, 10–27
  guardians
    and see Guardians
    alterations and termination, 11–68—11–83
    chief social work officer, 11–3—11–5
    concurrent, 11–6—11–7
    financial management, 11–39—11–67
    functions, actings and duties, 11–25—11–38
    individuals, 11–2
    interim, 11–19—11–21
    joint, 11–8—11–13

Guardianship—*cont.*
  guardians—*cont.*
    replacement, 11–17
    substitute, 11–14—11–16
    transitional, 11–18
  heritable property
    accommodation, 10–59
    amendment of registration, 10–57
    registration of orders, 10–55—10–56
    third party protection, 10–58
  inter-relationships, 10–70
  introduction, 10–1
  legal proceedings
    defence of proceedings, 10–43
    pursuit of proceedings, 10–43—10–44
    representation, 10–42
  liability, 10–62
  limitations, 10–31
  local authorities, and, 10–66—10–67
  management of resident's finances, and, 10–70
  management powers, and, 10–41
  Mental Welfare Commission, and, 10–65
  nominees, 10–47
  powers
    distinctions, 10–41
    generally, 10–37—10–40
  powers of attorney, and, 10–70
  procedure
    applicants, 10–47
    caution, 10–52—10–53
    introduction, 10–46
    nominees, 10–47
    notice, 10–47
    other orders and measures, 10–51
    registration with Public Guardian, 10–54
    reports, 10–48—10–50
  Public Guardian, and
    registration, 10–54
    supervision, 10–64
  recall
    local authorities powers, 11–76—11–79
    MWC's powers, 11–76—11–79
    Public Guardian's powers, 11–76—11–79
    sheriff's powers, 11–72
  records, 10–61
  registration, 10–54
  remuneration of guardian
    calculation, 11–35
    chief social work officer, 11–34
    forfeiture, 11–36
    individual, 11–33
    payment, 11–35
  renewal, 11–24
  reports
    generally, 10–48—10–50
    regulation, A2–09
  scope
    combinations, 10–30
    limitations, 10–31
    orders, 10–29
    summary, 10–32

Guardianship—*cont.*
  sheriff, and, 10–63
  Style, and
    application for order, A6–03
    application to replace, A6–02
  summary of measures, and, 3–9
  termination, 10–71
  third party protection, 10–68—10–69
  transitional provisions
    additional guardians, 11–101
    application of, 11–94
    continuation of pre-Act appointments, 11–92
    curators bonis, 11–102—11–103
    duration, 11–98—11–100
    former MHSA guardians, 11–97
    guardians with management powers, 11–95
    Guidance Notes, 11–96
    proceedings relating to pre-Act appointments, 11–93
    replacement guardians, 11–101
    substitute guardians, 11–101
  types of order
    combinations, 10–30
    generally, 10–29
    limitations, 10–31
    summary, 10–32
  uses, 10–37—10–40
  variation, 11–73
  welfare powers, and, 10–41

Handicap
  meaning, 1–3
Health-care decisions
  appeals, and, 5–19
  'appointee', 14–2
  appointee decision
    Code of Practice, 14–16
    general principles, and, 14–24
    generally, 14–13—14–14
    inter-relationships, 14–21—14–23
    limitations, 14–17—14–20
    source of authority, 14–15
  assault, and, 14–1
  authorisation
    introduction, 14–1
    necessity, 14–30—14–37
    parens patriae, 14–25—14–29
    Part X MHSA 1984, under, 14–38—14–39
  Code of Practice, A4–01
  consent, and
    appointee decision, 14–13—14–24
    introduction, 14–1
    patient's decision, 14–3—14–12
  guardianship, and, 10–70
  'health-care', 14–1
  Incapacity Act 2002, under
    intervention order, 14–40
    introduction, 14–1
    judicial determination, 14–58—14–62
    s.47(2), 14–41—14–47
    s.48(3), 14–48—14–53
    s.50(5), 14–54—14–58

Health-care decisions—*cont.*
  intervention order, and
    generally, 14–40
    introduction, 10–70
  introduction, 14–1
  judicial determination
    introduction, 14–58
    persons having an interest, 14–59
    s.50(3), under, 14–60
    s.50(6), under, 14–61
    s.52, under, 14–62
  medical certificates, A2–16
  'medical treatment', 14–2
  necessity
    application of Act, 14–34—14–37
    appointee decision, and, 14–22
    generally, 14–30—14–33
  parens patriae
    appointee decision, and, 14–21
    generally, 14–25—14–29
    intervention order, and, 14–21
    patient's decision, and, 14–8
  Part X MHSA 1984, under
    appointee decision, and, 14–21
    generally, 14–38—14–39
    necessity, and, 14–37
    patient's decision, and, 14–3
  patient's decision
    advance directives, and, 7–5—7–12
    generally, 14–3—14–10
    problem areas, 14–11—14–12
  powers of attorney, and, 6–42
  'practitioner, 14–2
  s.47(2) authority
    application of Act, 14–42
    appointee decision, and, 14–23
    duration, 14–43
    exclusions, 14–45—14–47
    general principles, and, 14–42
    generally, 14–41
    necessity, and, 14–34—14–35
    patient's decision, and, 14–3
    procedure, 14–43
    scope, 14–44
  s.48(3) authority
    appointee decision, and, 14–23
    emergencies, 14–53
    generally, 14–48
    treatments requiring certificate, 14–51—14–52
    treatments requiring court application, 14–49—14–50
  s.50(5) authority
    appointee decision, and, 14–23
    generally, 14–54—14–58
    patient's decision, and, 14–8
  specified treatments, A2–17
  summary of measures, and, 3–9
  terminology, 14–2
Heritable property
  guardianship and intervention orders, and
    accommodation, 10–59
    amendment of registration, 10–57
    registration of orders, 10–55—10–56
    third party protection, 10–58

Home, respect for
  human rights, and, 1–48
Hospital measures
  abolition of measures, and, 3–9
Human rights
  generally, 1–47—1–48
  inspection of registers, and, 5–23

Identification of client
  adult, 2–12—2–13
  hybrid situations, 2–15—2–18
  interested person, 2–14
  introduction, 2–11
  relative, 2–14
Identification of potential incapacity
  professional issues, and, 2–3—2–5
Impairment
  meaning, 1–3
Inability to communicate
  communication difficulties, and, 1–14
  'Incapable', meaning of
    criteria, 4–27—4–28
    generally, 4–23
    guardianship, and, 10–28
    intervention orders, and, 10–28
    'mental disorder', 4–24
    physical inability to communicate, 4–25—4–26
Incapable Adults (SLC Report)
  generally, 3–4
Incapacity
  appeals, and, 4–29
  criteria, 4–27—4–28
  definition
    generally, 4–23
    introduction, 3–10
    'mental disorder', 4–24
    physical inability to communicate, 4–25—4–26
  duty of care, and
    generally, 4–35
    introduction, 4–31—4–34
  fiduciary duty, and
    confidentiality, 4–38
    conflicts of interest, 4–37
    generally, 4–36
    introduction, 4–31—4–34
  good practice, 4–30
Income tax
  financial guardianship, and, 11–60
  powers of attorney, and, 6–48
  trusts, and
    discretionary trust, 13–22
    interest in possession, 13–20—13–21
    liferent trust, 13–20—13–21
    non-interest in possession, 13–22
Induced conditions
  intellectual impairments, and, 1–13
Informal voluntary arrangements
  responsive measures, and
    generally, 12–21—12–22
    good practice, 12–3
    joint bank accounts, 12–23
    summary of measures, and, 3–9
    third party measures, and, 13–39

Inheritance tax
  trusts, and, 13-26—13-30
Intellectual impairments and disabilities
  acute conditions, 1-13
  age-related conditions, 1-11—1-12
  brain injuries, 1-7
  distortions, and, 1-19
  effects, 1-15
  induced conditions, 1-13
  introduction, 1-5
  learning disabilities, 1-6
  legal significance
    anticipatory measures, 1-25
    facility and circumvention, 1-21
    introduction, 1-20
    modified liability, 1-24
    responsive measures, 1-26
    special benefits, 1-24
    supervening incapacity, 1-23
    third party measures, 1-27
    undue influence, 1-21
    validity of acts, 1-22
  mental illness, 1-8
  personality disorder, 1-9—1-10
  temporary conditions, 1-13
Inter vivos trusts
  summary of measures, and, 3-9
Interdict
  advance directives, and, 7-10
Interest in possession
  income tax, and, 13-20—13-21
Interim guardians
  generally, 11-19—11-21
Interim orders
  intervention order, and, 10-72
Intervention orders
  adult abroad, 10-45
  advance directives, and, 7-12
  application, 10-47
  authority to intromit, and, 10-70
  authority to treat, and
    generally, 14-40
    introduction, 10-70
  caution, 10-52—10-53
  change of address, 10-75
  combination orders, 10-30
  criminal procedure, and
    generally, 10-77—10-78
    statutory provision, A3-04
  criteria
    generally, 10-27
    'incapable', 10-28
    'likely to continue', 10-28
  death of adult, and, 10-71
  duty of care, and, 10-60
  fiduciary duty, and, 10-60
  generally, 10-26
  general principles, and
    duties, 10-60
    generally, 10-27
  health-care decisions, and
    generally, 14-40
    introduction, 10-70
  heritable property
    accommodation, 10-59

Intervention orders—*cont.*
  heritable property—*cont.*
    amendment of registration, 10-57
    registration of orders, 10-55—10-56
    third party protection, 10-58
  interim orders, 10-72
  inter-relationships, 10-70
  introduction, 10-1
  legal proceedings
    defence of proceedings, 10-43
    pursuit of proceedings, 10-43—10-44
    representation, 10-42
  liability, 10-62
  limitations, 10-31
  local authorities, and, 10-66—10-67
  management of resident's finances, and, 10-70
  management powers, and, 10-41
  Mental Welfare Commission, and, 10-65
  nominees, 10-47
  outlays, and, 10-74
  powers of attorney, and, 10-70
  procedure
    applicants, 10-47
    caution, 10-52—10-53
    introduction, 10-46
    nominees, 10-47
    notice, 10-47
    other orders and measures, 10-51
    registration with Public Guardian, 10-54
    reports, 10-48—10-50
  Public Guardian, and
    registration, 10-54
    supervision, 10-64
  recall, 10-73
  records, 10-61
  registration, 10-54
  reports
    generally, 10-48—10-50
    regulation, A2-11
  scope
    combinations, 10-30
    limitations, 10-31
    orders, 10-29
    summary, 10-32
  sheriff, and, 10-63
  Style, and, A6-01
  summary of measures, and, 3-9
  tax provisions, 10-76
  termination, 10-71
  third party protection, 10-68—10-69
  types of order
    combinations, 10-30
    generally, 10-29
    limitations, 10-31
    summary, 10-32
  uses and effects, 10-33—10-36
  variation, 10-73
  welfare powers, and, 10-41
Intervention, principles for
  application
    consequences of non-compliance, 4-4—4-5

Intervention, principles for—*cont.*
application—*cont.*
 intervention, 4–3
 introduction, 4–2
consequences of non-compliance,
 4–4—4–5
fifth principle, 4–22
financial guardianship, and
 generally, 11–39
 management plan, 11–48
first principle
 'benefit', 4–8
 introduction, 4–6
 'person responsible for authorising intervention', 4–7
 'such benefit not reasonably be achieved with intervention', 4–9
 wider application, 4–10—4–11
fourth principle, 4–20—4–21
guardianship, and
 duties, 10–60
 generally, 10–27
health-care decisions, and
 necessity, 14–34—14–37
 s.47(2) authority, 14–42
intervention, and, 4–3
intervention orders, and
 duties, 10–60
 generally, 10–27
introduction, 4–1
powers of attorney, and, 6–5
second principle
 choice of powers, 4–14
 choice of procedure, 4–13
 exercise of powers, 4–15
 introduction, 4–12
sheriffs, and, 5–8
third principle, 4–16—4–19
Intimation of applications
sheriffs, and, 5–9
Intromit, authority to
applications
 countersignature, 8–6—8–7
 introduction, 8–4
 medical certificate, 8–8
 Part A, 8–5
 Part B, 8–6—8–7
 post-receipt procedure, 8–9
certificate of authority, 8–10
duration, 8–15
guardianship, and, 10–70
intervention orders, and, 10–70
introduction, 8–1
limitations, 8–3
powers of attorney, and, 6–42
Public Guardian, and
 duration, 8–15
 intimation to adult, 8–9
 introduction, 8–1
 supervision, 8–14
 termination, 8–16
purposes, 8–11
related provisions
 joint accounts, 8–18
 managers of establishments, 8–19

Intromit, authority to—*cont.*
summary of measures, and, 3–9
supervision, 8–14
suspension, 8–16
termination, 8–16
terminology, 8–2
withdrawers
 actings and duties, 8–12—8–13
 generally, 8–1
Inventory
financial guardianship, and,
 11–42—11–43
Investigation of complaints
powers of attorney, and, 6–41
Investment
financial guardianship, and, 11–51

Joint bank accounts
authority to intromit, and, 8–18
generally, 7–1—7–2
informal voluntary arrangements, and, 12–23
powers of attorney, and, 6–42
summary of measures, and, 3–9
Joint guardians
actings, 11–10
additional appointment, 11–11—11–12
appointees, 11–9
consultation, 11–10
disagreements, 11–10
generally, 11–8
introduction, 11–6
liability, 11–10
removal, 11–13
resignation, 11–13
third party protection, 11–10
Judicial determination
introduction, 14–58
persons having an interest, 14–59
s.50(3), under, 14–60
s.50(6), under, 14–61
s.52, under, 14–62
Judicial factors
responsive measures, and, 12–25
Jurisdiction
generally, 3–20—3–21
sheriffs, and, 5–4

Learning disabilities
intellectual impairments, and, 1–6
Legal aid
generally, 3–30
regulatory amendments, A2–08
Legal incapacity
meaning, 1–4
minimising impairment, 1–16—1–18
Legal proceedings
guardianship and intervention orders, and
 defence of proceedings, 10–43
 pursuit of proceedings, 10–43—10–44
 representation, 10–42
Less favourable treatment
disability discrimination, and, 1–44

Liability
  joint guardians, and, 11–10
Liberty, right to
  human rights, and, 1–48
Liferent trust
  income tax, and, 13–20—13–21
'Likely to continue'
  guardianship and intervention orders, and, 10–28
Limited guardianship
  generally, 10–38
Limited registration
  management of resident's affairs, and, 9–4
Local authorities
  guardianship and intervention orders, and, 10–66—10–67
  role and function, 5–33—5–34
  supervision, and
    welfare attorneys, A2–03
    welfare guardians, A2–10
Local Authority Code
  introduction, 3–15

Management of resident's finances
  authority to intromit, and, 8–19
  changes in capacity
    resident leaves without regaining capacity, 9–21
    resident regains capacity, 9–20
    review of certificate, 9–19
  Code of Practice, 9–1
  guardianship, and, 10–70
  intervention orders, and, 10–70
  introduction, 9–1
  limited registration, 9–4
  management
    duties of managers, 9–10—9–11
    registered establishments, 9–13
    scope, 9–9
    withdrawal of funds, 9–12
  managers
    duties and functions, 9–10—9–11
    meaning, 9–3
  medical examination, 9–8
  opting out, 9–5
  powers of attorney, and, 6–42
  procedure
    generally, 9–6—9–7
    medical examination, 9–8
  Public Guardian
    introduction, 9–1
    supervision, 9–18
  registered establishments, 9–13
  summary of measures, and, 3–9
  supervision, 9–14—9–18
  terminology, 9–2
  transitional provisions, 9–22—9–24
  withdrawal of funds, 9–12
Management plan
  directions, 11–47
  general principles, 11–48
  introduction, 11–44
  pre-approval restrictions, 11–45
  review, 11–46

Management plan—*cont.*
  variation, 11–46
Management powers
  financial guardian, and
    accounting, 11–61—11–65
    audit, 11–63
    discharge of guardian, 11–66—11–67
    gifts, 11–55—11–60
    guardian's powers, 11–49—11–54
    introduction, 11–39—11–40
    inventory, 11–42—11–43
    management plan, 11–44—11–48
    Public Guardian's role, 11–41
  guardianship and intervention orders, and, 10–41
  tutors-dative, and, 10–25
Managing the Finances and Welfare of Incapable Adults (Consultation Paper)
  generally, 3–4
Manic depression
  intellectual impairments, and, 1–8
Means-tested benefits
  trusts, and, 13–31—13–35
Medical certificate
  authority to intromit, and, 8–8
  authority to treat, and, A2–16
  management of resident's affairs, and, 9–8
Medical practitioners
  certificates, A2–02
  meaning, 14–2
  role and function, 5–36
Medical research, authority for
  Ethics Committee, A2–15
  generally, 14–63—14–69
  'research', 14–70
  summary of measures, and, 3–9
  wrongful research, 14–71—14–72
Medical treatment decisions
  and see Health-care decisions
  appeals, and, 5–19
  generally, 14–2
'Mental disorder'
  incapacity, and, 4–24
Mental Health Act guardians
  abolition of measures, and, 3–9
  generally, 10–2—10–4
  transitional provisions, 11–97
Mental Health Act provisions
  responsive measures, and, 12–29—12–31
Mental health law
  advance directives, and, 7–11
  reform, 3–31
Mental health officers
  role and function, 5–37
Mental illness
  intellectual impairments, and, 1–8
Mental Welfare Commission
  guardianship and intervention orders, and, 10–65
  investigatory powers
    s.47(2) authority, 14–42
    s.48(3) authority, 14–48—14–53
    s.50(5) authority, 14–57
  powers of attorney, and, 6–41

Mental Welfare Commission—*cont.*
  role and function, 5–28—5–32
Mentally Disabled Adults (SLC Discussion Paper)
  generally, 3–4
MHSA guardians
  abolition of measures, and, 3–9
  generally, 10–2—10–4
  health-care decisions, and, 14–13
  transitional provisions, 11–97
MHSA provisions
  responsive measures, and, 12–29—12–31
Millan Committee
  brain injuries, and, 1–7
  construction of decisions, and, 15–18
  learning disabilities, and, 1–6
  mental illness, and, 1–8
  personality disorder, and, 1–9
Minimising impairment
  legal capacity, and, 1–16—1–18
Modified liability
  introduction, 1–24
Money
  financial guardianship, and, 11–50
Mortis causa trusts
  summary of measures, and, 3–9
Multiple sensory handicap
  intellectual impairments, and, 1–12

National Savings Bank
  responsive measures, and, 12–17
Nearest relative
  role and function, 5–38—5–39
  sheriffs, and, 5–16—5–17
Necessary medical treatment
  application of Act, 14–34—14–37
  appointee decision, and, 14–22
  generally, 14–30—14–33
  summary of measures, and, 3–9
Negotiorum gestio
  generally, 12–18—12–20
  good practice, 12–3
  summary of measures, and, 3–9
Neurosurgery for mental disorder
  patient's decision, and, 14–12
Neurotic disorders
  intellectual impairments, and, 1–8
Nominated practitioner
  meaning, 14–2
Nominations
  third party measures, and, 13–36
  summary of measures, and, 3–9
Nominees
  guardianship and intervention orders, and, 10–47
Non-compliance with welfare guardian's decisions
  generally, 11–37—11–38
  regulation, A2–13
Non-discrimination
  professional issues, and, 2–6—2–8

Obsessional disorders
  intellectual impairments, and, 1–8

"Old law"
  meaning, 3–1
  transitional arrangements, 3–2
Opting out
  management of resident's affairs, and, 9–5
Outlays
  intervention order, and, 10–74

Parens patriae
  good practice, 12–3
  health-care decisions, and
    appointee decision, and, 14–21
    generally, 14–25—14–29
    intervention order, and, 14–21
    patient's decision, and, 14–8
  management, 12–27
  personal welfare, 12–34
  summary of measures, and, 3–9
Part Codes
  introduction, 3–15
Part X MHSA 1984 authority
  appointee decision, and, 14–21
  generally, 14–38—14–39
  necessity, and, 14–37
  patient's decision, and, 14–3
Patient's decision
  advance directives, and, 7–5—7–12
  generally, 14–3—14–10
  problem areas, 14–11—14–12
Peaceable enjoyment of possessions, right to
  human rights, and, 1–48
Personal welfare
  criminal procedure, 12–32
  curators *ad litem*, 12–35
  intervention orders, and, 10–29
  introduction, 12–28
  MHSA provisions, 12–29—12–31
  parens patriae, 12–34
  removal under NAA 1948, 12–33
  summary of measures, 3–9
  undue influence, and, 1–40
Personality disorder
  intellectual impairments, and, 1–9—1–10
Physical inability to communicate
  incapacity, and, 4–25—4–26
Plenary guardianship
  generally, 10–38
  scope, 10–39
Powers of attorney
  advance directives, and, 7–9
  agency, and
    generally, 6–47
    income tax, 6–48
  applicable law, and, 6–53
  attorneys
    actings and duties, 6–33—6–36
    agents, as, 6–47
    duty of care, 6–5
    fiduciary duty, 6–5
    generally, 6–20—6–22
    indemnification, 6–37
  general principles, and, 6–5

Powers of attorney—cont.
  attorneys—cont.
    remuneration, 6–37
  authority to intromit, and, 6–42
  authority to treat, and, 6–42
  Books of Council, and, 6–18
  categories, 6–4
  certifiers, 6–12—6–14
  Code of Practice, 6–4
  contract, and, 6–7
  copies, 6–17
  creation
    certificates, 6–12—6–15
    certifiers, 6–12—6–14
    introduction, 6–11
  duty of care, 6–5
  enduring, 6–49—6–50
  English law, and, 6–49—6–50
  express powers, 6–25—6–126
  fiduciary duty, 6–5
  foreign law, and, 6–51—6–52
  general principles, and, 6–5
  gifts, and, 6–31
  good practice, 6–32
  grantor, 6–19
  guardianship, and, 10–70
  income tax, and, 6–48
  interpretation
    contract model, 6–7
    grant model, 6–8
    introduction, 6–6
  intervention orders, and, 10–70
  introduction, 6–1—6–5
  investigation of complaints, 6–41
  joint bank accounts, and, 6–42
  management of resident's finances, and, 6–42
  Mental Welfare Commission
    investigation of complaints, 6–41
  professional issues, and, 6–28—6–30
  Public Guardian
    general principles, and, 6–5
    investigation of complaints, 6–41
    registration, 6–16
  registration
    Books of Council, in, 6–18
    certificate, 6–17
    continuing attorney, 6–9
    generally, 6–16
    Public Guardian, with, 6–16
    welfare attorney, 6–10
  restrictions, 6–23—6–24
  sheriff, and
    general principles, and, 6–5
    powers, 6–38—6–40
  solicitor attorneys, and, 6–35
  Style, and
    form, A5–01
    generally, 6–28—6–30
  tax powers, 6–27
  termination
    effect, 6–46
    generally, 6–43—6–45
    transitional provisions, 6–54—6–58
Practitioner
  health-care decisions, and, 14–2
Premium bonds
  responsive measures, and, 12–17

Primary carer
  role and function, 5–40
Private international law
  generally, 3–20
Private life, respect for
  generally, 1–48
  inspection of registers, and, 5–23
Professional issues
  anticipatory measures
    gifts, 2–20
    taking instructions, 2–19
  construction of decisions, 15–1—15–28
  gifts, 2–20
  identification of client
    adult, 2–12—2–13
    hybrid situations, 2–15—2–18
    interested person, 2–14
    introduction, 2–11
    relative, 2–14
  identification of potential incapacity, 2–3—2–5
  introduction, 2–1—2–2
  non-discrimination, 2–6—2–8
  powers of attorney, and, 6–28—6–30
  principles, 2–9
  responsive measures, and, 2–10
Psychiatrists
  and see Approved psychiatrists
  role and function, 5–36
Psychologists
  role and function, 5–36
Psycho-neurotic disorders
  intellectual impairments, and, 1–8
Psychotic conditions
  intellectual impairments, and, 1–8
Psychotic disorders
  intellectual impairments, and, 1–8
Public Guardian
  authority to intromit, and
    duration, 8–15
    intimation to adult, 8–9
    introduction, 8–1
    supervision, 8–14
    termination, 8–16
  fees, A2–01
  financial guardianship, and
    generally, 11–41
    inventory, 11–43
    management plan, 11–44
  guardianship, and
    registration, 10–54
    supervision, 10–64
  intervention orders, and
    registration, 10–54
    supervision, 10–64
  management of resident's affairs, and
    introduction, 9–1
    supervision, 9–18
  powers of attorney, and
    general principles, and, 6–5
    investigation of complaints, 6–41
    registration, 6–16
    role and function, 5–23—5–27

Public hearing, right to
　human rights, and, 1–47
Public management
　excluded matters, and, 3–28
Purchase of accommodation
　guardianship, and, 11–53—11–54
　inventory order, and, 10–59

Reasonable adjustments
　disability discrimination, and, 1–45
Recall
　guardianship, and
　　local authorities powers,
　　　11–76—11–79
　　MWC's powers, 11–76—11–79
　　Public Guardian's powers,
　　　11–76—11–79
　　regulation, A2–12
　　sheriff's powers, 11–72
　intervention order, and, 10–73
Recognition of foreign measures
　generally, 3–26
Records
　guardianship and intervention orders,
　　and, 10–61
Registration of powers of attorney
　Books of Council, in, 6–18
　certificate, 6–17
　continuing attorney, 6–9
　generally, 6–16
　Public Guardian, with, 6–16
　welfare attorney, 6–10
Regulations
　generally, 3–12—3–13
Remits
　sheriffs, and, 5–20
Removal of guardians
　generally, 11–68
　introduction, 11–17
　joint guardians, 11–13
　sheriff's powers, 11–71
Removal under NAA 1948
　generally, 12–33
　summary of measures, and, 3–9
Remuneration of guardians
　calculation, 11–35
　chief social work officer, 11–34
　forfeiture, 11–36
　individual, 11–33
　payment, 11–35
Replacement guardians
　generally, 11–17
Replacement of guardians
　generally, 11–68
　introduction, 11–17
　joint guardians, 11–13
　sheriff's powers, 11–69—11–70
　transitional provisions, 11–101
Reports
　guardianship and intervention orders,
　　and
　　　generally, 10–48—10–50
　　　regulation, A2–09
Research, authority for
　Ethics Committee, A2–15

Research, authority for—*cont.*
　generally, 14–63—14–69
　'research', 14–70
　summary of measures, and, 3–9
　wrongful research, 14–71—14–72
Resident's finances, management of
　authority to intromit, and, 8–19
　changes in capacity
　　resident leaves without regaining
　　　capacity, 9–21
　　resident regains capacity, 9–20
　　review of certificate, 9–19
　Code of Practice, 9–1
　guardianship, and, 10–70
　intervention orders, and, 10–70
　introduction, 9–1
　limited registration, 9–4
　management
　　duties of managers, 9–10—9–11
　　registered establishments, 9–13
　　scope, 9–9
　　withdrawal of funds, 9–12
　managers
　　duties and functions, 9–10—9–11
　　meaning, 9–3
　medical examination, 9–8
　opting out, 9–5
　powers of attorney, and, 6–42
　procedure
　　generally, 9–6—9–7
　　medical examination, 9–8
　Public Guardian
　　introduction, 9–1
　　supervision, 9–18
　registered establishments, 9–13
　summary of measures, and, 3–9
　supervision, 9–14—9–18
　terminology, 9–2
　transitional provisions, 9–22—9–24
　withdrawal of funds, 9–12
Resignation of guardians
　generally, 11–80—11–83
　joint guardians, and, 11–13
Responsible doctor
　meaning, 14–2
Responsive measures
　and see under individual headings
　authority to intromit
　　applications, 8–4—8–10
　　duration, 8–15
　　introduction, 8–1—8–3
　　purposes, 8–11
　　related provisions, 8–18—8–19
　　supervision, 8–14
　　termination, 8–16
　　withdrawers actings and duties,
　　　8–12—8–13
　authority to transfer
　　generally, 8–17
　　introduction, 8–1
　　limitations, 8–3
　　terminology, 8–2
　bare trusts
　　generally, 12–24
　　good practice, 12–3

Responsive measures—*cont.*
  criminal injuries compensation
    generally, 12–16
    good practice, 12–3
  criminal procedure, 12–32
  curators *ad litem*
    good practice, 12–3
    management, 12–26
    personal welfare, 12–35
  damages payments
    good practice, 12–3
    other courts, in, 12–13
    sheriff court, in, 12–13—12–14
  guardianship
    criteria, 10–27—10–28
    distinctions, 10–42
    duties, 10–60
    further provisions, 10–72—10–78
    generally, 10–26
    heritable property, 10–55—10–59
    inter-relationships, 10–70
    introduction, 10–1
    legal proceedings, 10–42—10–45
    liability, 10–62
    procedure, 10–46—10–54
    records, 10–61
    scope, 10–29—10–32
    supervision, 10–63—10–67
    termination, 10–71
    third party protection, 10–68—10–69
    uses and powers, 10–37—10–40
  informal voluntary arrangements
    generally, 12–21—12–22
    good practice, 12–3
    joint bank accounts, 12–23
  intervention order
    criteria, 10–27—10–28
    distinctions, 10–42
    duties, 10–60
    further provisions, 11–1—11–104
    generally, 10–26
    heritable property, 10–55—10–59
    inter-relationships, 10–70
    introduction, 10–1
    legal proceedings, 10–42—10–45
    liability, 10–62
    procedure, 10–46—10–54
    records, 10–61
    scope, 10–29—10–32
    supervision, 10–63—10–67
    termination, 10–71
    third party protection, 10–68—10–69
    uses and effects, 10–33—10–36
  introduction, 1–26
  judicial factors, 12–25
  management of affairs
    bare trusts, 12–24
    criminal injuries compensation, 12–16
    curators *ad litem*, 12–26
    damages payments, 12–13—12–15
    informal voluntary arrangements, 12–21—12–23
    judicial factors, 12–25
    miscellaneous statutory methods, 12–17

Responsive measures—*cont.*
  management of affairs—*cont.*
    negotiorum gestio, 12–18—12–20
    parens patriae, 12–27
    social security benefits, 12–4—12–10
    vaccine damage payments, 12–11—12–12
  management of resident's finances
    changes in capacity, 9–19—9–21
    introduction, 9–1—9–5
    management, 9–9—9–13
    procedure, 9–6—9–8
    supervision, 9–14—9–18
    transitional provisions, 9–22—9–24
  MHSA provisions, 12–29—12–31
  National Savings Bank, and, 12–17
  negotiorum gestio
    generally, 12–18—12–20
    good practice, 12–3
  other
    good practice, 12–3
    introduction, 12–1—12–2
    management, 12–4—12–27
    personal welfare, 12–28—12–35
  parens patriae
    good practice, 12–3
    management, 12–27
    personal welfare, 12–34
  personal welfare
    criminal procedure, 12–32
    curators *ad litem*, 12–35
    introduction, 12–28
    MHSA provisions, 12–29—12–31
    parens patriae, 12–34
    removal under NAA 1948, 12–33
  Premium Bonds, and, 12–17
  professional issues, and, 2–10
  removal under NAA 1948, 12–33
  savings certificates, and, 12–17
  social security benefits
    generally, 12–4
    good practice, 12–3
    relevant regulations, 12–5—12–10
  summary, 3–9
  vaccine damage payments
    deed of trust, 12–12
    generally, 12–11
    good practice, 12–3

s.47(2) authority
  application of Act, 14–42
  appointee decision, and, 14–23
  duration, 14–43
  exclusions, 14–45—14–47
  general principles, and, 14–42
  generally, 14–41
  necessity, and, 14–34—14–35
  patient's decision, and, 14–3
  procedure, 14–43
  scope, 14–44
s.48(3) authority
  appointee decision, and, 14–23
  emergencies, 14–53
  generally, 14–48

s.48(3) authority—*cont.*
  treatments requiring certificate,
    14–51—14–52
  treatments requiring court application,
    14–49—14–50
s.50(5) authority
  appointee decision, and, 14–23
  generally, 14–54—14–58
  patient's decision, and, 14–8
Safeguarders
  sheriffs, and, 5–7
Savings certificates
  responsive measures, and, 12–17
Schizophrenia
  intellectual impairments, and, 1–8
Scottish Commission for the Regulation
    of Care, 9–1—9–5, 9–13—9–17
Security of person, right to
  human rights, and, 1–48
Sensory impairment
  communication difficulties, and, 1–14
Sheriff
  ancillary powers, 5–6
  appeals, and
    generally, 5–13
    incapacity decisions, 5–18
    medical treatment decisions, 5–19
    miscellaneous, 5–20
  applications, and, 5–21
  directions, 5–14—5–15
  expenses order, 5–10—5–12
  financial guardianship, and
    discharge of guardian, 11–67
    gifts, 11–59
  general principles, and, 5–8
  generally, 5–2—5–3
  guardianship, and, 10–63
  intervention orders, and, 10–63
  intimation of applications, and, 5–9
  jurisdiction, 5–4
  nearest relative, and, 5–16—5–17
  powers, 5–6
  powers of attorney, and
    general principles, and, 6–5
    powers, 6–38—6–40
  procedure, 5–5
  remits, and, 5–20
  safeguarders, and, 5–7
SLC Discussion Paper
  Mentally Disabled Adults (September
    1991), 3–4
SLC Report
  Incapable Adults (September 1995), 3–4,
    3–7, 3–28—3–29, 6–25
Social security benefits
  generally, 12–4
  good practice, 12–3
  relevant regulations, 12–5—12–10
  summary of measures, and, 3–9
Solicitor
  powers of attorney, and, 6–36
Special benefits
  introduction, 1–24
  management arrangements, 12–4
  means-tested state benefits, and, 13–31
  taxation of trusts, and, 13–19

Special protections
  disability discrimination, and, 1–41
  introduction, 1–24
Specialist nurses
  role and function, 5–36
Statement of wishes and feelings
  generally, 7–13
  introduction, 3–9
Statutory applications
  regulatory amendments, A2–09
Statutory guardians
  abolition of measures, and, 3–9
  generally, 10–2—10–4
Strokes
  intellectual impairments, and, 1–12
Substitute guardians
  caution, and, 11–15
  generally, 11–14
  transitional provisions, 11–101
  triggers for, 11–16
Substituted judgment
  construction of decisions, and,
    15–27—15–28
Summary applications
  regulatory amendments, A2–09
Supervening incapacity
  introduction, 1–23
Styles
  advance directives, and, 7–8
  guardianship, and
    application for order, A6–03
    application to replace, A6–02
  intervention orders, and, A6–01
  powers of attorney, and
    form, A5–01
    generally, 6–28—6–30

Taking decisions
  generally, 15–1—15–28
Taking instructions
  advance directives, and, 7–7
  anticipatory measures, and, 2–19
Tax powers
  financial guardianship, and, 11–60
  intervention order, and, 10–76
  powers of attorney, and, 6–27
Taxation of trusts
  capital gains tax, 13–23—13–25
  generally, 13–19
  income tax
    discretionary trust, 13–22
    interest in possession, 13–20—13–21
    liferent trust, 13–20—13–21
    non-interest in possession, 13–22
  inheritance tax, 13–26—13–30
Temporary conditions
  intellectual impairments, and, 1–13
Temporary insanity
  powers of attorney, and, 6–3
Third party measures
  bare trusts, 13–39
  bequests, 13–37
  formal private trusts
    and see Trusts
    accumulations, 13–17—13–18

Third party measures—*cont.*
  formal private trusts—*cont.*
    delivery, 13–10
    general, 13–2—13–9
    legal rights, 13–11—13–16
    means-tested benefits, 13–31—13–35
    taxation, 13–19—13–30
  generally, 13–1
  gifts, 13–37
  informal voluntary arrangements, 13–39
  introduction, 1–27
  management of particular assets, 13–38
  nominations, 13–36
Third party protection
  guardianship, and, 10–68—10–69
  intervention orders, and, 10–68—10–69
  joint guardians, and, 11–10
Transfer, authority to
  generally, 8–17
  introduction, 8–1
  limitations, 8–3
  terminology, 8–2
Transitional guardians
  generally, 11–18
Transitional provisions
  guardianship, and
    additional guardians, 11–101
    application of, 11–94
    continuation of pre-Act appointments, 11–92
    curators bonis, 11–102—11–103
    duration, 11–98—11–100
    former MHSA guardians, 11–97
    guardians with management powers, 11–95
    Guidance Notes, 11–96
    proceedings relating to pre-Act appointments, 11–93
    replacement guardians, 11–101
    substitute guardians, 11–101
Treat, authority to
  and see Health-care decisions
  guardianship, and, 10–70
  intervention orders, and, 10–70
  powers of attorney, and, 6–42
  summary of measures, and, 3–9
Trusts
  and see Bare trusts
  accumulations, and, 13–17—13–18
  capital gains tax, 13–23—13–25
  delivery, 13–10
  general, 13–2—13–9
  income tax
    discretionary trust, 13–22
    interest in possession, 13–20—13–21
    liferent trust, 13–20—13–21
    non-interest in possession, 13–22
  inheritance tax, 13–26—13–30
  legal rights of relatives
    beneficiary with impairment, 13–13—13–16
    calculation, 13–12
    introduction, 13–11
    means-tested benefits, 13–31—13–35

Trusts—*cont.*
  summary of measures, and, 3–9
  taxation
    capital gains tax, 13–23—13–25
    generally, 13–19
    income tax, 13–20—13–22
    inheritance tax, 13–26—13–30
Trusts for administration
  generally, 7–3
  summary of measures, and, 3–9
Tutors-at-law
  abolition of measures, and, 3–9
  generally, 10–11—10–12
  healthcare decisions, and, 14–13
Tutors-dative
  abolition of measures, and, 3–9
  appointees, 10–19—10–20
  comparative influences, 10–17
  generally, 10–13
  healthcare decisions, and, 14–13
  historical development, 10–14—10–16
  management powers, 10–25
  revival, 10–18
  welfare powers, 10–21—10–24

Undue influence
  criteria, 1–38—1–39
  generally, 1–36
  introduction, 1–21
  personal welfare, 1–40

Vaccine damage payments
  deed of trust, 12–12
  generally, 12–11
  good practice, 12–3
  summary of measures, and, 3–9
Validity of acts
  generally, 1–28—1–35
  introduction, 1–22
Variation of orders
  guardianship, and, 11–73
  intervention order, and, 10–73

Welfare guardians
  see Guardians
Welfare, personal
  criminal procedure, 12–32
  curators *ad litem*, 12–35
  intervention orders, and, 10–29
  introduction, 12–28
  MHSA provisions, 12–29—12–31
  parens patriae, 12–34
  removal under NAA 1948, 12–33
  summary of measures, 3–9
  undue influence, and, 1–40
Welfare powers
  and see Guardianship
  guardianship, and, 10–41
  intervention orders, and, 10–41
  meaning, 10–46
  tutors-dative, and, 10–21—10–24
Welfare powers of attorney
  and see Powers of attorney
  agency, 6–47—6–48

Welfare powers of attorney—*cont.*
  attorneys, 6-20—6-22, 6-33—6-37
  Code of Practice, 3-15
  creation and registration, 6-9—6-18
  good practice, 6-32
  grantor, 6-19
  introduction, 6-1—6-5
  nature, 6-6—6-8
  non-Scottish powers, 6-49—6-53
  other authorities, 6-41
  powers, 6-23—6-31
  sheriff, 6-38—6-40
  summary, 3-9
  termination, 6-43—6-46
  transitional provisions, 6-54—6-58

Wishes and feelings of adult
  constructing decisions, 15-1—15-28
  statement of, 3-9, 7-13
  taking into account, 4-16—4-19

Withdrawal of funds
  management of resident's affairs, and, 9-12

Withdrawal of life-preserving treatment
  excluded matters, and, 3-29

Withdrawers
  actings and duties, 8-12—8-13
  Code of Practice, 3-15
  generally, 8-1

Withholding of life-preserving treatment
  excluded matters, and, 3-29